North American Trees

North American Trees

Fifth Edition

Richard J. Preston, Jr.

Richard R. Braham

Department of Forestry
North Carolina State University

Iowa State Press
A Blackwell Publishing Company

Richard J. Preston, Jr., was Professor Emeritus of forestry,
North Carolina State University–Raleigh.
Richard R. Braham is Associate Professor of Forestry, College of Natural Resources,
North Carolina State University–Raleigh.

©1948, 1961, 1976, 1989 Iowa State University Press
©2002 Iowa State Press
A Blackwell Publishing Company

Cover and book design by Justin Eccles

Iowa State Press
2121 State Avenue, Ames, Iowa 50014

Orders:	1-800-862-6657
Office:	1-515-292-0140
Fax:	1-515-292-3348
Web site:	www.iowastatepress.com

∞ Printed on acid-free paper in the United States of America

First edition, 1948
Second edition, 1961
Third edition, 1976
Fourth edition, 1989
Fifth edition, 2002

Library of Congress Cataloging-in-Publication Data

Preston, Richard Joseph, 1905-2001
   North American trees. —5th ed./Richard J. Preston.
      p. cm.
   ISBN 0-8138-1526-6 (alk. paper)
   1. Trees—United States—Identification 2. Trees—Canada—Identification.
   I. Braham, Richard R. II. Title.
   QK110 .P74 2002
   582.16'097—dc21

                                                              2002009404

The last digit is the print number: 9 8 7 6 5 4 3 2 1

CONTENTS

PREFACE

About eight months before his death in April 2001, Richard J. Preston, Jr., asked me to prepare this new edition of his classic dendrology text. As his former graduate teaching assistant, I was honored by the opportunity. I have continued his original concept of a single comprehensive but readable account of the trees of North America, designed for the general public and beginning student. Toward this end, I have updated nomenclature, simplified terminology, expanded information on natural history, added keys, and expanded the background information on genera and families.

The scope and arrangement of this manual, the basic characters used in tree identification, and the highest classification categories of trees are discussed in the introduction. The process of identifying unknown trees and the keys to identify trees are provided in the first chapter, Identification of Unknown Specimens. The main body of this manual contains descriptions, natural history, and illustrations of the trees found in North America, excluding Central America, Mexico, tropical regions, the Arctic Archipelago, and Greenland. Technical terms and jargon are used only where accuracy and conciseness would be otherwise compromised. A glossary is also provided.

The illustrations used in this manual arise from several sources. Figures 1–9, 32, 33, 45, 71, 76, 78, 85, 87, 93, 102, 106, 108, 109, 111, 117, 141–144, 146, 149, 157, 159, 162, 164, 169, 171, 172, 181, 186, 193, 195, 196, 200, 202, 205, 211, 215–217, 219, 222, 239, 241, 243, 244, 246, 247, 249, 250, 252, 257, 261, 267, 269, 275, 277, 279, 281, 283, 285–287, 289, 292, 295, 299, 300, 304, 318, 319, 320, 329, 330, 333, 335, 336, 341, 343, 346, 351, 355, 359, 364, 369, 377, 380, 381, 388, 392, 393, 404, 405, 407, 409–412, 415, 421, 422, and 426 were drawn for the fifth edition by Theresa Workman from dried specimens found in the North Carolina State University, Department of Forestry Herbarium.

The remaining figures are from sources in the public domain, except two figures from *Trees in Kansas,* which are used with permission. Figures 10, 12, 14, 18–23, 25, 29, 31, 35, 39, 46, 48, 51, 53, 57, 59, 62, 63, 73, 75, 80, 82, 89, 91, 95, 99, 104, 113, 115, 116, 119, 121, 123, 125, 127, 130, 135, 137, 139, 147, 170, 173, 174, 192, 199, 208, 218, 226, 231, 235, 264, 270, 272, 274, 291, 323, 347, 354, 358, 360, 361, 363, 365, 370, 379, 383, 387, 395, 400, 408, and 419 are from *Forest Trees of the Pacific Slope* by George B. Sudworth (1908, U.S. Government Printing Office).

Figures 16, 83, 97, 153, 155, 161, 163, 166, 168, 179, 185, 203, 206, 210, 212, 214, 229, 230, 233, 236, 248, 253, 255, 262, 265, 293, 302, 306, 308, 310, 312, 314, 316, 327, 332, 342, 356, 368, 372, 374, 390, 401, 413, 417, and 424 are from *Pennsylvania Trees* by Joseph S. Illick (1914, Pennsylvania Department of Forestry, Bulletin 11).

Figures 27, 37, 41, 43, 55, 61, 65, 67, 69, 92, 100, 128, 131, 133, 151, 165, 177, 183, 187, 189, 191, 194, 197, 220, 223, 225, 227, 238, 242, 297, 321, 325, 337–339, 344, 349, 353, 362, 366, 371, 376, 378, 382, 385, 397, 398, 399, 406, 420, 427, and 429 are from *Michigan Trees: A Handbook of the Native and Most Important Introduced Species* by Charles H. Otis (1913, University of Michigan Bulletin, vol. 14, no. 16).

Figure 176 is from *Alaska Trees and Shrubs* by Leslie A. Viereck and E. L. Little (1972, Agriculture Handbook 410, Forest Service, U.S. Department of Agriculture). Figure 259 is from *Trees the Yearbook of Agriculture 1949* (U.S. Department of Agriculture, U.S. Government Printing Office). Figures 367 and 403 are from *Trees in Kansas* by A. Dickens, M. E. Whittemore, C. A. Scott, and F. C. Gates (1928, Report Kansas State Board of Agriculture, vol. 47, no. 186-A).

All range maps are from *Silvics of North America*, Vols. 1 (Conifers) and 2 (Hardwoods), by Russel M. Burns and Barbara H. Honkala (Tech. Coord.) (1990, Agriculture Handbook 654, Forest Service, U.S. Department of Agriculture). Timothy McKeand scanned all figures for publication. I wish to thank John W. Duffield, Jr., who kindly reviewed the section on gymnosperms.

I am grateful to have had the opportunity over the years to study trees with Roscoe R. Braham, Jr., Raymond Schulenberg, Burton V. Barnes, Warren H. Wagner, Jr., John W. Duffield, Jr., Richard J. Preston, Jr., Anne Margaret Hughes, Joel Smith, and thousands of students.

INTRODUCTION

PURPOSE AND SCOPE

This manual classifies, keys, and often describes the trees known to occur spontaneously in North America, north of Mexico and tropical Florida. Spontaneous trees are able to reproduce naturally without planting. These are the trees normally encountered in our natural forests and woodlands. Most trees covered in this manual are indigenous, but some have become naturalized (able to reproduce by themselves) largely from Europe or Asia after being planted. The amount of information provided for each species is directly related to the size of its geographic range and our knowledge of it. Important trees known to cultivation in our region or to worldwide commerce are mentioned under the appropriate genus or family, but with few exceptions they are not described or found in the keys.

ARRANGEMENT OF INFORMATION

This manual is divided into seven main sections: Introduction, Identification of Unknown Specimens, Gymnosperms, Angiosperms, Monocotyledons, Dicotyledons, Glossary, and Index. The main portions of this manual are the sections on gymnosperms, monocotyledons, and dicotyledons where individual trees are described. These sections are arranged alphabetically by family scientific name. Within each family, species are listed alphabetically by scientific name.

PHYLA, CLASSES, AND ORDERS

Except for tropical tree ferns, extant trees belong to one of two major phyla: gymnosperms (technically called the Pinophyta) or angiosperms (Magnoliophyta). Gymnosperms have naked seeds generally produced in cones but sometimes borne in the open air. Angiosperms have seeds enclosed within an ovary that develops into a fruit like a berry or a nut.

The largest group of gymnosperms is the conifers (Pinales), which contain trees that commonly grow in temperate climates. As the name suggests, conifers are cone-bearing trees such as pine, spruce, and cedar that have distinctive needlelike or scalelike leaves. Conifers are sometimes called evergreens or softwoods, but these names are not ideal. Some conifers, such as larch and baldcypress, are not evergreen and shed their leaves annually. Some conifers do not have soft wood. Longleaf pine, for example, often has a wood density comparable to white ash or red oak.

Conifers are currently further subdivided into two families: the Pine Family (Pinaceae) and the Cypress Family (Cupressaceae). Older books recognize a third family, the Redwood Family (Taxodiaceae), but more modern classifications combine this family with the Cupressaceae.

Angiosperms are divided into two classes: monocotyledons or monocots (Liliopsida) and dicotyledons or dicots (Magnoliopsida). Monocots are characterized by a single seed leaf, parallel veins in leaves, flower parts in threes or multiples of three, and vascular bundles scattered throughout the stem. Monocot stems do not grow in diameter each year from divisions of a vascular cambium, and therefore monocots are not truly woody. But because some monocots are treelike in habit, some monocots are classified as trees.

Dicot trees are most frequently called hardwoods or broadleaved trees. Dicots differ from monocots in having two seed leaves, netlike branched veins in the leaves, floral parts often in fours or fives, and vascular bundles arranged in a ring around the pith.

DEFINITION OF TREE

Trees are woody vascular plants that grow to large sizes and live for many years, growing in height and diameter each year from aboveground parts. Lianas (vines) and shrubs are also woody plants that grow annually from aboveground parts. Lianas differ from trees because lianas do not grow as large in diameter, do not stand erect without support, and employ specialized mechanisms, usually tendrils or rootlets, to assist with climbing on other plants. Shrubs are smaller than trees at maturity, have several to many aboveground stems, and often produce new stems from the root collar at irregular intervals. Unfortunately, the distinction between trees and shrubs in size and number of stems is not universally accepted, because a complete gradation exists among species between large shrubs and small trees. To complicate matters, the form may change within a species. Some species are trees in a portion of their geographic range or on very favorable sites, but shrubs elsewhere. Therefore, the distinction is somewhat arbitrary. In this manual a tree is defined as a woody plant with one to four well-defined, self-supporting stems that at maturity grow to at least 25 feet in height and 3 inches in diameter.

CLASSIFICATIONS

The basic unit of tree classification is the species. A species is a collection of individuals with a common parentage that shares a common appearance, ecology, and reproductive biology. By definition, members of the same species can potentially reproduce with one another.

A group of closely related species constitute a genus (plural, genera), and related genera are grouped into families. When a species has no living close relatives it is monotypic—the only species in the genus or in the family or both.

ENTRIES IN THIS MANUAL

In this manual, the individual characteristics of trees are discussed by a combination of common and technical terms. Complicated terms have been avoided whenever possible. Technical terms are used whenever common words will not produce reasonably concise descriptions. When identifying trees, remember that characters are variable and sometimes overlap with those of closely related trees. Identification should be based on as many characteristics as possible.

The main entry for each species contains some or all of the following information: common name, scientific name, nomenclature, form, leaves, flowers, cones or fruits, twigs and buds, bark, wood, natural history, varieties, hybrids, and range. Some entries lack some of this information because it is not adequately known. To help new students, the information provided in each entry and many technical terms are explained below. Additional help is provided in the glossary.

COMMON NAMES

Over the centuries most trees have been given one or more common names by ordinary people. Common names generally describe some attribute of the tree, particularly folk use, color, appearance, or ecology. For example, the names post oak and lodgepole pine describe a common use; yellow birch and whitebark pine describe bark color; and subalpine fir and river birch describe the ecology.

Unfortunately, common names have many limitations. Some trees have more than one common name. For example, *Liriodendron tulipifera* is called tuliptree in the Lake States, tulip-poplar in the Middle Atlantic States, and yellow-poplar in the South. *Carpinus caroliniana* is called musclewood, American hornbeam, blue-beech, and ironwood. The same common name is sometimes used for different species. For example, the name scrub pine, scrub oak, or nut pine each applies to several species. Common names also change over time. Many years ago, loblolly pine was called shortleaf pine, a name now applied to an entirely different species. Sometimes common names apply to entirely different genera. In North America, for example, the name gum is applied to *Nyssa* or *Liquidambar*, but in Australia gum is *Eucalyptus*. For these reasons, this manual often provides multiple common names. The common names used in this manual are those most widely applied. But because of these problems scientists decided that each species should have a scientific name, a name recognized throughout the world that cannot be applied to any other species.

SCIENTIFIC NAMES

The scientific names used in this manual are the names currently accepted by most tree experts. With few exceptions they follow *Flora North America* (New York: Oxford University Press, 1993, 1997, and 2000), when available, or *Checklist of United States Trees* (Agriculture Handbook 541, Forest Service, U.S. Department of Agriculture, 1979) by E. L. Little, Jr.

Scientific names are latinized forms of root words, usually either Greek or Latin. Scientific names consist of three parts: (1) the genus, the first word, which is italicized and always begins with a capital letter; (2) the specific epithet, the second word, which is italicized and begins with a small letter; and (3) the author citation, the full or abbreviated name of the person or persons who named the plant. Author citations provide a bibliographic reference useful when the same name is inadvertently proposed by two different people for two different plants, or when different people give the same plant different names. For example, the complete scientific name of white oak is *Quercus alba* L. The genus is *Quercus*; all true oaks belong to *Quercus*. The specific epithet is *alba,* which references a particular oak. Since the scientific name for white oak was proposed by Linnaeus, either the capital letter L. or the full name Linnaeus follows the epithet.

When the author citation consists of the names of two people and the first name is enclosed within parentheses, the tree was originally named by the first person but placed in a different genus. The second person transferred the tree to the current genus. For example, western hemlock was first named *Abies heterophylla* by Constantine Samuel Rafinesque. But Charles Sargent recognized later that this tree was better classified in the genus *Tsuga*. Thus, the current scientific name is *Tsuga heterophylla* (Raf.) Sarg. In common practice, author citations are used principally when scientific names are used in publications, and they are rarely memorized by nonspecialists. This manual provides the full scientific name for all main entries, but to improve readability, the author citation is usually omitted in the text.

FORM

The form of a tree refers to the overall shape, especially the main stem and branches. When the main stem extends from the ground to the top of the tree without forking, the form is excurrent. Most pines, Douglas-fir, sweetgum, and yellow-poplar are excurrent. If the main stem repeatedly divides into large branches, the form is deliquescent or decurrent. American elm is typically deliquescent. But form of a species may vary. A tree growing in the open will be more deliquescent than forest-grown trees. At old age, excurrent trees often become more deliquescent. Trees subject to the harsh conditions at timberline are often stunted and leaning, compared to trees of the same species growing under better conditions at lower elevations. The German word *krummholz*, meaning crooked-wood, is used to describe the form of windswept trees growing at timberline.

NOMENCLATURE

Former or alternative scientific names, if any, are provided to assist with cross-referencing to older manuals.

LEAVES

Since leaves of the same species look more-or-less alike, they are useful organs in identifying trees. Leaves consist of a flat green portion called the blade or lamina. Leaves of most trees have a supporting stalk, the petiole. Leaves borne directly on the twig without stalks are sessile. Species that keep some live leaves throughout the year are evergreen, while species that are leafless for part of the year are deciduous. Note that the term "evergreen" is not restricted to a particular genus or family of trees. For this reason conifers should not be called evergreens. Some leaves develop stipules, small scaly or hairlike structures attached *in pairs* at the base of the petiole or on the adjacent twig. Leaves without stipules are called estipulate.

Leaves are attached to the twig at a position called the node. When one leaf is found per node, the leaf arrangement is alternate or spiral; two leaves per node are opposite; and more than two leaves per node are whorled (fig. 1). In pines, the leaves are spirally arranged in a very tight cluster called a fascicle (fig. 1).

Leaves composed of a single blade are simple. If a leaf is divided into several

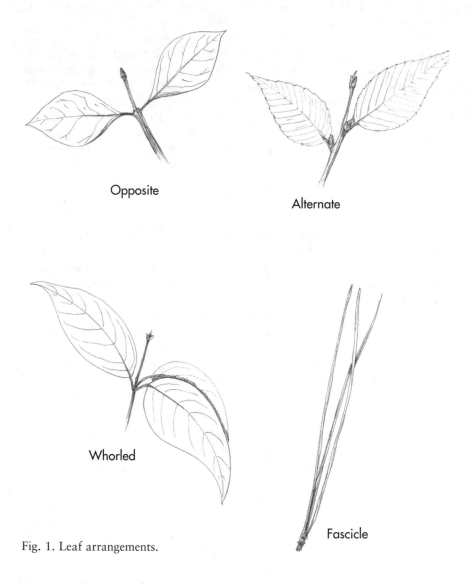

Opposite

Alternate

Whorled

Fascicle

Fig. 1. Leaf arrangements.

individual parts called leaflets, the leaf is compound. If the leaflets are arranged along each side of a common axis, the rachis, the leaf is pinnately compound, like ashes and hickories. If the leaflets arise fanlike from the tip of the petiole, the leaf is palmately compound, like buckeyes (fig. 2). Other characters commonly used in identification are overall leaf shape (fig. 3), leaf edge or margin (fig. 4), and leaf tip and base (fig. 5). Leaf texture—either hairless (glabrous) or hairy (pubescent)—is also useful.

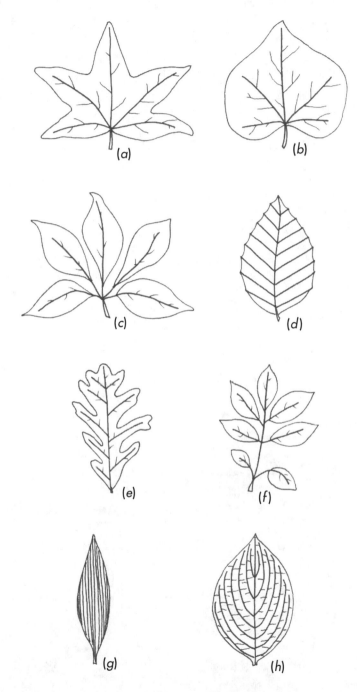

Fig. 2. Leaf composition: (*a*) simple lobed with palmate veins, (*b*) simple not lobed with palmate veins, (*c*) palmately compound with five leaflets, (*d*) simple with pinnate veins, (*e*) simple lobed with pinnate veins, (*f*) pinnately compound, (*g*) parallel veins, and (*h*) arcuate veins.

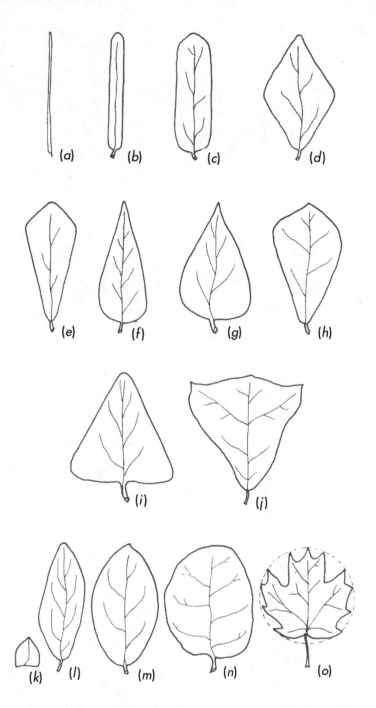

Fig. 3. Leaf shapes: (*a*) needlelike or acicular, (*b*) linear, (*c*) oblong, (*d*) rhomboid, (*e*) oblanceolate, (*f*) lanceolate, (*g*) ovate, (*h*) obovate, (*i*) triangular or deltate, (*j*) obdeltate, (*k*) scalelike, (*l*) narrowly elliptical, (*m*) elliptical, (*n*) oval, (*o*) round or orbicular.

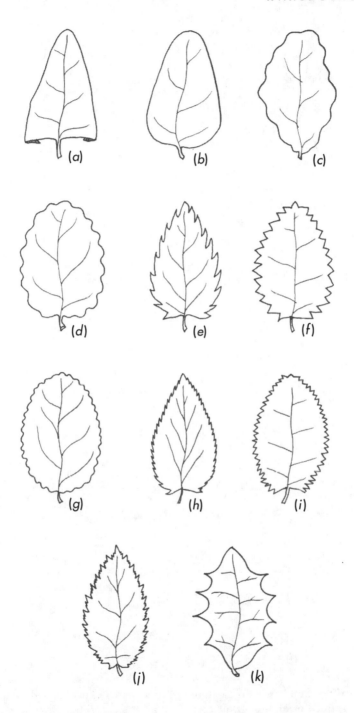

Fig. 4. Leaf margins: (*a*) rolled under or revolute, (*b*) smooth or entire, (*c*) wavy or sinuate, (*d*) crenate, (*e*) serrate, (*f*) dentate, (*g*) crenulate, (*h*) serrulate, (*i*) denticulate, (*j*) doubly serrate, (*k*) spiny or aculeate.

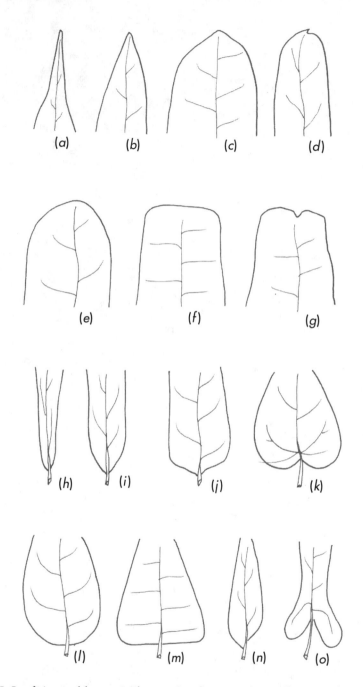

Fig. 5. Leaf tips and bases: (*a*) long-pointed or acuminate; (*b*) pointed or acute; (*c*) blunt-pointed or obtuse; (*d*) mucronate; (*e*) rounded; (*f*) flat or truncate; (*g*) notched or emarginated; (*h*) wedge-shaped or cuneate; (*i*) acute; (*j*) obtuse; (*k*) heart-shaped or cordate; (*l*) rounded; (*m*) flat or truncate; (*n*) asymmetrical, inequilateral, or oblique; (*o*) earlike or auriculate.

CONES

All conifers bear their reproductive parts in unisexual cones, either male or female. Cones are composed of several to many scales, which may be either flat as in pines, or mushroom-shaped (peltate) as in baldcypress and redwood (fig. 6). All scales of one cone are alike, either all flat or all peltate. Male cones are papery and produce pollen. After pollen release, male cones wither and fall off. Typically woody but sometimes fleshy, female cones produce seeds. One to three years after pollination, the female cone is mature. In most cases the cones dry and open in the fall to release seeds, most of which have attached wings. These winged seeds are dispersed by wind. In many junipers the cone is fleshy and resembles a blueberry. Fleshy cones are eaten and dispersed by animals, especially birds. In a few cases, most notably jack, knobcone, pond, and some sand and lodgepole pines, the cones are serotinous, opening years after maturity generally from the heat of fire to release the seed to a well-prepared seed bed.

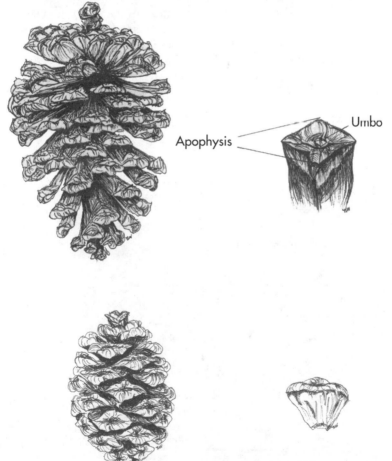

Apophysis   Umbo

Fig. 6. Conifer cones: (*top*) flat-scaled and (*bottom*) peltate-scaled.

Two parts of the individual cone scale are often useful for identification (fig. 6). The apophysis is the upper portion of the cone scale that is exposed when the cone is closed. It is generally lighter in color. The apophysis of pine cones contains a small rectangular projection called the umbo. The umbo is located either on the external face of the apophysis (dorsal) or at the tip (terminal). If cones are armed, the prickle always arises as a prolongation of the umbo.

FLOWERS

Angiosperms bear their reproductive parts in flowers (fig. 7). (By definition, gymnosperms do not flower.) Flowers are marginally useful for identification since they are usually inconspicuous and the period of flowering is brief. Flowers vary greatly in structure and size. A complete flower contains leaflike sepals (collectively the calyx); brightly colored petals (collectively the corolla); stamens (collectively the androecium), the male organs that bear pollen in saclike anthers; and the carpel(s) (collectively the pistil or gynoecium), the female organ consisting of a terminal stigma that catches the pollen, a style, and an ovary. The ovary may consist of one or more compartments that support one to many ovules that mature into seeds. If the ovary is located on top of the other flower parts, it is superior. If the ovary appears below the sepals, petals, and stamens, it is inferior.

Flowers may be either bisexual (perfect) or unisexual (imperfect). Plants having unisexual flowers can either have both sexes present in different structures on the same plant (a condition called monoecious), or each sex borne on a different plant

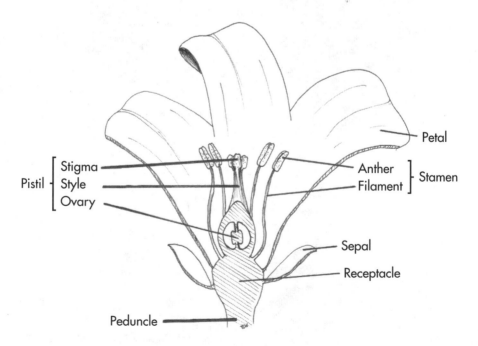

Fig. 7. Flower anatomy.

(dioecious). This latter condition provides male and female trees. Plants that bear both bisexual and unisexual flowers are polygamous. Flowers may appear singly or in clusters called inflorescences.

FRUIT

A fruit is a mature ovary. Only angiosperms produce fruits since all gymnosperms lack an ovary. Three basic groups of fruit are found in trees: fleshy, dry-dehiscent, and dry-indehiscent (fig. 8). Fleshy fruits are drupes when they have a single hard pit in the center, berries when they are fleshy throughout, and pomes when they have a papery core. Peaches are drupes, tomatoes are berries, and apples are pomes. Dry-dehiscent fruits split open naturally at maturity. Dehiscent fruits with a single carpel are follicles when they split along one line, but legumes when they split along two lines. Dehiscent fruits with two or more carpels are capsules when they split along two or more lines. Magnolias have follicles, redbud and mesquite have legumes, and sourwood and rhododendron have capsules. Dry-indehiscent fruits are distinguished mostly by size and partly by anatomy. Large indehiscent fruits are nuts like acorns, but smaller fruits are nutlets. Even smaller fruits are achenes when the seed is not fused to the ovary wall. When the seed is fused to the ovary wall, the fruit is a grain (caryopsis) found only in the Grass Family. The type of fruit produced is often characteristic of a particular group and fruits are therefore useful in identification. Pome fruits for example are limited to the Rose Family (Rosaceae), and all members of the Legume Family (Fabaceae) produce legumes.

TWIGS

The color, stoutness, and surface markings of twigs may be useful in identifying trees, especially deciduous trees in winter (fig. 9). The center of the twig is the pith, and several types of pith are found in trees. Most commonly the pith is solid and homogeneous. Sometimes the pith is solid, but divided at regular intervals by partitions, a condition called diaphragmed. Magnolia, yellow-poplar, and blackgum are characterized by a diaphragmed pith. Rarely, the pith is chambered, hollow but divided by solid partitions at regular intervals. Because of its rarity, chambered twigs, found in walnuts and sweetleaf, are very useful for identification. When leaves fall off they frequently leave characteristically shaped scars on the twig. The size, shape, and arrangement of buds are also helpful in identification. Most trees have a terminal bud located at the tip of each twig. In roughly one-third of our angiosperm trees, the terminal bud aborts at the end of each growing season, leaving a small bump beside the upper-most (last-formed) lateral bud. The following year the upper-most lateral bud, called a pseudoterminal bud, substitutes for the true terminal bud. The same pattern of growth and abortion continues the next fall. The presence or absence of terminal buds is very useful in tree identification.

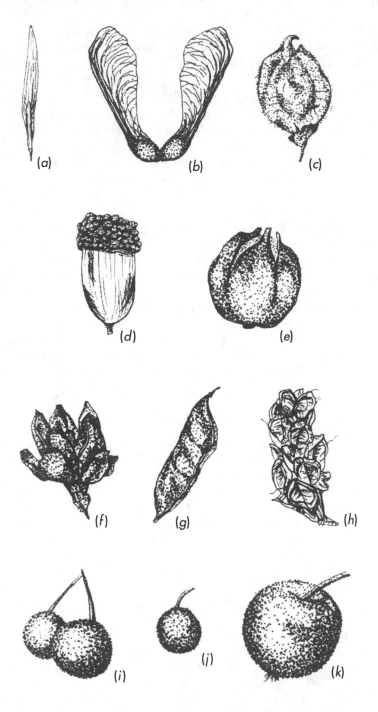

Fig. 8. Fruit types. Dry-indehiscent:(*a–c*) winged fruit or samara, (*d*, *e*) nut; dry-dehiscent: (*f*) capsule, (*g*) legume, (*h*) conelike cluster of follicles; fleshy: (*i*) drupe, (*j*) berry, (*k*) apple or pome.

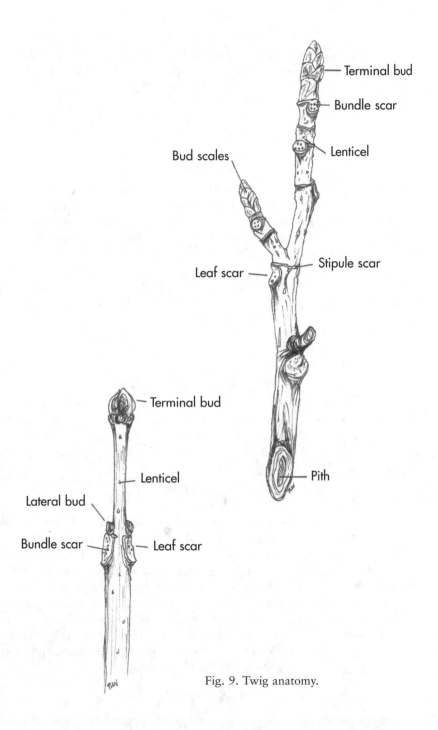

Terminal bud

Bundle scar

Lenticel

Bud scales

Stipule scar

Leaf scar

Pith

Terminal bud

Lenticel

Lateral bud

Bundle scar

Leaf scar

Fig. 9. Twig anatomy.

BARK

The appearance of bark while varying with age is useful in tree identification. Bark ranks among the most useful characters for identification of hardwoods especially in winter, but considerable practice is required. Color, texture, and odor are useful characters. The bark of all small trees is smooth, but with increasing age the bark of most trees becomes thicker and rougher. Bark texture is commonly either ridged with peaks and valleys (furrows), plated with large plateaus separated by furrows, scaly with flaky chips, or smooth.

WOOD

Wood anatomy is a separate means of identification that often requires magnification. Wood anatomy is more conservative than external characters since the wood anatomy of related species is often remarkably similar, making anatomy useful for identification to genus or family only. Most wood cells die shortly after formation. The outer portions of the stem, the sapwood, contain a few live cells. But in the inner portion, the heartwood, all cells are dead. The sapwood is generally lighter in color, sometimes markedly, than the heartwood. The sapwood of black walnut, for example, is cream colored, but the heartwood is chocolate colored. The heartwood is generally more decay resistant and more valuable commercially. In this manual, only outstanding macroscopic wood characters are given, particularly color, weight, and commercial use.

NATURAL HISTORY

The natural history is provided for many species, but the information varies greatly by species, a reflection of what is known about each species. Natural history includes tolerance to shade, growth rate and longevity, reproductive biology, damaging agents, typical host sites and locations, associate species, and wildlife and folk use.

VARIETIES

Individuals *within a species* that exhibit minor but consistent differences are often further classified as subspecies or varieties. Varieties and subspecies differ somewhat from the typical species in appearance, ecology, or size at maturity. In all cases, however, the differences are not sufficient to recognize separate species. Although subspecies technically exhibit greater differences than varieties, in practice these categories are the same. When a species is divided into varieties, the varietal name follows the specific epithet. For clarity, the abbreviation "var." precedes the varietal name. For example, ponderosa pine is often divided into varieties based upon needle length and the number of needles per fascicle. The variety with shorter and fewer needles is *Pinus ponderosa* var. *scopulorum*.

HYBRIDS

Some tree species can potentially reproduce with other related species to create hybrids. The closer the relationship between or among species, the greater the number of hybrids produced. Tree hybrids are usually intermediate in appearance between the parents. Hybrids cause confusion in identification because they will not reasonably match the description of either parent. A list of known hybrids is provided to assist with understanding the relationships among species, and with the identification of trees that do not reasonably match any description.

RANGE

The geographic range of native species is provided either verbally or in figures. In mountain regions the elevation where a species is found is often provided. The native homeland of exotic naturalized species is provided, but the range of exotics in our region is described only in general terms since our knowledge of this information is usually incomplete.

North American Trees

Fifth Edition

CHAPTER 1
IDENTIFICATION OF
UNKNOWN
SPECIMENS

The process of identifying an unknown tree begins with determining what information is available and what is already known, if anything about the species. Collect as many parts from the unknown as possible including leaves attached to twigs, flowers, and fruits or cones. Also observe the bark and habitat. Similar looking species can sometimes be completely identified only when all parts are present.

If the identity of the tree is completely unknown, begin with the keys found below. If the unknown tree can be identified to genus, turn to the appropriate page in this manual and follow the paired statements in the generic key.

USE OF KEYS

Keys contain a series of paired statements. Decide which statement more closely describes the unknown. Rarely, the first selected statement will provide the identity of the unknown. More commonly, the selected statement will lead to other paired statements identified by number or letter. Follow the numbers or letters. Each time select the statement that more closely describes the unknown until the identity of the genus is given at the end of the chosen statement. Turn to the page where the indicated genus is discussed, and use the generic key to identify the species.

Sometimes neither statement reasonably describes the unknown. This situation usually indicates that the wrong statement was previously selected. In this case, begin again but follow a different pathway by selecting at least one different statement. Alternatively, continue the process, but note the number where neither statement seemed appropriate. If the final determination is not correct, return to the paired statements immediately preceding the noted statement and select the other statement.

After determining the possible name of the unknown, compare the unknown to the written description and figure, if available. If the determination is correct, the description and figure should reasonably match the specimen. If not, repeat the process.

KEYS TO TAXA

Because of the large number of trees contained in this manual, the keys have been subdivided to simplify use. To select the appropriate subkey, begin with the Key to Subkeys below.

KEY TO SUBKEYS

I. Seeds naked, not contained within an ovary (Gymnosperms) . . . . .Go to Subkey A
I. Seeds borne in an ovary (Angiosperms) . . . . .Go to II
    II. Leaves with parallel veins (Monocots) . . . . .Go to Subkey B
    II. Leaves (rarely absent) with netted veins (Dicots) III
III. Leaves opposite or whorled IV
III. Leaves alternate V
    IV. Leaves compound . . . . .Go to Subkey C
    IV. Leaves simple . . . . .Go to Subkey D
V. Leaves compound . . . . .Go to Subkey E
V. Leaves simple VI
    VI. Leaves evergreen . . . . .Go to Subkey F
    VI. Leaves deciduous VII
VII. Leaves scalelike or falling quickly . . . . .Go to Subkey G
VII. Leaves not scalelike or not falling quickly VIII
    VIII. Leaves lobed . . . . .Go to Subkey H
    VIII. Leaves not lobed IX
IX. Leaf margin entire . . . . .Go to Subkey J
IX. Leaf margin toothed . . . . .Go to Subkey K

SUBKEY A. GYMNOSPERMS

1. Leaves needlelike in clusters of 1–5 . . . . .pine, *Pinus,* pg. 73
1. Leaves linear or scalelike; borne singly 2
    2. Leaves alternate; linear 3
    2. Leaves opposite or whorled; scalelike or awl-shaped 13
3. Seeds dry; borne in cones 4
3. Seeds with fleshy covering 12
    4. Cone scales flat. Seeds terminally winged; 2 per scale 5
    4. Cone scales peltate. Seeds laterally winged; 2–9 per scale 10
5. Twigs with spur shoots 6
5. Twigs without spur shoots 7
    6. Cones less than 1.5 in. long . . . . .larch, *Larix,* pg. 57
    6. Cones more than 3 in. long . . . . .cedar, *Cedrus,* pg. 42
7. Leaves borne on twigs on peglike projections (sterigmata) 8
7. Leaves borne on smooth or nearly smooth twigs 9
    8. Leaves without stalks; prickly . . . . .spruce, *Picea,* pg. 62
    8. Leaves with tiny stalks; soft . . . . .hemlock, *Tsuga,* pg. 128
9. Leaves with rounded bases; buds rounded . . . . .fir, *Abies,* pg. 42
9. Leaves pointed at base; buds pointed . . . . .Douglas-fir, *Pseudotsuga,* pg. 125
    10. Eastern; cones spherical . . . . .cypress, *Taxodium,* pg. 35
    10. Western; cones longer than wide 11
11. Cone 1–1.5 in. long; Pacific coastal . . . . .redwood, *Sequoia,* pg. 32

11. Cone 2–3 in. long; Sierra Nevada ......giant sequoia, *Sequoiadendron,* pg. 34
    12. Leaves 0.5–1 in. long; seed largely enclosed by red flesh ..yew, *Taxus,* pg. 134
    12. Leaves 1–3 in. long; seed enclosed in green or purple flesh ....
    ....torreya, *Torreya,* pg. 136
13. Cones berrylike ....juniper, *Juniperus,* pg. 23
13. Cone woody or leathery 14
    14. Cones spherical; scales peltate 15
    14. Cones longer than wide; scales flat 16
15. Cones over 0.5 in. wide ....cypress, *Cupressus,* pg. 19
15. Cone less than 0.5 in. wide ....cedar, *Chamaecyparis,* pg. 14
    16. Cones with 4–6 scales ....incense-cedar, *Calocedrus,* pg. 13
    16. Cones with 6–12 scales ....cedar, *Thuja,* pg. 38

SUBKEY B. MONOCOTYLEDONS

1. Leaves lanceolate; fruit a capsule ....yucca, *Yucca,* pg. 137
1. Leaves fan-shaped; fruit fleshy ....Go to 2
    2. Leaf stalks without prickles ....palmetto, *Sabal,* pg. 141
    2. Leaf stalks with prickles 3
3. Leaf stalk prickles more-or-less straight ....saw-palmetto, *Serenoa,* pg. 143
3. Leaf stalks with recurved prickles ....washingtonia, *Washingtonia,* pg. 143

SUBKEY C. DICOTYLEDONS WITH OPPOSITE COMPOUND LEAVES

1. Leaves palmately compound ....buckeye, *Aesculus,* pg. 323
1. Leaves pinnately compound or 3-foliate ....Go to 2
    2. Fruit a samara 3
    2. Fruit fleshy or capsule 4
3. Leaflets with small teeth ....ash, *Fraxinus,* pg. 371
3. Leaflets with large teeth, nearly lobed ....boxelder, *Acer negundo,* pg. 151
    4. Leaves with 3 leaflets ....bladdernut, *Staphylea,* pg. 449
    4. Leaves with 5–9 leaflets 5
5. Fruit drupelike ....elderberry, *Sambucus,* pg. 197
5. Fruit a capsule ....trumpetflower, *Tecoma stans,* pg. 192

SUBKEY D. DICOTYLEDONS WITH OPPOSITE OR WHORLED SIMPLE LEAVES

1. Leaves evergreen; thick ....devilwood, *Osmanthus,* pg. 383
1. Leaves deciduous; thin ....Go to 2
    2. Leaves palmately lobed ....maple, *Acer,* pg. 145
    2. Leaves not lobed 3
3. Leaves entire 4
3. Leaves toothed 10
    4. Leaves heart-shaped; 5–12 in. long 5
    4. Leaves linear to ovate; less than 5 in. long 6
5. Leaves densely hairy below; fruit 1–2 in. long ....paulownia, *Paulownia,* pg. 445
5. Leaves hairless or slightly hairy below; fruit 8–20 in. long ....
    ....catalpa, *Catalpa,* pg. 192
    6. Leaves linear to lanceolate ....desertwillow, *Chilopsis,* pg. 194
    6. Leaves nearly rounded or elliptical 7

SUBKEY E. LEAVES ALTERNATE AND COMPOUND

SUBKEY F. LEAVES ALTERNATE, SIMPLE, AND EVERGREEN

3. Fruit an acorn . . . . .oak, *Quercus* (in part), pg. 259
3. Fruit a hairy capsule . . . . .fremontia, *Fremontodendron,* pg. 450
   4. Lower leaf surface dotted with scales or glands 5
   4. Lower leaf surface without scales or glands 8
5. Leaves covered with yellow scales below . . . . . . .chinkapin, *Chrysolepis,* pg. 255
5. Leaves glandular—dotted below 6
   6. Leaves aromatic . . . . .waxmyrtle, *Myrica,* pg. 368
   6. Leaves without odor 7
7. Fruit with 2–4 wings .buckwheat-tree, *Cliftonia,* pg. 213
7. Fruit without wings . . . . .fetterbush, *Lyonia,* pg. 221
   8. Fruit with a long hairy (plumelike) tip . . . . .cercocarpus, *Cercocarpus,* pg. 395
   8. Fruit without a plumelike tip 9
9. Fruit an acorn 10
9. Fruit not an acorn 11
   10. Acorn cap with flat scales . . . . .oak, *Quercus* (in part), pg. 259
   10. Acorn cap with long spiny scales . . . . .tanoak, *Lithocarpus,* pg. 258
11. Leaves entire (rarely toothed on vigorous shoots) 12
11. Leaves toothed 25
   12. Leaves aromatic 13
   12. Leaves not aromatic 16
13. Fruit woody 14
13. Fruit fleshy 15
   14. Fruit shaped like a pinwheel . . . . .anise-tree, *Illicium,* pg. 327
   14. Fruit shaped like a top . . . . .eucalypt, *Eucalyptus,* pg. 369
15. Calyx lobes persistent on fruit; Southeast . . . . .redbay, *Persea,* pg. 347
15. Calyx lobes deciduous; California and Oregon . . . . .laurel, *Umbellularia,* pg. 352
   16. Sap milky . . . . .fig, *Ficus,* pg. 363
   16. Sap watery 17
17. Fruit a conelike cluster of follicles . . . . .magnolia, *Magnolia,* pg. 356
17. Fruit simple; not a cluster 18
   18. Fruit a 5-parted capsule 19
   18. Fruit fleshy or dry drupe or berry 20
19. Leaves 3–4 in. long; flat . . . . .mountain laurel, *Kalmia,* pg. 221
19. Leaves 4–10 in. long; cupped . . . . .rhododendron, *Rhododendron,* pg. 223
   20. Twigs spiny 21
   20. Twigs not spiny 22
21. Leaves 1–3 in. long; drupe black . . . . .bumelia, *Bumelia,* pg. 443
21. Leaves 0.5–0.7 in. long; drupe red . . . . .bluewood, *Condalia,* pg. 388
   22. Fruit a dry drupe . . . . .titi, *Cyrilla,* pg. 215
   22. Fruit a fleshy drupe or berry 23
23. Stipules or their scars present . . . . .holly, *Ilex,* pg. 166
23. Stipules and their scars absent 24
   24. Fruit black; lustrous; Southeast . . . . .blueberry, *Vaccinium,* pg. 225
   24. Fruit orange; glandular-coated; Western . . .Pacific madrone, *Arbutus,* pg. 219
25. Leaves 3-nerved from base . . . . .ceanothus, *Ceanothus,* pg. 387
25. Leaves with pinnate veins 26
   26. Stipules absent 27
   26. Stipules or their scars present 28
27. Leaves 1–2 in. long; entire or finely toothed . . . . . .blueberry, *Vaccinium,* pg. 225
27. Leaves 3–6 in. long; toothed . . . . .loblolly-bay, *Gordonia,* pg. 455

28. Leaves narrowly lanceolate . . . . .vauquelinia, *Vauquelinia*, pg. 416
28. Leaves wider than lanceolate 29
29. Fruit a pome . . . . .toyon, *Heteromeles*, pg. 399
29. Fruit a drupe 30
    30. Twigs spiny; leaves nearly round . . . .
    . . . . .hollyleaf buckthorn, *Rhamnus crocea*, pg. 391
    30. Twigs not spiny; leaves lanceolate to ovate 31
31. Leaf scar with single bundle scar . . . . .holly, *Ilex*, pg. 166
31. Leaf scar with 3 or more bundle scars . . . . . . .cherry, *Prunus* (in part), pg. 402

SUBKEY G. LEAVES ALTERNATE, SIMPLE, DECIDUOUS AND SCALELIKE, INCONSPICUOUS, OR FALLING QUICKLY

1. Plants succulent (cacti) with clustered spines 2
1. Plants woody 3
    2. Branches columnar . . . . .saguaro, *Cereus*, pg. 196
    2. Branches flattened; jointed . . . . .prickly-pear, *Opuntia*, pg. 196
3. Leaves scalelike . . . . .tamarisk, *Tamarix*, pg. 454
3. Leaves falling quickly; trees appearing leafless 4
    4. Twigs with triangular glands at most nodes . . . . . . .canotia, *Canotia*, pg. 202
    4. Twigs lacking triangular glands 5
5. Fruit a legume . . . . .smokethorn, *Dalea*, pg. 229
5. Fruit a berry . . . . .allthorn, *Koeberlinia*, pg. 346

SUBKEY H. LEAVES ALTERNATE, SIMPLE, DECIDUOUS, LOBED

1. Leaves 4-lobed; buds with valvate scales . . . .yellow-poplar, *Liriodendron*, pg. 354
1. Leaves not 4-lobed; bud scales not valvate . . . . .Go to 2
    2. Leaves strongly aromatic . . . . .sassafras, *Sassafras*, pg. 351
    2. Leaves not strongly aromatic 3
3. Leaves palmately 3–7 lobed 4
3. Leaves not palmately lobed 5
    4. Leaves with rounded teeth . . . . . .sweetgum, *Liquidambar styraciflua*, pg. 322
    4. Leaves coarsely spiny toothed . . . . .sycamore, *Platanus*, pg. 383
5. Terminal bud absent; sap milky 6
5. Terminal bud present; sap watery 7
    6. Leaves velvety-hairy below . . . . .paper-mulberry, *Broussonetia*, pg. 365
    6. Leaves hairless or hairy below . . . . .mulberry, *Morus*, pg. 366
7. Twigs with sharp thorns . . . . .hawthorn, *Crataegus*, pg. 397
7. Twigs lacking sharp thorns 8
    8. Leaf scars with many bundle scars . . . . .oak, *Quercus*, pg. 259
    8. Leaf scars with 3 bundle scars 9
9. Leaves toothed . . . . .crab apple, *Malus*, pg. 400
9. Leaves entire . . . . .poplar, *Populus*, pg. 421

SUBKEY J. LEAVES, ALTERNATE, SIMPLE, DECIDUOUS, ENTIRE

1. Leaves, twigs, and fruit silver-scaly 2
1. Plants not silver-scaly 3

2. Leaves elliptic to oblong . . . . .buffaloberry, *Shepherdia,* pg. 217
2. Leaves lanceolate . . . . .elaeagnus, *Elaeagnus,* pg. 217
3. Leaves heart-shaped . . . . .redbud, *Cercis,* pg. 235
3. Leaves not heart-shaped 4
   4. Sap milky . . . . .Osage-orange, *Maclura,* pg. 365
   4. Sap watery 5
5. Leaves obovate-elliptical; 10–12 in. long . . . . .pawpaw, *Asimina,* pg. 165
5. Leaves not as above 6
   6. Terminal bud present 7
   6. Terminal bud absent 14
7. Twigs with encircling stipular scars . . . . .magnolia, *Magnolia,* pg. 365
7. Twigs lacking encircling stipular scars 8
   8. Stipules present . . . . .oak, *Quercus* (in part), pg. 259
   8. Stipules absent 9
9. Leaves with arcuate veins . . . . .dogwood, *Cornus,* pg. 203
9. Leaves with pinnate veins 10
   10. Twigs aromatic when crushed . . . . .smoketree, *Cotinus,* pg. 161
   10. Twigs lacking odor 11
11. Twigs with large circular lenticels . . . . .corkwood, *Leitneria,* pg. 353
11. Leaves with few small lenticels 12
   12. Pith diaphragmed . . . . .blackgum, *Nyssa,* pg. 207
   12. Pith homogeneous 13
13. Leaves hairy below . . . . .elliottia, *Elliottia,* pg. 221
13. Leaves hairless below . . . . .titi, *Cyrilla,* pg. 215
   14. Leaves unequal at base . . . . .hackberry, *Celtis,* pg. 461
   14. Leaves symmetrical at base 15
15. Stipules or their scars present 16
15. Stipules absent 19
   16. Buds with single caplike scale .willow, *Salix,* pg. 436
   16. Buds scaly or naked 17
17. Sap milky; twigs stout . . . . .sumac, *Rhus,* pg. 162
17. Sap watery; twigs slender 18
   18. Leaves 0.5–0.7 in. long . . . . .bluewood, *Condalia,* pg. 388
   18. Leaves 1–7 in. long . . . . .buckthorn, *Rhamnus,* pg. 389
19. Leaves nearly round; margin with widely spaced bristlelike teeth . . . .
   . . . . .snowbell, *Styrax,* pg. 451
19. Leaves much longer than wide; margin entire or with rounded teeth 20
   20. Lateral twigs usually spiny . . . . .bumelia, *Bumelia,* pg. 443
   20. Lateral twigs not spiny 21
21. Leaves hairless below . . . . .persimmon, *Diospyros,* pg. 215
21. Leaves very hairy below . . . . .anacahuita, *Cordia,* pg. 195

SUBKEY K. LEAVES ALTERNATE, SIMPLE, DECIDUOUS, NOT LOBED, TOOTHED

1. Leaves unequal at base with 6–10 coarse rounded teeth on each side . . . .
   . . . . .witchhazel, *Hamamelis,* pg. 321
1. Leaves otherwise 2
   2. Fruit a nut, partly or completely enclosed by scaly cap or spiny bur 3
   2. Fruit not a nut, or if a nut not enclosed by scaly cap or spiny bur 5

3. Lateral leaf veins not strongly pinnate and not ending at the margin as a bristle . . . . .oak, *Quercus,* pg. 259

3. Lateral leaf veins prominent, pinnate, and ending at the margin as a bristle 4

    4. Terminal bud present . . . . .beech, *Fagus,* pg. 255

    4. Terminal bud absent . . . . .chestnut, *Castanea,* pg. 249

5. Fruit a nut or nutlets subtended by leafy bracts or borne in a cone 6

5. Fruit a samara, capsule, pome, or drupe 10

    6. Lateral twigs developing into pronounced spur shoots . . .birch, *Betula,* pg. 177

    6. Lateral twigs more-or-less shorter versions of terminal shoots 7

7. Nutlets borne in small (0.5–1.5 in. long) woody cone . . . . . . .alder, *Alnus,* pg. 170

7. Nut or nutlet subtended by leafy bracts 8

    8. Nut 0.5–1 in. long . . . . .hazelnut, *Corylus,* pg. 189

    8. Nutlet 0.1–0.2 in. long 9

9. Nutlet enclosed in bladderlike sac . . . . .hophornbeam, *Ostrya,* pg. 190

9. Nutlet subtended by 3-lobed leafy bract . . . . .hornbeam, *Carpinus,* pg. 188

    10. Fruit a capsule 11

    10. Fruit a samara, pome, or drupe 13

11. Terminal bud present . . . . .cottonwood, *Populus,* pg. 421

11. Terminal bud absent 12

    12. Capsules borne in spikes or aments . . . . .willow, *Salix,* pg. 436

    12. Capsules borne in large clusters (panicles) . .sourwood, *Oxydendrum,* pg. 223

13. Fruit a waferlike samara . . . . .elm, *Ulmus,* pg. 467

13. Fruit a pome or drupe 14

    14. Fruit a nutlike drupe attached to a straplike leafy bract . . . . .basswood, *Tilia,* pg. 457

    14. Fruit otherwise 15

15. Leaves with gland-tipped teeth . . . . .planertree, *Planera,* pg. 467

15. Leaves not gland-tipped 16

    16. Sap milky . . . . .mulberry, *Morus,* pg. 366

    16. Sap watery 17

17. Terminal bud absent 18

17. Terminal bud present 19

    18. Leaves white hairy below, at least along the veins . .snowbell, *Styrax,* pg. 451

    18. Leaves hairless below . . . . .buckthorn, *Rhamnus,* pg. 389

19. Twig pith chambered 20

19. Twig pith solid 21

    20. Leaves leathery; fruit smooth . . . . .sweetleaf, *Symplocos,* pg. 453

    20. Leaves thin; fruit 2–4 winged . . . . .silverbell, *Halesia,* pg. 451

21. Leaf scars with 1 bundle scar . . . . .holly, *Ilex,* pg. 166

21. Leaf scars with 3 bundle scars 22

    22. Fruit a drupe . . . . .cherry, *Prunus,* pg. 402

    22. Fruit a pome 23

23. Twigs with sharp thorns that lack leaves . . . . .hawthorn, *Crataegus,* pg. 397

23. Twigs without thorns or with thorns with leaves 24

    24. Fruit pear-shaped . . . . .pear, *Pyrus,* pg. 413

    24. Fruit spherical 25

25. Pome over 0.7 in. long . . . . .crab apple, *Malus,* pg. 400

25. Pome 0.3–0.5 in. long . . . . .serviceberry, *Amelanchier,* pg. 393

CHAPTER 2
GYMNOSPERMS

Except for tropical tree ferns, extant trees in the world belong to one of two phyla: gymnosperms (Pinophyta) or angiosperms (Magnoliophyta). Gymnosperms are characterized by the absence of an ovary. Their seeds are borne naked, generally in cones but sometimes in the open air. The name gymnosperm means naked seed. Compared to angiosperms, gymnosperms produce wood that contains fewer cell types, especially the absence or near absence of vessel elements. Gymnosperms first appear in the fossil record about 350 million years ago in the Devonian. Among vascular plants, only ferns and related families (the Pteridophytes) are more primitive.

CONIFERS: THE ORDER PINALES

Conifers are currently subdivided into two families, the Pine Family (Pinaceae) and the Cypress Family (Cupressaceae). The number of conifer families has varied over the years. In the distant past, all conifers were placed in a single family, Pinaceae. Subsequently, the Pinaceae was split into three families, Pinaceae, Cupressaceae, and Taxodiaceae. Many older tree books, including the previous edition of this manual, recognize these three families. Today consensus is building to recognize only two families by expanding the Cupressaceae to include the Taxodiaceae. Increasing evidence shows that the old Cupressaceae arose from within the Taxodiaceae.

Fourteen genera of conifers containing about 95 species are native to North America. In addition, cedar (*Cedrus*) is sometimes planted. Conifers are sometimes called evergreens or softwoods, but these names are not ideal. Some conifers, such as larch and baldcypress, are not evergreen since they shed their leaves annually. Some conifers do not have soft wood. Longleaf pine, for example, sometimes has a wood density comparable to white ash or red oak.

THE CYPRESS FAMILY: CUPRESSACEAE

The Cypress Family contains about 120 species in 25–30 genera growing throughout the world in both the Northern and Southern Hemispheres. In our area, about 35 tree-sized species in 8 genera grow naturally. In addition, 4 exotic species are commonly cultivated. Among the species in North America, the geographic range of a few is large (e.g., eastern redcedar), but many more species have small distributions (e.g., giant sequoia, Arizona cypress, and Port Orford-cedar). No members of the Cypress Family have immense transcontinental ranges, unlike some members of the Pine Family.

The Cypress Family usually contains trees but some are shrubs. The leaves are linear or scalelike, often contain resin glands, are generally evergreen but deciduous in baldcypress (*Taxodium*), and are usually spiral or decussate. Reproductive parts are produced in unisexual cones, but both sexes may (monoecious) or may not (dioecious) be present on each tree. Male cones are simple with overlapping scales that bear two to ten pollen sacs on the underside. Female cones are compound with either overlapping or adjacent scales, and they are wind pollinated. Each female scale bears 1–20 winged or wingless seeds that mature in one to two years. The female scale and bract are fused into a single structure. Economically, the Cypress Family provides lumber, paneling, shingles, shakes, siding, furniture, landscaping mulch, pet bedding, and flavoring for gin. The heartwood of most genera is aromatic, either killing insects or resisting termite and fungal attack.

Members of the Cypress Family are often commonly called cedar. Based upon consistency, these common names are unfortunate because true cedars belong to the genus *Cedrus*, a member of the Pine Family. To complicate matters, the name cedar is also applied not only to tropical hardwoods (some Meliaceae and Fabaceae) but also to other gymnosperms (*Torreya*) and even to lichens (*Cetraria*). The name cedar is traditional in the Cypress Family, but it is not very discriminating.

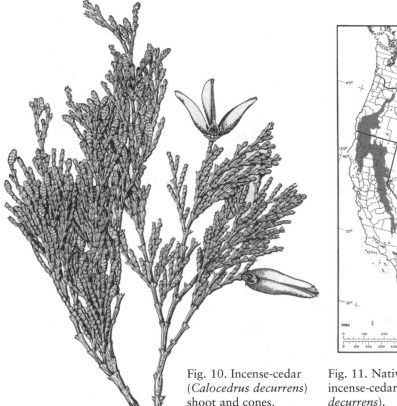

Fig. 10. Incense-cedar (*Calocedrus decurrens*) shoot and cones.

Fig. 11. Native range of incense-cedar (*Calocedrus decurrens*).

INCENSE-CEDAR: THE GENUS *CALOCEDRUS*

The genus *Calocedrus* contains three species worldwide, but only one occurs in the region covered by this manual. Members of this genus are large evergreen trees, having scalelike whorled leaves with resin glands. Reproductive structures are contained in unisexual cones, and each tree contains both sexes (monoecious). Female cones are flat scaled and wind pollinated and mature in one year. The wind-dispersed seeds have two large lateral wings of different sizes. The wood is nonporous and very resistant to decay.

Incense-cedar, Pencil-cedar

Calocedrus decurrens (Torr.) Florin (fig. 10)

Nomenclature. Older manuals place this species in the genus *Libocedrus*, a genus now applied only to trees of New Caledonia and New Zealand following subdivision of the genus.

Form. Excurrent, medium-sized tree growing 80–120 ft in height and 3–4 ft in diameter (largest known 230 ft by 13 ft); bole tapering often fluted at base, covered for up to half its length with branches.

Leaves. Whorled in fours; much longer than wide; facial leaves flattened; lateral leaves keeled and almost sheathing the facial leaves; lustrous; oblong-ovate; 0.1–0.5 in. long; persisting 3–5 years; glandular; aromatic when crushed; long-decurrent at base.

Cones. Male cones oblong; light brown. Young female cones oblong; yellow-green. Mature female cones pendent; 0.7–1.5 in. long; oblong; red-brown; 6-scaled; outer scales reflexed at maturity. Seeds 0.3–0.5 in. long; 2 per scale; straw colored.

Twigs. Slender; flattened; covered with leaves when young; often held vertically.

Bark. On young trees, thin, smooth or scaly, gray-green. On old trees becoming 3–8 in. thick, yellow-brown to cinnamon-red, divided into long, rectangular ridges separated by deep furrows.

Wood. Valuable commercially. Sapwood white. Heartwood red-brown to brown, sometimes with purple tint; pungent odor; even grained; lightweight. Used for posts, shakes, siding, landscape timbers, woodenware, interior trim, sashes, mothproof chests and closets, and doors. Principal current source of wood used in pencils.

Natural History. Tolerant of shade. Slow growing; lacking the spring growth flush typical of many trees. Characterized by almost continuous shoot growth that proceeds in different seasons at different rates. Reaches maturity in 300 years (extreme age 900 years). Reproduction abundant; seed production dependable with heavy seed crops every 3–6 years. Root system moderately deep. Wildfire, mistletoe, and pecky rot cause the most damage. Found on a wide variety of soils, including serpentine, because it is able to absorb calcium and phosphorus while excluding extra magnesium. Tolerant of dry summers. Found almost always as a canopy subdominant in mixed stands with sugar pine, ponderosa pine, Jeffrey pine, western white pine, white fir, giant sequoia, and Douglas-fir.

Range. See figure 11. Elevation: 200–9,700 ft.

WHITECEDAR OR FALSECYPRESS: THE GENUS *CHAMAECYPARIS*

This genus contains six or seven species in the world, but only three are native to our region. Two Japanese species are cultivated and rarely escape, hinoki (*Chamaecyparis obtusa*) and sawara (*Chamaecyparis pisifera*).

Trees in this genus have evergreen, scalelike, decussate leaves. The reproductive structures are borne in unisexual cones. Both sexes are found on the same tree (monoecious) but generally on different branches. Female cones are spherical, wind pollinated, mature in one or two years, and have peltate scales. Each seed has two lateral wings. The genus *Chamaecyparis* is sometimes merged with the genus *Cupressus*.

KEY TO WHITECEDARS

1. Leaves green, lacking white markings . . . . .Go to 2
1. Leaves on the undersides of branches with white markings . . . . Go to 3
    2. Female cone 0.2 in. long; Maine to Mississippi . . . .
    . . . . .Atlantic whitecedar, *Chamaecyparis thyoides*
    2. Female cone 0.2–0.5 in. long; Pacific Northwest . . . .
    . . . . .Alaska-cedar, *Chamaecyparis nootkatensis*
3. Leaves conspicuously glandular on the back . . . .
    . . . . Port Orford-cedar, *Chamaecyparis lawsoniana*
3. Leaves without glands or glands indistinct 4
    4. Female cones 0.3–0.4 in. long; orange-brown . . . .
    . . . . .hinoki-cypress, *Chamaecyparis obtusa*
    4. Female cones 0.2 in. long; dark brown . . . . . .sawara, *Chamaecyparis pisifera*

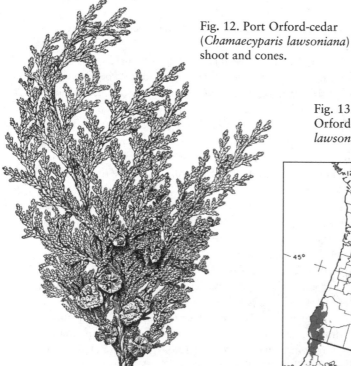

Fig. 12. Port Orford-cedar
(*Chamaecyparis lawsoniana*)
shoot and cones.

Fig. 13. Native range of Port Orford-cedar (*Chamaecyparis lawsoniana*).

Port Orford-cedar, Lawson-cypress

Chamaecyparis lawsoniana (A. Murr.) Parl. (fig. 12)

Nomenclature. Numerous cultivars have been developed where it is sold under the name Port Orford-cypress or Lawson-cypress.

Form. Large excurrent tree growing 140–180 ft in height and 4–6 ft in diameter (largest known 230 ft by 16 ft). Bole clear; often fluted at base. Crown short-conical with many branches.

Leaves. Scalelike; blunt; 0.1 in. long; entire; yellow-green to blue-green; glandular; distinctive x-pattern to the white stomate bands on leaves on the undersides of branches.

Cones. Male cones oblong; bright red. Female cone 0.3–0.5 in. long; spherical; red-brown to purple-brown; sometimes white-waxy; not resinous; maturing in 1 year; persist long after the seed is released. Scales decussate; 6–8. Umbo thin, acute, reflexed. Seeds 0.1 in. long; 2–5 per scale; ovoid; chestnut-brown. Seed wings broad.

Twigs. Slender; flattened; leaf covered when young; forming horizontal feathery sprays.

Bark. Grows 6–10 in. thick; red-brown to silver-brown; thin and scaly on young trees; fibrous and furrowed on old trees.

Wood. Valuable commercially. Sapwood nearly white. Heartwood yellow-white to yellow-brown; sapwood and heartwood often not distinct. Gingerlike odor when fresh cut; very durable; moderately lightweight; easily worked. Used for sashes, interior trim, boat planking, arrowshafts, and woodenware. Used to line closets, because of a reputed value in repelling moths; but new closets should first be aired to reduce condensation of volatile oils on buttons and closet hardware. Recent cutting rates far exceed growth. Formerly used for battery separators. The Japanese buy most sawlogs, because the wood resembles their native Hinoki-cypress. Coupled with a limited source high demand makes Port Orford-cedar lumber more expensive than any other western species.

Natural History. Moderately tolerant of shade; able to grow in either full sunlight or partial shade. Growth rate moderate; reaches maturity in 250–300 years (extreme age 560 years). Reproduction aggressive on disturbed sites. Seed released from cones throughout the year. Seed wings may be more effective in water dispersal than wind dispersal; about 50 percent of seed is sound. Large seed crops every 3–5 years.

A serious root rot disease (*Phytophthora*) was introduced about 1952. Carried by water or mud on vehicle tires, the deadly disease has spread rapidly decimating many stands. Since naturally resistant trees and effective management treatments have not been identified, the future of this useful species is not clear. Restricted to soils with constant water seepage, it develops best in places with moisture-laden winds. It grows in pure stands in Coos County, Oregon, but in other places grows mixed with Douglas-fir, Sitka spruce, western red-cedar, western hemlock, white fir, and red alder. Over 240 cultivars have been developed from this species.

Range. See figure 13. Elevation: sea level–5,000 ft.

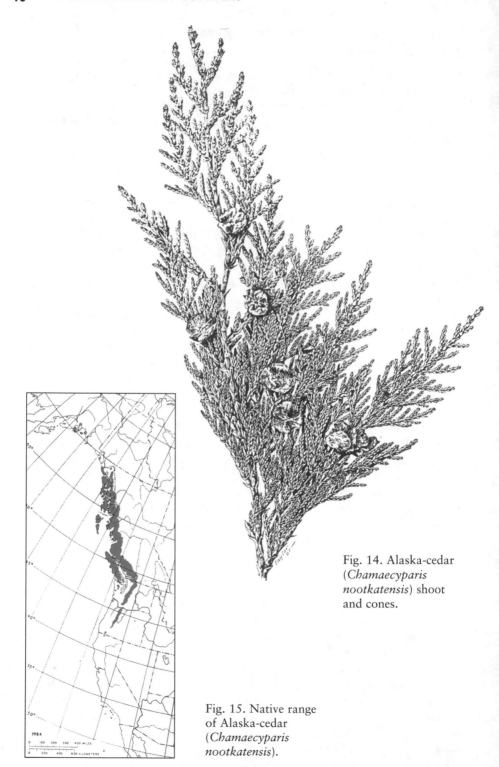

Fig. 14. Alaska-cedar
(*Chamaecyparis
nootkatensis*) shoot
and cones.

Fig. 15. Native range
of Alaska-cedar
(*Chamaecyparis
nootkatensis*).

Alaska-cedar, Alaska yellow-cedar

Chamaecyparis nootkatensis (D. Don) Spach (fig. 14)

Nomenclature. A recent proposal classifies this species and a newly discovered conifer in Vietnam in a new genus, *Xanthocyparis*, in which case Alaska-cedar would be called *Xanthocyparis nootkatensis*. Numerous cultivars have been developed.

Form. Excurrent medium-sized tree growing 75–125 ft in height and 2–3 ft in diameter (largest known 200 ft by 14 ft); shrublike at timberline. Bole clear; fluted at base. Crown conical; branches drooping.

Leaves. Scalelike; acute; 0.1 in. long; blue-green to gray-green; prickly; persisting 2–3 years; occasionally with glands; emitting pungent odor when bruised. Leaf tips slightly reflexed.

Cones. Male cones bright yellow. Immature female cones green with purple dots; soft. Mature female cones spherical; 0.2–0.5 in. long; yellow-green with brown dots; hard; white-waxy; resinous; maturing in 1 year in the southern portions of the distribution and 2 years in the northern portions. Cone scales decussate, 4–6; 2–4 seeds. Umbo pointed. Seeds 0.2 in. long; broad wings.

Twigs. Pendulous; limp.

Bark. Thin; gray-brown; scaly on young trees; fibrous with crisscrossing flat ridges on old trees; ridges sometimes spiraling down the tree.

Wood. Valuable commercially; extremely durable; moderately heavy; even-grained. Sapwood white to yellow-white. Heartwood bright yellow, darkening over time; fresh-cut wood smells like raw potatoes. Used for boats, sashes, poles, marine pilings, doors, canoe paddles, oars, interior trim, marine buoys, acid tanks, and sounding boards for musical instruments. Used by Native Americans for making ceremonial masks. Most high-quality logs are exported to Japan.

Natural History. Tolerant of shade. One of the slowest-growing conifers in the West; reaches maturity in 600 years (extreme age not known, possibly 3,500 years). Because of the slow growth little interest exists in managing the species. Reproduction sparse; small amounts of seed produced each year; heavy crops produced every 4–5 years; only 10–30 percent of the seed is sound. Low branches in contact with the soil may root (layering). Since 1880 at least, Alaska-cedar has suffered severe decline in southeast Alaska. The cause is not understood, but it is thought to be abiotic. Found on moist sites in generally thin organic soils overlying bedrock. Occurs sometimes in pure stands, but more commonly mixed with western hemlock, Pacific silver fir, noble fir, Sitka spruce, western redcedar, subalpine fir, western white pine, Engelmann spruce, and mountain hemlock.

Hybrids. Hybridizes with Monterey cypress to produce Leyland cypress (x *Cupressocyparis leylandii*), a common ornamental tree.

Range. See figure 15. Grows from sea level in Alaska to 7,500 ft in the Cascades.

Fig. 16. Atlantic whitecedar
(*Chamaecyparis thyoides*)
shoot and cone.

Fig. 17. Native range of
Atlantic whitecedar
(*Chamaecyparis thyoides*).

Atlantic whitecedar, Southern whitecedar
Chamaecyparis thyoides (L.) B.S.P. (fig. 16)

Form. Excurrent small to medium-sized tree growing 60–80 ft in height and 1–2 ft in diameter (largest known 120 ft by 5 ft). Bole clear of branches, cylindrical. Crown conical; often short.

Leaves. Scalelike; 0.1 in. long; blue-green; keeled; glandular.

Cones. Male cones yellow; scales peltate. Mature female cones spherical; 0.2–0.3 in. long; purple to red-brown; sometimes white-waxy; maturing in 1 year. Scales 5–7. Umbo pointed; reflexed. Seeds 0.1 in. long; slightly compressed; 1–2 per scale.

Bark. Thin; gray to red-brown; fibrous with intersecting flat ridges; sometimes spiraling along the stem.

Wood. Very valuable commercially but little remains. Sapwood white. Heartwood light brown tinged with red; aromatic; slightly oily; decay resistant; even-grained; lightweight; overall similar to northern whitecedar. Used for posts, poles, shingles, shakes, siding, and water tanks. A long-time favorite for East Coast boat builders but the supply is nearly exhausted.

Natural History. Moderately tolerant of shade. Slow growing; reaches maturity in 150–200 years (extreme age 1,000 years). Reproduction vigorous on bare soil or rotting wood. Seed production begins at age 3–5 years; adequate seed crops produced most years; seed viability highly variable from 10–90 percent. Seedlings and saplings sprout from suppressed buds. Roots shallow. Windthrow and wildfire cause the most damage. Found mostly in swamps and bogs in muck soils but sometimes in wet sand. Grows in dense, even-aged, pure stands or mixed with red maple, sweetbay, pondcypress, pond pine, swamp blackgum, titi, and redbay. White-tailed deer browse the foliage.

Varieties. Populations along the Gulf Coast are sometimes separated as var. *henryae* because the bark is smoother, the leaves are more appressed and often lack glands, and the cones and seeds are slightly larger. Some authors recognize these same populations as a distinct species, *Chamaecyparis henryae*.

Range. See figure 17. Elevation generally from 3-350 ft but one stand in New Jersey occurs at 1,500 ft.

CYPRESS: THE GENUS *CUPRESSUS*

The genus *Cupressus* contains 10–26 species found naturally in the Northern Hemisphere, but only 7 species occur in our region. Our species all grow in western states in small disjunct populations. Considerable disagreement exists on how our trees should be classified, and additional study is needed. The treatment here is conservative; as many as 15 species have been proposed. Italian cypress (*Cupressus sempervirens*), native to the Mediterranean region, is sometimes cultivated in the warmer parts of our region because of the pleasing upright form.

Cypresses are either trees or shrubs. The leaves are evergreen, decussate, scale-like, and often glandular. The reproductive parts are borne in unisexual cones, and both sexes occur on each tree (monoecious). Female cones contain 4–14 peltate scales each containing 2–20 seeds. They are wind pollinated. The seeds are laterally winged, and they mature in one or two seasons. The wood is nonporous, aromatic, light colored, and durable.

KEY TO CYPRESSES

1. Leaves white-waxy, pale blue to silver-green . . . . .Go to 2
1. Leaves dark or bright green . . . . Go to 4
    2. Twigs bright red . . . . .Tecate cypress, *Cupressus guadalupensis*
    2. Twigs brown or gray 3
3. Leaves with conspicuous resinous gland . . . Arizona cypress, *Cupressus arizonica*
3. Leaves with inconspicuous dry gland . . . . . . .Sargent cypress, *Cupressus sargentii*
    4. Leaves conspicuously glandular on back 5
    4. Leaves without glands or obscurely glandular 6
5. Cones with prominent hornlike umbos . .MacNab cypress, *Cupressus macnabiana*
5. Cones with short, conical umbos . . . . .Modoc cypress, *Cupressus bakeri*
    6. Cones with 6–8 scales; 0.5–0.7 in. long . .Gowen cypress, *Cupressus goveniana*
    6. Cones with 8–14 scales; 0.7–1.5 in. long 7
7. Cone scale umbo thick; native . . . . . . .Monterey cypress, *Cupressus macrocarpa*
7. Cone scale umbo thin; planted ornamental . . . .
    . . . . .Italian cypress, *Cupressus sempervirens*

Fig. 18. Gowen cypress (*Cupressus goveniana*) shoot and cones.

Arizona cypress
Cupressus arizonica Greene

Form. Excurrent tree growing 50–60 ft in. height and 1–2 ft in diameter (largest known 80 ft by 4 ft). Bole short, limby, sharply tapering. Crown dense; very conical.

Leaves. Scalelike; pointed, 0.1 in. long; silver-green to gray-green; conspicuous pit-like resin glands; releasing skunklike odor when bruised.

Cones. Male cones oblong; yellow. Mature female cone nearly spherical; 0.7–1 in. wide; gray; on stout stalks; maturing after 2 years, but persisting for many years. Scales 6–8. Umbo stout; raised; incurved. Seeds 0.1 in. long; 6–20 per scale; oblong to triangular; light or dark brown; sometimes white-waxy; laterally winged. Seed wings thin; narrow.

Twigs. Square in cross section; dark gray. Terminal buds minute; naked.

Bark. Loose gray or purple scales on young trees and branches; flaking off to reveal the nonweathered inner bark of red-purple or yellow-green creating a mottled appearance. Fibrous and furrowed on old trees; dark red-brown or gray.

Wood. The only cypress utilized for wood production. Slightly aromatic; durable. Sapwood straw colored. Heartwood light brown; lightweight, splitting easily; used locally for fence posts and mine timbers.

Natural History. Tolerant of shade throughout life; slow growing; reaches maturity in 200–300 years (extreme age 400 years). Reproduction sparse, even though seeds are produced every year, because the harsh environment allows few seedlings to become established. Best growth on moist, gravelly, north-facing slopes; but also found on dry, rocky sites. Planted as an ornamental.

Varieties. Bark differences have been used by some authors to delineate 4 varieties.

Range. Most of the geographic range occurs in Mexico, but is found in scattered areas in extreme southern Texas, southern New Mexico, central and southern Arizona, and southern California. Elevation: 4,500–8,000 ft.

Modoc cypress, Baker cypress
Cupressus bakeri Jepson

Excurrent tree growing to 90 ft in height. Leaves scalelike; slightly white-waxy; conspicuous pitlike resin gland. Female cones spherical; 0.5–1 in. long; gray; generally covered with resin blisters. Umbo raised; prominent. Rare; the conservation of this species is a matter of concern. Found in scattered areas in southern Oregon and northern California. Elevation: 3,600–6,600 ft in mixed evergreen forests.

Gowen cypress
Cupressus goveniana Gordon (fig. 18)

Shrub or small tree growing to 30 ft in height. Leaves scalelike; green not white-waxy; very small or no resin glands. Female cones spherical; 0.4–1.2 in. long; gray-brown. Umbo flat, not raised. This species is sometimes subdivided into 3 varieties or 3 distinct species. Found in scattered coastal areas of central and northern California. Elevation: 200–2,600 ft on dry soils.

Tecate cypress

Cupressus guadalupensis var. *forbesii* (Jepson) Little

Shrub or small tree growing to 30 ft in height. Leaves scalelike; with inconspicuous dry gland. Female cones spherical; 1–1.4 in. long; brown. Umbo flat or raised. Grows in chaparral. Rare; the conservation of this variety is a concern. The typical variety grows only on Guadalupe Island, Baja California, Mexico. Found in scattered areas of southwestern California, and south into Baja California. Elevation: 1,500–3,300 ft.

MacNab cypress

Cupressus macnabiana A. Murray (fig. 19)

Small tree growing to 30 ft in height. Leaves scalelike; sometimes white-waxy with a conspicuous pitlike gland that produces resin. Female cones spherical; 0.6–1 in. long; brown or gray. Umbo erect; conic. Grows in chaparral or woodland forests. Often found on serpentine soils. Hybridizes with Sargent cypress. Found in scattered areas in northern California. Elevation: 1,000–2,800 ft.

Fig. 19. MacNab cypress
(*Cupressus macnabiana*)
shoot and cones.

Fig. 20. Monterey cypress
(*Cupressus macrocarpa*)
shoot and cones.

Monterey cypress

Cupressus macrocarpa Hartweg (fig. 20)

Deliquescent tree growing to 80 ft in height. Leaves scalelike; dark green, not white-waxy; lacking glands or with small, inconspicuous glands that do not produce resin. Female cones oblong; 1–2 in. long; gray-brown. Umbo nearly flat. Commonly planted because of the graceful crown shape. Hybridizes with Alaska-cedar to produce Leyland cypress, a fast-growing ornamental tree. Rare in nature on coastal bluffs; known only in 2 areas near Monterey, California; also naturalized along the Pacific coast and in subtropical areas around the world.

Sargent cypress

Cupressus sargentii Jepson

Excurrent or deliquescent tree or shrub growing 20–80 ft in height. Leaves scalelike; often white-waxy with inconspicuous dry glands. Female cones spherical; 0.7–1 in. long; gray or brown; scattered resin blisters. Umbo small; inconspicuous. Grows in chaparral, woodland, and montane forests; may grow on serpentine soils. Hybridizes with MacNab cypress. Found in western California. Elevation: 700–3,600 ft.

JUNIPER: THE GENUS *JUNIPERUS*

The genus *Juniperus* contains about 60 species of trees and shrubs widely scattered through the Northern Hemisphere. Only 11 tree-sized species are indigenous to our region. Only eastern redcedar is commercially valuable. Identifying junipers is sometimes difficult, because the distinguishing characters are small and slight. This situation has contributed to taxonomic confusion especially in the claims of hybridization.

Juniper leaves are evergreen, scalelike or awl shaped, and decussate or whorled. Except for common juniper, scalelike leaves are found on mature branches while awl shaped leaves occur on young branches. In common juniper, all leaves are awl shaped. Branchlets are held at various angles, but never in flat sprays. The reproductive parts occur in unisexual cones, and most trees contain only one sex (dioecious). Female cones are wind pollinated. Each scale bears one to three wingless seeds. Female cones mature in one to two years, and the scales become fleshy or leathery. Resembling a berry, the cones are dispersed by animals, especially birds. This characteristic possibly explains the large distribution of several members of this genus. The aromatic heartwood is nonporous and very durable.

KEY TO JUNIPERS

1. Leaves all awl shaped; shrub to small tree . .common juniper, *Juniperus communis*
1. Leaves on mature branches scalelike, but awl shaped on juvenile shoots . . .Go to 2
    2. Bark thick, square plates . . . . .alligator juniper, *Juniperus deppeana*
    2. Bark fibrous and shaggy 3
3. Cone bright red to brown, covered with white wax 4
3. Cone blue to blue-black 8

4. Cone red or copper-red . . . . .Pinchot juniper, *Juniperus pinchotii*
4. Cone dull blue-brown to purple-brown 5
5. Seeds 4–12 per cone; branchlets drooping . . . .drooping juniper, *Juniperus flaccida*
5. Seeds 1–2 per cone; branchlets seldom drooping 6
 6. Cone 0.1–0.3 in. diameter; maturing in 1 year . . . .
 . . . . .one-seed juniper, *Juniperus monosperma*
 6. Cone 0.2–0.7 in. diameter; maturing in 2 years .7
7. Leaves in whorls of threes, rarely opposite; California . . . .
. . . . .California juniper, *Juniperus californica*
7. Leaves opposite, rarely in threes; Rocky Mountains . . . .
. . . . .Utah juniper, *Juniperus osteosperma*
 8. Leaf margin smooth; heartwood red 9
 8. Leaf margin with minute teeth (as seen under hand lens); heartwood brown .10
9. Cone maturing in 2 years; western . . . .
. . . . .Rocky Mountain juniper, *Juniperus scopulorum*
9. Cone maturing in 1 year; eastern . . . . .eastern redcedar, *Juniperus virginiana*
 10. Cone with 2–3 thick-shelled seeds; maturing in 2 years . . . .
 . . . . .western juniper, *Juniperus occidentalis*
 10. Cone with 1–2 thin-shelled seeds, maturing in 1 year 11
11. Seeds 1 (rarely 2); leaves gray-green; Nevada to California . . . .
. . . . .one-seed juniper, *Juniperus monosperma*
11. Seeds 1–2; leaves blue-green; Missouri to Texas and Mexico . . . .
. . . . .Ashe juniper, *Juniperus ashei*

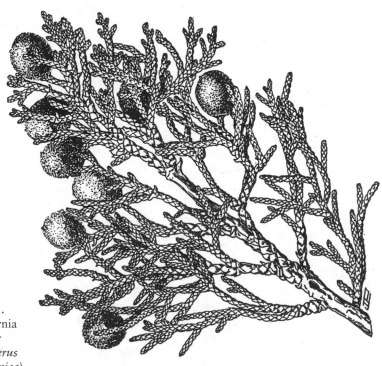

Fig. 21.
California
juniper
(*Juniperus
californica*)
shoot and
fleshy cones.

Ashe juniper
Juniperus ashei Buchholz

Small tree growing to 40 ft in height. Leaf glands dome shaped. Cones dark blue; white-waxy. Found on rocky bluffs and limestone glades in Missouri, Arkansas, Oklahoma, Texas (mostly), and south into Mexico.

California juniper
Juniperus californica Carr. (fig. 21)

Small deliquescent tree growing to 30 ft in height. Leaves scalelike; conspicuously glandular on back. Margin denticulate. Mature female cone spherical; blue-brown; white-waxy; 0.4–0.7 in. long; maturing in 1 year. Seeds 1–2 per cone. Grows on dry, rocky slopes and flats. Found largely in California but also in extreme southern Utah, western Arizona, and south into Baja California.

Common juniper
Juniperus communis L. (fig. 22)

Small tree growing to 30 ft in height. Leaves awl-like in whorls of 3; sometimes white-waxy; elongated glands on back. Mature seed cones spherical to ovoid; 0.2–0.5 in. diameter; blue-black; white-waxy; maturing in 2 years; used to flavor gin. Var. *depressa* is distinguished from the typical variety by the upturned leaves and a shrubby habit. Found in New England and the Lake States, north into Canada, and south to South Carolina in scattered areas. Absent from the Great Plains, but found in all western states and provinces.

Fig. 22. Common juniper
(*Juniperus communis*)
shoot and fleshy cones.

Alligator juniper
Juniperus deppeana Steud.

Spreading shrub or small tree. Crown broad. Leaves scalelike; 0.1 in. long; acute; blue-green; conspicuously glandular. Margin toothed. Cones unisexual with both sexes found on each tree (monoecious). Mature female cone white-waxy; dark red-brown; 0.3–0.5 in. long; maturing in 2 years. Seeds distinctly grooved; 1–4 (usually 4) in each cone; conspicuously swollen on back. Bark deeply furrowed into square plates, 1–2 in. wide; red-brown. Heartwood brown. Drought resistant; grows commonly mixed with nut pines and oaks. Found in New Mexico and Arizona, and south into Mexico.

Drooping juniper
Juniperus flaccida Schlect

Small excurrent tree growing to 35 ft in height. Leaves scalelike; green; glandular. Mature female cone spherical; brown to purple-brown; white-waxy; slightly woody. Branchlets drooping. Found largely in Mexico but extending north into Big Bend National Park, Texas.

One-seed juniper
Juniperus monosperma (Engelm.) Sarg.

Small tree growing to 30 ft in height, or shrublike as a result of large branches developing from the root collar. Leaves scalelike; 0.1 in. long; acute; gray-green; denticulately fringed; usually glandular. Cone copper colored (rarely blue); white-waxy; 0.1–0.2 in. long; maturing in 1 year. Seeds ovoid; 1 (rarely 2) in each cone. Wood used locally for posts and fuelwood. Grows on dry rocky slopes in pure stands or mixed with pinyon and ponderosa pine. Found in northern and western Texas, southern Colorado, New Mexico, Arizona, and south into Mexico.

Western juniper, Sierra juniper
Juniperus occidentalis Hook (fig. 23)

Form. Moderate-sized tree growing to 30–60 ft in height (largest known 90 ft by 13 ft), but often much smaller in arid regions. Crown broad; rounded; extending nearly to ground.

Leaves. Scalelike; adjacent pairs often not overlapping; 0.1 in. long; acute or acuminate; gray-green; conspicuously glandular on back. Margin denticulate.

Cones. Unisexual with both sexes found either on each tree (monoecious) or on separate trees (dioecious). Mature female cone nearly spherical to ellipsoid; blue-black; 0.2–0.3 in. in diameter; white-waxy; resinous; maturing in 2 years. Seeds 2–3 in each cone.

Bark. Smooth on young trees. Fibrous on older trees with thin shaggy strips; red-brown to brown.

Wood. Little or no commercial value. Sapwood white; thick. Heartwood pale brown tinged with red; exceedingly durable. Used locally for fence posts, rails, and fuelwood, but sometimes for furniture, interior paneling, and novelty items.

Natural History. Intolerant of shade. Growth rate slow; reaches maturity in 200–400 years (extreme age 1,000 years). Reproduction vigorous on bare mineral soil; good seed crops occur almost every year. Seeds dispersed by birds and coyotes. Fire causes the most damage, but since most fires are suppressed the abundance of western juniper has increased. Generally found in shallow rocky soils on mountain slopes and on dry high plains. Most abundant in central Oregon. Grows in pure stands or mixed with mountain-mahogany, ponderosa pine, Jeffrey pine, lodgepole pine, and Douglas-fir.

Varieties. Found on dry slopes in California, var. *australis* has slightly larger seed cones and is mostly dioecious.

Range. See figure 24.

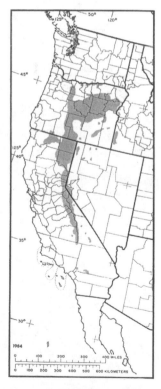

Fig. 23. Western juniper (*Juniperus occidentalis*) shoot and fleshy cones.

Fig. 24. Native range of western juniper (*Juniperus occidentalis*).

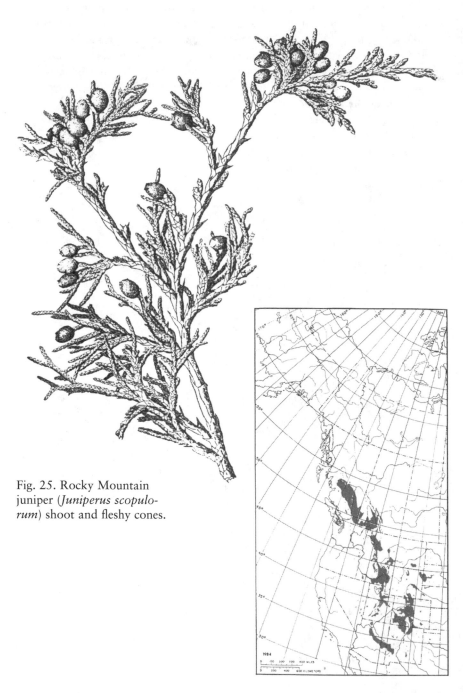

Fig. 25. Rocky Mountain
juniper (*Juniperus scopulorum*) shoot and fleshy cones.

Fig. 26. Native range of
Rocky Mountain juniper
(*Juniperus scopulorum*).

Utah juniper
Juniperus osteosperma (Torr.) Little

Spreading shrub or small tree. Bole single or many stemmed, forking immediately above the ground. Leaves scalelike; 0.1 in. long; acute; yellow-green; usually glandular. Margin minutely toothed. Usually monoecious, sometimes dioecious. Female cone white-waxy; red-brown; 0.2–0.7 in. long; maturing in 2 years. Seeds ovoid; 1 (rarely 2) in each cone; sharply angled; marked to the middle by a conspicuous white spot (hilum). Heartwood light yellow-brown; very durable; used locally for fence posts and fuelwood. Grows on dry rocky slopes in pure stands or mixed with one-seed juniper, pinyon, and desert shrubs. Found in southern Montana, Wyoming, eastern Idaho, western Colorado, Utah, Nevada, extreme northwestern New Mexico, Arizona, and eastern California.

Pinchot juniper, Redberry juniper
Juniperus pinchotii Sudw.

Older manuals may include *Juniperus erythrocarpa*, a tree now believed to be simply a Pinchot juniper with unusually red cones. Large shrub or small tree. Leaves scalelike; decussate, barely overlapping the adjacent pair; yellow-green; elliptical glands with white resin exudate. Mature female cone spherical to ovoid; copper-red; not white-waxy; not resinous; maturing in 1 year. Seeds 1 (rarely 2) per cone. Found in Texas (mostly), western Oklahoma, and southeastern New Mexico.

Rocky Mountain juniper
Juniperus scopulorum Sarg. (fig. 25)

Form. Shrub (on exposed sites) or excurrent tree growing 40–55 ft in height and 1–2 ft in diameter. Bole sometimes forked. Crown typically irregular; rounded.

Leaves. Scalelike; 0.1 in. long; acute or acuminate; light green, dark green, or blue-green; white-waxy; glandular on back; barely overlapping the adjacent pair. Margin entire.

Cones. Unisexual with the sexes borne on separate trees (dioecious). Mature female cone blue (brown when immature); 0.2–0.3 in. in diameter; white-waxy; maturing in 2 years. Seeds 1–2 per cone; angled; grooved.

Bark. Smooth or flaky on young trees. Fibrous and shaggy on older trees, exfoliating in thin strips; brown.

Wood. Sapwood white. Heartwood dull red or bright red; durable.

Natural History. Very drought resistant. Grows in pure stands or mixed with pinyon and ponderosa pine.

Hybrids. Hybridizes with eastern redcedar.

Range. See figure 26. Largest distribution of any western juniper.

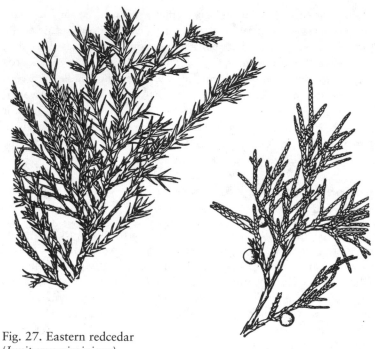

Fig. 27. Eastern redcedar
(*Juniperus virginiana*)
shoot and fleshy cone.

Fig. 28. Native range of
eastern redcedar
(*Juniperus virginiana*).

Eastern redcedar, Juniper

Juniperus virginiana L. (fig. 27)

Form. Small to medium-sized excurrent tree growing 30–40 ft in height and 1–2 ft in diameter (largest known 100 ft by 4 ft). Crown dense; pyramidal.

Leaves. On adult branches scalelike; decussate; closely appressed; dark green, blue-green, or yellow-green; acute; 0.1 in. long; glandular. Margin entire. On juvenile branches awl shaped; sharp pointed; 0.2–0.5 in. long; whorled.

Cones. Unisexual with the sexes borne on separate trees (dioecious), sometimes polygamo-dioecious. Mature female cones nearly spherical; white-waxy; dark blue; berrylike; 0.2–0.3 in. in diameter; maturing in 1 year. Seeds angled; 1–4 in each cone; requiring 1–2 years to germinate.

Twigs. Slender; square in cross section. Buds naked; minute; leaf covered.

Bark. Thin (0.1–0.2 in. thick); red-brown to gray-brown; fibrous, shaggy with long, narrow strips.

Wood. The most commercially valuable juniper. Sapwood nearly white. Heartwood purple to red sometimes streaked with included white sapwood; aromatic; very durable; easily worked; moderately heavy. Growth rings often eccentric; false rings sometimes present. Used mostly for fence posts, but also for chests, closet linings, interior trim, pencils, pet bedding, and novelty items. The wood reputedly repels moths, but the aromatic compounds released by the wood actually kill moth larvae. Cedarwood oil used in perfume. Wide defect-free lumber is increasingly scarce.

Natural History. Intermediate in tolerance to shade. Slow growing; reaches maturity in 300 years. Roots deep; many fibrous laterals. Reproduction abundant and vigorous especially in old pastures, along roads and edges of woods, along fences, under power lines, and in open hardwood stands. Some seed produced each year, but heavy seed crops occur every 2–3 years. Fire causes the most damage. Alternate host for cedar-apple rust. Adapted to a wide variety of sites, but typical of glades, thin rocky soils with frequent rock outcrops; drought resistant. Found in pure stands or mixed with Virginia pine, shortleaf pine, post oak, white oak, and hickory. Numerous ornamental cultivars have been developed; commonly planted for shelterbelts. Planted for Christmas trees and wreaths. Dense crowns provide nesting sites for songbirds. Eastern redcedar is the most widely distributed conifer in the United States.

Varieties. Found from South Carolina to eastern Texas, an ecotype of wet coastal dunes, Indian shell middens, sea islands, dredge spoil islands, abandoned rice field dikes, and low ridges separating coastal rivers, is sometimes separated as var. *silicicola*, southern redcedar. It has slightly smaller female cones, blunt leaf tips, and drooping branchlets. Southern redcedar commonly grows with live oak, laurel oak, cabbage palmetto, loblolly pine, slash pine, and redbay. Older manuals make this variety a distinct species, *Juniperus silicicola*.

Range. See figure 28.

REDWOOD: THE GENUS *SEQUOIA*

Only one species is currently classified in this genus although older manuals include a second species, giant sequoia. Redwoods are very large trees limited to the coastal fog belts of the West Coast. Reproductive parts are borne in unisexual cones, and each tree contains both sexes (monoecious). Each pollen cone scale contains two to six pollen sacs. Female cones are wind pollinated, mature in one season, and contain 15–30 peltate scales. Each scale produces two to seven seeds. Each seed has two narrow lateral wings. The wood is nonporous and very resistant to decay and termites. Older manuals place this genus in the family Taxodiaceae.

Fig. 29. Redwood
(*Sequoia sempervirens*)
shoot and cones.

Fig. 30. Native range
of redwood (*Sequoia
sempervirens*).

Redwood, California redwood, Coast redwood

Sequoia sempervirens (D. Don) Endl. (fig. 29)

Form. Excurrent tall tree commonly growing 200–275 ft in height and 8–12 ft in diameter (largest known 370 ft by 23 ft). Likely the tallest tree in the world. Reports exist of even taller Douglas-fir and eucalypt trees, but the claims cannot be documented. Crown short; irregularly conical. Bole clear; straight. Due to sprouting, multiple-stemmed trees or circles of young trees may be found growing from old stumps.

Leaves. Leaves spiral; dimorphic; usually flattened; 0.5–1 in. long; decurrent; linear; becoming gradually shorter at both ends of twigs; 2-ranked. Leaves on terminal shoots and cone-bearing branches awl-like; sharp; 0.3–0.5 in. long; held in several ranks. Persisting several years leaves and twigs shed intact. Yellow-green above; 2 white stomatal bands below. Tip acute; petiole short. Perfume is made from a leaf extract.

Cones. Male cone oblong. Female cone ovoid; pendent; 0.7–1.2 in. long; red-brown; scales wrinkled. Seeds 0.1 in. long; light brown. Seed wings as broad as seed body.

Twigs. Slender; green; smooth. Buds small; spherical; covered by acute, overlapping scales.

Bark. Fibrous with long deep furrows; 6–12 in. thick; red-brown to cinnamon-brown. Sold for landscaping mulch and insulation.

Wood. Very valuable commercially. Sapwood white. Heartwood light red to red-brown; lightweight; very durable; lacks oily materials. Used for laminated structural beams, paneling, siding, signs, outdoor furniture, blinds, caskets and coffins, cooling towers, water tanks, wine vats, greenhouses, fences, and hot tubs. A single tree yielded 480,000 board feet. Burls are sliced to produce veneer, turned into bowls and trays, or sold as novelties.

Natural History. Very tolerant of shade. Fast growing but only in full sunlight. Reaches maturity in 400–1,800 years (extreme age 2,200 years). Reproduces from seeds; prolific seed crops produced most years but seed viability is only 15 percent. Seeds lack internal dormancy and germinate shortly after falling. Sprouts from root crowns and stumps. Root system widespread. Remarkably free of biotic damaging agents; fire and catastrophic flooding cause the most damage. Restricted to a belt of abundant winter rain and summer fog in California and southern Oregon. Best development on stream bottoms, terraces, and valley slopes of rivers that flow into the Pacific Ocean. Occurs commonly in pure stands, but may be mixed with Douglas-fir, Sitka spruce, grand fir, western hemlock, tanoak, red alder, and Pacific madrone. Preservation of the remaining old-growth redwoods has long been a goal of many organizations especially since the 1960s. The only conifer with 6 sets of chromosomes (hexaploid).

Range. See figure 30. Elevation: sea level–3,000 ft.

GIANT SEQUOIA: THE GENUS *SEQUOIADENDRON*

This genus contains one species listed below found in montane forests on the west side of the Sierra Nevada. Reproductive parts are borne in unisexual cones, and both sexes occur on each tree (monoecious). Male cones contain 12–20 scales, each scale with two to five pollen sacs. Female cones are wind pollinated, mature in two years, and contain 25–45 peltate scales. Each scale contains two to nine seeds. Each seed contains two lateral wings of unequal size. This genus was split from the genus *Sequoia* about 1940, but not all authorities accept this division. Formerly classified in the family Taxodiaceae.

Giant sequoia, Bigtree, Sierra-redwood

Sequoiadendron giganteum (Lindl.) Buchholz. (fig. 31)

Nomenclature. Formerly called *Sequoia gigantea*.

Form. Excurrent tree commonly growing 250–280 ft in height and 10–15 ft in diameter (largest known 293 ft by 37 ft); the most massive tree on earth. Crown scraggly and open; flat and irregular in old trees. Bole clear with short thick branches. Often fire scarred at base.

Leaves. Spirally arranged; blue-green; dimorphic. Leaves on terminal branches lanceolate; spreading; triangular in cross section; 0.5 in. long; decurrent. Leaves on lateral and lower branches ovate; appressed and thickly covering the twig; 0.1–0.2 in. long; rigid; sharp pointed; turning brown in 2–3 years, but persisting several years.

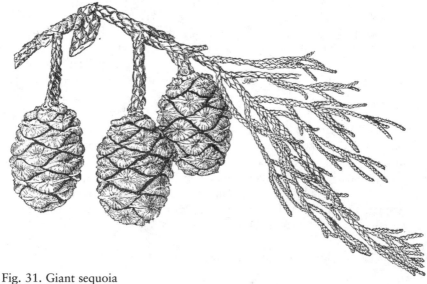

Fig. 31. Giant sequoia
(*Sequoiadendron giganteum*)
shoot and cones.

Cones. Mature female cones ovoid-oblong; pendent; 2–3.5 in. long; red-brown to brown. Reaching full size the first year but not maturing until the second year; remaining green and closed as long as 20 years. Scales wrinkled. Seeds 0.2 in. long; light brown; wings broader than seed. Seeds shed only after the cone dies or falls from the tree. Dark red pigment used in ink obtained from the cone.

Twigs. Slender; often leaf covered. Winter buds small; naked.

Bark. Fibrous; 12–24 in. thick; cinnamon-red; deeply furrowed between broad, rounded ridges.

Wood. No commercial value, because most stands are not managed for wood production. Giant sequoia stands were generally not subject to logging partly because felled trees were too large to move. Sapwood white. Heartwood dark red-brown with a purple cast; resistant to decay. Similar overall to redwood, but more brittle.

Natural History. Intermediate in tolerance of shade. Fast growing; reaches maturity in 4,000–5,000 years. Reproduction sparse; bare mineral soil needed for seed germination; does not sprout. Root system shallow with wide-spreading laterals. Few natural enemies aside from lightning and fire. Grows on a variety of soils but adequate soil moisture in summer is critical. In former geologic periods, this genus was widely scattered throughout the forests of the Northern Hemisphere. Grows with sugar pine, ponderosa pine, Jeffrey pine, white fir, red fir, and incense-cedar.

Range. Found naturally only on about 36,000 acres in 75 groves along the western slopes of the Sierra Nevada of California. Elevation: 4,600–7,000 ft.

BALDCYPRESS: THE GENUS *TAXODIUM*

This genus is found only in North America where one to three species are recognized. This manual recognizes one species with three varieties. In prehistoric times, the genus occurred much more widely in Europe and North America. The genus was formerly placed in the family Taxodiaceae.

Dawn redwood (*Metasequoia glyptostroboides*) is sometimes confused with baldcypress. Known from fossils from many places in North America and Eurasia, dawn redwood was thought to be extinct until it was found growing in China in 1945. Today it is sometimes planted in our region, and it is included in the key below. The foliage resembles baldcypress, but the twigs appear opposite. The cones resemble redwood, but they are gray-brown and not wrinkled. The base of even young trees becomes highly fluted.

Baldcypresses are large trees. The leaves are deciduous or evergreen, linear, and spirally arranged. Leaves on terminal twigs fall individually, but leaves on lateral twigs fall as a unit with the twig. Reproductive parts are borne in unisexual cones, and both sexes are present on each tree (monoecious). Male cones contain 10–20 scales, and each scale has two to ten pollen sacs. They are found in drooping clusters (panicles). Female cones are wind pollinated, mature in one season, glandular inside, and contain five to ten peltate scales. Each scale has one to two seeds. The seeds are wingless, irregularly shaped, and released when the entire cone shatters. The wood is nonporous and lacks resin ducts.

KEY TO BALDCYPRESSES

1. Small twigs opposite . . . . .dawn redwood, *Metasequoia glyptostroboides*
1. Small twigs alternate . . . . .Go to 2
   2. Leaves spreading; small twigs held at various angles . . . .
   . . . . .baldcypress, *Taxodium distichum*
   2. Leaves held at a steep upward angle, touching the twigs; small twigs held upward
   . . . . .pondcypress, *Taxodium distichum* var. *imbricarium*

Baldcypress, Southern-cypress

Taxodium distichum (L.) Rich. (fig. 32)

Form. Large excurrent tree growing 100–120 ft in height and 3–5 ft in diameter (largest known 150 ft by 17 ft). Young crown narrowly pyramidal becoming

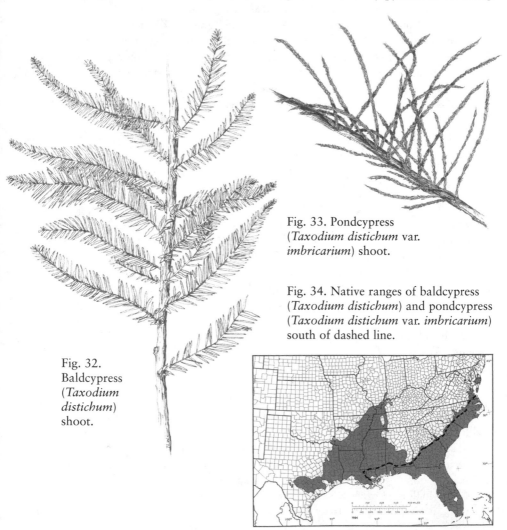

Fig. 33. Pondcypress
(*Taxodium distichum* var.
imbricarium) shoot.

Fig. 34. Native ranges of baldcypress
(*Taxodium distichum*) and pondcypress
(*Taxodium distichum* var. *imbricarium*)
south of dashed line.

Fig. 32.
Baldcypress
(*Taxodium
distichum*)
shoot.

irregular and flat topped with age. Bole strongly tapered on young trees becoming cylindrical on old trees. Base fluted. Peculiar conical or rounded upward growth of the roots, called knees, rise above the soil level and grow 1–8 ft tall.

Leaves. Linear; 0.5–1 in. long; yellow-green; mostly 2-ranked; decurrent; shorter and nearly scalelike on fertile branches. Leaves and short shoots look like small feathers. Fall color bronze.

Cones. Female cones spherical; 0.7–1 in. long; light brown; pendent. Seeds 0.7 in. long; brown; irregularly triangular in cross section. Dispersed by floating on water.

Twigs. Held at various angles. Terminal twigs bearing axillary buds and persistent; lateral twigs deciduous, with needles still attached. Buds small; nearly spherical; scales overlapping.

Bark. Thin; 1 in. thick; fibrous or slightly scaly; red-brown to ash-gray.

Wood. Extremely valuable commercially. Sapwood yellow-white merging gradually into the heartwood. Heartwood varies in color either yellow, light brown, dark brown, or almost black; dark wood more common farther south and more decay resistant; greasy; coarse grain; moderately heavy; very durable. Used for siding, beams, posts, dock and bridge timbers, railroad ties, coffins, shingles, shakes, doors, blinds, vats, silos, water tanks, greenhouses, boat planking, and bird houses. Wood of old trees riddled with friable decayed wood called pecky rot.

Natural History. Intolerant of shade. Growth rapid on imperfectly drained sites but very slow growing on sites long flooded. May form false rings. Reaches maturity in 250–300 years (extreme age 1,000–1,700 years). The oldest known trees in eastern North America, 1,700-year-old baldcypress trees were recently found along the Black River in North Carolina. Reproduces well from seed and sprouts vigorously from smaller stumps. Root system shallow; wide-spreading. Surprisingly windfirm even on wet soils. For many years the knees were thought to help aerate the root system, especially since the knees often grow slightly taller than the average high-water level. But research has failed to confirm this function. Most typical of river sloughs and oxbow lakes, where pure stands develop; becoming increasingly less common as the drainage improves in first bottoms where it is generally mixed with water tupelo, swamp blackgum, red maple, American elm, and Carolina ash. Planted as an ornamental in uplands where it may still develop knees.

Varieties. Two varieties are recognized. Var. *imbricarium*, pondcypress (fig. 33), differs in having short shoots held vertically from larger branches and leaves tightly appressed against the twigs. Pondcypress grows only in water that lacks suspended sediment like blackwater rivers, pocosins, Carolina bays, and shallow depressions in flatwoods. Pondcypress was formerly incorrectly called var. *nutans*. It is sometimes considered to be a completely separate species, *Taxodium ascendens*. Var. *mexicanum*, Montezuma baldcypress, grows in Mexico and extends north into southern Texas. It differs from typical baldcypress in having evergreen needles. This variety is also sometimes considered to be a separate species, *Taxodium mucronatum*.

Range. See figure 34.

CEDAR OR ARBORVITAE: THE GENUS *THUJA*

Worldwide *Thuja* contains five species, but only two are indigenous to our region. The other species are native to Asia. Long classified as *Thuja orientalis*, Oriental arborvitae is now generally classified separately as *Platycladus orientalis*. This widely planted exotic is locally naturalized in our region. It differs from *Thuja* by vertically held branchlets, slightly fleshy spherical cones with hooked umbos, and wingless seeds.

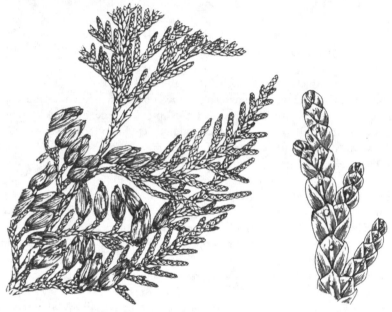

Fig. 35. Northern whitecedar
(*Thuja occidentalis*) shoot and cones.

Fig. 36. Native range of
northern whitecedar
(*Thuja occidentalis*).

Cedar trees are evergreen with decussate scalelike leaves. The branchlets are often flattened into sprays, a characteristic that helps separate this genus from others in the family. At maturity looking like small rose buds, the female cones are wind pollinated, ovoid-cylindrical, held erect, mature in one season, and contain 8–12 more-or-less flat scales. The seeds have two lateral wings of equal size. The wood is nonporous and decay resistant, and it lacks resin ducts.

KEY TO CEDARS

1. Cone spherical with hooked, hornlike umbo
. . . . .Oriental arborvitae, *Platycladus orientalis*
1. Cone oblong with minute umbo . . . . .Go to 2
    2. Leaves on the undersides of branches with white triangular splotches . . . .
    . . . . .western redcedar, *Thuja plicata*
    2. Leaves on the undersides of branches uniformly light green . . . .
    . . . . .northern whitecedar, *Thuja occidentalis*

Northern whitecedar, Arborvitae

Thuja occidentalis L. (fig. 35)

Form. Small to moderate-sized excurrent tree growing 40–60 ft in height and 1–2 ft in diameter (largest known 120 ft by 6 ft). Bole often curved and tapering abruptly. Crown dense; compact.

Leaves. Scalelike; 0.1 in. long; dull green; glandular on main shoots and sometimes elsewhere. Settlers in eastern Canada and northern New England steeped leaves in hot water to produce a tea high in vitamin C. Since the drink cured scurvy, the tree was called arborvitae, the tree of life. Cedar leaf oil used in perfume.

Cones. Flat scaled; 0.3–0.5 in. long; yellow-brown, turning brown; oblong-cylindrical. Cone apex rounded with a minute prickle. Seeds light brown; 0.2 in. long.

Bark. Thin; gray; fibrous with interconnecting flat ridges; ridges sometimes spiraling along the bole.

Wood. Sapwood yellow-white. Heartwood yellow-brown; aromatic; even grained; very lightweight. Used for posts, poles, shingles, log cabins, rustic furniture, water tanks, canoe ribs, fishnet floats, and imitation minnows.

Natural History. Moderately tolerant of shade. Slow growth rate, reaches maturity in 250–300 years (extreme age 400 years). Reproduction moderate on bare soil or decaying logs and stumps. Cone production begins at age 6–8 years; large seed crops produced every 2–5 years; seeds remain viable for only 1 year. Also reproduces by layering. Grows on a wide variety of sites, but generally found on cool, moist, nutrient-rich soils; often in seepage areas on limestone-derived soils, fens, or muck swamps; absent from very wet or very dry soils. Found in pure stands or mixed with balsam fir, black spruce, eastern larch, eastern hemlock, eastern white pine, black ash, and red maple. Probably the first North American species to be introduced to Europe. Often planted in cemeteries in the East. Provides winter cover and browse for white-tailed deer.

Range. See figure 36. Elevation: 500–2,000 ft.

Fig. 37. Western redcedar (*Thuja plicata*) shoot and cones.

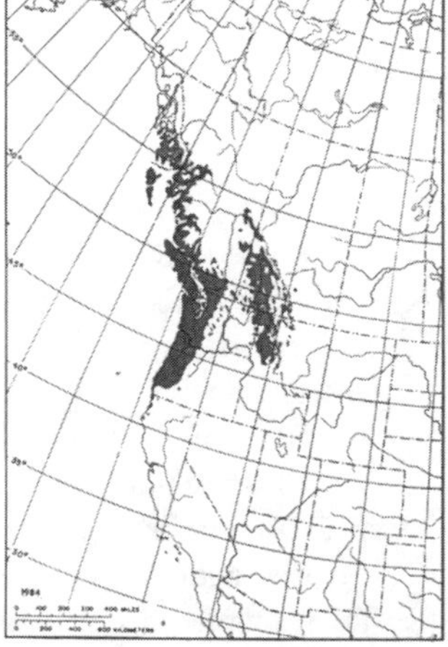

Fig. 38. Native range of western redcedar (*Thuja plicata*).

Western redcedar, Giant arborvitae

Thuja plicata Donn ex D. Don. (fig. 37)

Form. Large excurrent tree growing 150–200 ft in height and 4–8 ft in diameter (largest known 270 ft by 21 ft). Bole tapering; fluted at base; often forked toward the top. Crown irregular; with horizontal or drooping branches.

Leaves. Scalelike; lustrous; dark yellow-green; generally lacking glands; persisting 2–5 years. Leaves on the undersides of branches with triangular splotches. Facial leaves flat; grooved; lateral leaves rounded or keeled. Perfume, deodorant, insecticides, veterinary soap, and shoe polish are made from leaf oils.

Cones. Female cones terminal; dark brown; 8–12 scales but only 6 are fertile; 0.5–0.7 in. long; ovoid-oblong; spine tipped. Sometimes held pointing away from branch tips. Seeds 0.1 in. long; red-brown; lenticular. Seed wings each about as wide as seed body.

Twigs. Slender; flattened; leaf covered in drooping sprays when young.

Bark. On young trees, smooth; green; lacking resin blisters. On old trees, fibrous with narrow interlacing ridges; cinnamon-red to gray-brown. Inner bark used by Native Americans to make clothing, blankets, rope, baskets, mats, and fishing nets.

Wood. Highly valuable commercially. Sapwood yellow-white. Heartwood red to red-brown; soft; fragrant; very durable; lightweight; even grained. Used for shingles, shakes, siding, interior trim, boat planking, poles, coffins, greenhouse equipment, and outdoor decks. Nearly all wooden shingles are now made from this species. Once used extensively by Native Americans for totem poles, lodges, and dug-out seagoing boats, because the wood is easily worked with simple tools.

Natural History. Tolerant of shade. Rather slow growing; reaches maturity in 300–400 years (extreme age 1,200 years). Reproduction generally plentiful on either bare mineral soil or rotten wood; large seed crops common. Also reproduces by layering, rooting of fallen branches or branches on fallen trees. The large buttresses at the base of trees requires leaving tall stumps. Roots shallow and widespread. Fire, windthrow, and pecky heart rot cause the most damage. Found on a wide variety of soils, but typically only those with abundant moisture. Found nearly always in mixed stands with Douglas-fir, western hemlock, Sitka spruce, grand fir, Pacific silver fir, black cottonwood, bigleaf maple, and red alder. Foliage often eaten by deer and elk.

Range. See figure 38. Elevation: sea level–7,500 ft.

THE PINE FAMILY: PINACEAE

The Pine Family is the most important gymnosperm family in North America and the Northern Temperate Zone. Members of this family dominate forests that cover large areas. Worldwide about 200 species in 10 genera are known, but our region contains only about 65 native species in 6 genera. In addition, cedar (*Cedrus*) is commonly planted in the Southeast and West.

Cedrus is the true cedar. Four species occur in the world, but none are native to our region. Cedars have linear needles arranged in loose spirals on new shoots and in dense spirals or tufts on lateral spur shoots. The foliage strongly resembles larch (*Larix*), but cedar needles are evergreen, not deciduous. Mature female cones are borne upright, and they completely disintegrate (shatter) at maturity. Pollination occurs in autumn. Atlas cedar (*Cedrus atlantica*) and deodar or Himalayan cedar (*Cedrus deodara*) are widely planted in the warmer sections of the United States. Cedar-of-Lebanon (*Cedrus libani*) is much less commonly planted.

Members of this family are generally excurrent trees that live hundreds of years, and grow large or very large in size. Reproductive parts are borne in unisexual cones, and both sexes occur on each tree (monoecious). The male cone is simple, composed of spirally arranged scales that bear two pollen sacs on the underside of each scale. Female cones are compound and wind pollinated, and are composed of spirally arranged scales, each subtended by a bract. Unlike in the Cupressaceae, the scale and bract remain separate structures. Each female cone scale bears two seeds, which mature in one to three years. Most seeds have one terminal wing, which forms from the cone scale, and they are wind dispersed. Economically this family provides many products that sustain our lives or culture including lumber, plywood, pulpwood, turpentine and rosin, mulch, garlands, Christmas trees, and pine nuts. Several species are also used in shelterbelts and ornamental plantings.

FIR: THE GENUS *ABIES*

This genus contains about 40 species widely scattered through North and Central America, Europe, Asia, and northern Africa. Ten species occur in our region. Fir trees are pyramidal in shape with dense, spirelike crowns. They are often counted among the most beautiful of trees, a feeling reflected in their names noble, grand, *magnifica*, and *amabilis* (lovely).

Fir leaves are evergreen, spirally arranged, linear, sessile, single, usually flat, and blunt. They extend from all sides of the twig, but often appear two-ranked by twisting near their base. The leaves are usually grooved above with white lines (stomates) below. After falling from the twigs, they leave a smooth circular scar. This manner of leaf attachment separates fir from spruce, hemlock, and Douglas-fir. The branching on young twigs appears opposite.

Male cones are oval or cylindrical; yellow to scarlet and borne on the lower sides of lower branches. Female cones are wind pollinated, borne erect on the upper side of upper branches, and oblong. They mature in one season. The cone scales are thin and fan shaped. The cone bracts are shorter (inserted) or longer (exserted) than the cone scales, and this character is often useful for identification. Seeds are covered with resin vesicles and released when the cone disintegrates, the scales and bracts falling from the central axis that may persist for many years. The bark of younger trees is generally thin and smooth with numerous blisterlike resin pockets. The wood is nonporous and lacks resin ducts. The lumber is often mixed with hemlock and sold under the name Hem-Fir. Fir trees generally grow on moist, cool sites. They are quite tolerant of shade, and often become established beneath other trees.

KEY TO FIRS

1. Female cone bracts spiny; long exserted with a long bristle; found only in Monterey County, California . . . . .bristlecone fir, *Abies bracteata*
1. Female cone bracts not spiny tipped; exserted or included . . . . .Go to 2
   2. Needles held erect, crowded toward the upper side of the twigs 3
   2. Needles held out, spreading; not crowded, often 2-ranked 7
3. Needles flattened; dark green above, with 2 distinct white bands (stomata) on lower surface . . . . .Pacific silver fir, *Abies amabilis*
3. Needles 4-sided, white-waxy; stomata (covered with white dots) on all sides 4
   4. Needles with longitudinal groove on upper surface . . . .noble fir, *Abies procera*
   4. Needles lacking longitudinal groove on upper surface 5
5. Cone bracts exserted . . . . .Shasta red fir, *Abies magnifica* var. *shastensis*
5. Cone bracts inserted 6
   6. Needles L-shaped; twigs red-brown . . . . . . .California red fir, *Abies magnifica*
   6. Needles straight; twigs green . . . . .subalpine fir, *Abies lasiocarpa*
7. Cone bracts exserted, Southern Appalachian Mts. . . . . .Fraser fir, *Abies fraseri*
7. Cone bracts inserted 8
   8. Needles 0.7–1.7 in. long; cone scales slightly longer than broad 9
   8. Needles 1–3 in. long; cone scales slightly broader than long 11
9. Needles dark green above; 2 distinct white bands (stomata) below . . . .
   . . . . .balsam fir, *Abies balsamea*
9. Needles with white stomata on both surfaces 10
   10. Mature bark hard; smooth; gray . . . . .subalpine fir, *Abies lasiocarpa*
   10. Mature bark soft; corky; yellow-white . . . .
   . . . . .corkbark fir, *Abies lasiocarpa* var. *arizonica*
11. Needles dark green above; 2 white bands of stomata below . . . .
   . . . . .grand fir, *Abies grandis*
11. Needles gray-green; stomata on both surfaces 12
   12. Top side of needles white-waxy with 7 rows of stomata . . . .
   . . . . .white fir, *Abies concolor*
   12. Top side of needles green with 12 rows of stomata . . . .
   . . . . .Sierra white fir, *Abies lowiana*

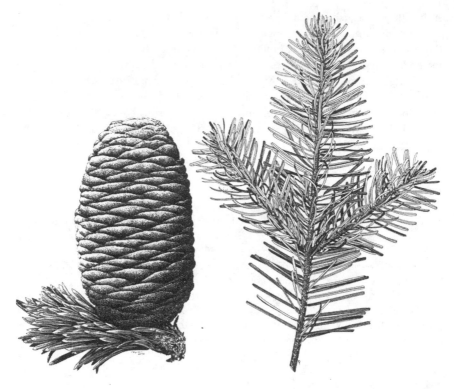

Fig. 39. Pacific silver
fir (*Abies amabilis*)
shoot and cone.

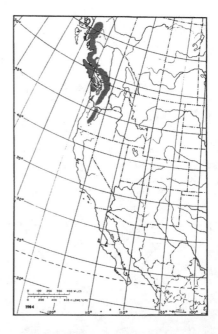

Fig. 40. Native range
of Pacific silver fir
(*Abies amabilis*).

Pacific silver fir, Silver fir

Abies amabilis Dougl. ex Forbes. (fig. 39)

Form. Excurrent tree growing 140–160 ft in height and 2–4 ft in diameter (largest known 220 ft by 8 ft). Crown spirelike or pyramidal; bole clear when forest grown, but covered to the ground with short branches when open grown.

Leaves. Linear; 0.7–1.5 in. long; held erect and out from the top and sides, but not the bottom, of the twigs; slightly pointing toward the terminal bud; flat; shiny, dark green above; grooved above; silvery white with lines of stomata below. Apex notched. Top side of leaves of fertile branches with a few silvery stomates near the apex.

Cones. Male cones red. Young female cones lustrous purple. Mature female cones 3–6 in. long; cylindric-barrel-shaped; deep purple. Scales slightly broader than long. Bracts spiny tipped; inserted. Seeds 0.5 in. long; light yellow-brown. Wings pale brown; 0.7 in. long.

Twigs. Stout; orange-brown; opposite; slightly hairy the first year, becoming red-brown. Winter buds nearly spherical; 0.2 in. long; sharp pointed; dark purple; resinous at tip.

Bark. Thin; smooth; silver-white to light gray; white blotches common; covered with resin blisters when young. Large trees become scaly.

Wood. Yellow-brown to light brown; sapwood not distinct from heartwood. Used for lumber, plywood, and pulpwood. Lumber formerly sold as larch.

Natural History. Very tolerant of shade. Growth rate moderate; reaches maturity in 250 years (extreme age 700 years). Reproduction sometimes problematic; large seed crops every 3–6 years, but many seeds are not viable. Balsam woolly adelgid, fire, windthrow, and dwarf mistletoe cause the most damage. Grows on a wide variety of sites, but best developed on deep, moist soils with southern or western exposure. Occurs in pure stands or mixed with Sitka spruce, Douglas-fir, grand fir, western hemlock, and western redcedar. Planted as an ornamental, including in Europe, because of the handsome crown shape and dense shiny foliage.

Range. See figure 40. Elevation: sea level–6,000 ft, but mostly a tree of mountains.

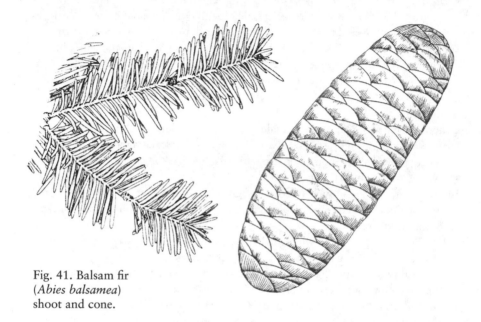

Fig. 41. Balsam fir
(*Abies balsamea*)
shoot and cone.

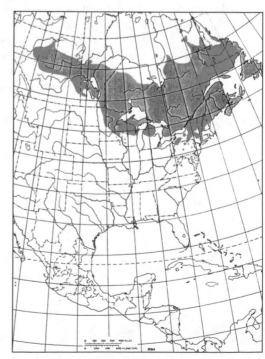

Fig. 42. Native range of
balsam fir (*Abies balsamea*).

Balsam fir, Balsam, Canadian balsam

Abies balsamea (L.) Mill. (fig. 41)

Form. Medium-sized excurrent tree growing 40–60 ft in height and 1–1.5 ft in diameter (largest known 90 ft by 3 ft). Crown dense; dark green; narrowly pyramidal with a slender spirelike tip.

Leaves. Linear; 0.7–1.5 in. long; dark green above; two white bands of stomata below; flat; tip rounded or notched. On lower branches, 2-ranked and widely spaced; On upper branches, spreading and crowded.

Cones. Male cones yellow, red, purple, or green. Female cones dark purple turning brown; 2–4 in. long; oblong-cylindric. Scales longer than broad; apex rounded. Bracts inserted. Seeds 0.2 in. long. Seed wing broad; purple-brown.

Twigs. Slender; finely hairy; often opposite; yellow-green; becoming smooth and gray to purple. Winter buds nearly spherical; resinous; 0.1–0.2 in. long; scales orange-green.

Bark. Thin; ash-gray; smooth except for numerous fragrant resin blisters on young trees. Becoming 0.5 in. thick; red-brown; breaking into thin scales. Resin in bark blisters is source of Canada balsam, used in microscope slide mounts and varnishes.

Wood. Soft; white to yellow-white. Used mostly for pulpwood and boxes, especially cheese boxes. Formerly used for sugar and butter tubs.

Natural History. Very tolerant of shade; recovering well from suppression. Short-lived tree reaches maturity in 150 years. Reproduction plentiful generally in the shade of other species. Heavy seed crops every 2–4 years. Shallow root system; branches lying on the ground sometimes take root producing new trees. Wildfire, spruce budworm, and balsam woolly adelgid cause the most damage. Found only on moist to wet soils. Found in swamps on organic soils; either in pure stands or mixed with black spruce and tamarack; also found on upland sites with mineral soils mixed with white spruce, red spruce, eastern hemlock, eastern white pine, paper birch, trembling aspen, yellow birch, and sugar maple. Used for Christmas trees, garlands, and wreaths. Dried needles used in potpourri.

Varieties. Divided into 2 varieties depending upon the length of the cone bracts and geographic location. Var. *balsamea* with a large distribution has inserted cone bracts. Var. *phanerolepis*, found only in northern Virginia and West Virginia, has the cone bracts slightly exserted and reflexed. The trees in West Virginia are sometimes called Canaan fir. The relationship of these two taxa is not settled. The latter variety has been considered a hybrid between balsam and Fraser fir or recognized as a separate species, *Abies phanerolepis*. This taxonomy probably results from changes in tree distributions following the last glacial period.

Range. See figure 42. Elevation: sea level–6,000 ft (on Mt. Washington, New Hampshire).

Bristlecone fir

Abies bracteata D. Don ex Poiteau

Excurrent tree growing 40–80 ft in height and 2–3 ft in diameter. Leaves linear; 1–2 in. long; upper surface dark green; lower surface with white stomatal bands; flat; arranged in several ranks. Apex sharp pointed. Mature female cones 3–4 in. long; purple-brown. Bracts with a long spiny bristle; much longer than the scales; not reflexed. Grows in dry coastal forests. A very aromatic resin obtained from bark blisters used by the Spanish for incense. Found only to the Santa Lucia Mountains of Monterey County, California. Elevation: 2000–3000 ft.

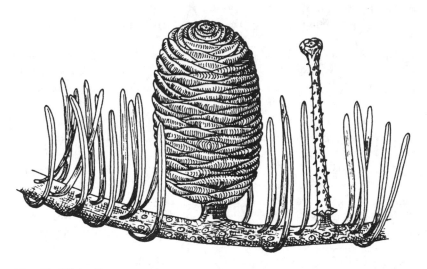

Fig. 43. White fir
(*Abies concolor*)
shoot and cone.

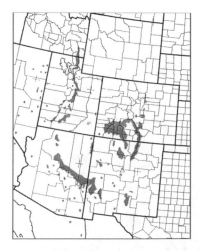

Fig. 44. Native
range of white fir
(*Abies concolor*).

White fir

Abies concolor (Gord. & Glend.) Hildebr. (fig. 43)

Form. Excurrent tree growing 120–150 ft in height and 3–4 ft in diameter (largest known 250 ft by 9 ft). Crown dense; conical; long-persisting, short branches.

Leaves. Linear; 2–3 in. long on young branches; 0.7–1.5 in. long on fertile branches and old trees; silver-blue to silver-green; white-waxy; flat; thick; slightly curved; slightly grooved above; crowded close together; 2-ranked or held upward at an angle to form a U- or V-shape; stomate lines above and below. Apex acute, rounded, or rarely notched.

Cones. Male cones red, purple, or green. Female cones 3–5 in. long; oblong; olive-green or purple. Scales hairy; much broader than long. Bracts inserted. Seeds 0.3–0.5 in. long; yellow-brown. Seed wings light red; broad.

Twigs. Moderately stout; hairless or with yellow hairs; opposite; yellow-green to brown-green when young, turning gray-brown with age. Buds nearly spherical; resinous; 0.1–0.2 in. long; yellow-brown.

Bark. Thin on young trees; gray; smooth, except for numerous resin blisters; becoming 4–7 in. thick on old trees; ash-gray; sometimes corky with deep furrows and wide ridges.

Wood. Once considered worthless, the wood is moderately valuable today. Yellow-brown to light brown; sapwood not distinct from heartwood. Used for lumber, plywood, and pulpwood.

Natural History. Tolerant of shade; moderate growth rate, reaches maturity in 250–300 years (extreme age 350 years). Reproduction generally abundant in light shade; adequate seed crops occur every 2–5 years. Requires less moisture than all other western firs; sensitive to high soil-moisture levels. Found on a wide range of soil conditions, including serpentine. Mistletoe, dwarf mistletoe, annosum root rot, and the fir engraver beetle cause the most damage. Seldom found in pure stands, usually grows mixed with ponderosa pine, lodgepole pine, Douglas-fir, Engelmann spruce, and trembling aspen. Commonly planted for Christmas trees or as ornamentals, because of the pleasing silvery foliage. Trees sold in nurseries sometimes labeled concolor fir.

Varieties. A variable species containing many geographically and genetically distinct populations. Trees in southern Oregon and California are classified as either var. *lowiana* or as a completely separate species, *Abies lowiana*. In either case, these trees differ in having longer 2-ranked needles with a notched apex.

Hybrids. Var. *lowiana* hybridizes easily with grand fir, and the separation of these two taxa is sometimes difficult. Trees difficult to classify are sometimes nick-named *grandicolor*.

Range. See figure 44. Elevation: 6,000–11,000 ft.

Fraser fir, Southern balsam, She balsam

Abies fraseri (Pursh) Poir. (fig. 45)

Fraser fir is very similar to balsam fir, except for the exserted cone scale bracts, which are strongly reflexed. See the comments provided under balsam fir. Restricted to the fog belt of the high mountains. First discovered in 1957 on Mt. Mitchell, North Carolina, the balsam woolly adelgid has caused very severe damage to older trees, but regeneration has appeared beneath the dead parents. Acid precipitation probably also causes damage. The future of Fraser fir in natural stands is uncertain. Fraser fir is commonly grown as an ornamental in the southern Appalachians, and also grown commercially for Christmas trees, garlands, and wreaths. Owing to the sensitive location of natural stands, Fraser fir is not harvested for fiber. Found naturally only in the Appalachian Mountains of southern Virginia, North Carolina, and Tennessee. Elevation: mostly above 5,000 ft.

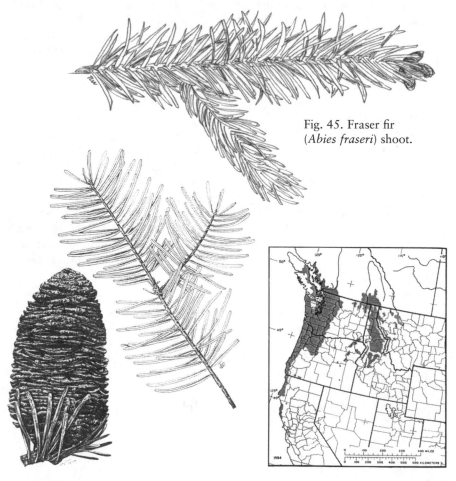

Fig. 45. Fraser fir (*Abies fraseri*) shoot.

Fig. 46. Grand fir (*Abies grandis*) shoot and cone.

Fig. 47. Native range of grand fir (*Abies grandis*).

Grand fir, Lowland white fir

Abies grandis (Dougl. ex D. Don) Lindl. (fig. 46)

Form. Excurrent tree, growing 140–160 ft in height and 2–4 ft in diameter (largest known 250 ft by 6 ft). Crown open; conical; old trees become domelike with long branches in the middle of the crown and drooping lower branches. Old trees with broken tops develop vigorous upturned branches that look like miniature trees sitting in the crown of the old tree.

Leaves. Linear; 1–2 in. long; 2-ranked or held in a wide V-shape, except on some fertile branches where the needles may be held erect; flat; lustrous; yellow-green to dark green; grooved above; 2 white stomate bands below. Apex blunt or notched.

Cones. Male cones pale yellow. Female cones light yellow-green; 2–4 in. long; cylindrical; yellow-green to green-purple. Scales broader than long. Bracts inserted. Seeds 0.4 in. long; light brown. Seed wings straw colored; about 0.7 in. long.

Twigs. Slender; yellow-green to orange-brown; opposite; slightly hairy, becoming hairless the second year. Buds nearly spherical; 0.1–0.2 in. long; brown or purple; resinous.

Bark. Thin; gray-brown; smooth, except for resin blisters; chalky white blotches on young trees. Becoming 2–3 in. thick on old trees; gray; divided into small blocky ridges separated by furrows.

Wood. Moderately valuable; yellow-brown to light brown; sapwood not distinct from heartwood. Used for lumber, plywood, and pulpwood. Has a disagreeable odor that provides the local name stinking fir.

Natural History. Moderately tolerant but less tolerant than associated firs. Growth rate fast; reaches maturity in 200–250 years (extreme age 300 years). Reproduction abundant given sufficient moisture and protection from frost. Good seed crops produced every 2–3 years; seed viability averages 50 percent. Windfirm with deep spreading roots. Spruce budworm, balsam woolly adelgid, Douglas-fir tussock moth, and stringy brown-rot fungus cause the most damage. Grows along streams, in valleys with deep, moist, alluvial soils, or on mountain slopes. Found occasionally in pure stands, but more frequently mixed with red alder, black cottonwood, bigleaf maple, Douglas-fir, western hemlock, western larch, western redcedar, subalpine fir, Engelmann spruce, ponderosa pine, western white pine, and lodgepole pine. Grown for Christmas trees. Planted for timber production in Europe. The Indian Paint fungus commonly found on older trees was used as a source of red pigment by Native Americans.

Hybrids. Hybridizes with white fir, making differentiation difficult.

Range. See figure 47. Elevation: sea level–6,000 ft; the only true fir found in the lowlands of Washington, Oregon, and California.

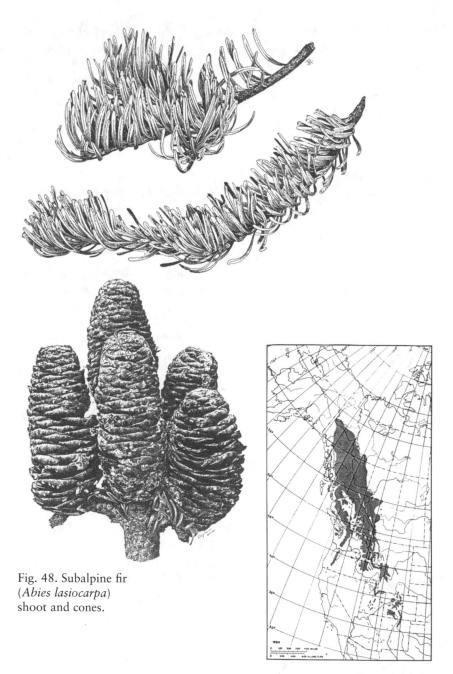

Fig. 48. Subalpine fir
(*Abies lasiocarpa*)
shoot and cones.

Fig. 49. Native range of subalpine
fir (*Abies lasiocarpa*).

Subalpine fir, Alpine fir

Abies lasiocarpa (Hook.) Nutt. (fig. 48)

Nomenclature. Sometimes subdivided into 2 species, *Abies lasiocarpa* and *Abies bifolia*, based largely upon wood and resin chemistry, but this subdivision is not universally accepted.

Form. Excurrent tree, growing 45–100 ft in height and 1–2 ft in diameter (largest known 160 ft by 3 ft); smallest of the western firs. Crown dense; narrowly pyramidal; very spirelike; often extending to the ground. A prostrate shrub (*krummholz*) at timberline.

Leaves. Linear; flat; 0.7–1.7 in. long; blue-green; white-waxy; held uniformly erect; stomate lines on both surfaces, but less conspicuous above. Apex rounded or notched.

Cones. Male cones dark indigo blue. Female cones dark purple or black; 2–4 in. long; oblong-cylindrical; resinous. Scales hairy; mostly longer than broad; bracts included. Seeds 0.2 in. long; seed wings dark; lustrous.

Twigs. Stout; hairy, becoming hairless; pale orange-brown, gray, or silver-white. Buds nearly spherical; resinous; 0.1–0.2 in. long. Scales orange-brown.

Bark. Thin; gray; smooth; resin blisters on young trees and in inner bark; becoming shallowly fissured on old trees. The only fir with resin pockets located inside the bark.

Wood. Moderately valuable commercially. The sapwood and heartwood are not distinctly colored. Both range from yellow-brown to red-brown; sometimes tinged with purple. Used for lumber, plywood, and especially pulpwood.

Natural History. Tolerant of shade; survival of young trees enhanced by shade. Growth rate moderate or slow. Reaches maturity in 150–200 years (extreme age 250 years). Reproduction abundant and vigorous; adequate seed crops produced most years with heavy crops produced every 3 years. Shallow root system; branches touching the ground sometimes develop roots. Restricted to cold but humid sites; otherwise found on a wide range of soils. Windthrow, wildfire, and the balsam woolly adelgid cause the most damage. Engelmann spruce is the constant associate, but subalpine fir also grows with white spruce, Sitka spruce, lodgepole pine, whitebark pine, limber pine, western larch, alpine larch, western hemlock, mountain hemlock, paper birch, and trembling aspen.

Varieties. Populations in New Mexico, Arizona, and southern Colorado, with soft, corky, yellow-white to ash-gray bark are separated as corkbark fir, *Abies lasiocarpa* var. *arizonica*.

Range. See figure 49. Elevation: sea level in the north to 12,000 ft in the south.

Sierra white fir, California white fir

Abies lowiana (Gordon) A. Murray

Form. Excurrent tree, growing 150–180 ft in height and 4–6 ft in diameter. Branches borne at right angles or somewhat drooping.

Leaves. Linear; 0.8–2.5 in. long; 2-ranked flat; green and grooved above; white-waxy or green below with 10–16 rows of stomates. Tip notched.

Cones. Young female cones olive-green. Mature female cones yellow-brown; cylindrical; 3–3.5 in. long; 1.5–1.7 in. wide. Scales included; hairy.

Twigs. Yellow-green; hairy or hairless. Buds rounded; light brown; not resinous.

Bark. Smooth and gray when young; becoming deeply furrowed with vertical ridges. Inner bark yellow-brown.

Wood. Similar to other firs.

Natural History. Grows in mixed stands.

Varieties. Sometimes classified as a variety of white fir, *Abies concolor* var. *lowiana*.

Range. See figure 50. Elevation: 3,000–7,500 ft.

Fig. 50. Native range of Sierra white fir (*Abies lowiana*).

Fig. 51. California red fir (*Abies magnifica*) shoot and cone.

Fig. 52. Native range of California red fir (*Abies magnifica*).

California red fir

Abies magnifica A. Murr. (fig. 51)

Form. Excurrent tree growing 150–180 ft in height and 4–5 ft in diameter (largest known 230 ft by 10 ft). Crown narrow; round topped; bole clear for much of its length. Lateral branches short.

Leaves. Linear; 0.7–1.5 in. long; blue-green; white-waxy on new shoots; stomate lines on all sides. Leaves on lower branches somewhat flattened; somewhat 2-ranked. Leaves on upper fertile branches almost square in cross section; held erect and crowded; short callous tips. Apex rounded.

Cones. Male cones red-purple. Young female cones green. Mature female cones 6–9 in. long; cylindrical to barrel shaped; dark purple-brown. Scales longer than broad. Bracts spiny tipped; inserted. Seeds 0.5–0.7 in. long; dark brown. Seed wings large; broad; rose colored.

Twigs. Stout; yellow-green; slightly rusty-hairy the first year, becoming hairless and light red-brown. Buds ovoid; 0.2 in. long; dark brown; slightly resinous at the tip.

Bark. Smooth and chalk-gray on young trees; becoming divided into rough rectangular ridges on old trees; distinctly red to red-brown; 4–6 in. thick.

Wood. Yellow-brown to light brown; sapwood not distinct from heartwood. Used for lumber, plywood, boxes and crates, sashes, doors, interior trim, and pulpwood.

Natural History. Moderately intolerant of shade. Growth rather slow, reaches maturity in 250–300 years (extreme age 500 years). Reproduction abundant on moist mineral soil; adequate seed crops produced every 1–4 years. Root system deep; spreading; adjacent trees sometimes form root grafts. Generally found on cool or cold, moist sites. Annosus root rot and fir engraver beetle cause the most damage. Grows in dense pure stands or mixed with California white fir, Douglas-fir, sugar pine, ponderosa pine, lodgepole pine, incense-cedar, and mountain hemlock. John Muir, a naturalist who worked for the creation of national parks, called red fir the most charmingly symmetrical tree in the Sierras. Grown for Christmas trees, and sold as silvertip fir.

Varieties. Shasta red fir, var. *shastensis*, is found in northern California and southern Oregon. It differs from the typical variety by the cone bracts that are exserted and strongly reflexed and by the buds that are almost free of resin. Some people think Shasta red fir is a hybrid between California red fir and noble fir, and that it represents either the merging or the splitting of these 2 species.

Range. See figure 52. Elevation: 4,600–9,000 ft.

Noble fir
Abies procera Rehd. (fig. 53)

Nomenclature. Older references use the name *Abies nobilis*, a name now rejected.

Form. Large excurrent tree, growing 150–200 ft in height and 4–6 ft in diameter (largest known 280 ft by 9 ft). The largest species of fir; only Douglas-fir, giant sequoia, and California redwood grow taller. Crown broad and rounded. Bole clear of branches for much of its length.

Leaves. Linear; 1–1.5 in. long; slightly L-shaped; grooved on upper surface; blue-green; stoma lines on all sides. Leaves on lower branches flattened; notched at the apex; slightly 2-ranked. Leaves on upper, fertile branches square in cross section; callous tips; held erect or upcurved.

Fig. 53. Noble fir (*Abies procera*) shoot.

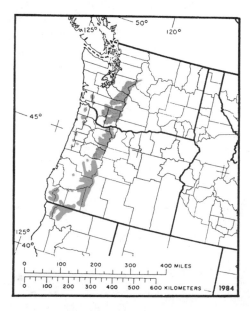

Fig. 54. Native range of noble fir (*Abies procera*).

Cones. Male cones red-purple. Female cones 4–6 in. long; cylindrical; purple or olive-brown. Scales wider than long. Bracts green; tip prolonged; exserted and strongly reflexed, almost completely covering the cone scales. Seeds 0.5 in. long; red-brown. Seed wings short; lustrous; light brown.

Twigs. Slender; red-brown; rusty-hairy. Buds oblong-conic; 0.1 in. long; slightly resinous at tip; red-brown; blunt.

Bark. 1–2 in. thick; red-brown; smooth and gray on young trees; prominent resin blisters. Old trees develop narrow, parallel, rectangular ridges separated by fissures; purple-gray to red-brown.

Wood. Produces the highest quality fir lumber; yellow-brown to light brown; sapwood not distinct from the heartwood; stronger than other firs; straight grained; not durable. Used for lumber, plywood, doors, interior trim, ladder rails, aircraft, and pulpwood. Formerly sold commercially under the name larch to avoid the prejudice associated with other fir lumber.

Natural History. Intermediate in tolerance of shade; the least tolerant of all western firs. Noble fir will not regenerate in a closed stand. Growth is rather rapid, after a period of slow growth as a seedling; reaches maturity in 300–350 years (extreme age 600 years). Reproduction success variable; most years the cone crop is too sparse. Adequate seed produced at 3–6 year intervals, but only about 10 percent is sound. Highly self-fertile; no evidence that selfed-seed is inferior. Planted for timber production in Washington and Oregon. Stands on good sites develop very high standing timber volumes that may exceed the volumes produced by Douglas-fir. Wildfire and dwarf mistletoe cause the most damage. Grows best on cool moist sites with deep soils, but acceptable growth occurs on thin, rocky soils if the moisture level is sufficient. Found in pure stands, but more commonly in mixed stands with Douglas-fir, Pacific silver fir, grand fir, subalpine fir, western hemlock, mountain hemlock, western larch, western white pine, lodgepole pine, western redcedar, and Alaska-cedar. Planted for Christmas trees.

Hybrids. Noble fir hybridizes with California red fir and subalpine fir.

Range. See figure 54. Elevation: 2,000–5,500 ft.

LARCH: THE GENUS *LARIX*

This genus contains ten species scattered through the Northern Hemisphere. In North America, three species are native. In addition, European larch (*Larix decidua*.), native to northern and eastern Europe, is planted and sometimes escapes.

Larches are generally excurrent pyramidal trees with open lacy crowns. The leaves are spirally arranged and needlelike. On older twigs the needles are borne in a tight spiral on distinctive short shoots, forming roselike clusters. (In our region only *Cedrus* develops similar short shoots.) The leaves turn yellow in autumn and are shed for the winter (deciduous). The cones are unisexual, but both sexes occur on each tree (monoecious). Wind-pollinated and maturing in one season, the female cones are borne erect with two winged seeds per cone scale. The cone bract may (exserted) or may not (inserted) be longer than the cone scale. The wood is strong, oily, and nonporous with small scattered resin ducts.

KEY TO LARCHES

1. Cones with bracts shorter than the scales . . . . Go to 2
1. Cones with bracts longer than the scales . . . . Go to 3
   2. Cones 0.3–0.7 in. long; composed of 12–15 hairless scales . . . .
   . . . . .tamarack, *Larix laricina*
   2. Cones 0.7–1.5 in. long, composed of 40–50 hairy scales . . . .
   . . . . .European larch, *Larix decidua*
3. Twigs slightly hairy; needles triangular in cross section . . . .
   . . . . western larch, *Larix occidentalis*
3. Twigs densely woolly; needles square in cross section . . . alpine larch, *Larix lyallii*

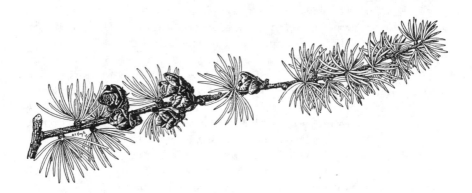

Fig. 55. Eastern larch (*Larix laricina*) shoot and cones.

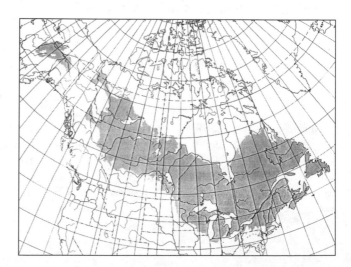

Fig. 56. Native range of eastern larch (*Larix laricina*).

Tamarack, Eastern larch

Larix laricina (Du Roi) K. Koch (fig. 55)

Nomenclature. Disjunct populations in Alaska are sometimes designated as a separate species, *Larix alaskensis*, but most authorities do not recognize this separation.

Form. Strongly excurrent small to medium-sized tree, growing 50–75 ft in height and 1–2 ft in diameter (largest known 115 ft by 3 ft). Bole clear; cylindrical. Crown open; pyramidal; slender horizontal branches.

Leaves. Linear; triangular in cross section; 0.7–1.2 in. long; blue-green to yellow-green.

Cones. Male cones nearly spherical; sessile. Young female cones oblong; yellow-green with pink scale margins. Mature female cones 0.5–0.7 in. long; short stalked; nearly spherical; chestnut-brown; falling the second year. Cone scales fewer than 20; slightly longer than broad; hairless; lustrous. Margin toothed. Bracts inserted. Seeds 0.1 in. long. Seed wings about 0.2 in. long; light chestnut-brown.

Twigs. Slender; smooth; hairless; white-waxy at first, turning brown. Buds spherical; small; lustrous; dark red.

Bark. Smooth and gray on young stems. Red-brown and scaly on mature stems; 0.5–0.7 in. thick. Formerly used as a source of tannin.

Wood. Sapwood white, narrow. Heartwood yellow-brown to red-brown; strong; moderately heavy; durable. Used for posts, poles, railroad ties, dog sled runners, rough lumber, and pulpwood.

Natural History. Very intolerant of shade; reaches maturity in 150–180 years (extreme age 335 years). Reproduction vigorous on favorable sites; shallow root system. Larch sawfly, larch casebearer, and wildfire cause the most damage. In the southern part of its range, generally found in sphagnum bogs or swamps. Farther north it grows on lake shores, low ridges, and well-drained uplands, where growth is faster. Generally grows in pure stands or mixed with black spruce, but balsam fir, trembling aspen, paper birch, and jack pine are also associates. Extends north to the limits of tree growth in our region, where the tree is stunted and shrublike.

Range. See figure 56. Elevation: sea level to 4,000 ft.

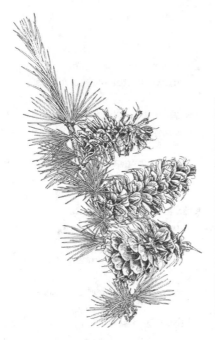

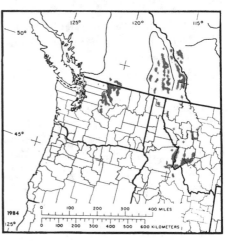

Fig. 57. Alpine larch (*Larix lyallii*) shoot and cones.

Fig. 58. Native range of alpine larch (*Larix lyallii*).

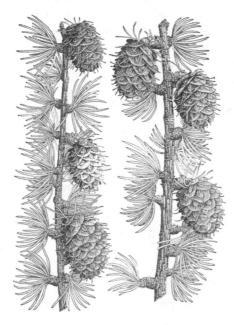

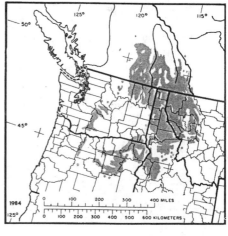

Fig. 59. Western larch (*Larix occidentalis*) shoot and cones.

Fig. 60. Native range of western larch (*Larix occidentalis*).

Alpine larch, Subalpine larch, Lyall larch

Larix lyallii Parl. (fig. 57)

Similar in general appearance to western larch. Needles linear; square in cross section; twigs and cone scales hairy. Cone scale bracts with a long awn that extends beyond the cone scale (exserted). The wood is not important commercially. Very slow growing; reaches maturity in 400–500 years (extreme age 1,000 years). Large seed crops infrequent. Grows at timberline and in alpine meadows in open, park-like stands. Except for the North Cascades, the geographic range of alpine larch lies within the range of western larch. For range see figure 58. Elevation: 5,000–9,900 ft.

Western larch

Larix occidentalis Nutt. (fig. 59)

Form. The largest larch in the world. Excurrent tree growing 140–180 ft in height and 3–4 ft in diameter (largest known 200 ft by 7 ft). Bole long; clear; cylindrical; often with a swollen base. Crown open; short; small horizontal branches.

Leaves. Linear; triangular in cross section; 1–1.7 in. long; light green.

Cones. Male cones oblong; sessile. Mature female cones oblong; 0.7–1.5 in. long; short stalked; yellow-brown to red-brown; falling the first year. Cone scales 40 or more per cone; broader than long. Margin smooth or wavy; sometimes reflexed. Bracts terminated with a long narrow awn that extends beyond the cone scale. Awn easily broken, giving a misrepresentation of its length. Seeds 0.2 in. long. Seed wings 0.5 in. long.

Twigs. Stout; brittle; pale hairy when young, soon becoming hairless and orange-brown. Buds 0.2 in. long; nearly spherical; chestnut-brown.

Bark. Scaly on young stems; with time developing scaly plates; 4–6 in. thick; cinnamon-brown to yellow-brown; separated by deep furrows.

Wood. Sapwood white to straw-brown; narrow. Heartwood red-brown; moderately heavy; straight-grained. Used for lumber, plywood, poles, laminated beams, flooring, interior trim, railroad ties, boxes and crates, pallets, and fuelwood. Contains water-soluble gum (arabinogalactan) used in making paint, ink, and baking soda.

Natural History. Very intolerant of shade. Fastest growing conifer in the northern Rockies; reaches maturity in 300–400 years (extreme age 900 years). Fair to good seed crops occur every 2 years. Seedlings require bare mineral soil to become established. Reproduction vigorous, sometimes dense after clearcutting or wildfire. Windfirm with deep, wide-spreading root system. Dwarf mistletoe, larch casebearer, and western spruce budworm cause the most damage. Occurs on a wide variety of sites, but best development is on deep, moist soils. Grows in pure stands, or mixed with Douglas-fir, western white pine, ponderosa pine, lodgepole pine, western hemlock, Engelmann spruce, grand fir, and subalpine fir.

Range. See figure 60. Elevation: 1,500–5,000 ft.

SPRUCE: THE GENUS *PICEA*

Worldwide spruce includes about 35 species, largely restricted to cool moist regions of the Northern Hemisphere. In our region, 7 indigenous species occur. Norway spruce (*Picea abies*), a European species, is naturalized in scattered localities.

Spruces are evergreen trees with sharp-pointed, pyramidal crowns, and straight boles. They sometimes become stunted and shrubby at timberline. The stiff linear leaves (needles) extend out from all sides of the twigs. Each needle is borne on a peglike projection of the twig (sterigma), a character that easily separates spruce from fir (*Abies*). The cones are unisexual, but both sexes occur on each tree (monoecious). Female cones are wind pollinated, mature in one season, found mostly at the top of the crown, and pendent at maturity. Each cone scale bears two winged seeds. The cone bract is always shorter than the scale at maturity (inserted). The bark is thin and scaly. The lustrous wood is nonporous, resinous, very strong for its weight, and valuable commercially. Spruce is easy to identify to genus, but difficult to identify to species from foliage alone. Cones or knowledge of the native range are sometimes needed for positive identification.

Fig. 61. Norway spruce (*Picea abies*) shoot and cone.

Fig. 62. Brewer spruce (*Picea breweriana*) shoots and cones.

KEY TO SPRUCES

1. Cone scales rounded at tip; margin smooth or wavy (erose) . . . . .Go to 2
1. Cone scales wedge shaped at tip, margin wavy (erose) . . . . .Go to 5
   2. Cones under 3 in. long; needles 4-sided 3
   2. Cones 3–6 in. long; needles flattened . . . . . . .Brewer spruce, *Picea breweriana*
3. Cones 1–1.5 in. long; ovoid; purple-brown; scales stiff; margin wavy; Trans-Canada
   and northern . . . . black spruce, *Picea mariana*
3. Cones 2–2.5 in. long; oblong; brown; scales pliable; margin rounded 4
   4. Twigs hairy; northeastern United States and Canada, and Appalachians . . . . . .
   . . . . .red spruce, *Picea rubens*
   4. Twigs hairless; Trans-Canada and northern . . . . . . .white spruce, *Picea glauca*
5. Cones 4–7 in. long; red-brown; branchlets drooping; exotic . . . .
   . . . . .Norway spruce, *Picea abies*
5. Cones rarely over 4.5 in. long; yellow-brown; native and western 6
   6. Needles flattened or triangular in cross section; yellow-green . . . .
   . . . . .Sitka spruce, *Picea sitchensis*
   6. Needles square in cross section; blue-green 7
7. Cones 1–2 in. long; twigs usually hairy . . . .
   . . . . .Engelmann spruce, *Picea engelmannii*
7. Cones 2–4 in. long; twigs hairless . . . . .blue spruce, *Picea pungens*

Norway spruce
Picea abies (L.) Karst. (fig. 61)

Excurrent tree with drooping branchlets. Leaves linear; square in cross section; 0.5–1 in. long; dark green. Twigs red-brown; hairless. Mature female cones 4–7 in. long; short stalked to sessile; brown; cylindrical; the only spruce cone in our region that cannot be crushed between the fingers and palm. Cone scales very stiff; diamond-shaped; cone margin jagged with a slight notch at the apex. Bark on young trees orange-brown; smooth. Bark on older trees turning gray-brown; scaly. Usually grows faster than our native species, except Sitka spruce. Native to Europe; occasionally planted for lumber in the East, but more commonly planted as an ornamental tree throughout the cooler portions of our region; naturalized in New England, the Lake States, the southern Appalachians, and Canada.

Brewer spruce, Weeping spruce
Picea breweriana S. Wats. (fig. 62)

Excurrent tree growing 70–80 ft in height and 1–2 ft in diameter. Bole often fluted at base. Needles linear; flat or triangular in cross section; 1–2 in. long; slightly ridged above; blunt at tip; dark green; pointing toward tip of twig. Cones 3–6 in. long. Cone scales rounded; entire; sometimes slightly reflexed. Twigs finely hairy; thin, weeping branchlets. Bark red-brown. Uncommon subalpine species, restricted to the Siskiyou Mountains of southern Oregon and northern California. Elevation: 3,300–7,500 ft.

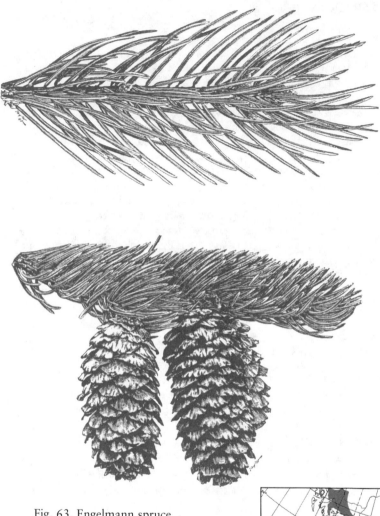

Fig. 63. Engelmann spruce
(*Picea engelmannii*) shoot
and cones.

Fig. 64. Native range of
Engelmann spruce (*Picea
engelmannii*).

Engelmann spruce

Picea engelmannii Parry ex Engelm. (fig. 63)

Form. Excurrent tree growing 60–120 ft in height and 1–3 ft in diameter (largest known 220 ft by 8 ft). Bole long but limby; cylindrical. Crown compact; pyramidal; branches moderately long. Becomes shrublike (*krummholz*) near timberline.

Leaves. Linear; held upward at a 30-degree angle; 0.7–1.2 in. long; square in cross section; blue-green, occasionally white-waxy; blunt or acute tips (not sharp to touch); flexible.

Cones. Male cones dark purple. Young female cones bright scarlet. Mature female cones 1–2 in. long; oblong-cylindrical; sessile or short stalked; yellow-brown to brown. Cone scales flexible almost like stiff paper. Margin jagged at apex. Seeds 0.1 in. long; nearly black. Seed wing oblique; 0.5 in. long.

Twigs. Minutely hairy (visible with 10× hand lens); rather stout; orange-brown to gray-brown; often held upward. Buds 0.1–0.2 in. long; broadly ovoid to conic; pale chestnut-brown. Bud scales usually appressed.

Bark. Thin; 0.2–0.5 in. thick; cinnamon-red to purple-brown; broken into thin, loosely attached scales arranged without a pattern.

Wood. Similar to white spruce, but weaker with lighter weight and longer fibers. Used for pulpwood, lumber, telephone poles, railroad ties, mine timbers, ladders, paddles, oars, and fuel.

Natural History. Tolerant of shade; recovers well from prolonged suppression; generally rather slow growing because of the short growing season. Long-lived; reaches maturity in 350–500 years (extreme age 800 years). Reproduction abundant and vigorous. Roots shallow; spreading. Windthrow, white pine weevil, and spruce beetle cause the most damage. Grows on rich loamy soils with abundant moisture. Found in pure stands or mixed with subalpine fir, lodgepole pine, and other conifers at high elevations. The foliage of Engelmann spruce and blue spruce is often confounded, because needle color alone is not reliable. The most reliable vegetative characteristics are crown form, needle angle, branch angle, and arrangement of bark scales.

Hybrids. Freely hybridizes with white spruce where their ranges overlap, making separation of the 2 species impossible.

Range. See figure 64. Elevation: 1,500–5,000 ft in the Canadian Rockies and 10,000–12,000 ft in the southern Rockies. The principal spruce throughout the interior portions of western North America.

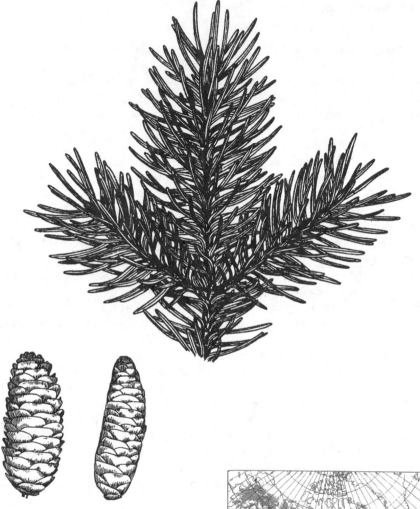

Fig. 65. White spruce (*Picea glauca*) shoot and cones.

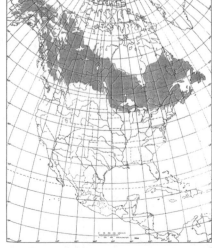

Fig. 66. Native range of white spruce (*Picea glauca*).

White spruce

Picea glauca (Moench) Voss (fig. 65)

Form. Excurrent tree growing 60–70 ft in height and 1–2 ft in diameter (largest known 180 ft by 4 ft). Crown narrowly to broadly pyramidal.

Leaves. Linear; 0.4–0.7 in. long; crowded on upper side of branch by twisting of leaves on lower side; square in cross section; blue-green occasionally white-waxy; rigid acute tips; odor pungent when crushed.

Cones. Male cones pale red to yellow. Young female cones red or yellow-green. Mature female cones 1–2.5 in. long; oblong-cylindrical; nearly sessile. Cone scales flexible; rounded at apex; light green or red-brown before shedding seed, but turning light brown soon after. Seeds 0.1 in. long; pale brown; seed wings 0.2–0.4 in. long.

Twigs. Hairless, or slightly hairy in the far Northwest; orange-brown; skunklike odor when bruised. Buds 0.1–0.2 in. long; ovoid; obtuse; chestnut-brown.

Bark. Thin, less than 0.5 in. thick; gray-brown; inner bark silver; separated into irregular thin plates or scales.

Wood. Valuable commercially. Sapwood not distinct from heartwood; both white to yellow-brown; lustrous; moderately lightweight. Used mostly for pulp, but also for poles, mine props, general construction lumber, boxes and crates, laminated beams, doors, ladders, paddles and oars, and musical sounding boards.

Natural History. Tolerant of shade; recovers from suppression well. Slow growing but faster than black spruce. Reaches maturity in 250–300 years. Reproduction abundant on moist sites. Root system shallow and spreading; roots used by Native Americans to weave baskets and bind canoes. Found on a wide range of soils, but most typical of moist soils, stream banks, and lake shores. Generally more demanding in site requirements than associated conifers. Replaced by black spruce and tamarack on wetter sites and lodgepole pine on drier sites. Often forms pure, dense stands, but also grows mixed with balsam fir, paper birch, trembling aspen, red pine, and eastern white pine.

Hybrids. White spruce hybridizes freely with Engelmann spruce, and the species cannot be separated where their ranges overlap.

Varieties. Western white spruce, var. *albertiana*, grows in the Rocky Mountain region and in the Black Hills. It has longer needles, shorter and broader cones, and a narrower crown. This variety has become popular in landscaping, where it is called Alberta spruce. Var. *porsildii* has smooth bark with resin blisters, hairy twigs, and shorter, more pointed cone scales.

Range. See figure 66. Elevation: sea level–5,000 ft.

Fig. 67. Black spruce (*Picea mariana*) shoot and cones.

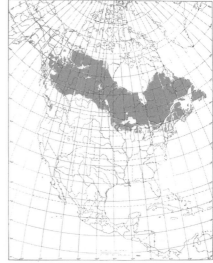

Fig. 68. Native range of black spruce (*Picea mariana*).

Black spruce
Picea mariana (Mill.) B.S.P. (fig. 67)

Form. Excurrent tree growing 40–65 ft in height and 1 foot in diameter (largest known 100 ft by 2 ft); shrublike at the limits of tree growth in northern Canada and Alaska. Bole short; slender; usually retaining dead branches. Crown open; conical; more-or-less irregular.

Leaves. 0.5–0.7 in. long; square in cross section; blue-green; white-waxy; blunt at apex; more or less incurved; white bands of stomata above; lustrous bands of stomata below.

Cones. Male cones 0.5 in. long; red. Young female cones purple. Mature female cones 0.7–1.5 in. long; ovoid; on short curved stalks. Cone scales stiff; rounded to jagged at apex; slightly hairy; purple-brown; persisting for many years. Seeds 0.1 in. long; dark brown. Seed wings 0.2–0.3 in. long; pale brown; oblique.

Twigs. Rusty-hairy; at first green turning yellow-brown. Buds 0.1 in. long; ovoid; acute; light red-brown; slightly hairy. Branches lying on the soil surface may develop roots (layering) and turn upward, forming a new tree.

Bark. Thin; gray-brown; separated into thin, closely appressed scales; inner bark olive-green.

Wood. The most important pulpwood species in Canada.

Natural History. Tolerant of shade, recovering from suppression at an advanced age. Slow growing; slower than most associate trees. Rather short-lived; reaches maturity in 150–200 years (extreme age 280 years). Roots shallow; spreading. Reproduction good on moist sites especially following catastrophic wildfire. Seeds produced almost every year, with heavy crops every 4 years. Dwarf mistletoe, European spruce sawfly, and girdling by snowshoe hares provide the most damage. Typical of sphagnum bogs and other organic swamps, but also found on upland glacial till. Grows to the northern limit of tree growth where sites are underlain by permafrost. Forms dense, pure stands; or grows with tamarack, balsam fir, white spruce, white birch, balsam poplar, trembling aspen, and lodgepole pine.

Hybrids. Hybridizes with red spruce where their ranges overlap, often making identification difficult.

Range. See figure 68. Elevation: sea level–6,000 ft.

Blue spruce, Colorado blue spruce

Picea pungens Engelm. (fig. 69)

Form. Excurrent tree growing 80–100 ft in height and 1–2 ft in diameter (largest known 150 ft by 4 ft). Crown typically dense and conical.

Leaves. Linear; held nearly at right angles to the twig; 1–1.5 in. long; square in cross section; blue-green frequently covered with white-wax; stiff. Tip long; sharp.

Cones. Mature female cones 2–4 in. long; yellow-brown; oblong-cylindrical; sessile or short stalked. Cone scales stiff spreading with jagged margins; often held until the second season.

Twigs. Hairless to slightly hairy; stout and rigid; orange-brown to gray-brown; often held at right angles to the main stem.

Bark. Thin with scales in vertical rows on young trees; becoming 0.7–1.5 in. thick; deeply furrowed with rounded ridges; orange-brown to gray-brown.

Wood. Limited commercial value. Similar to white spruce, but brittle and knotty.

Natural History. Moderately tolerant of shade, but the least tolerant of the spruces. Slow growing; moderately long-lived. Reproduction generally scant. Windfirm. Grows on rich moist soils, typically on stream banks. Never abundant; grows in small groves or mixed with ponderosa pine, Douglas-fir, white fir, alpine fir, Engelmann spruce, and trembling aspen. Widely planted as an ornamental; many trees have been selected for their blue color. The foliage of blue spruce and Engelmann spruce is commonly confused. See the comments provided under Engelmann spruce.

Range. See figure 70. Elevation: 6,000–9,000 ft in the north and 8,000–11,000 ft in the south; generally at lower elevation than Engelmann spruce.

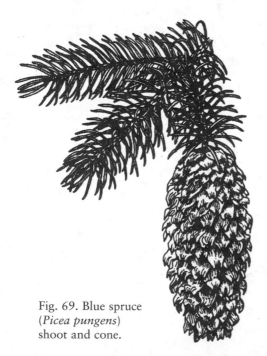

Fig. 69. Blue spruce
(*Picea pungens*)
shoot and cone.

Fig. 70. Native range of blue
spruce (*Picea pungens*).

Red spruce
Picea rubens Sarg. (fig. 71)

Form. Excurrent tree growing 60–75 ft in height and 1–2 ft in diameter (largest known 120 ft by 4 ft).

Leaves. Linear; extending at nearly right angles from all sides of twig; 0.5–0.7 in. long; square in cross section; dark yellow-green; prickly; blunt or pointed at apex.

Cones. Mature female cones 1.5–2 in. long; ovoid-oblong; nearly sessile. Cone scales rigid; rounded at apex; red-brown.

Twigs. Slightly hairy on young twigs becoming hairless; orange-brown.

Bark. Thin; 0.2–0.5 in. thick; gray-brown to red-brown; separating into irregular scales.

Wood. Valuable commercially; lightweight; even grained; lustrous. Used for lumber, pulp, organ pipes, and musical sounding boards. Formerly used for airplane frames. Resin formerly used in making chewing gum.

Natural History. Tolerant of shade. Moderately long-lived; reaches maturity in 200–250 years (extreme age 430 years). Reproduction vigorous. Wildfire and windthrow cause the most damage. Grows under a wide variety of conditions ranging from swamps and bogs to mountaintops. Best growth on well-drained uplands and mountain slopes in the Appalachians. Found in pure or mixed stands. Throughout the central and southern Appalachians, red spruce is declining, possibly the result of a warming climate and air pollution.

Hybrids. Red spruce hybridizes with black spruce, making identification difficult.

Range. See figure 72. Elevation: sea level in the north to 6,600 ft in the southern Appalachians. The common native spruce of New England, the mountains of New York, and south to North Carolina.

Fig. 71. Red spruce
(*Picea rubens*) cone.

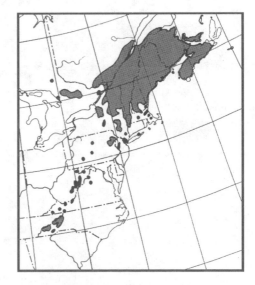

Fig. 72. Native range of
red spruce (*Picea rubens*).

Fig. 73. Sitka spruce
(*Picea sitchensis*)
shoot and cones.

Fig. 74. Native range
of Sitka spruce (*Picea
sitchensis*).

Sitka spruce

Picea sitchensis (Bong.) Carr. (fig. 73)

Form. Very large excurrent tree growing 180–200 ft in height and 3–4 ft in diameter (largest known 290 ft by 17 ft); largest spruce in the world. Bole often clear of branches for 100 ft. Crown pyramidal; short; open.

Leaves. Linear; often held nearly at right angles to the twig; 0.6–1 in. long; flat or triangular in cross section; yellow-green to blue-green; white-waxy below; very sharp pointed.

Cones. Male cones dark red. Female cones 2–4 in. long; yellow-brown to brown; oblong-cylindrical; short stalked; falling the first season. Cone scales thin, like stiff paper; wedge-shaped at apex; margin jagged. Seeds 0.1 in. long; red-brown; seed wings 0.4 in. long.

Twigs. Hairless; orange-brown to gray-brown. Buds 0.2–0.5 in. long; ovoid; red-brown.

Bark. Thin; 0.5–1 in. thick; yellow-brown to gray-brown; broken into thin concave scales.

Wood. Very valuable commercially. Sapwood white to light yellow. Heartwood yellow to pale brown, sometimes tinged with purple; lightweight; very strong; straight grained; lustrous. Sometimes confused for eastern white pine. Among spruce, Sitka produces the strongest wood; pound-for-pound stronger than steel. Used for pulpwood, lumber, plywood, poles, sailing ship masts and spars, oars, turbine blades, laminated beams, sound boards of musical instruments, ladder rails, and warehouse and garage doors. Formerly used in wooden aircraft; the Spruce Goose, a large, boatlike airplane with 8 engines designed and flown once for 1 mile in 1947 by Howard Hughes, is made from Sitka spruce.

Natural History. Moderately tolerant of shade. Fairly fast growing; reaches maturity in 400–500 years (extreme age 900 years). Reproduction vigorous on either mineral or organic soils, provided it is not droughty or waterlogged; may establish itself on rotten fallen trees (nurse logs) or stumps. Roots shallow. Windthrow, white pine weevil, and spruce beetle cause the most damage. Best development on deep moist loams in areas with abundant moisture, mild winters, and cool summers. Grows in pure stands or mixed with western hemlock, Douglas-fir, western redcedar, red alder, Alaska-cedar, black cottonwood, and bigleaf maple.

Hybrids. Intergrades and hybridizes with white spruce in north coastal British Columbia.

Range. See figure 74. Elevation: sea level–3,000 ft; rarely found more than 130 miles from the Pacific Coast.

PINES: THE GENUS *PINUS*

Worldwide this genus contains about 100 species, but only about 37 species are indigenous to North America, 13 in the East, 23 in the West, and one transcontinental (jack pine). In addition, Japanese black pine (*Pinus thunbergii*) and Japanese red pine (*Pinus densiflora*) of Asia and the following European species are planted in our region: Canary Island pine (*Pinus canariensis*), mugo pine (*Pinus mugo*),

Austrian pine (*Pinus nigra*), Italian stone pine (*Pinus pinea*), and Scotch pine (*Pinus sylvestris*). The genus is subdivided into two major subgenera, Soft Pines (with 13 species) and Hard Pines (with 24 species).

Pines are moderate to large trees, nearly always excurrent in form. The leaves are spirally arranged, evergreen, and needlelike (acicular). Juvenile leaves are single, but adult leaves are borne in clusters (fascicles) of one to eight, enclosed in a deciduous (in Soft Pines) or persistent (in Hard Pines) sheath. Reproductive structures are borne in unisexual cones, and both sexes occur on each tree (monoecious). During pollination the cone bract is always longer than the cone scale, but at maturity the bract is always shorter. Female cones are wind pollinated and mature in two (rarely three) years. The seeds (commonly called pine nuts) are edible. The wood is nonporous and resinous, and it is used for numerous products, including lumber, plywood, and pulpwood. The resin of several species has been tapped for naval stores (turpentine and rosin). Some species are used for Christmas trees and landscape plantings, and foliage of some is used for landscape mulch, wreaths, and garlands.

KEY TO PINES

1. Fascicle sheath deciduous, or nearly deciduous (mostly Soft Pines) . . . . . .Go to 2
1. Fascicle sheath persistent (Hard Pines) . . . . .Go to 15
   2. Needles in fascicles of 1–4; Western species 3
   2. Needles in fascicles of 5; Eastern or Western species 7
3. Needles one per fascicle . . . . .singleleaf pinyon, *Pinus monophylla*
3. Needles in fascicles of 2–4 4
   4. Needles in fascicles of 2 . . . .pinyon, *Pinus edulis*
   4. Needles in fascicles of 3 or 4 5
5. Needles in fascicles of 4; southern California . . . . .pinyon, *Pinus quadrifolia*
5. Needles in fascicles of 3 6
   6. Cone scale apophysis keeled . . . . .Mexican pinyon, *Pinus cembroides*
   6. Cone scale apophysis not keeled . . . .
      . . . . .Chihuahua pine, *Pinus leiophylla* var. *chihuahuana*
7. Cone scales thin, without prickles 8
7. Cone scales thick, with or without prickles 10
   8. Cones 4–8 in. long; Eastern species . . . . . . .eastern white pine, *Pinus strobus*
   8. Cones 5–18 in. long; Western species 9
9. Cones 5–11 in. long; many cone scales reflexed . . . .
      . . . . .western white pine, *Pinus monticola*
9. Cones 12–20 in. long; most cone scales straight . . . .sugar pine, *Pinus lambertiana*
   10. Cone scales without prickles; seed wing absent or short 11
   10. Cone scales with prickles; seed wing long 13
11. Cones 1.5–3 in. long; closed at maturity . . . . . . .whitebark pine, *Pinus albicaulis*
11. Cones 3–10 in. long, opening at maturity 12
   12. Cone scales not or slightly reflexed; scattered throughout West . . . .
      . . . . .limber pine, *P. flexilis*
   12. Cone scales reflexed; found near Mexican border . . . .
      . . . . .southwestern white pine, *Pinus strobiformis*
13. Cones with long, straight prickles . . . . .bristlecone pine, *Pinus aristata*
13. Cones with short, incurved prickles 14

14. Needles lacking median groove . . . . .foxtail pine, *Pinus balfouriana*
14. Needles with pronounced median groove . . . .
. . . . .intermountain bristlecone pine, *P. longaeva*
15. Eastern species 16
15. Western species 30
16. Needles 3 per fascicle 17
16. Needles 2 or 2 and 3 per fascicle 20
17. Terminal bud white . . . . .longleaf pine, *Pinus palustris*
17. Terminal bud brown or yellow 18
18. Open cones cylindrical, longer than broad . . . . . . .loblolly pine, *Pinus taeda*
18. Open cones spherical, about as long as broad .19
19. Coastal swamps; Delaware south to Florida and west to Alabama . . . .
. . . . .pond pine, *Pinus serotina*
19. Upland sites north of Delaware or coastal swamps in Delaware . . . .
. . . . .pitch pine, *Pinus rigida*
20. Needles 2 and 3 per fascicle 21
20. Needles 2 per fascicle 22
21. Needles 8–12 in. long . . . . .slash pine, *Pinus elliottii*
21. Needles 3–5 in. long . . . . .shortleaf pine, *Pinus echinata*
22. Needles 4–6 in. long 23
22. Needles 1–3 in. long 26
23. Terminal buds white; introduced 24
23. Terminal buds brown or yellow; native 25
24. Cone sessile; buds resinous . . . . .Austrian pine, *Pinus nigra*
24. Cone stalked; buds not resinous . . . . . .Japanese black pine, *Pinus thunbergii*
25. Cones lacking prickles; opening at maturity; East Canada to Minnesota and West Virginia . . . . .red pine, *Pinus resinosa*
25. Cones armed, often serotinous; Florida and Alabama . . . .sand pine, *Pinus clausa*
26. Cone scales pyramidally thickened; exotic . . . . . .Scotch pine, *Pinus sylvestris*
26. Scales not pyramidally thickened; native 27
27. Cones with hooked prickles . . . . .Table-mountain pine, *Pinus pungens*
27. Cones with straight prickles or lacking prickles .28
28. Cones asymmetrical, generally serotinous . . . . . . .jack pine, *Pinus banksiana*
28. Cones symmetrical, opening at maturity 29
29. Cones with long prickle; upper side of scale with purple stripe . . . .
. . . . .Virginia pine, *Pinus virginiana*
29. Cones with short, often deciduous, prickle; upper side of scale with brown stripe
. . . . .spruce pine, *Pinus glabra*
30. Needles in fascicles of 4 and 5, or 5 31
30. Needles in fascicles of 2 and 3, or 3 32
31. Needles 5–7 in. long; Arizona and New Mexico . . . .
. . . . .Arizona pine, *Pinus ponderosa* var. *arizonica*
31. Needles 8–13 in. long; southern costal California . .Torrey pine, *Pinus torreyana*
32. Cones massive with clawlike spines 33
32. Cones not massive; with small or straight spines 34
33. Cones yellow-brown, 10–14 in. long; seeds shorter than wings . . . .
. . . . .Coulter pine, *Pinus coulteri*
33. Cones red-brown, 6–10 in. long; seeds longer than wings . . . .
. . . . .digger pine, *Pinus sabiniana*

34. Cones asymmetrical with thickened scales, often serotinous. 35
34. Cones symmetrical with thin scales, opening at maturity 41
35. Needles 1–3 in. long; cones under 2 in. long 36
35. Needles 3–7 in. long; cones 2–6 in. long 37
36. Cones with knoblike scales and moderate prickles; Western . . . .
. . . . .lodgepole pine, *Pinus contorta*
36. Cones with thin scales and minute or no prickles; Canada and northeastern
United States . . . . .jack pine, *Pinus banksiana*
37. Needles 2 per fascicle; cones 2–3 in. long 38
37. Needles 2–3 or 3 per fascicle; cones 3–7 in. long 40
38. Terminal buds yellow-green or brown . . . . .bishop pine, *Pinus muricata*
38. Terminal buds white 39
39. Cones sessile; buds resinous. . . . . .Austrian pine, *Pinus nigra*
39. Cones stalked; buds nonresinous . . . . . . .Japanese black pine, *Pinus thunbergii*
40. Cone scales flattened, pyramidal . . . . .knobcone pine, *Pinus attenuata*
40. Cone scales rounded, domelike . . . . .Monterey pine, *Pinus radiata*
41. Cones 2–3 in. long; northern California and western Nevada . . . .
. . . . .Washoe pine, *Pinus washoensis*
41. Cones 3–15 in. long 42
42. Cones 5–15 in. long; twigs with pineapple odor . . .Jeffrey pine, *Pinus jeffreyi*
42. Cones 3–6 in. long; twigs with turpentine odor .43
43. Needles 4–11 (mostly 5–7) in. long, needles 2 or 3 per fascicle . . . .
. . . . .ponderosa pine, *Pinus ponderosa*
43. Needles 8–15 in. long, needles 3 per fascicle . . . .Apache pine, *Pinus engelmannii*

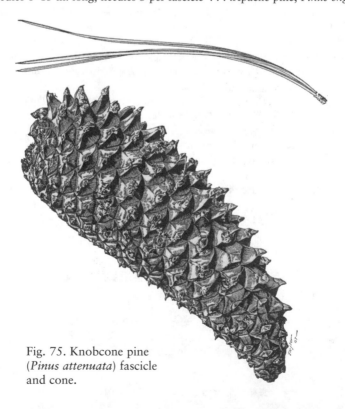

Fig. 75. Knobcone pine
(*Pinus attenuata*) fascicle
and cone.

HARD PINES: SUBGENUS *PINUS*

Hard Pines are sometimes called Yellow Pines. Over 60 species of Hard Pine are found throughout the world. Twenty-four hard pines occur naturally in our region, 11 species grow in the East, 12 species grow in the West, and 1 species (jack pine) is transcontinental in Canada.

Hard Pines generally bear needles in clusters (fascicles) of two or three. The fascicle sheath is persistent except on Chihuahua pine. Cone scales generally have prickles. The sapwood is white to yellow-white. The heartwood is yellow, orange, red-brown, or light brown, and typically harder and less uniform than Soft Pines. The transition between springwood and summerwood is abrupt.

Knobcone pine
Pinus attenuata Lemm. (fig. 75)

Form. Excurrent to deliquescent tree growing 20–60 ft in height and 1–2 ft in diameter (largest known 100 ft by 3 ft). Crown open; sparse.

Leaves. Fascicles of 3; 3–7 in. long; yellow-green; slender; twisted; persisting 4–5 years. Margin with minute teeth. Sheath persistent.

Cones. Male cones orange-brown. Young female cones purple. Mature female cones short stalked; 3–6 in. long; ovoid-conic; light red-brown; strongly asymmetrical with outer basal scales knoblike; remaining closed (serotinous) and persisting for 20 or more years; sometimes becoming overgrown by wood when the supporting branch grows in diameter. Found in clusters encircling the stems of even small trees. Cone scales have wide purple-red stripe on inner surface. Umbo with a short prickle. Seeds 0.2 in. long; remain viable in cones for over 50 years; seed wing 1 in. long.

Twigs. Slender; smooth; orange-brown. Buds 0.5 in. long; brown.

Bark. Thin; gray-brown; low scaly ridges. Upper bole nearly smooth.

Wood. Limited commercial value; soft and weak; used locally for fuel.

Natural History. Intolerant of shade; short lived and fast growing. Reproduction vigorous and abundant after wildfires that reduce competition from other species and open the serotinous cones. Grows on dry mountain slopes, generally in pure stands but sometimes in mixed stands with ponderosa pine, Digger pine, and various scrub oaks.

Range. Found in southwestern Oregon, northern and central California, and south in scattered areas to Baja California. Elevation: 1,000 to 5,000 ft.

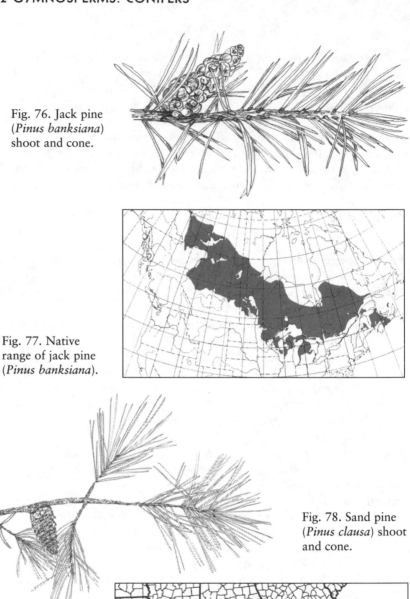

Fig. 76. Jack pine (*Pinus banksiana*) shoot and cone.

Fig. 77. Native range of jack pine (*Pinus banksiana*).

Fig. 78. Sand pine (*Pinus clausa*) shoot and cone.

Fig. 79. Native range of sand pine (*Pinus clausa*).

Jack pine, Scrub pine
Pinus banksiana Lamb. (fig. 76)

Form. Excurrent small tree, growing 55–65 ft in height and 1 ft in diameter (largest known 100 ft by 2 ft). Crown open, irregular, scraggly. Dead branches persist along the bole.

Leaves. Fascicles of 2; 1–2 in. long; divergent; stout; twisted; yellow-green; persisting 2–3 years. Margins with minute teeth. Sheath persistent.

Cones. Male cones yellow to orange-brown. Young female cones dark purple. Mature female cones clustered; sessile; dull yellow; slick; 1–2 in. long; oblong-conic; asymmetrical; often pointing toward branch tips; remaining closed for years (serotinous), sometimes becoming embedded in wood when branches grow in diameter. Umbo not armed or with minute deciduous prickle. Seeds 0.1 in. long, black. Seed wings about 0.3 in. long.

Twigs. Thin; rough; flexible; orange-red to red-brown. Buds 0.3 in. long; ovoid; pale cinnamon-brown; very resinous.

Bark. Thin; orange-brown to yellow-brown; scaly.

Wood. Moderately important commercially. Sapwood nearly white. Heartwood light brown; moderately heavy. Used for pulpwood, posts, rough construction, and mine timbers. The knotty lumber is considered inferior to other pines.

Natural History. Very intolerant of shade. Short lived; reaches maturity in 60–80 years (extreme age 200 years). Wide-spreading roots with a taproot. Reproduction vigorous after catastrophic wildfire, forming dense, even-aged, pure stands. Grows on dry sterile soils, especially glacial outwash plains. Found with northern pin oak, aspens, red pine, and paper birch. Young stands with branches that extend to the ground provide habitat for the Kirtland's warbler, an endangered bird.

Range. See figure 77. Elevation: sea level to 2,000 ft. Extends farther north than any other American pine.

Sand pine, Scrub pine
Pinus clausa (Chapm. ex Engelm.) Vasey ex Sarg. (fig. 78)

Small to moderate-sized tree growing 70–80 ft in height and 1–2 ft in diameter (largest known 100 ft by 2 ft). Leaves in fascicles of 2; slightly twisted; slender. Margin with minute teeth. Sheath persistent. Female cones short stalked or sessile; 2–3 in. long; red-brown; opening at maturity or serotinous; serotinous cones turning silver-gray with age. Scales with a purple-brown marginal stripe on the upper surface. Umbo with a short, sharp, often deciduous prickle. Dead branches persist on the main stem. Bark divided into small scaly rectangular plates; red-brown; upper stem scaly. Used for pulpwood and Christmas trees. Regenerates aggressively after catastrophic wildfire, forming dense even-aged stands. Grows with myrtle oak, Chapman oak, and tree lyonia. Generally divided into 2 varieties, both found on dry infertile sandy soils. Choctawhatchee sand pine (var. *immuginata*) is common in the Florida panhandle, where the cones are largely nonserotinous. Ocala sand pine (var. *clausa*) is abundant in the Big Scrub of central Florida where the cones are largely serotinous. For range see figure 79.

Lodgepole pine

Pinus contorta Dougl. ex Loud. (fig. 80)

Form. Highly variable; small to large tree depending upon variety. Excurrent or somewhat deliquescent growing 30–80 ft in height and 1–2 ft in diameter (largest known 150 ft by 3 ft). Bole slender and straight or bent and contorted.

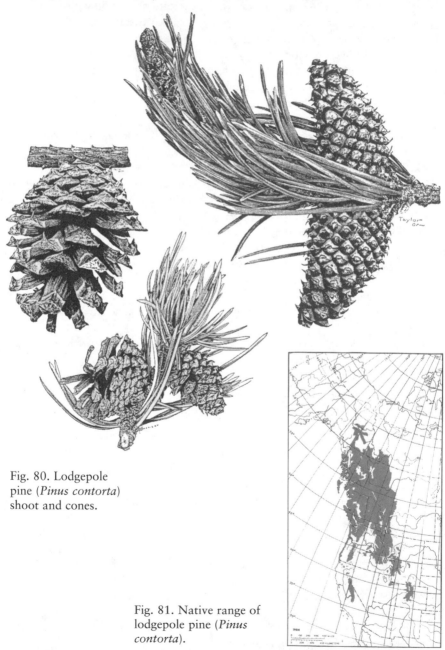

Fig. 80. Lodgepole pine (*Pinus contorta*) shoot and cones.

Fig. 81. Native range of lodgepole pine (*Pinus contorta*).

Bole clear of dead branches or covered with persistent dead branches. Crown conical or irregular and scraggly.

Leaves. Fascicles of 2; 1–3 in. long; stout; twisted; yellow-green to dark green; persisting 3–8 years. Margins with minute teeth. Sheath persistent.

Cones. Male cones orange-red. Mature female cones vary according to variety. Cones clustered; subsessile; 1.5–2.5 in. long; light brown; ovoid to spherical; often asymmetrical at the base; often curved; remaining closed (serotinous) and persisting on the tree for many years or opening and falling. Scales knoblike. Umbo armed with a slender often deciduous prickle. Seeds 0.1–0.2 in. long; thin; red-brown; mottled with black. Seed wings 0.5 in. long.

Twigs. Stout; light orange-brown, becoming black with time. Buds 0.2 in. long; ovoid; dark chestnut-brown; resinous.

Bark. Moderately thick; red-brown to black and furrowed on coastal trees. Elsewhere thin, rarely over 0.5 in. thick; orange-brown to gray; covered by thin, loosely appressed scales.

Wood. Moderately important commercially. Sapwood white to pale yellow. Heartwood yellow-brown, often not distinct from the sapwood; moderately lightweight; fine textured. Used for pulpwood, low-grade lumber, plywood, poles, posts, and mine timbers. Used locally for orchard props, corral rails, and rustic furniture.

Natural History. Intolerant of shade. Generally slow growing; reaching maturity in 200–300 years (extreme age 600 years). Root system shallow. Reproduction vigorous in full sunlight; typically following catastrophic wildfires or clearcutting. One of the principal fire species of the American West, many lodgepoles store seed in serotinous cones until heat from fire opens the cones and releases the seed. These seed are then available to regenerate the area. Fire, bark beetles, and dwarf mistletoe cause the most damage. Grows under a broader range of site conditions than any other tree in North America, ranging from dry sands at low elevations to seasonally wet meadows at high elevations. Found in pure, dense, even-aged stands, or in mixture with other conifers. At lower elevations it grows with ponderosa pine, Douglas-fir, and western larch. At higher elevations, it grows with Engelmann spruce, subalpine fir, red fir, Jeffrey pine, and limber pine.

Varieties. Three or 4 geographical varieties are distinguished. Var. *contorta*, often called shore pine, is a small, crooked or leaning tree with serotinous cones that grows at lower elevations in the maritime fog belt along the Pacific Coast or in bogs in Alaska and British Columbia. Shore pine trees in Mendocino County, California are further subdivided into var. *bolanderi* by some authorities. Var. *latifolia* is a moderate to large tree generally with serotinous cones. It occupies the most area growing throughout the Rocky Mountains, often to timberline. Var. *latifolia* produces the most timber. Var. *murrayana*, called Sierra lodgepole pine, grows in montane forests from Washington to Baja California. Largest of the 3 varieties it has nonserotinous cones.

Range. See figure 81. Elevation: sea level to 11,000 ft. Widely distributed in western North America.

Coulter pine
Pinus coulteri D. Don (fig. 82)

Form. Excurrent tree growing 40–50 ft in height and 1–2 ft in diameter (largest known 140 ft by 5 ft). Crown large; open; asymmetrical; ends of branches often upturned.

Leaves. Fascicles of 3; 6–12 in. long; dark blue-green; stiff; held outward; persisting 3–4 years. Margin with minute teeth. Sheath persistent.

Cones. Male cones purple-brown. Young female cones dark red-brown. Mature female cones massive, the heaviest cone in North America; short stalked; 10–14 in. long; oblong-ovoid; generally opening at maturity, but sometimes remaining closed and persisting several years; light yellow-brown. Scales thick; resinous. Umbo terminating in large, curved claw, especially at the base of the cone. Be careful not to be hit by falling cones, which may weigh over 5 pounds. Seeds 0.5 in. long; thick shelled. Seed wings about 1 in. long.

Twigs. Stout and rough; purple-brown, often white-waxy. Buds 0.5 in. long; red-brown; resinous.

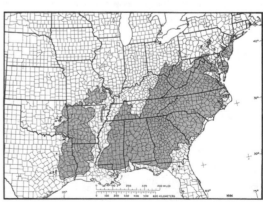

Fig. 82. Coulter pine (*Pinus coulteri*) leaves and cone.

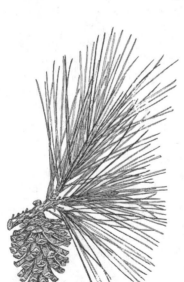

Fig. 83. Shortleaf pine (*Pinus echinata*) shoot and cone.

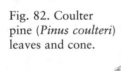

Fig. 84. Native range of shortleaf pine (*Pinus echinata*).

Bark. Gray-brown to nearly black; 1–2 in. thick; furrowed with scaly ridges.

Wood. Low commercial value. Soft and weak; used locally for fuel.

Natural History. Intolerant of shade. Slow growing, reaches maturity in about 150 years. Roots deep with wide-spreading laterals. Reproduction sparse. Found on dry, rocky slopes in pure stands or mixed with California live oaks, ponderosa pine, Jeffrey pine, and incense-cedar.

Hybrids. Hybridizes with Jeffrey pine.

Range. Found in scattered areas in western California, and south into Baja California. Elevation: 1,000–7,000 ft.

Shortleaf pine, Shortleaf

Pinus echinata Mill. (fig. 83)

Form. Strongly excurrent, growing 80–100 ft in height and 2–3 ft in diameter (largest known 130 ft by 4 ft). Bole long; clear, except for occasional small branches. Crown narrow when young, but becoming broad crowned in old age. One of the straightest of the Southern Pines.

Leaves. Fascicles of 2 but sometimes 3; 3–5 in. long; slender; flexible; yellow-green; persisting 2–4 years. Margin with minute teeth. Sheath persistent.

Cones. Male cones pale purple. Young female cones pale pink. Mature female cones short stalked; 1–2 in. long; oblong to conic; opening at maturity and persisting several years; red-brown to light brown. Scales thin; lacking marginal stripe on inner face. Umbo armed with short prickle. Seeds 0.2 in. long; brown with black marks; seed wings 0.5 in. long.

Twigs. Slender; flexible; rough; red-brown; vigorous twigs white-waxy. Buds 0.2 in. long; red-brown to gray-brown; somewhat resinous.

Bark. Dark gray to black and scaly on young trees; later developing irregular plates, separated by furrows; the face of each plate flaking; gray to red-brown with yellow splotches on flake undersides. Resin pockets usually present, appearing as small rounded depressions. The only Southern Pine with yellow splotches and resin pockets.

Wood. Very valuable commercially. Sapwood pale yellow. Heartwood red-brown. Moderately heavy to heavy. Used for pulpwood, lumber, high-density beams, plywood, poles, and pilings. Sold as southern yellow pine.

Natural History. Intolerant of shade. Moderate growth rate roughly 10 percent slower than loblolly pine; reaches maturity in 150–170 years (extreme age 400 years). Windfirm with deep taproot and extensive lateral roots. Young trees capable of sprouting, sometimes producing trees with 2 stems. Littleleaf disease, Nantucket pine tip moth, southern pine beetle, root rot, and ice storms cause the most damage. Best developed in the Piedmont. Found on a wide variety of sites, but most common on drier, less-fertile upper slopes. Generally not found on basic soils. Grows in pure stands or mixed with loblolly pine, Virginia pine, pitch pine, white oak, black oak, post oak, southern red oak, sweetgum, yellow-poplar, blackgum, and hickories.

Range. See figure 84. Elevation: 10–3,000 ft. The most widely distributed southeastern pine.

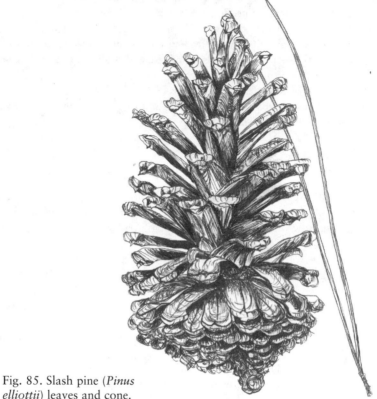

Fig. 85. Slash pine (*Pinus elliottii*) leaves and cone.

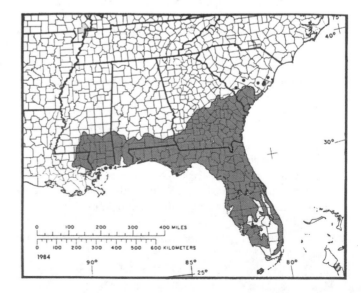

Fig. 86. Native range of slash pine (*Pinus elliottii*).

Slash pine
Pinus elliottii Engelm. (fig. 85)

Nomenclature. Until 1824, slash pine was not recognized as distinct from other Southern Pines. It was also commonly misidentified as *Pinus caribaea*, a species of the West Indies and Central America.

Form. Excurrent tree growing 80–100 ft in height and 2–3 ft in diameter (largest known 150 ft by 4 ft). Bole long; clear. Crown rounded, dense.

Leaves. Mostly in fascicles of 3, but a few in fascicles of 2; fascicles of 2 most common in the extreme northern and southern portions of the range; 8–12 in. long; stout; glossy; dark green; evenly distributed along young branches; less tufted than longleaf and loblolly pine; persisting 2 years. Margin with minute teeth. Sheath persistent.

Cones. Male cones dark purple. Young female cones pink. Mature female cones stalked; 4–6 in. long; ovoid-conic; opening at maturity and falling with or without the stalk the following year; chocolate-brown, shining as if varnished. Scales thin. Umbo armed with small sharp prickle. Seeds 0.2 in. long; black. Seed wings about 1 in. long.

Twigs. Stout; rough; orange-brown. Buds 0.5–0.7 in. long. Bud scales red-brown; free at the tips. Bud color is an excellent characteristic to separate slash pine from longleaf pine, which has white buds.

Bark. Scaly on young trees but developing irregular bark plates; bright orange-brown to purple-brown; flaking off in thin layers, which maintains the bright color and causes accumulations at the base of old trees.

Wood. Very valuable commercially. Used for pulpwood, lumber, plywood, poles, and pilings. Formerly used for railroad ties and naval stores. Sold as southern yellow pine.

Natural History. Intolerant of shade. Very fast growing when young; reaches maturity in 80–100 years (extreme age 150–200 years). Windfirm with a small taproot and extensive laterals. Reproduction generally abundant after major disturbances, especially logging and wildfire. Frequently planted in southeastern Georgia and northern Florida, where it is the most important commercial species. Open stands with grassy understories are often used for grazing cattle. Fusiform rust causes the most damage, but annosum root rot and pitch canker are also important. Resistant to fire only after age 10–12 years. Originally confined to poorly drained flats, pond edges, bays, and small drainages, slash pine has replaced longleaf pine on uplands, owing to fire suppression. Found in extensive pure stands or mixed with longleaf pine, loblolly pine, pond pine, red maple, swamp blackgum, laurel oak, pondcypress, sweetbay, redbay, loblolly-bay, and cabbage palm.

Varieties. In the southern half of Florida, South Florida slash pine (*Pinus elliottii* var. *densa.*) occurs. It differs from typical slash pine by having a swollen base, more fascicles with 2 needles, slightly reflexed cone scales, heavier wood, and a grass stage. It is also smaller at maturity, tends to develop forked stems, and grows on dry sandy flats and limestone outcrops.

Range. See figure 86.

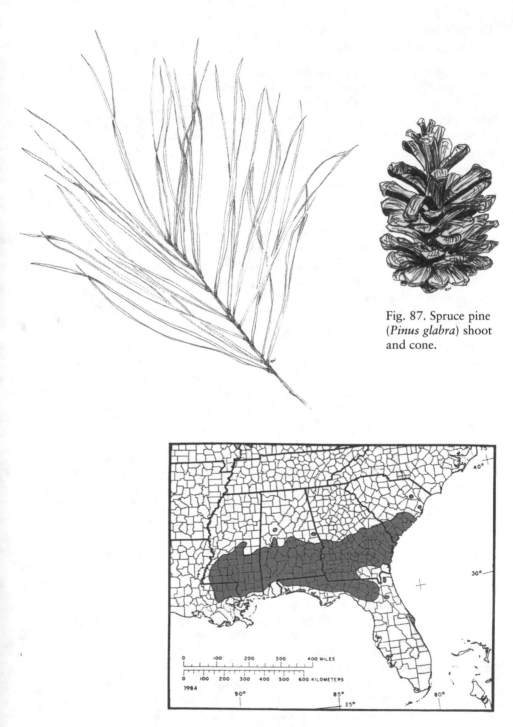

Fig. 87. Spruce pine (*Pinus glabra*) shoot and cone.

Fig. 88. Native range of spruce pine (*Pinus glabra*).

Apache pine
Pinus engelmannii Carr.

Similar in overall appearance to ponderosa pine. Excurrent tree growing 50–90 ft in height and 1–2 ft in diameter (largest known 75 ft by 3 ft). Limited height growth the first few years (grass stage). Leaves in fascicles of 3 (occasionally 2–5); 8–15 in. long; dark green; persisting 2 years; often clustered at the ends of twigs and drooping under their own weight. Margin with small teeth. Sheath persistent; 0.7–1 in. long. Mature female cones short stalked to sessile; light brown; ovoid; 3–4 in. long. Umbo elongated into a curved claw. Grows most commonly on dry mountain slopes, but also found in valleys and on high mesas. Largely found in the Sierra Madre Occidental of Mexico, Apache pine reaches its northern limit in extreme southern Arizona and New Mexico. Elevation: 5,500–8,200 ft.

Spruce pine
Pinus glabra Walt. (fig. 87)

Excurrent tree growing 80–100 ft in height and 2–3 ft in diameter (largest known 125 ft by 5 ft). Resembling shortleaf pine in foliage and cone. Leaves in fascicles of 2; 2–4 in. long; slender. Cones 2–3 in. long; red-brown. Umbo with a short, weak prickle. Young twigs smooth; gray. Bark tight; dark gray to black; divided into long narrow ridges; not the typical plated red-brown bark of other Southern Pines. Nowhere abundant spruce pine always grows mixed with hardwoods in bottomlands or on fertile uplands. Bark and site are the best characteristics to separate spruce pine from shortleaf pine. Little commercial value; the close-grained wood is brittle. Limbs subject to ice breakage, if planted north of its natural range. Sometimes grown for Christmas trees. For range see figure 88.

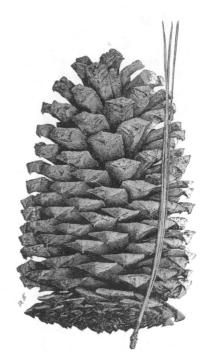

Fig. 89. Jeffrey pine (*Pinus jeffreyi*) leaves and cone.

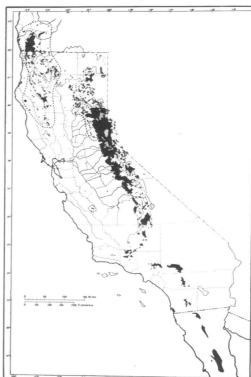

Fig. 90. Native range of Jeffrey pine (*Pinus jeffreyi*).

Jeffrey pine

Pinus jeffreyi Grev. & Balf. (fig. 89)

Form. Excurrent tree growing 90–140 ft in height and 3–4 ft in diameter (largest known 200 ft by 8 ft); smaller than ponderosa pine.

Leaves. Fascicles of 3, or 2 and 3; 4–9 in. long; blue-green; persisting 5–9 years. White-waxy around stomata. Generally extending along the twigs, not tufted.

Cones. Mature female cone 5–15 in. long. Scales thin; borne closer together than ponderosa pine. Umbo with stout J-shaped prickle.

Twigs. Stout; purple; generally white-waxy; producing a vanilla or pineapple odor when bruised. Buds not resinous. Bud scales fringed.

Bark. Similar to ponderosa pine but red-brown and sulfur-yellow on scale undersides.

Wood. Nearly identical to ponderosa pine; color redder and essential oils 90–95 percent heptane. Sold as western yellow pine or ponderosa pine.

Natural History. Found largely in the mountains of California, Jeffrey pine is similar in general appearance to ponderosa pine. Jeffrey pine competes well on cold, dry, infertile sites. It is also one of the few trees that can grow well on serpentine soils with high levels of calcium and magnesium. Very windfirm. Jeffrey pine beetle, dwarf mistletoe, and flooding cause the most damage. Incense-cedar is the most common associate on serpentine soils. Elsewhere, ponderosa pine, Douglas-fir, sugar pine, Port Orford-cedar, western white pine, Coulter pine, and knobcone pine are common associates.

Hybrids. Hybridizes with Coulter pine and ponderosa pine.

Range. See figure 90. Elevation: 400–10,000 ft.

Chihuahua pine

Pinus leiophylla Schiede & Deppe var. *chihuahuana* (Engelm.) Shaw

Small tree. Leaves in fascicles of 3 (rarely 2, 4 or 5); 2–5 in. long; persisting 2–4 years; clustered at the tips of twigs. Margin with minute teeth. Sheath deciduous (even though the species is a hard pine). Cones 2–3 in. long; stalked; dark brown; ovoid. Female cones mature in 3 years, rather than the usual 2 years; often remaining closed (serotinous). Umbo with a small often deciduous prickle. Found on dry slopes. Essentially Mexican in distribution reaching its northern limit in extreme southern Arizona and southern New Mexico. Var. *leiophylla* is confined to Mexico.

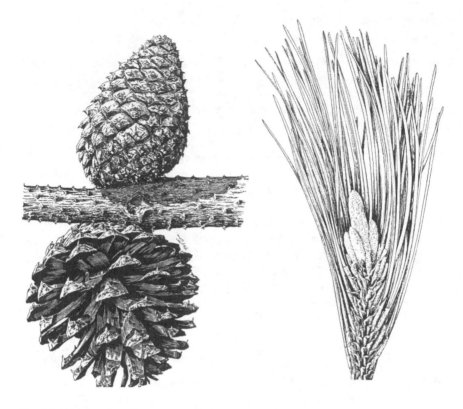

Fig. 91. Bishop pine (*Pinus muricata*)
shoot and cones.

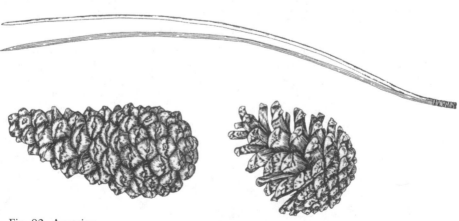

Fig. 92. Austrian
pine (*Pinus nigra*)
leaves and cones.

Bishop pine
Pinus muricata D. Don (fig. 91)

Small to moderate-sized tree growing 30–80 ft in height and 1–3 ft in diameter; handsome rounded crown of dense tufted foliage. Leaves in fascicles of 2; 4–6 in. long; dark yellow-green; thick; rigid; persisting 2–3 years. Sheath persistent. Mature female cones sessile; in clusters of 3–7; 2–4 in. long; ovoid; yellow-brown; asymmetrical, with outer basal scales knoblike and extended into spurlike spines; often remaining closed and persisting for years. Bark thick; purple-brown; rough; furrowed. Wood used locally for lumber and fuel. Moderately tolerant of shade; short lived and fast growing. Reproduction abundant and aggressive following catastrophic wildfire. Found on a variety of sites, ranging from wet clays and peat bogs to dry sandy ridges. Forms pure stands or mixed with lodgepole pine, madrone, and oaks. Commonly planted as an ornamental. Occurs locally along the California coast, on Santa Crux and Santa Rosa islands, and in Baja California.

Austrian pine, European black pine
Pinus nigra Arnold (fig. 92)

Similar to red pine and Japanese black pine in general characteristics. Leaves in fascicles of 2; bending not breaking when bent; dark green. Buds light brown; covered with white resin. Cones 2–3 in. long; shiny yellow-brown; sessile. Umbo armed with a minute prickle. Tolerant of pollution and salt spray. Native to southern Europe; cultivated as early as 1760 in the United States; rarely escaping. Mostly used in ornamental plantings in eastern Canada, New England, the Lake States, and British Columbia.

Longleaf pine, Longstraw

Pinus palustris Mill. (fig. 93)

Form. Excurrent tree growing 80–120 ft in height and 2–3 ft in diameter (largest known 150 ft by 4 ft). Bole straight; clear; less taper than some other pines. Crown open with needles in dense tufts at ends of branches. With age, trees become decidedly flat topped, a characteristic used to help locate old trees. One of the straightest Southern Pines.

Leaves. Fascicles of 3; 8–18 in. long; slender; flexible drooping under their own weight; bright green; persisting 2 years. Margin with minute teeth. Sheath persistent; 0.3–0.5 in. long. Dead needles raked from the forest floor, baled, and

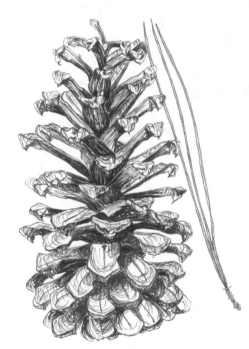

Fig. 93. Longleaf pine (*Pinus palustris*) leaves and cone.

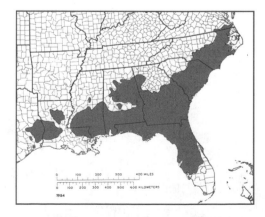

Fig. 94. Native range of longleaf pine (*Pinus palustris*).

sold for landscaping mulch. Selling mulch can provide more income to landowners than cutting the trees and selling the wood.

Cones. Male cones purple-blue. Young female cone dark purple. Mature female cone sessile; 6–10 in. long; ovoid-cylindrical; opening at maturity. Falling readily leaving basal scales attached to twig; brown. Scales thin; wide. Umbo with incurved prickle. Seeds 0.5 in. long; pale with dark blotches; germinating in the fall, which is unusual for a Southern Pine. The largest Southern Pine cone, sometimes used in decorations and crafts. Seed wings 1.5 in. long.

Twigs. Very stout; up to 1 in. in diameter; upturned at tips; very rough; orange-brown to black. Buds 0.5–1 in. long; white; covered by silvery fringed scales that increase fire resistance. The only native pine in the Southeast with white buds.

Bark. Developing very quickly to provide insulation from fire; 1–3 in. thick on old trees; bright orange-brown; forming irregular flaky plates, separated by black fissures. Flaking off and remaining brightly colored.

Wood. Very valuable commercially. Sapwood yellow. Heartwood orange-red; heavy; strong; high resin content, 7–15 percent. Decay resistant owing to the high resin content. Resin-soaked wood sold as lighter wood, used to start fires. Used for timbers, lumber, plywood, railroad ties, posts, and poles. Wood from old growth trees called heart pine, which is sometimes recycled from old buildings. Formerly used for paving blocks, flooring, and the principal source of naval stores. Sold as southern yellow pine.

Natural History. Intolerant of shade. Slow to fast growth depending upon site conditions. Forms a grass stage for the first 1–10 years, where aboveground growth is extremely limited and the tree resembles a tuft of grass. Extremely resistant to fire while in the grass stage. When the stem becomes about 1 in. in diameter, a period of rapid height growth begins. After 1–3 more years when the tree is 10–15 ft in height and 1–2 in. in diameter, the tree is again very resistant to fire. Reaches maturity in 160–180 years (extreme age 400 years). Windfirm with deep taproot system. Reproduction limited to infrequent heavy seed crops. Seeds eaten by humans and wildlife. Originally found on nearly all upland mineral soils, but today found largely on droughty, sandy or sandy loam sites. Eliminated from 95 percent of the original range by fire suppression, foraging by hogs, loss of trees to navel stores, brown spot disease, establishment of loblolly pine plantations, and site conversion to agriculture. Brown spot needle blight of seedlings and lightning strikes to large trees cause the most damage. In the Coastal Plain, found in pure stands or mixed with other pines (loblolly, pond pine, and slash pine) and hardwoods, especially turkey oak, sand post oak, bluejack oak, persimmon, sweetgum, and sassafras. In the Piedmont mixed with post oak, blackjack oak, white oak, southern red oak, and mockernut hickory. Trees over 60 years old with stem decay provide the best habitat for the red-cockaded woodpecker, an endangered bird.

Hybrids. Hybridizes with loblolly pine (*Pinus* x *sondereggeri*). See the entry under loblolly pine for additional information.

Range. See figure 94. Elevation: sea level–2,200 ft (in Alabama).

Ponderosa pine, Western yellow pine
Pinus ponderosa Laws. (fig. 95)

Form. Large excurrent tree growing 90–180 ft in height and 3–4 ft in diameter (largest known 250 ft by 9 ft). Bole clear of branches for much of its length. Crown conical when young, but becoming flat topped with age. Basal fire scars common on old trees.

Leaves. Fascicles of 3, or 2 and 3 (rarely 4 or 5); 3–11 in. long (mostly 4–7 in.); stout; dark green to yellow-green; persisting 2–7 years (usually 4–6 years); often tufted at the ends of twigs. Margin with minute teeth. Sheath persistent.

Cones. Male cones yellow. Young female cones red. Mature female cone short stalked or sessile; 2–6 in. long; red-brown to yellow-brown; ovoid; opening at maturity; basal scales remain attached to twig. Cone scales thin. Umbo armed with short stout prickles. Seeds 0.2 in. long; purple-brown; often mottled. Seed wings 1 in. long.

Twigs. Stout; orange; occasionally white-waxy; turpentine odor when bruised. Buds about 0.5 in. long; often resinous; scales white-fringed.

Bark. Black and furrowed on young trees, which are locally called black pine, blackjack, or bull pine. Later turning yellow-brown to orange-brown; develop-

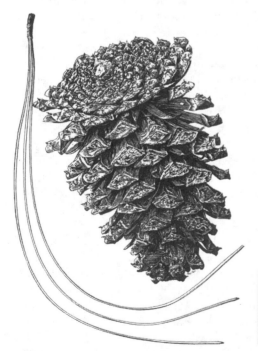

Fig. 95. Ponderosa
pine (*Pinus ponderosa*)
leaves and cone.

Fig. 96. Native range
of ponderosa pine
(*Pinus ponderosa*).

ing large rectangular plates separated by black fissures. The surface of each plate is covered with small flakes that fall and accumulate at the base of large trees. Each flake resembles a jigsaw puzzle piece. Older trees with cinnamon-red bark are locally called punkins.

Wood. Very valuable commercially. One of the most heavily utilized species in North America. Sapwood wide (up to 80 rings), white to pale yellow. Heartwood light red to orange-brown; moderately heavy. Somewhat similar to white pine. Extensively used for pulpwood, construction lumber, plywood, posts and pilings, boxes and crates, interior trim, paneling, millwork, porch columns, stair rails, coffins, furniture, shade rollers, and toys. Sold as western yellow pine or ponderosa pine.

Natural History. Slow growing; reaches maturity in 300–500 years (extreme age 700 years). Reproduction sporadic, generally occurring every 3–8 years when above-average summer rainfall follows a moderate to heavy cone crop; seedlings require full sunlight. Usually occurs as a mosaic of small even-aged groups that establish themselves after fires. Fire, several kinds of bark beetles, heart rot, and dwarf mistletoe cause the most damage. Owing to the large geographic range, ponderosa pine grows under a wide range of conditions, and is not exacting in its soil requirements. With a long taproot, the species is exceedingly drought resistant. Most commonly grows on droughty sites, where it occurs in pure parklike stands with grassy understories and little or no midstory. Open stands are maintained by periodic surface fires, which eliminate associate species with thin bark. Recent fire suppression policies have created much denser stands and have also allowed understory fuels to accumulate. Wildfires today are consequently crown fires, which consume the entire stand and not just the understory. Associate species on droughty sites include trembling aspen, lodgepole pine, California black oak, several species of pinyon, and several species of juniper. In the wetter parts of its range (especially the west side of the Cascades) where fire is less frequent, ponderosa pine grows in much denser mixed stands with Douglas-fir, grand fir, lodgepole pine, western larch, and sugar pine. Birds and small mammals eat large numbers of seeds, consuming nearly every seed in years with low numbers of cones.

Varieties. Generally subdivided into 3 varieties, but not all authorities agree with this division. Var. *ponderosa*, found in mixed stands in British Columbia, Washington, Oregon, and California, has needles borne in fascicles of 3 (rarely 2); 5–10 in. long; and cones 3–6 in. long. Rocky Mountain ponderosa pine (var. *scopulorum*), found throughout the interior portions of the West, has needles in fascicles of 2 or 3; 3–7 in. long; and cones 2–4 in. long. Arizona pine (var. *arizonica*) found in southern New Mexico and southern Arizona has needles borne in fascicles of 3, 4, or 5 (3–7 in. long) and small cones 2–3 in. long. Var. *ponderosa* grows in mixed stands, but vars. *scopulorum* and *arizonica* usually grow in pure stands. Arizona pine is sometimes classified as a completely separate species, *Pinus arizonica*.

Range. See figure 96. Elevation: sea level (near the Pacific coast) to 10,000 ft (in the Rocky Mountains). One of the most widely distributed trees in western North America.

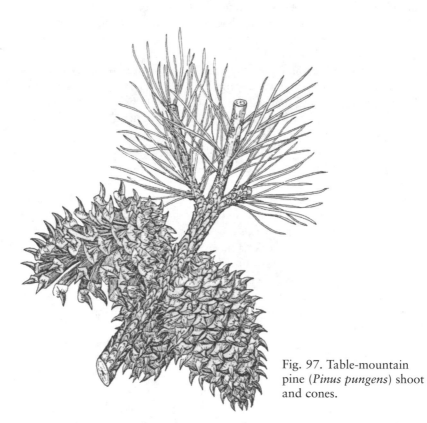

Fig. 97. Table-mountain pine (*Pinus pungens*) shoot and cones.

Fig. 98. Native range of Table-mountain pine (*Pinus pungens*).

Table-mountain pine
Pinus pungens Lamb. (fig. 97)

Small tree growing 30–60 ft in height. Crown open; often with branches as long as the tree is tall. Needles in fascicles of 2; 1–3 in. long; yellow-green; very stout; twisted. Cones sessile; light brown; ovoid; remaining closed (serotinous) for several years but persisting on the tree for many years; often in clusters that encircle the branch. Cone scales thick. Umbo with large hooked prickles. Wood with very little commercial value. Intolerant of shade. Growth rate slow. Regenerates from seed after severe wildfire or disturbance. Found on dry ridges and rock ledges. Grows with pitch pine, scarlet oak, and chestnut oak. For range see figure 98.

Monterey pine, Radiata pine
Pinus radiata D. Don (fig. 99)

Tree growing 70–100 ft in height and 2–3 ft in diameter (largest known 125 ft by 5 ft); often crooked, windswept, and irregular. Crown open; rounded. Needles in fascicles of 3, sometimes 2; 4–6 in. long; dark green; slender; flexible; persisting 3 years. Sheath persistent. Mature female cones short stalked; 3–7 in. long; ovoid; yellow-brown; asymmetrical, with outer basal scales round, thickened, and dome-like; remaining closed (serotinous) and persistent. Bark thick; red-brown to nearly black; furrowed. Moderately tolerant of shade; fast growing. Commonly grown as an ornamental in coastal California. No timber value in the United States, but the most widely planted pine in the world for wood products. Extensive plantations occur in Australia, New Zealand, Spain, Kenya, South Africa, Argentina, Chile, and Uruguay. Found naturally in only 4 coastal counties (San Mateo, Santa Cruz, Monterey, and San Luis Obispo) in California and on two islands off the coast of Baja California.

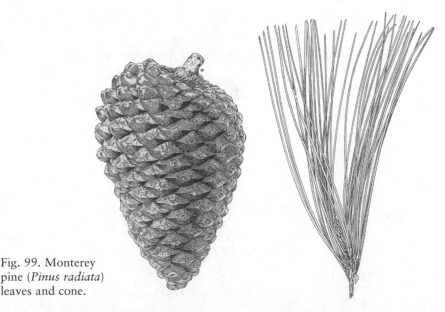

Fig. 99. Monterey pine (*Pinus radiata*) leaves and cone.

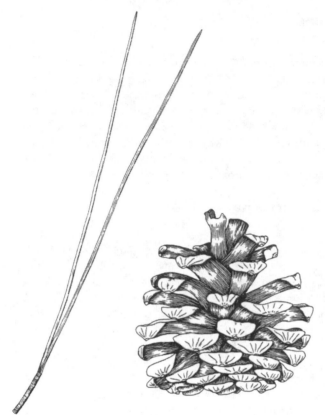

Fig. 100. Red pine (*Pinus resinosa*) leaves and cone.

Fig. 101. Native range of red pine (*Pinus resinosa*).

Red pine, Norway pine
Pinus resinosa Ait. (fig. 100)

Form. Excurrent slender tree growing 70–80 ft in height and 2–3 ft in diameter (largest known 150 ft by 5 ft). Bole with little taper and generally clear of small branches. Crown narrow and open, but broad and flat topped on old trees.

Leaves. Fascicles of 2; 4–6 in. long; slender; straight; brittle generally snapping when bent; dark yellow-green; persisting 4–5 years. Margins with minute teeth. Sheath persistent.

Cones. Male cones red-purple. Young female cones scarlet. Mature female cones subsessile; 1–2 in. long; ovoid-conic; chestnut-brown. Umbo without a prickle. Seeds 0.2 in. long; brown; seed wings 0.7 in. long.

Twigs. Stout; rough; orange to red-brown. Buds 0.5–0.7 in. long; scales red-brown with white fringed margins.

Bark. 1–1.5 in. thick; red-brown; broken into large rectangular plates with a scaly surface.

Wood. Valuable commercially. Sapwood white to yellow. Heartwood light red to orange-brown. Used for pulp, lumber, poles, pilings, and railroad ties.

Natural History. Intolerant of shade. Moderate growth rate; reaches maturity in 150 years (extreme age 300 years). Roots wide-spreading with taproot. Reproduction vigorous. One of the few forest trees to produce sound seed from self-pollination. Generally free of serious insect and disease problems. Extensively planted in northern United States and adjacent Canada for timber; also planted for shelterbelts and Christmas trees. Generally occurs on sandy soils in pure stands; associated with white pine on better sites, and jack pine and aspen on poorer sites.

Range. See figure 101.

Fig. 102. Pitch pine (*Pinus rigida*) shoot and cone.

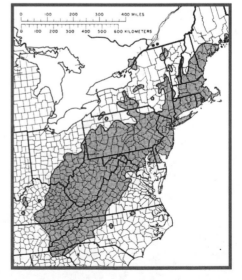

Fig. 103. Native range of pitch pine (*Pinus rigida*).

Pitch pine

Pinus rigida Mill. (fig. 102)

Form. Excurrent to deliquescent tree growing 50–80 ft in height and 1–2 ft in diameter (largest known 100 ft by 4 ft). Best form and largest sizes found in Pennsylvania. Crown open; irregular with large branches. Bole sometimes covered with small branches.

Leaves. Fascicles of 3; 3–5 in. long; stout; stiff; usually twisted; held nearly at right angles to twig; yellow-green; persisting 2–3 years; often found in tufts on bole. Margins with minute teeth. Sheath persistent.

Cones. Male cones yellow. Young female cones red-green. Mature female cones short stalked; 2–3 in. long; ovoid-conic to spherical; often occurring in clusters of 4–20; opening at maturity in most places but serotinous in the coastal regions from Maryland north to New Jersey. Umbo with short rigid prickle. Seeds 0.2 in. long; dull black.

Twigs. Stout; rough; gray-brown. Buds 0.5–0.7 in. long; scales chestnut-brown; fringed; resinous.

Bark. Thick; dark red-brown; flat irregular plates separated by furrows.

Wood. Sapwood white to pale yellow. Heartwood red-brown to light brown; coarse grained; moderately dense; very resinous. Used for rough lumber, railroad ties, mine props, and fuel. The high resin content makes the wood resistant to decay. Formerly used in the Northeast to produce tar hence the common name. Resin-impregnated knots or bundles of splinters burned for illumination.

Natural History. Very intolerant of shade. Reaches maturity in 150–200 years (extreme age 350 years). Reproduces after wildfire; young trees sprout from the root collar when the stem is killed by wildfire. Large branches susceptible to breaking in wind or ice storms. Pitch pine looper causes the most damage. Typically found on infertile, droughty sites with either shallow, sandy, or gravelly soil. In New Jersey found on imperfectly drained sands, gravels, or muck soils with Atlantic whitecedar. In mountainous areas, most common on south- and west-facing slopes. Forms pure or mixed stands with chestnut oak, scarlet oak, post oak, blackgum, red maple, gray birch, and Table-mountain pine.

Varieties. Some authorities classify pond pine as a variety of pitch pine, *Pinus rigida* var. *serotina*. The varieties are difficult to separate where their ranges overlap in the East's Delmarva Peninsula, owing to hybridization.

Range. See figure 103. Elevation: sea level–4,500 ft.

Fig. 104. Digger pine (*Pinus sabiniana*) leaves and cone.

Fig. 105. Native range of Digger pine (*Pinus sabiniana*).

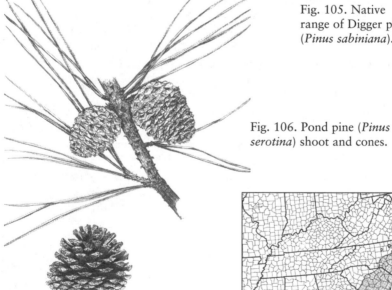

Fig. 106. Pond pine (*Pinus serotina*) shoot and cones.

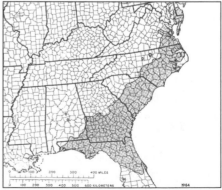

Fig. 107. Native range of pond pine (*Pinus serotina*).

Digger pine, Gray pine
Pinus sabiniana Dougl. (fig. 104)

Form. Excurrent when young but becoming deliquescent with age; growing 40–80 ft in height and 2–3 ft in diameter (largest known 160 ft by 5 ft). Bole often forked. Crown open; sparse.

Leaves. Fascicles of 3; 7–12 in. long; blue-green; flexible; drooping; persisting 3–4 years. Margin with minute teeth. Sheath persistent. Needles formerly woven into baskets by Native Americans.

Cones. Male cones yellow. Young female cones dark purple. Mature female cone similar to Coulter pine but smaller (6–10 in. long) and darker (chocolate-brown); persisting 5–7 years. Seeds 0.7 in. long; thick shelled; eaten by Native Americans, western gray squirrels, woodpeckers, and scrub jays. Seed wings 0.4 in. long.

Twigs. Stout; rough; purple-brown; white-waxy.

Bark. Dark brown to black; irregular scaly ridges separated by deep furrows.

Wood. Moderately heavy with an unusually high resin content. Used for railroad ties and pallets. Used during the California gold rush for fuel and rough construction.

Natural History. Found in the transition between grasslands of the California central valley and montane forests. Grows on exceedingly dry infertile sites in the Coast Ranges and on the west slope of the Sierra Nevada. Formerly found in moist valleys, but largely eliminated from these sites by agriculture. Fire and dwarf mistletoe cause the most damage. Found in pure stands or mixed with Coulter pine, California buckeye, western juniper, blue oak, California black oak, and interior live oak.

Range. See figure 105. Elevation: 100–7,000 ft.

Pond pine
Pinus serotina Michx. (fig. 106)

Some authorities classify pond pine as a variety of pitch pine (*Pinus rigida* var. *serotina*). See entry for pitch pine for additional information. Closely resembles pitch pine. Cones generally serotinous; shaped like a top when closed and nearly spherical when open; stalked. Umbo with a weak prickle or not armed. Grows in fire-maintained subclimaxes in wet flats and pocosins, generally in wet sandy loam or muck soil. Numerous suppressed buds in the bole and branches. Fire-scorched trees recover by sprouting from buds. Red heart is the most damaging agent. Grows in pure stands or mixed with loblolly pine, longleaf pine, red maple, swamp blackgum, pondcypress, sweetbay magnolia, and loblolly-bay. The stalked serotinous cones and sprouts distinguish pond pine from loblolly pine with which it is sometimes confused. Range: see figure 107.

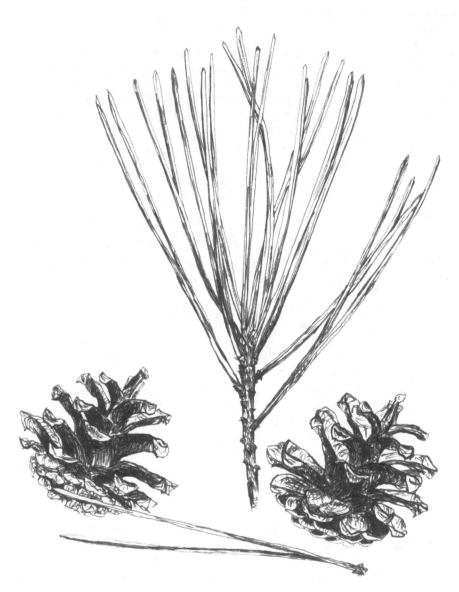

Fig. 108. Scots pine (*Pinus sylvestris*) shoot and cones.

Scotch pine, Scots pine

Pinus sylvestris L. (fig. 108)

Form. Excurrent to somewhat deliquescent tree growing 60–80 ft in height and 1–2 ft in diameter in the United States (largest known 100 ft by 2 ft). Highly variable in stem straightness, depending upon the original Eurasian seed source; may be straight, crooked, or leaning.

Leaves. Fascicles of 2; 2–3 in. long; strongly twisted; yellow-green to blue-green; persisting for 2–4 years; white stoma lines on all needle surfaces. Margins with or without minute teeth. Sheath persistent.

Cones. Male cones yellow or light pink. Young female cones red. Mature female cones short stalked; dull yellow-brown; 1–2 in. long; ovoid-spherical; apophysis pyramidally thickened. Umbo with a small generally deciduous prickle. Seeds gray to black.

Twigs. Slender; orange-brown when young; rough. Buds red-brown; 0.5 in. long; resinous.

Bark. Gray to brown; developing irregular furrows. Upper portions of tree scaly; bright orange.

Wood. Similar to red pine. Used for pulp, lumber, and poles.

Natural History. Intolerant of shade. Favored for Christmas trees in the Northeast and Lake States. Wildfire, pine root collar weevil, and pine root tip weevil cause the most damage. Widely used in landscaping and plantations in the Northeast, Lake States, and Pacific Northwest. Plantations do not develop well unless the proper seed source is used. The most widely distributed pine in the world. Native to Eurasia stretching from Scotland nearly to the Pacific Ocean. Naturalized in New England and the Lake States.

Fig. 109. Loblolly pine (*Pinus taeda*) leaves and cone.

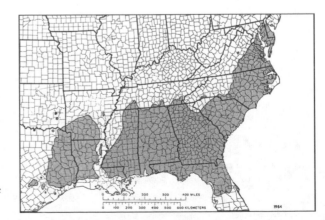

Fig. 110.
Native range
of loblolly pine
(*Pinus taeda*).

Loblolly pine, Loblolly

Pinus taeda L. (fig. 109)

Form. Large excurrent tree growing 90–120 ft in height and 2–3 ft in diameter (largest known 160 ft by 5 ft). Bole long; clear; wild trees somewhat crooked but tree breeding has greatly increased the straightness of trees in plantations. Crown rounded; dense.

Leaves. Fascicles of 3 (rarely 2 or 4); 5–8 in. long; slender; yellow-green; persisting 3 years. Margin with minute teeth. Sheath persistent.

Cones. Male cones yellow. Young female cones yellow, edges of scales and bracts tinged with red. Mature female cones sessile; 3–6 in. long; oblong-cylindrical; dull yellow-brown; opening at maturity. Cones firmly attached to branches, falling the next year, and leaving the basal scales attached to the twig. Scales thin. Umbo armed with a stout sharp spine, especially near the base of the cone. Seeds 0.2 in. long; brown with black markings; seed wings 0.7 in. long.

Twigs. Moderately slender; roughened; yellow-brown to red-brown. Buds 0.5 in. long; scales red-brown with free tips.

Bark. Scaly and nearly black on young trees; becoming red-brown to gray-brown; divided into rectangular flat plates with scaly surfaces. Scales not flaking off; accumulating to a depth of 2–3 in. on old trees. Resin pockets lacking.

Wood. Very valuable commercially; the most important timber species in the South. Sapwood yellow. Heartwood red-brown to orange-brown. Moderately heavy. Used for pulpwood, lumber, plywood, poles, and pilings. Sold as southern yellow pine.

Natural History. Somewhat tolerant of shade; reaches maturity in 150–180 years (extreme age 250 years). Very fast growing; producing 2–3 times more volume than associated hardwoods. Windfirm with wide-spreading lateral roots. Reproduction very aggressive forming dense stands. Not resistant to fire when young but developing resistance by age 12–15 years. Southern pine beetle, pine engraver beetle, and fusiform rust cause the most damage. Red heart causes damage in old trees. Confined largely to bottomlands in precolonial times, but now found on a wide variety of sites; absent only from very infertile and very wet sites. Responds well to management; planted extensively in the Southeast including on deep organic soils. Accounts for about one-half of the southern pine timber volume. Also planted in South Africa, New Zealand, and Central and South America. Grows naturally in pure or mixed stands with very many associates including longleaf pine, slash pine, shortleaf pine, pond pine, sweetgum, red maple, swamp chestnut oak, water oak, willow oak, laurel oak, cherrybark oak, southern red oak, white oak, northern red oak, white ash, yellow-poplar, American elm, and cabbage palmetto.

Hybrids. A natural hybrid between loblolly and longleaf pines, Sonderegger pine (*Pinus* x *sondereggeri*) may occur whenever both parents are present. Most commonly found when abundant loblolly pine trees pollinate isolated longleaf pine trees. Hybrid trees generally key to loblolly pine.

Range. See figure 110. Elevation: sea level to 1,200 ft.

Japanese black pine

Pinus thunbergii Parl.

Similar to red pine or Austrian pine in general characteristics. Needles in fascicles of 2; 3–4 in. long; bending not breaking when folded; dark green. Buds silver-gray; not resinous; fringed. Cones 2–3 in. long; brown; short stalked. Umbo armed with a minute prickle. Native to Japan and Korea. Used in ornamental plantings, especially on barrier islands in the Southeast.

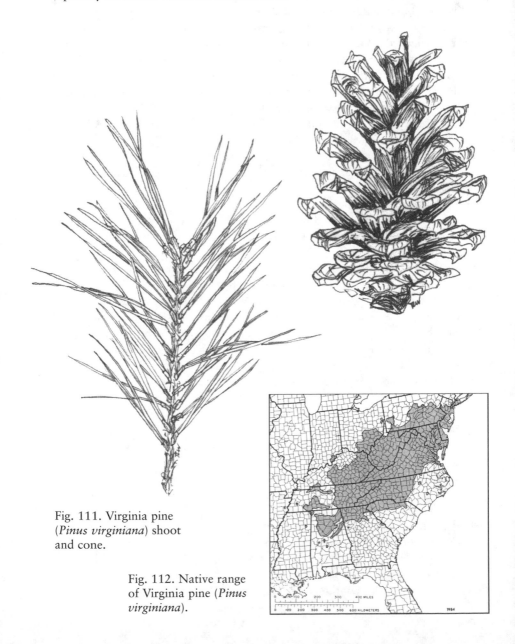

Fig. 111. Virginia pine
(*Pinus virginiana*) shoot
and cone.

Fig. 112. Native range
of Virginia pine (*Pinus
virginiana*).

Torrey pine
Pinus torreyana Parry ex Carr.

Small tree growing 25–60 ft in height and 1 ft in diameter, but growing to 100 ft in cultivation. Branches few; stout. Needles in fascicles of 5; 7–13 in. long; dark yellow-green; rigid; persisting 3–4 years. Sheath persistent. Mature female cones long stalked; 4–6 in. long; broad-ovoid; chocolate-brown; persisting 3–4 years. Scales thick. Umbo with a prickle. Bark red-brown; rough; furrowed. Very rare; the smallest range of any American pine. Found only in California in San Diego County and on Santa Rosa Island.

Virginia pine, Scrub pine
Pinus virginiana Mill. (fig. 111)

Form. Excurrent tree growing 70–80 ft in height and 1–2 ft in diameter (largest known 120 ft by 3 ft). Crown open; irregular; scraggly. Bole often covered with dead branches.

Leaves. Fascicles of 2; 1–3 in. long; divergent; stout; strongly twisted; yellow-green; persisting 3–4 years. Margins with minute teeth. Sheath persistent. Foliage similar to jack pine and lodgepole pine.

Cones. Male cones orange-brown. Young female cones pale green tinged with rose. Mature female cones short stalked; 2–3 in. long; ovoid-conic; symmetrical; dark red-brown; opening at maturity but persisting 3–4 years. Scales with sharp thin prickle; dark purple-red marginal stripe on inner face. Seeds 0.2 in. long; red-brown; seed wing about 1 in. long.

Twigs. Slender; purple-red; white-waxy on vigorous shoots.

Bark. Thin; scaly; orange-brown when young; gray-brown when old.

Wood. Very similar to jack pine. Used for rough construction and pulpwood. The knotty lumber is less valuable than other Southern pines.

Natural History. Very intolerant of shade; early growth rapid; reaches maturity in 60–80 years. Shallow rooted; not windfirm. Reproduction vigorous after catastrophic disturbance especially clearcutting and fire, forming dense, even-aged, pure stands. Common pioneer on old fields. Requires bare mineral soil; seed viability about 50 percent. Fire, girdling by rodents, windthrow, and southern pine beetle cause the most damage. Older dense stands subject to windthrow following partial harvests. Grows on a wide variety of soils; very competitive on dry soils; not tolerant of wet sites. Used for Christmas trees. Common associates include shortleaf pine, white oak, southern red oak, scarlet oak, red maple, and mockernut hickory.

Range. See figure 112. Elevation: near sea level to 3,300 ft.

Fig. 113. Whitebark
pine (*Pinus albicaulis*)
shoot and cones.

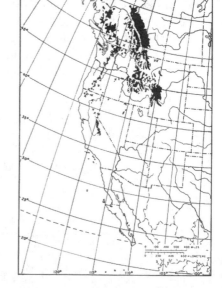

Fig. 114. Native range
of whitebark pine (*Pinus
albicaulis*).

Washoe pine

Pinus washoensis Mason & Stock.

Similar in overall appearance to Jeffrey pine or ponderosa pine and sometimes lumped into a single species with ponderosa pine. Needles in fascicles of 3 (rarely 2); 4–6 in. long; gray-green; slightly twisted. Margin finely toothed. Sheath persistent. Mature female cones sessile; light brown to red-brown; 3–4 in. long; broadly ovoid; inner side of cone scale much lighter than outer side. Umbo with a small reflexed prickle. Conservation of this rare and local species is a concern; known only from 3 mountain ranges in northern California and adjacent Nevada at the western edge of the Great Basin.

SOFT PINES: SUBGENUS *STROBUS*

Over 30 species of Soft Pine are found throughout the world, but only 13 species occur in our area. One species (eastern white pine) grows in the East; the remainder are western. Soft Pines generally bear needles in clusters (fascicles) of five, although the pinyons have clusters of one to four. The fascicle sheath is always deciduous. (A few exceptional Hard Pines also have a deciduous sheath.) Cones scales generally lack prickles. The wood is softer and more uniform in composition than that found in the Hard Pines.

Whitebark pine

Pinus albicaulis Engelm. (fig. 113)

Short subalpine tree similar in overall appearance to limber pine except for its cones. Cones short stalked; 1–3 in. long; nearly spherical; remaining closed at maturity (serotinous); often falling intact and opening by disintegrating at the axis; purple-brown. Scales thick. Umbo stout; pointed. White pine blister rust and mountain pine beetles provide the most damage. Seeds commonly eaten and disseminated by Clark's nutcracker, small mammals, bears, and sometimes humans. For range: see figure 114.

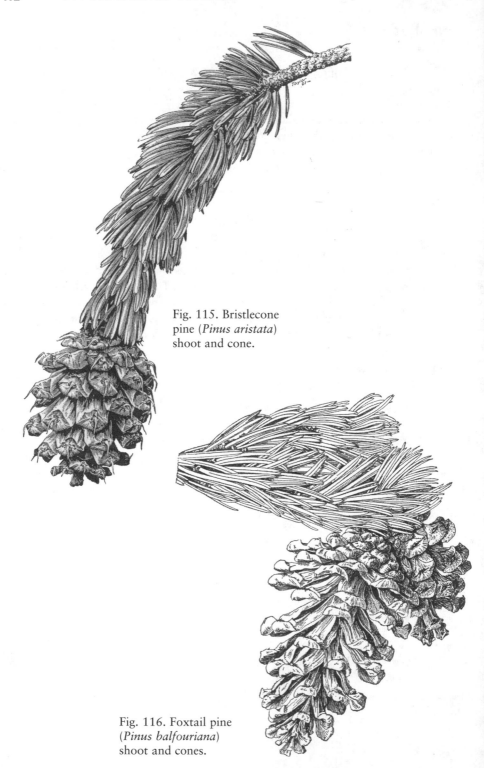

Fig. 115. Bristlecone pine (*Pinus aristata*) shoot and cone.

Fig. 116. Foxtail pine (*Pinus balfouriana*) shoot and cones.

Bristlecone pine, Colorado bristlecone pine
Pinus aristata Engelm. (fig. 115)

Form. Short tree growing 30–40 ft in height and 1–2 ft in diameter (largest known 60 ft by 3 ft). Bole short; stocky; commonly twisted. Crown dense; irregular; bushy; frequently clothing the stem nearly to the ground.

Leaves. Fascicles of 5; 1–2 in. long; stout and curved; needles in each fascicle often held together; dark green; persisting 10–17 years; lustrous on back; inner surfaces marked by numerous rows of stomata; outer surface with continuous medial groove; conspicuous white resin exudations. Sheath deciduous.

Cones. Male cones dark orange-red. Young female cones purple. Mature female cones short stalked; 3–4 in. long; ovoid-oblong; opening at maturity. Scales moderately thick with dark chocolate-brown apophysis; umbo dorsal; long, bristlelike, incurved prickles, which are easily broken. Seeds 0.2 in. long; seed wing 0.5 in. long.

Twigs. Stout; orange becoming nearly black; foliage held like a bottlebrush on young twigs. Buds 0.3 in. long; brown.

Bark. Thin; smooth; gray-white on young stems. On mature stems, 0.5–1 in. thick; red-brown; furrowed.

Wood. Little or no commercial value. Moderately soft. Heartwood pale red-brown; used locally for fuel and mine props. The location of these trees in sensitive ecological areas limits commercial value.

Natural History. Very intolerant of shade; slow growing; reaches maturity in 200–250 years; attains great age, some trees living over 2,400 years; reproduction sparse and scattered. Windfirm. Typical of exposed sites. Grows alone or mixed with limber pine, subalpine fir, and Engelmann spruce.

Range. Found locally near timberline in Colorado, northern New Mexico, and Arizona. Elevation: 7,500–10,800 ft.

Foxtail pine
Pinus balfouriana Grev. & Balf. (fig. 116)

Strongly resembles intermountain bristlecone pine. Some scientists argue that the two species should be combined. The leaves and ecology of these two species are essentially identical; only the cones differ. Foxtail pine has a rounded apophysis; depressed umbo; and a weak sometimes deciduous prickle. Found only at timberline and in alpine meadows in California.

Mexican pinyon, Nut pine
Pinus cembroides Zucc.

Needles in fascicles of 3 (rarely 2 or 4). Most seeds are thick shelled; but thin shelled seeds are found on trees in the Edwards Plateau, Texas. Seeds eaten by humans. Wood used locally for fuel and construction. Found in southern Arizona, New Mexico, and Texas; most of the range lies in Mexico in the Sierra Madre Occidental and Sierra Madre Oriental.

Fig. 117. Pinyon (*Pinus edulis*) shoot, leaves, and cone.

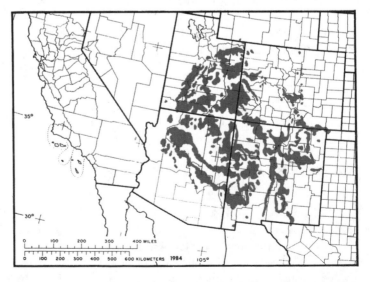

Fig. 118. Native range of pinyon (*Pinus edulis*).

Pinyon
Pinus edulis Engelm. (fig. 117)

Form. Excurrent or deliquescent small tree growing 20–50 ft in height and 1–2 ft in diameter (largest known 70 ft by 5 ft). Bole tapers rapidly; often dividing to form a spreading rounded crown.

Leaves. Fascicles of 2 (rarely 1 or 3); 1–2 in. long; moderately slender; needles in a fascicle held together; blue-green; curved; sharp pointed; persisting 4–6 years; marked with stomate bands. Margins with or without minute teeth. Fascicle sheath only partially deciduous.

Cones. Male cones yellow or red-brown. Mature female cones 1.5–2 in. long; ovoid to spherical; yellow or tan. Scales few; thickened; unarmed; resinous; 2 prominent seed cavities on each scale. Seeds 0.5 in. long; wingless; edible; thin shelled, easily cracked with teeth.

Twigs. Moderately stout; light brown to red-brown. Often persist nearly to the ground.

Bark. Divided into irregular ridges separated by shallow fissures; red-brown.

Wood. Low commercial value. Heartwood yellow; heavy. Used locally for fuel because the wood is heavy (only oak is heavier in the area) and burns with a pleasant aroma. Sometimes used for posts, railroad ties, and rough construction, but the small size of most trees limits use.

Natural History. Intolerant of shade. Growth extremely slow; reaches maturity in 200–400 years (extreme age 1,000 years). Windfirm. Grows on arid rocky plateaus, gravelly slopes, and mesas. Common associates include junipers, scrub oaks, sagebrush, and mountain-mahogany. Seeds called pine nuts are collected and eaten by humans. Small trees used locally for Christmas trees. Planted as an ornamental in the Southwest.

Range. See figure 118.

Fig. 119. Limber pine (*Pinus flexilis*) shoot and cone.

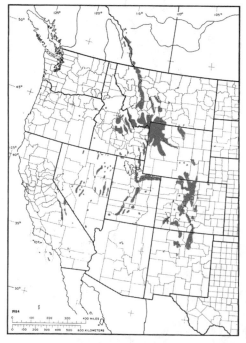

Fig. 120. Native range of limber pine (*Pinus flexilis*).

Limber pine, White pine
Pinus flexilis James (fig. 119)

Form. Excurrent to deliquescent tree growing 25–50 ft in height and 1–2 ft in diameter (largest known 85 ft by 6 ft). Crown broad; open; often crooked with large, plumelike branches; branches often extend to the ground.

Leaves. Fascicles of 5; 1–3 in. long; stiff; dark green; persisting 5–6 years; often turning upward; rows of stomata on all sides. Margins with or without minute teeth. Sheath is deciduous.

Cones. Male cones red. Young female cones red-purple. Mature female cones short stalked; 3–8 in. long; yellow; often clustered; nearly cylindrical; opening at maturity. Scales greatly thickened and often slightly reflexed. Umbo terminal; not armed. Seeds 0.5 in. long; wingless; thick; light brown.

Twigs. Flexible; smooth; silver-white or gray. Buds 0.5 in. long; broadly ovoid; pointed.

Bark. Thin; smooth; white-gray.

Wood. Little or no commercial value; close grained; used locally for mine props and railroad ties.

Natural History. Very intolerant of shade. Slow growing; reaches maturity in 200–300 years (extreme age 1,700 years). Very windfirm with long taproot. Wildfires, white pine blister rust, and bark beetles cause the most damage. Adapted to many sites but most often found on rocky foothills and windswept summits. Generally found in pure stands, but may grow at lower elevations with Douglas-fir, trembling aspen, and lodgepole pine, and at higher elevations with Engelmann spruce and subalpine fir.

Range. See figure 120. Elevation: 3,000–12,500 ft.

Sugar pine
Pinus lambertiana Dougl. (fig. 121)

Form. The largest American pine. Reaching massive sizes on good sites, commonly growing 175–200 ft in height and 3–6 ft in diameter (largest known 250 ft by 10 ft) with a long clear bole and large often contorted branches.

Leaves. Fascicles of 5; 2–4 in. long; thicker than western and eastern white pine; slightly twisted; blue-green to gray-green; persisting 2–4 years; white lines of stomata on each side of each needle. Margin with minute teeth. Sheath deciduous.

Cones. Male cones yellow. Young female cones bright pink with purple scale margins. Mature female cones long stalked; 10–24 in. long; the longest cone of any pine in the world; cylindrical; golden brown; resinous. Cone scales thicker and more rigid than western and eastern white pine. Umbo terminal; not armed. Well-formed cones used for decorations and crafts. Seeds 0.5 in. long; dark brown to black; seed wings 1–2 in. long.

Twigs. Slender to stout; at first rusty-hairy later hairless and orange-brown. Buds 0.3 in. long; sharp pointed; chestnut-brown; resinous.

Fig. 121. Sugar pine (*Pinus lambertiana*) shoot and cone.

Fig. 122. Native range of sugar pine (*Pinus lambertiana*).

Bark. On young trees thin; smooth; gray-green. On mature trees 1–4 in. thick; divided into flat plates covered with purple-red scales.

Wood. Very valuable commercially. Sapwood white to yellow-white frequently discolored by blue stain. Heartwood light brown to red-brown similar to white pine but coarser in texture. Used for window sashes, interior and exterior trim, pattern work, pulpwood, plywood, piano keys, and organ pipes. A sugary substance called pinite exudes from wounds or freshly cut wood, giving the tree its common name.

Natural History. Intolerant of shade. Reaches maturity in 200–350 years (extreme age 600 years). Reproduction generally sparse. Windfirm with well-developed tap and lateral root system. White pine blister rust and bark beetles cause the most damage. Generally found on moister sites than other western pines. Sometimes in small pure groves but more commonly mixed with ponderosa pine, Jeffrey pine, Douglas-fir, western hemlock, incense-cedar, and western red-cedar.

Range. See figure 122. Elevation: 1,000 to 10,000 ft; best developed on the west slopes of Sierra Nevada at 4,500–5,500 ft.

Intermountain bristlecone pine

Pinus longaeva D. K. Bailey

Nomenclature. Sometimes classified as a variety of bristlecone pine, *Pinus aristata* var. *longaeva*. Some authorities think this species and foxtail pine should be combined into a single species.

Form. Small tree growing 30–50 ft in height and 1–2 ft in diameter. Bole strongly tapered; commonly twisted. Crown irregular; often sheared by wind.

Leaves. Fascicles of 5; 0.5–1.5 in. long; upturned; needles in fascicle often held together; yellow-green; persisting 10–30 years; outer surface lacking medial groove; little or no white resin exudate. Sheath deciduous.

Cones. Male cones dark orange-red. Young female cones purple. Mature female cones nearly sessile; 2.5–3.5 in. long; ovoid; opening at maturity. Scales thick; apophysis red-brown; sharply keeled. Umbo dorsal and raised; with a short slender prickle. Seeds 0.2 in. long; seed wing 0.5 in. long.

Twigs. Stout; often twisted; red-brown. Foliage held like a bottlebrush on young twigs. Buds 0.4 in. long; red-brown.

Bark. Red-brown and furrowed.

Wood. Very low commercial value. Heartwood red-brown. The location of these trees in sensitive ecological areas limits commercial value.

Natural History. Very intolerant of shade; very slow growing. Reaches the greatest known age of any tree up to 5,000 years. Windfirm.

Range. Found locally at or near timberline in Utah, Nevada, and eastern California. Elevation: 5,600–11,100 ft.

Singleleaf pinyon, Pinyon, Nut pine

Pinus monophylla Torr. & Frem. (fig. 123)

Small deliquescent tree. Needles in fascicles of 1 (rarely 2); the only pine with 1 needle per fascicle; stiff; 0.7–1.5 in. long; green-white-waxy; curved; round in cross section; often with 2 grooves. Cone broadly ovoid; 1.5–2 in. long; prickles incurved. Seed wing lacking. Wood used locally for fuel and fence posts. Intolerant of shade. Very slow growing; trees only 7 ft tall may be 60 years old. Reaches maturity in 300 years (extreme age 600 years). Seed production highly variable; good seed crops occur every 3–7 years. Taproot long; large. Grows on extremely dry slopes and ridges; rarely found in valleys; the most drought-tolerant pine in North America. Found in pure stands or mixed with Utah juniper, western juniper, Jeffrey pine, ponderosa pine, and mountain-mahogany. Used for Christmas trees; seeds eaten by humans. For range see figure 124; abundant in the Great Basin. Elevation: 3,300–10,000 ft.

Western white pine, Idaho white pine

Pinus monticola Dougl. ex D. Don (fig. 125)

Form. Excurrent tree growing 90–180 ft in height and 2 ft in diameter (largest known 200 ft by 8 ft). Develops a long bole with narrow symmetrical crown. Occasional long branches produced near the apex of the crown give distinctive form.

Fig. 123. Singleleaf pinyon (*Pinus monophylla*) shoot and cone.

Fig. 124. Native range of single-leaf pinyon (*Pinus monophylla*).

Leaves. Fascicles of 5; 2–4 in. long; slender; slightly twisted; blue-green; persisting 3–4 years; white stomata lines on only the inner 2 sides of each needle. Margin with minute teeth. Sheath deciduous.

Cones. Male cones yellow. Young female cones red-purple in clusters. Mature female cones 5–12 in. long; cylindrical; yellow-brown; often slightly curved; resinous. Cone scales thin; slightly reflexed at the base of the cone. Umbo terminal; not armed. Seeds 0.25 in. long; seed wings about 1 in. long; red-brown.

Twigs. Slender; at first rusty-hairy, later smooth and red-brown to purple-brown. Buds 0.5 in. long; oblong-ovoid.

Bark. On young stems thin; smooth; light gray. On mature trees rarely over 1 in. thick; developing square or rectangular flat plates; dark gray.

Wood. Very important commercially. Sapwood white to yellow-white. Heartwood light brown; very similar to eastern white pine. Used for building construction, siding, interior and exterior trim, sashes, doors, caskets, matches, and pulpwood.

Natural History. Tolerant of shade when young but becoming intolerant with age. Reaches maturity in 200–400 years (extreme age 500 years). Windfirm with well-developed tap and lateral root system. Wildfires, white pine blister rust, and bark beetles cause the most damage. Development best on rich, porous, but moist soils. Formerly occurred in extensive pure stands in Idaho and adjacent Washington and British Columbia; severely reduced by white pine blister rust, fire suppression, and logging; occupies less than 5 percent of original distribution. Elsewhere grows mixed with grand fir, western larch, ponderosa pine, Douglas-fir, western redcedar, and western hemlock.

Range. See figure 126. Elevation: sea level–7,000 ft.

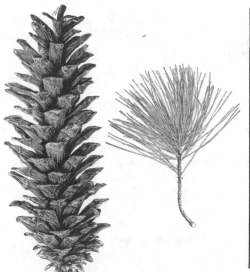

Fig. 125. Western white pine (*Pinus monticola*) shoot and cone.

Fig. 126. Native range of western white pine (*Pinus monticola*).

Parry pinyon, Nut pine
Pinus quadrifolia Parl. ex Sudw. (fig. 127)

Small deliquescent tree growing to 35 ft in height. Needles in fascicles of 4 (rarely 3 or 5); 1.2–2.2 in. long; blue-green; stiff; inner faces white with lines of stomata. Cone nearly spherical; yellow-brown; apophysis raised and diamond-shaped; prickle recurved. Twigs slender; orange-brown turning gray-brown; glandular hairy. Buds red-brown; slightly resinous. Found locally in the mountains of southern California. Most of the distribution of this tree lies in Baja California Norte, Mexico.

Fig. 127. Parry pinyon (*Pinus quadrifolia*) shoot and cone.

Southwestern white pine, Mexican white pine
Pinus strobiformis Engelm.

Classified by some authorities as a variety of limber pine, *Pinus flexilis* var. *reflexa*. Very similar to limber pine but having longer (2–4 in.), thinner needles and strongly reflexed cone scales. Found mostly in Mexico at high elevations in the Sierra Madre Oriental and Sierra Madre Occidental. This species reaches its northern limit in west Texas, New Mexico, and Arizona.

Eastern white pine, Northern white pine, Weymouth pine
Pinus strobus L. (fig. 128)

Form. Excurrent tree growing 80–120 ft in height and 3–4 ft in diameter (largest known 200 ft by 6 ft). Rivals yellow-poplar for the tallest tree in the East. Bole long; clear. Crown open; with horizontal branches. As found in other white pines, some branches grow much longer than others, producing a layered appearance.

Leaves. Fascicles of 5; 2–5 in. long; slender; green to blue-green; persisting 2–3 years; white stomata bands only on the inner surfaces. Margin with widely spaced minute teeth.

Cones. Male cones yellow. Mature female cones 4–8 in. long; short stalked; cylindrical; sometimes slightly curved; very resinous. Scales thin; tan-brown. Umbo terminal; not armed.

Twigs. Smooth; slender; pliable; hairless; red-brown to tan-brown. Buds 0.2 in. long; red-brown to chestnut-brown. Lateral branches borne in tight spirals (called whorls); one whorl produced each year.

Bark. On young trees, smooth, olive-green or gray. On mature trees, becoming furrowed with rectangular flat ridges; light gray.

Wood. Valuable commercially. Sapwood white to pale yellow. Heartwood light brown to red-brown; soft; lightweight. Used for sashes, interior trim, toys, novelties, signs, caskets, matches, venetian blinds. Formerly used extensively in home construction.

Natural History. Somewhat tolerant of shade when young. Until about 1890 this species ranked among the most important timber trees in North America. Reaches maturity in 200–250 years (extreme age 450 years). Formerly tapped by French settlers for naval stores. Prized by the British for ship masts during the colonial period. Currently used for Christmas trees, garlands, and ornamental plantings. Widely planted outside its natural range including in Europe. Wildfire and white pine weevil cause the most damage. Trees on wet sites killed by root rot. Grows on dry to moist soils; absent from wet soils. Common pioneer on old agricultural fields especially in New England. Grows in pure stands or mixed with red pine, northern red oak, white oak, eastern hemlock, balsam fir, red maple, paper birch, sugar maple, beech, and yellow birch.

Range. See figure 129. Elevation: sea level–4,500 ft.

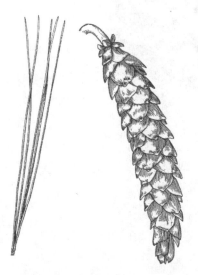

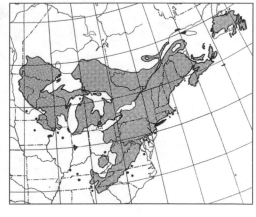

Fig. 128. Eastern white pine (*Pinus strobus*) leaves and cone.

Fig. 129. Native range of eastern white pine (*Pinus strobus*).

Fig. 130. Bigcone Douglas-fir
(*Pseudotsuga macrocarpa*)
shoot and cone.

DOUGLAS-FIR: THE GENUS *PSEUDOTSUGA*

The genus *Pseudotsuga* contains five species worldwide, but only two species occur in our area. Douglas-firs are evergreen trees with slightly drooping irregularly placed branches. The leaves are linear, spirally arranged, and borne on the twig on small raised mounds. The buds are red-brown and sharp pointed. Reproductive parts are borne in unisexual cones, and both sexes are present on each tree (monoecious). Female cones are wind pollinated, pendent at maturity, and require one year to mature. Each cone scale bears two winged seeds, and no umbo is present. The cone bract is three-pronged at the tip and always longer than the scale. The bract turns from green to brown when the seed is mature. The wood is nonporous, contains resin ducts, and varies by geographic region between moderately light and moderately heavy. Douglas-fir is not a true fir (of the genus *Abies*), and thus a hyphen should be used in the common name. The foliage is sometimes confused with spruce or fir, but the small mounds on twigs and sharp-pointed buds are reliable characters for Douglas-fir.

KEY TO DOUGLAS-FIRS

1. Cones 2–4 in. long; leaf tip obtuse to acute . . . .Douglas-fir, *Pseudotsuga menziesii*
1. Cones 4–7 in. long; leaf tip mucronate . . . .
. . . . .bigcone Douglas-fir, *Pseudotsuga macrocarpa*

Bigcone Douglas-fir, Bigcone-spruce
Pseudotsuga macrocarpa (Vasey) Mayr (fig. 130)

Excurrent tree growing 30–100 ft in height and 2–3 ft in diameter (largest known 145 ft by 7 ft). Crown generally extends to the ground. Leaves linear with mucronate tips. Cones 4–7 in. long. Cone scales stiff; rounded at tip. Cone bracts only slightly longer than the cone scales. Limited commercial value; wood used locally for rough construction and fuel. Reaches maturity in 250–300 years (extreme age 600 years). Grows on dry rocky slopes. Found mostly in small groups, but also mixed with canyon live oak in the transition zone between chaparral and higher elevation mixed conifer forests. Trees damaged by fire develop a new crown by sprouting along the upper surface of branches in the upper crown. Does not sprout from stumps. Found only in the mountains of southwestern California. Elevation: 900–7,900 ft.

Douglas-fir, Doug-fir, Oregon-pine
Pseudotsuga menziesii (Mirb.) Franco (fig. 131)

Form. Moderate to very large excurrent tree depending upon geographic region; growing 230–250 ft in height (largest known 330 ft tall) and 5–6 ft in diameter west of the Cascades, but only 130 ft in height in the Rocky Mountains. Trees 400 ft tall have been reported, but the reports cannot be confirmed. Crown compact; pyramidal.

Leaves. Linear; 0.7–1.2 in. long; more-or-less flat; blunt to pointed; petiolate; grooved above; 2 white stomata lines below; persisting 5–8 years.

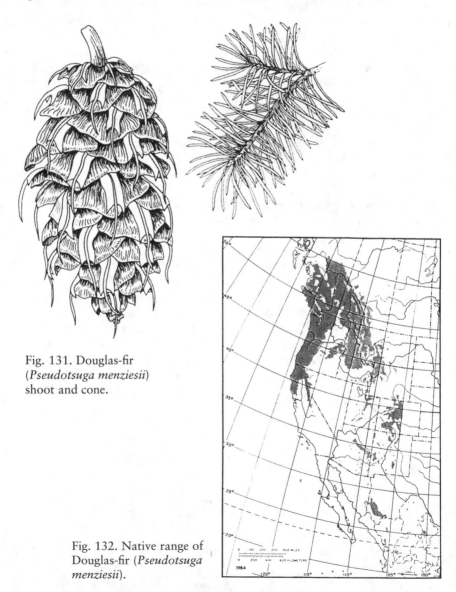

Fig. 131. Douglas-fir
(*Pseudotsuga menziesii*)
shoot and cone.

Fig. 132. Native range of
Douglas-fir (*Pseudotsuga
menziesii*).

Cones. Male cones orange-red or yellow. Young female cones red-green. Mature female cones 2–4 in. long; oblong-ovoid. Scales thin; rigid; rounded. Bracts 3-pronged; much longer than the scales (exserted). Seeds 0.2 in. long. Seed wing large; rounded.

Twigs. Slender; hairy; orange-brown becoming gray-brown. Covered with resin blisters when young. Buds 0.2 in. long; conical; sharp pointed; lustrous; brown.

Bark. Smooth on young stems; gray-brown; resin blisters present; becoming very thick (6–24 in.) on old trees; long rectangular ridges separated by deep furrows; red-brown to gray-brown.

Wood. Very valuable commercially in the Pacific Northwest; much less valuable in the Rocky Mountains. One of 2 leading timber species in the United States. (The other species is loblolly pine of the South.) Sapwood white, yellow, or red-white. Heartwood very variable in color depending upon growth rate; yellow or red-yellow when slow grown; orange-red or dark red when fast grown. Weight dependent upon geographic region; moderately light in the Rocky Mountains, but moderately heavy in the Pacific Northwest. Used for lumber, timbers, poles, plywood, laminated beams and arches, silos and tanks, sashes, doors, flooring, railroad cars, railroad ties, ships, and containers for corrosive chemicals. Leading pulpwood species in the Pacific Northwest.

Natural History. Intermediate in tolerance to shade. Fast growing; maintains fast diameter growth for over 100 years. Long-lived; reaches maturity in 600–700 years (extreme age 1,400 years). Reproduction abundant and vigorous on disturbed sites especially after clearcutting and wildfire. Extensive pure even-aged stands occur in northern Oregon, Washington, and British Columbia, owing to recurrent wildfires and more recently to clearcutting. Seed production somewhat irregular; moderate to heavy seed crops produced every 3–4 years. Extensively planted for wood products in Oregon, Washington, and British Columbia. Well-developed taproot with wide-spreading laterals; root grafts common. Dwarf mistletoe, windthrow, red ring rot, Douglas-fir tussock moth, Swiss needle cast, and western spruce budworm cause the most damage. Adapted to a variety of soils, but development is best on moist, deep, well-aerated soils. Poorly drained or compacted soils are not suitable. Able to endure drought in the Rocky Mountains. In the Pacific Northwest, Douglas-fir grows with western hemlock, western redcedar, Sitka spruce, and ponderosa pine. Where regeneration after wildfire or logging has been incomplete, red alder is a common associate. In the Rocky Mountains, ponderosa pine and Engelmann spruce are common associates. Commonly planted in the United States for Christmas trees, and in Europe, Australia, New Zealand, and Chile for timber. Many songbirds eat the seeds, and old trees provide critical habitat for the Northern spotted owl, an endangered bird.

Varieties. In the Rocky Mountains region, Rocky Mountain Douglas-fir, *Pseudotsuga menziesii* var. *glauca*, is recognized. It differs from the typical variety by having white-waxy needles, generally smaller cones, and cone bracts that extend outward at right angles to the cone.

Range. See figure 132. Elevation varies by region: sea level–7,500 ft in the Pacific Northwest, and 1,800–10,700 ft in the Rocky Mountains.

HEMLOCK: THE GENUS *TSUGA*

This genus contains 14 species widely scattered through North America and Asia. In our area 4 native species occur: 2 in the West and 2 in the East. Hemlocks are broadly pyramidal evergreen trees with slender, horizontal, pendulous branches. The terminal shoot characteristically droops. Leaves are evergreen, linear, spirally arranged, grooved above, have small petioles, and two white stomata bands on the underside. Borne on small woody pegs (sterigmata), the leaves are often arranged on opposite sides of the twig by twisting the petioles. The leaves are deciduous in drying. Reproductive parts are borne on twigs of the previous season in unisexual cones, and both sexes occur on each tree (monoecious). Female cones are wind pollinated, pendent, and mature in one year. Cone bracts are shorter than the scales. Each scale contains two terminally winged seeds dotted with small resin vesicles. The bark contains high levels of tannin. The wood is nonporous, moderately soft, and normally lacking resin ducts. Hemlocks are generally very tolerant of shade and require abundant moisture. *Tsuga* is one of the few scientific names to be adapted from a Japanese word (*tsugi*) instead of a Greek or Latin word.

KEY TO HEMLOCKS

1. Needles rounded or keeled above; 2 white bands above and 2 below . . . .
. . . . .mountain hemlock, *Tsuga mertensiana*
1. Needles flat, grooved above, with 2 white bands only below . . . . .Go to 2

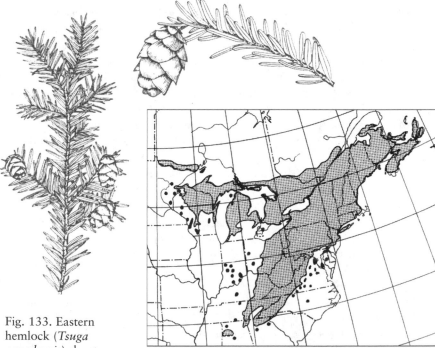

Fig. 133. Eastern hemlock (*Tsuga canadensis*) shoots and cones.

Fig. 134. Native range of eastern hemlock (*Tsuga canadensis*).

2. Needle margins entire; needles spreading in all directions . . . .

. . . . Carolina hemlock, *Tsuga caroliniana*

2. Needle margins finely toothed; needles mostly 2-ranked 3

3. Needles tapering from base to apex . . . . .eastern hemlock, *Tsuga canadensis*

3. Needles of uniform width from base to apex . . . .

. . . . .western hemlock, *Tsuga heterophylla*

Eastern hemlock, Canada hemlock

Tsuga canadensis (L.) Carr. (fig. 133)

Form. Excurrent large tree growing 80–100 ft in height and 3–4 ft in diameter (largest known 170 ft by 7 ft). Crown dense; pyramidal; horizontal branches extending to the ground in open-grown trees. Terminal leader flexible; drooping.

Leaves. Linear; flattened; 0.3–0.7 in. long; tapering from base to apex; dark yellow-green; 2 narrow well-defined white bands of stomata below; appearing 2-ranked; rounded or notched at apex. Shorter needles generally lie upside down parallel to the twig. Margin with minute teeth. Petiole short.

Cones. Male cones yellow. Young female cones pale green. Mature female cones 0.5–0.7 in. long; oblong-ovoid; light brown. Scales nearly rounded; margin smooth; scales of open cones held at 45 degree angle. Seeds 0.1 in. long; seed wing about 0.3 in. long; light brown.

Twigs. Slender; light brown; hairy the first year later becoming gray-brown and hairless. Buds ovoid; 0.1 in. long.

Bark. Scaly on young trees becoming deeply furrowed and ridged; red-brown to gray with purple streaks on freshly cut surfaces. In the late 1800s and early 1900s trees were felled only for their bark, which was boiled in water to extract tannin used in tanning leather.

Wood. Lumber production peaked about 1900, when the wood was used for lumber, sheathing, roofing, subflooring, boxes, and crates. Current commercial value low. Sapwood light brown. Heartwood red-brown. Moderately lightweight; coarse grained; often spiral grained. Used for pulpwood and lower grades of lumber; knotty, the result of persistent branches.

Natural History. The most shade-tolerant eastern tree; able to survive suppression for very long periods. Slow growing; reaches maturity in 250–350 years (extreme age 900 years). Reproduction abundant but only in the shade of other trees. Moderate to large seed crops produced about every other year, but seed viability is only about 25 percent. Trees less than 3 ft tall easily killed by drought. Root system shallow; wide-spreading; occasional root grafts. Lightning, drought, hemlock looper, browsing by white-tailed deer, and hemlock woolly adelgid cause the most damage. The hemlock woolly adelgid is becoming a serious problem in some areas. Found on cool moist sites; sometimes in small pure groves, but more commonly mixed with white pine, yellow birch, sweet birch, black cherry, American beech, red maple, sugar maple, white ash, and basswood. Commonly planted as an ornamental tree. Foliage browsed by white-tailed deer.

Range. See figure 134.

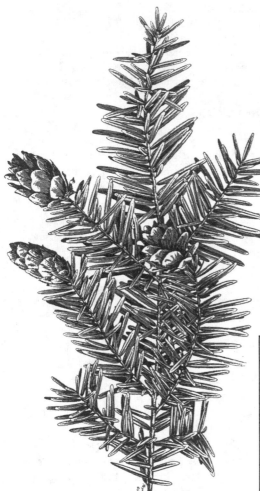

Fig. 135. Western hemlock (*Tsuga heterophylla*) shoot and cones.

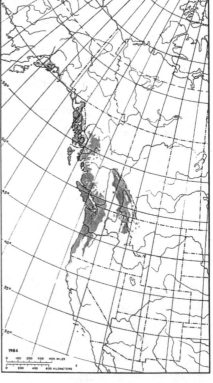

Fig. 136. Native range of western hemlock (*Tsuga heterophylla*).

Carolina hemlock

Tsuga caroliniana Engelm.

Excurrent tree growing 50–80 ft in height and 2–3 ft in diameter. Leaves linear; yellow-green; extending from the twig in all directions. Margin entire. Mature female cones 0.7–1.5 in. long; brown; cone scales of open cones held at right angles to the cone axis or sometimes reflexed. Wood has no commercial value. Found on rocky slopes and ledges of the Appalachian Mountains from Virginia to northern Georgia.

Western hemlock

Tsuga heterophylla (Raf.) Sarg. (fig. 135)

Form. Large excurrent tree growing 140–200 ft in height and 3–4 ft in diameter (largest known 260 ft by 9 ft). Bole long; clear. Crown short; open; pyramidal. Terminal shoot typically flexible; drooping.

Leaves. Linear; flat; 0.2–0.7 in. long; dark shiny green and grooved above; 2 white stomatal bands below; mostly 2-ranked. Apex rounded or blunt.

Cones. Male cones yellow. Young female cones red or purple. Mature female cones 0.7–1 in. long; ovoid; light brown. Scales nearly rounded; wavy margined. Seeds 0.1 in. long; ovoid; as long as wide. Seed wing straw colored.

Twigs. Slender; hairy; pale yellow-brown becoming dark red-brown; drooping. Resin blisters lacking. Buds ovoid; 0.1 in. long; blunt; bright chestnut-brown.

Bark. Thin (1–1.5 in.) even on large trees. Scaly on young trees; russet-brown. On old trees, hard; dark russet-brown; wide, flat ridges separated by furrows; inner bark dark red streaked with purple. Formerly boiled to obtain tannin used in tanning leather.

Wood. Once considered a worthless weed, western hemlock now produces commercially very valuable wood. Sapwood white to yellow-brown. Heartwood red-brown; frequently with dark streaks or white spots. Moderately light in weight; straight grained. Used for pulpwood, lumber, plywood, ladder rails, slack cooperage, paneling, boxes, and crates. Superior to eastern hemlock in overall quality.

Natural History. Very tolerant of shade. Fast growing competing well with Douglas-fir, and sometimes producing 25–40 percent more volume. Reaches maturity in 350–425 years (extreme age 700 years). Reproduction abundant and vigorous; often becomes established on decaying logs (nurse trees) and stumps. Some seed is produced each year, and heavy seed crops occur every 3–4 years. Seed viability is about 50 percent. Root system shallow; wide-spreading; taproot absent. Wildfire, windthrow, sulfur dioxide pollution, dwarf mistletoe, western hemlock looper, and western blackheaded budworm cause the most damage. Grows on a variety of soils provided the soil is moist and well aerated with a deep litter layer. Planted for fiber production. Grows in pure dense stands, or mixed at lower elevations with Douglas-fir, silver fir, grand fir, Sitka spruce, western red-cedar, redwood, and bigleaf maple, and at higher elevations with noble fir, Alaska-cedar, mountain hemlock, western white pine, and lodgepole pine. Roosevelt elk and black-tailed deer commonly browse the foliage.

Range. See figure 136. Elevation: sea level–7,000 ft.

Fig. 137. Mountain hemlock (*Tsuga mertensiana*) shoot and cones.

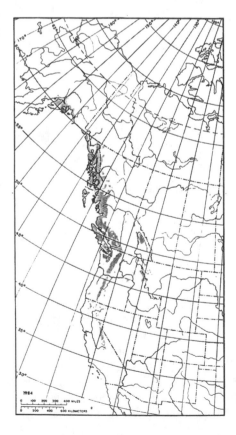

Fig. 138. Native range of mountain hemlock (*Tsuga mertensiana*).

Mountain hemlock
Tsuga mertensiana (Bong.) Carr. (fig. 137)

Form. Excurrent tree growing 75–100 ft in height and 2–3 ft in diameter (largest known 150 ft by 7 ft). Bole long and clear, or knotty and malformed. Crown short; pyramidal; with slender drooping branches and drooping terminal shoot. Becomes a sprawling shrub (*krummholz*) at timberline.

Leaves. Linear; semicircular in cross section; 0.5–1 in. long; pale gray-green; white stomatal bands above and below; upper surface often grooved; base abruptly narrowed into straight or twisted petiole; extending from all sides of twig or crowded toward upper side. Tip blunt.

Cones. Male cones purple. Young female cones purple or green. Mature female cones 1.5–3.5 in. long; oblong-cylindrical; yellow-green to purple. Scales oblong-obovate; held at right angles to the axis or reflexed. Seeds 0.1 in. long; ovoid. Seed wings straw colored.

Twigs. Slender or stout; hairy for 2–3 years; light red-brown becoming gray-brown and scaly. Buds conical; 0.1 in. long; acute; red-brown; outer scales with awl-like tip.

Bark. Thin (at most 1.5 in.) on all trees; dark purple to red-brown; narrow furrows separate narrow rounded ridges. Contains large quantities of tannin.

Wood. Similar to western hemlock but seldom used owing to the sensitive location of most stands.

Natural History. Tolerant of shade. Growth slow; reaches maturity before 500 years. Reproduction develops slowly; sometimes requiring 100 years to develop fully stocked stands. Adequate seed crops produced every 3–4 years, but other years can be complete failures. Root system shallow. Restricted to north-facing slopes and cirque basins in the southern portions of the range. Found on loose coarse-textured soils or thick organic matter. Grows in pure stands or mixed with subalpine fir, alpine larch, Engelmann spruce, whitebark pine, lodgepole pine, and western white pine.

Hybrids. Hybridizes occasionally with western hemlock forming *Tsuga* x *jeffreyi*. Formerly thought by some authorities to be a hybrid between spruce and hemlock.

Range. See figure 138. Elevation: sea level (in Alaska) to 10,000 ft; found mostly at or near timberline on snowy subalpine sites.

YEWS: THE ORDER TAXALES

Until about 1920, yews were classified with the conifers. But based on the reproductive differences noted below, universal agreement now exists to place them in their own order.

THE YEW FAMILY: TAXACEAE

Worldwide the Taxaceae contains 17–20 species in five genera, but in our area only 4 species in two genera grow large enough to sometimes be considered trees. Members of the Yew Family are small trees or shrubs with profuse branching and leaves that are spirally arranged, linear, evergreen, decurrent, and more-or-less two-ranked. The spherical pollen cones are composed of either flat (*Torreya*) or peltate (*Taxus*) scales, each with two to eight pollen sacs. The solitary seeds terminate short branches, and they are subtended by small decussate bracts. The seed becomes partly or completely overgrown by a fleshy or leathery sac (the aril), which develops from the base of the seed. At maturity the seed looks more like a berry than the seed of a gymnosperm. The wood is nonporous and lacks resin ducts.

YEW: THE GENUS *TAXUS*

The genus *Taxus* contains six to ten species in the world. Three species occur in our area, but only two become trees. Two light green stripes occur on the underside of each leaf. Unlike the tips in *Torreya*, leaf tips are not sharp. The reproductive parts are unisexual, and each tree contains only one sex (dioecious). The seeds mature in one year and are nearly covered by a bright red aril. The foliage, bark, and seeds, but not the aril, are poisonous. All six to ten species are very similar in appearance, and knowledge of native range is useful in identification. Originally all taxa were classified as varieties of a single worldwide species.

KEY TO YEWS

1. Leaves straight; yellow-green above . . . . .western yew, *Taxus brevifolia*
1. Leaves sickle-shaped; dark green above   . . . . .Florida yew, *Taxus floridana*

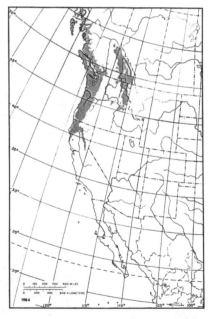

Fig. 139. Pacific yew (*Taxus brevifolia*) shoot and seed.

Fig. 140. Native range of Pacific yew (*Taxus brevifolia*).

Pacific yew, Western yew
Taxus brevifolia Nutt. (fig. 139)

Form. Small tree or large shrub growing 20–50 ft in height and 1–2 ft in diameter (largest known 60 ft by 5 ft); becomes a sprawling shrub near timberline. Bole with large limbs; often fluted. Crown large; lopsided.

Leaves. Linear-lanceolate; 0.5–1 in. long; persisting 5–12 years; petiolate; yellow-green above with 2 pale stripes beneath.

Seeds. Male cones in spherical heads; yellow. Seed single; erect; ovoid-oblong; covered with hard shell; 0.3 in. long; enclosed except at the tip by scarlet aril; maturing in one season. Native Americans believed that eating the aril would prevent conception.

Twigs. Slender; drooping. Buds small; ovoid; obtuse; numerous overlapping scales.

Bark. Very thin (largest 0.2 in.); scaly; dark red-purple. Contains taxol, useful in treating cancer.

Wood. Commercial lumber value limited by the small size of the tree and scarce supplies. Sapwood light yellow. Heartwood bright orange to red; even-textured; heavy; very hard; strong; durable. Provides the heaviest lumber of all gymnosperms. Used for archery bows, canoe paddles, tool handles, splitting wedges, boat decking, musical instruments, fence posts, and novelty items. Native Americans obtained red paint from the wood. Many logs are sent to Japan, where they are used for carvings and toko poles.

Natural History. The most shade-tolerant tree in the Pacific Northwest; usually dies from exposure when left after logging. Slow growing; reaches maturity in 250–350 years. Reproduction adequate but only in shade; seeds produced prolifically but the frequency of heavy crops is not known. Germination slow. Also reproduces by stump sprouts and layering. Fire causes the most damage. Grows on deep, moist, gravelly soils; best development near springs, along mountain streams, or in coves and shady canyons. Found in small groups or as an occasional understory tree growing with grand fir, white fir, subalpine fir, western redcedar, western larch, Engelmann spruce, western hemlock, Douglas-fir, black cottonwood, red alder, and Oregon ash. Pacific yew was largely considered to be a weed, until the use in treating cancer was discovered.

Range. See figure 140. Elevation: 2,000 to 8,000 ft.

Florida yew
Taxus floridana Nutt.

Shrub or small tree growing 20–30 ft in height. Leaves linear; 0.5–1 in. long; slightly sickle-shaped; dark green above with 2 gray stripes below. Bark thin; scaly; purple-brown. Found only on shady limestone bluffs along the Apalachicola River in Florida.

TORREYA: THE GENUS *TORREYA*

The genus *Torreya* contains four to six species found in eastern Asia and North America. Only two species occur in our area: one in California and one in Georgia and Florida. The unisexual reproductive parts are borne on separate trees (dioecious). Both species are rare in nature.

KEY TO TORREYAS

1. Leaves 1–3 in. long; older twigs red-brown . . . .
. . . . .California torreya, *Torreya californica*
1. Leaves 0.6–1.5 in. long; older twigs yellow-green . . . .
. . . . .Florida torreya, *Torreya taxifolia*

California torreya, California-nutmeg
Torreya californica Torr.

Small tree growing 15–70 ft in height and 1–2 ft in diameter. Crown pyramidal with slender spreading branches. Leaves linear-lanceolate; 1–3 in. long; rigid; dark green and lustrous above; paler below with 2 narrow white bands of stomata. Leaf tip acuminate; often bristle tipped. The seed is ellipsoidal; 1–1.5 in. long; aril green with purple streaks; maturing in 2 years but requiring an additional year to germinate. Older twigs red-brown; drooping. Buds small; ovoid; acute; composed of a few overlapping opposite scales. Bark thin (0.5 in.); gray-brown; divided into narrow, scaly ridges. Wood varies from moderately lightweight to moderately heavy; little color difference between sapwood and heartwood, both yellow. Little or no commercial value; used locally for fence posts, models, and novelty items. Tolerant of shade; slow growing; long-lived; reproduction sparse, but stumps sprout vigorously. Grows only on moist sites in dense thickets or mixed with hardwoods. Found in scattered areas in the Sierra Nevada and coast ranges of California.

Florida torreya, Stinking-cedar, Gopherwood
Torreya taxifolia Arn.

Small tree growing 20–40 ft in height and 1 ft in diameter. Leaves linear-lanceolate; 0.6–1.5 in. long; 2 gray stomatal stripes below; fetid odor when bruised. Leaf tip sharp. Seed ellipsoidal; 1–1.5 in. long; aril dark green with purple streaks. Older twigs yellow-green; drooping. Wood fine grained; strong; durable. Formerly used for fence posts. Little is known about seed reproduction, seed germination, and seedling establishment. Also reproduces from stump sprouts. Grows with American beech, yellow-poplar, American holly, loblolly pine, spruce pine, white oak, and sweetgum. Formerly used for Christmas trees. Once thriving in the wild, most populations have declined severely owing to fungal disease. Federally listed as endangered. Found largely on shady limestone bluffs along the Apalachicola River in Florida and southern Georgia.

CHAPTER 3
ANGIOSPERMS:
MONOCOTYLEDONS

Angiosperms, technically called the Magnoliophyta, are characterized by seeds contained within an ovary. At maturity the ovary develops into a fruit. Whereas gymnosperms are always woody, angiosperms may be either woody or herbaceous. Angiosperms also differ from gymnosperms in having a much more complex wood structure, containing many more types of cells especially vessel elements. Worldwide the angiosperms include about 250,000 species in about 400 families. Thus there are about 300 times as many species of angiosperms as gymnosperms. Angiosperms also appeared about 210 million years later in the fossil record (in the Lower Cretaceous) and are universally considered more advanced. Angiosperms are subdivided into two classes, monocotyledons and dicotyledons.

MONOCOTYLEDONS: THE CLASS LILIOPSIDA

Monocotyledons, generally called monocots, are characterized by leaves (usually alternate and entire) with parallel veins, flower parts borne in multiples of three, scattered closed vascular bundles, and generally one seed leaf (hence the name monocot). Authorities agree that monocots arose from primitive dicots. About one-quarter of all angiosperms are monocots. Most monocots are herbs, but the families listed below include species that grow tall enough to be considered trees. Tree-sized monocots never form the annual increments of wood (secondary xylem) found in gymnosperms and angiosperms.

THE CENTURY-PLANT FAMILY: AGAVACEAE

Worldwide this family contains about 200–300 species in 8–13 genera found in arid regions of the Americas especially Mexico. Yucca is the only tree-sized genus in our region. Older manuals include this family within the Liliaceae.

Members of this family have alternate, linear leaves, borne closely spaced in clusters. The flowers are bisexual and usually showy. The ovary is either inferior or superior. It contains carpels that usually mature into a capsule, but sometimes into a berry. The flowers are pollinated by birds, bats, or insects. Economically the family provides twine (*Agave* and *Yucca*), medicine (*Agave* and *Yucca*), liquor (*Agave*), and ornamental plants.

YUCCA OR SPANISH-BAYONET: THE GENUS *YUCCA*

Worldwide this genus contains about 35 species found in Mexico, the West Indies, and the southern portions of our region. The tallest species in our region are keyed below, and the most treelike are described.

KEY TO YUCCAS

1. Native to the Southeast . . . . .Go to 2
1. Native to the Southwest . . . . .Go to 3
   2. Leaves toothed; fruit soft . . . . .aloe yucca, *Yucca aloifolia*
   2. Leaves nearly entire; fruit dry . . . . .moundlily yucca, *Yucca gloriosa*
3. Fruit held erect . . . . .soaptree yucca, *Yucca elata*
3. Fruit pendent 4

Fig. 141. Joshua-tree
(*Yucca brevifolia*) form.

4. Fruit with thin dry flesh; leaves toothed . . . . .Joshua-tree, *Yucca brevifolia*
4. Fruit with soft flesh; leaves entire or nearly so 5
5. Leaf margin lacking loose fibers . . . . .Schotts yucca, *Yucca schottii*
5. Leaf margins with loose filamentous fibers 6
   6. Leaves 2–4 ft long; dark green 7
   6. Leaves 1–2 ft long; yellow-green 8
7. Leaves concave . . . . .Trecul yucca, *Yucca treculeana*
7. Leaves flat . . . . Faxon yucca, *Yucca faxoniana*
   8. Flower style elongated .Torrey yucca, *Yucca torreyi*
   8. Flower style short . . . . .Mohave yucca, *Yucca schidigera*

Joshua-tree

Yucca brevifolia Engelm. (fig. 141)

Small tree growing to 35 ft in height and 2–3 ft in diameter. Single stem dividing into multiple branches. Branches retain dead leaves. Leaves alternate in crowded radiating clusters; evergreen; serrate; 8–15 in. long; 0.4–0.6 in. wide; tapering to a sharp spine. Flowers light yellow; 1–1.5 in. long; opening at night; borne in erect terminal clusters (panicles). Fruit a capsule; 2.5–5 in. long; 2 in. wide; dry. Found in groves in deserts and dry mesas in southwestern Utah, southern Nevada, western Arizona, and southern California.

Soaptree yucca, Soapweed

Yucca elata Engelm.

Small tree sometimes growing to 30 ft in height and 0.5–1 ft in diameter. Main stem branched or not branched; covered with persistent dead leaves. Leaves alternate in crowded radiating clusters; simple; 15–30 in. long; 0.1–0.5 in. wide; tapering to a sharp spine; hairless; yellow-green; flat above; rounded below. Leaf margin entire; splitting into stringlike white fibers. Flowers white or green; 3–4 in. wide; borne in terminal clusters (panicles) on a stalk 4–6 ft tall. Fruit a capsule; oblong; 1.5–2 in. long; 3-valved; light brown; edible; held erect. Grows on desert plateaus, arid grasslands, and dry mesas. Roots used for soap. Fibers used for string. Found in western Texas, southern New Mexico, central and southeastern Arizona, and south into Mexico; disjunct in southwestern Utah.

Faxon yucca

Yucca faxoniana Sarg.

Large shrub or small tree growing 6–40 ft in height and 1–2 ft in diameter. Stem not branched or few branched near top. Leaves alternate in radiating clusters; 2–4 ft long; 2–3 in. wide; narrowed at base, widening to the middle, and tapering to a sharp point. Leaf margin entire but separating into stringlike gray or brown fibers. Flowers white or green; 2–3.5 in. long; borne in large terminal clusters (panicles) 3–4 ft long. Fruit a capsule; 3–4 in. long; 3-valved; orange-brown turning black; bitter. Found on high desert plateaus in western Texas and Mexico.

Fig. 142. Cabbage palmetto
(*Sabal palmetto*) form.

THE PALM FAMILY: ARECACEAE OR PALMAE

Worldwide this family contains about 2,780 species in 200 genera, found mostly in tropical and subtropical areas. Our region contains 6 species in 3 genera, but only 3 species are tree-sized. Compared to other families palms are little known. The taxonomy and natural history of palms require more study.

Palms are shrubs or trees usually without branches. The leaves are alternate and simple, but they often appear pinnately or palmately compound because of splitting. The leaves usually occur in a tuft at the end of the main stem. The flowers are small and bisexual or unisexual with three sepals, three petals, six stamens, and 1-3 carpels. They are pollinated mostly by insects. The fruit is a drupe or nutlike drupe. Economically the palm family provides food (*Areca*, *Cocus*, and *Phoenix*), wax (*Copernica*), and rattan (*Calamus*).

KEY TO PALMS

1. Leaf stalks lacking prickles . . . . .cabbage palmetto, *Sabal palmetto*
1. Leaf stalks with prickles . . . . .Go to 2
    2. Prickles straight or nearly so . . . . .saw-palmetto, *Serenoa repens*
    2. Prickles strongly recurved . . . . .washingtonia, *Washingtonia filifera*

PALMETTO: THE GENUS *SABAL*

Worldwide this genus contains about 14 species, all found in tropical and subtropical America. Our region contains 4 species. Dwarf palmetto (*Sabal minor*) of wet or flooded soil and scrub palmetto (*Sabal etonia*) of droughty sandy soil are usually shrubs. Mexican palmetto (*Sabal mexicana*) is tree-sized, but in our area it is rarely encountered since it occurs naturally in only one county (Cameron) in southern Texas.

Members of this genus have alternate, evergreen, simple leaves that appear fanlike or palmately compound, because they split into segments. The petiole is continued into the leaf base (costa-palmate), causing the leaf to bend. The petioles lack prickles. The flowers are bisexual with three petals.

Cabbage palmetto
Sabal palmetto (Walt.) Lodd. ex J.A. & J. H. Schult (fig. 142)

Small tree growing 40–60 ft in height and 1–2 ft in diameter (tallest known 98 ft). The stem almost never branches. Leaves alternate but found in tight clusters; simple but splitting and appearing fanlike (costa-palmate); split into 40–90 segments; evergreen; margin with loose fibers; blade 2–4 ft long and arched; falling when the petiole breaks, leaving the base attached (the boot). Petiole stout; 2–4 ft long; extending into the blade; base splitting forming a V-shaped gap. Fruit drupelike; spherical; 0.3–0.5 in. wide; shiny black. Grows on a wide variety of sites from dry sands to wet bottomlands. Found in a narrow band along the coast in extreme southern North Carolina, South Carolina, Georgia, and in most of Florida.

Fig. 143. Saw-palmetto
(*Serenoa repens*) leaf.

SAW-PALMETTO: THE GENUS *SERENOA*

Worldwide this genus contains only the species of our region.

Saw-palmetto
Serenoa repens (Bartr.) Small (fig. 143)

Usually a prostrate shrub, rarely growing into a small tree. Usually found in dense thickets. Leaves alternate but found in clusters; simple but splitting into 25–35 segments and appearing fanlike; evergreen; sometimes slightly white-waxy; blade 2 ft long and wide. Petiole ending at leaf base; 18–36 in. long; with sharp slightly curved spines. Flowers bisexual; light yellow; three petals. Fruit drupelike; nearly spherical to pear-shaped; blue-black to black. Grows on a variety of sites from dry sands to seasonally wet silts and clays. Found in the Coastal Plain from southern South Carolina to Florida, and west to southeastern Louisiana.

WASHINGTONIA: THE GENUS *WASHINGTONIA*

Worldwide this genus contains two species, one in Mexico and one in our region. The Mexican species (*Washingtonia robusta*) with hooklike prickles extending throughout the petiole is cultivated in the warmer portions of our region.

Washingtonia, California washingtonia, California palm
Washingtonia filifera (Linden ex Andre) H. Wendl.

Moderate-sized tree growing 50–75 ft in height and 2–3 ft in diameter. Columnar stem clothed with thatchlike mass of hanging dead leaves. Leaves alternate; simple but appearing fanlike or costa-palmate, the result of splitting into 40–70 segments; 3–6 ft long and wide; margins separating into threadlike filaments. Petioles 3–5 ft long; 1–3 in. wide; armed below the middle with stout hooked prickles. Flowers bisexual; minute; white; borne in clusters 8–10 ft long. Fruit drupelike; 0.4 in. long; black; ellipsoidal; thin sweet pulp; produced in large quantities. Bark smooth with circular grooves; gray. Moderately tolerant of shade when young, becoming intolerant. Reproduction plentiful from seed. Grows in small groves on alkaline soils in dry warm canyons. Found in southern California and southwestern Arizona.

CHAPTER 4
ANGIOSPERMS:
DICOTYLEDONS

THE CLASS MAGNOLIOPSIDA

Dicotyledons, generally called dicots, are a diverse group of plants characterized by leaves with netlike veins, flower parts mostly borne in groups of four or five, primary vascular bundles arranged in a circle, and generally two seed leaves (hence the name dicot). About three-quarters of all angiosperms are dicots.

MAPLE FAMILY: ACERACEAE

Worldwide the Maple Family contains 115–200 species in two genera, all trees or shrubs. Found largely in northern temperate areas and tropical mountains, most species are found in Asia. The genus *Dipteronia* contains only two species, both native to China. All other species are maples (*Acer*). The Aceraceae is sometimes placed within the family Sapindaceae.

Flowers in the Maple Family are bisexual or unisexual, and most species have both flower types and both sexes on each tree (polygamous). Each flower has either five petals or no petals, and two carpels. The flowers appear before or as the new leaves are expanding in the spring. They are wind or insect pollinated, and some people are allergic to the pollen. The fruit is a samara. The samara wing completely surrounds the seed in *Dipteronia*, forming a waferlike structure. In maple the wing grows only from one side. The wood is diffuse-porous.

MAPLE: THE GENUS *ACER*

In our region 14 species of maple occur, but only 12 species regularly become tree-sized. Vine maple (*Acer circinatum*) and Rocky Mountain maple (*Acer glabrum*) are normally large shrubs. Norway maple (*Acer platanoides*) of Europe, planetree maple (*Acer pseudoplatanus*) of Europe and western Asia, and Japanese maple (*Acer palmatum*) of Asia are cultivated. On rare occasion, Norway maple and planetree maple escape from cultivation.

Maple leaves are opposite, simple or compound (in boxelder and sometimes Rocky Mountain maple), and lack stipules except for black maple. The venation is usually palmate. The leaves often turn bright red, orange, or yellow in fall. In some species the flowers are complete, and in others they are highly reduced. The sex of individual trees may change over time. The fruit is a double samara (sometimes called keys) united at the base. The seeds are usually solitary by abortion. The bud scales are valvate or overlapping (imbricate).

KEY TO MAPLES

1. Leaves compound . . . . Go to 2
1. Leaves simple . . . . .Go to 3
    2. Lateral buds white hairy . . . . .boxelder, *Acer negundo*
    2. Lateral buds hairless; red . . . . Rocky Mountain maple, *Acer glabrum*
3. Leaf lobes toothed; sinus base V- or L-shaped 4
3. Leaf lobes entire; sinus base U-shaped 9
    4. Fruits mature in late spring; buds with 4–8 externally visible scales 5
    4. Fruits mature in late summer; buds with 2 (rarely 4) externally visible scales 6

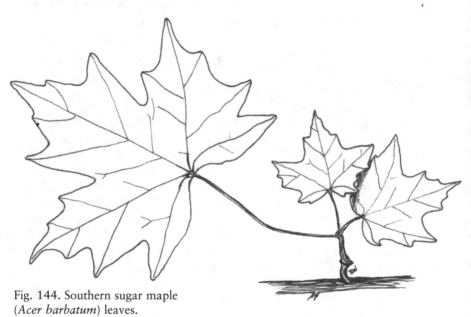

Fig. 144. Southern sugar maple
(*Acer barbatum*) leaves.

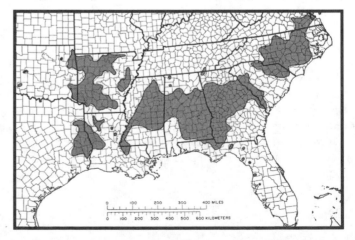

Fig. 145.
Native range
of southern
sugar maple
(*Acer barbatum*).

5. Sides of middle leaf lobe diverging . . . . silver maple, *Acer saccharinum*
5. Sides of middle leaf lobe parallel or converging . . . . red maple, *Acer rubrum*
    6. Leaves hairless or nearly so below; Western 7
    6. Leaves hairy below; Eastern 8
7. Leaves 7–9 lobed . . . . vine maple, *Acer circinatum*
7. Leaves 3–5 lobed . . . . Rocky Mountain maple, *Acer glabrum*
    8. Leaves with large rounded teeth . . . . mountain maple, *Acer spicatum*
    8. Leaves with small pointed teeth . . . . striped maple, *Acer pensylvanicum*
9. Fruit wings diverging nearly at 180 degrees . . . . . Norway maple, *Acer platanoides*
9. Fruit wings diverging at or less than 90 degrees 10
    10. Bud scales red; Western 11
    10. Bud scales brown; Eastern 12
11. Leaves 6–12 in. wide . . . . bigleaf maple, *Acer macrophyllum*
11. Leaves 2–5 in. wide . . . . canyon maple, *Acer grandidentatum*
    12. Leaves 1–3 in. wide; Southeastern 13
    12. Leaves 3–6 in. wide; mostly northern and southern Appalachians 14
13. Leaves whitened below . . . . Florida maple, *Acer barbatum*
13. Leaves yellow-green below . . . . chalk maple, *Acer leucoderme*
    14. Leaves lacking stipules; 3–5 lobed . . . . sugar maple, *Acer saccharum*
    14. Leaves with stipules; mostly 3 lobed . . . . black maple, *Acer nigrum*

Southern sugar maple, Florida maple

Acer barbatum Michx. (fig. 144)

Nomenclature. Formerly called *Acer floridanum*. Sometimes considered a variety or subspecies of sugar maple (*Acer saccharum* var. *floridanum*), a treatment with considerable merit. Regardless of treatment, closely related to sugar maple.

Form. Moderate-sized tree growing 60–70 ft in height and 1–2 ft in diameter (largest known 120 ft by 3 ft).

Leaves. Opposite; simple; 3–5 lobes; 12–14 points; margin entire; slightly whitened and hairy below at least on the main veins. Leaf stalks of varying lengths.

Flowers. Red or yellow; bisexual and either male or female on each tree (polygamo-dioecious); appearing in the spring before or with the new leaves.

Fruit. Double samara; wings U-shaped; 1–1.5 in. long; mature in summer or fall.

Twigs. Light brown.

Bark. Light brown or gray; smooth when young; developing shallow fissures that separate low flat ridges; 1 side of the ridges sometimes turning outward forming a fluted ridge.

Wood. Low commercial value; used occasionally for furniture, flooring, and paneling.

Natural History. Very tolerant of shade usually developing in the shade of other trees. Grows on fertile moist soils of well-drained bottomlands, coves, and lower slopes; development best on limestone or marl soils. Usually found in small groves, growing with sweetgum, willow oak, red maple, yellow-poplar, northern red oak, bitternut hickory, and eastern redcedar. Not tapped for maple syrup. Commonly planted as a street tree in the South.

Range. See figure 145.

Canyon maple, Bigtooth maple
Acer grandidentatum Nutt. (fig. 146)

Classified by some authorities as a variety of sugar maple, *Acer saccharum* var. *grandidentatum*. Large shrub or small tree growing to 50 ft in height and 1 ft in diameter. Leaves simple; opposite; 3–5 lobes; 2–5 in. wide; margin wavy to dentate, sometimes entire; base of sinus U-shaped. Petiole 1.5–2 in. long. Flowers yellow; appearing in the spring with new leaves. Fruit a double samara; about 1 in. long; mature in late summer. Twigs red-brown turning gray; numerous small lenticels. Terminal buds red-brown; slightly hairy. Bark brown or gray; smooth at first, developing large scales. Wood used mostly for fuel. Grows in mountain valleys and along streams. Found in south central Montana and southeastern Idaho, and south to Mexico; southern Texas, and local in southwestern Oklahoma. Elevation: to 6,000 ft.

Chalk maple
Acer leucoderme Small

Sometimes classified as a variety or subspecies of sugar maple (*Acer saccharum* var. *leucoderme*); in either case closely related to it. Small tree growing to 40 ft in height. Bole often crooked. Leaves simple; opposite; about 3 in. long; 3–5 lobes; 6–8 points; tip of upper lobes long pointed; hairy and green or yellow-green below; not whitened below. Flowers appearing in the spring with new leaves. Fruit a double samara; red-brown; 0.5–0.8 in. long. Bark light gray to white. Grows sporadically and locally. Found in the Piedmont from North Carolina to Alabama, and disjunct in all other southern states.

Bigleaf maple, Broadleaf maple, Oregon maple
Acer macrophyllum Pursh (fig. 147)

Form. Moderate-sized tree growing 50–80 ft in height and 3–4 ft in diameter (largest known 160 ft by 9 ft). Burls often form at base.

Leaves. Simple; opposite; palmately 5-lobed; entire or slightly wavy toothed; terminal lobe narrowed at base; 6–12 in. wide; base heart-shaped. Petiole as long as the blade; milky sap.

Fig. 146. Canyon maple (*Acer grandidentatum*) leaf.

Flowers. Yellow; aromatic; appearing in spring with new leaves.

Fruit. Double samara; 2–3 in. long; seed densely hairy; wings slightly to widely diverging.

Twigs. Stout; green-brown to red-brown; lenticels common. Terminal buds 0.3 in. long; blunt; red-green; scales with hairy margin.

Bark. Red-brown or gray; shallow furrows with interlacing ridges.

Wood. Sapwood red-white. Heartwood pink-brown; moderately heavy and hard; growth rings not distinct. Wood used for furniture, piano frames, handles, wooden-ware, and fuel; burls prized for furniture.

Natural History. Moderately tolerant of shade. Reaches maturity in 200 years. Reproduces well from seed in moist soil; usually becomes established under a light canopy or in forest openings; large seed crops produced most years; seedling height growth rapid, up to 6 ft the first year. Reproduces profusely from stump sprouts. Verticillium wilt and carpenter worm cause the most damage. Found on a wide variety of soils; development best on moist gravelly soils; absent from soils high in boron. Leaf litter high in nutrients. Found in small groves or mixed with Douglas-fir, Pacific madrone, Pacific dogwood, black cottonwood, red alder, Sitka spruce, and western hemlock. Twigs browsed by deer, elk, and beaver. Seeds eaten by songbirds and squirrels. Tapped for maple syrup in January and February but syrup is lower in quality compared to sugar maple.

Range. See figure 148. Generally found below 1,100 ft.

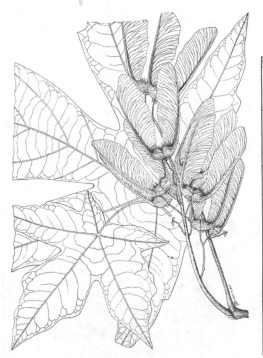

Fig. 147. Bigleaf maple (*Acer macrophyllum*) leaf and fruit.

Fig. 148. Native range of bigleaf maple (*Acer macrophyllum*).

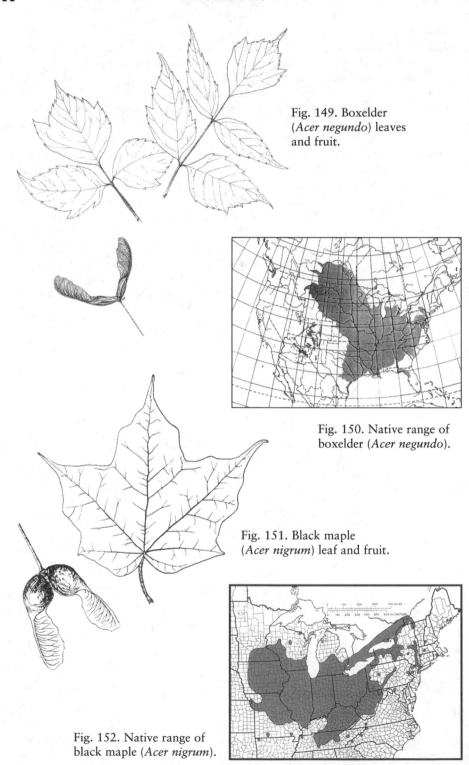

Fig. 149. Boxelder (*Acer negundo*) leaves and fruit.

Fig. 150. Native range of boxelder (*Acer negundo*).

Fig. 151. Black maple (*Acer nigrum*) leaf and fruit.

Fig. 152. Native range of black maple (*Acer nigrum*).

Boxelder
Acer negundo L. (fig. 149)

Form. Moderate-sized tree growing 50–70 ft in height and 2–3 ft in diameter. Bole often leaning, forked near ground and covered with sprouts.

Leaves. Pinnately compound; 4–6 in. long; 3–7 leaflets; seedlings and saplings usually have 3 leaflets; terminal leaflet shallow-lobed at tip; basal leaflets shallow lobed at base; hairless or hairy above; hairy on the veins below; margin coarsely toothed.

Flowers. Unisexual with only one sex on each tree (dioecious); yellow-green; wind pollinated; appearing in the spring before or with the new leaves.

Fruit. Paired samara; 1–2 in. long; seeds narrowed at ends; matures in late summer.

Twigs. Moderately stout; green to purple; sometimes covered with white wax; leaf scars touching. Terminal and lateral buds white hairy.

Bark. Thin; light brown or gray; divided by shallow furrows into narrow flat ridges.

Wood. Little or no commercial value; heartwood yellow-white to yellow-brown; sometimes used for crates and pallets.

Natural History. Moderately tolerant of shade. Short-lived; reaches maturity in 60 years (extreme age 100 years). Reproduces well from seeds; becomes established under light canopies or in old fields; adequate seed crops produced most years; seed dispersal period extended, lasting from fall to spring. Reproduces from stump and root sprouts. Verticillium wilt causes the most damage. Found on nearly all types of soils from sands to heavy clays; most common on moist alluvial soils along rivers; tolerant of drought. Planted in the West for shelterbelts. Often considered to be a weed in the East. Seeds eaten through the winter by songbirds and small mammals.

Varieties. As many as 14 forms and varieties have been named, but they intergrade with the typical variety. Many authorities no longer recognize these forms and varieties.

Range. See figure 150.

Black maple
Acer nigrum Michx. f (fig. 151)

Sometimes considered to be a variety or subspecies of sugar maple (*Acer saccharum* var. *nigrum*); in any case closely related to it. Moderate to large tree growing 80–100 ft in height and 2–3 ft in diameter. Leaves opposite; simple; 4–6 in. long and wide; 3–5 lobed; 12–14 blunt points; mostly 3-lobed; tips of lobes long pointed; the blade drooping along the midvein especially in autumn; hairy below. Margin entire or undulating. Petiole hairy; stipules present sometimes large and leafy; base swollen and partly enclosing the lateral buds. Flowers green-yellow; appearing in the spring when new leaves are about one-half expanded; male and female flowers borne on separate trees (dioecious). Fruit a paired samara; 0.7–1.2 in. long; seed hairless; mature in autumn. Twigs orange-brown or gray. Terminal buds hairy. Bark nearly black; sharp furrows dividing long, narrow ridges. Found in seasonally wet woods and swamps. Tapped for maple syrup. For range see figure 152.

Fig. 153. Striped maple (*Acer pensylvanicum*) leaves and fruit.

Fig. 154. Native range of striped maple (*Acer pensylvanicum*).

Striped maple, Moosewood

Acer pensylvanicum L. (fig. 153)

Form. Large shrub or small tree growing to 35 ft in height and 0.5–1 ft in diameter (tallest known 50 ft). Bole often dividing near the base.

Leaves. Simple; opposite; rounded; 3–5 shallow palmate lobes; juvenile leaves not lobed; 5–6 in. long; sharply doubly toothed; hairless.

Flowers. Yellow-green; unisexual either with both sexes found on each tree (monoecious) or on different trees (dioecious); sex expression may change annually; female trees about 10 times more abundant; flowers appear in the spring after the new leaves have nearly expanded.

Fruit. Double samara; wings widely divergent; red turning light brown; borne in pendent racemes; mature in autumn.

Twigs. Slender; smooth; red to green-brown; hairless. Terminal buds red.

Bark. Thin; red-brown to green; marked on small branches and stems with vertical white stripes.

Wood. Little or no commercial value.

Natural History. Tolerant of shade. Very slow growing, sometimes only 1 in. per year; but responds quickly to release. Short-lived; reaches maturity in 80–100 years. Seed production of females varies considerably by tree; seeds dispersed by wind or blowing across crusted snow; seeds germinate in 1–2 years. May rarely reproduce by stump sprouting and branch layering. Sometimes considered a nuisance when large numbers of small trees crowd the growing space of more marketable hardwoods. Verticillium wilt causes the most damage. Usually found on cool moist sites. Foliage browsed by moose and white-tailed deer. Rabbits, beaver, and porcupine eat the inner bark. Fruits eaten by grouse. Dried foliage formerly used for winter fodder.

Range. See figure 154.

Fig. 155. Red maple
(*Acer rubrum*) shoot
and fruit.

Fig. 156. Native
range of red maple
(*Acer rubrum*).

Red maple, Soft maple

Acer rubrum L. (fig. 155)

Form. Moderate-sized tree growing 60–90 ft in height and 2–3 ft in diameter (largest known 125 ft by 5 ft).

Leaves. Opposite; simple; 2–4 in. wide; palmately 3–5 lobed; sides of terminal lobe parallel or converging toward apex; sinus base V- or L-shaped; lobe margins toothed; hairless or nearly so.

Flowers. Bisexual and either male or female flowers on the same tree (polygamo-dioecious), or unisexual with both sexes on the same tree (monoecious); red, rarely yellow; petals present; appearing before the new leaves in the spring.

Fruit. Paired samaras; wings slightly divergent; 0.5–1 in. long; ripens in spring.

Twigs. Slender; red; marked with white dots (lenticels); odorless. Terminal bud scales red; flower buds more rounded and clustered.

Bark. Thin; gray; smooth on young trees; on older trees developing shallow furrows that separate flat ridges; becoming slightly shaggy on very large trees.

Wood. Sapwood white; wide. Heartwood light brown, sometimes with gray, green, or purple tint; moderately heavy. Used for frames of upholstered furniture, boxes, crates, pallets, core stock for hardwood plywood, and pulpwood.

Natural History. Tolerant of shade, but may become established in full sunlight. Fast growing when young, but growth rate declines greatly with age. Responds well to thinning. Reaches maturity in 70–80 years (extreme age 150 years). Reproduces well from seed; adequate seed crops produced most years; large crops produced every 2 years. Seeds lack internal dormancy, and germinate shortly after release in spring. Hardwood litter does not limit germination and seedling survival. Black cherry allelopathy may limit seedling development. Sprouts prolifically from the stump. Root system shallow and spreading. Heart rot resulting from physical injury and fire cause the most damage. Probably our most ecologically diverse eastern species; found on sites ranging from dry ridges to wet sloughs; very tolerant of flooding. Grows in pure stands or in mixed stands with more than 70 species; loss of American elm and American chestnut from disease, fire suppression, and preferential removal of more marketable species have increased the abundance of red maple. White-tailed deer and elk browse the twigs in winter. Fruits eaten by songbirds and fox. Tapped for maple syrup, but only before spring bud break, which spoils the flavor.

Hybrids. Hybridizes with silver maple.

Varieties. Trees of southern swamps with smaller, 3-lobed leaves are sometimes separated as var. *trilobum*.

Range. See figure 156.

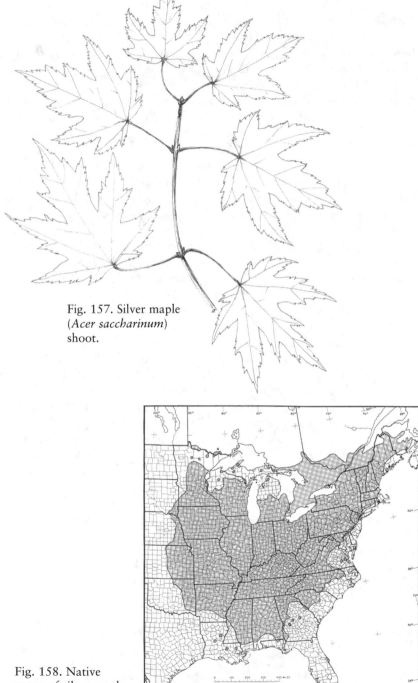

Fig. 157. Silver maple (*Acer saccharinum*) shoot.

Fig. 158. Native range of silver maple (*Acer saccharinum*).

Silver maple, Soft maple

Acer saccharinum L. (fig. 157)

Form. Moderate-sized tree growing 70–90 ft in height and 2–3 ft in diameter (largest known 120 ft by 7 ft). Bole often dividing into several upright branches.

Leaves. Simple; opposite; round; 4–6 in. wide; deeply palmately 5-lobed; silver-white below. Terminal lobe diverging toward apex; base of sinus V-shaped; lobe margins sharply toothed.

Flowers. Bisexual and unisexual on same tree (polygamous), or male and female flowers borne on separate trees (dioecious); type of flowers produced may change from year to year. May form viable seed from self-pollination. Borne in crowded clusters; lacking petals; green-yellow; appearing in the spring well before the new leaves.

Fruit. Double samara; wings widely divergent; 2–3 in. long; yellow-brown; hairless; mature in late spring.

Twigs. Slender; dark red; lustrous; fetid odor when bruised. Terminal buds blunt; dark red; 2–4 pairs of externally visible scales with ciliate margins.

Bark. Smooth and light gray on young stems; on older trees developing shallow furrows that separate flat scaly plates.

Wood. Sapwood white; wide. Heartwood light brown; moderately heavy; moderately hard. Used when the supply of sugar maple is inadequate.

Natural History. Moderately tolerant of shade on high-quality sites, but intolerant on low-quality sites. Fast growing; rather short-lived reaching maturity in 110–130 years. Seed production prolific; lacking internal dormancy, seeds germinate quickly after release. Root system shallow and extensive; notorious for clogging underground water pipes and drains. Verticillium wilt and breakage from ice or wind cause the most damage. Found along lakes or rivers in alluvial soil. Grows most commonly with American elm, but also found with sweetgum, pin oak, swamp white oak, sycamore, and eastern cottonwood. Flower buds eaten in spring by squirrels. Seeds eaten by songbirds, fox, and small mammals. Inner bark eaten by beaver. Commonly planted for ornamental purposes. Tapped for maple syrup but sugar content is low.

Hybrids. Hybridizes readily with red maple, when red maple is the female parent.

Range. See figure 158.

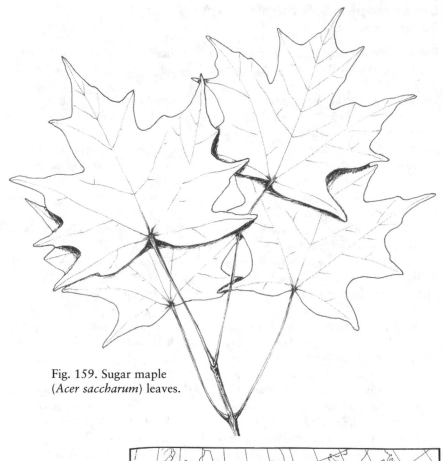

Fig. 159. Sugar maple
(*Acer saccharum*) leaves.

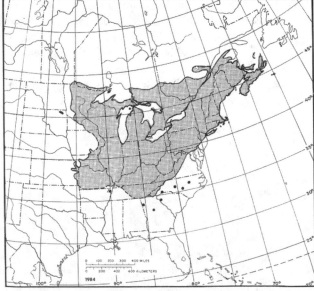

Fig. 160. Native
range of sugar
maple (*Acer
saccharum*).

Sugar maple, Hard maple

Acer saccharum Marsh. (fig. 159)

Nomenclature. The classification of our 5 sugar maples (southern sugar maple, black maple, chalk maple, sugar maple, and canyon maple) has varied over the years. As few as one species or as many as 97 different combinations of species, subspecies, varieties, and forms have been proposed. Most studies have found continuous variation in characters, suggesting that recognizing a single species is most appropriate.

Form. Large tree growing 90–120 ft in height and 2–3 ft in diameter (largest known 135 ft by 5 ft). Crown dense; broad.

Leaves. Simple; opposite; rounded; palmately 5-lobed (rarely 3-lobed); 3–5 in. long; margin entire; 16–24 points; base of sinus U-shaped.

Flowers. Bisexual and unisexual on each tree (polygamous); borne on long stalks in clusters; petals lacking; yellow-green; appearing in the spring with the new leaves.

Fruit. Double samara; U-shaped with nearly parallel wings; 1 in. long; red-brown; hairless; matures in autumn shortly before leaf fall.

Twigs. Slender; smooth; red-brown; shiny. Terminal bud 0.2–0.3 in. long; acute; red-brown; nearly hairless; 4–8 pairs of externally visible scales.

Bark. Smooth and gray on young trees; becoming dark gray with shallow furrows that separate long flat ridges; one side of the ridge sometimes turning outward, producing a fluted appearance.

Wood. Very valuable commercially. Sapwood white with red tinge; narrow. Heartwood light red-brown; heavy; hard; even-grained; sometimes with curly grain or bird's eye figure. High amount of defect in standing trees, 35–50 percent. Used for furniture, musical instruments (especially violins and piano frames), bowling pins, pool cues, croquet balls and mallets, dumbbells, flooring, farm vehicles, handles, shuttles, spools, toys, butcher blocks, woodenware, novelties, pulpwood, and fuelwood.

Natural History. Very tolerant of shade; highest growth rate occurs in 65 percent shade. Slow growing; reaches maturity in 300–400 years. Reproduces well from seed; good seed crops produced every 1–4 years. Seed viability averages 95 percent; optimum germination temperature is 34 degrees F; little germination occurs above 50 degrees F. Reproduces vegetatively from stump sprouts and layering. Young roots able to penetrate leaf litter. Root system extensive; many fine roots grow into the litter layer; root grafting to other sugar maples common. Allelopathy from aster and goldenrod reduce germination and growth rate of sugar maple; allelopathy from sugar maple reduces growth of yellow birch. Bud miners, scale insects, road salt, and air pollution cause the most damage. Grows on soils ranging from sands to silt loam; growth best on loam with abundant organic matter; absent from shallow droughty soils and swamps. Found in pure stands or mixed with basswood, yellow birch, American beech, black cherry, northern red oak, yellow-poplar, eastern white pine, and eastern hemlock. White-tailed deer browse the foliage. Squirrels eat the fruit and buds. Sapsuckers frequently peck the bark. Commonly planted as an ornamental. Spring sap averages 2.5 percent sugar; tapped for maple syrup and sugar.

Range. See figure 160.

Mountain maple
Acer spicatum Lam. (fig. 161)

Shrub or small tree occasionally growing to 35 ft in height and 0.5 ft in diameter. Branches upright forming a compact crown. Leaves simple; opposite; palmately 3-lobed (rarely 5-lobed); 3–5 in. long; large blunt or rounded teeth; dark green and hairless above; white hairy below. Flowers bisexual and unisexual on the same tree (polygamous); borne in erect terminal racemes; yellow-green; appearing in the spring after the new leaves. Fruit a double samara; wings widely divergent; 0.5–1 in. long; hairless; bright red; mature in autumn. Twigs slender; slightly hairy; red to brown. Terminal bud 0.1–0.2 in. long; bright red; more or less hairy. Bark thin; red-brown; smooth or slightly furrowed. Wood without commercial value. Tolerant of shade. Found on cool moist sites from Newfoundland to eastern Saskatchewan, south to Pennsylvania and Iowa; and south along the Appalachians at progressively higher elevations to northern Georgia.

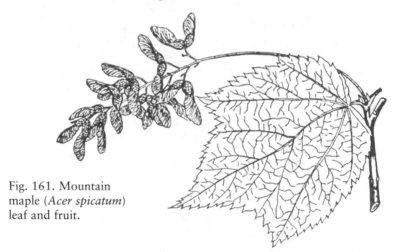

Fig. 161. Mountain maple (*Acer spicatum*) leaf and fruit.

CASHEW FAMILY: THE ANACARDIACEAE

The Cashew Family contains 600–800 species in 70 genera in the world, mostly in tropical and subtropical areas. Our region contains 15 species in 4 genera, but only 1 species in each genus becomes tree-sized. In addition, peppertree (*Schinus molle*), native to South America, has become naturalized in the southwestern portion of our region. Worldwide this family produces many useful products including food from cashew (*Anacardium*), pistachio (*Pistacia*); and mango (*Mangifera*); various plums (*Spondias* and *Harpephyllum*); lumber from zebrawood (*Astronium*) and quebracho (*Schinopsis*); resins from mastic (*Pistacia*); varnish (*Toxicodendron*); and tannic acid from several genera (*Cotinus*, *Pistacia*, *Rhus*, and *Schinopsis*).

The leaves of the Cashew Family are alternate, deciduous or evergreen, and either trifoliate, pinnately compound, or simple. Usually no stipules are produced. The flowers are radially symmetrical, and may be either bisexual or unisexual.

Pollinated by insects, each flower contains five sepals, five petals, and three carpels. The fruit is either a drupe or a drupelike nut. Some members of this family produce latex or resin that cause skin rashes in some people.

SMOKETREE: THE GENUS *COTINUS*

Worldwide three species of smoketree are found. Our region contains the single species listed below, although some authorities question whether it is actually native. The remaining two species are found in Eurasia. The European smoketree (*Cotinus coggygria*) is planted in our region and often mistaken for our native species. The European species has white leaf margins and more hairs on the fruiting stalks.

American smoketree
Cotinus obovatus Raf. (fig. 162)

Shrub or small tree sometimes growing to 35 ft in height and 1 ft in diameter. Leaves simple; alternate; deciduous; 2–6 in. long; oval to obovate; entire; dark green. Leaf tip rounded or notched. Flowers dioecious; borne in loose terminal clusters (panicles); borne on long purple-hairy stalks giving the tree its common name. Fruit a drupe; dry; compressed; kidney-shaped; light brown; 0.1–0.2 in. long. Bark gray or black; smooth at first but becoming scaly. Wood durable; used locally for fence posts; contains yellow dye. Sprouts vigorously from stumps. Often found on limestone soils. Rare and local in the highlands of Tennessee, Alabama, Arkansas, Missouri, Oklahoma, and Texas.

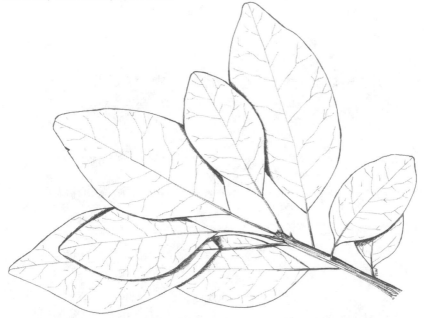

Fig. 162. American smoketree
(*Cotinus obovatus*) shoot.

PISTACHE: THE GENUS *PISTACIA*

Found in Mexico, Central America, North America, and Eurasia about 10 species of pistache occur in the world, but our region contains only the species described below. Pistachio nuts and pastachio nut oil are obtained from *Pistacia vera*, native to the Mediterranean region and west Asia. Other *Pistacia* provide livestock forage, ink, dye, varnish, and lumber.

Texas pistache, American pistachio

Pistacia texana Swingle

Shrub or small tree sometimes growing to 35 ft in height. Usually found in clumps. Leaves alternate; 2–4 in. long; evergreen; pinnately compound, sometimes lacking a terminal leaflet. Leaflets 10–16; slightly curved; spatulate; entire; 0.3–1 in. long. Rachis slightly winged. Flowers unisexual with the sexes borne on different trees (dioecious); lacking sepals and petals. Fruit a drupe; red-brown. Very intolerant of shade. Grows in limestone stream beds, on limestone cliffs, and on alluvial soils. Found in south Texas and south into Mexico.

SUMAC: THE GENUS *RHUS*

Worldwide about 150 species of sumac are found, mostly in temperate and subtropical areas of Asia, Europe, North America, and Africa. Our region contains 14

Fig. 163. Staghorn sumac (*Rhus typhina*) leaves, twig, flowers, and fruit.

species. The tallest species are keyed below, but only staghorn sumac becomes tree-sized. Formerly the poison-sumacs (*Toxicodendron*) were placed with the sumacs in *Rhus*.

KEY TO SUMACS

1. Leaves simple or trifoliate . . . . .Go to 2
1. Leaves pinnately compound with 5 or more leaflets . . . . .Go to 5
   2. Leaves broadly ovate . . . . .sugar sumac, *Rhus ovata*
   2. Leaves oval to ovate 3
1. Fruit white . . . . .laurel sumac, *Rhus laurina*
1. Fruit red 4
   4. Leaves toothed and entire . . . . .mahogany sumac, *Rhus integrifolia*
   4. Leaves entire only . . . . .Kearney sumac, *Rhus kearneyi*
1. Fruits in clusters of 2–15 6
1. Fruits in clusters of more than 20 7
   6. Rachis winged; fruit red . . . . .littleleaf sumac, *Rhus microphylla*
   6. Rachis not winged; fruit white . . . . .poison-sumac, *Toxicodendron vernix*
1. Twigs and petioles densely velvety hairy . . . . .staghorn sumac, *Rhus typhina*
1. Twigs and petioles hairless or nearly so 8
   8. Rachis not winged . . . . .smooth sumac, *Rhus glabra*
   8. Rachis winged. 9
1. Leaflets ovate-lanceolate, not curved . . . . .shining sumac, *Rhus copallina*
1. Leaflets narrow-lanceolate, often curved . . . . . . .prairie shining sumac, *Rhus lanceolata*

Staghorn sumac

Rhus typhina L. (fig. 163)

Form. Shrub or small tree sometimes growing to 40 ft in height and 1 ft in diameter. Commonly forming thickets.

Leaves. Alternate; deciduous; pinnately compound with a terminal leaflet; 8–24 in. long; contain white sap. Leaflets 11–31; lanceolate; middle leaflets the longest; serrate; 2–5 in. long; whitened and hairy on the veins below. Petiole hairy.

Flowers. Unisexual with one sex per tree (dioecious) or sometimes with unisexual and bisexual flowers (polygamous); appearing after the new leaves have expanded. Fruit a drupe; hairy; 0.2 in. wide; dark red; borne in large terminal cluster (panicle).

Twigs. Stout; velvety hairy; sap milky; pith large. Terminal bud absent. Lateral buds conical; brown; hairy; covered by base of petiole.

Bark. Thin; dark brown; large lenticels; smooth becoming scaly with age.

Wood. No commercial value; soft and weak; ring-porous.

Natural History. Intolerant of shade; becomes established after disturbance in forest openings, forest edges, roadsides, and fencerows. Fast growing but short-lived. Female trees produce large fruit crops every 1–3 years. Sprouts vigorously from the roots producing clones of several to many individuals. Fruits remain on plant well into winter, providing food for songbirds, white-tailed deer, opossum, turkey, and quail. Inner bark eaten by rabbits when other food is scarce. The common name refers to the resemblance of the leafless twigs to the velvet-covered antlers of white-tailed deer.

Range. Found from Nova Scotia to Minnesota, and south to western North Carolina.

POISON-SUMAC: THE GENUS *TOXICODENDRON*

Prior to about 1970, this genus was commonly classified within the genus *Rhus*. Today most authorities separate the nonpoisonous sumacs (*Rhus*) from the poisonous sumacs (*Toxicodendron*). Worldwide this genus contains about 15 species, found in North and South America and east Asia. Only one species is tree-sized in our region, but several shrubs or vines are well known for the skin rashes they cause in many people: poison-ivy (*Toxicodendron radicans*), eastern poison-oak (*Toxicodendron pubescens*), and western poison-oak (*Toxicodendron diversilobium*).

Poison-sumac

Toxicodendron vernix (L.) Kuntze (fig. 164)

Mostly a tall shrub, rarely becoming tree-sized. Bole short with few branches. Leaves alternate; pinnately compound; deciduous. Leaflets ovate or elliptical; 7–15; entire; often held upward in a shallow V-shape; hairy on the veins. Rachis and main veins often purple-red. Fruit a drupe; 0.2–0.3 in. wide; green-yellow to dull yellow; borne hanging in clusters (panicle); persisting into winter. Twigs stout; red turning light brown; hairless; lenticels present. Bark smooth; brown or gray. Grows in non-alluvial swamps, bogs, pocosins, and wet flats. Fruits eaten by many songbirds. Range fragmented; disjuncts common. Found from southern Maine to eastern Minnesota, and south to central Florida and east Texas.

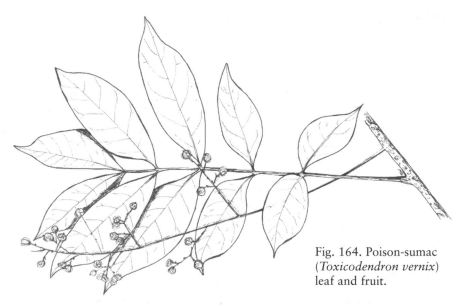

Fig. 164. Poison-sumac (*Toxicodendron vernix*) leaf and fruit.

CUSTARD-APPLE FAMILY: ANNONACEAE

This family contains about 2,300 species in 130 genera, mostly found in the lowlands of tropical regions. Our region contains only pawpaw (*Asimina*).

Members of this family are either trees or shrubs, and they are considered to be primitive among the angiosperms. The leaves are alternate, simple, and entire, and they lack stipules. The leaves are aromatic (often smelling like motor oil) due to ethereal oil cells. The flowers are bisexual, usually nodding, showy, radially symmetrical, and usually pollinated by beetles. Each flower has three sepals, six petals, and numerous distinct carpels. The fruit is a single berry or cluster of fused berries that are further fused to the expanded tip of the flower stalk (receptacle). The family produces edible fruits from *Annona* (cherimoya, soursop, sweetsop, and custard-apple) and *Asimina* (pawpaw), and perfume from *Cananga*.

PAWPAW: THE GENUS *ASIMINA*

This genus contains eight species of trees and shrubs found in the southeastern United States, especially Florida. Only the specie listed below becomes tree-sized.

Pawpaw, Papaw

Asimina triloba (L.) Dunal (fig. 165)

Large shrub or small tree growing 25–40 ft in height and 0.5–1 ft in diameter. Often found in colonies. Leaves alternate; simple; deciduous; entire; elliptical to obovate; 10–12 in. long; 4–6 in. wide; aromatic, smelling like motor oil. Tip acute. Base wedge-shaped. Flowers purple-red; about 2 in. wide; appearing after new leaves have expanded. Fruit is a berry; oblong; yellow-brown; 3–5 in. long; when yellow, the pulp is sweet and edible. Seeds large; dark brown; flattened. Twigs slender; brown; pith diaphragmed. Terminal bud present; naked; slender; brown hairy, appearing like an artists paint brush. Bark thin; brown to gray with blotches; smooth or smooth with warts. Wood with no commercial value; soft and weak; yellow-green. Moderately tolerant of shade. Short-lived. Fruit rarely produced; most reproduction from root sprouts. Usually found in moist bottomlands, but occasionally found in the understory of mesic hardwoods. Grows in small pure groves, or mixed with bottomland hardwoods. Fruit eaten by humans, turkey, squirrel, raccoon, opossum, and fox. Ignored by commerce for hundreds of years, interest in growing pawpaw for commercial fruit production is beginning. Range from Pennsylvania to eastern Kansas, and south to central Georgia and east Texas.

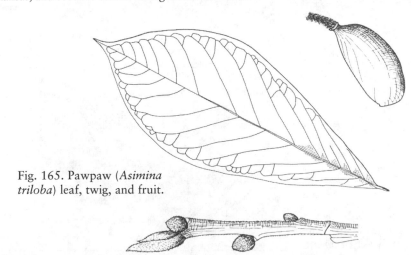

Fig. 165. Pawpaw (*Asimina triloba*) leaf, twig, and fruit.

HOLLY FAMILY: AQUIFOLIACEAE

Worldwide this family of trees and shrubs contains about 420 species in four genera, although some authors subdivide it by placing each genus in a separate family. The family occurs widely in both hemispheres in temperate and tropical areas. Our region contains 18 species in two genera, holly (*Ilex*) and mountain-holly (*Nemopanthus*).

A few hollies become tree-sized, but mountain-hollies are usually medium to large shrubs. Leaves in this family are simple, alternate, and evergreen or deciduous. The flowers are small, often unisexual, green or white, with four to five petals and four to seven carpels, and borne in small axillary clusters. The fruit is a drupe with several stones. The wood is diffuse-porous. Economically the family provides tea with very high caffeine content (*Ilex*) and shrubs for ornamental planting (*Ilex*).

HOLLY: THE GENUS *ILEX*

Our region contains 16 native species. The 5 species keyed below may occasionally become tree-sized, but only American holly is regularly tree-sized. Numerous cultivars and hybrids of native and Asian species are commonly planted, but none have escaped. Hollies have either evergreen or deciduous leaves. The drupe fruits contain several stones rather than the usual single stone, a feature that prompts some authorities to classify them as either berrylike or berrylike drupes. If eaten by humans, the fruits of all hollies induce vomiting.

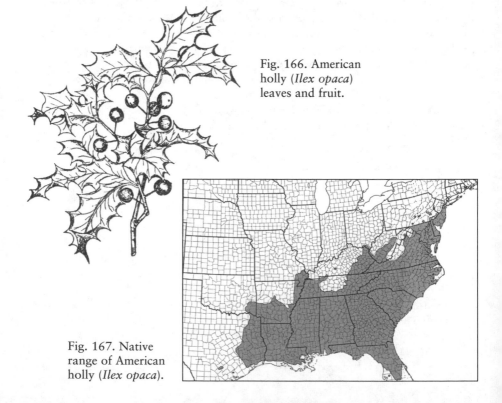

Fig. 166. American holly (*Ilex opaca*) leaves and fruit.

Fig. 167. Native range of American holly (*Ilex opaca*).

KEY TO HOLLIES

1. Leaves deciduous; not leathery . . . . .Go to 2
1. Leaves evergreen; thick and leathery . . . . .Go to 3
    2. Leaves sharply toothed. Leaf tip pointed . .mountain winterberry, *Ilex montana*
    2. Leaves with few rounded teeth. Leaf tip obtuse . . . . .possumhaw, *Ilex decidua*
3. Leaves with spiny teeth or a spiny tip 4
3. Leaves lacking spiny teeth or tips; margin smooth or toothed 5
    4. Leaves 1–2 times longer than wide . . . . .American holly, *Ilex opaca*
    4. Leaves 4 or more times longer than wide . . . . .dahoon, *Ilex cassine*
5. Leaves entire; oblanceolate . . . . .dahoon, *Ilex cassine*
5. Leaves with rounded teeth; oval .yaupon, *Ilex vomitoria*

American holly

Ilex opaca Ait. (fig. 166)

Form. Small tree growing 40–60 ft in height and 1–2 ft in diameter (largest known 100 ft by 4 ft). Crown dense.

Leaves. Alternate; simple; persisting 3 years; elliptical; 2–4 in. long; thick and leathery. Margin usually spiny toothed, but sometimes entire, especially in the tops of large trees. Leaf tip always spiny, a character that distinguishes American holly from dahoon, which has rounded leaf tips.

Flowers. Appearing with the leaves; unisexual with the sexes borne on separate trees (dioecious). Pollinated by insects, usually bees, wasps, yellow-jackets, ants, and nocturnal moths.

Fruit. Drupe; persisting into winter; bright red or orange, rarely yellow; 0.2–0.5 in. long; borne in leaf axils.

Twigs. Slender; hairless. Leaf scar with single bundle trace. Terminal buds present; 0.1–0.2 in. long; ciliate.

Bark. Thin; smooth; gray-white; sometimes with splotches or warts.

Wood. Limited commercial value. Sapwood white. Heartwood ivory-white; often with blue streaks; hard and heavy; fine textured, the growth rings barely visible. Used locally for inlay work, handles, turning stock, and novelties. Occasionally stained black to imitate ebony (*Diospyros* and *Maba*) and used for piano keys and violin pegs.

Natural History. Very tolerant of shade but reproducing in shade and sun alike. Slow growing. Reproduction by seed common; some fruits produced on female plants most years; late spring frosts may cause fruit failure. Reproduces well from stump sprouts. Wildfire and leaf miner cause the most damage. Found on a wide variety of sites but only those lacking fire; grows on beach dunes, uplands, and bottomlands. Tolerant of salt spray; will not tolerate flooding for more than 1–2 weeks in the growing season. The largest trees develop in the rich bottomlands along the lower Mississippi River. Fruits eaten by songbirds, turkey, quail, white-tailed deer, and squirrels. Common and favorite Christmas decoration, a practice started by the English during the colonial period owing to the resemblance to the traditional symbol of Christmas in England, English holly.

Hybrids. Hybridizes with dahoon.

Range. See figure 167. Elevation: to 3,000 ft in the southern Appalachians.

GINSENG FAMILY: ARALIACEAE

The Ginseng Family contains about 1,200 species in about 50 genera, widespread in tropical and subtropical areas with a few species in temperate areas. In our region only the species described below becomes tree-sized. The family is sometimes included within the Apiaceae.

The Ginseng Family contains herbs, vines, shrubs, and trees. The leaves are usually alternate, either simple or compound, and usually with stipules. The flowers are bisexual or unisexual often borne in clusters of heads or umbels and insect pollinated. The ovary is inferior, and the fruit is usually a berry or drupe. Economically the family provides ginseng (*Panax*) and rice paper (*Tetrapanax*).

ARALIA: THE GENUS *ARALIA*

Worldwide the genus *Aralia* contains about 30 species found mostly in Asia. Our region contains about 6 species, but only devils-walkingstick becomes tree-sized.

Devils-walkingstick, Hercules' club
Aralia spinosa L. (fig. 168)

Large shrub or small tree occasionally growing to 35 ft in height and 0.5 ft in diameter (tallest known 51 ft). Bole often not branched; palmlike in habit. Leaves alternate; bi- or tripinnately compound; deciduous; 2–4 ft long; pinnae usually with

Fig. 168. Devils-walkingstick (*Aralia spinosa*) pinna of compound leaf and twig.

10–12 leaflets each. Leaflets ovate; serrate; 2–3 in. long; prickly on leaf stalks and veins. Petiole base expanded. Flowers bisexual and male; green-white; small; borne in many-flowered terminal clusters (panicles); appearing in late summer. Fruit is a berry; juicy; purple-black; 0.2–0.3 in. wide; tipped with persistent style; borne on red stalks. Twigs stout (1–1.5 in. thick); covered with many stout prickles. Terminal bud present; conical. Intolerant of shade; short-lived. Reproduces from bird-dispersed seeds and root sprouts. Found on a wide range of soil conditions, on roadsides, edges of woods, and disturbed areas. Fruits eaten by songbirds and small mammals. Range: New York southwest to Arkansas and south to central Florida and east Texas.

SUNFLOWER OR COMPOSITE FAMILY: ASTERACEAE OR COMPOSITAE

Worldwide this family contains over 19,000 species in 1,160 genera, found throughout both hemispheres especially in temperate and dry areas. It is one of the largest plant families in the world. Our region contains about 2,700 species in 345 genera, but only several are woody. Sagebrush (*Artemisia*) and groundsel-tree (*Baccharis*) grow the largest, but both rarely become tree-sized.

Leaves in this family are alternate (usually) or opposite and always simple, but sometimes they are very deeply lobed and appear compound. Stipules are lacking, and some members produce milky sap. The flowers are bisexual or unisexual, and usually borne in headlike clusters subtended by bracts (phyllaries). They are usually pollinated by insects but sometimes by wind. The sepals are absent or reduced to hairs or scales (pappus). The five petals are fused into a tube, but sometimes this tube is split open along one line and lies flat. The ovary is inferior and contains two carpels. The fruit is an achene. Economically the family provides oils (*Helianthus* and *Carthamus*), leafy vegetables (*Lactuca* and *Cichorium*), insecticides (*Chrysanthemum*), medicine (*Anthemis* and *Artemisia*), and numerous ornamental plants.

BIRCH FAMILY: BETULACEAE

Worldwide the Birch Family contains about 150 species in six genera, found mostly in northern temperate regions. Our region contains 33 species in five genera, but not all are trees. Only the Chinese genus *Ostryopsis* is absent from our region. Older manuals call this family the Hazel Family (Corylaceae). Many European manuals subdivide this family into the Corylaceae (with *Carpinus*, *Corylus*, *Ostrya*, and *Ostryopsis*) and the Betulaceae (with *Alnus* and *Betula*).

Members of the Birch Family are either trees or shrubs. The leaves are alternate, deciduous, simple, and serrate or dentate. Stipules are present. The flowers are highly reduced, unisexual with both sexes found on each plant (monoecious), and wind pollinated. Male flowers are found in aments, and they become evident the preceding autumn. The sepals and petals are minute or absent, and the pollen is allergenic. The ovary is inferior with two carpels. Fruits are nuts, nutlets, or samaras, all subtended or enclosed by bracts. Economically the family provides filberts and hazelnuts (*Corylus*) and wood products (*Alnus* and *Betula*).

ALDER: THE GENUS *ALNUS*

This genus contains about 30 species of shrubs and trees scattered through the cooler portions of the Northern Hemisphere and extending into the mountains of South America. Seven native species occasionally grow large enough to be considered trees. Only red alder is commercially valuable. European alder (*Alnus glutinosa*) is naturalized in the eastern United States.

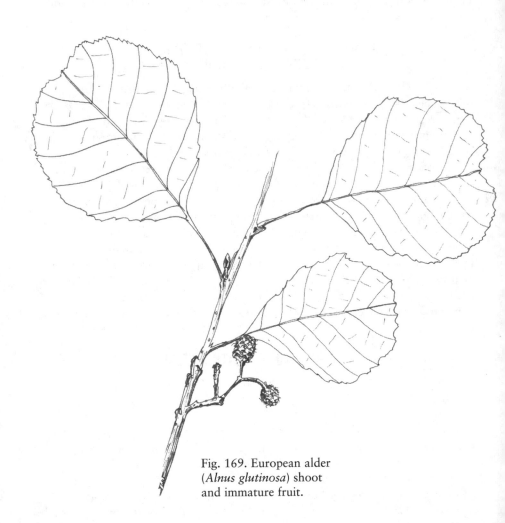

Fig. 169. European alder (*Alnus glutinosa*) shoot and immature fruit.

Alders are shrubs to medium-sized trees. The leaves are alternate, simple, deciduous, usually serrate or dentate, and pinnately veined with stipules. They fall without changing color. The flowers are unisexual. Male flowers occur in pendent scaly aments. Each scale bears three to six flowers subtended by three to five bracts. Female flowers are borne in pairs in erect aments subtended by two to four bracts. The fruit is a nutlet that matures in one season. It is borne in a semiwoody cone. Each cone scale bears two to four nutlets. The twig pith is homogeneous and triangular in cross section. Terminal buds are absent, and the lateral buds are usually stalked with two to three (rarely six) scales. Nodules found on the roots fix nitrogen. The wood is diffuse-porous. Alders occur mostly on moist or wet sites.

KEY TO ALDERS

1. Lateral buds stalkless; 3–6 scales . . . . .green alder, *Alnus viridis*
1. Lateral buds stalked; 2–3 scales . . . . .Go to 2
   2. Leaves with 5–6 pairs of lateral veins; naturalized . . . .
   . . . . .European alder, *Alnus glutinosa*
   2. Leaves with 8–15 pairs of lateral veins; native 3
3. Leaves with small serrated lobes 4
3. Leaves not lobed; finely or coarsely serrated 6
   4. Leaf margin revolute . . . . .red alder, *Alnus rubra*
   4. Leaf margin flat, not revolute 5
5. Twigs with orange lenticels . . . . .thinleaf alder, *Alnus incana* subsp. *tenuifolia*
5. Twigs with white lenticels . . . . .speckled alder, *Alnus incana* subsp. *rugosa*
   6. Leaves coarsely toothed; Western 7
   6. Leaves finely toothed; Eastern 8
7. Leaves oval to ovate . . . . .white alder, *Alnus rhombifolia*
7. Leaves oblong-lanceolate . . . . .Arizona alder, *Alnus oblongifolia*
   8. Leaves with straight veins .hazel alder, *Alnus serrulata*
   8. Leaves with arching veins . . . . .seaside alder, *Alnus maritima*

European alder, Black alder, European black alder
Alnus glutinosa (L.) Gaertn. (fig. 169)

Large shrub or small tree growing 60–70 ft in height. Leaves obovate to round; 2–3.5 in. long; leathery; dark green above; hairless or slightly hairy below especially along the major veins; both surfaces covered with resin; tip notched or rounded. Margin flat not rolled under; doubly serrate. Cones nearly spherical; 0.5–1 in. long; nutlets lack lateral wings. Terminal buds ellipsoid; 0.2–0.5 in. long; resin coated. Bark dark brown; smooth at first, developing shallow fissures; lenticels horizontal. Planted for ornamental purposes and on mine spoil banks, because of its tolerance for acid soils and ability to fix nitrogen. In the 1970s and 1980s, research was conducted in the Southeast on the suitability of European alder for high-yield plantations, but the idea was abandoned owing to low survival of planted seedlings. Native to Europe, north Africa, and Asia Minor. Originally introduced to our region for charcoal production. Naturalized locally in northeastern United States and eastern Canada.

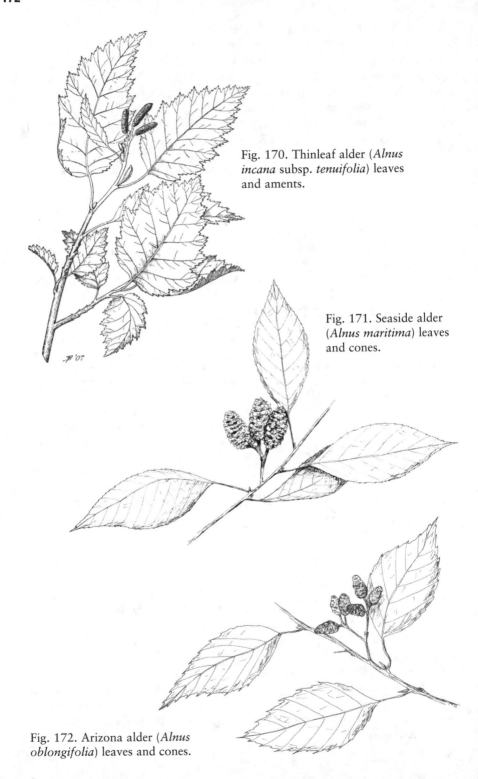

Fig. 170. Thinleaf alder (*Alnus incana* subsp. *tenuifolia*) leaves and aments.

Fig. 171. Seaside alder (*Alnus maritima*) leaves and cones.

Fig. 172. Arizona alder (*Alnus oblongifolia*) leaves and cones.

Thinleaf alder, Mountain alder

Alnus incana (L.) Moench subsp. *tenuifolia* (Nutt.) Breit.(fig. 170)

Sometimes considered a separate species, *Alnus tenuifolia*. Multiple-stemmed shrub or sometimes a small tree reaching 30 ft in height. Crown narrow; round. Leaves ovate-oblong; 1.5–4 in. long; small acute lobes; doubly serrate; dark green and hairless above; pale yellow-green below; margin flat, not rolled under; tip and base acute. Petiole stout; orange-yellow. Nutlet nearly circular; wing reduced to membranous border. Cones 0.3–0.5 in. long; obovoid-oblong; scales flattened and thickened; 3-lobed at apex. Twigs slender; large orange-colored lenticels. Lateral buds stalked; 0.2–0.3 in. long; red; slightly hairy. Bark thin; smooth; red-brown; becoming scaly on old trees. Tolerant of shade when young becoming intolerant with age. Found on banks of mountain streams. Range from western Saskatchewan northwest to central Alaska, and south to New Mexico and central California. The common alder of the Rocky Mountains.

Seaside alder, Brook alder

Alnus maritima Muhl. ex Nutt. (fig. 171)

Thicket-forming shrub or small tree growing to 30 ft in height. Leaves narrowly elliptical to ovate sometimes obovate; 2–4 in. long; leathery; nearly hairless and resin coated below; tip acute to acuminate; base acute; margin flat not rolled under; with widely spaced teeth. Petiole grooved; flat. Cones ovoid; 0.5–1.2 in. long; nutlet wings reduced to ridges. Buds with 2–3 scales of unequal size. Bark smooth; gray; very small lenticels. Grows along and in ponds and streams. Occurs in disjunct populations in Delaware, Maryland, and Oklahoma; possibly remnants of a larger more continuous distribution.

Arizona alder

Alnus oblongifolia Torr. (fig. 172)

Moderate-sized tree growing 30–40 ft in height. Often in clumps of 2–4 stems. Leaves ovate to lanceolate; 2–4 in. long; leathery; hairless or slightly hairy below; covered with resin on both surfaces; tip acuminate; margin flat, not rolled under; sharply and coarsely doubly serrate; petiole grooved. Cones ellipsoid; 0.5–1 in. long; nutlet wings smaller than body. Bark smooth; gray turning black; developing thin plates; lenticels very small. Found only at high elevation in Arizona and New Mexico, and south into Mexico.

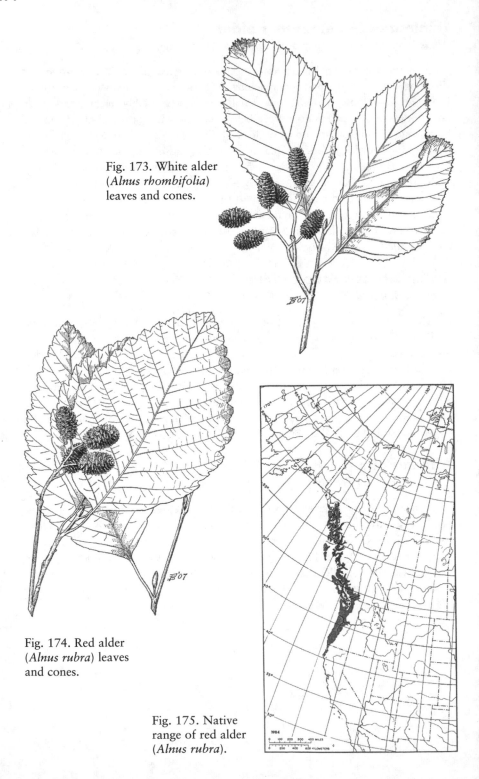

Fig. 173. White alder (*Alnus rhombifolia*) leaves and cones.

Fig. 174. Red alder (*Alnus rubra*) leaves and cones.

Fig. 175. Native range of red alder (*Alnus rubra*).

White alder, California alder
Alnus rhombifolia Nutt. (fig. 173)

Moderate-sized tree growing 70–80 ft in height. Often in clumps. Leaves elliptical to rhomboid; 2–5 in. long; 1–2 in. wide; slightly to very hairy below; base rounded to wedge-shaped; margin flat not rolled under; singly and finely serrate. Cones ovoid to cylindrical; 0.5–1 in. long; nutlet wings smaller than body. Buds with 2 bud scales; resinous. Bark smooth becoming scaly plated near the ground; light gray with splotches; small lenticels. Found on rocky stream banks and lower slopes. Range from western Idaho to Washington, and south to western Nevada and southern California.

Red alder, Oregon alder
Alnus rubra Bong. (fig. 174)

Form. Medium-sized excurrent tree growing 90–100 ft in height and 2–3 ft in diameter (largest known 130 ft by 7 ft). Crown narrow; rounded; pendulous branches.

Leaves. Ovate to elliptical; 3–6 in. long; 1–3 in. wide; dark green and hairless above; paler and rusty hairy below. Tip acute. Base obtuse or rounded. Margin slightly lobed with doubly dentate gland-tipped teeth; rolled under (revolute). Petiole grooved; 0.2–0.7 in. long.

Fruit. Borne in cones 0.4–1.3 in. long; woody; persistent; ovoid to oblong; with orange stalks or, rarely, stalkless; scales truncate with thick wrinkled tips. Nutlet nearly circular with encircling membranous wing or 2 lateral wings.

Twigs. Slender to stout; light green and densely hairy at first becoming bright red and lustrous the second year. Lateral buds 0.3–0.6 in. long; stalked; dark red; scurfy hairs; resinous.

Bark. Thin; smooth; outer bark white to blue-gray with black splotches; sometimes roughened by small warts. Inner bark turns bright red when exposed; formerly mixed with water by children to imitate blood.

Wood. The principal alder used for wood products and the most utilized hardwood in the Pacific Northwest. Sapwood white or nearly white but turning light brown tinged with red when exposed. Heartwood not distinct from sapwood in color; moderately lightweight; soft; straight grained. Used for pulpwood, furniture, the central layers in plywood, sashes, doors, paneling, bowls, and novelties.

Natural History. Intermediate in shade tolerance. Fast growing; may grow from seed to 32 ft tall in 5 years. Short-lived, reaching maturity in 60–70 years (extreme age 100 years). Reproduction by seed aggressive; requires bare mineral soil and full sunlight; often dominates burned or logged areas. Begins producing seed at age 3–4 years; seed production consistent and prolific. Reproduces vegetatively from stump sprouts and cuttings; investigated for short rotation energy plantations. Root system extensive; fibrous. Found mostly on soils with restricted drainage, especially in summer, including stream banks and swamps. Grows in pure even-aged stands or mixed with Douglas-fir, western redcedar, western hemlock, Sitka spruce, grand fir, black cottonwood, and bigleaf maple. Sometimes planted on Douglas-fir sites infested with root rot to help recovery and add nitrogen. Beavers eat the bark of twigs and small trees in the fall.

Range. See figure 175. Elevation: sea level to 3,600 ft.

Sitka alder

Alnus viridis (Villars) de Candolle subsp. *sinuata* (Regel) A. Love & D. Love (fig. 176)

Sometimes classified as a separate species, *Alnus sinuata*. Shrub or small tree rarely growing to 40 ft in height. Crown narrow and open. Leaves ovate; 3–6 in. long; acute; numerous small lateral lobes; finely toothed; yellow-green above, pale below. Nutlet oval about as wide as the wings. Cones borne in elongated leafy clusters (panicles); 0.5–0.7 in. long; about 0.3 in. wide; scales flattened; thickened at apex; stalk slender. Twigs slender; pale lenticels. Terminal buds stalkless; 0.5 in. long; acuminate; dark purple; finely hairy. Bark thin; blue-gray; inner bark bright red. Tolerant of shade when young, becoming intolerant with age. Found on moist flats and along streams. Range from Yukon to central Alaska, and south to central Montana and northwestern California; also in northeastern Asia.

Fig. 176. Sitka alder (*Alnus viridis* subsp. *sinuata*) leaves, cones, and twigs.

BIRCH: THE GENUS *BETULA*

This genus contains 35–50 species of trees and shrubs scattered through the cooler portions of North America, Asia, and Europe. Eighteen species are native to the region covered by this manual, but only 11 are trees. In addition, 2 European species (*Betula pendula* and *Betula pubescens*) are planted and sometimes naturalized. Birches are sometimes difficult to identify because many species hybridize. Indeed, Murray birch noted below arose from hybridization.

Birch leaves are alternate, simple, and usually strongly pinnate veined. The flowers are unisexual, and both sexes are found on each tree (monoecious). They appear in the spring before or with the new leaves. Male flowers occur in aments, which become evident the previous autumn. Female flowers are also borne in aments in clusters of three. The fruit is classified as either a winged nutlet or a samara. The fruit matures in autumn after one growing season, except river birch, which matures after a few weeks in the spring. The fruits are subtended by three-pronged bracts that are aggregated into small cones. The twig pith is homogeneous and triangular in cross section. The branches are generally specialized into long and short shoots. Terminal buds are absent. The bark is smooth or papery, usually resinous, often peeling in thin layers, and sometimes marked by horizontal rows of lenticels. The wood is diffuse-porous.

KEY TO BIRCHES

1. Twigs with wintergreen odor . . . . .Go to 2
1. Twigs lacking wintergreen odor . . . . .Go to 5
   2. Bark yellow-bronze; separating into thin, papery layers . . .yellow birch, *Betula alleghaniensis*
   2. Bark gray-brown or red-brown; smooth not separating into papery layers . . .3
3. Leaves with more than 12 pairs of lateral veins . . . . .sweet birch, *Betula lenta*
3. Leaves with 2–10 pairs of lateral veins 4
   4. Leaf tip nearly round . . . . .roundleaf birch, *Betula uber*
   4. Leaf tip pointed . . . . .Murray birch, *Betula murrayana*
5. Bark red-brown or chestnut-brown 6
5. Bark white or silver-white, except sometimes black at base of tree 11
   6. Leaf entire near base 7
   6. Leaf toothed to or nearly to the base 8
7. Bark smooth; western .water birch, *Betula occidentalis*
7. Bark peeling in thin sheets; eastern . . . . .river birch, *Betula nigra*
   8. Leaf base heart-shaped . . . . .heartleaf birch, *Betula cordifolia*
   8. Leaf base rounded, flat, or wedge-shaped 9
9. Twigs lacking resin glands; naturalized . . .European white birch, *Betula pubescens*
9. Twigs with sparse to dense resin glands; native 10
   10. Twigs hairless with conspicuous resin glands . . .resin birch, *Betula neoalaska*
   10. Twigs slightly hairy with only a few scattered resin glands . . . .
   . . . . .Kenai birch, *Betula kenaica*
11. Bark black at base of tree; not separating into papery layers . . . .
   . . . . .gray birch, *Betula populifolia*
11. Bark white at base of tree; separating into papery layers 12
   12. Twigs hairy, nearly nonglandular . . . . .paper birch, *Betula papyrifera*
   12. Twigs hairless and resinous-glandular . .European silver birch, *Betula pendula*

Yellow birch

Betula alleghaniensis Britt. (fig. 177)

Nomenclature. Some older manuals incorrectly call this species *Betula lutea*, a name published later.

Form. Medium-sized excurrent tree growing 60–80 ft in height and 1–2 ft in diameter (largest known 110 ft by 4 ft).

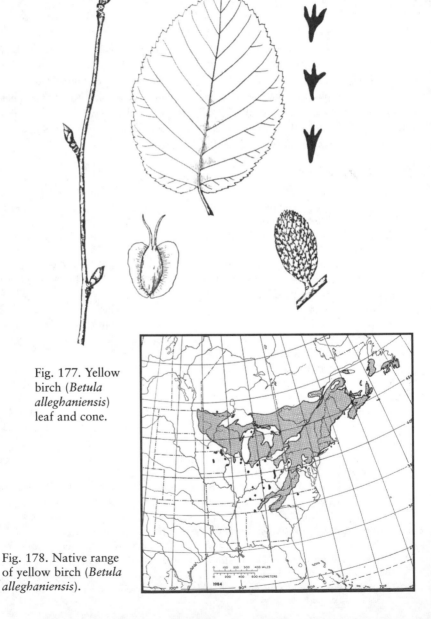

Fig. 177. Yellow birch (*Betula alleghaniensis*) leaf and cone.

Fig. 178. Native range of yellow birch (*Betula alleghaniensis*).

Leaves. Ovate to oblong-ovate; 3–5 in. long; slightly aromatic; 8–12 or more pairs of veins. Base rounded; unequal. Margin sharply doubly serrate. Petiole hairy.

Fruit. Cones ovoid-cylindrical; erect; nearly stalkless; 1–1.5 in. long. Scales hairy; longer than broad; lateral lobes ascending; tardily deciduous. Nutlet light brown; about as wide as wing.

Twigs. Smooth; lustrous; yellow-brown or gray; slight wintergreen odor. Terminal buds ovate; acute; chestnut-brown; ciliate on scale margins. Spur shoots prominent; 2 leaves per shoot.

Bark. Thin; yellow-bronze; separating horizontally into thin papery strips; with horizontal rows of lenticels. Papery strips useful as fire tinder, lighting with a match even when wet.

Wood. Most commercially valuable birch. Sapwood white to pale yellow. Heartwood brown to red-brown; heavy to very heavy; hard. Used for pulpwood, railroad ties, furniture, kitchen cabinets, flooring, audio-video cabinets, toys, doors, spools and bobbins, butcher blocks, and musical instruments. Also used to make wood alcohol and acetate of lime.

Natural History. Intermediate in tolerance to shade; our most shade-tolerant birch. Moderately fast growing; reaches maturity in 150 years. Reproduction from seed vigorous; seed production prolific; good seed crops occur every 2–3 years; seeds mature in August but fall during the winter; dispersed by wind including blowing across crusted snow; seed viability low, about 20 percent; seeds require stratification and germinate on bare soil or rotten logs; roots of seedlings not able to penetrate hardwood leaf litter. Found with stilt roots when seedlings become established on old stumps. Sprouts only from small stumps. Windthrow, fire, and the bronze birch borer cause the most damage. Grows on a wide variety of soils; especially common on cool mesic flats and lower slopes. Found in small, pure groves of even-aged trees or mixed in even-aged or uneven-aged stands with eastern hemlock, sugar maple, American beech, eastern white pine, red maple, yellow-poplar, and red spruce. Twigs eaten by rabbits and white-tailed deer; ruffed grouse and songbirds eat the aments and seeds.

Hybrids. Hybridizes with paper birch and with bog birch forming purpus birch, *Betula* x *purpusii*.

Range. See figure 178.

Heartleaf birch, Mountain white birch
Betula cordifolia Regel

Formerly thought to be a fertile hybrid between yellow birch and paper birch. Sometimes treated as a variety of paper birch (*Betula papyrifera* var. *cordifolia*), which it closely resembles. Heartleaf birch differs in having fewer chromosomes, more lateral leaf veins, darker bark, and host sites at higher elevations. Large shrubs to moderate-sized trees growing 60–70 ft in height and 1–2 ft in diameter. Often with several stems growing in a clump. Leaves ovate; 2.5–5 in. long; 9–12 pairs of lateral veins; slightly to very hairy below. Leaf tip acute. Leaf base heart-shaped. Margin doubly serrated. Twigs hairless or slightly hairy; often with resin glands. Bark tan to cinnamon-brown; lustrous; separating in thin papery sheets. Found from Newfoundland to central Ontario, and south to northern New York and northern Iowa; also at higher elevations in the southern Appalachians of North Carolina.

Kenai birch

Betula kenaica W.H. Evans

Closely related to paper birch and sometimes considered a variety, *Betula papyrifera* var. *kenaica*. Small trees grow to 40 ft in height. Leaves broadly ovate;

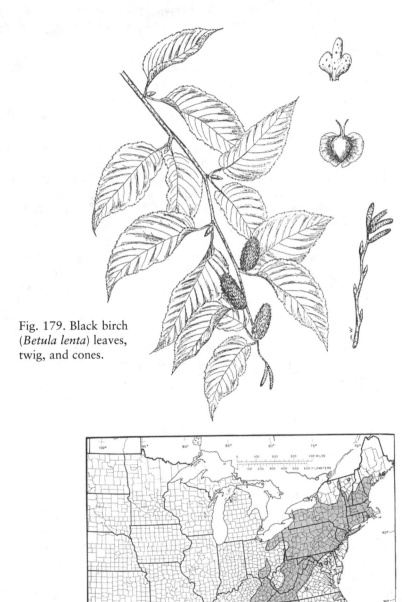

Fig. 179. Black birch (*Betula lenta*) leaves, twig, and cones.

Fig. 180. Native range of black birch (*Betula lenta*).

2–3 in. long; hairy below, especially along the major veins; sometimes with scattered resin glands. Base rounded to wedge-shaped. Margin coarsely serrate to doubly serrate. Twigs hairy with scattered resin glands. Bark red-brown to pink-white; separates into thin papery sheets. Grows on rocky slopes in subalpine areas of Alaska.

Black birch, Sweet birch, Cherrybark birch
Betula lenta L.(fig. 179)

Form. Medium-sized excurrent tree growing 60–70 ft in height and 1–2 ft in diameter (largest known 100 ft by 5 ft). Crown rounded; open; pendulous branchlets.

Leaves. Ovate to oblong-ovate; 2–4 in. long; usually singly serrate; teeth small; hairless above; aromatic; 12 or more pairs of lateral veins. Base heart-shaped or unequally rounded.

Fruit. Cones oblong-ovoid; held erect; nearly stalkless; 1–1.5 in. long. Scales hairless; longer than wide. Nutlet about as wide as wing.

Twigs. Smooth; lustrous; light red-brown; strong wintergreen odor; small resin glands present. Terminal buds 0.5–0.7 in. long; conical; acute; red-brown; mostly hairless. Spur shoots prominent; 2 leaves per shoot.

Bark. Thin; 0.5–0.7 in. thick; red-brown, gray-brown, or nearly black; smooth not papery; breaking into small chiplike plates in old trees; prominent horizontal rows of lenticels. Source of birch oil.

Wood. Similar to yellow birch. With time, wood darkens to resemble mahogany; used as inexpensive substitute. Source of wintergreen oil, methyl salicylate.

Natural History. Intolerant of shade. Grows moderately fast; reaches maturity in 120–150 years (extreme age 260 years). Reproduces well from seeds released in autumn; seeds dispersed by wind, including blowing over crusted snow; large seed crops produced every 1–2 years. Reproduces as sprouts from small stumps. Wildfire causes the most damage. Development best on fertile well-drained soils in coves of the southern Appalachians, but also hardy on infertile dry soils. Generally found mixed with yellow-poplar, red maple, basswood, white ash, yellow birch, northern red oak, and eastern hemlock.

Range. See figure 180.

Murray birch
Betula murrayana B.V. Barnes and Dancik

Small tree growing to 50 ft in height. Leaves ovate; 2–4 in. long; hairless or slightly hairy below; 7–10 pairs of lateral veins. Base wedge-shaped. Margin sharply toothed; sometimes doubly serrate. Cones held erect; 1–2 in. long; scales hairless or slightly hairy; scale lobes ascending. Grows in swamps with bog birch. A rare natural polyploid (octoploid) derivative of the hybrid between yellow birch and bog birch. Currently known only in Michigan, but possibly occurs wherever the parents grow together.

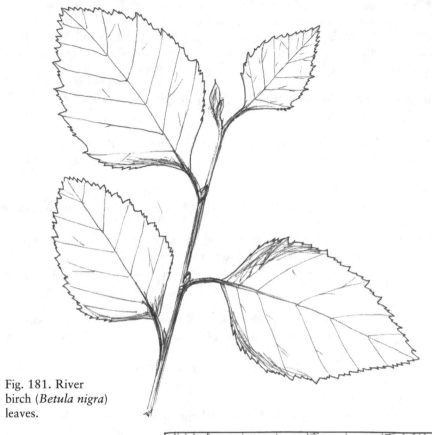

Fig. 181. River birch (*Betula nigra*) leaves.

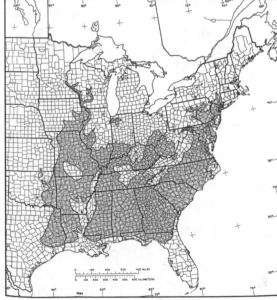

Fig. 182. Native range of river birch (*Betula nigra*).

Resin birch, Paper birch
Betula neoalaskana Sarg.

Formerly thought to be related to paper birch, and sometimes made a variety, *Betula papyrifera* var. *neoalaskana*. Now thought to be related to gray birch and European silver birch. Moderate-sized tree growing to 75 ft in height. Leaves ovate to deltate; 1–3 in. long; hairy along the major veins below; resinous glands present; 5–18 pairs of lateral veins. Tip long-acuminate. Base rounded to broadly wedge-shaped. Margin coarsely doubly serrate. Fruit cones pendent; 1–2 in. long; scales hairless with marginal cilia. Twigs hairless; covered with resin glands. Bark red-brown to pink-white; separating in thin papery sheets. Grows near the northern limit of trees. Range from northwest Mackenzie to northwest Alaska, and south to Saskatchewan and British Columbia.

River birch
Betula nigra L.(fig. 181)

Form. Medium-sized tree growing to 60–80 ft in height and 2–3 ft in diameter. Often grows in clumps.

Leaves. Rhombic-ovate; 2–4 in. long; more-or-less hairy below; 5–12 pairs of lateral veins. Base broadly wedge-shaped; entire at base. Margin coarsely doubly serrate.

Fruit. Cones oblong; held erect on stout stalks. Scale lobes narrow; ascending; hairy. Mature in spring.

Twigs. Red-brown; hairless to slightly hairy; lacking wintergreen odor; often with scattered resin glands. Terminal buds 0.2 in. long; woolly becoming hairless.

Bark. Thin; on young trees salmon-pink to red-brown; separating into thin papery layers. On older trees gray-brown to dark yellow; divided into flat scaly ridges with black furrows.

Wood. Similar to yellow birch but not as heavy.

Natural History. Intolerant of shade. Fast growing. Found on stream banks and second bottoms in alluvial soils with abundant moisture all year; not tolerant of flooding in the growing season. Reproduces abundantly from seeds; large seed crops produced almost every year; only birch to mature and release seeds in spring; seeds dispersed by wind and floating on water; seeds germinate quickly on bare soil after release. Flooding and floating ice blocks cause the most damage. Grows in mixed stands with sweetgum, sycamore, red maple, black willow, yellow-poplar, American elm, bitternut hickory, eastern cottonwood, swamp chestnut oak, and boxelder. Planted for strip mine reclamation. Used in ornamental planting because of the pleasing bark and natural resistance to the bronze birch borer.

Range. See figure 182.

Water birch, River birch
Betula occidentalis Hook.

Nomenclature. Formerly called *Betula fontinalis*.

Form. Shrub to small tree reaching 25 ft in height and 1 ft in diameter. Crown broad; open with ascending branches. Frequently found in dense thickets.

Leaves. Broadly ovate; 1–2 in. long and 0.7–1 in. wide; sharply and often doubly serrate, but entire at base; sometimes slightly lobed; hairless; dark green above; yellow-green and minutely glandular below; 2–6 pairs of lateral veins. Tip acute to acuminate. Petioles stout; 0.3–0.5 in. long; light yellow; glandular-dotted. Stipules bright green; slightly ciliate.

Fruit. Cones cylindrical; pendent or erect; long-stalked; 1–1.2 in. long; scales ciliate; nutlet narrower than wings.

Twigs. At first, light green becoming dark red-brown; abundant red resin glands; lenticels present; lacking wintergreen odor. Terminal buds 0.2 in. long; ovoid; acute; very resinous; chestnut-brown.

Bark. Thin (0.2 in. thick); smooth; lustrous; dark bronze; not separating in papery layers; marked by long rows of pale horizontal lenticels.

Wood. Used locally for fencing and fuel.

Natural History. Intolerant of shade. Reproduction abundant in moist, mineral soil. Commonly found in the Rocky Mountains along streams in moist mountain valleys and canyons.

Hybrids. Hybridizes with paper birch sometimes making separation of the 2 species difficult. These hybrids were formerly called *Betula papyrifera* var. *subcordata*. Also hybridizes with dwarf birch, forming Yukon birch (*Betula* x *eastwoodiae*).

Range. Southern Manitoba to northeastern British Columbia, and south to northern New Mexico and Oregon; also in the Sierra Nevada of California.

Paper birch, White birch, Canoe birch
Betula papyrifera Marsh. (fig. 183)

Form. Moderate-sized tree growing 50–60 ft in height and 1–2 ft in diameter (largest known 120 ft by 4 ft). Old trees with open crowns and pendulous branches. Sometimes found in clumps of 2–4 stems.

Leaves. Ovate; 2–5 in. long; coarsely and usually doubly serrate; dark green and hairless above; yellow-green, slightly hairy, and covered with resin glands below; fewer than 9 pairs of lateral veins. Base flat, rounded, or wedge-shaped.

Fruit. Cones cylindrical; pendent; stalk slender; 1–1.5 in. long. Scales about as long as wide; hairless or slightly hairy; lateral lobes held nearly at right angles to axis. Nutlet narrower than wings.

Twigs. At first green; slightly hairy; scattered orange lenticels; turning dark orange-brown; scattered resin glands; lustrous; lacking wintergreen odor. Terminal buds 0.2 in. long; obovoid; acute; dark chestnut-brown; hairless; gummy. Spur shoots prominent; 3 leaves per shoot.

Bark. Red-brown on very young trees turning cream-white; separating into thin, papery layers; marked by rows of lenticels. Inner bark orange.

Wood. Similar to yellow birch but not as heavy. In addition to uses listed above also used for tooth picks, clothes pins, and ice cream sticks.

Natural History. Very intolerant of shade. Fast growing, but short-lived. Reproduction vigorous covering extensive areas following fire. Grows on fertile loam or sandy soils.

Hybrids. Hybridizes with bog birch forming *Betula* x *sandbergii.* The blue birches (*Betula* x *caerulea* and *Betula caerulea-grandis*), once thought to be hybrids with paper birch, are hybrids between heartleaf birch and gray birch.

Varieties. Other manuals may recognize 5 varieties. Three varieties (var. *cordifolia,* var. *kenaica,* and var. *neoalaskana*) are now classified as separate species, and are described above. Var. *subcordata* is now thought to be a hybrid between paper birch and water birch. The nonpeeling brown bark of the remaining variety, var. *commutata,* is apparently environmentally induced and not worthy of naming.

Range. See figure 184.

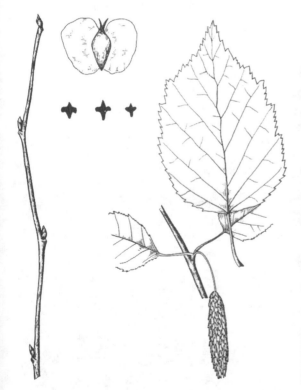

Fig. 183. Paper birch (*Betula papyrifera*) leaf, twig, cone, cone bracts, and fruit.

Fig. 184. Native range of paper birch (*Betula papyrifera*).

Weeping birch, European white birch

Betula pendula Roth

Formerly called *Betula verrucosa*. Moderate-sized tree growing to 75 ft in height. Leaves broadly ovate; 1–2 in. long; hairless to slightly hairy below; small resin glands present; 5–18 pairs of lateral veins. Margin coarsely doubly serrate. Cones held erect or pendent; 0.7–1.5 in. long; cylindric. Scales hairy; middle lobe shorter than the laterals. Twigs drooping; hairless; small resin glands present. Bark white to silver white; separates in long papery sheets; long rows of lenticels. Native to Eurasia. Commonly cultivated and sometimes escaping, especially in New England.

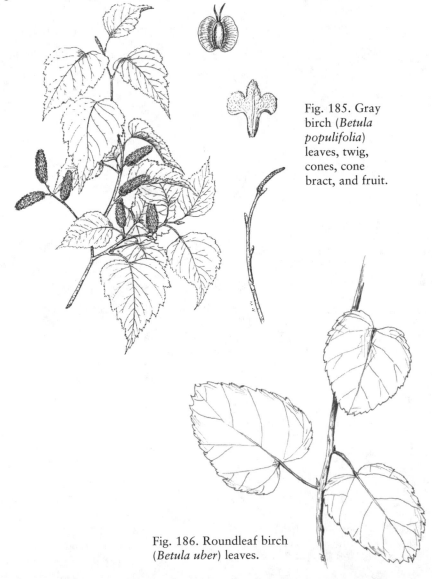

Fig. 185. Gray birch (*Betula populifolia*) leaves, twig, cones, cone bract, and fruit.

Fig. 186. Roundleaf birch (*Betula uber*) leaves.

Gray birch
Betula populifolia Marsh. (fig. 185)

Small excurrent tree growing to 40 ft in height; often leaning. Sometimes found in clumps of 2–4 stems. Leaves deltate to rhombic; doubly serrate; hairless or hairy below; 5–18 pairs of lateral veins. Tip long acuminate. Cones cylindrical; erect or pendent; on slender stalks. Scales about as long as wide; very hairy above; middle lobe shorter than laterals; lateral lobes recurved. Nutlet much narrower than wings. Twigs with tiny resin glands; red-brown; lacking wintergreen odor. Terminal buds 0.2 in. long; ovoid; chestnut-brown; gummy. Bark thin; smooth; gray-white; not separating into papery sheets; black and furrowed at base of larger trees and below larger branches. Common pioneer on disturbed sites and abandoned agricultural fields. Found on rocky infertile soils. Twigs and bark used by Native Americans and settlers to treat infected cuts. The blue birches (*Betula* x *caerulea* and *Betula caerulea-grandis*), formerly thought to be either species or hybrids with paper birch, have been shown to be hybrids between gray birch and heartleaf birch. Range from Nova Scotia to southern Ontario, and south to New Jersey and central Pennsylvania. Local in northern Ohio, northwestern Indiana, and northern Virginia.

European white birch
Betula pubescens Ehrhart

Large shrub or small tree. Leaves ovate; 1.5–2 in. long; slightly to densely hairy below especially along the veins; resin glands lacking. Tip acute. Margin serrate. Cones pendent; cylindrical; scales hairless to slightly hairy. Twigs covered with short hairs; no wintergreen odor. Bark on young trees red-brown; turning light red-brown, tan, or gray-white; smooth or separating into papery sheets. Powdered bark used to treat chafed skin or mixed with maple syrup to relieve stomach cramps. Var. *tortuosa* has smaller leaves and twigs with resin glands. Native to Greenland, Iceland, and Eurasia. Planted in our region, and occasionally escaped.

Roundleaf birch;
Betula uber (Ashe) Fern. (fig. 186)

The taxonomic status of roundleaf birch is not settled. Some authorities classify it as a separate species, while others think it is a mutant form of black birch. The issue needs further study. Small slender tree growing to 30 ft in height. Leaves nearly round; hairless or slightly hairy below, especially along the major veins; 2–6 pairs of lateral veins. Tip rounded. Base rounded or heart-shaped. Cones held erect; ellipsoid-cylindrical. Scales hairless; middle lobe shorter than laterals. Twigs covered with small resin glands; wintergreen odor present. Bark smooth; dark brown; not separating into papery layers; with rows of horizontal lenticels. Grows on mesic stream banks and floodplains. Known only from Smyth County, Virginia. The only known population of roundleaf birch was first described in 1918, but the location of the population was lost. It was rediscovered in 1974.

HORNBEAM: THE GENUS *CARPINUS*

Worldwide the genus *Carpinus* contains about 25 species, found mostly in the north temperate zones in North America, Europe, and Asia. Only the species listed below occurs in our region. The European species (*Carpinus betulus*) is frequently planted in North America, but it has not escaped.

Hornbeams are small to large trees. The flowers appear in the spring with the new leaves. The flowers are unisexual, and both sexes are found on each tree (monoecious). Male flowers are borne in aments. Female flowers are found in loose

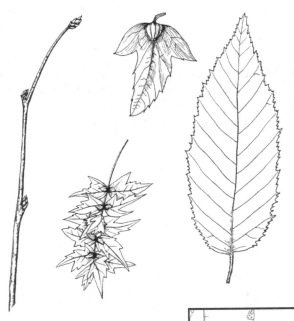

Fig. 187. American hornbeam (*Carpinus caroliniana*) leaf, twig, fruit cluster, and nutlet with bract.

Fig. 188. Native range of American hornbeam (*Carpinus caroliniana*).

aments. The fruit is a nutlet, maturing in one season, subtended by a three-pronged bract, and borne in racemelike clusters. The terminal bud is absent. The wood is diffuse-porous.

American hornbeam, Musclewood, Blue-beech, Ironwood
Carpinus caroliniana Walt. (fig. 187)

Form. Small tree rarely growing over 30–40 ft in height and 1 ft in diameter (largest known 65 ft by 2 ft). Often occurs in clumps of 2–3 stems.

Leaves. Ovate to elliptical; 2–4 in. long; dark green and glossy above; paler and slightly to moderately hairy below; 2-ranked; lateral veins rarely branching. Tip acute. Margin sharply doubly serrate.

Fruit. Nutlet ovoid; flat; brown; subtended by 3-pronged bract.

Twigs. Slender; round; pale green at first becoming lustrous and red-brown; leaf scars with 3 bundle scars. Lateral buds 0.1 in. long; brown; acute; flower buds square in cross section.

Bark. Thin; smooth; blue-gray; often mottled with light or dark patches; often fluted.

Wood. Little or no current commercial value. Sapwood white. Heartwood light yellow to brown-white; heavy; hard. Used locally for tool handles, splitting wedges, farm vehicle parts, and fuel.

Natural History. Very tolerant of shade. Slow growing. Reproduces in shade from seed lying on leaf litter; dispersed by wind and birds; large seed crops occur every 3–5 years. Fire causes the most damage. Tolerant of a wide range of moisture conditions, but usually found on moist to wet-mesic sites; moderately tolerant of flooding in the growing season. Almost always found in the understory; grows with black cherry, sugar maple, American beech, eastern hemlock, yellow birch, red maple, yellow-poplar, sweetgum, American elm, northern red oak, swamp chestnut oak, laurel oak, cherrybark oak, river birch, and bitternut hickory. Seeds, buds, and aments eaten by songbirds, ruffed grouse, quail, turkey, fox, and gray squirrel. Inner bark eaten by beaver and rabbits.

Subspecies. Some authors recognize 2 subspecies, which hybridize and intergrade. Subsp. *caroliniana* of the southeast has a blunt leaf apex and lacks brown glands on leaf undersurfaces. Subsp. *virginiana* of the Northeast and Lake States has a long acuminate leaf apex with brown glands on leaf undersurfaces.

Range. See figure 188.

HAZELNUT: THE GENUS *CORYLUS*

This genus contains about 15 species worldwide, but only 3 are native to our region. All are shrubs except California hazel, which may occasionally become tree-sized. Giant filbert (*Corylus maxima*) and European filbert (*Corylus avellana*) of Europe are planted in the United States for the edible nuts.

Hazelnuts are characterized by deciduous, alternate, simple, ovate to nearly round, doubly serrate leaves. The ovoid nuts surrounded by leafy toothed bracts mature in one season. Sometimes sold as filberts, the nuts are also a favorite food for many small mammals.

California hazel

Corylus cornuta Marsh. subsp. *californica* (A. DC) E. Murray

Sometimes treated as a variety, instead of a subspecies. Large shrub occasionally a small tree growing to 45 ft in height. Open and spreading with multiple stems. Leaves broadly elliptical to nearly round; 2–4 in. long; leathery; hairy below and very hairy on the major veins. Tip obtuse or acute. Base rounded or cordate. Margin coarsely doubly serrate. Petiole hairy often with glandular hairs. Nuts borne in clusters of 2–4; enclosed in long tubular bracts; bracts sticky. Twigs glandular hairy. Found along streams and on moist mountain slopes in California, Oregon, Washington, and British Columbia.

HOPHORNBEAM: THE GENUS *OSTRYA*

This genus contains five to eight species worldwide, and three species occur in our area. The remaining species grow in Europe and Asia.

Hophornbeams are small trees. The flowers appear in the spring with the new leaves. The fruits are nutlets enclosed within bladderlike sacs. The fruit clusters somewhat resemble the fruits of hops, providing the basis of the common name. Terminal buds are absent. The wood is very hard, heavy, and diffuse-porous.

KEY TO HOPHORNBEAMS

1. Leaves 3–5 in. long . . . . .eastern hophornbeam, *Ostrya virginiana*
1. Leaves 1–3 in. long . . . . .Go to 2

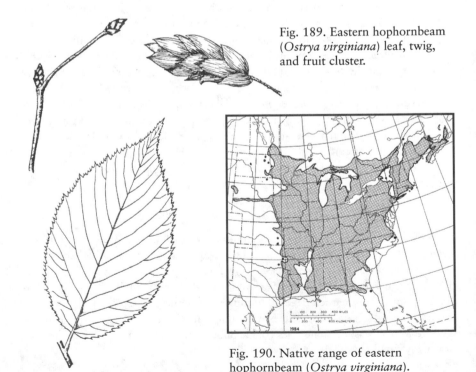

Fig. 189. Eastern hophornbeam (*Ostrya virginiana*) leaf, twig, and fruit cluster.

Fig. 190. Native range of eastern hophornbeam (*Ostrya virginiana*).

2. Petiole with stipitate glands . . . . .Knowlton hophornbeam, *Ostrya knowltonii*
2. Petiole hairy, but lacking stipitate glands . . . .
. . . . .Chisos hophornbeam, *Ostrya chisosensis*

Chisos hophornbeam
Ostrya chisosensis Correll

Small tree growing to 40 ft in height. Leaves elliptical to lanceolate; 1.5–2.5 in. long; slightly hairy below especially along the veins. Margin finely doubly serrate. Petiole lacking stipitate glands. Twigs hairy but lacking stipitate glands. Known only in Big Bend National Park in west Texas along streams and on moist slopes.

Knowlton hophornbeam, Western hophornbeam
Ostrya knowltonii Coville

Small tree growing to 30 ft in height. Leaves ovate to broadly elliptical; 1–3 in. long; hairy below especially on the veins; 5–8 pairs of lateral veins. Margin doubly serrate. Petiole covered with stipitate glands. Twigs hairy; often with stipitate glands. Found sporadically along streams in canyons or on rocky but moist mountain slopes in western Texas, southeastern New Mexico, northern Arizona, and southeastern Utah.

Eastern hophornbeam, Ironwood, Leverwood
Ostrya virginiana (Mill.) K. Koch (fig. 189)

Form. Small excurrent tree growing 30–40 ft in height and 0.5–1 ft in diameter (largest known 70 ft by 3 ft). Crown round; slender.

Leaves. Oblong-ovate; 3–5 in. long; thin; dull yellow-green above; somewhat hairy below; 11–15 pairs of lateral veins; lateral veins sometimes branching near leaf base. Tip acuminate. Margin sharply doubly serrate.

Fruit. Borne in a loose drooping cluster. Nutlet ovoid; flat; enclosed in pale sacs; sacs 1 in. long.

Twigs. Slender; round; red-brown becoming dark brown; slightly to very hairy; leaf scars with 3 bundle scars. Lateral buds 0.1–0.2 in. long; ovoid; acute; bud scales green with brown margins.

Bark. Thin; gray-brown; divided into long, narrow, flat ridges separated by shallow fissures; with age, the ends of the ridges separate from the tree and look shaggy.

Wood. Little or no commercial value currently. Sapwood white. Heartwood white to light brown; very heavy; hard. Formerly used for sled runners, axles, tool handles, levers, mallets, splitting wedges, airplane propellers, and fuel.

Natural History. Tolerant of shade. Slow growing. Reproduces from seeds released in autumn; wind and bird dispersed; seeds germinate the following spring on a wide variety of seed beds. Reproduces from stump sprouts. Relatively free of serious insect and fungus disease problems but sensitive to air pollution. Grows on dry-mesic slopes or mesic valleys. Occurs as a scattered understory tree, growing with white oak, black oak, northern red oak, southern red oak, sugar maple, American beech, eastern hemlock, white ash, flowering dogwood, pignut hickory, and yellow-poplar. Buds and aments eaten in winter by ruffed grouse.

Range. See figure 190. Elevation: 250–3,200 ft.

TRUMPET-CREEPER FAMILY: BIGNONIACEAE

Worldwide this family contains 650–750 species in about 110 genera, found mostly in the tropics. Our region contains 4 species in 3 genera. Found naturally in the Southwest and naturalized in Florida, trumpetflower (*Tecoma stans*) is normally a shrub with pinnately compound leaves and showy, yellow, tubelike flowers.

The Trumpet-Creeper Family contains trees, shrubs, and especially lianas that climb by rootlets or tendrils. The leaves are opposite (sometimes whorled), often glandular, and pinnately or palmately compound (sometimes simple). If compound, the leaflets are sometimes modified into tendrils. Stipules are lacking. The flowers are usually large, showy, bisexual, tubelike, and bilaterally symmetrical. Each flower contains five fused sepals, five fused petals, and two carpels, and they are pollinated by insects or birds. The fruit is usually a capsule with winged seeds, but sometimes a berry. The wood is ring-porous. Economically the family provides wood products (*Catalpa*, *Cybistax*, *Stereospermum*, and *Tabebuia*) and numerous ornamentals.

CATALPA: THE GENUS *CATALPA*

Worldwide this genus contains about 11 species, found in temperate Asia, the West Indies, and our region. Our 2 similar species are often misidentified.

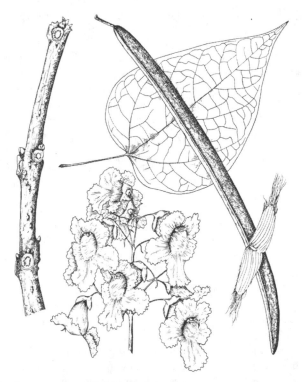

Fig. 191. Northern catalpa (*Catalpa speciosa*) leaf, twig, flowers, fruit, and seed.

KEY TO CATALPA

1. Seed wings narrowing to a point covered with short hairs . . . .
. . . . southern catalpa, *Catalpa bignonioides*
1. Seed wings rounded but tipped with long hairs . . . .
. . . . northern catalpa, *Catalpa speciosa*

Southern catalpa
Catalpa bignonioides Walt.

Moderate-sized tree growing 30–40 ft in height and 1–2 ft in diameter. Leaves simple; whorled or opposite; deciduous; 6–12 in. long; heart-shaped, entire, but sometimes with a large tooth near the tip. Flowers white with large purple spots and yellow stripes inside; tubelike; 1.5–2 in. wide; borne in early summer in many-flowered terminal clusters (panicles). Fruit a cigarlike capsule; 6–12 in. long; 0.3–0.4 in. wide; borne in clusters of 1–6; mature in autumn and releasing seeds into the winter. Seeds winged; flat; narrowing to a point and covered with short hairs. Twigs stout; terminal bud lacking; hairless. Leaf scar large; round. Bark brown to gray-brown; divided by shallow furrows into narrow ridges. Grows naturally in moist soil along streams and in well-drained bottomlands, but planted on many sites. Original range uncertain; probably found from southwest Georgia and northwest Florida to Mississippi; planted and naturalized from New England to southern Michigan, and south to northeastern Florida and east Texas.

Northern catalpa, Cigar-tree
Catalpa speciosa Warder ex Engelm. (fig. 191)

Form. Medium-sized tree growing 40–60 ft in height and 1–3 ft in diameter (largest known 120 ft by 6 ft).

Leaves. Whorled or opposite; simple; deciduous; 6–12 in. long; heart-shaped; entire; sometimes with a large tooth above the middle; hairy below.

Flowers. Showy; white with small purple spots and yellow lines inside; 2–2.5 in. wide; borne in few-flowered clusters (panicles); appearing in late spring or early summer.

Fruit. Cigarlike capsule; 8–20 in. long; 0.5–0.6 in. wide; mature in autumn and persistent through winter. Seeds winged; numerous; flat; rounded but long-fringed at ends.

Twigs. Very stout; brown; hairless; leaf scar round. Terminal bud lacking. Lateral buds small; sunken into twig; pith solid.

Bark. Rather thin; brown; broken into short ridges or thick scales.

Wood. Light; soft; weak; brown; durable; used for fence posts and railroad ties.

Natural History. Intolerant of shade. Fast growing on fertile sites. Found on moist fertile soil, but widely planted on many sites. Planted for fence posts or to attract catalpa worms, large defoliating larvae used for fish bait.

Range. Original range uncertain; probably found in the Mississippi River Valley from southwestern Indiana to Tennessee, possibly Louisiana. Naturalized through all but coldest portions of United States.

Desertwillow

Chilopsis linearis (Cav.) Sweet (fig. 192)

Shrub or small tree rarely growing to 30 ft in height. Lower stem often lying on soil surface. Leaves opposite, becoming alternate at the ends of long shoots; simple; linear or linear-lanceolate; 5–12 in. long; 0.2–0.3 in. wide. Tip pointed. Flowers showy; white; tubelike; 5-lobed; yellow-spotted inside; 0.7–1.5 in. long. Fruit a capsule; slender; elongated; thin-walled; 7–12 in. long; 0.2 in. wide; splitting into 2 parts; persistent into the winter. Twigs slender; hairless or very hairy; light brown. Terminal bud absent. Lateral buds minute; scaly. Intolerant of shade. Short-lived. Grows on banks of watercourses in desert and low mountain areas. Found from southwest Texas to southern Nevada, and south into Mexico.

Fig. 192. Desertwillow (*Chilopsis linearis*) leaves, flowers, and fruit.

BORAGE FAMILY: THE BORAGINACEAE

Worldwide this family contains about 2,400 species in 117 genera. It is sometimes subdivided into as many as five separate families. Members of this family occur around the world. Most species are herbs, but a few are shrubs or trees.

CORDIA: THE GENUS *CORDIA*

Worldwide this genus contains about 250 species, found mostly in the tropical portions of South America, Central America, and the West Indies. The genus is sometimes placed in the segregate family Ehretiaceae. Our region contains 1 species.

Anacahuite

Cordia boissieri A. DC.

Large shrub or small tree sometimes growing to 25 ft in height. Leaves alternate; simple; oval to oblong-ovate; 4–5 in. long; entire or with widely spaced teeth; thick and firm; dark green above; very hairy below; falling slowly. Flowers bisexual; showy; funnel-shaped; 2 in. wide; white with yellow spots inside. Fruit drupelike; ovoid; 1 in. long; 0.7 in. wide; lustrous; bright red-brown; enclosed by orange-brown hairy sepals. Twigs stout; dark gray or brown; slightly hairy; marked by occasional large lenticels. Leaf scars elevated. Intolerant of shade. Planted as an ornamental. Found on dry limestone ridges and depressions in extreme south Texas, and south into Mexico.

EHRETIA: THE GENUS *EHRETIA*

Worldwide this genus contains about 50 species, found mostly in the Old World tropics. The genus is sometimes placed in the segregate family Ehretiaceae. Our region contains 1 species.

Anacua

Ehretia anacua (Teran & Berland.) I. M. Johnst.

Large shrub or small tree growing to 50 ft in height. Leaves simple; alternate; semi-evergreen; elliptical to oblong; entire or toothed above the middle; olive-green and sandpapery above; hairless or slightly hairy below. Flowers white; bell-shaped; 5-lobed; 0.3–0.5 in. wide; appearing in the spring and again later after rain. Fruit is a drupe or berrylike drupe; stone separating into 2 parts; 0.3–0.5 in. wide; yellow-orange; juicy; edible. Twigs zigzag; brown hairy at first, becoming hairless. Bark red-brown to nearly black; divided into small scaly plates that peel in layers. Wood hard; heavy; difficult to split; used locally for fence posts, tool handles, and wagon parts. Planted as an ornamental. Found in central and south Texas and Mexico.

TORCHWOOD FAMILY: THE BURSERACEAE

Worldwide this family contains about 500 species in about 16 genera, all found in tropical or subtropical areas. Our region contains only the genus *Bursera* with 2 species of the Southwest, but both are rarely tree-sized. Elephant-tree (*Bursera microphylla*) with alternate bipinnately compound leaves, each with 20–40 leaflets, occurs on desert mountains in southwest Arizona and extreme southern California. Fragrant bursera [*Bursera fagaroides*) occurs in Pima County, Arizona, and south into Mexico. In the tropics, this family provides useful resins.

CACTUS FAMILY: CACTACEAE

Worldwide this family contains roughly 1,500 species in about 90 genera. The family occurs naturally only in the Americas especially in Mexico and Central America, but it has been introduced elsewhere in the world. The classification of cacti has varied over the years. Cacti are problematic to study. They are difficult to preserve as dried specimens, and comparative study is difficult. The number of recognized genera has varied from 30 to 300. In addition, commercial breeders and growers have increased the number of names without providing suitable documentation. In our region only saguaro (*Cereus*) is always tree-sized. Jumping cholla (*Opuntia fulgida*) is usually a large shrub, and Indian-fig (*Opuntia ficus-indica*), probably native to Mexico, persists from cultivation or occasionally escapes in the Southwest.

Most cacti are shrubs, but a few species may grow to 40–60 ft in height and 1–2 ft in diameter. The stems are succulent and adapted for storing water. Owing to an enlarged pith, comparatively little wood is produced usually in the form of a hollow or meshed cylinder. The treelike species in our region have either flattened stems (*Opuntia*) or columnar stems (*Cereus*).

The leaves are alternate, simple, and generally reduced to spines or scales. The scale leaves are quickly shed, and most photosynthesis occurs in green fleshy stems. The flowers are bisexual, large and showy, and usually borne singly. Numerous petals and stamen are produced, and the ovary is inferior. The flowers are pollinated by insects, birds, and bats. The fruit is a berry that is edible but not always tasty.

KEY TO CACTI

1. Stems columnar; vertically ribbed . . . . .saguara, *Cereus giganteus*
1. Stems flattened; segments jointed . . . . .jumping cholla, *Opuntia fulgida*

Saguaro

Cereus giganteus Engelm.

Also classified as *Carnegiea gigantea*. Moderate-sized tree growing 30–40 ft in height and 1–2 ft in diameter (largest known 52 ft tall with 52 branches). Stem fluted with 12–24 ribs; not branched or with 2–10 upright branches. Spines borne on ribs in clusters of 10–25; 0.5–2 in. long; gray; straight not hooked. Flowers opening at night; white or yellow-white; 3–4 in. wide; borne in clusters near the tips of branches. Fruit a berry; egg-shaped; usually lacking spines; 2.5–3.5 in. long; red or purple; mature in midsummer. Slow growing; reaches maturity in 150–200 years (extreme age 235 years). Found on warmer microsites, especially gravelly slopes; usually absent from valleys. Fruit eaten fresh or dried by Native Americans or used to make preserves and syrup. Found in Arizona; formerly also found locally in southern California. Elevation: 700–3,500 ft.

CAESALPINIA FAMILY: CAESALPINIACEAE

Sometimes recognized as a separate family, the Caesalpiniaceae is included within the Legume Family (Fabaceae) in this manual. As a separate family the Caesalpiniaceae of our region would contain redbud (*Cercis*), honeylocust (*Gleditsia*), coffeetree (*Gymnocladus*), parkinsonia (*Parkinsonia*), paloverde (*Cercidium*), and caesalpinia (*Caesalpinia*).

HONEYSUCKLE FAMILY: CAPRIFOLIACEAE

Worldwide the Honeysuckle Family contains about 450 species in 12 genera, found largely in east Asia and eastern North America. Most species are shrubs or lianas although a few herbs are found also. Our region contains 11 species in 2 genera that sometimes become tree-sized.

Leaves in this family are opposite and simple (usually) or compound, and they usually lack stipules. The flowers are bisexual and showy with four to five petals fused into a tube or bell. The ovary is inferior with two to five carpels. The fruit is either a drupe, berry, achene, or capsule. Economically the family provides fruit (*Sambucus*) and many ornamental plants (*Lonicera* and *Viburnum*).

ELDERBERRY: THE GENUS *SAMBUCUS*

About 30 species of elderberry occur in the world, mostly in subtropical and temperate areas. Our region contains 5 species that are usually shrubs but may become tree-sized under very favorable conditions. The 2 species with the largest distributions are described below.

KEY TO ELDERBERRIES

1. Found naturally in eastern and central North America . . . .
. . . . .American elder, *Sambucus canadensis*
1. Found naturally in western North America . . . . .Go to 2
   2. Fruit red . . . . Pacific red elder, *Sambucus callicarpa*
   2. Fruit blue-black, often covered with white wax 3
3. Twigs and leaf undersides hairy . . . . velvet elder, *Sambucus velutina*
3. Twigs and leaves hairless or nearly so 4
   4. Leaves evergreen; leaflets 3–5 . . . . Mexican elder, *Sambucus mexicana*
   4. Leaves deciduous; leaflets 5–9 . . . . blue elder, *Sambucus cerulea*

American elder, Elderberry

Sambucus canadensis L. (fig. 193)

In Florida and along the Gulf Coast, plants with the lower leaflets becoming tri-foliate are sometimes called var. *laciniata*. Some older books make this variety a species, *Sambucus simpsonii*. Large shrub or small tree growing to 25 ft under ideal conditions. Usually growing in multistemmed clumps. Leaves opposite; pinnately

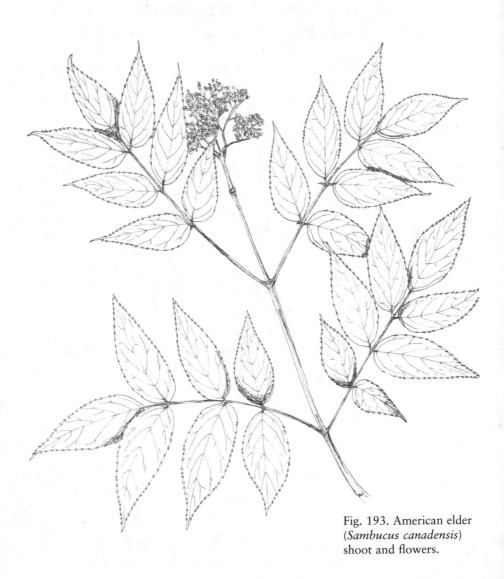

Fig. 193. American elder (*Sambucus canadensis*) shoot and flowers.

compound; deciduous; 5–9 in. long; rachis grooved above near base. Leaflets 7–9; elliptical to ovate; short stalked or stalkless; hairy above and below on the veins. Flowers white; petals 5; ovary inferior; borne in large nearly flat-topped terminal clusters (cyme). Fruit a drupe or berrylike drupe with several stones; dark blue; sometimes covered with white wax. Twigs rather stout; tan; marked with large dots (lenticels); pith white. Intolerant of shade. Seeds usually germinating on bare soil or grass. Sprouts from stumps. Found in moist to wet soil; often in roadside ditches and along streams. Leaves and twigs poisonous when eaten. Fruit eaten by songbirds. Range from Nova Scotia to eastern North Dakota, and south to southern Florida and southern Texas. Naturalized in the West Indies and Central America.

Blue elder
Sambucus cerulea Raf.

Formerly called *Sambucus glauca*. Shrub or small tree growing 30–40 ft in height and 0.5–1.5 ft in diameter. Leaves opposite; pinnately compound; deciduous; 5–7 in. long. Leaflets 5–9; ovate to narrowly oblong; 2–3 in. long; coarsely toothed; hairless or slightly hairy below. Flowers small; yellow-white; borne in nearly flat-topped terminal clusters (cymes). Fruit drupelike berry; blue. Twigs stout; somewhat angled; somewhat hairy at first, becoming hairless; red-brown. Terminal bud absent. Lateral buds scaly; green. Bark thin; dark brown tinged with red. Wood with no commercial value. Intolerant of shade. Short-lived. Sprouts well from stumps. Grows on moist porous soils along streams, in ravines, or on moist hillsides. Range from western Montana to southern British Columbia, and south to west Texas and southern California.

VIBURNUM: THE GENUS *VIBURNUM*

Worldwide this genus contains 150–200 species found in north temperate and subtropical areas, and south in the mountains of South America. About 21 species occur in our region, but many are shrubs. Wayfaringtree (*Viburnum lantana*), native to Eurasia, is cultivated in our region. The 7 tallest species are keyed below, and the 3 most treelike are further described.

KEY TO VIBURNUMS

1. Leaves 3-lobed . . . . .American cranberrybush, *Viburnum trilobum*
1. Leaves not lobed . . . . .Go to 2
   2. Buds lacking scales; fruit red . . . . .wayfaringtree, *Viburnum lantana*
   2. Buds 2-scaled; fruit blue or black 3
3. Leaves entire or teeth rounded 4
3. Leaves with pointed teeth 5
   4. Flower and fruit clusters long stalked . . . . .possumhaw, *Viburnum nudum*
   4. Flower and fruit clusters short stalked .Walter viburnum, *Viburnum obovatum*
5. Buds red-woolly; buds oblong . . . . .rusty blackhaw, *Viburnum rufidulum*
5. Buds nearly hairless; buds slender or flask-shaped 6
   6. Leaves ovate; long pointed . . . . .nannyberry, *Viburnum lentago*
   6. Leaves elliptical; obtuse or slightly pointed . . .blackhaw, *Viburnun prunifolium*

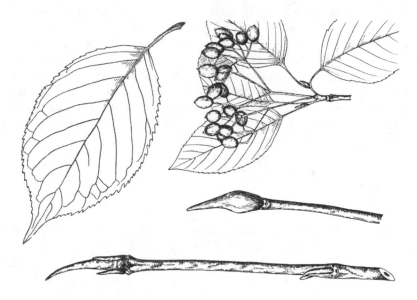

Fig. 194. Nannyberry (*Viburnum lentago*) leaf, twigs, and fruit cluster.

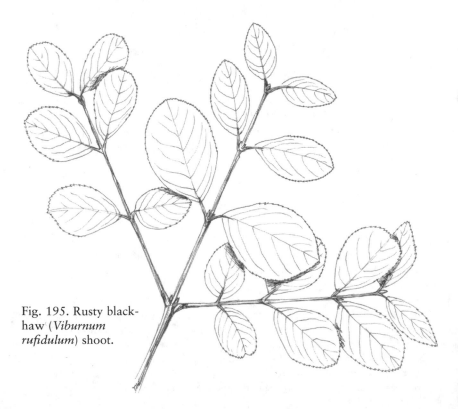

Fig. 195. Rusty black-haw (*Viburnum rufidulum*) shoot.

Nannyberry
Viburnum lentago L. (fig. 194)

Shrub or small tree growing occasionally to 30 ft height and 0.5–0.8 ft in diameter. Usually found growing in a clump of several crooked stems. Leaves opposite; simple; deciduous; ovate; 2–4 in. long; 1–2 in. wide; sharp incurved teeth; marked with minute black dots below. Leaf tip long pointed. Leaf stalk grooved; slightly winged. Flowers white or yellow-white; fragrant; borne in terminal flat-topped clusters (cymes). Fruit a drupe; juicy; edible; blue-black; flattened; sometimes covered with white wax; borne in red-stalked clusters. Twigs slender; light green and hairy becoming dark red-brown. Terminal buds enclosed by 2 valvate scales; thin; hairy; long pointed. Flower buds swollen at base. Bark red-brown; broken into small scaly plates. Moderately tolerant of shade. Fast growing. Sprouts from the roots. Found on moist often basic soil on stream banks, lower slopes, and bottomlands. Fruit eaten by songbirds and small mammals. Range from New Brunswick to southeastern Saskatchewan, and south to West Virginia and eastern Nebraska; also local in southwestern Virginia.

Walter viburnum
Viburnum obovatum Walt.

Shrub or small tree growing to 30 ft in height. Leaves simple; opposite; deciduous; oblanceolate to obovate; 1–2 in. long; entire or finely toothed above the middle; stalkless or short stalked; hairless above; red-brown dotted on the midvein above; red-brown dotted below. Leaf tip obtuse to rounded. Fruit a drupe; spherical; red turning black; lacking white wax. Twigs rusty hairy; slightly winged. Terminal buds with 2 scales. Grows in moist to wet soil on stream banks, floodplains, and flatwoods. Range from coastal South Carolina, south to central and northwestern Florida.

Rusty blackhaw
Viburnum rufidulum Raf. (fig. 195)

Large shrub or small tree growing to 30 ft in height and 0.5 ft in diameter. Single or few stemmed. Leaves opposite; simple; elliptical to nearly round; 1.5–2.5 in. long; 1–1.5 in. wide; teeth small and sharp; lustrous above; paler with scattered red hairs below. Leaf tip acute. Fruit a drupe; dark blue; sometimes covered with white wax; borne in terminal clusters (cymes). Twigs often rusty hairy. Terminal buds rusty hairy. Bark gray; divided into small square ridges (cobbled). Found in well-drained soils. Range from southeastern Virginia to central Missouri, and south to northern Florida and east Texas.

BITTERSWEET FAMILY: CELASTRACEAE

Worldwide the Bittersweet Family contains about 850 species in 55 genera, all either trees, shrubs, or vines. Most species occur in tropical or subtropical areas, but some species are found in temperate areas. In our region no species regularly become tree-sized. Three species in 2 genera may rarely become tree-sized under ideal conditions: Canotia (*Canotia holacantha*), a southwestern species with spiny usually leafless twigs; eastern wahoo (*Euonymus atropurpureus*) of eastern North America; and western wahoo (*Euonymus occidentalis*) of Washington, Oregon, and California. Both wahoos have simple, opposite leaves and square or winged twigs.

PEPPERBUSH FAMILY: CLETHRACEAE

This family contains a single genus (*Clethra*) containing about 100 species in the world. Our region contains 3 species; all are shrubs except the species described below. The Clethraceae is sometimes included within the Ericaceae.

Fig. 196. Cinnamon clethra (*Clethra acuminata*) shoots.

Cinnamon clethra, Pepperbush

Clethra acuminata Michx. (fig. 196)

Tall shrub or small tree rarely growing to 30 ft in height. Usually found in 2–4 stemmed clumps. Leaves alternate; simple; deciduous; finely serrated; obovate to oval; 3–6 in. long; tip long pointed. Flowers white; borne in racemes; appearing in summer. Fruit a capsule; 3-valved; enclosed by the sepals. Bark red-brown; flaky to slightly shaggy. Grows on dry-mesic to mesic sites. Found in the Appalachians from western Virginia to eastern Kentucky, and south to northern Georgia.

DOGWOOD FAMILY: CORNACEAE

Worldwide this family contains 100–120 species in 12–16 genera. Found in the Southern Hemisphere, tropical mountains, and especially in the Northern Hemisphere, the Dogwood Family contains trees, shrubs, and herbs. The family is sometimes subdivided into two families by placing tupelo (*Nyssa*) in the Nyssaceae. Our region contains 3 native genera, but only dogwood (*Cornus*) and tupelo (*Nyssa*) regularly become tree-sized. The other genus, silk-tassel (*Garrya*), contains mostly shrubs. Found in coastal mountains from Oregon to southern California waveyleaf silk-tassel (*Garrya elliptica*) grows tallest, rarely becoming a small tree with evergreen opposite leaves that are wavy and 2–4 in. long.

Members of this family have simple, evergreen or deciduous, opposite (rarely alternate) leaves. The flowers are small with 4–5 petals and an inferior ovary. They are pollinated by insects. The fruit is usually a drupe, but sometimes a berry. Economically the family produces the edible Cornelian-cherry (*Cornus mas*) and wood products (*Cornus* and *Nyssa*).

DOGWOOD: THE GENUS *CORNUS*

Worldwide this genus contains 45–65 species, found in the Northern Hemisphere except for a few species in Peru. Our region contains 16–17 species, but only the 2 described below regularly become tree-sized. Native to Asia kousa dogwood (*Cornus kousa*) is increasingly planted in our region because it is more resistant to disease.

Dogwoods are mostly shrubs, sometimes trees, and rarely herbs. The leaves are simple, usually opposite, but sometimes alternate or whorled. The leaf veins are curved following the margin, which is usually entire. The flowers are small and bisexual with four petals. In our tree-sized species, groups of flowers are subtended by showy white or pink bracts that are often mistaken for petals. The fruit is a drupe that matures in one growing season. The wood is diffuse-porous.

KEY TO DOGWOODS

1. Flower bracts strongly notched at tip; Eastern . . . .
. . . . .Flowering dogwood, *Cornus florida*
1. Flower bracts rounded or nearly so at tip; Western . . . .
. . . . .Pacific dogwood, *Cornus nuttallii*

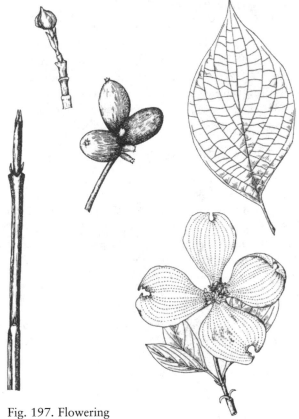

Fig. 197. Flowering dogwood (*Cornus florida*) leaf, twigs, flower, and fruit.

Fig. 198. Native range of flowering dogwood (*Cornus florida*).

Flowering dogwood
Cornus florida L. (fig. 197)

Form. Small deliquescent tree growing 30–40 ft in height and 0.5–1 ft in diameter (largest known 55 ft by 2 ft). Bole usually dividing into 2–6 stems at 1–4 ft above the ground level.

Leaves. Opposite; simple; deciduous; 3–6 in. long; oval; entire. Veins curved along the margin (arcuate). Turning dark red in autumn. Tip abruptly pointed.

Flowers. Small; bisexual; yellow; borne in tight clusters, surrounded by 4 showy white (rarely pink) bracts; the entire complex 2–4 in. wide. Bracts decidedly notched at tip; appearing in the spring before the new leaves.

Fruit. Drupe; ovoid; red; 0.5 in. long; in clusters of 3–4; bitter.

Twigs. Slender; dark green or purple. Terminal bud present; 0.1 in. long; narrow conical; covered with 2 valvate scales. Flower buds terminal; almost spherical.

Bark. Dark red-brown; broken into small square blocks (cobbled).

Wood. Sapwood light tan to pink-brown; wide. Heartwood dark brown; very heavy and hard; fine textured. Little current commercial value; occasionally used for spools, pulleys, mallet heads, and jeweler's blocks; formerly widely used for weaving shuttles.

Natural History. Very tolerant of shade; photosynthesis maximum at one-third of full sunlight. Reaches maturity in 60–80 years (extreme age 125 years). Height growth rate moderate for 20–30 years then declining rapidly. Large fruit crops usually produced every other year. Seeds from isolated trees are usually empty. Reproduces well from stump sprouts and layering. Root growth rapid forming extensive shallow root system. Drought, fire, basal stem canker, and anthracnose cause the most damage. Introduced from Asia about 1975, anthracnose is killing many dogwoods in areas with high daytime humidity, especially the southern Appalachians. Found along small streams and lower slopes in light-textured constantly moist soils; often on slightly acid or neutral soils; does not tolerate flooding. Leaf litter high in calcium. Grows mixed with a wide variety of species, especially yellow poplar, white ash, sweetgum, northern red oak, white oak, black oak, southern red oak, loblolly pine, Virginia pine, and long-leaf pine. Extremely valuable wildlife food plant. Fruit eaten by many songbirds, grouse, quail, turkeys, chipmunks, black bear, foxes, white-tailed deer, skunks, beavers, and squirrels. Foliage browsed by white-tailed deer and rabbits.

Range. See figure 198.

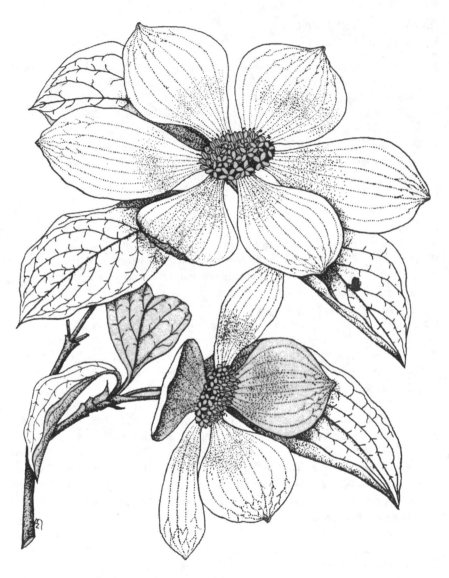

Fig. 199. Pacific dogwood (*Cornus nuttallii*) leaves and flowers.

Pacific dogwood
Cornus nuttallii Audubon (fig. 199)

Small tree growing 30–40 ft in height (tallest known 80 ft). Leaves opposite; ovate to elliptical; 3–5 in. long; veins curving along the margin; margin smooth but wavy. Flowers small; nearly white; borne in tight clusters; surrounded by 4–6 white bracts, which are often confused for petals. Bract tip rounded or pointed but not notched. Often producing a second crop of flowers in late summer. Fruit a drupe; flattened; red; borne in dense clusters. Bark smooth; gray; becoming slightly scaly on old trees. Wood characteristics and use similar to flowering dogwood. Tolerant of shade. Found in valleys and on moist slopes. Wildfire and anthracnose cause the most damage. Fruits eaten by songbirds. Range from southwestern British Columbia, and south to southern California; also local in Idaho.

TUPELO: THE GENUS *NYSSA*

This genus contains about seven species of trees or shrubs, native to Asia and Eastern North America. Our region contains four species, all tree-sized. The genus *Nyssa* is placed in the family Nyssaceae by some authors.

Tupelo leaves are alternate, simple, and entire. The flowers on each tree are bisexual and either male or female (polygamo-dioecious). They appear in the spring before the new leaves have expanded. The fruit is a drupe. Terminal buds are present, and the pith is diaphragmed. Stipules are lacking. The leaf scar contains three vascular bundles. The wood is diffuse-porous. Tupelo shoots are sometimes confused with persimmon (*Diospyros*), but persimmons lack terminal buds and have a single bundle scar.

KEY TO TUPELOS

1. Fruit red at maturity . . . . .Ogeechee tupelo, *Nyssa ogeche*
1. Fruit red-purple to black at maturity . . . . .Go to 2
   2. Leaves 4–8 in. long; usually toothed . . . . .water tupelo, *Nyssa aquatica*
   2. Leaves 2–4 in. long; usually not toothed 3
3. Leaves oblanceolate; bottomlands . . . . .swamp blackgum, *Nyssa biflora*
3. Leaves obovate; uplands . . . . .blackgum, *Nyssa sylvatica*

Fig. 200. Water tupelo
(*Nyssa aquatica*) leaves.

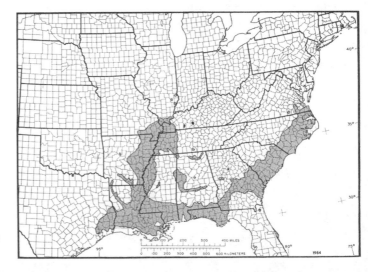

Fig. 201.
Native range
of water
tupelo (*Nyssa
aquatica*).

Water tupelo

Nyssa aquatica L. (fig. 200)

Form. Moderately large excurrent tree growing 70–90 ft in height and 3–4 ft in diameter (largest known 110 ft by 8 ft). Base often swollen.

Leaves. Alternate; simple; 4–8 in. long; oblong-obovate; yellow-green; usually with irregular triangular teeth; more-or-less hairy below. Tip acuminate.

Flowers. Bisexual and either male or female on each tree (polygamo-dioecious); small; green-white; appearing in the spring before or with the new leaves. Pollinated by wind and possibly bees.

Fruit. Drupe; dark purple with light spots; oblong; 1–1.5 in. long; borne singly on long stalks; pit strongly ribbed. Mature in fall and dispersed by water.

Twigs. Terminal bud present; yellow-brown; 0.1–0.2 in. long; somewhat rounded.

Bark. Gray-brown; deep furrows that separate long flat ridges.

Wood. Sapwood white to gray-white. Heartwood green to brown-gray; moderately heavy; moderately hard; growth rings not distinct; grain usually interlocked. May form false rings. Commercially valuable; used for pulpwood, furniture, kitchen cabinets, boxes, crates, factory flooring, and trim and molding. Formerly used for cigar and fruit boxes.

Natural History. Intolerant of shade. Reproduces well from seed; large seed crops produced most years; seeds tolerate submersion for about 1 year. Sprouts prolifically from stumps. Wildfire and forest tent caterpillar cause the most damage. Found in sloughs and deep swamps on very wet sites; sometimes flooded all year. Soils on the best sites remain saturated all year. Occurs in pure stands or mixed with baldcypress, swamp cottonwood, red maple, overcup oak, American elm, Carolina ash, and green ash. Flowers provide nectar for honey. White-tailed deer browse the foliage. Fruit eaten by wood duck, squirrels, raccoon, and white-tailed deer.

Range. See figure 201.

Fig. 202. Swamp blackgum (*Nyssa biflora*) shoot and immature fruit.

Swamp blackgum, Swamp tupelo
Nyssa biflora Walt. (fig. 202)

Nomenclature. Sometimes classified as a variety of blackgum, *Nyssa sylvatica* var. *biflora*.

Form. Moderate-sized tree growing 70–80 ft in height and 2–3 ft in diameter (largest known 120 ft by 4 ft). Base usually swollen.

Leaves. Simple; alternate; lanceolate, oblanceolate, narrowly elliptical, or rounded; 1–3 in. long; 1–2 in. wide; leathery; usually entire but sometimes with a few coarse teeth on juveniles and sprouts.

Fruit. Drupe; 0.4–0.5 in. long; ellipsoid; dark blue to black; borne singly or in clusters of 2–3 at tip of long stalk.

Bark. Gray-black; furrows create long, narrow ridges.

Wood. Sapwood white to gray-white. Heartwood green or brown-gray; moderately heavy; moderately hard; interlocking grain. Used for pulpwood, furniture, railroad ties, crates, pallets, woodenware, and novelties. Formerly used for cigar and fruit boxes.

Natural History. Intolerant of shade. Produces abundant fruits; dispersed in late summer to early winter. Seed viability 40–60 percent. Fruits do not float; germination occurs when water level drops to the soil surface. Sprouts prolifically from stumps and roots. Wildfire, forest tent caterpillar, sapsucker, and salt spray cause the most damage. Grows on a variety of bottomland soils as long as they flood regularly, including mucks, heavy clay, and sands; tolerates extended flooding in the growing season provided the water does not stagnate. Also found as scattered trees in localized wet depressions in Coastal Plain pine stands. Seedlings do not tolerate prolonged submergence in summer. Found in very dense pure stands or growing with baldcypress, pondcypress, red maple, water hickory, American elm, overcup oak, swamp cottonwood, laurel oak, and cabbage palmetto. Fruits eaten by songbirds, fox, and bear. Flowers provide nectar for honey.

Range. Found mostly in the Coastal Plain from Delaware to southern Florida, west to east Texas, and north in the Mississippi River valley to Tennessee.

Ogeechee tupelo, Ogeechee-lime
Nyssa ogeche Bartr. ex Marsh.

Large shrub to small tree growing 25–35 ft in height and 1–2 ft in diameter (tallest known 65 ft). Often found as a clump of small crooked stems. Leaves alternate; simple; 4–6 in. long; elliptical, oblong, or obovate; margin entire or with a few coarse teeth; gray and hairy below. Leaf tip pointed. Petiole hairy. Flowers bisexual and unisexual on the same tree; green-yellow; appearing after the new leaves are fully expanded. Probably pollinated by bees. Fruit a drupe; red; oblong to obovate; 1–1.5 in. long; mature in mid- to late summer; edible. Fruit pit with papery wings. Twigs hairy. Wood with no commercial value. Reproduces well from sprouts. Grows in very wet alluvial soils; very tolerant of flooding; also found on wet flats. Flowers provide nectar for honey. Fruit used in making preserves and drinks. Found in the Coastal Plain from extreme southern South Carolina to northwestern Florida especially along the Ogeechee, Altamaha, and Suwannee rivers.

Fig. 203. Blackgum
(*Nyssa sylvatica*)
leaves, fruit, and twig.

Fig. 204. Native range of
blackgum (*Nyssa sylvatica*).

Blackgum, Black tupelo, Sourgum

Nyssa sylvatica Marsh. (fig. 203)

Form. A medium-sized tree growing 50–80 ft in height and 1–3 ft in diameter (largest known 139 ft by 5 ft). Lateral branches frequently held at right angles to the main stem.

Leaves. Alternate; simple; deciduous; 2–5 in. long; 1–2 in. wide; obovate, elliptical, or nearly round; usually entire, but sometimes with a few coarse teeth on sprouts and juveniles; lustrous; hairy or hairless below; turning scarlet to dark red in autumn. Tip acute to short-acuminate.

Flowers. Each tree contains bisexual and either male or female flowers (polygamo-dioecious); small; green-white; appearing in the spring with the new leaves.

Fruit. Drupe; egg-shaped; blue-black; 0.4–0.5 in. long. Pit indistinctly ribbed. Mature in autumn. Edible but tart.

Twigs. Slender; red-brown; smooth; pith diaphragmed; leaf scars with 3 bundle scars. Terminal bud present; light-brown.

Bark. Thick; light gray; becoming deeply furrowed to create rectangular or square ridges (cobbled).

Wood. Sapwood white to gray-white. Heartwood green or brown-gray; moderately heavy; moderately hard; grain interlocking; growth rings indistinct. Little commercial value; sometimes used for pulpwood, railroad ties, pallets, and rarely furniture. Larger trees usually hollow; formerly used whole as water pipes or split longitudinally and used as feeding and water troughs.

Natural History. Moderately tolerant of shade. Reproduces from seeds and stump and root sprouts. Wildfire causes the most damage. Grows on a wide variety of sites, ranging from moist lower slopes to droughty ridges. Usually found as scattered single trees, growing with black oak, white oak, southern red oak, northern red oak, chestnut oak, sourwood, yellow-poplar, pitch pine, shortleaf pine, Virginia pine, and loblolly pine. Extremely valuable wildlife species; fruit eaten by songbirds, wild turkeys, black bear, foxes, and opossums. Sprouts eaten by white-tailed deer; tree cavities used as den by insects, birds, bats, and other mammals.

Range. See figure 204.

CYRILLA FAMILY: THE CYRILLACEAE

This family contains about 13 species in three genera, all confined to the New World especially Cuba. Our region contains 2–3 species in two genera: buckwheat-tree (*Cliftonia*) and swamp cyrilla (*Cyrilla*). Buckwheat-tree is a thicket-forming tall shrub with two- to four-winged fruits, found on wet sites in the Gulf States and Georgia. Swamp cyrilla occasionally becomes tree-sized.

Fig. 205. Swamp cyrilla (*Cyrilla racemiflora*) shoot with fruit.

Swamp cyrilla, Titi
Cyrilla racemiflora L. (fig. 205)

Large shrub occasionally becoming a small tree 30 ft in height and 0.5–1 ft in diameter (tallest known 52 ft). Often crooked, leaning, and in clumps of 2–4 stems. Leaves simple; alternate; semi-evergreen and falling slowly through the winter; narrowly elliptical to oblanceolate; entire; 2–3 in. long; 0.5 in. wide; lacking stipules. Tip rounded to obtuse. Base long tapering. Flowers small; bisexual; white, rarely pink; borne in slender axillary racemes; racemes usually in clusters. Fruit a drupe; spherical to ovoid; subtended by persistent bracts; persisting through the winter. Twigs angled below each leaf. Bark gray; often with white blotches; smooth. Intolerant of shade. Fruits abundantly produced most years. May form thickets from root sprouts. Grows on wet sites in flatwoods, along nonalluvial streams, in seepage areas, and in pocosins. Numerous varieties of swamp cyrilla have been described, and some varieties have been considered separate species most notably *Cyrilla parvifolia* with smaller leaves. None warrant recognition. Found in the Coastal Plain from southeastern Virginia to central Florida, and west to southeastern Texas; also south into Central America and the West Indies.

EBONY FAMILY: EBENACEAE

Worldwide the Ebony Family contains about 485 species in two genera. Our region contains only *Diospyros*. Economically the family provides fruit (*Diospyros*) and ebony lumber from various species of *Diospyros*.

PERSIMMON: THE GENUS *DIOSPYROS*

This genus contains about 400 species found mostly in tropical areas. Our region contains the 2 species listed below. In addition, Japanese persimmon (*Diospyros kaki*) is planted for the large edible fruits in the warmer portions of our region. Persimmon is the name used by Native Americans.

KEY TO PERSIMMONS

1. Leaf tip flat, rounded, or notched . . . . .Texas persimmon, *Diospyros texana*
1. Leaf tip pointed . . . . .persimmon, *Diospyros virginiana*

Texas persimmon
Diospyros texana Scheele

Large shrub or small tree growing to 40 ft in height. Leaves alternate; simple; evergreen; leathery; oblong or obovate; densely hairy below. Leaf tip flat, rounded, or notched. Flowers unisexual with only one sex found on each tree (dioecious); green-white; urn-shaped; about 0.3 in. long. Fruit a berry; black; nearly spherical; 0.7–1 in. wide. Bark gray; smooth but sloughing off in sheets. Sapwood yellow. Heartwood black; heavy. Found in central and west Texas, and south into Mexico.

Fig. 206. Persimmon (*Diospyros virginiana*) leaves, fruit, and twig.

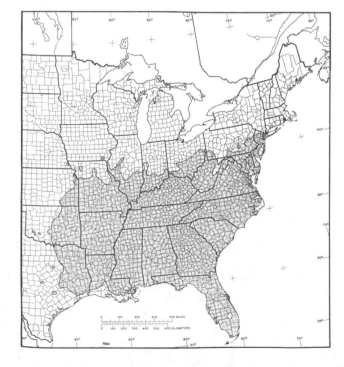

Fig. 207. Native range of persimmon (*Diospyros virginiana*).

Persimmon, Simmon
Diospyros virginiana L. (fig. 206)

Form. Medium-sized excurrent tree growing 30–80 ft in height and 1–2 ft in diameter (largest known 130 ft by 4 ft).

Leaves. Alternate; simple; deciduous; 3–6 in. long; 1.5–2.5 in. wide; oblong-ovate to oval; entire; slightly whitened between the green veins below and appearing somewhat mottled. Tip pointed; base rounded.

Flowers. Unisexual with one sex found on each tree (dioecious); sometimes also with a few bisexual flowers (polygamo-dioecious); green-yellow; 0.3–0.5 in. long; urn-shaped or tubular; appearing in the spring with the leaves; insect-pollinated.

Fruit. A berry; nearly spherical; dull orange, yellow, or dark red; sometimes white-waxy; 0.8–2 in. wide; subtended by 4-lobed woody calyx; developing in 1 growing season. Flesh very astringent until fully ripe supposedly after the first frost, then edible. But fruits of some trees never completely lose the astringent taste. Seeds 1–8; brown; flat.

Twigs. Slender; gray-brown; leaf scar with single bundle scar. Terminal buds absent; lateral buds nearly black with 2 overlapping scales. Pith homogeneous or chambered.

Bark. Thick; hard; gray-black; divided by furrows into square blocks (cobbled).

Wood. Moderate commercial value. Sapwood cream-white; wide; most lumber is all sapwood. Heartwood brown-black to black; very heavy; very hard; semi-ring-porous. Used for weaving shuttles, spools, golf-club heads, billiard cues, and brushes.

Natural History. Tolerant of shade but also developing well in full sunlight. Growth rate slow. Large seed crops produced every other year. Sprouts from stumps and prolifically from roots often forming thickets; sometimes considered a pest in pastures. Fall webworm and persimmon wilt cause the most damage. Adaptable; grows on a wide variety of sites ranging from droughty ridges to well-drained bottomlands where the largest trees develop; not tolerant of sites flooded for more than several days in the growing season. Found singly or in small thickets mixed with yellow-poplar, northern red oak, white oak, cherrybark oak, white ash, sycamore, sugarberry, sassafras, red maple, sweetgum, Virginia pine and loblolly pine.

Range. See figure 207.

OLEASTER FAMILY: ELAEAGNACEAE

Worldwide this family contains 45–50 species in three genera found in tropical and subtropical areas. Several species in two genera are native to our region, but none regularly become tree-sized. Among our species silver buffaloberry (*Shepherdia argentea*) grows tallest with opposite silvery-scurfy leaves. Native to Europe and Asia, Russian-olive (*Elaeagnus angustifolia*) with alternate silvery-scurfy leaves occasionally escapes from cultivation.

The family is distinct owing to the brown or silvery hairs or scales (lepidote) found on the twigs, leaf undersides, and sometimes the fruit. The leaves are simple, alternate or opposite, deciduous or evergreen, and they lack stipules. The flowers are bisexual or unisexual, and petals are lacking. The fruit is an achene although it looks like a drupe, because it becomes completely enveloped by fleshy sepals.

HEATH FAMILY: ERICACEAE

Worldwide the Heath Family contains about 3,400 species in about 100 genera. Commonly associated with very acidic mineral or organic soils the family occurs throughout the temperate zones especially in western China and southern Africa. Most members are shrubs or small trees but herbs occur also. Our region contains about 200 species but only 7–9 become tree-sized. Heather (*Calluna*) and heath (*Erica*) of Europe belong to this family.

Members of the Heath Family have simple, alternate, deciduous or evergreen leaves that lack stipules. The leaf margin is either entire or finely toothed, and it is sometimes rolled under. The leaves and twigs of some members (especially *Rhododendron* and *Kalmia*) are toxic to stock animals and humans if eaten or inhaled in smoke. The flowers are bisexual, usually white or pink, showy, and often borne in small clusters. The petals of each flower are fused into bell- or urn-shaped structures with four to five lobes at the tip. The ovary is usually five-parted, inferi- or or superior, and it produces numerous seeds. The fruit is usually a capsule, but sometimes a berry or drupe. The family is usually absent from limestone soils.

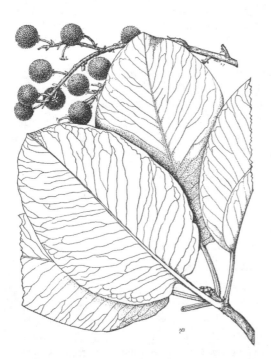

Fig. 208. Pacific madrone (*Arbutus menziesii*) leaves and fruit cluster.

Fig. 209. Native range of Pacific madrone (*Arbutus menziesii*).

MADRONE: THE GENUS *ARBUTUS*

Arbutus contains 15–20 species in the world, found in North and Central America, western Europe and western Asia. Our region contains 3 species but only Pacific madrone occurs widely. Texas madrone (*Arbutus texana*) is a small tree on dry sites in southern Texas and southeastern New Mexico. Arizona madrone (*Arbutus arizonica*) is found mostly in Mexico, but it extends north into southeastern Arizona and southwestern New Mexico.

Madrones have simple evergreen leaves. The bark often peels in thin sheets or scales to reveal the lighter under bark. The fruit is berrylike with a wrinkled surface. The wood is diffuse-porous.

KEY TO MADRONES

1. Leaves 3–6 in. long .Pacific madrone, *Arbutus menziesii*
1. Leaves 1–3 in. long . . . . .Go to 2
    2. Secondary leaf veins prominent below . . . .Arizona madrone, *Arbutus arizonica*
    2. Secondary leaf veins not visible below . . . . . . .Texas madrone, *Arbutus texana*

Pacific madrone
Arbutus menziesii Pursh (fig. 208)

Form. Medium-sized tree growing 30–100 ft in height and 1–4 ft in diameter (largest known 125 ft by 9 ft). Often leaning and crooked.

Leaves. Alternate; simple; evergreen; 3–6 in. long; oval to oblong; usually entire but finely toothed on sprouts and vigorous growth; leathery; hairless; dark green and lustrous above; white-waxy below.

Flowers. White; bisexual; borne in terminal clusters (panicles); pollinated by bees.

Fruit. Berrylike; spherical; orange-red; semifleshy; glandular-coated; 0.3–0.5 in. long; mature in autumn.

Twigs. Slender; green to red-brown; hairless. Terminal buds present; ovoid; scaly; bright brown.

Bark. Thin; orange to red-brown; flaking off to expose the tan to green inner bark.

Wood. Sapwood white to cream with pink tinge. Heartwood red-brown; heavy; hard; growth rings barely visible. Low commercial value. Used locally for furniture, fuelwood, and charcoal for gunpowder. Formerly used for shuttles, bobbins, flooring, and cargo rollers on ships.

Natural History. Tolerant of shade when young; requiring sun as mature trees. Growth slow; reaches maturity in 200–250 years (extreme age 500 years). Produces abundant fruit most years but most reproduction occurs from stump sprouts. Wildfire and madrone canker cause the most damage. Found on a wide range of soil textures, but most common on shallow rocky soils with good internal drainage on south- and west-facing slopes. Grows in mixed stands with Douglas-fir, western hemlock, ponderosa pine, Port Orford-cedar, tanoak, Oregon white oak, California black oak, and sugar pine. Fruit eaten by birds, deer, and small mammals.

Range. See figure 209. Elevation: sea level to 4,500 ft.

MANZANITA: THE GENUS *ARCTOSTAPHYLOS*

Worldwide this genus contains about 60 species, found mostly in the western United States and Mexico. Most species are shrubs, but 2 species from the western United States may rarely become tree-sized under favorable conditions. Bigberry manzanita (*Arctostaphylos glauca*), found from the coast ranges of central California to Mexico, has white-waxy leaves, fruit stalks with sticky hairs, and fruit with a single stone. Whiteleaf manzanita (*Arctostaphylos viscida*), found from southwestern Oregon to central California, is similar, but the fruit has multiple stones.

Fig. 210. Mountain-laurel (*Kalmia latifolia*) leaves, flowers, and fruit.

Fig. 211. Tree lyonia (*Lyonia ferruginea*) shoot with flower buds.

Worldwide this genus contains only 1 specie listed below. Found in Japan, two closely related species are usually placed in the genus *Tripetaleia*.

Elliottia, southern-plume

Elliottia racemosa Muhl. ex Ell.

Small tree. Leaves simple; alternate; oblong; entire; deciduous; 3–4 in. long. Flowers bisexual with four straplike petals. Fruit a capsule; globular. Rare and local in eastern Georgia.

Worldwide this genus contains about 7 species, all found in our region or Cuba. Only the species listed below becomes tree-sized.

Mountain-laurel, Ivy

Kalmia latifolia L. (fig. 210)

Large shrub (usually) or small tree rarely growing 25–30 ft in height. Often crooked and contorted. Leaves alternate; simple; evergreen; lustrous; 2–4 in. long; 1–2 in. wide; elliptical; midrib light colored; lateral veins not evident; margin entire; hairless above and below. Flowers showy; white to pink; angular bowl-shaped; found in terminal clusters; stalks and sepals sometimes sticky glandular. Fruit a capsule; 5-parted; seeds slightly curved. Bark red-brown; developing shallow vertical furrows that separate the narrow ridges; ridges coming loose and shaggy. Moderately tolerant of shade but developing best in full sun. Sprouts from stumps. Grows on rocky knolls, outcrops, ledges, or in thin organic accumulations over bedrock. Range from southern Maine to southeastern Mississippi and northwestern Florida; but largely absent from the Southeastern Coastal Plain.

Worldwide this genus contains about 40 species, found mostly in the West Indies and eastern Asia. Our region contains 5 species, but only 1 occasionally becomes tree-sized.

Tree lyonia, Staggerbush, Crookedwood

Lyonia ferruginea (Walt.) Nutt. (fig. 211)

Large shrub or small tree sometimes growing to 30 ft in height (tallest known 40 ft); usually crooked and leaning. Leaves simple; alternate; evergreen; elliptical to obovate; 0.5–2.5 in. long; gray- and brown-scaly below. Margin entire; rolled under (revolute). Flowers in axillary clusters; white; appearing in the spring before the new leaves. Fruit a capsule; ovoid; 0.3 in. long; 5-angled. Young twigs gray hairy; sometimes with scales. Usually grows in sandy soil with myrtle oak and Chapman oak. Found in coastal areas from southeastern South Carolina to Florida; common in the Big Scrub of central Florida.

Fig. 212. Sourwood
(*Oxydendrum arboreum*)
leaves, twig, and flower cluster.

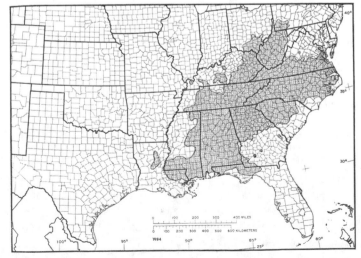

Fig. 213.
Native range
of sourwood
(*Oxydendrum
arboreum*).

SOURWOOD: THE GENUS *OXYDENDRUM*

Worldwide this genus contains only the one specie found in our region (monotypic).

Sourwood, Lily-of-the-valley-tree
Oxydendrum arboreum (L.) DC. (fig. 212)

Form. Small tree growing 20–50 ft in height and 1 ft in diameter (largest known 80 ft by 2 ft). Often leaning and crooked.

Leaves. Alternate; simple; deciduous; 5–7 in. long; 1–2.5 in. wide; oblong to lanceolate; thin; finely toothed; sour tasting; scattered bristle hairs below on the midvein; turning scarlet in autumn.

Flowers. Bisexual; white; petals fused into urn shapes; borne in terminal clusters (panicles); appearing in summer. Pollinated by insects.

Fruit. A capsule; 5-valved; 0.3–0.5 in. long; borne in terminal clusters (panicles) and usually falling in clusters; often persisting through the winter.

Twigs. Slender; hairless; yellow-green to red-brown; leaf scar with a single bundle scar. Terminal bud absent; lateral buds small; red-brown; partially embedded in twig.

Bark. Thick; red-brown; hard; developing deep vertical furrows that separate flat or pointed ridges.

Wood. No commercial value. Sapwood yellow-brown to pink-brown; wide. Heartwood brown tinged with red; hard; heavy; diffuse-porous. Used locally for fuel, tool handles, and sled runners.

Natural History. Tolerant of shade but also thriving in full sun. Growth rapid when young but slowing markedly with age. Reproduces well from seeds and stump sprouts. Grows most commonly on moderate to droughty sites; absent from limestone soils. Fall webworm causes the most damage. Found in mixed stands with scarlet oak, chestnut oak, white oak, black oak, blackgum, Virginia pine, shortleaf pine, and loblolly pine. Nectar prized for honey.

Range. See figure 213.

RHODODENDRON AND AZALEA: THE GENUS *RHODODENDRON*

Worldwide this genus contains 600–800 species found mostly in Asia. Our region contains about 20 species found mostly in the Southeast. Only 2 species become tree-sized. Rarely Catawba rhododendron (*Rhododendron catawbiense*) with white leaf undersurfaces and buds without subtending bracts is also tree-sized. Years ago this genus was subdivided. Species with evergreen leaves and ten or more stamen were classified in *Rhododendron*, and species with deciduous leaves and generally five stamen were placed in *Azalea*. Additional study found that no character dependably separates rhododendrons from azaleas. As a result rhododendrons and azaleas are currently lumped together in *Rhododendron*.

KEY TO RHODODENDRONS

1. Terminal buds subtended by long, narrow bracts . . . .
. . . . .rosebay rhododendron, *Rhododendron maximum*
1. Terminal buds without subtending bracts . . . . .Go to 2
    2. Leaves white below; Eastern . . . .
. . . . .Catawba rhododendron, *Rhododendron catawbiense*
    2. Leaves green or brown below; Western . . . .
. . . . .Pacific rhododendron, *Rhododendron macrophyllum*

Fig. 214. Rosebay rhododendron (*Rhododendron maximum*) leaves, flowers, and fruit.

Pacific rhododendron, California rosebay
Rhododendron macrophyllum D. Don ex G. Don

Formerly called *Rhododendron californicum*. Large shrub or small tree growing under favorable conditions to 30 ft in height. Leaves alternate; simple; evergreen; leathery; oblong to elliptical; 2.5–5.5 in. long; green above; light green or brown below. Flowers light red to purple; bell-shaped and 5-lobed; lobe tips scalloped; upper lobe green dotted inside; stamens not extending beyond the lobes (inserted); ovary red, hairy. Fruit a capsule; 5-parted; 0.5–1.5 in. long. Sprouts prolifically from stumps. Grows in moist to dry soil often forming dense thickets. Foliage poisonous to livestock. Found along the coast from southern British Columbia to California; abundant along the Mendocino and Humboldt coasts.

Rosebay rhododendron, Great rhododendron
Rhododendron maximum L. (fig. 214)

Form. Large shrub or rarely a small tree growing to 35 ft in height and 1 ft in diameter. Bole short; crooked.

Leaves. Alternate; simple; evergreen persisting 2–3 years; 4–10 in. long; 1–2 in. wide; oblong to obovate; leathery; margin entire; dark green above; green-white below. Base wedge-shaped tapering to petiole.

Flowers. Bisexual; showy; white to purple; petals fused and bell-shaped; 1 in. wide; sticky; appearing from late spring to summer; borne in terminal clusters.

Fruit. Capsule; 5-parted; woody; oblong-ovoid; red-brown; sticky with glandular hairs. Seeds small; numerous.

Twigs. Dark green to red-brown. Terminal bud present; green; subtended by narrow bracts. Flower buds 1–1.5 in. long; conical.

Bark. Thin; red-brown; smooth at first becoming scaly or shaggy.

Wood. Little or no commercial value; heavy; hard; diffuse-porous; fine textured. Used locally for walking sticks, tool handles, and crafts.

Natural History. Very tolerant of shade. Slow growing. Sprouts from stumps. Grows on moist shady sites; forms dense thickets along creeks in the southern Appalachians. Foliage and twigs toxic to humans if eaten; smoke inhaled from fires toxic. Wildfire causes the most damage usually killing the aboveground portions.

Range. Found in the Appalachian Mountains and adjacent foothills from southern Maine to northern Georgia.

BLUEBERRY: THE GENUS *VACCINIUM*

Worldwide about 250–300 species of blueberry are known, mostly in the north temperate zone and tropical mountains. Our region contains about 30 species, but only the species listed below is tree-sized. This genus includes the cranberries, which are tiny shrubs.

Sparkleberry, Farkleberry
Vaccinium arboreum Marsh. (fig. 215)

Large shrub or small tree occasionally growing to 25–30 ft in height. Stems contorted. Often found in colonies. Leaves simple; alternate; deciduous or semi-evergreen; obovate to oval; 1–2 in. long; leathery; dark green and lustrous above; paler beneath and hairy on the veins. Margin entire or minutely toothed and slightly rolled under. Flowers white; urn-shaped; either solitary or in racemes; each flower subtended by an oblong bract. Fruit a berry; black; spherical; 0.3–0.5 in. wide; pulpy, usually not eaten by humans. Bark red-brown; flaky and sloughing on small branches; developing shallow furrows that separate very narrow ridges. Moderately

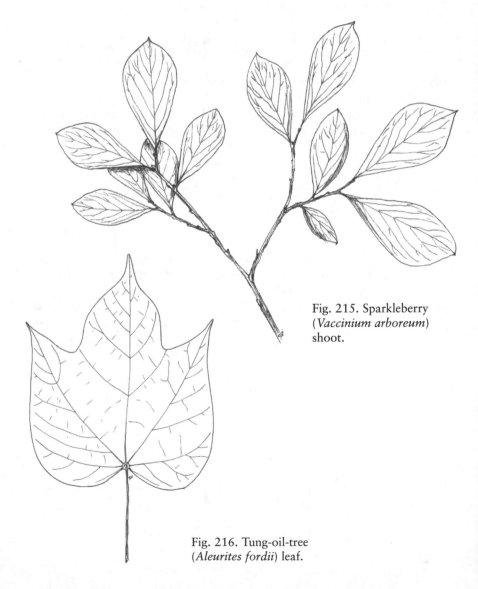

Fig. 215. Sparkleberry
(*Vaccinium arboreum*)
shoot.

Fig. 216. Tung-oil-tree
(*Aleurites fordii*) leaf.

tolerant of shade. Sprouts from roots. Grows on dry-mesic sites. Range from Virginia to southern Missouri, south to central Florida and east Texas; but largely absent from the Mississippi River floodplain.

SPURGE FAMILY: EUPHORBIACEAE

Found mostly in the tropics, the Spurge Family contains over 7,000 species in about 330 genera in the world. Our region barely includes 1 native tree species, jumping-bean sapium (*Sapium biloculare*), but many herbs occur. In addition, two naturalized exotics, tung-oil-tree and Chinese tallowtree, are regularly tree-sized. Castorbean (*Ricinus communis*), native to Africa, is widely planted, and sometimes escapes in the warmer parts of our region.

Members of this family are either trees, shrubs, or herbs. Some species become succulent and look like a cactus. The leaves are either simple or compound, and alternate, opposite, or whorled. The leaves and stems usually contain milky sap. The flowers vary widely, but are often highly reduced and sometimes subtended by brightly colored bracts. They are usually pollinated by insects, particularly flies but sometimes by wind. The fruit is usually a three-lobed schizocarp or a capsule. Economically the family provides rubber (*Hevea*), castor oil (*Ricinus*), cassava and tapioca (*Manihot*), waxes and resins (*Euphorbia*), oils and resins (*Croton*), and tung-oil and waxes (*Aleurites*).

TUNG-OIL-TREE: THE GENUS *ALEURITES*

This genus contains about six species of trees found in Japan, China, Southeast Asia, the Philippines, Australia, and India. None are native to our region, but the species listed below is cultivated and sometimes escapes.

Tung-oil-tree
Aleurites fordii Hemsl. (fig. 216)

Small tree growing 30–40 ft in height. Leaves simple; alternate; ovate; entire; palmately veined; not lobed or 3–5 lobed; containing milky sap; brown, hairy above; hairy or hairless below. Leaf base flat or heart-shaped. Petiole with 2 red glands at apex. Flowers unisexual with male and female flowers borne on each tree (monoecious). Fruit a capsule; 1–3 in. long; nearly spherical; smooth; dark red or green-red; borne on a stalk 1–5 in. long. Seeds large; smooth; thick shelled; oily; very poisonous. Twigs stout; hairless; brown or gray. Bark light gray; smooth. Oil from the seeds used in paint, wood finishes, and soap. Native to China; cultivated in subtropical regions for the oil in the seeds. Grown in plantations in the Coastal Plain from Georgia to Texas; locally naturalized.

SAPIUM: THE GENUS *SAPIUM*

Worldwide this genus contains about 100 species, found mostly in the tropical and subtropical areas of the Americas. Our region contains 1 native species and 1 exotic species. Found mostly in northwest Mexico, the northern limit of jumping-bean sapium (*Sapium biloculare*) extends into southern Arizona.

KEY TO SAPIUMS

1. Capsule with 2 seeds each . . . . .jumping-bean sapium, *Sapium biloculare*
1. Capsule with 3 seeds each . . . . .Chinese tallowtree, *Sapium sebiferum*

Chinese tallowtree, Popcorn-tree

Sapium sebiferum (L.) Roxb. (fig. 217)

Small tree growing 30–40 ft in height and 1 ft in diameter. Leaves simple; alternate; 1–3 in. long; containing milky sap; entire; broadly ovate; somewhat resembling trembling aspen. Flowers small; green; borne in spikes. Fruit a capsule; 3-celled; 0.5 in. wide; containing black seeds covered with white wax; wax used in candle making. Invasive on old fields and bottomlands. Native to China; naturalized in the Coastal Plain from southern North Carolina to Florida, and west to Texas.

LEGUME, PEA, OR BEAN FAMILY: FABACEAE OR LEGUMINOSAE

The Legume Family contains about 18,000 species in 630 genera in the world, the second or third largest plant family. Our region contains about 28 species in 13

Fig. 217. Chinese tallowtree
(*Sapium sebiferum*) shoot
with flower spike.

genera that may become trees. Based on flower characteristics, this family is some-times subdivided into three families: the Caesalpiniaceae with ten or fewer stamen and unequal-sized distinct (not fused) petals, the Mimosaceae with numerous sta-men and equal-sized generally tubelike petals, and the Fabaceae (in the narrow sense) with ten stamen and unequal-sized partly fused petals.

The Legume Family is characterized by alternate compound leaves. Pinnately compound or bipinnately compound leaves are most common, but the leaves may be palmately compound or unifoliate (as in *Cercis*) the result of reduction to a sin-gle leaflet. Stipules are present, and the base of each leaf or leaflet or both is gener-ally swollen by a pulvinus, a structure that allows leaf or leaflet movement as a result of changes in turgor pressure. The flowers are either radially or bilaterally symmetrical, usually bisexual, and showy. Each flower has five petals, either not fused, all fused, or only the two lower petals fused. The flowers are usually polli-nated by insects or birds. Each flower has one carpel that develops into a usually flattened and often twisted legume. The roots of some species develop nitrogen-fixing nodules.

Second only to the Grass Family in worldwide economic importance, the Legume Family includes important food plants (various beans, chickpeas, soybeans, peanuts, peas, lentils, and cow peas) and forage plants (alfalfa, clover, lupine, vetch, and sweet clover). It also provides insecticide (rotenone), Acacia gum, resins, indi-go dye, and numerous ornamentals. Large-scale wood production is limited to two genera, rosewood (*Dalbergia*) of the tropics and black locust (*Robinia*) of our region.

Tree-sized species of our region are listed in the key and described below. Shrubs of our region that may rarely become tree-sized are included in the key. Many of these shrubby species either are found primarily in Mexico or are occasional escapees from cultivation.

KEY TO LEGUMES

1. Leaves unifoliate (appearing simple) or pinnately compound . . . . Go to 2
1. Leaves bipinnately compound or both pinnately and bipinnately compound . . . . . .
. . . . .Go to 9
    2. Leaves unifoliate, appearing simple 3
    2. Leaves pinnately compound 4
3. Leaves heart-shaped; twigs lacking thorns . . . . .redbud, *Cercis canadensis*
3. Leaves oblong or absent; twigs modified into thorns . . .smokethorn, *Dalea spinosa*
    4. Leaflets less than 1 in. long 5
    4. Leaflets 1–4 in. long 6
5. Leaflets with glandular dots . . . . .kidneywood, *Eysenhardtia polystachya*
5. Leaflets lacking glandular dots . . . . .tesota, *Olneya tesota*
    6. Leaves trifoliate; flowers red . . . . .coralbean, *Erythrina flabelliformis*
    6. Leaves many foliate; flowers white, yellow, or blue 7
7. Leaflets 3–4 in. long, alternate along rachis . . . . .yellowwood, *Cladrastis kentukea*
7. Leaflets 1–2.5 in. long; opposite along rachis 8
    8. Legume flattened, not constricted between each seed . . . . . .locust, *Robinia* sp.
    8. Legume round, constricted between each seed . . . .
. . . . .mescal bean, *Sophora secundiflora*

9. Flowers or fruits in racemes 10
9. Flowers or fruits single, in rounded heads or cylindrical spikes 14
  10. Flowers green-white; small and inconspicuous 11
  10. Flowers yellow; large and showy 12
11. Leaves 1–3 ft long; basal pinnae simple ....coffeetree, *Gymnocladus dioicus*
11. Leaves 0.5–1 ft long; basal pinnae compound ....honeylocust, *Gleditsia* sp.
  12. Stamen extending beyond petals ....poinciana, *Caesalpinia* sp.
  12. Stamen shorter than petals, not extending beyond 13
13. Leaflets quickly falling leaving spine-tipped rachis ....
  ....Jerusalem-thorn, *Parkinsonia aculeata*
13. Entire leaf quickly falling, leaving green twig ....paloverde, *Cercidium* sp.
  14. Twigs armed with spines 15
  14. Twigs lacking spines 17
15. Legumes dehiscent; stamen filaments united .....blackbead, *Pithecellobium* sp.
15. Legumes indehiscent; stamen filaments free except at base 16
  16. Flowers yellow or white; petioles not glandular ....acacia, *Acacia* sp.
  16. Flowers green-white; petioles glandular at tip ....mesquite, *Prosopis* sp.
17. Flowers pink; stamen numerous ....mimosa, *Albizia julibrissin*
17. Flowers white; stamen 10–20 18
  18. Stamen 12–20, extending beyond the petals ....lysiloma, *Lysiloma* sp.
  18. Stamen 10, shorter than the petals ....leadtree, *Leucaena* sp.

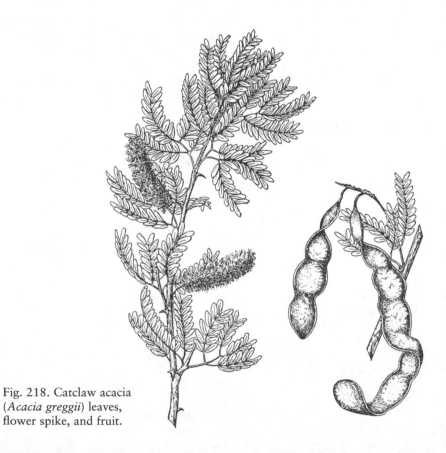

Fig. 218. Catclaw acacia
(*Acacia greggii*) leaves,
flower spike, and fruit.

ACACIA: THE GENUS *ACACIA*

Worldwide the genus *Acacia* is very large containing 800–1,200 species. Most species are subtropical. Australia and Africa contain the most species. In our region most are shrubs or sporadically small trees; only the 3 species listed below regularly become tree-sized. Acacia leaves are deciduous, bipinnately compound with small leaflets. The flowers are usually yellow, borne in heads or spikes. The stamen are numerous and extend well beyond the petals. The fruit is a legume often constricted between the seeds.

KEY TO ACACIAS

1. Spines straight . . . . .sweet acacia, *Acacia farnesiana*
1. Spines hooked, clawlike . . . . .Go to 2
  2. Legume about 0.5 in. wide . . . . .catclaw acacia, *Acacia greggii*
  2. Legume about 1 in. wide . . . . .Wright catclaw, *Acacia wrightii*

Sweet acacia, Huisache
Acacia farnesiana (L.) Willd.

Large shrub to small tree occasionally growing to 30 ft in height and 1.5 ft in diameter. Leaves alternate; 1–4 in. long; bipinnately compound; 2–8 pairs of pinnae; each pinna with 20–50 leaflets. Each leaflet 0.1–0.3 in. long. Flowers yellow; very fragrant; in heads about 0.6 in. wide; heads in clusters of 2–5. Fruit a legume; 2–3 in. long; straight or curved; red-brown, purple, or black. Twigs armed with paired stipular spines; 1–1.5 in. long. Wood used locally for fence posts and woodenware. Dye and ink obtained from inner bark and fruit. Widely cultivated in tropical gardens. Found in southern Texas and Mexico; rare disjuncts in southern Arizona and California; also in West Indies, Central America, and South America.

Catclaw acacia, Gregg catclaw
Acacia greggii Gray (fig. 218)

Shrub or small tree occasionally growing to 30 ft in height and 1 ft in diameter. Often forming dense thickets. Leaves alternate; bipinnately compound; 1–3 in. long; 1–3 pairs of pinnae; each pinna with 6–14 leaflets. Leaflets 0.1–0.3 in. long; 2–3 veined. Petiole short; brown, glandular near middle. Flowers bright yellow; fragrant; in dense hairy spikes 1–2.5 in. long. Stamens numerous; longer than the petals. Fruit a legume; linear-oblong; flat; curved and contorted; indehiscent; light brown; 2–6 in. long; 0.5–0.7 in. wide; contracted between the seeds. Seeds dark brown; lustrous; 0.2 in. long. Twigs slender; angled; hairless or slightly hairy. Armed with stout recurved spines; 0.2–0.3 in. long, giving tree its common name. Bark thin; furrowed; scaly; light gray-brown; astringent. Wood used for fuel; very heavy; hard; durable; ring porous; sapwood light yellow; heartwood red-brown. Intolerant of shade. Grows in dry infertile soils on gravelly mesas or sides of arroyos and canyons. Seeds eaten by quail. Honey obtained from nectar. Native Americans ground the legumes into flour. Found in the southern portions of Texas, New Mexico, Arizona, Utah, and California, and in northern Mexico.

Wright catclaw, Wright acacia

Acacia wrightii Benth.

Large shrub or small tree sometimes reaching 30 ft in height. Leaves bipinnately compound; 1–2 in. long; often clustered; 1–3 pairs of pinnae; each pinna with 4–10 leaflets. Petiole hairy. Flowers yellow; in cylindrical spikes 0.7–2 in. long. Fruit a legume; 2–4 in. long; 1 in. wide; straight or curved; edge thick. Twigs with hooklike spines. Wood used locally for fuel and fence posts. Grows on droughty rocky soils. Found in Texas and south into Mexico.

MIMOSA: THE GENUS *ALBIZIA*

Worldwide this genus contains between 100 and 150 species, all native to the warmer regions of the Old World. The species listed below has become naturalized in our region.

Mimosa leaves are alternate, deciduous, pinnately or bipinnately compound, and they lack a terminal leaflet. The petiole contains a gland, and tiny stipules are produced. The flowers are either bisexual or unisexual with numerous long-exserted

Fig. 219. Mimosa (*Albizia julibrissin*) leaf.

stamen. The stamen filaments are brightly colored and function to attract pollinators, at least some of which are hummingbirds. The fruit is a legume that does not crack open at maturity. Outside our region many varied products are obtained from this genus including gum, resin, dye, soap, medicine, and lumber.

Mimosa, Silktree

Albizia julibrissin Durazz. (fig. 219)

Small deliquescent tree growing 30–35 ft in height and 0.5 ft in diameter (largest known 40 ft by 3 ft). Crown open; lacy. Leaves bipinnately compound; 8–24 pinnae; 4–11 in. long; 4–5 in. wide; closing at night; terminal leaflets lacking. Leaflets about 0.3–0.6 in. long; hundreds per leaf; base inequilateral. Petiole slightly hairy; with circular gland near base. Flowers with numerous long, pink-stalked stamen; in crowded heads. Legume flat; light tan; 4–6 in. long; 0.7–1.5 in. wide; outline of seeds visible on surface. Twigs stout with large lenticels; terminal bud lacking. Leaf scar 3-lobed. Bark smooth; green-gray or gray. Short-lived. Fungal blight causes the most damage sometimes quickly killing the tree. Found in open pine stands, edges of woods, roadsides, fencerows, and waste places. Native to Asia; widely planted and naturalized from Maryland to Indiana and south.

CAESALPINIA: THE GENUS *CAESALPINIA*

Worldwide this genus contains 100–200 species, found mostly in tropical and subtropical areas. Our region contains only 1 native species, Mexican caesalpinia (*Caesalpinia mexicana*), found mostly in Mexico but extending north into extreme southern Texas. In addition, paradise caesalpinia (*Caesalpinia gilliesii*), native to South America, occasionally escapes in the Southwest.

PALOVERDE: THE GENUS *CERCIDIUM*

Worldwide seven species of paloverde occur, all in our region, Mexico, or Venezuela. Our region contains three species, all large shrubs or small trees. Our species intergrade possibly the result of hybridization, and further study is needed. Yellow paloverde (*Cercidium microphyllum*), found in extreme southeastern California, southern Arizona, and south into Mexico, is rarely tree-sized.

The leaves of *Cercidium* occur below a spine, and they are bipinnately compound with an even number of pinnae. The leaves usually fall quickly, and the trees are leafless through much of the year. The flowers are yellow and borne in axillary clusters. The petals are clawed, and the stamen are longer than the petals. The wood is soft and diffuse-porous.

KEY TO PALOVERDES

1. Pinnae with 4–8 pairs of leaflets . . . . . .yellow paloverde, *Cercidium microphyllum*
1. Pinnae with 1–3 pairs of leaflets . . . . .Go to 2
    2. Legume tip narrowing abruptly to a point . . . .
    . . . . .Texas paloverde, *Cercidium texanum*
    2. Legume tip rounded . . . . .blue paloverde, *Cercidium floridum*

Blue paloverde
Cercidium floridum Benth. ex Gray

Thorny shrub or small tree sometimes growing to 30 ft in height. Leaves alternate; bipinnately compound; 1 pair of pinnae each with 2–3 pairs of leaflets. Leaflets obtuse; white-waxy; 0.1–0.2 in. long; falling soon but frequently bearing a second crop during the rainy season. Flowers in clusters of 4–5; bright yellow; 0.7 in. wide; petals glandular at base. Fruit a legume; oblong; compressed; 3–4 in. long; 0.2–0.3 in. wide; straight or somewhat contracted between the 2–8 seeds. Twigs stout; hairless; white-waxy; light yellow or pale olive-green. Spines thin; 0.2 in. long. Wood with little or no commercial value; used locally for fuelwood. Intolerant of shade. Grows on sandy or gravelly soil in desert sinks, canyons, and depressions. Found in southeastern California, southern Arizona, and south into Mexico.

Texas paloverde
Cercidium texanum Gray

Formerly subdivided into 2 species, *Cercidium texanum* and *Cercidium macrum*. Large shrub or small deliquescent tree sometimes growing to 30 ft in height. Leaves alternate; bipinnately compound with 2 pinnae; 0.5–0.7 in. long. Leaflets 0.1–0.2 in. long; 1–3 pairs per pinna. Flowers yellow; sepals reflexed; claw-petal red spotted. Fruit a legume; 1–2.5 in. long; 0.2 in. wide. Twigs green to olive-green; thorns numerous. Bark thin; smooth; light or dark green. Grows on gentle slopes often in limestone soils. Found in south Texas and south into Mexico.

REDBUD: THE GENUS *CERCIS*

A total of eight species of redbud occur in the world. Only two species occur in our region, but California redbud (*Cercis occidentalis*) only occasionally becomes tree-sized.

Redbud leaves are somewhat unusual among legumes because they are unifoliate containing a single leaflet and appearing simple as a result of reduction. The flowers are pink or red appearing in the spring before the new leaves on larger branches or the bole (cauliflory). The wood is ring-porous.

KEY TO REDBUDS

1. Leaf tip pointed . . . . .eastern redbud, *Cercis canadensis*
1. Leaf tip rounded or notched . . . . .California redbud, *Cercis occidentalis*

Eastern redbud, Judas-tree
Cercis canadensis L. (fig. 220)

Form. Small deliquescent tree growing to 40 ft in height and 1–2 ft in diameter.

Leaves. Alternate; unifoliate (appearing simple); broadly ovate to reniform; 3–5 in. in diameter; hairless above and below. Tip acute. Base heart-shaped. Margin entire. Stipules small; membraceous.

Fruit. Legume; flat; oblong; red-brown; 2–4 in. long; 0.5 in. wide. Seeds 0.2 in. long; ovoid or oblong; compressed; red-brown.

Twigs. Slender; round; not armed; marked by numerous pale lenticels. Leaf scars with 3 bundle scars; often fringed above. Terminal bud absent; chestnut-brown.

Bark. Thin; brown or gray; smooth but becoming scaly on older trees.

Wood. No commercial value. Heavy; hard; sapwood white; heartwood dark red-brown.

Natural History. Tolerant of shade. Short-lived; reaches maturity in 75 years. Reproduces well from seeds; good fruit crops produced most years. Self-pollinated by bees. Seed germination irregular and delayed; seeds remain viable in the litter for several years. Found on a wide variety of sites from moist to dry; most common on moist well-drained sites, lower south-facing slopes, or bottomlands. Often on limestone-based soils. Does not tolerate long periods of flooding. Commonly used in ornamental plantings. Songbirds, pheasants, and squirrels eat the seeds. Flowers eaten fresh by humans in salads or fried.

Varieties. Var. *texensis,* the Texas redbud with more rounded leaf tips occurs in southern Oklahoma, east Texas, and south into Mexico.

Range. See figure 221.

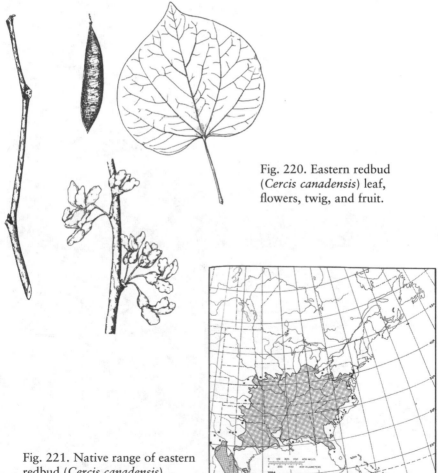

Fig. 220. Eastern redbud (*Cercis canadensis*) leaf, flowers, twig, and fruit.

Fig. 221. Native range of eastern redbud (*Cercis canadensis*).

YELLOWWOOD: THE GENUS *CLADRASTIS*

Worldwide the genus *Cladrastis* contains four species, three species in Asia and one in our region.

The flowers are white, bisexual, showy, and borne in clusters (either racemes or panicles) that droop from branch tips. The upper petal is large, rounded, and reflexed. The wood is semi-ring-porous or diffuse-porous.

Yellowwood

Cladrastis kentukea (Dum.-Cours.) Rudd

Formerly called *Cladrastis lutea*. Moderate-sized tree growing 40–50 ft in height. Leaves alternate; deciduous; pinnately compound; 6–10 in. long. Leaflets 5–11; 3–4 in. long; ovate; entire; abruptly pointed at tip, yellow-green; almost always alternate along the rachis. Petiole base hollow, enclosing the bud. Legume

Fig. 222. Waterlocust (*Gleditsia aquatica*) shoot with thorns and fruit.

flat; short stalked; linear; 2–3 in. long; containing 4–6 seeds. Twigs slender; hairless. Terminal buds lacking; lateral buds naked; yellow hairy. Bark thin; smooth; gray; marked with brown vertical streaks. Wood with little or no commercial value; occasionally used for gun stocks, woodenware, fuelwood, and dye. Sapwood yellow-white. Heartwood yellow turning brown with exposure; heavy; hard; sometimes with gum deposits. Rare in nature; occasionally cultivated for the showy flowers. Grows on moist slopes, stream banks, and limestone bluffs. Found in small disjunct areas in southern Indiana, southern Illinois, Kentucky, Tennessee, western Virginia, western North Carolina, southern Missouri, and Arkansas.

HONEYLOCUST: THE GENUS *GLEDITSIA*

Worldwide the genus *Gleditsia* contains 14 species found in North America, Central and East Asia, South America, and tropical Africa. Only 2 species occur in our region.

Honeylocusts have alternate, pinnately compound or bipinnately compound, deciduous leaves. Small stipules are present. The flowers appear after the new leaves are completely expanded, and they are small, green-yellow, and radially symmetrical with three to five petals. Each tree has both bisexual and unisexual flowers (polygamous). Nectar from the flowers is used in honey making. Maturing in a single season and sometimes persisting through the winter, the fruit is a legume. Some twigs are modified into stout, branched thorns that occasionally occur in large clusters on the lower bole, but thorns are completely lacking on some trees. The wood is ring-porous.

KEY TO HONEYLOCUSTS

1. Legume 1–2 in. long; leaflets hairless below . . . . . . .waterlocust, *Gleditsia aquatica*
1. Legume 6–14 in. long; leaflets slightly hairy below . . . .
. . . . .honeylocust, *Gleditsia triacanthos*

Waterlocust
Gleditsia aquatica Marsh. (fig. 222)

Large shrub to moderate-sized tree growing 70–80 ft in height and 1–2 ft in diameter (largest known 90 ft by 2 ft in diameter). Leaves pinnately or bipinnately compound; leaflets 18–40; hairless or nearly hairless. Leaf rachis and rachilla hairless or nearly hairless. Fruit a legume; oval; 1–2 in. long; 1–1.5 in. wide; flat; lacking sugary green pulp inside. Seeds 1–3. Thorns not branched or 2–3 branched. Bark gray to nearly black; smooth or warty with occasional narrow furrows. Grows as scattered trees in bottomlands and wet flats. Hybridizes with honeylocust to form the Texas honeylocust (*Gleditsia* x *texana*), characterized by a legume 4–5 in. long. Found in the coastal region from South Carolina to Texas, and in the Mississippi River valley to southern Indiana.

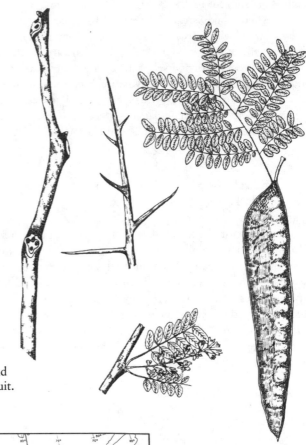

Fig. 223. Honeylocust
(*Gleditsia triacanthos*)
bipinnately compound
leaf, pinnately compound
leaf, twig, thorn, and fruit.

Fig. 224. Native range
of honeylocust (*Gleditsia
triacanthos*).

Honeylocust, Sweet-locust
Gleditsia triacanthos L. (fig. 223)

Form. Medium-sized tree growing 70–80 ft in height and 2–3 ft in diameter (largest known 140 ft by 6 ft). Crown open. Bole and branches sometimes armed with clusters of straight or branched thorns growing up to 16 in. long. Dead branches often retained.

Leaves. Alternate; pinnately or bipinnately compound; 6–12 in. long; rachis and rachilla hairy. Leaflets 0.5–1.5 in. long; smaller on bipinnately compound leaves; lanceolate-oblong; entire or slightly scalloped; slightly hairy below at least along the veins. Found in clusters on older twigs.

Fruit. A legume; strap-shaped; red-brown to purple-brown; usually twisted or curved or both; shiny; 6–16 in. long; 1 in. wide; not splitting open. Seeds 12–14; dark brown.

Twigs. Slender to stout. Thorns straight or 3-branched; produced on young trees and the lower portions of mature trees; 3–16 in. long; green to red-brown. Terminal bud absent; lateral buds minute; nearly submerged in leaf scar; brown; usually stacked in a row of 3.

Bark. Smooth and gray on young trees. On older trees divided into wide flat ridges separated by shallow vertical furrows; 1 side of the ridge sometimes turning outwards producing a fluted appearance; gray to nearly black.

Wood. Low commercial value largely owing to scarcity. Sapwood yellow; wide. Heartwood red-brown or light red; heavy; hard; often with a pleasing figure. Used locally for interior trim, bows, novelties, fence posts and rails, and fuelwood.

Natural History. Intolerant of shade; requires full or nearly full sunlight to reproduce. Fast growing; reaches maturity in 125 years. Some fruit produced most years; heavy crops occur every 2–3 years. Seed germination highly irregular owing to a thick seed coat; some seeds germinate in 1–2 years while others remain dormant in the soil for many years. Germination possibly hastened after passing through the gut of birds or mammals. Sprouts from stumps and roots. Root system deep with a well-developed taproot. Grows on a wide variety of conditions but development is best on slightly acidic to alkaline soils; typical of fertile bottomlands; generally absent on thin soils. Salt and drought tolerant. Often planted in shelterbelts, for erosion control, and for shade in cities. Found as widely scattered trees, growing with sweetgum, sugarberry, boxelder, willow oak, water oak, bur oak, American elm, red maple, persimmon, black walnut, green ash, and white ash. Fruit eaten by hogs, cattle, squirrels, fox, white-tailed deer, opossum, quail, and crows. Light green pulp in fruits formerly used as sugar substitute or fermented into beer.

Varieties. The thornless form commonly planted in cities is *forma inermis*.

Hybrids. Hybridizes with water locust, forming Texas honeylocust (*Gleditsia* x *texana*) with fruits 4–5 in. long.

Range. See figure 224.

COFFEETREE: THE GENUS *GYMNOCLADUS*

Worldwide the genus *Gymnocladus* contains four species. Our region has one species; the remaining three are found in Asia.

The leaves of coffeetrees are alternate, deciduous, and bipinnately compound. Small stipules are produced. The flowers on one tree are unisexual and bisexual (polygamous), and they appear after the new leaves are fully expanded. Pollinated by insects, each flower is nearly radially symmetrical with five purple-white petals. The fruit is a thick legume requiring one growing season to mature. The wood is ring-porous, and often mistaken for honeylocust.

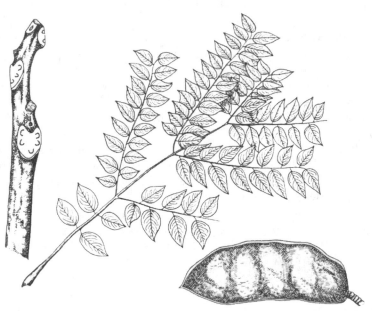

Fig. 225. Kentucky coffeetree
(*Gymnocladus dioicus*) leaf,
twig, and fruit.

Kentucky coffeetree
Gymnocladus dioicus (L.) K. Koch (fig. 225)

Some authors use the original spelling, *dioica*. Medium-sized tree growing 60–80 ft in height and 2–3 ft in diameter (largest known 110 ft by 4 ft). Leaves alternate; bipinnately compound except for 1–2 pairs of simple basal pinnae; pinnae lacking a terminal leaflet; 40 or more leaflets; 1–3 ft long; appearing late in the spring. Leaflets 2–2.5 in. long; ovate; acute; entire; short stalked; hairless. Fruit a thick legume; short stalked; red-brown; 4–8 in. long; 1–2 in. wide; pulp sugary. Seeds 6–9; ovoid; 0.7 in. long; seed coat thick; formerly roasted and used as substitute for coffee; raw seeds and pulp are poisonous. Twigs very stout; lacking thorns; red hairy when young becoming hairless; large leaf scars. Terminal bud absent. Lateral buds small; 2 stacked on top of the other; depressed in craters; brown; silky hairy. Bark on young trees smooth; brown to gray. Bark on older trees gray; divided into narrow flat ridges by shallow furrows; edges of ridges turning outward appearing fluted. Wood with little commercial value. Sapwood yellow; narrow. Heartwood light red, red, or red-brown; heavy; hard; used locally for fence posts and rails, railroad cross ties, interior trim, cabinets, and fuelwood. Intolerant of shade. Fast growing. Some fruits produced most years on female trees; seed germination irregular and delayed, the result of a thick seed coat; some seeds remain dormant in the soil for several years. Found as widely scattered trees in bottomlands. Seeds used by Native Americans in dicelike games; trees found near former villages, the result of seeds lost from games. Range from extreme southern Ontario to extreme eastern Nebraska, and south to northern Kentucky and Oklahoma; disjuncts in New York, Pennsylvania, West Virginia, Virginia, Tennessee, Wisconsin, and Minnesota; infrequent throughout its range.

LEUCAENA OR LEADTREE: THE GENUS *LEUCAENA*

This genus contains about 50 species found mostly in the American tropics and subtropics. In our region, great leucaena becomes a moderate-sized tree. A second species, littleleaf leucaena, rarely becomes tree-size. In addition, leucaena (*Leucaena leucocephala*), probably native to southeast Mexico, has become naturalized in south Texas.

KEY TO LEUCAENAS

1. Each leaf pinna with 6–12 leaflets . . . . .littleleaf leucaena, *Leucaena retusa*
1. Each leaf pinna with 30–120 leaflets . . . .great leucaena, *Leucaena pulverulenta*

Fig. 226. Jerusalem-thorn (*Parkinsonia aculeata*) leaves, flowers, and fruit.

Great leucaena, Great leadtree
Leucaena pulverulenta (Schlecht.) Benth.

Moderate-sized tree growing to 60 ft in height. Leaves alternate; bipinnately compound; pinnae 20–36. Leaflets 30–120 per pinna; linear; 0.1–0.2 in. long. Petiole with dark, round gland. Flowers white; borne in rounded heads. Fruit a legume 5–14 in. long; 0.5–0.8 in. wide; flat; thin. Twigs white hairy becoming hairless. Bark red-brown; smooth becoming scaly. Sapwood yellow. Heartwood dark brown; heavy; hard; locally used for fence posts. Planted in cities. Found along streams in south Texas, and south into Mexico.

PARKINSONIA: THE GENUS *PARKINSONIA*

Worldwide this genus contains two species. One species native to tropical America has become naturalized in the warmer portions of our region. The other species grows in Africa.

Jerusalem-thorn
Parkinsonia aculeata L. (fig. 226)

Large shrub or small tree growing to 35 ft in height. Leaves pinnately compound; 8–16 in. long. Leaflets 50–80; linear; 0.2–0.3 in. long; falling early leaving the rachis. Stipules spiny. Flowers yellow; 1 petal larger than the other 4; produced from spring to late summer often after rain. Fruit a legume; 2–4 in. long; brown to orange-red; hairy or hairless; narrowed between the seeds; long pointed at tip. Bark smooth and green at first, becoming red-brown with small scales. Wood heavy; hard; used locally for fuelwood. Cattle, horses, and deer eat the fruit. Native Americans ground the seeds into flour. Found from Texas to southern Arizona, and south to South America. Planted in California and Florida, and possibly escaping.

BLACKBEAD: THE GENUS *PITHECELLOBIUM*

Worldwide this genus contains 150–200 species found mostly in tropical regions. Our region contains the 2 species keyed below, but huajillo of south Texas and Mexico rarely becomes tree-sized.

KEY TO BLACKBEADS

1. Leaf pinnae with 14–40 leaflets; legume thin and membraceous . . . .
. . . . .huajillo, *Pithecellobium pallens*
1. Leaf pinnae with 6–10 leaflets; legume thick and woody . . . .
. . . . .ebony blackbead, *Pithecellobium flexicaule*

Ebony blackbead, Texas-ebony, Ebony apes-earring

Pithecellobium flexicaule (Benth.) Coult.

Large shrub or small tree growing to 40 ft in height. Leaves alternate; evergreen; bipinnately compound; 2–3 in. long; 1–3 pairs of pinnae; 6–10 leaflets per pinna. Leaflets 0.2–0.5 in. long; nearly stalkless. Petiole often glandular at or above middle. Stipules spiny. Flowers fragrant; yellow; borne in cylindrical spikes. Fruit a legume 4–6 in. long; dark brown or black; straight or curved; thick; very hard. Seeds bright red-brown. Twigs stout but flexible; green to red-brown; hairy becoming hairless. Wood extremely heavy, usually sinking in water; very durable. Found along the Gulf Coast of Texas, along the lower Rio Grande, and south into Mexico.

MESQUITE: THE GENUS *PROSOPIS*

Worldwide the genus *Prosopis* contains about 45 species of trees and shrubs, found mostly in warm and dry areas of our region, Mexico, and central and South America. Our region contains 4 species, but only 3 are trees. The wood is ring-porous.

KEY TO MESQUITES

1. Legume 1–2 in. long; tightly spiraled; leaf pinnae each with 10–16 leaflets . . . .
. . . . .screwbean mesquite, *Prosopis pubescens*
1. Legume 4–9 in. long; not spiraled; leaf pinnae each with 22–40 leaflets . . . .Go to 2
   2. Leaves and twigs hairy . . . . .velvet mesquite, *Prosopis velutina*
   2. Leaves and twigs hairless . . . . .honey mesquite, *Prosopis glandulosa*

Honey mesquite

Prosopis glandulosa Torr.

Formerly called *Prosopis juliflora*. Large shrub or small tree rarely 50 ft in height and 4 ft in diameter. Crown open; straggling. Leaves alternate; bipinnately compound. Pinnae each with 22–40 leaflets. Leaflets linear to linear-oblong; 0.5–2 in. long. Rachis spine tipped. Fruit a legume; 4–9 in. long; 0.2–0.5 in. wide; flat to nearly rounded; not splitting open at maturity; yellow; straight or curved; edible. Seeds oblong; compressed; light brown. Twigs slender; smooth; usually with stipular spines; 0.5–2 in. long. Terminal bud absent; lateral buds small; brown. Bark thick; dark red-brown; furrowed and scaly. Wood very heavy and hard. Sapwood yellow. Heartwood red to dark brown; durable. Intolerant of shade. Long-lived; adapted to droughty desert sites by a long taproot descending 40–50 ft into the soil. Found from Texas to southern Nevada and south into Mexico.

Screwbean mesquite
Prosopis pubescens Benth.

Large shrub or small tree sometimes reaching 30 ft in height and 1 ft in diameter. Leaves bipinnately compound; 1.5–3 in. long; pinnae 2 or 4; rachis extending as a small spine. Each pinna with 10–16 leaflets; 1.5–2 in. long. Fruit a legume; 1–2 in. long; yellow-brown; twisted by 12–20 turns into a spiral; not cracking open at maturity. Twigs with single or paired stipular spines. Wood durable; used locally for fence posts and fuelwood. Seeds ground into flour by Native Americans, also steeped in water to make a drink. Seeds eaten by roadrunner and quail. Found from Texas to California, north into Nevada and Utah, and south into Mexico.

Velvet mesquite
Prosopis velutina Woot.

Very similar to honey mesquite and sometimes considered a variety of it. Distinguished by the hairy leaves and twigs. Found in west Texas, New Mexico, central Arizona, and south into Mexico.

LOCUST: THE GENUS *ROBINIA*

About ten species of locust occur in the world; all are native to North America. One species (black locust, *Robinia pseudoacacia*) regularly becomes tree-sized, but three additional species may grow to tree-size in favorable environments.

Locust leaves are alternate, pinnately compound, and deciduous. The stipules are hardened into two spines on young plants and epicormic branches. Locust flowers are bisexual, showy, and insect pollinated. The flowers are red or white, borne in a raceme, appear shortly after the new leaves are expanded, and are bilaterally symmetrical with five petals. The wood is ring-porous.

KEY TO LOCUSTS

1. Legume and stalk smooth; hairless . . . . .black locust, *Robinia pseudoacacia*
1. Legume and stalk hairy . . . . .Go to 2
   2. Twigs hairless; usually a shrub . . . . .Kelsey locust, *Robinia kelseyi*
   2. Twigs hairy 3
3. Hairs not sticky . . . . .New Mexican locust, *Robinia neomexicana*
3. Hairs sticky . . . . .clammy locust, *Robinia viscosa*

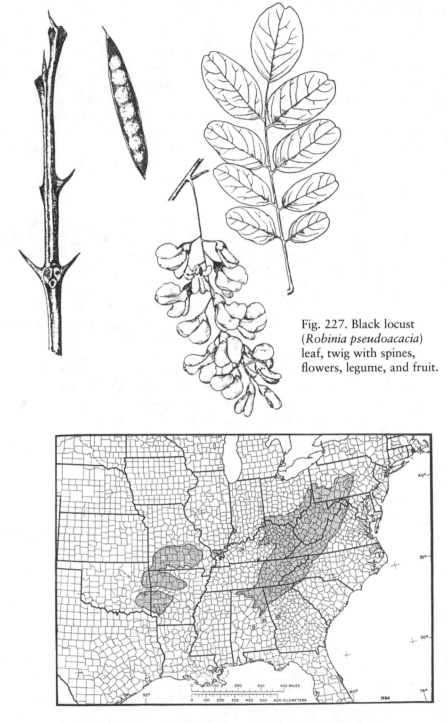

Fig. 227. Black locust (*Robinia pseudoacacia*) leaf, twig with spines, flowers, legume, and fruit.

Fig. 228. Native range of black locust (*Robinia pseudoacacia*).

Black locust, Yellow locust, Locust

Robinia pseudoacacia L. (fig. 227)

Form. Medium-sized tree growing 50–70 ft in height and 1–2 ft in diameter (largest known 100 ft by 4 ft). Crown open; irregular.

Leaves. Alternate; pinnately compound; 6–12 in. long. Leaflets 7–21; ovate-oblong; entire; hairless.

Fruit. Legume; smooth; brown; flat; oblong; 2–4 in. long. Seeds 4–8; flat; brown; 0.2–0.3 in. long.

Twigs. Rather stout; red-brown; angular; hairless; juvenile trees usually armed with 2 stipular spines; spines 0.5–1 in. long. Terminal bud absent. Lateral buds minute; 3–4 stacked in a row; submerged in the leaf scar and thereby usually not visible.

Bark. Red-brown, gray, or nearly black; soft corky; deeply furrowed into crisscrossing ridges.

Wood. Commercial value varies considerably; sometimes considered nonmerchantable and other times merchantable. Sapwood yellow-white; narrow. Heartwood green-yellow, dark yellow, or golden brown; very heavy and hard; very durable; used for posts, mine props, railroad ties, machine parts, woodenware, and novelties. Formerly used for pins (tree nails) placed in other woods; the wood shrinks less than others and pin joints tighten over time.

Natural History. Very intolerant of shade; requires full sunlight. Fast growing but short-lived; growth declines considerably after age 30; reaches maturity in about 80 years. Reproduces sometimes from seeds; large seed crops produced every 1–2 years. Most regeneration occurs from stump and root sprouts. Heavily damaged by insects and disease sometimes making the trees useless for wood products; locust borer, heart rot, locust leafminer, and locust twig borer cause the most damage. Survives well on a very wide range of site conditions; development best on moist loams or limestone soils. Will not tolerate poorly drained soils or eroded, compacted, clayey soils. Owing to adaptability, planted on mine spoil banks and shelterbelts; naturalized throughout much of eastern North America. Widely planted in Europe, Asia, and north Africa where genetic selections have been made. Found in pure stands often on old fields; also found mixed with yellow-poplar, white oak, northern red oak, pignut hickory, black birch, eastern white pine, and shortleaf pine. Foliage poisonous to livestock, but browsed by white-tailed deer. Quail eat the seeds. Trees with heart rot provide cavities for woodpeckers. Flowers provide nectar for honey production.

Hybrids. Hybridizes with Kelsey locust, New Mexican locust, and clammy locust.

Varieties. A clone of this species called shipmast locust (var. *rectissima*) is planted for its straight bole and darker heartwood.

Range. See figure 228.

SOPHORA: THE GENUS *SOPHORA*

Worldwide *Sophora* contains 50–70 species, found in tropical and warm temperate regions. Our region contains 1 species that often becomes tree-sized. A second species, Texas sophora, only rarely becomes tree-sized. In addition, the Japanese pagodatree (*Sophora japonica*) with the flowers borne in large terminal clusters (panicles) is planted for ornament.

The leaves of sophora are alternate, evergreen or deciduous, and they lack a terminal leaflet. Small stipules are produced. The flowers are bilaterally symmetrical, bisexual, fragrant, showy, and they appear with the new leaves. The fruit is a legume compressed between each seed.

KEY TO SOPHORAS

1. Leaves deciduous; leaflets mostly 13–15 per leaf . . .Texas sophora, *Sophora affinis*
1. Leaves evergreen; leaflets mostly 5–9 per leaf . . . .mescalbean, *Sophora secundiflora*

Mescalbean, Coralbean
Sophora secundiflora (Gomez Ortega) Lag. ex DC.

Large shrub or small tree growing 30 ft in height and 0.5 ft in diameter; commonly thicket forming. Leaves alternate; evergreen; bipinnately compound but lacking a terminal leaflet. Leaflets 7–13; 0.7–2 in. long; elliptical; leathery; shiny; entire; sometimes notched at tip; hairy above when young but becoming hairless; hairy or hairless below. Fruit a legume; 1–7 in. long; oblong; terete; does not crack open at maturity; contracted between the seeds; hairy. Seeds bright scarlet; very poisonous. Twigs slender; round; lacking spines and thorns; lateral buds minute. Wood with no commercial value; heartwood orange-yellow; heavy; hard. Range from central Texas to southeastern New Mexico, and south into Mexico.

BEECH FAMILY: FAGACEAE

The Beech Family contains 700–800 species in nine genera. Found mostly in the Northern Hemisphere, the family is widespread in temperate and tropical areas, often dominating forests. Our region contains five genera and about 100 species, but only about half are tree-sized.

The Beech Family contains shrubs or trees. It has simple, alternate leaves with stipules. The flowers are highly reduced, lack petals, and are unisexual with four to six sepals. Both sexes are found on each tree (monoecious). Male flowers are borne in aments. The wind-dispersed pollen is allergenic to most people. Female flowers have an inferior ovary and are borne singly or in small groups. The fruits are nuts that mature in one or two years, and they are always subtended by a cupule, a complex fusion of leaf and stem tissue. The cupule becomes the familiar acorn cap of oaks or the spiny bur of chestnuts. Terminal buds are present or absent. Economically the family provides cork (*Quercus*), tannin (*Quercus* and *Castanea*), nuts (*Castanea*, *Fagus*, and *Quercus*), and especially wood products (*Fagus*, *Quercus*, and formerly *Castanea*).

CHESTNUT: THE GENUS *CASTANEA*

Worldwide the genus *Castanea* contains eight to ten species found in North America, Europe, and Asia. In our area three species occur naturally and one Chinese species is commonly planted.

Chestnuts are trees or large shrubs. The leaves are simple, alternate, and deciduous with unbranched lateral veins that terminate in bristlelike teeth in the margin. The flowers are unisexual and appear after the leaves have expanded. Male flowers have white hairs, and are borne in a more-or-less rigid spike. Female flowers are found in a cluster of one to three at the base of some male spikes. They are pollinated by a combination of wind and insects. The nut fruits occur in clusters of one to three, mature in one growing season, and are completely enclosed by a very spiny burlike cupule. The wood is ring-porous. All chestnuts including European and Asian species are interfertile, and may hybridize when grown in close proximity. Chinese chestnut (*Castanea mollissima*) may be seen persisting from cultivation. It is generally a wide-spreading multiple-stemmed tree with hairy leaves 6–9 in. long, hairy yellow-brown twigs, and hairy spines on the fruit bur.

KEY TO CHESTNUTS

1. Vigorous twigs hairless . . . . .Go to 2
1. Vigorous twigs hairy . . . . .Go to 3
    2. Nuts 1 per bur; round on all sides . . . . .Ozark chinkapin, *Castanea ozarkensis*
    2. Nuts 2–3 per bur; flattened on 1–2 sides .American chestnut, *Castanea dentata*
3. Leaves 3–5 in. long; nut 1 per bur . . . . .chinkapin, *Castanea pumila*
3. Leaves 6–9 in. long; 2–3 nuts per bur . . . . .Chinese chestnut, *Castanea mollissima*

Fig. 229. American chestnut (*Castanea dentata*) leaves, twig, flowers, and fruit.

American chestnut

Castanea dentata (Marsh.) Borkh. (fig. 229)

Form. Formerly a moderate to large tree growing 60–90 ft in height and 2–4 ft in diameter (largest known 120 by 10 ft); currently reduced by disease to a small tree or large shrub growing to 30 ft in height and 0.5 ft in diameter. Often found as clumps of stump sprouts.

Leaves. Oblanceolate to obovate; 5–10 in. long; coarsely toothed with bristlelike recurved teeth; yellow-green; hairless below except for occasional hairs on the major veins. Tip acuminate. Base wedge-shaped or acute.

Fruit. Nut flattened on 1–2 sides; chestnut-brown; 0.5–1 in. long; edible. Cupule spherical; 2–2.5 in. wide; with 2–4 valves; composed of branched spines that lack hairs. Nuts eaten by humans; formerly sold hot roasted in cities by street vendors.

Twigs. Round in cross section; lustrous; chestnut-brown; hairless; oval leaf scars with many bundle scars. Pith stellate. Pseudoterminal buds ovoid; acute; brown; 0.2 in. long; with 2–3 visible scales.

Bark. Smooth on young trees; divided into broad flat ridges on old trees; gray-brown. Former source of tannin.

Wood. Formerly provided very valuable lumber from cut trees; currently extremely valuable but only very limited quantities are available from recycled lumber from old barns and houses. Sapwood light brown; narrow. Heartwood gray-brown to brown; darkening with age; moderately lightweight; astringent taste; very durable. Formerly used for poles, fence posts, railroad ties, furniture, caskets, doors, sashes, and paneling. Standing dead trees were harvested until about 1960 and sold as wormy chestnut. Former principal source of tannin obtained by soaking wood chips in hot water.

Natural History. Intermediate in tolerance to shade. Formerly reproduced from nuts or more commonly from stump sprouts. Current regeneration limited to sprouting. Throughout the original range, the aboveground portions of essentially all trees have been killed by chestnut blight, a Chinese disease introduced to New York about 1904. Trees seen today are stump sprouts from the original trees. Efforts to find naturally disease-resistant trees have failed. Creating resistance by hybridizing American chestnut with the disease-resistant Chinese chestnut followed by repeated backcrosses to American chestnut looks promising. Originally found on a wide range of sites, ranging from mesic lower slopes to dry ridges; most abundant on middle and upper slopes. Today found mostly on dry upper slopes growing in mixed stands with chestnut oak, scarlet oak, white oak, northern red oak, pignut hickory, sourwood, blackgum, Table-mountain pine, and pitch pine. Nuts formerly eaten by bear, deer, small mammals, wild pigs, and wild boar. Formerly collected by settlers and either eaten or sold to vendors who resold the nuts in East Coast cities.

Range. Southern Maine to extreme southern Illinois, and south to southwest Georgia and southern Mississippi; apparently extirpated from northwest Florida.

Fig. 230. Chinkapin
(*Castanea pumila*)
shoot, twig, flower
spikes, and fruit.

Ozark chinkapin
Castanea ozarkensis Ashe

Some references combine Ozark chinkapin and chinkapin into a single species, *Castanea pumila*. Formerly a moderate-sized tree growing to 70 ft in height; reduced by disease to a small tree or large shrub growing to 30 ft in height; often growing in clumps of stump sprouts. Leaves narrowly obovate to oblanceolate; 5–9 in. long; bristle tipped; hairless or brown-white hairy below. Tip acuminate. Base rounded or wedge-shaped. Twigs hairless. Burs spiny; 2-valved; 1 nut per bur; 1 in. wide; nut rounded. Found locally in the Ozark plateau and the mountains of southern Missouri, Arkansas, and eastern Oklahoma.

Chinkapin, Dwarf chinkapin, Chinquapin
Castanea pumila Mill. (fig. 230)

Coastal Plain populations with few spines on the fruit bur are sometimes designated as a separate species, *Castanea alnifolia*. Shrubs or occasionally small trees growing to 40 ft in height. Leaves narrowly elliptical to oblanceolate; 3–5 in. long; short teeth widely spaced; generally very hairy below but sometimes hairless. Fruit bur 2-valved; about 2 in. in diameter; needle-sharp spines; 1 nut per bur; nut rounded. Twigs hairy sometimes becoming hairless. Found from New Jersey to Arkansas, and south to central Florida and east Texas.

WESTERN CHINKAPIN: THE GENUS *CHRYSOLEPIS*

This genus contains only two species worldwide. Both occur in our region, but only the species listed below is a tree. The remaining species (*Chrysolepis sempervirens*) is a low alpine shrub of the Coast Range and Sierra Nevada. This genus was formerly included within *Castanopsis*, but was separated to accommodate differences in the cupules. With this separation, *Castanopsis* is restricted to Asia.

Chrysolepis contains evergreen trees and shrubs with simple, alternate, leathery leaves. Stipules are present. The flowers appear in early summer, and are similar to chestnut. The large shiny nut fruit matures in two growing seasons. Borne singly or in clusters of two to three, the nuts are completely enclosed in a spiny bur. Terminal buds are present, and the wood is ring-porous.

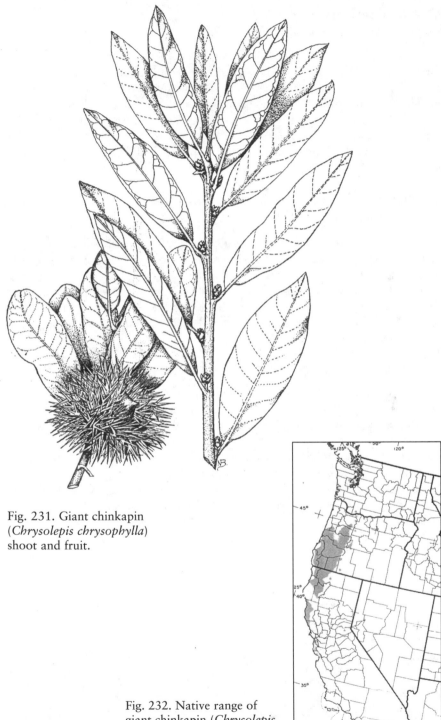

Fig. 231. Giant chinkapin
(*Chrysolepis chrysophylla*)
shoot and fruit.

Fig. 232. Native range of
giant chinkapin (*Chrysolepis
chrysophylla*).

Giant chinkapin, Golden chinkapin

Chrysolepis chrysophylla (Dougl. ex Hook.) Hjelm. (fig. 231)

Nomenclature. Formerly called *Castanopsis chrysophylla.*

Form. Tall shrub to medium-sized tree growing 60–80 ft in height and 2–3 ft in diameter (largest known 130 ft by 5 ft). When tree-sized, bole clear. Crown dense; rounded; with stout, spreading branches.

Leaves. Lanceolate to oblong-ovate; 2–6 in. long; pinnate venation; entire and often revolute; dark green and lustrous above; covered with golden-yellow scales below. Tip acuminate.

Fruit. Nut broadly ovoid, yellow-brown; 0.5 in. long; edible. Bur 4-valved; spherical; 1–1.5 in. in diameter; covered with prickly irregularly branched spines.

Twigs. Slender; round in cross section; covered with golden-yellow scales but turning red-brown. Pith stellate. Buds ovoid; 0.2 in. long; light brown; numerous overlapping scales.

Bark. Thick; dark red-brown; long linear ridges separated by deep furrows.

Wood. Little or no commercial value. Sapwood light brown tinged with pink. Heartwood not easily distinguished from sapwood; moderately heavy. Used locally for paneling, furniture, and novelties.

Natural History. Tolerant of shade but requiring sunlight for fast growth. Growth rather rapid; reaches maturity in 130–150 years (extreme age 500 years). Reproduces well from seed; good seed crops produced every 2–5 years; seeds dispersed by gravity, birds, and squirrels. Sprouts prolifically from stumps. Generally free of damaging agents; not affected by chestnut blight. Often found in pure stands on infertile dry sites, or as an understory tree growing with redwood, Douglas-fir, incense-cedar, sugar pine, ponderosa pine, white fir, western redcedar, western hemlock, and Pacific madrone. Nuts eaten by birds and mammals.

Varieties. A shrubby form with leaves folded upward along the midvein is designated var. *minor.*

Range. See figure 232.

BEECH: THE GENUS *FAGUS*

This genus contains eight to ten species scattered through the Northern Hemisphere, but only the one species listed below is native to our region. Sometimes planted in the Northeast, European beech (*Fagus sylvatica*) has smaller leaves (2–4 in. long), smaller teeth, and 4–8 pairs of lateral veins.

Beech leaves are deciduous and pinnately veined. Each vein ends in the margin as a tooth. The nuts mature in one growing season. Terminal buds are absent. The lateral buds contain numerous overlapping bud scales. The wood is diffuse-porous.

American beech

Fagus grandifolia Ehrh. (fig. 233)

Form. Medium-sized tree growing 60–80 ft in height and 2–3 ft in diameter (largest known 160 ft by 5 ft); grows largest in the lower Ohio and Mississippi River valleys and in the southern Appalachians. Crown rounded; deep with slender spreading branches.

Fig. 233. American beech (*Fagus grandifolia*) leaves, twig, and fruit.

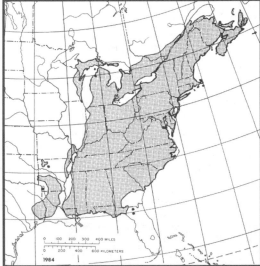

Fig. 234. Native range of American beech (*Fagus grandifolia*).

Leaves. Elliptical to oblong-ovate; 2.5–6 in. long; hairless or hairy below; 9–14 pairs of lateral veins. Margin with widely spaced bristlelike teeth. Tip acuminate; base wedge-shaped; petiole short. Dead leaves retained over winter on small branches.

Flowers. Appearing after the leaves have expanded. Male flowers in spherical heads; 1 in. in diameter; calyx 4–8 lobes; stamens 6–16. Female flowers 2–4 in spikes; calyx with 4–5 lobes; carpels 3.

Fruit. Nut; triangular in cross section; 0.5–0.7 in. long; edible if cooked; 2–3 nuts completely enclosed in a woody bur (cupule) covered with weak unbranched spines.

Twigs. Slender; round in cross section; lustrous; olive-green to red-brown turning gray; hairless or with silky hairs; somewhat zigzag. Pith round; leaf scars small with many bundle scars. Pseudoterminal bud 0.7–1 in. long; sharp pointed; slender; cigarlike.

Bark. Thin (to 0.7 in.); smooth; gray; often mottled with white; sometimes with scattered warts.

Wood. Commercial value strongly depends upon local manufacturing facilities; often not commercially valuable. Sapwood nearly white. Heartwood red-white to red-brown; strong; heavy; hard; light brown; not durable. Used for flooring, furniture, railroad ties, baskets, cutting boards, spoons and bowls, fuelwood, yeast slats for brewing beer, and pulpwood.

Natural History. Very tolerant of shade; often a climax species. Growth rate slow; reaches maturity in 200–250 years (extreme age 400 years). Roots shallow often growing on soil surface. Reproduces in shade from seed; large seed crops occur every 2–8 years; dispersed short distances by gravity and bouncing downhill; dispersed long distances by bluejays. Fire, flooding, sucking insects, and beech bark disease cause the most damage; the latter disease is problematic in the Adirondack Mountains. Reproduces from stump sprouts and especially from root sprouts, which provide nearly all the regeneration in mountain saddles (beech gaps). Found on cool, moist, or seasonally wet sites; does not tolerate flooding in the growing season; generally on coarse-textured soils. Grows in small pure groves or mixed with sugar maple, red maple, yellow birch, black cherry, eastern hemlock, yellow-poplar, basswood, bitternut hickory, northern red oak, and white oak. Nuts eaten by many small mammals, white-tailed deer, black bear, fox, ruffed grouse, ducks, and bluejays.

Varieties. Some references recognize var. *caroliniana*, southern beech, which has rounded or heart-shaped leaf bases, fewer and shorter prickles on the cupule, and a more southerly distribution. Other references recognize 3 races: gray beech (found in the North and the southern Appalachians at high elevations), white beech (found on the Coastal Plain), and red beech (found everywhere else).

Range. See figure 234.

TANOAK: THE GENUS *LITHOCARPUS*

Worldwide tanoak contains 100–200 species growing in North America and Asia, but our region contains only the 1 species listed below.

Tanoaks are evergreen trees and shrubs. The leaves are simple, alternate, and leathery with parallel lateral veins extending to the margin. Large often persistent stipules are produced. The flowers are similar to chestnut appearing in the summer. The nut fruit matures after the second growing season. It is covered at the base by a cupule composed of reflexed scales with hooked tips. The fruit superficially resembles an oak acorn, but *Lithocarpus* is more closely related to chestnut and golden chinkapin. Terminal buds are present. The wood is semi-ring-porous.

Tanoak, Tanbark-oak
Lithocarpus densiflorus (Hook. & Arn.) Rehd.

Form. Shrub to medium-sized excurrent or deliquescent tree growing 50–90 ft in height and 2–3 ft in diameter (largest known 210 ft by 6 ft). Bole clear. Crown rounded; ascending branches.

Leaves. Oblong to oblong-lanceolate; 3–6 in. long; brittle; irregularly toothed to entire; pale green and hairless above; veins sunken above; woolly brown hairs below in spring becoming blue-white and nearly hairless; sometimes covered with white wax below; persistent 3–4 years; often curved downward. Tip acute or rounded. Stipules persistent on upper leaves. Petiole densely hairy.

Fruit. Nut; oval; bitter; yellow-brown; 0.7–1 in. long; enclosed at base by a shallow cap lined with lustrous red hairs.

Twigs. Stout; round in cross section; covered for 1–3 years with thick yellow hairs becoming red-brown; sometimes covered with white wax. Buds ovoid; obtuse; 0.2 in. long; covered by a few long, hairy scales.

Bark. Red-brown; deeply furrowed with broad, rounded, scaly ridges. Formerly used as a source of tannin, which provides the common name. Bark infusions formerly used to treat sores.

Wood. Little commercial value. Sapwood thick; light red-brown turning darker with age and becoming difficult to distinguish from heartwood. Heartwood light brown tinged with red, turning dark red; heavy; hard. Used locally for pulpwood, fuelwood, furniture, mine timbers, and baseball bats.

Natural History. Tolerant of shade. Growth moderate; reaches maturity in 200 years; maximum age not known because underground tubers repeatedly sprout. Reproduces well from seeds in shade; heavy seed crops occur every other year; mostly dispersed by gravity and rolling downhill. Seedlings quickly develop belowground tubers, which produce many vigorous sprouts with or without injury of the original stem. Wildfire causes the most damage. Grows on gravelly, sandy, or loamy soils, but not clay. Also found on serpentine soils. Occurs in pure stands along the inland side of the redwood belt; also grows mixed with redwood, Douglas-fir, Pacific madrone, California black oak, California white fir, sugar pine, ponderosa pine, western hemlock, and Sitka spruce. Nuts eaten by birds, rodents, deer, bear, goats, hogs, and cattle.

Varieties. A shrubby form with flat leaves that lack sunken veins is separated as var. *echinoides*.

Range. Found in coastal areas of southern Oregon and California; also in the Sierra Nevada of California. Elevation: sea level to 6,000 ft.

OAK: THE GENUS *QUERCUS*

Worldwide about 500 species of oak occur. About 90 species occur in our area, but only about 60 are tree sized. In addition, varieties are recognized in several species, and oaks hybridize more commonly than most other groups of trees. These factors increase the difficulty of identifying oaks. Ten tree-sized oaks in our area have tiny natural distributions often in only a few counties. Among the white oaks, this list includes Carmen oak (*Quercus carmenensis*), Engelmann oak (*Quercus engelmannii*), Sonoran blue oak (*Quercus oblongifolia*), and netleaf white oak (*Quercus polymorpha*). Among the red oaks, the list includes mapleleaf oak (*Quercus acerifolia*), silverleaf oak (*Quercus hypoleucoides*), Chisos oak (*Quercus robusta*), lateleaf oak (*Quercus tardifolia*), Channel Island oak (*Quercus tomentella*), and scrub oak (*Quercus viminea*). These species are not treated below, because most users will not encounter them. The common oak of Europe, English oak (*Quercus robur*), is occasionally planted and sometimes escapes, but it is also not included. English oak leaves resemble white oak leaves, but the acorn stalk is much longer, up to 2 in.

Oaks are deciduous or evergreen trees or shrubs. The leaves are alternate and simple, and stipules are present. Young deciduous species often retain dead leaves over winter. The flowers are unisexual, but both sexes are borne on the same tree (monoecious). Flowering occurs in the spring as the new leaves are expanding. Male flowers are clustered in drooping aments; individual flowers have a calyx with four to seven lobes that encloses 2–12 stamens. Female flowers occur in one- to many-flowered spikes; individual flowers have a calyx with six lobes that surround a three-celled (rarely 4- to 5-celled) ovary. The fruit is a nut commonly called an acorn, which matures in one or two years, and it is completely or partly enclosed by a cupule. At maturity the cupule becomes the familiar acorn cap. The twigs have a star-shaped pith. Terminal buds are present, and lateral buds are found clustered at ends of most twigs. The bark is either gray and scaly (in many white oaks) or dark and furrowed (in many red oaks). The wood is ring-porous (semi-ring-porous in live oaks) with large rays.

Oaks are subdivided into two subgenera, the Cycle-Cap Oaks (subgenus *Cyclobalanopsis*) and the Scale-Cap Oaks (subgenus *Quercus*). Cycle-Cap Oaks occur naturally only in Asia, but the Scale-Cap Oaks occur in many places in the Northern Hemisphere including our area. Scale-Cap Oaks are further subdivided into three sections: Red Oaks (section *Erythrobalanus*), White Oaks (section *Leucobalanus*) and Intermediate Oaks (*Protobalanus*). Knowledge of the sections is useful for identification purposes, and each section is described in greater detail below.

KEY TO OAKS

Owing to the large number of species, this key is subdivided into six subkeys. Use the key below to determine the appropriate subkey.

I. Mature acorns found on 1 year-old twigs . . . . .Go to II
I. Mature acorns found on 2 year-old twigs . . . . .Go to IV
    II. Leaves evergreen; thick and leathery . . . . .Subkey #1
    II. Leaves deciduous; thin and papery III
III. Leaves without lobes or with shallow lobes or margin wavy or coarsely toothed . .
. . . . .Subkey #2
III. Leaves with regular moderate to deep lobes .Subkey#3
    IV. Leaves evergreen; thick and leathery . . . . .Subkey #4
    IV. Leaves deciduous or tardily deciduous; thin and papery V
V. Leaves not lobed (except on sprouts and juveniles) . . . . .Subkey #5
V. Leaves lobed . . . . .Subkey#6

SUBKEY #1. ACORNS MATURING IN 1 YEAR; LEAVES EVERGREEN.

1. Southeastern species occurring in and east of east Texas . . . . .Go to 2
1. Southwestern species occurring in and west of Central Texas . . . . .Go to 4
    2. Leaves with golden glands below . . . . .Chapman Oak, *Quercus chapmannii*
    2. Leaves with white wooly hairs below 3
3. Leaves flat with rolled margin. . . . . .live oak, *Quercus virginiana*
3. Leaves canoe-shaped . . . . .sand live oak, *Quercus geminata*
    4. Acorn stalk 0.2 in. long or less 5
    4. Acorn stalk at least 0.5 in. long. 7
5. Leaves densely hairy below 6
5. Leaves hairless below, except for tufts in vein axils 8
    6. Leaves dark green and smooth above . . . . .Vasey oak, *Quercus vaseyana*
    6. Leaves yellow-green and sandpapery above . . . .pungent oak, *Quercus pungens*
7. Tips of scales of acorn cap loose, almost fringelike; California . . . .
. . . . .coast live oak, *Quercus agrifolia*
7. Tips of scales of acorn cap appressed, smooth; Arizona, New Mexico, Texas . . . . .
. . . . .Emory oak, *Quercus emoryi*
    8. Leaf veins not raised below . . . . .Texas live oak, *Quercus fusiformis*
    8. Leaf veins raised below 9
9. Leaf broadly obovate . . . . .netleaf oak, *Quercus rugosa*
9. Leaf elliptical to oblanceolate . . . . .Arizona oak, *Quercus arizonica*

SUBKEY #2. ACORNS MATURING IN 1 YEAR; LEAF WITHOUT LOBES OR WITH SHALLOW LOBES OR MARGIN WAVY OR COARSELY TOOTHED.

1. Tree of California . . . . .blue oak, *Quercus douglasii*
1. Tree of eastern, central, or southeastern North America 2
    2. Leaves with golden glands below . . . . .Chapman oak, *Quercus chapmannii*
    2. Leaves lacking golden glands below 3

3. Leaf margin smooth, not lobed, wavy, or toothed . . . .
. . . . .Oglethorpe oak, *Quercus oglethorpensis*
3. Leaves with shallow lobes or margin wavy or toothed 4
    4. Leaves regularly toothed from tip to base 5
    4. Lower third of leaf not lobed or toothed 7
5. Leaves with feltlike hairs below . . . . .swamp chestnut oak, *Quercus michauxii*
5. Leaves with few or no hairs below 6
    6. Bark light gray; scaly or flaky . . . . .chinkapin oak, *Quercus muhlenbergii*
    6. Bark brown or dark gray; tight with furrows . .chestnut oak, *Quercus montana*
7. Acorn stalk 1.5–2 in. long . . . . .swamp white oak, *Quercus bicolor*
7. Acorn stalk less than 1 in. long. 8
    8. Acorn cap saucer-shaped; 7–11 pairs of lateral leaf veins . . . .
    . . . . .bastard oak, *Quercus sinuata*
    8. Acorn cap goblet-shaped; 4–8 pairs of lateral leaf veins . . . .
    . . . . .bluff oak, *Quercus austrina*

SUBKEY #3, ACORNS MATURING IN 1 YEAR; LEAVES WITH MODERATE TO DEEP LOBES.

1. Tree of Pacific Coast or Rocky Mountains 2
1. Tree of central plains or eastern North America 5
    2. Leaf sinus reaching much less than half way to the midvein . . . .
    . . . . .blue oak, *Quercus douglasii*
    2. Leaf sinus reaching at least half way to the midvein 3
3. Acorn at least 0.7 in. long; cap covers less than half of nut 4
3. Acorn less than 0.7 in. long; cap covers at least half of nut . . . .
. . . . .Gambel oak, *Quercus gambelii*
    4. Acorn cap saucerlike; nut rounded at tip . . . .
    . . . . .Oregon white oak, *Quercus garryana*
    4. Acorn cap cuplike; nut pointed at tip . . . . .valley oak, *Quercus lobata*
5. Rim of acorn cap conspicuously fringed with curly hairlike scales . . . .
. . . . .bur oak, *Quercus macrocarpa*
5. Rim of acorn cap not fringed 6
    6. Acorn cap nearly or completely covering the nut . .overcup oak, *Quercus lyrata*
    6. Acorn cap covering half or less of the nut 7
7. Acorn stalk at least 1.5 in. long . . . . .swamp white oak, *Quercus bicolor*
7. Acorn stalk less than 1 in. long 8
    8. Some or all lateral leaf lobes square 9
    8. Lateral leaf lobes tapering to a rounded point 10
9. Twigs hairless; small trees in a colony . . . . . . .dwarf post oak, *Quercus margaretta*
9. Twigs hairy; single large trees . . . . .post oak, *Quercus stellata*
    10. Terminal buds hairless 11
    10. Terminal buds hairy 12
11. Leaves with 3–7 pairs of lateral veins . . . . .white oak, *Quercus alba*
11. Leaves with 7–11 pairs of lateral veins . . . . .bastard oak, *Quercus sinuata*
    12. Leaves hairless below, except along the major veins . . . .
    . . . . .bluff oak, *Quercus austrina*
    12. Leaves sparsely hairy below with branched hairs . . . .
    . . . . .swamp post oak, *Quercus similis*

SUBKEY #4, ACORNS MATURING IN 2 YEARS; LEAVES EVERGREEN.

1. Tree of the southeast, including east Texas 2
1. Tree of the southwest, including west Texas 4
    2. Leaves 0.5–2 in. long; broadly obovate . . . . . . .Myrtle oak, *Quercus myrtifolia*
    2. Leaves 2–4 in. long; narrowly elliptical to oblanceolate 3
3. Leaf tip narrowly pointed; bottomlands . . . . .swamp laurel oak, *Quercus laurifolia*
3. Leaf tip blunt pointed to rounded; sandy uplands . . . .
    . . . . .laurel oak, *Quercus hemisphaerica*
    4. Twigs and petiole densely hairy . . . . .canyon live oak, *Quercus chrysolepis*
    4. Twigs and petiole hairless to slightly hairy . . .Sierra live oak, *Quercus wislizeni*

SUBKEY #5, ACORNS MATURING IN 2 YEARS; LEAVES DECIDUOUS; NOT LOBED.

1. Leaves obovate to obdeltate 2
1. Leaves linear, oblong, or spatulate 3
    2. Terminal buds red-brown; hairless . . . . .Arkansas oak, *Quercus arkansana*
    2. Terminal buds light brown; hairy . . . . .blackjack oak, *Quercus marilandica*
3. Leaves spatulate; hairless below . . . . .water oak, *Quercus nigra*
3. Leaves linear or oblong; hairy or hairless below 4
    4. Leaves hairy below 5
    4. Leaves hairless below. 6
5. Leaves white-hairy below; petiole very hairy . . . . . . .bluejack oak, *Quercus incana*
5. Leaves green-hairy below; petiole hairless . . . . . . .shingle oak, *Quercus imbricaria*
    6. Leaves uniformly linear-lanceolate; tip tapering to bristle . . . .
    . . . . willow oak, *Quercus phellos*
    6. Leaves variable: rhombic, lanceolate, oblanceolate, or narrow elliptical;
    tip acute, obtuse, or rounded. 7
7. Leaf tip acute; bottomlands. . . . . .swamp laurel oak, *Quercus laurifolia*
7. Leaf tip obtuse or rounded; sandy uplands. . . . .laurel oak, *Quercus hemisphaerica*

SUBKEY #6, ACORN MATURING IN 2 YEARS; LEAVES DECIDUOUS; LOBED.

1. Tree of California and Oregon . . . . .California black oak, *Quercus kelloggii*
1. Tree found east of the Rocky Mountains 2
    2. Leaves shallowly 3-lobed at tip 3
    2. Leaves deeply lobed 6
3. Leaves distinctly hairy below 4
3. Leaves hairless below 5
    4. Leaves gray or red hairy below . . . . .southern red oak, *Quercus falcata*
    4. Leaves brown hairy below . . . . .blackjack oak, *Quercus marilandica*
5. Leaf base rounded . . . . .Arkansas oak, *Quercus arkansana*
5. Leaf base narrowly wedge-shaped . . . . .water oak, *Quercus nigra*
    6. Leaves uniformly white or red hairy below 7
    6. Leaves hairless below or hairy only in vein axils .9

7. Leaf base flat or wedge-shaped 8
7. Leaf base rounded or U-shaped . . . . .southern red oak, *Quercus falcata*
   8. Buds hairless . . . . .cherrybark oak, *Quercus pagoda*
   8. Buds gray hairy . . . . .black oak, *Quercus velutina*
9. Acorn cap saucer-shaped, covering only the basal one-quarter or less of the nut .10
9. Acorn cap cup-shaped covering more than the basal one-quarter of the nut 13
   10. Leaf sinuses extending about half the distance to the midvein . . . .
. . . . .northern red oak, *Quercus rubra*
   10. Leaf sinuses extending more than half way to midvein 11
11. Leaves 6–8 in. long; many veins ending in bristle tips . . . .
. . . . .Shumard oak, *Quercus shumardii*
11. Leaves 2–5 in. long; only major veins ending in bristle tips 12
   12. Leaves with 5–7 lobes; bottomlands . . . . .pin oak, *Quercus palustris*
   12. Leaves with 3–5 lobes; rocky slopes and hills . . . .
. . . . .Georgia oak, *Quercus georgiana*
13. Acorn cap scales fringed on rim 14
13. Acorn cap scales not fringed on rim 15
   14. Leaf base obtuse to flat; buds gray hairy . . . . . . .black oak, *Quercus velutina*
   14. Leaf base long pointed; buds red hairy . . . . .turkey oak, *Quercus laevis*
15. Leaf lobes triangular, lacking secondary lobes . . . . .Graves oak, *Quercus gravesii*
15. Leaf lobes often with secondary lobes 16
   16. Dry slopes and ridges 17
   16. Moist slopes and bottomlands 18
17. Nut about as long as wide . . . . .scarlet oak, *Quercus coccinea*
17. Nut longer than wide . . . . .northern pin oak, *Quercus ellipsoidalis*
   18. Buds hairless or slightly ciliate at tip; bottomlands along lower
   Mississippi River . . . . .Texas red oak, *Quercus texana*
   18. Buds distinctly ciliate at tip; limestone slopes and
   creeksides in Texas and Oklahoma . . . . .Buckley oak, *Quercus buckleyi*

RED OAKS, THE SECTION *ERYTHROBALANUS*

Sometimes called the Black Oak Section. Large veins of red oak leaves extend beyond the margin as bristle tips. In some species (e.g., willow oak), only the midvein extends as a terminal bristle. In others (e.g., blackjack oak and water oak), the bristles may be very short or limited to juvenile leaves. The acorns generally require two growing seasons to reach maturity, but coast live oak, Emory oak, silverleaf oak, and runner oak require only one year. Acorns germinate in the spring, and contain more tannin than white oaks, making them less desirable for consumption by wildlife and humans. The sapwood is white or cream colored, and the heartwood is pink to red-brown. The thick-walled late wood pores are rounded. The transition from early wood to late wood is gradual and the pores lack tyloses making the wood unsuitable for barrels used in storing liquids (slack cooperage). Lumber from all species in this section is generally sold under the name red oak. The bark is brown, gray, or black; tight; and develops ridges and furrows with age.

Fig. 235. Coast live oak (*Quercus agrifolia*) shoots.

Coast live oak, California live oak

Quercus agrifolia Nee (fig. 235)

Form. Medium-sized tree growing 50–75 ft in height and 2–4 ft in diameter (largest known 90 ft by 12 ft). Bole dividing near ground into several large horizontal limbs that often turn downward and rest on the ground. Crown broad, up to 150 ft wide.

Leaves. Semi-evergreen dropping as the new leaves appear; oval, oblong, or nearly round; 1–3 in. long. Margin entire to spiny toothed; rolled under; leathery; shiny and dark green above; paler and hairy or hairless below.

Fruit. Maturing in 1 year; stalkless or nearly so. Acorn 0.7–1.5 in. long; chestnut-brown; tapering to a point at the tip. Cap bowl-shaped; enclosing less than one-third of the nut; narrow overlapping scales.

Twigs. Slender; gray-brown. Buds 0.1 in. long; spherical.

Bark. Smooth on young trees. On mature trees becoming thick; nearly black; deeply furrowed with scaly ridges.

Natural History. Intolerant of shade; slow growing. Grows in valleys and on dry-mesic slopes.

Varieties. Leaves densely hairy below are classified as var. *oxyadenia*.

Hybrids. Hybridizes with California black oak and interior live oak.

Range. Found below 3,000 ft in the Coast Ranges of central and southern California; also on Santa Cruz and Santa Rosa Islands, and south into Mexico.

Arkansas oak

Quercus arkansana Sarg.

Small understory tree growing to 45 ft in height and 1 ft in diameter. Leaves 2–6 in. long; rhombic to obovate; with 2–3 shallow lobes at tip or not lobed; hairy or hairless below except for tufts in vein axils. Leaf tip broadly obtuse or rounded. Leaf base acute or heart-shaped. Acorn maturing in 2 years; 0.2–0.5 in. long. Acorn cap goblet- to saucer-shaped; hairy; covering one-quarter of the nut. Nut nearly spherical; hairy. Twigs gray, hairy. Bark black with irregular ridges separated by deep furrows. Shade tolerant, usually found in the understory. Found on well-drained sandy soil or in seepages. Hybridizes with bluejack oak and water oak. Found mostly in the Coastal Plain of southwest Georgia, northwest Florida, Alabama, southeast Louisiana, and southwest Arkansas.

Fig. 236. Scarlet oak (*Quercus coccinea*) shoots, aments, and acorns.

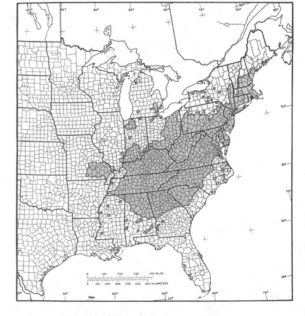

Fig. 237. Native range of scarlet oak (*Quercus coccinea*).

Buckley oak

Quercus buckleyi Nixon & Dorr

Formerly incorrectly classified as Texas red oak, or as varieties of northern red oak or Shumard oak. Small tree growing to 45 ft in height. Leaves 2–4 in. long; round to broadly elliptical; with 7–9 deep lobes extending more than half the distance to the midrib; shiny above; light green or copper-green and hairless below. Acorn maturing in 2 years; 0.5–0.7 in. long. Acorn cap cup-, goblet-, or occasionally saucer-shaped; covering less than one-half the nut. Twigs gray-brown or red-brown; buds hairy at tip. Bark smooth and gray when young; becoming black and furrowed with age. Grows on limestone-based soils on ridges, slopes, and along streams. Found in Oklahoma and Texas.

Scarlet oak

Quercus coccinea Muenchh. (fig. 236)

Form. Medium-sized mostly excurrent tree growing 60–80 ft in height and 2–3 ft in diameter (largest known 100 ft by 4 ft). Crown open; rounded; often with persistent dead branches. The base of the tree often swollen.

Leaves. Deciduous; obovate to oval; 3–7 in. long; hairless below except for tufts in vein axils; turning brilliant scarlet in autumn; deeply 5–9 lobed with wide circular or C-shaped sinuses. Lobes toothed and bristle tipped. Petioles 1–2 in. long; slender.

Fruit. Maturing in 2 years; acorn 0.6–1.0 in. long; stalkless or nearly so; red-brown; subspherical; sometimes with concentric rings near apex. Cap thick; turbanlike; enclosing about one-half of the nut; scale tips sometimes arranged in vertical rows.

Twigs. Slender; smooth; red-brown. Terminal buds 0.1–0.3 in. long; conical; red-brown; sometimes gray hairy at the tip.

Bark. Smooth and gray with black vertical fissures on young trees. With age the lower 8 ft of the bole becomes completely furrowed or warty and black; the upper portions develop wide vertical black furrows, separated by smooth vertical gray streaks.

Wood. Low to moderate commercial value, owing to the large number of knots. Defect-free lumber used for the same products as northern red oak, but most lumber used for cross ties and fuelwood.

Natural History. Intolerant of shade. Grows faster initially than many other oaks, but growth rate declines greatly with age. Reproduces from acorns that generally die back and re-sprout several times, each time growing larger; large acorn crops produced every 3–5 years. Stumps sprout at greater age and larger size than most other oaks. Wildfire, oak wilt, oak decline, and defoliation by walkingsticks cause the most damage. Generally found on middle and upper south-facing slopes on droughty infertile soils. May form pure stands in the Ozarks, but more commonly grows in mixed stands with chestnut oak, black oak, white oak, northern red oak, blackgum, sourwood, shortleaf pine, Virginia pine, pitch pine, and Table-mountain pine.

Hybrids. Hybridizes with black oak, pin oak, and bear oak.

Range. See figure 237.

Fig. 238. Northern pin oak (*Quercus ellipsoidalis*) twig, shoot with ament, leaf, and fruit.

Northern pin oak, Upland pin oak, Hill oak
Quercus ellipsoidalis E. J. Hill (fig. 238)

Some manuals classify this species as a variety of scarlet oak. Moderate-sized excurrent tree growing 50–60 ft in height and 1–2 ft in diameter (largest known 85 ft by 4 ft); often with persistent dead branches at base of crown. Leaves 3–5 in. long; 5–7 deep lobes extending more than half the distance to the midrib; hairless below, except sometimes for tufts of hairs in vein axils; in general, similar to scarlet oak but smaller. Leaf base flat or broadly wedge-shaped. Acorn maturing in 2 years; 0.5–1 in. long; short stalked or stalkless. Nut round, ellipsoidal, or bullet-shaped; sometimes striped when young. Cap cup-shaped; slightly hairy; covering one-third to one-half of the nut. Twigs red-brown; covered with light brown hairs. Bark smooth; gray or dark brown; with vertical black fissures. Wood quality generally low owing to numerous knots and the small size of mature trees; used mostly for railroad ties and fuelwood. Intolerant of shade; moderately fast-growing but short-lived. Found on droughty, infertile, sandy soils. Grows mixed with black oak, bigtooth aspen, red pine, and jack pine. Hybridizes with northern red oak and black oak. Found from Michigan and northern Ohio, west to extreme eastern North Dakota and extreme northern Missouri.

Emory oak
Quercus emoryi Torr.

Large shrub or small tree occasionally reaching 70 ft in height. Crown round with stout, drooping branches. Leaves more-or-less evergreen, dropping with the growth of new leaves; narrowly oblong to lanceolate; 1–3 in. long; entire or remotely spiny toothed; leathery; dark green above; tuft of hairs below along the base of the midrib. Leaf base heart-shaped. Acorn maturing in 1 year; 0.5–0.7 in. long; stalkless or nearly so; ellipsoid to oblong. Acorn cap brown; cup-shaped; hairy; covering about one-quarter of the nut. Nut nearly black. Twigs slender; red and hairy at first becoming dark brown and hairless. Bark thick; nearly black; deeply furrowed with scaly plates. Intolerant of shade; sprouts profusely from stumps. Found on dry foothills in pure or mixed stands. Acorns eaten by humans and animals. Hybridizes with Chisos oak and Graves oak. Found in western Texas, southern New Mexico, central and southeastern Arizona, and south into Mexico.

Fig. 239. Southern
red oak (*Quercus
falcata*) leaves.

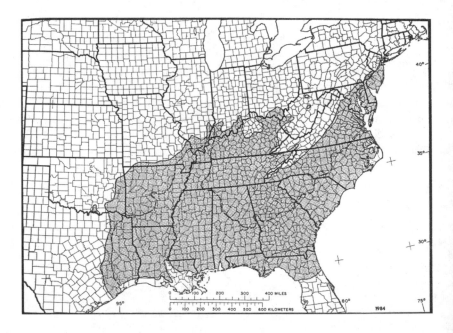

Fig. 240. Native range
of southern red oak
(*Quercus falcata*).

Southern red oak, Spanish oak

Quercus falcata Michx. (fig. 239)

Form. Medium-sized excurrent tree growing 70–80 ft in height and 2–3 ft in diameter (largest known 120 ft by 7 ft). Naturally prunes dead branches.

Leaves. Obovate to ovate; 5–10 in. long; lobing variable; juvenile trees shallowly 3-lobed at apex; adult trees deeply 3–5 lobed; terminal lobe often much longer than the laterals; lateral lobes triangular; all lobes sometimes curved; slightly to densely red-hairy below. Leaf base rounded.

Fruit. Maturing in 2 years; stalkless or nearly so; 0.3–0.5 in. long; subspherical; brown. Acorn cap saucer-shaped; slightly hairy; covering only the base of the nut. Scales tightly appressed.

Twigs. Red-brown; hairy. Terminal buds 0.2–0.3 in. long; red-brown; hairy.

Bark. Variable depending upon growth rate. On slow-growing trees, nearly black; furrowed throughout with warty ridges resembling black oak. On fast-growing trees, smooth with gray vertical streaks separated by wide black furrows resembling northern red oak.

Wood. Moderately valuable commercially. Sold as red oak. Used for the same products as northern red oak.

Natural History. Intolerant to moderately tolerant of shade; reaches maturity in 150 years. Reproduces by acorns or stump sprouts. Wildfire causes the most damage. Grows on dry to mesic sites on sandy, loamy, or clayey soils. Grows in mixed stands with many other species, especially Virginia pine, loblolly pine, shortleaf pine, longleaf pine, white oak, black oak, scarlet oak, post oak, blackjack oak, sweetgum, blackgum, sourwood, yellow-poplar, mockernut hickory, and pignut hickory.

Varieties. Treated as a separate species in this manual, cherrybark oak, *Quercus falcata* var. *pagodifolia,* is sometimes classified as a variety of southern red oak. Some manuals recognize var. *triloba,* a form having leaves with 3 shallow lobes at the tip, but this variety may only be trees with juvenile leaves.

Hybridization. Hybridizes with bear oak, turkey oak, blackjack oak, bluejack oak, willow oak, black oak, shingle oak, Shumard oak, and water oak.

Range. See figure 240. Generally found below 2,800 ft.

Graves oak

Quercus gravesii Sudw.

Small tree growing to 40 ft in height. Leaves resembling southern red oak; 2–5 in. long; ovate to narrowly elliptical; 3–5 shallow pointed lobes; light-green or copper-green and hairless or with tufts of hairs along the midrib below. Leaf base rounded to wedge-shaped. Acorn maturing in 2 years; 0.3–0.5 in. long. Acorn cap cup- or goblet-shaped; hairless; covering one-third to one-half of the nut. Nut ovoid to elliptical; sometimes hairy at tip; sometimes striped when young. Found above 3,500 ft in the mountains of southwestern Texas and adjacent Mexico.

Georgia oak

Quercus georgiana M. A. Curtis (fig. 241)

Small tree growing to 45 ft in height. Leaves elliptical to obovate; 2–6 in. long; 3–5 triangular lobes; hairless below, except for tufts of hairs in vein axils. Leaf base narrowly to broadly wedge-shaped. Acorn maturing in 2 years; 0.3–0.5 in. long. Acorn cap saucer-shaped; hairy; covering one-third of nut. Twigs dark red; hairless; terminal bud red-brown; hairless or slightly hairy. Bark scaly; gray to brown. Grows on rocky outcrops and knolls. Hybridizes with blackjack oak and possibly with water oak. Found locally in South Carolina, northern Georgia, and northern Alabama.

Fig. 241. Georgia oak (*Quercus georgiana*) leaf.

Fig. 242. Shingle oak (*Quercus imbricaria*) shoot with fruit.

Laurel oak, Darlington oak
Quercus hemisphaerica Bartr. ex Willd.

Sometimes lumped with swamp laurel oak and considered a single species; see additional comments provided under swamp laurel oak. Large excurrent tree growing 90–110 ft in height and 2–3 ft in diameter. Leaves leathery; evergreen or slowly deciduous over the winter; narrowly elliptical to oblanceolate; widest at or above the middle; 2–4 in. long; without lobes or with 1–3 shallow lobes (or large teeth) near the tip; leaves on young trees more commonly lobed; hairless above and below. Leaf tip acute to obtuse. Leaf base obtuse to rounded. Acorn maturing in 2 years; 0.4–0.7 in. long. Acorn cap saucer-shaped; hairy; covering less than one-third of the nut often only the base; scales tightly appressed. Twigs brown to red-brown; buds red-brown; hairless or slightly hairy. Bark smooth; gray to nearly black; with shallow black vertical furrows. Found on upland sites on dry sandy soils, sandhills, or occasionally in ravines. Found from North Carolina to east Texas.

Shingle oak
Quercus imbricaria Michx. (fig. 242)

Medium-sized excurrent tree growing 50–60 ft in height and 2–3 ft in diameter. Leaves narrowly elliptical to oblong; widest near the middle; 3–7 in. long; never lobed; 1 bristle at the tip; dark green and lustrous above; pale and white, hairy below with slender yellow veins. Acorn matures in 2 years; usually short stalked; 0.3–0.5 in. long; chestnut-brown; ovoid; sometimes green-striped when young. Acorn cap cup-shaped; hairy; yellow-brown to red-brown; scales tightly appressed. Twigs green-brown; slightly hairy. Terminal bud 0.2–0.3 in. long; conical; chestnut-brown to red-brown; slightly hairy; distinctly angled in cross section. Bark gray-brown; smooth when young; developing shallow furrows with age. Intolerant of shade. Grows rapidly; reaches maturity in 200–250 years. Found on moist, fertile, lower slopes and bottomlands and in ditches. Grows in mixed stands with American elm, green ash, red maple, shagbark hickory, and eastern cottonwood. Hybridizes with many red oaks, northern red oak, southern red oak, scarlet oak, bear oak, blackjack oak, black oak, pin oak, willow oak, and Shumard oak. Hybrids between shingle oak and other red oaks with lobed leaves are possibly more easily noticed owing to the great differences between parents in leaf shape. Leaves of the hybrid with black oak resemble adult leaves of southern red oak. Range from Pennsylvania to southern Iowa, and southwest to central Tennessee and northern Arkansas; disjunct populations in Michigan, Maryland, Virginia, North Carolina, Alabama, and Kansas.

Bluejack oak

Quercus incana Bartr. (fig. 243)

Small tree growing to 40 ft in height. Leaves narrowly elliptical; widest near the middle; 2–3 in. long; adult leaves without lobes and 1 bristle at the apex; juvenile leaves sometimes with 1–3 lobes and bristle tips; blue-green above; densely white hairy below. Petiole hairy. Acorn maturing in 2 years; 0.3–0.5 in. long. Acorn cap

Fig. 243. Bluejack oak (*Quercus incana*) leaves.

Fig. 244. California black oak (*Quercus kelloggii*) leaf.

Fig. 245. Native range of California black oak (*Quercus kelloggii*).

cup- to saucer-shaped; hairy; covering one-quarter of the nut. Nut ovoid; sometimes striped when young. Twigs brown to red-brown; very hairy to slightly hairy. Terminal buds light brown to red-brown; often red- or silver hairy at tip. The wood has little or no commercial value. Grows on dry, sandy Coastal Plain sites. Hybridizes with southern red oak, laurel oak, turkey oak, blackjack oak, water oak, willow oak, black oak, and possibly myrtle oak. Found from Virginia to Florida, west to Texas, and north to Arkansas and Oklahoma.

California black oak
Quercus kelloggii Newb. (fig. 244)

Nomenclature. Formerly called *Quercus californica.*

Form. Medium-sized tree growing 70–80 ft in height and 2–3 ft in diameter (largest known 125 ft by 9 ft); generally leaning. Tree bases often scared by fire. Crown large; open; rounded.

Leaves. Elliptical to obovate; 3–8 in. long; 7–11 deep lobes; sinuses rounded and narrow; lobes usually toothed; dark yellow-green above; paler and hairless or hairy below. Petiole hairless or densely hairy.

Fruit. Acorn; mature in 2 years; short stalked; 1–1.5 in. long; ellipsoidal; light chestnut-brown. Acorn cap bowl-shaped; covering one-half to two-thirds of the nut; chestnut-brown; scale tips fringelike along the rim. Nut oblong; slightly hairy at tip. Nuts often stored in holes drilled in the bark by woodpeckers.

Twigs. Slender or stout; red-brown. Terminal buds 0.2 in. long; ovoid; chestnut-brown; hairless or hairy.

Bark. Light brown and smooth on young trees. On older trees nearly black; divided by deep furrows into wide irregular ridges.

Wood. Limited commercial value even though the wood resembles northern red oak, an eastern species of very high value. Occasionally used for furniture, flooring, molding, and mulch. Prized for fuelwood, a characteristic that is nearly eliminating stands near urban areas. Forked trees and curved branches were formerly used for the keel and ribs of ships.

Natural History. Moderately tolerant of shade when young becoming intolerant with age. Reaches maturity in 300 years (extreme age 500 years). Found on sites subject to frequent fires; most reproduction from stump sprouts. Reproduction from acorns infrequent and uncertain. Acorn production quite variable by tree and location. Older trees and trees at lower elevations produce more acorns. Production very sporadic before age 75 years; some trees rarely produce acorns; other trees bear large crops every 2–3 years; still others produce acorns nearly every year. Wildfire and heart rot cause the most damage. Found only on well-drained soils with sandy or loamy texture; rarely found on clay soils. Most common on rocky slopes with thin soils. Grows in even-aged pure stands or in mixed stands with ponderosa pine, incense-cedar, tanoak, and Douglas-fir. Foliage and acorns eaten by deer; acorns eaten by woodpeckers and Native Americans.

Hybrids. Hybridizes with coast live oak and interior live oak.

Range. See figure 245. Elevation: from 200–8,000 ft.

Turkey oak, Scrub oak

Quercus laevis Walt. (fig. 246)

Formerly called *Quercus catesbaei*. Small understory tree growing 20–50 ft in height and 0.5–1 ft in diameter (largest known 80 ft by 2 ft). Often found in clumps of 2–4 stems. Crown open; irregular. Leaves 3–8 in. long; round or broadly elliptical; 3–7 deep lobes; 3-lobed leaves resemble a turkey foot and provide the common name; lustrous yellow-green above; paler and hairless below except for tufts of hairs in vein axils. Leaf lobes spreading; curved. Leaf base long, wedge-shaped. Acorn maturing in 2 years; short stalked; 1 in. long. Acorn cap goblet-shaped; light brown; covering one-half of the nut. Cap scales loose at rim; also present on the inside of the cap, the only eastern species with this characteristic. Twigs stout; red-brown; hairless or slightly hairy. Terminal buds 0.5 in. long; tapering from the base to the tip; chestnut-brown; red hairy. Bark rather thick; gray to black; warty or furrowed into small irregular ridges. Wood with little commercial value; used locally for fuelwood. Intolerant of shade. Reproduces from acorns on droughty sites only when the acorn is covered by leaf litter; internal seed dormancy only about 2 months. Sprouts vigorously from stumps. Leaves held vertically on hot summer

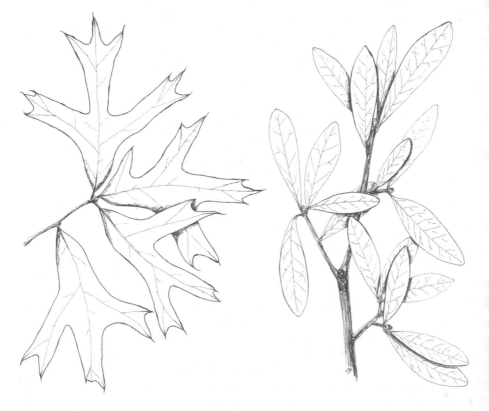

Fig. 246. Turkey oak
(*Quercus laevis*) leaves.

Fig. 247. Swamp laurel oak
(*Quercus laurifolia*) leaves.

days to reduce exposure. Generally grows on dry sandy soils of sandhills, pinelands, and old dunes. Found in small pure groves, when the commercially valuable overstory longleaf pine have been selectively harvested; otherwise found mixed with longleaf pine, blackjack oak, bluejack oak, dwarf post oak, sand live oak, sand hickory, sassafras, and persimmon. Acorns eaten by white-tailed deer, black bear, turkey, and quail. Hybridizes with southern red oak, blackjack oak, bluejack oak, scarlet oak, Shumard oak, black oak, Arkansas oak, myrtle oak, willow oak, laurel oak, and water oak. Range from southeastern Virginia to central Florida, and west to southeastern Louisiana.

Swamp laurel oak, Diamondleaf oak
Quercus laurifolia Michx. (fig. 247)

Nomenclature. The classification of this taxa has long been debated. Many authorities combine this species with laurel oak (*Quercus hemisphaerica*). When combined the correct name is also *Quercus laurifolia*, a situation that causes confusion when the classification system is not clear. Once thought to be a hybrid between willow oak and water oak, swamp laurel oak is currently regarded as a separate species by most authorities.

Form. Medium-sized excurrent tree growing 60–80 ft in height and 2–3 ft in diameter (largest known 120 ft by 8 ft). Bole often straight and clear of branches.

Leaves. Deciduous or nearly evergreen, falling in early spring just before the new leaves appear; narrowly elliptical, oblanceolate, or diamond-shaped; often widest at or near the middle; 2–4 in. long; margin entire or wavy; occasionally lobed, especially on young trees and sprouts; yellow-green above; paler and hairless below. Leaf tip bristled or rounded.

Fruit. Acorn maturing in 2 years; stalkless or nearly so; 0.3–0.5 in. long. Acorn cap saucer-shaped; tan; covering one-quarter or less of the nut; scales hairy and tightly appressed. Nut brown to nearly black; hemispherical.

Twigs. Slender; red-brown; hairless. Terminal buds 0.1–0.3 in. long; dark red-brown; angled in cross section; sometimes red hairy at tip.

Bark. Smooth and gray on young trees. With age developing shallow black fissures but retaining many gray smooth streaks.

Wood. Moderate commercial value; considered inferior in quality to most other red oaks; used mostly for pulpwood.

Natural History. Tolerant of shade; often becoming a member of the canopy by growing up through the understory. Wildfire causes the most damage. Grows in moist to wet bottomlands, often on sandy soils; does not tolerate prolonged flooding in the growing season. Found in mixed stands with loblolly pine, slash pine, sweetgum, red maple, baldcypress, overcup oak, swamp chestnut oak, Nuttall oak, and cabbage palmetto. Acorns eaten by white-tailed deer, turkey, wood ducks, quail, raccoons, and squirrels.

Hybrids. Hybridizes with southern red oak, bluejack oak, water oak, blackjack oak, willow oak, Shumard oak, and myrtle oak.

Range. Found from southeastern Virginia to southern Florida, and west to southeastern Texas. Local in southern Arkansas and southern Tennessee.

Fig. 248. Blackjack oak (*Quercus marilandica*) twig, leaves, and fruit.

Fig. 249. Myrtle oak (*Quercus myrtifolia*) leaves.

Blackjack oak

Quercus marilandica Muenchh. (fig. 248)

Small tree growing 20–30 ft in height and 0.5–1 ft in diameter (largest known 50 ft by 2 ft). Crown rounded; often contorted. Leaves deciduous but leathery; broadly obovate to obdeltate; more-or-less 3-lobed at apex; 3–6 in. long; lobes entire, toothed, or bristle tipped; dark-green and lustrous above; paler and red hairy below. Leaf base flat or heart-shaped. Acorn maturing in 2 years; stalkless or nearly so; 0.7 in. long. Acorn cap cup-shaped; covering one-half of the nut; scales red-brown and shaggy. Twigs stout; gray-brown to red-brown; hairy or very hairy. Terminal buds 0.2–0.5 in. long; angled in cross section; rusty brown hairy; conical. Bark nearly black; divided into warty or square blocks. Wood with little commercial value; used mostly for railroad ties and fuelwood. Grows on droughty sites in mixed stands with longleaf pine, shortleaf pine, Virginia pine, mockernut hickory, post oak, southern red oak, and white oak. Trees in the western portion of the range are sometimes separated as var. *ashei*, having leaves 2–3 in. long and gray hairy below. Hybridizes with Buckley oak, southern red oak, northern red oak, pin oak, turkey oak, Georgia oak, bear oak, shingle oak, bluejack oak, myrtle oak, willow oak, water oak, swamp laurel oak, and laurel oak. Found from southern New York to southern Iowa, and south to northern Florida and central Texas. Local in southern Michigan.

Myrtle oak

Quercus myrtifolia Willd. (fig. 249)

Large dense shrub or small tree growing to 30 ft in height. Leaves nearly evergreen; old leaves dropping when new leaves form in the spring; elliptical to obovate; 1–2 in. long; margin entire; sometimes cupped downward; hairless above and below. Acorn maturing in 2 years; 0.3–0.5 in. long. Acorn cap saucer- to goblet-shaped; covering one-third of the nut; slightly hairy. Twigs red-brown; some thorn-like; usually hairy. Buds brown; hairy at tip. Bark smooth and gray; shallow fissures developing near the base of larger trees. Wood has no commercial value. Found on old sand dunes, sandy ridges, and sandy plains. Grows in mixed stands with sand pine, Chapman oak, and tree lyonia. Found from southern South Carolina to southern Florida, and west to southern Mississippi. Common in the Big Scrub in central Florida.

Fig. 250. Water oak
(*Quercus nigra*) adult
and juvenile leaves.

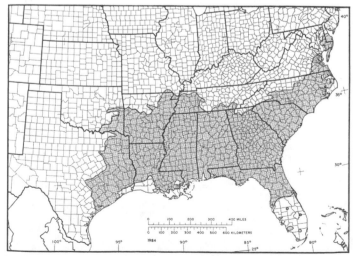

Fig. 251.
Native range
of water oak
(*Quercus nigra*).

Water oak

Quercus nigra L. (fig. 250)

Form. Medium-sized tree growing 70–90 ft in height and 2–3 ft in diameter (largest known 125 ft by 6 ft).

Leaves. Mostly deciduous but sometimes retaining a few green leaves until late winter; spatulate or obovate; shallowly 3-lobed at tip on adult trees; often lacking bristles; 2–6 in. long; dull green above; paler and hairless below except for tufts of hairs in vein axils. On juveniles and sprouts, the leaves are deeply 3- to 7-lobed.

Fruit. Maturing in 2 years; stalkless or nearly so; acorn 0.3–0.5 in. long; brown to nearly black; subspherical. Acorn cap saucer-shaped; covering less than one-quarter of the nut; scales appressed and hairy.

Twigs. Slender; red-brown; hairless. Terminal buds 0.1–0.2 in. long; angled in cross section; sharp; red-brown; hairy especially at the tip.

Bark. Rather thin; gray-black; smooth when young. With age developing shallow furrows that separate wide smooth ridges.

Wood. Moderately valuable commercially. Uses similar to northern red oak but used more for pulpwood.

Natural History. Intolerant of shade. Grows rapidly; reproduces well from acorns or stump sprouts; large acorn crops occur every 2–3 years. Planted in southern bottomlands on a large scale for pulpwood. Wildfire causes the most damage. Originally found in silty clay or loamy soils on moist bottomlands sites; will not tolerate prolonged flooding. Current fire suppression policies have allowed the species to become widely established on uplands. Grows naturally in bottomlands in mixed stands with willow oak, swamp laurel oak, Nuttall oak, swamp chestnut oak, sweetgum, American elm, pecan, green ash, American hornbeam, sugarberry, loblolly pine, slash pine, and spruce pine. Commonly planted as a shade tree in the Southeast.

Varieties. A form with narrow pointed leaf bases has been named var. *tridentifera*.

Hybrids. Hybridizes with southern red oak, turkey oak, bluejack oak, willow oak, blackjack oak, black oak, northern red oak, pin oak, Shumard oak, Arkansas oak, Georgia oak, laurel oak, swamp laurel oak, myrtle oak, and Texas red oak.

Range. See figure 251.

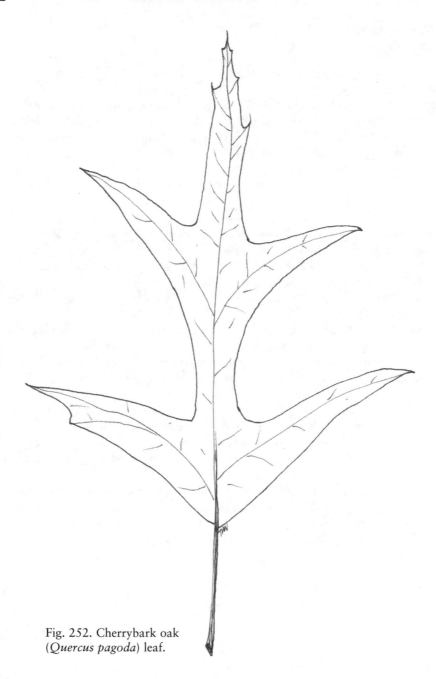

Fig. 252. Cherrybark oak
(*Quercus pagoda*) leaf.

Cherrybark oak
Quercus pagoda Raf. (fig. 252)

Nomenclature. Formerly called *Quercus pagodifolia*. Often considered to be a variety of southern red oak, *Quercus falcata* var. *pagodifolia*. Formerly spelled *pagodaefolia*.

Form. Tall excurrent tree growing 90–130 ft in height and 3–4 ft in diameter (largest known 150 ft by 9 ft). Lower bole straight and clear of branches.

Leaves. Ovate, elliptical, or obovate; 4–9 in. long; 5–9 triangular lobes; lobes generally straight and the terminal lobe generally the same length as the laterals; lustrous and hairless above; pale and hairy below. Leaf tip acute. Leaf base generally wedge-shaped sometimes rounded. Leaves turned with the petiole at the top resemble Oriental pagodas hence the scientific name.

Fruit. Acorn maturing in 2 years; 0.3–0.7 in. long. Cap saucer-shaped to cup-shaped; covering one-third of the nut; hairy. Nut nearly round; brown but sometimes green striped when young; slightly hairy. Identical to southern red oak.

Twigs. Yellow-brown; hairy. Terminal buds red-brown; angled in cross section; hairy.

Bark. When young, gray; smooth; slightly glossy. With age, remaining gray or turning nearly black; developing shallow black furrows that separate smooth gray streaks in the upper bole; forming short narrow ridges throughout the lower bole; some ridges becoming loose and slightly scaly. Resembling black cherry but not as scaly and never red-brown.

Wood. Extremely valuable commercially; produces the highest quality red oak lumber in our region. Sold as red oak. Used for the same products as northern red oak.

Natural History. Intolerant of shade; generally found only in the upper canopy. Fast growing particularly when competing vegetation is controlled. Reproduces very well from acorns in large open areas or old fields; direct seeding reasonably successful. Unlike most other oaks reproduction from stump sprouts is not reliable. Growth of planted seedlings less than natural seedlings. Wildfire and windthrow cause the most damage. Found in well-drained first bottoms and terraces on silt loams and loam soils; not common on clay soils. Absent from waterlogged soils or sites with prolonged flooding in the growing seasons. Found in mixed stands with swamp chestnut oak, Shumard oak, willow oak, water oak, white ash, shagbark hickory, sweetgum, yellow-poplar, bitternut hickory, American beech, and American elm. Acorns eaten by squirrels, turkeys, blue jays, wood ducks, woodpeckers, grackles, raccoons, and white-tailed deer.

Hybrids. Hybridizes with southern red oak and willow oak.

Range. Found in the Coastal Plain from southeastern Virginia to northern Florida, west to east Texas, and north in the Mississippi River valley to southwestern Indiana.

Fig. 253. Pin oak (*Quercus palustris*) shoot with fruit.

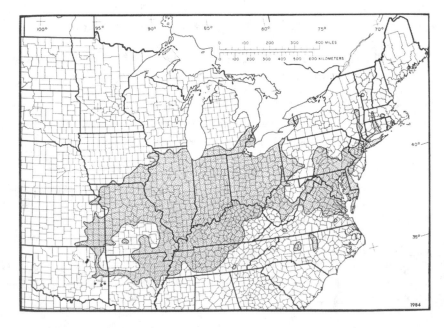

Fig. 254. Native range of pin oak (*Quercus palustris*).

Pin oak

Quercus palustris Muenchh. (fig. 253)

Form. Medium-sized excurrent tree growing 80–90 ft in height and 2–3 ft in diameter (largest known 120 ft by 5 ft). Crown pyramidal; upper branches ascending and lower branches drooping; dead branches retained.

Leaves. Elliptical; 2–5 in. long; 5–7 deep lobes; bright green and lustrous above; paler and hairless below, except for tufts of hairs in vein axils. Sinuses rounded; extending well over half the distance to the midvein.

Fruit. Acorn maturing in 2 years; stalkless or nearly so; 0.5 in. long. Acorn cap saucer-shaped; covering less than one-quarter of the nut; hairless or hairy; scales tightly appressed. Nut hemispherical; light brown; often green striped when young.

Twigs. Slender; smooth; red-brown; many short pinlike branches hence the common name. Terminal buds 0.1–0.2 in. long; red-brown; shiny; sharp pointed; angled in cross section; slightly hairy.

Bark. Thin; gray-brown; smooth when young and in the upper bole of older trees; with age developing shallow fissures that separate tight narrow ridges.

Wood. Moderate commercial value; numerous knots limit the value. Used for fuelwood and some of the same products as northern red oak.

Natural History. Intolerant of shade. Fast growing but short-lived; reaches maturity in 90–100 years (extreme age 140 years). Reproduces well from acorns or stump sprouts. Wildfire causes the most damage. Grows on clay soils in poorly drained bottomlands or glacial till flats. Very tolerant of flooding in winter; seedlings tolerate complete submersion; moderately tolerant of flooding in summer. Very commonly planted as a shade tree in the South. Acorns eaten by mallards, wood ducks, blue jays, woodpeckers, squirrels, turkeys, and white-tailed deer.

Hybrids. Hybridizes with scarlet oak, shingle oak, water oak, willow oak, blackjack oak, Shumard oak, black oak, and northern red oak.

Range. See figure 254.

Fig. 255. Willow oak
(*Quercus phellos*)
shoot with fruit.

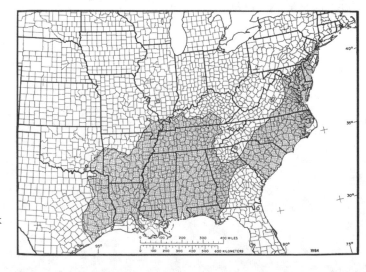

Fig. 256.
Native
range of
willow oak
(*Quercus
phellos*).

Willow oak

Quercus phellos L. (fig. 255)

Form. Medium-sized excurrent tree growing 80–100 ft in height and 2–4 ft in diameter (largest known 130 ft by 7 ft). Crown dense; rounded; dead branches often retained.

Leaves. Linear; the sides nearly parallel; never lobed, including juvenile plants; 2–5 in. long; margin entire or wavy; bright green above; paler and hairless or hairy below. Leaf tip acute with bristle tip.

Fruit. Maturing in 2 years; stalkless or nearly so; acorn 0.5 in. long; green-brown to yellow-brown; hemispherical. Acorn cap thin; hairy; covering less than one-third of the nut; scales red-brown. Identical to water oak.

Twigs. Slender; red-brown; hairless. Terminal buds 0.1–0.2 in. long; sharp pointed; chestnut-brown; hairless.

Bark. Gray to nearly black; smooth and shiny on young trees; broken by shallow furrows into low narrow ridges on older trees.

Wood. Commercially valuable; currently used mostly for pulpwood.

Natural History. Moderately tolerant of shade. Very fast growing; moderately long-lived reaches maturity in 150–200 years. Reproduces following disturbance from advance regeneration, saplings established earlier from acorns. Large acorn crops produced nearly every year. Sprouts well from small stumps. Planted in southern bottomlands. Owing to similar site requirements, industrial foresters do not distinguish between water oak and willow oak, calling them both water willow. Wildfire causes the most damage. Found originally on a wide variety of moderately well-drained bottomland sites and soils; intolerant of prolonged soil saturation or flooding in the growing season. Best development on deep silty or loamy soils. Current policies of fire suppression allow willow oak to become established also on upland sites. Grows in mixed stands with water oak, Shumard oak, swamp chestnut oak, cherrybark oak, sweetgum, sugarberry, green ash, red maple, and American hornbeam. Commonly planted shade tree in the South. Acorns eaten by ducks, woodpeckers, blue jays, grackles, turkeys, squirrels, and white-tailed deer.

Hybrids. Hybrids between willow oak and other red oaks with lobed leaves are easily noticed because of the great difference in leaf shape. Hybridizes with water oak, black oak, northern red oak, southern red oak, Shumard oak, bear oak, blackjack oak, and pin oak.

Range. See figure 256.

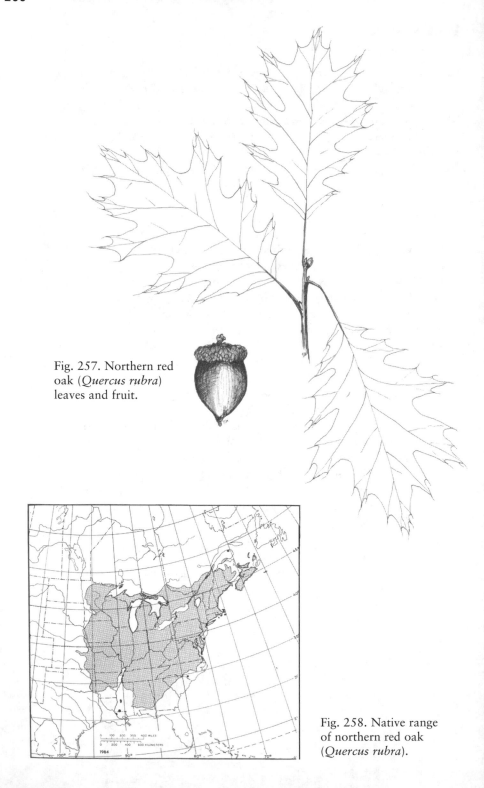

Fig. 257. Northern red oak (*Quercus rubra*) leaves and fruit.

Fig. 258. Native range of northern red oak (*Quercus rubra*).

Northern red oak

Quercus rubra L. (fig. 257)

Nomenclature. Formerly called *Quercus borealis* or *Quercus maxima.*

Form. Medium-sized mostly excurrent tree growing 80–90 ft in height and 2–4 ft in diameter (largest known 150 ft by 6 ft).

Leaves. Elliptical, ovate, or obovate; 5–9 in. long; 7–11 lobes; dull green above; paler and hairless below except for tufts of hairs in vein axils. Lobes more-or-less triangular pointing upward; toothed. Sinuses shallow; U-shaped; extending halfway to midrib. Leaf base widely wedge-shaped.

Fruit. Maturing in 2 years; stalkless or nearly so; acorn 0.5–1 in. long. Acorn cap saucer- to cup-shaped; brown; covering a variable amount of the nut from less than one-quarter to one-half; hairless. Nut oblong to round; red-brown; slightly hairy.

Twigs. Red-brown; lustrous; hairless. Terminal buds 0.2–0.3 in. long; circular in cross section; lustrous; red-brown; hairless or slightly hairy.

Bark. On young trees smooth; green-brown or gray on young trees. Older trees gray to black; developing shallow black furrows that separate long, wide, smooth streaks. Some streaks extend nearly to ground level.

Wood. Very valuable commercially producing high-quality lumber, second only to cherrybark oak. Sold as red oak. The most valuable wood-producing species in the southern Appalachians. Used for many products: furniture, cabinets, flooring, molding, barrels, railroad ties, and fuelwood. Not as decay resistant as white oak, owing to the lack of tyloses.

Natural History. Moderately tolerant of shade. Moderate to fast growing; reaches maturity in 150–200 years (extreme age 300 years). Regenerates from advance regeneration by sprouting from small stumps because seedlings never grow fast enough to compete with sprouts. Acorns must be covered with leaf litter to survive and become established. Acorn production variable by tree; some trees regularly produce large crops and other trees almost never produce acorns. Wildfire, oak wilt, and gypsy moth cause the most damage. Found on a wide variety of soil types but always on moist soils. Most common on concave-shaped middle and lower slopes with northern or eastern aspects. Occasionally found in pure stands, especially above 4,000 ft in the southern Appalachians; more commonly found mixed with eastern white pine, eastern hemlock, black oak, white oak, chestnut oak, southern red oak, red maple, sugar maple, American beech, yellow birch, basswood, black cherry, white ash, trembling aspen, and bigtooth aspen.

Hybrids. Hybridizes with pin oak, northern pin oak, willow oak, black oak, Shumard oak, shingle oak, bear oak, and blackjack oak.

Range. See figure 258.

Shumard oak

Quercus shumardii Buckl. (fig. 259)

Form. Moderate to large excurrent tree growing 90–100 ft in height and 3–4 ft in diameter (largest known 180 ft by 8 ft). Bole straight and clear of branches. Crown open; widespreading.

Leaves. Obovate to oblong; 6–8 in. long; 5–9 lobes; dark green above; paler and hairless below except for tufts of hairs in vein axils. Lobes many toothed with more bristles than other red oaks; upper lobes becoming wider toward the tip and sometimes overlapping the tip of the lobe below. Sinuses extend more than halfway to midvein. Petiole slender. Often confused for northern red oak or scarlet oak.

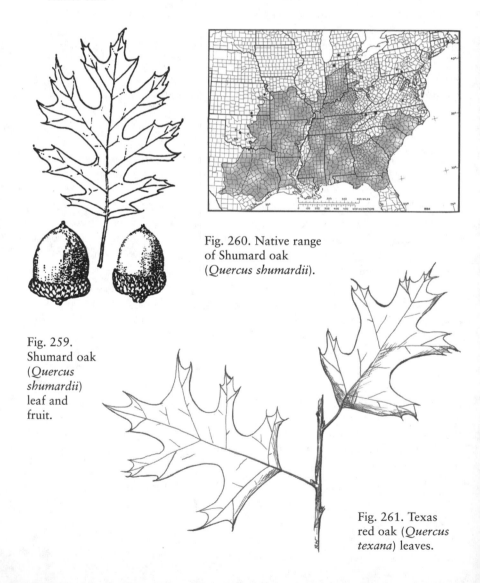

Fig. 260. Native range of Shumard oak (*Quercus shumardii*).

Fig. 259. Shumard oak (*Quercus shumardii*) leaf and fruit.

Fig. 261. Texas red oak (*Quercus texana*) leaves.

Fruit. Acorn maturing in 2 years; stalkless or nearly so; 0.7–1.2 in. long; silver-green turning red-brown; oblong-ovoid; often confused with northern red oak. Acorn cap saucer-shaped; covering less than one-quarter of the nut; brown hairy; scales appressed.

Twigs. Yellow-brown; hairless. Terminal buds 0.2 in. long; straw colored; often angled in cross section; hairless or hairy.

Bark. Smooth and brown-green on young trees. With age, turning gray-brown or gray; developing shallow black furrows that separate wide, smooth, vertical streaks. Mature bark similar to northern red oak.

Wood. Commercially valuable; sold as red oak. Many trees provide high-quality wood. Used for the same products as northern red oak.

Natural History. Intolerant of shade; requires open areas to become established. May suppress competing vegetation by allelopathy. Good seed crops produced every 2–3 years. Found on well-drained loam soils associated with bottomland terraces. Sometimes found on basic soils. Grows in mixed stands with cherry-bark oak, swamp chestnut oak, willow oak, white ash, green ash, American beech, southern sugar maple, American elm, sugarberry, yellow-poplar, loblolly pine, and spruce pine.

Hybrids. Hybridizes with southern red oak, water oak, willow oak, laurel oak, swamp laurel oak, shingle oak, blackjack oak, turkey oak, northern red oak, and black oak.

Varieties. Some manuals classify Texas red oak as a variety of Shumard oak, *Quercus shumardii* var. *texana*.

Range. See figure 260.

Texas red oak, Nuttall oak

Quercus texana Buckley (fig. 261)

The correct classification of Texas red oak has long puzzled authorities. Sometimes thought to be a form of pin oak or Shumard oak or a hybrid between Shumard oak and water oak. Additional study is needed. Formerly called *Quercus nuttallii*. The name *Quercus texana* has long been incorrectly used for Buckley oak. Moderate-sized tree growing to 80 ft (largest known 120 ft by 5 ft). Leaves elliptical or obovate; 3–7 in. long; 5–9 deep lobes; sinuses extend more than half the distance to the midvein; hairless below except for tufts of yellow hairs in vein axils. Lobes wider at tip than base. Leaf base broadly wedge-shaped to almost flat. Acorn maturing in 2 years; 0.5–1 in. long; stalked. Acorn cap goblet-shaped; constricted at base; covering one-third to one-half of nut. Nut ovoid to oblong; red-brown sometimes green-striped; hairless or slightly hairy. Twigs red-brown to gray; hairless. Terminal buds gray to gray-brown; hairless or slightly hairy at tip. Bark dark brown; shallow fissures separate flat ridges. Moderately tolerant of shade; fast growing; reproduces well from acorns. Found in poorly drained bottomlands growing with American elm, red maple, green ash, overcup oak, water oak, and willow oak. Found in the Mississippi River valley from southern Illinois to Louisiana; also in southern Alabama and east Texas.

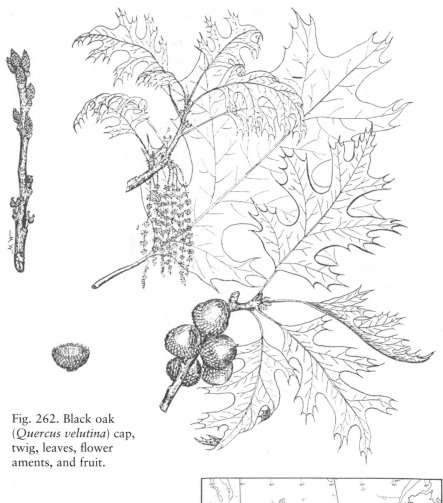

Fig. 262. Black oak (*Quercus velutina*) cap, twig, leaves, flower aments, and fruit.

Fig. 263. Native range of black oak (*Quercus velutina*).

Black oak, Quercitron

Quercus velutina Lam. (fig. 262)

Form. Medium-sized tree excurrent to somewhat deliquescent growing 60–80 ft in height and 2–3 ft in diameter (largest known 150 ft by 8 ft). Crown irregular.

Leaves. Obovate to oblong; 5–9 in. long; 5–7 lobes; lustrous and dark green above; paler or coppery and hairless or hairy below. Amount of hair and depth of sinuses variable; leaves on juvenile trees and sprouts are hairy below with shallow sinuses. Leaves on adult trees are hairless below with deep sinuses extending more than half the distance to the midvein.

Fruit. Acorn; maturing in 2 years; stalkless or nearly so; 0.5–0.7 in. long. Acorn cap cup-shaped; covering about half of the nut. Cap scales gray-brown; dull; free at tips providing a fringe along the rim. Nut red-brown; often green-striped when young; ovoid.

Twigs. Red-brown; hairless. Terminal buds 0.2–0.5 in. long; angled in cross section; gray woolly.

Bark. Smooth and gray-black when young. With age becoming nearly black and furrowed throughout with narrow ridges; larger trees lack smooth streaks. Compared to other red oaks the inner bark is brighter orange-yellow and much more bitter to the taste.

Wood. Commercially valuable; sold as red oak; some trees provide low-quality lumber while others provide high-quality lumber. Wood use similar to northern red oak.

Natural History. Moderately tolerant of shade. Moderate growth rate; reaches maturity in 150–175 years. Generally becomes a member of the canopy by sprouting from the stump of small trees already established in the understory. Seedlings grow too slowly to compete with sprouts of this and other species. Large acorn crops produced every 2–3 years. Wildfire, oak wilt, and gypsy moth provide the most damage. Found on a wide variety of sites including all aspects. Most abundant in droughty infertile soil on middle- and upper-slopes and ridges. Grows only in mixed stands with white oak, post oak, northern red oak, scarlet oak, southern red oak, chestnut oak, blackjack oak, pitch pine, Virginia pine, shortleaf pine, loblolly pine, eastern white pine, yellow-poplar, pignut hickory, mockernut hickory, white ash, black cherry, and sassafras. Acorns eaten by squirrels, mice, turkeys, and white-tailed deer.

Hybrids. Hybridizes with scarlet oak, southern red oak, upland pin oak, shingle oak, bluejack oak, blackjack oak, pin oak, Shumard oak, northern red oak, pin oak, and water oak.

Range. See figure 263. Elevations: to 4,000 ft.

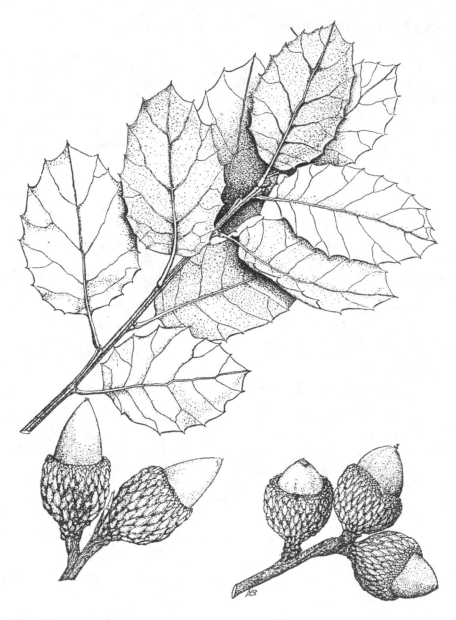

Fig. 264. Interior live
oak (*Quercus wislizeni*)
shoot and fruit.

Interior live oak, Sierra live oak

Quercus wislizeni A. DC. (fig. 264)

This taxon is sometimes split into 2 species, *Quercus wislizeni* and *Quercus parvula*; the latter species with larger leaves and abruptly tapering nuts. Commonly a shrub but in selected areas becoming a medium-sized tree growing 60–80 ft in height and 1–2 ft in diameter (largest known 90 ft by 7 ft). Crown round; wide with large spreading branches. Leaves evergreen persisting 2 years; oblong to broadly elliptical; 1–3 in. long (mostly about 1.5 in); leathery; lustrous dark green and hairless above; paler and hairless below. Margin entire on adult trees, but with spiny teeth that look like American holly on young trees. Acorn maturing in 2 years; stalkless or short stalked; 1–1.5 in. long. Acorn cap cup-shaped; covering less than half of the nut; slightly hairy; scale tips loose. Nut chestnut-brown; narrowly oblong; tapering to the tip; hairless or slightly hairy. Twigs slender; dark brown; hairless or slightly hairy. Terminal buds chestnut brown to red-brown; 0.1–0.2 in. long; ovoid; hairless or slightly hairy at tip. Bark thick; nearly black; deeply furrowed with wide scaly ridges. Intolerant of shade; slow growing. Found in dry river bottoms and on slopes with fertile but droughty soil. Grows in pure stands or mixed with Digger pine. Shrubby plants having oval leaves with entire or coarsely toothed margins are classified as var. *frutescens*. Hybridizes with coast live oak and California black oak. Found from northern to southern California mostly in the Coast Ranges and foothills of the Sierra Nevada; also south into Baja California.

WHITE OAKS, THE SECTION *LEUCOBALANUS*

White oak leaves generally lack bristle tips on the margin. The acorns always mature in a single growing season, and they generally germinate either while still on the mother tree or shortly after falling. (Some white oaks in cold climates germinate in the spring.) The wood is light or dark brown with thin-walled more-or-less angular late wood pores. The transition from early wood to late wood is abrupt, and the wood pores become naturally plugged with tyloses. This latter property makes the wood watertight and suitable for making barrels used to store liquids (tight cooperage). The lumber from all species in this section is generally sold under the name white oak. The acorns contain less tannin than the acorns of other sections making them superior food for wildlife and humans. Even so, raw acorns are bitter contrary to the description of sweet found in many references. Native Americans and settlers normally soaked the acorns in water to remove the tannin before grinding them into flour. The bark is often ash-gray and somewhat scaly or flaky.

Fig. 265. White oak (*Quercus alba*) leaves, flower aments, and fruit.

Fig. 266. Native range of white oak (*Quercus alba*).

White oak

Quercus alba L. (fig. 265)

Form. Medium-sized tree growing 80–100 ft in height and 3–4 ft in diameter (largest known 150 ft by 8 ft). Crown rounded with large branches.

Leaves. Deciduous; oblong to obovate; 5–9 in. long; 7–9 lobes; lobes either broad with shallow sinuses or narrow with deep sinuses extending nearly to the midrib; hairless above and below. Tip of lobes rounded.

Fruit. Acorn; maturing in 1 year; stalkless or short stalked; 0.5–0.7 in. long; light brown; oblong; enclosed for about one-quarter of length in bowllike cap with warty scales.

Twigs. Rather stout; red-brown. Terminal buds 0.1–0.3 in. long; ovoid to spherical; obtuse; red-brown; nearly hairless.

Bark. Light ash-gray; narrow scaly ridges separated by shallow furrows; becoming somewhat shaggy along the middle and upper stem.

Wood. The most commercially valuable white oak. Sapwood nearly white to light brown. Heartwood light to dark brown; straight grained; heavy to very heavy; durable. Used for railroad ties, tight and slack cooperage, fence posts, mine timbers, furniture (especially desks, tables, and chairs), flooring, doors, interior trim, wainscoting, cabinets, coffins, handles, sled runners, pulpwood, and fuel-wood.

Natural History. Moderately tolerant of shade; able to withstand suppression for over 90 years. Moderately slow growing but long-lived; reaches maturity in 250–300 years (extreme age 600 years). Reproduces well in shade from acorns; good seed crops irregular occurring every 4–10 years; germination occurs short-ly after release in the fall, but shoot growth delayed until the following spring; seeds dispersed by gravity, skipping down slope, and rodents. Trees up to 12 in. in diameter sprout vigorously from stumps. Gypsy moth, oak wilt, and decay induced by fire scars cause the most damage. Found on a wide variety of soils except on the shallowest dry soils and wet bottomlands; most abundant on south- and west-facing slopes, but development is best on north- and east-facing slopes. The abundance of white oak is due largely to its adaptability and ability to survive suppression and outlive many competitors. Grows in small pure groves or mixed with numerous species especially northern red oak, black oak, scarlet oak, post oak, yellow-poplar, white ash, basswood, sweetgum, blackgum, American beech, sugar maple, red maple, shortleaf pine, Virginia pine, loblolly pine, eastern white pine, pignut hickory, and mockernut hickory. Possibly the single most important wildlife food species; acorns eaten by small mammals, blue jays, woodpeckers, turkeys, quail, wood ducks, deer, bear, and raccoons. Foliage browsed by white-tailed deer.

Hybrids. Hybridizes most commonly with chestnut oak and swamp chestnut oak but also with swamp white oak, bur oak, chinkapin oak, and post oak.

Range. See figure 266.

Arizona oak, Arizona white oak

Quercus arizonica Sarg.

Small to moderate-sized tree growing to 60 ft in height and 3 ft in diameter. Branches often horizontal and twisted. Leaves essentially evergreen falling when the

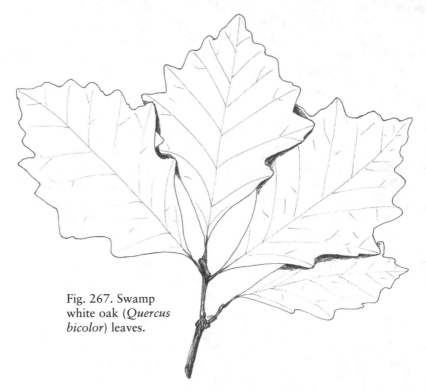

Fig. 267. Swamp white oak (*Quercus bicolor*) leaves.

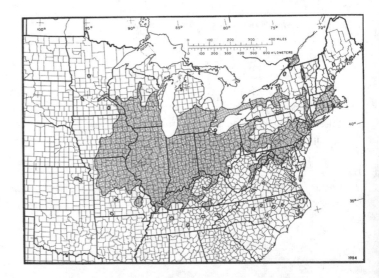

Fig. 268. Native range of swamp white oak (*Quercus bicolor*).

new leaves appear; leathery; elliptical to obovate; 2–4 in. long; often slightly cupped; blue-green and shiny above; slightly to very curly hairy below. Margin entire or coarsely toothed near the tip. Acorn 0.3–0.5 in. long; light brown; cap cup-shaped; covering about half the nut; cap scales hairy. Twigs yellow with feltlike hairs. Bark gray with scaly ridges. Found in pinyon woodlands and arroyos in Arizona, New Mexico, and west Texas.

Bastard white oak

Quercus austrina Small

Moderate-sized tree growing to 75 ft in height. Leaves deciduous; elliptical to obovate; 3–5 in. long; hairy below at first becoming hairless except on the main veins. Margin irregularly shallowly lobed. Acorn ovoid; 0.7 in. long; short stalked; cap cup- to goblet-shaped covering nearly half the nut. Bark similar to white oak. Often confused with bluff oak, but becoming hairless on the undersurfaces of leaves. Local on moist soil in the Coastal Plain and lower Piedmont from North Carolina to central Florida, and west to Mississippi.

Swamp white oak

Quercus bicolor Willd. (fig. 267)

Form. Medium-sized tree growing 60–70 ft in height and 2–3 ft in diameter (largest known 100 ft by 7 ft). Crown irregular; open.

Leaves. Deciduous; obovate to oblong obovate; 5–7 in. long; 2–4 in. wide; irregular margins with large glandular teeth or shallow lobes; white and slightly to very hairy below.

Fruit. Acorn; 0.7–1.5 in. long; often paired; ovoid; light brown; enclosed about one-third by cap; light brown. Cap slightly fringed along rim; hairy. Acorn stalk 1.2–3.2 in. long (among eastern oaks only swamp white oak, live oak, and English oak have long stalks).

Twigs. Slender to rather stout; dark brown. Terminal buds 0.1 in. long; orange-brown; spherical; nearly hairless.

Bark. Young trees have curly papery scales. On old trees thick; ash-gray to brown; deeply furrowed into short or long scaly ridges.

Wood. Uses similar to white oak but less valuable commercially.

Natural History. Moderately tolerant of shade. Moderately fast growing; reaches maturity in 200–250 years (extreme age 350 years). Regeneration similar to white oak, but good seed crops occur more frequently every 3–5 years. Found on imperfectly to poorly drained sites with either mineral or organic soils. Grows as scattered individuals in mixed stands with sweetgum, pin oak, red maple, silver maple, American elm, black ash, green ash, sycamore, and black willow.

Hybrids. Hybridizes with white oak, overcup oak, bur oak, chinkapin oak, live oak, and chestnut oak.

Range. See figure 268.

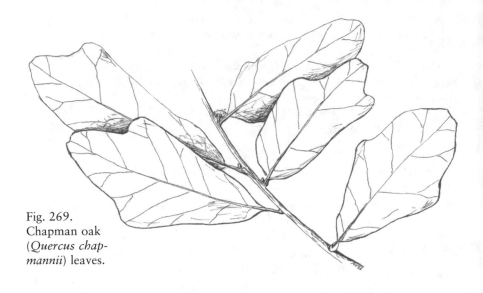

Fig. 269.
Chapman oak
(*Quercus chap-
mannii*) leaves.

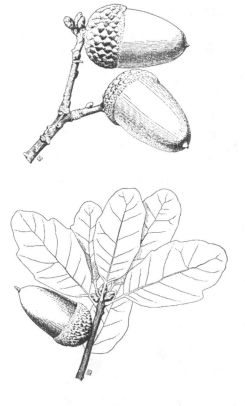

Fig. 270. Blue oak (*Quercus
douglasii*) leaves and fruit.

Fig. 271. Native range of blue
oak (*Quercus douglasii*).

Chapman oak
Quercus chapmannii Sarg. (fig. 269)

Small tree growing to 30 ft in height. Leaves semi-evergreen falling slowly over the winter; obovate to oblong; yellow glands below especially prominent in spring. Margin entire or with 1–4 shallow lobes mostly above the middle; slightly revolute. Petiole 0.1–0.2 in. long. Acorn 0.5–0.7 in. long; cap cup-shaped covering about half the nut; cap gray and slightly hairy. Bark brown to gray; scaly. Grows on dry sandy soils. Found in coastal regions of South Carolina and Georgia, and south to central Florida. Abundant in the Big Scrub of central Florida.

Blue oak
Quercus douglasii Hook. & Arn. (fig. 270)

Form. Shrub to medium-sized tree growing 50–80 ft in height and 2–3 ft in diameter. Crown dense; irregular. Small branches common on lower bole.

Leaves. Deciduous; oblong to obovate; 2–5 in. long; blue-green above; lighter and hairy below. Margin entire, coarse toothed, or shallowly and irregularly 4–5 lobed especially near the tip; teeth and lobes rounded with callous tips.

Fruit. Stalkless or nearly so; nut 0.7–1.2 in. long; chestnut-brown; ellipsoidal. Cap shallow; hairy.

Twigs. Stout; red-brown. Buds 0.1–0.2 in. long; bright red.

Bark. Thin; gray; scaly.

Wood. Little or no commercial value. Used locally for fence posts and fuelwood.

Natural History. Intolerant of shade. Growth slow; reaches maturity in 200–250 years (extreme age 400 years). Formerly reproduced well from seed but current reproduction sparse probably owing to overconsumption by stock animals; seeds must be covered by soil or leaf litter to survive; good seed crops produced every 2–3 years. Reproduces poorly from sprouts. Found on dry foothills with shallow rocky soils and abundant surface rock; absent from poorly drained clay soils. Grows in pure savannalike stands or mixed with Digger pine, ponderosa pine, knobcone pine, or Coulter pine. Basic biology little known. Nuts eaten by Native Americans, acorn woodpeckers, scrub jays, quail, squirrels, and stock animals.

Hybrids. Hybridizes with Oregon white oak and valley oak.

Range. See figure 271.

Texas live oak
Quercus fusiformis Small

Sometimes considered a variety of live oak, *Quercus virginiana* var. *fusiformis*. Large shrubs or moderate-sized trees growing to 70 ft in height. Leaves very similar to live oak; differing by leaf tips acute and leaf bases more commonly flat or heart-shaped. Found in Oklahoma and central and southwestern Texas, and south into Mexico.

Gambel oak

Quercus gambelii Nutt.

Shrub or small tree growing 25–35 ft in height and 1 ft in diameter (largest known 60 ft by 5 ft). Sometimes found in clumps or colonies. Crown open with

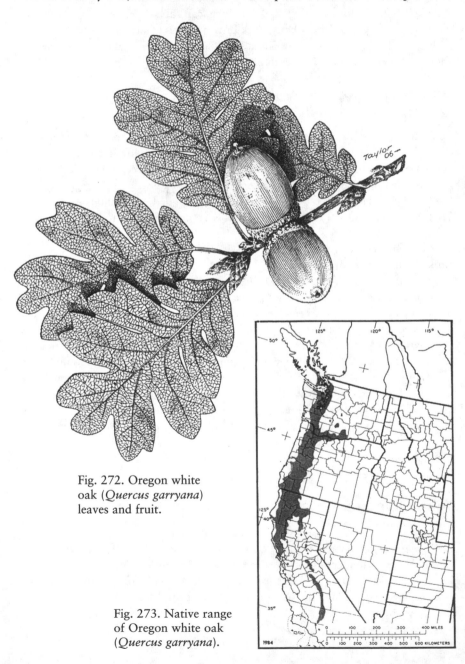

Fig. 272. Oregon white oak (*Quercus garryana*) leaves and fruit.

Fig. 273. Native range of Oregon white oak (*Quercus garryana*).

thick erect branches. Leaves deciduous; oblong to obovate; 2–7 in. long; lobes 5–8 extending more than half the distance to the midvein; shiny above; light green, hairy, and sometimes white-waxy below. Tips of lobes rounded. Acorn stalkless or nearly so; 0.6–0.8 in. long; brown; ovoid. Cap cup-shaped; hairy; enclosing less than half the nut. Twigs orange-brown to red-brown; hairy or hairless. Buds 0.1–0.2 in. long; brown; slightly hairy. Bark gray; scaly. Wood with little or no commercial value; used locally for fuelwood. Grows on dry foothills and canyon walls. Hybridizes with various shrubby oaks forming hybrid swarms that have traditionally been called the *Quercus* x *undulata* complex. Found in extreme southern Wyoming to Utah, and south to west Texas and southeastern Arizona; also in northern Mexico. The only common deciduous oak at low elevations in the Rocky Mountains.

Oregon white oak, White oak

Quercus garryana Dougl. ex Hook. (fig. 272)

Form. Moderate-sized tree growing 50–90 ft in height and 2–3 ft in diameter (largest known 120 ft by 8 ft). Crown broad; with age, developing twisted and gnarled branches. Shrubby at high elevations.

Leaves. Deciduous; oblong to obovate; 3–6 in. long. Lobes 5–9; rounded; extending more than half way to the midvein; largest lobes with sublobes; thick and leathery; dark green and slightly sandpapery above; pale and hairy below.

Fruit. Stalkless or nearly so; nut 1–1.2 in. long; ovoid; rounded at tip; hairless or hairy. Cap saucer- to cup-shaped covering less than one-fourth of the nut; yellow-brown to red-brown; hairy.

Twigs. Stout; hairy and orange at first becoming red–brown and hairless. Buds 0.3–0.5 in. long; densely hairy.

Bark. Light gray; scaly or divided into small ridges; shaggy on old trees.

Wood. Little or no commercial value even though the wood is often good quality. Used locally for fence posts and fuelwood, and occasionally for flooring, furniture, interior trim, railroad ties, ships, and barrels.

Natural History. Moderately tolerant of shade. Growth rate slow; reaches maturity in 250–300 years (extreme age 500 years). Reproduces well from seeds; basic biology little known; acorns dispersed by gravity and animals; must be covered by leaves or soil to become established. Recovers and reproduces well from sprouts after wildfire. Current fire suppression policies allow Oregon white oak stands to be replaced by bigleaf maple and Douglas-fir. Taproot long. Found along rivers but most common on sites too dry or exposed for other species. Grows in pure stands or mixed with Douglas-fir, Port Orford-cedar, tanoak, Pacific madrone, ponderosa pine, knobcone pine, blue oak, and California black oak. Acorns formerly eaten by Native Americans and collected by ranchers for hog feed.

Varieties. Two varieties are recognized; both clonal shrubs of higher elevations: Var. *semota* with leaves short hairy below and var. *breweri* with longer hairs below.

Hybrids. Hybridizes with blue oak and valley oak.

Range. See figure 273. Elevation: sea level to 2,600 ft.

Sand live oak

Quercus geminata Small

Sometimes considered a variety of live oak, *Quercus virginiana* var. *geminata*, a classification with considerable merit. Small tree growing to 40 ft in height and 1 ft in diameter. Often leaning and contorted with an irregular crown. Leaves evergreen; leathery; elliptical; not lobed except for juveniles and sprouts; shiny and dark green above; white with wooly hairs below. Leaves similar to live oak but curled and cupped. Fruit, twigs, and bark the same as live oak. Grows in deep sands usually on drier sites compared to live oak. Found throughout Florida and in the coastal regions from South Carolina to Mississippi.

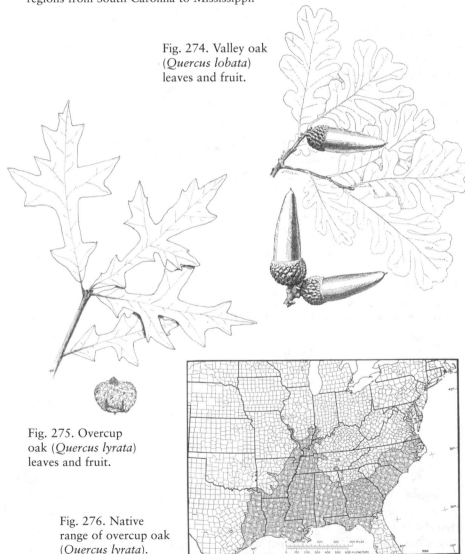

Fig. 274. Valley oak (*Quercus lobata*) leaves and fruit.

Fig. 275. Overcup oak (*Quercus lyrata*) leaves and fruit.

Fig. 276. Native range of overcup oak (*Quercus lyrata*).

Valley oak, California white oak
Quercus lobata Nee (fig. 274)

Form. Moderately large excurrent to deliquescent tree growing 80–100 ft in height and 3–5 ft in diameter (largest known 125 ft by 9 ft). Bole single; massive; sometimes dividing near the ground into large spreading limbs.

Leaves. Deciduous; elliptical to obovate; 2–4 in. long; 7–11 rounded lobes extending more than half the distance to the midvein; dark green and slightly sandpapery above; light green or white hairy below.

Fruit. Stalkless or nearly so; acorn 1–2 in. long; elongate-conic tapering to a point; green becoming brown. Cap cup-shaped; enclosing one-quarter of nut; hairy; scales slightly fringed along rim.

Twigs. Slender; yellow-gray to red-brown; hairy. Terminal buds 0.2 in. long; yellow-brown; ovoid; very hairy.

Bark. Thick; light gray; scaly or divided into square plates.

Wood. Little or no commercial value.

Natural History. Found in valleys, along streams, and on lower slopes on a variety of soils ranging from fertile and moist to infertile and dry.

Range. Found from northern to southern California; also on Santa Cruz and Santa Catalina Islands.

Overcup oak
Quercus lyrata Walt. (fig. 275)

Form. Medium-sized excurrent tree growing 70–90 ft in height and 2–3 ft in diameter (largest known 100 ft by 5 ft). Crown open with large branches.

Leaves. Deciduous; oblong to obovate; 5–8 in. long; 4–8 irregular pointed lobes; uppermost lobes often reduced to large teeth; hairless or white-hairy below. Base tapering to a point.

Fruit. Acorn; stalkless or nearly so; 0.5–1 in. long; chestnut-brown; subspherical. Cap gray; nearly enclosing the entire nut; nut released when cap splits open.

Twigs. Rather stout; gray-brown; usually hairless. Buds 0.1 in. long; rounded; hairy.

Bark. Light gray; developing rectangular plates separated by deep furrows.

Wood. Little or no commercial value because it has the reputation of being difficult to season and having ring-shake (growth rings that separate in standing trees). Produces the lowest quality white oak lumber.

Natural History. Moderately tolerant of shade. Moderately slow growth rate reaches a maximum age of 400 years. Reproduces well from acorns, which germinate in the spring owing to winter flooding; good seed crops produced every 3–4 years. Our wettest-site oak; found on poorly drained alluvial soils in first bottoms and along the edges of sloughs. Tolerant of late spring flooding, which often kills competing trees. Typically grows in small pure groves or mixed with water hickory, American elm, laurel oak, green ash, red maple, and willow oak. Acorns eaten by wildlife, but less valuable than other white oaks.

Hybrids. Hybridizes with white oak, bluff oak, swamp white oak, bur oak, post oak, and live oak.

Range. See figure 276.

Fig. 277. Bur oak (*Quercus macrocarpa*) leaves.

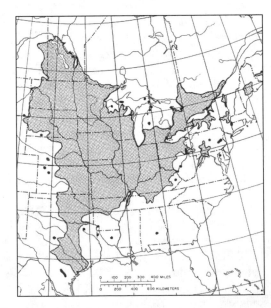

Fig. 278. Native range of bur oak (*Quercus macrocarpa*).

Bur oak

Quercus macrocarpa Michx. (fig. 277)

Form. Medium-sized tree growing 60–80 ft in height and 2–3 ft in diameter (largest known 170 ft by 7 ft). Trees on dry ridges may only grow to 25 ft in height. Crown rounded with large branches.

Leaves. Deciduous; oblong to obovate; 6–8 in. long; 5–9 rounded lobes; the upper sinuses often very shallow and the middle sinuses very deep forming a fanlike top; dark green and shiny above; light green or green-white and hairy below. Leaves in shade often with shallow sinuses only.

Fruit. Stalkless or short stalked; acorn; 0.6–2 in. long; ellipsoidal. Cap gray hairy; with curly fringed margin.

Twigs. Stout; yellow-brown to gray; often with corky wings. Buds 0.2–0.4 in. long; hairless.

Bark. Thick; gray-brown; long flat ridges separated by deep furrows.

Wood. Similar to white oak.

Natural History. Moderately tolerant of shade. Growth rate slow; reaches maturity in 200–300 years (extreme age 400 years). Good seed crops produced every 2–3 years; acorns germinate in the fall but in the spring in northern trees. Small trees reproduce well from stump sprouts. Seedlings quickly develop large root system with long taproot. Oak lacebug, oak wilt, and Strumella canker cause the most damage; resistant to air pollution. Grows on a wide variety of soils and sites ranging from moist bottomlands to dry hills; often on limestone soils. Found in oak savannas in the transition from forest to prairie. Grows with sweetgum, red maple, American elm, green ash, white oak, shagbark hickory, chestnut oak, scarlet oak, post oak, and pignut hickory. Used for shelterbelt plantings. Acorns eaten by red squirrels, wood ducks, white-tailed deer, and ground squirrels.

Hybrids. Hybridizes frequently with white oak forming Bebb oak (*Quercus* x *bebbiana*); also hybridizes with swamp white oak, Gambel oak, overcup oak, swamp chestnut oak, post oak, chinkapin oak, and live oak.

Range. See figure 278. Extends farther west than other Eastern oaks.

Dwarf post oak, Sand post oak

Quercus margaretta (Ashe) Ashe

Trees in the Cross Timbers area of east Texas are intermediate between dwarf post oak and post oak, and sometimes called Drummond post oak (*Quercus drummondii*). Sometimes made a variety of post oak (*Quercus stellata* var. *margaretta*). Small tree growing to 35 ft in height. Generally forming small colonies from root sprouts. Leaves elliptical to obovate; 2–4 in. long; moderately to deeply lobed; middle lobes somewhat square forming a lopsided cross; velvet hairy below; overall similar to post oak but smaller and middle lobes not as square. Acorn cap cup-shaped; gray hairy. Twigs hairless. Bark gray-white; scaly. Grows on dry sandy or gravelly soils; often in oak scrub or pine savanna. Found from southeastern Virginia to western Missouri, and south to central Florida and central Texas. Local in eastern Massachusetts.

Fig. 279. Swamp chestnut oak (*Quercus michauxii*) shoot.

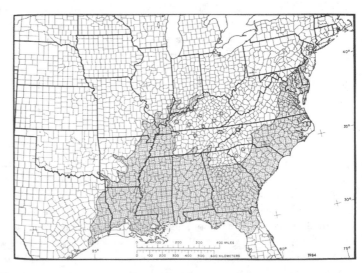

Fig. 280. Native range of swamp chestnut oak (*Quercus michauxii*).

Swamp chestnut oak, Cow oak, Basket oak

Quercus michauxii Nutt. (fig. 279)

Form. Medium-sized tree growing 60–80 ft in height and 2–3 ft in diameter (largest known 120 ft by 10 ft).

Leaves. Deciduous; obovate or elliptical; 5–8 in. long; 3–4 in. wide; coarse rounded or pointed teeth; teeth often gland tipped; light green and velvet hairy below; lateral veins straight with 15–20 pairs.

Fruit. Acorn; stalkless or nearly so; 1–1.5 in. long; ovoid; brown. Cap cup-shaped; encloses less than half of the nut. Cap scales wedge-shaped; not fused together.

Twigs. Brown to red-brown; slightly hairy or hairless. Buds 0.2 in. long; ovoid; acute; red; hairy or hairless.

Bark. Ash-gray to white-gray; scaly or irregularly furrowed with scaly small ridges.

Wood. Similar to white oak.

Natural History. Intolerant of shade. Good seed crops produced every 3–5 years with few acorns produced in other years; germinates in fall. Sprouts somewhat from stumps and roots. Roots may produce allelopathic substances. Grows in well-drained bottomlands on loamy to silty clay soils. Found mixed with loblolly pine, red maple, cherrybark oak, laurel oak, sweetgum, white ash, green ash, and American elm. Acorn eaten by white-tailed deer, feral hogs, and squirrels.

Hybrids. Hybridizes with overcup oak, bur oak, and especially with white oak forming *Quercus* x *beadlei*.

Range. See figure 280.

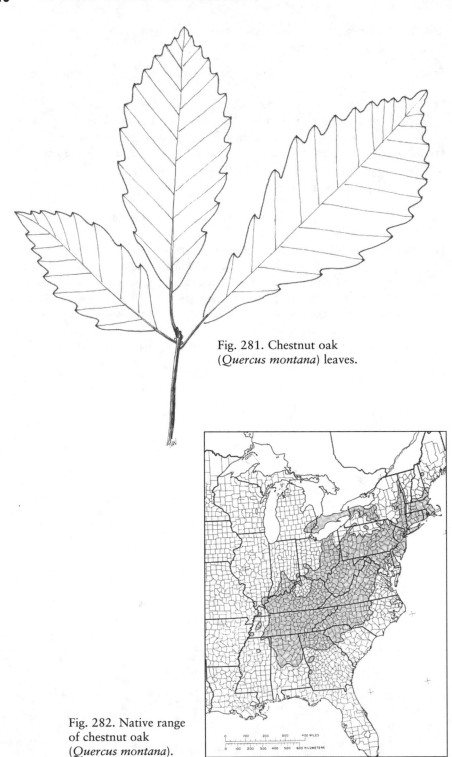

Fig. 281. Chestnut oak (*Quercus montana*) leaves.

Fig. 282. Native range of chestnut oak (*Quercus montana*).

Chestnut oak, Rock oak, Rock chestnut oak

Quercus montana Willd. (fig. 281)

Nomenclature. The appropriate scientific name for this species has long been disputed. Many manuals use *Quercus prinus*, a name with priority that is also sometimes used for swamp chestnut oak. The dispute arises because no agreement exists on which species Linnaeus was naming, since the correct identity of his type specimen is not clear. To avoid confusion, some manuals have completely abandoned the name *Quercus prinus*, the practice followed here.

Form. Medium-sized tree growing 60–80 ft in height and 2–3 ft in diameter (largest known 100 ft by 6 ft). Often with 2–4 stems, growing in a clump. Crown broad; open.

Leaves. Deciduous; elliptical to obovate; 4–9 in. long; 1–3 in. wide; teeth coarse and pointed or rounded; yellow-green above; paler and hairy below.

Fruit. Acorn; stalk short; 1–1.5 in. long; oval to ovoid; chestnut-brown. Cap bowl-shaped; thin; encloses less than half the nut; scales fused.

Twigs. Stout; orange to red-brown. Buds 0.2–0.5 in. long; conical; acute; chestnut-brown; soft hairy; ciliate.

Bark. Thick; dark gray-brown to black; elongated flat ridges, separated by deep furrows. Formerly used as a source of tannin.

Wood. Similar to white oak.

Natural History. Moderately tolerant of shade. Growth rate slow; reaches maturity in 200–250 years (extreme age 400 years). Acorns mature 2–5 weeks earlier than other oaks; produces fewer acorns than other oaks; large nut crops occur every 4–5 years; survival increased when covered by leaf litter. Sprouts prolifically from stumps; most stands develop from sprouts. Wildfire and gypsy moth cause the most damage. Most abundant on infertile dry ridges and south- or west-facing upper slopes; occasionally found in well-drained soil along streams. Grows in pure stands or mixed with white oak, scarlet oak, black oak, blackgum, sourwood, pitch pine, Table-mountain pine, and Virginia pine. Acorns eaten by white-tailed deer, turkeys, black bears, wild boars, and small mammals.

Hybrids. Hybridizes with swamp white oak and post oak, but most often with white oak.

Range. See figure 282.

Fig. 283. Chinkapin oak (*Quercus muhlenbergii*) leaves.

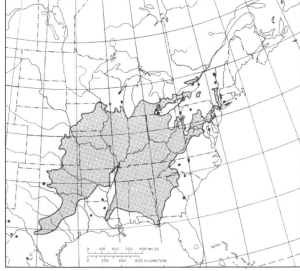

Fig. 284. Native range of chinkapin oak (*Quercus muhlenbergii*).

Chinkapin oak

Quercus muhlenbergii Engelm. (fig. 283)

Nomenclature. The epithet is sometimes spelled *muehlenbergii*.

Form. Medium-sized excurrent tree, growing 60–80 ft in height and 2–3 ft in diameter (largest known 160 ft by 4 ft). Crown narrow; rounded with ascending branches.

Leaves. Deciduous; obovate to oblong-lanceolate; 4–7 in. long; yellow-green above; paler and hairy below. Teeth coarse; pointed; gland tipped.

Fruit. Stalkless or nearly so; acorn 0.5–0.7 in. long; chestnut-brown to black; ovoid. Cap hairy; scales small; encloses about half of the nut.

Twigs. Slender; orange to gray-brown; hairless. Buds 0.1 in. long; orange-brown; acute; conical.

Bark. Thin; ash-gray; scaly or flaky.

Wood. Similar to white oak.

Natural History. Intolerant of shade. Details on seed production not known. Sprouts readily from stumps. Generally found on weakly acid to basic soils developed from limestone. Often on dry sites. Almost never found in pure stands; grows scattered among white oak, northern red oak, black oak, pignut hickory, white ash, sugar maple, sourwood, and eastern redcedar.

Varieties. Intergrades with a shrubby form, dwarf chinkapin oak (var. *prinoides*). Dwarf chinkapin oak is sometimes made a separate species, *Quercus prinoides*.

Hybrids. Hybridizes with white oak, swamp white oak, bur oak, and Gambel oak.

Range. See figure 284.

Oglethorpe oak

Quercus oglethorpensis Duncan

Medium-sized tree growing to 70 ft in height. Leaves linear to oblanceolate; 3–6 in. long; dark green and sandpapery above; yellow-green and hairy below. Margin entire; not lobed but becoming wavy at the tip of leaves on sprouts. Nut ovoid; 0.4 in. long; gray-brown; cap tan hairy; constricted at base; covering less than half of the nut. Twigs red-brown; slightly hairy or hairless. Bark light gray; scaly. Little known. Possibly affected by chestnut blight when stressed. Found in widely scattered but locally abundant populations along streams and in bottomlands in South Carolina, Georgia, Mississippi, and Louisiana. First discovered in 1940; a species whose conservation is problematic.

Pungent oak, Sandpaper oak

Quercus pungens Liebm. (fig. 285)

Large shrub to moderate-sized tree. Leaves evergreen to semi-evergreen; elliptical to oblong; 0.5–1.5 in. long; stiff; leathery; 5–8 pairs of lateral veins; glossy and sandpapery above; densely hairy, sandpapery, or nearly hairless below; margin

Fig. 285. Pungent oak
(*Quercus pungens*) leaves.

Fig. 286. Bluff oak
(*Quercus sinuata*) leaves.

coarsely toothed or spiny. Acorn 0.5 in. long; ovoid. Acorn cap cup-shaped covering about one-quarter of the nut. Cap scales red-brown; dense gray hairy. Twigs gray; hairy becoming hairless. Bark tan; papery. Hybridizes extensively with Vasey oak in west Texas making separation almost impossible. Found on dry slopes in pinyon-juniper woodlands and desert in west Texas, New Mexico, Arizona, and Mexico.

Netleaf oak
Quercus rugosa Nee

Large shrub to moderate-sized tree. Leaves evergreen; broadly obovate to nearly round; 3–4 in. long; stiff and leathery; often cupped; shiny and dark green above; white waxy to densely brown hairy below; 8–10 pairs of lateral veins; secondary veins raised. Leaf base heart-shaped. Leaf margin with spiny teeth near tip; edge rolled under (revolute). Acorn to 1 in. long. Cap saucer- to cup-shaped; covering half the nut. Cap scales loose; slightly hairy. Found above 6,500 ft in west Texas, southern New Mexico, Arizona, and south to Guatemala.

Swamp post oak, Delta post oak
Quercus similis Ashe

Sometimes classified as a variety of post oak, *Quercus stellata* var. *paludosa*. Moderate-sized tree growing to 80 ft in height. Leaves deciduous; obovate; 3–5 in. long; 2–3 small rounded lobes on each side; not cross-shaped; shiny and dark green above; gray and slightly hairy below. Acorn 0.5–0.7 in. long. Cap scales loose; fine gray hairs. Twigs gray; slightly hairy. Bark brown; scaly. Grows in fine sandy loam soils on terraces along rivers. Grows with cherrybark oak, water oak, willow oak, swamp chestnut oak, sweetgum, American elm, and loblolly pine. Found from Mississippi to east Texas, and north to Arkansas.

Bluff oak, Bastard oak
Quercus sinuata Walt. (fig. 286)

The correct scientific name for this species has been debated, since the original plant specimens on which the name is based have been lost. Many manuals use *Quercus durandii*, a name published over 70 years later. Moderate-sized tree growing 50–70 ft in height and 1–2 ft in diameter. Leaves deciduous; oblanceolate to oblong; 2–5 in. long; dull green and hairless above; small star-shaped hairs below. Margin with irregular widely spaced teeth, shallow lobes, or wavy. Tip rounded or slightly 3-lobed. Acorn 0.5 in. long; ovoid to oblong. Acorn cap saucer-shaped; covering less than one-quarter of the nut. Twigs slightly hairy or hairless. Bark gray; flaky and peeling. Grows in moist soil along rivers and in bottomlands. A shrubby clonal form found on dry limestone soils in Oklahoma and Texas with shorter leaves is separated as var. *breviloba*. Found from southern North Carolina to central Florida, and west to east Texas.

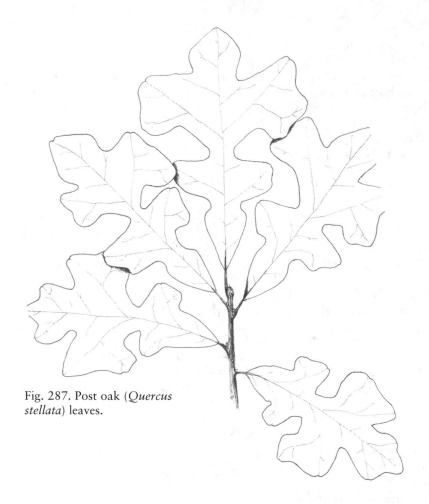

Fig. 287. Post oak (*Quercus stellata*) leaves.

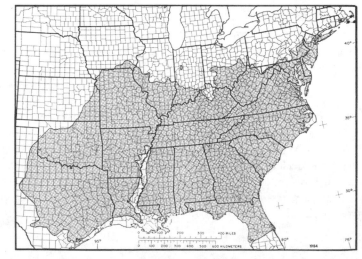

Fig. 288. Native range of post oak (*Quercus stellata*).

Post oak

Quercus stellata Wangenh. (fig. 287)

Form. Small to medium-sized tree growing 50–70 ft in height and 1–2 ft in diameter (largest known 100 ft by 4 ft). Crown rounded; branches large.

Leaves. Deciduous; oblong to obovate; 4–6 in. long; shape variable but typically deeply 5-lobed; middle lobes opposite forming a cross; thick; shiny and dark green above; star-shaped hairs below.

Fruit. Acorn; stalkless or nearly so; 0.5–0.7 in. long; oval; often borne in clusters. Acorn cap bowl-shaped; gray; encloses about half of the nut.

Twigs. Stout; more-or-less hairy. Buds 0.1–0.2 in. long; hairy; chestnut-brown.

Bark. Gray-brown to gray; divided into narrow ridges, separated by furrows; tight not becoming flaky or shaggy.

Wood. Similar to white oak but usually lower quality.

Natural History. Intolerant of shade. Growth rate slower than nearly all other associates. Acorn production variable by tree; some trees rarely produce acorns; good seed crops occur every 2–3 years. Sprouts well from stumps. Seedlings have large taproots. Generally found on infertile dry soils on ridges and upper slopes facing south or west. Grows with white oak, black oak, scarlet oak, Virginia pine, blackgum, sourwood, and eastern redcedar. Acorns eaten by turkeys, white-tailed deer, and small mammals.

Varieties. Two taxa treated as separate species in this manual are sometimes classified as varieties of post oak: dwarf post oak (*Quercus stellata* var. *margaretta*) and swamp post oak (*Quercus stellata* var. *paludosa*).

Hybrids. Hybridizes with many species, white oak, swamp white oak, bluff oak, overcup oak, bur oak, chestnut oak, and live oak.

Range. See figure 288. Elevation: to 3,000 ft in the southern Appalachians.

Fig. 289. Live oak (*Quercus virginiana*) adult and juvenile leaves.

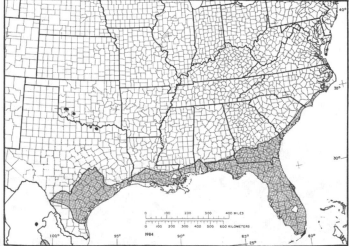

Fig. 290. Native range of live oak (*Quercus virginiana*).

Live oak, Southern live oak

Quercus virginiana Mill. (fig. 289)

Form. Moderate-sized deliquescent tree growing 50–70 ft in height and 2–3 ft in diameter. Open-grown trees dividing near the ground into several large horizontal branches that curve downward to the ground and turn upward again. In Georgia and Florida, branches often covered with Spanish moss (*Tillandsia usneoides*) and ballmoss (*Tillandsia recurvata*). Crown dense; rounded; open-grown trees with a span of up to 170 ft.

Leaves. Essentially evergreen; the old leaves dropping when the new leaves appear; oval to oblong; 2–3 in. long; flat; dark green above; dense white woolly below. Margin rolled under (revolute); generally lacking teeth but spiny toothed on second flushes, sprouts, and young trees. Petiole 0.1–0.2 in. long; hairy.

Fruit. Acorn; 0.7–1 in. long; oblong; dark brown to black; stalk 1–2 in. long. Cap goblet-shaped; gray; covering less than half the nut; scales gray hairy.

Twigs. Light brown or gray; hairy or hairless. Buds 0.1 in. long; ovoid; chestnut brown; slightly hairy.

Bark. Black; tight; rough throughout with small ridges and shallow furrows; lacking smooth streaks even on branches.

Wood. Current commercial value low. Sapwood white-brown to gray-brown. Heartwood brown; very heavy and hard; sometimes sinking in water. Differs from other oaks in being semi-ring-porous. Formerly prized for the structural members of sailing ships.

Natural History. Moderately tolerant of shade. Reproduces well from acorns; large nut crops produced most years; seedlings may form underground tubers, but details on seedling establishment and growth not known. Also reproduces from stumps and root sprouts. Wildfire causes the most damage; fire suppression policies have increased the abundance of live oak. Live oak decline causes damage in Texas. Nearly always found on sandy soil; resistant to salt spray and high soil-salinity levels. Typical of barrier islands and coastal dunes. Grows with laurel oak, water oak, southern magnolia, sweetgum, waxmyrtle, yaupon, American holly, cabbage palmetto, and saw-palmetto. Traditional ornamental shade tree in the South. Underground tubers formerly eaten like potatoes.

Varieties. Three other live oaks treated here as separate species are sometimes classified as varieties of live oak: Texas live oak (var. *fusiformis*), sand live oak (var. *geminata*), and dwarf live oak (var. *minima*). Dwarf live oak is a shrub.

Hybrids. Hybridizes with post oak, bur oak, and overcup oak.

Range. See figure 290.

INTERMEDIATE OAKS, THE SECTION *PROTOBALANUS*

Sometimes called golden oaks. Leaves of intermediate oaks are evergreen, whitened below, and never lobed. The leaf margin is entire or spiny toothed particularly in juveniles. Like white oaks, the bark is scaly, but the acorns require two years to mature. Scales of the acorn cap are covered with thick hairs that allow only the tips of each scale to protrude. Five species of intermediate oaks are known in the world, one in Mexico and four in our region. Of these four species, only canyon live oak, listed below, is tree-sized.

Canyon live oak

Quercus chrysolepis Liebm. (fig. 291)

Form. Shrub to medium-sized tree growing 60–80 ft in height and 1–2 ft in diameter (largest known 100 ft by 12 ft). Crown large and spreading; usually dividing above ground into large horizontal branches. May form dense thickets on dry slopes.

Leaves. Evergreen; persisting 3–4 years; oblong-ovate to elliptic; 1–4 in. long; mostly entire on old trees; coarsely spiny toothed and looking like American holly on young trees, but both forms may be present; leathery; slightly cupped along the midvein; 12 or more pairs of lateral veins; yellow-green with small starlike hairs above; covered with blue-white wax and starlike hairs on new leaves but nearly hairless on old leaves below. Margin rolled under (revolute).

Fruit. Acorn; maturing in 2 years; stalkless or nearly so; 0.5–2 in. long; chestnut-brown; ellipsoidal to ovate. Acorn cap saucer-shaped; covering less than one-quarter of the nut; rim often corky; scales covered with golden, woolly hairs. Native Americans considered the nuts to be poisonous.

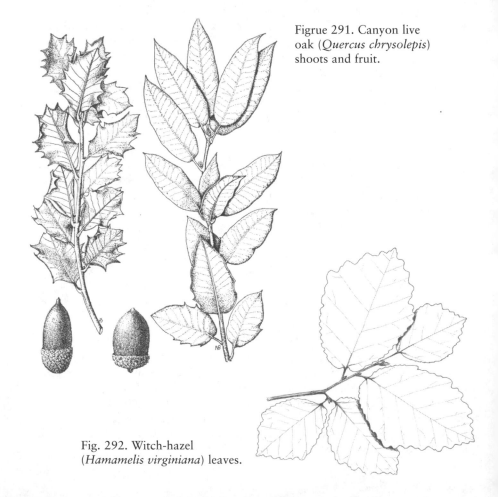

Figrue 291. Canyon live oak (*Quercus chrysolepis*) shoots and fruit.

Fig. 292. Witch-hazel (*Hamamelis virginiana*) leaves.

Twigs. Slender; yellow-brown; woolly hairy on new growth. Terminal buds 0.1 in. long; chestnut-brown; slightly hairy.

Bark. Gray-brown tinged with red; smooth when young becoming scaly on old trees.

Wood. Little or no current commercial value. Formerly used for wagon wheels, axles, and splitting mauls.

Natural History. Tolerant of shade when young; long-lived. Found on hot dry canyon sides and bottoms.

Varieties. Canyon live oak is extremely variable in leaf and fruit, and several varieties have been named over the years. Recent study suggests that recognizing varieties is not warranted.

Range. Found from southwestern Oregon to southern California, and south into Baja California. Local in western Nevada and Arizona.

WITCH-HAZEL FAMILY: HAMAMELIDACEAE

This family contains about 110 species in 30 genera in the world. They occur in temperate and subtropical areas mostly in east Asia but also in eastern North America, Mexico, Australia, and Africa. Our area contains 5 species in 3 genera (*Fothergilla, Hamamelis, Liquidambar*), but only 2 species are tree-sized. Economically the family provides gum-resin (*Altingia* and *Liquidambar*), liniment (*Hamamelis*), and wood products (*Altingia* and *Liquidambar*).

The Hamamelidaceae contains trees or shrubs often with starlike hairs. The leaves are simple, alternate, and deciduous or evergreen with stipules. The flowers are usually small, bisexual or unisexual, with the perianth reduced or absent. They are pollinated by wind or insects. The ovary is usually half-inferior, and it develops into a capsule fruit. The wood is diffuse-porous.

WITCH-HAZEL: THE GENUS *HAMAMELIS*.

Worldwide this genus contains six species found in eastern Asia, Mexico, and eastern North America. Our region contains two species, witch-hazel, a small tree, and a shrub, *Hamamelis vernalis*.

Witch-hazel
Hamamelis virginiana L. (fig. 292)

Large shrub or rarely a small tree growing to 30 ft in height. Often found growing in clumps 3 to many stems. Leaves simple; alternate; deciduous; 3–7 in. long; broadly elliptical; margin coarsely scalloped. Flowers yellow (rarely red); appearing in the autumn after the leaves have fallen; pollinated by bumblebees. Petals 4; yellow; linear. Fruit a capsule; 2–valved; seeds ejected. Buds tan; hairy; nearly naked. Bark smooth; gray. Moderately tolerant of shade. Sprouts from the stump. Usually found on dry-mesic to mesic sites in well-drained bottomlands, coves, and side slopes. Leaves and twigs provide witch-hazel liniment. Forked twigs formerly used for divining rods to locate underground aquifers. Found from Nova Scotia to eastern Iowa, and south to central Florida and southeastern Texas.

SWEETGUM: THE GENUS *LIQUIDAMBAR*

Worldwide this genus contains three species, two in Asia and one in our region.

Sweetgum, Redgum

Liquidambar styraciflua L. (fig. 293)

Form. Large excurrent tree growing 80–120 ft in height and 2–4 ft in diameter (largest known 200 ft by 7 ft). Bole quickly sheds dead branches.

Leaves. Deciduous; palmately 5–7 lobed looking star-shaped; 4–7 in. long; slightly aromatic; hairless below except for tufts of hairs in vein axils. Margin serrate.

Flowers. Unisexual; borne in heads; each tree contains both sexes (monoecious); appearing with the new leaves in the spring. Male flowers in heads in terminal

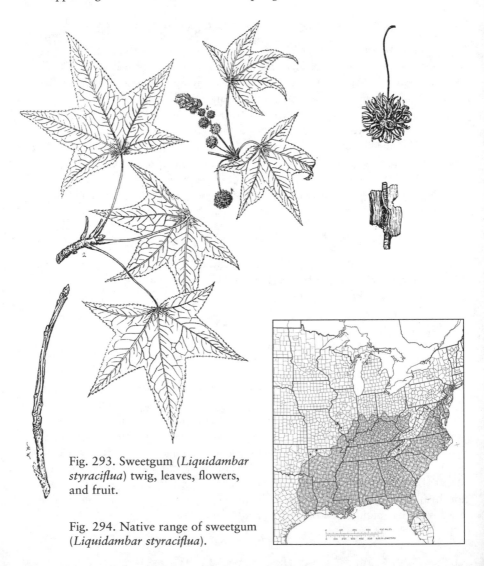

Fig. 293. Sweetgum (*Liquidambar styraciflua*) twig, leaves, flowers, and fruit.

Fig. 294. Native range of sweetgum (*Liquidambar styraciflua*).

racemes; 2–3 in. long; calyx and corolla lacking. Female flowers in solitary long-stalked heads; calyx minute. Wind pollinated.

Fruit. Beaked capsules borne in a head commonly called a sweetgum ball; head 1–1.5 in. wide. Maturing in 1 year but persisting through the winter. Seeds 0.3 in. long; short wing terminal; 2 per capsule.

Twigs. Slender to stout; round or slightly angled; sometimes developing corky wings on young trees and sprouts; green to red-brown. Pith angled and homogeneous. Terminal bud present; 0.2–0.5 in. long; scaly.

Bark. Gray-brown; furrowed with narrow and somewhat scaly ridges. Storax gum used in drugs and soaps obtained from the inner bark.

Wood. Commercially very valuable. Sapwood white, often tinged with pink and discolored with blue stain. Heartwood red-brown to gray; often with dark streaks; moderately heavy; grain interlocked and will not split easily; gum canals sometimes present. Currently used mostly for pulpwood, hardwood ply-wood for furniture, and the interior plys of pine plywood; sometimes used for paneling, fruit baskets, cigar boxes, barrels, mine props, railroad ties, and cabinets. High grades marketed as satin walnut.

Natural History. Intolerant of shade. Growth rate rapid. Reproduces well from seeds on old fields and bare ground; adequate seed crops produced most years; large seed crops produced about every 3 years. The most commonly planted hardwood in the Southeast. Reproduces from root sprouts. Fire and girdling by beaver, mice, and rabbits cause the most damage. Adapted to a wide range of sites except very droughty and infertile soils. Growth fastest on silt loams and silty clay loams of first bottoms. Not tolerant of long periods of flooding in the growing season. Grows in pure stands or mixed with willow oak, swamp laurel oak, cherrybark oak, swamp chestnut oak, pin oak, white oak, northern red oak, sycamore, yellow-poplar, river birch, American elm, slash pine, loblolly pine, red maple, sugarberry, and cabbage palmetto.

Range. See figure 294.

BUCKEYE FAMILY: HIPPOCASTANACEAE

Worldwide the Buckeye Family contains 15 species in 2 genera found in tropical America and temperate areas of the Northern Hemisphere. Our region contains only buckeye (*Aesculus*). The other genus (*Billia*) occurs naturally in southern Mexico and South America. Some authorities place the Hippocastanaceae within the Sapindaceae.

BUCKEYES AND HORSECHESTNUT: THE GENUS *AESCULUS*

Found in temperate forests of the Northern Hemisphere, this genus contains 13 species in the world. Our region contains 6 species, but only 3 species regularly become tree-sized. Horsechestnut (*Aesculus hippocastanum*), native to the Balkans, is widely planted and occasionally escapes. Buckeyes hybridize frequently. Red horsechestnut (*Aesculus* x *carnea*), a hybrid of horsechestnut and red buckeye, is planted for the red flowers.

Buckeyes are shrubs or medium-sized trees. The leaves are opposite, deciduous, and palmately compound. The petiole is as long as or longer than the leaflets, and stipules are lacking. The flowers are showy, somewhat tubelike, borne in large terminal clusters (panicles), and both bisexual and unisexual flowers occur on the same tree (polygamous). The flowers appear after the new leaves are fully expanded, and they are pollinated by insects. Each flower contains four to five petals, which are either yellow, red, or white. The fruit is a smooth or spiny capsule containing one to six seeds. Sometimes mistaken for nuts because of their large size, each seed is lustrous, brown, poisonous, and marked by a large white spot (the hilum). The seeds were used in taxidermy before glass eyes were widely available, a practice that provided the common name. Terminal buds are present. The wood is diffuse-porous.

KEY TO BUCKEYES

1. Winter buds coated with sticky resin . . . . .Go to 2
1. Winter buds lacking sticky resin . . . . .Go to 3
    2. Fruit covered with short prickles . . . . .horsechestnut, *Aesculus hippocastanum*
    2. Fruit smooth . . . . .California buckeye, *Aesculus californica*
3. Fruit husk prickly 4
3. Fruit husk smooth 5

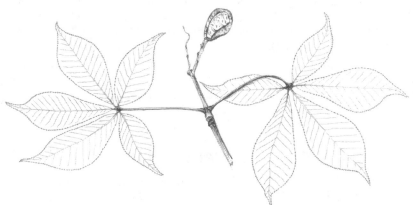

Fig. 295. Yellow buckeye (*Aesculus flava*) leaves and fruit wall.

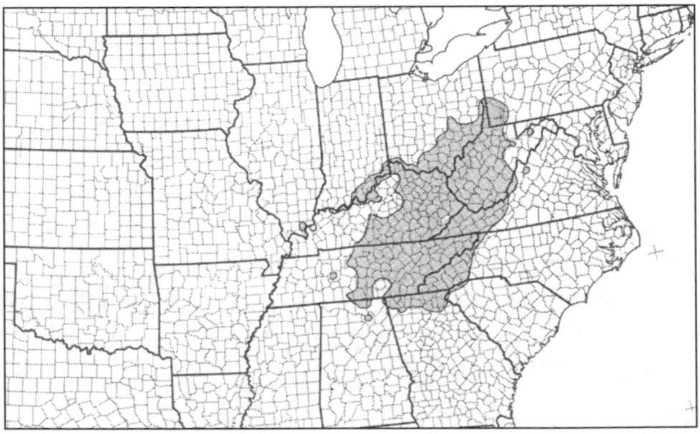

Fig. 296. Native range of yellow buckeye (*Aesculus flava*).

4. Leaflets 5 per leaf . . . . .Ohio buckeye, *Aesculus glabra*
4. Leaflets 7–11 per leaf . . . . .Texas buckeye, *Aesculus glabra* var. *arguta*
5. Moderately large tree . . . . .yellow buckeye, *Aesculus flava*
5. Shrub 6
    6. Flowers white; found mostly in Alabama . . . .
    . . . . .bottlebrush buckeye, *Aesculus parviflora*
    6. Flowers usually red or yellow 7
7. Petals hairless but glandular on margin; usually red sometimes yellow . . . .
    . . . . .red buckeye, *Aesculus pavia*
7. Petals hairy but not glandular on margin; always yellow . . . .
    . . . . .painted buckeye, *Aesculus sylvatica*

California buckeye
Aesculus californica (Spach) Nutt.

Large shrub or occasionally a small tree growing to 35 ft in height. Leaves opposite; palmately compound. Leaflets 5 sometimes 7; oblong to lanceolate; toothed; usually hairy. Flowers white to light pink. Fruit a capsule; nearly pear-shaped; smooth. Seeds usually 1. Terminal bud sticky resinous. Grows on dry slopes or in canyons. Found from northern to southern California below 4,000 ft.

Yellow buckeye
Aesculus flava Soland. (fig. 295)

Nomenclature. Formerly known as *Aesculus octandra*, a name published later.
Form. Medium-sized tree growing 60–90 ft in height and 2–3 ft in diameter (largest known 140 ft by 4 ft).
Leaves. Opposite; palmately compound; 4–10 in. long. Leaflets 5; elliptical; hairless or hairy; toothed.
Flowers. Yellow to white-yellow; stalks glandular hairy; stamens shorter than the petals. Each tree develops bisexual and male flowers (polygamo-dioecious); bisexual flowers limited to base of flower cluster; appearing after the new leaves have expanded.
Fruit. Capsule; 3-parted; pale brown; 2–3 in. long; smooth. Seeds 1–4, but usually 1; light to dark brown; smooth; lustrous; poisonous if eaten by humans; dispersed in autumn by gravity, animals, or water.
Twigs. Stout; hairy at first becoming smooth; red-brown to gray. Terminal bud 0.6–1 in. long; hairless; pale brown; nonresinous; scales not prominently keeled.
Bark. Light gray; separating into rectangular flakes.
Wood. Sapwood white to gray-white gradually changing to heartwood. Heartwood yellow-white with gray streaks; lightweight; ranks among the softest hardwoods in our region. Formerly used for artificial limbs; currently used for cigar boxes, toys, woodenware, travel trunks, drawing boards, boxes, crates, and pulpwood.
Natural History. Tolerant of shade; usually becoming established in small canopy openings. Found in river bottoms, stream banks, north-facing slopes, and coves. Young shoots and seeds poisonous to livestock.
Hybrids. Hybridizes with Ohio and painted buckeye; sometimes backcrossing to either parent and making identification difficult.
Range. See figure 296. Elevation in the southern Appalachians to 5,000 ft.

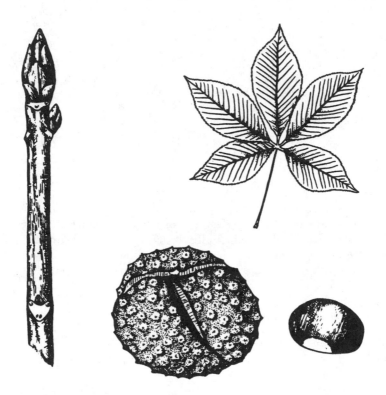

Fig. 297. Ohio buckeye
(*Aesculus glabra*) leaf,
twig, fruit, and seed.

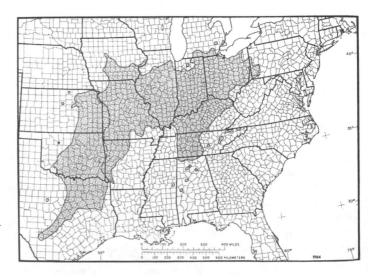

Fig. 298.
Native range
of Ohio buck-
eye (*Aesculus
glabra*).

Ohio buckeye

Aesculus glabra Willd. (fig. 297)

Form. Small tree usually growing 30–40 ft in height and 1 ft in diameter; sometimes growing to 70 ft in height and 2 ft in diameter (largest known 145 ft by 4 ft). Crown with large branches.

Leaves. Opposite; palmately compound with 5 leaflets (rarely 7); 3–6 in. long. Leaflets ovate to oval; hairless; finely toothed; ill-scented when bruised.

Flowers. Yellow or green-yellow; stalks smooth lacking glandular hairs; stamens longer than the petals; appearing after the leaves have expanded. Each tree has bisexual and male flowers (polygamo-dioecious); bisexual flowers found only at base of flower cluster.

Fruit. Capsule; red-brown; 1–2 in. long; usually short-prickly; containing 1–3 seeds. Seeds light or dark brown; smooth; lustrous; dispersed by gravity, animals, and water.

Twigs. Stout; hairy at first becoming smooth; red-brown to gray; disagreeable odor when bruised. Terminal buds 0.6 in. long; red-brown; nonresinous; scales prominently keeled.

Bark. Ash-gray; ill scented; deep fissures that separate flat scaly plates.

Wood. Same as yellow buckeye.

Natural History. Tolerant of shade becoming established in small canopy openings. Found on moist sites: valley flats, slopes, or stream sides, and on limestone soils. Grows in mixed stands with chinkapin oak, sugar maple, white ash, American beech, basswood, black cherry, shagbark hickory, American elm, and black walnut. If eaten, the young shoots, bark, and seeds are poisonous to livestock.

Varieties. Var. *arguta* found in Missouri, Kansas, Oklahoma, Arkansas, and Texas has 7–11 leaflets and is usually a shrub; sometimes considered a separate species, *Aesculus arguta*.

Hybrids. Hybridizes with yellow and red buckeye; sometimes backcrossing to either parent and making taxonomic classification problematic.

Range. See figure 298.

STAR-ANISE FAMILY: ILLICIACEAE

Found mostly in eastern Asia, the Star-Anise Family contains about 40 species, all in a single genus (*Illicium*). Only 2 species are found in our area. Seldom encountered in nature, swamp star-anise (*Illicium parviflorum*) occurs in only a few counties in central Florida and southwest Georgia although it is often cultivated as an ornamental. *Illicium* is sometimes placed in the family Magnoliaceae.

KEY TO STAR-ANISES

1. Leaf tip rounded or notched . . . . .swamp star-anise, *Illicium parviflorum*
1. Leaf tip pointed . . . . .Florida anise, *Illicium floridanum*

Florida anise, Stink-bush

Illicium floridanum Ellis (fig. 299)

Large shrub or small tree. Leaves evergreen; leathery; alternate; entire; ellipti-cal; 3–6 in. long; gland-dotted below; aromatic (sweet-smelling to some people but foul-smelling to others). Leaf tip acute to acuminate. Flowers showy; bisexual; 1–2 in. wide. Petals red or purple-red; 20–30. Fruit a radiating aggregate of 10–15 fol-licles that resemble a pinwheel. Tip of each follicle hooklike. Young twigs red turn-ing gray; leaf scar U-shaped. Grows in moist wooded ravines or along and in streams. Found in the Coastal Plain from northwest Florida to southeastern Louisiana.

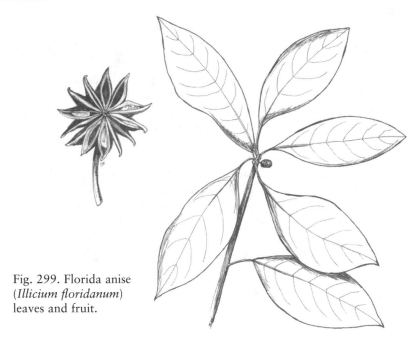

Fig. 299. Florida anise
(*Illicium floridanum*)
leaves and fruit.

THE WALNUT FAMILY: JUGLANDACEAE

Worldwide the Walnut Family contains about 60 species in nine genera. Hickory (*Carya*) and walnut (*Juglans*) are the largest genera, and the only two that occur naturally in our region.

Members of this family are usually trees with alternate pinnately compound leaves that are usually gland-dotted below and lack stipules. The tiny flowers are unisexual with both sexes found on each tree (monoecious). Flowering occurs in the spring as the leaves are expanding. Most people are allergic to the wind-dispersed pollen. The ovary is inferior and develops into a nut. It is enclosed in a husk that develops from the involucre and calyx. Our genera are easily separated. Hickory fruits have suture lines and walnut lacks sutures. The twig pith of hickory is solid homogeneous and walnut is chambered.

HICKORY: THE GENUS *CARYA*

The genus *Carya* contains 18 species in the world, all restricted to eastern North America, Mexico, and eastern Asia. With 11, eastern North America contains most of the species. Hickories are subdivided into two sections, true hickories (*Eucarya*) and pecan hickories (*Apocarya*). Each section is described below.

Hickory leaves are alternate, pinnately compound, and deciduous. The number of leaflets varies from 3–17 per leaf. Stipules are not produced. The flowers are unisexual with both sexes produced on each tree (monoecious). Flowers lack petals and appear in the spring after the new leaves are expanded. The male flowers occur in three-branched aments. The female flowers contain four sepals and usually two carpels, and they occur in spikes of two to ten. The fruit is a drupelike nut enclosed in a semiwoody husk. It matures in one growing season. The husk is four-parted and partly or completely dehiscent. The bark is smooth or shaggy and very hard. The wood is heavy and either semi-ring-porous (pecan hickories) or ring-porous (true hickories).

KEY TO HICKORIES

1. Leaflets 7–17 each about the same size . . . .(pecan hickories) Go to 2
1. Leaflets 3–9; upper leaflets much larger . . . .(true hickories) Go to 5
   2. Nuts about twice as long as wide . . . . .pecan, *Carya illinoinensis*
   2. Nuts about as long as wide 3
3. Leaflets silver-white or bronze below . . . . . .nutmeg hickory, *Carya myristiciformis*
3. Leaflets pale green below 4
   4. Terminal buds red-brown to yellow-brown; leaflets 9–11 . . . .
   . . . . .water hickory, *Carya aquatica*
   4. Terminal buds bright sulfur yellow; leaflets 7–9 . . . .
   . . . . .bitternut hickory, *Carya cordiformis*
5. Fruit husk 0.2–0.5 in. thick; terminal buds 0.5–1 in. long 6
5. Fruit husk 0.1 in. thick; terminal buds 0.2–0.5 in. long 8
   6. Rachis densely covered with strongly aromatic hairs . . . .
   . . . . .mockernut hickory, *Carya tomentosa*
   6. Rachis hairless or slightly covered with mildly aromatic hairs 7
7. Fruit 2–3 in. long; leaflets usually 7 . . . . .shellbark hickory, *Carya laciniosa*
7. Fruit 1–1.5 in. long; leaflets 3 or 5 . . . . .shagbark hickory, *Carya ovata*
   8. Leaf undersides nearly hairless . . . . .pignut hickory, *Carya glabra*
   8. Leaf undersides with numerous scales 9
9. Leaf undersides with silver scales . . . . .sand hickory, *Carya pallida*
9. Leaf undersides with red or brown scales 10
   10. Sandy soils in Florida . . . . .scrub hickory, *Carya floridana*
   10. Rocky hillsides, sandy uplands, and creek banks in Indiana, Illinois, and states west of Mississippi River .black hickory, *Carya texana*

PECAN HICKORIES (*APOCARYA*)

Four species in our area are classified as pecan hickories characterized by 4–6 valvate bud scales, 5–17 (mostly more than 7) curved leaflets, and winged fruit husks. The leaflets are approximately the same size.

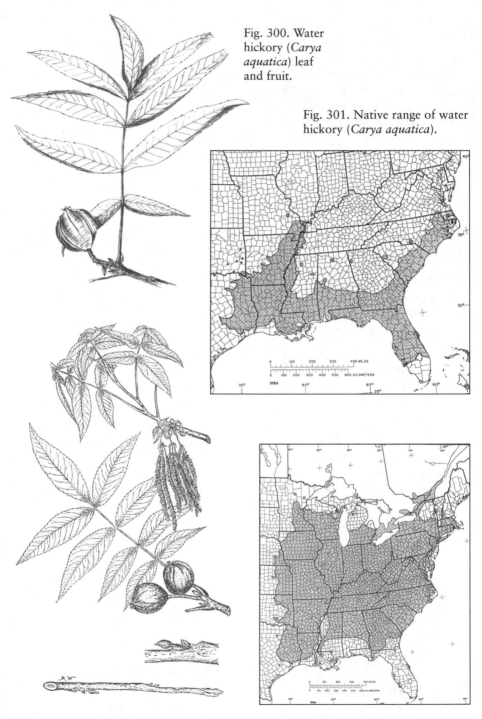

Fig. 300. Water hickory (*Carya aquatica*) leaf and fruit.

Fig. 301. Native range of water hickory (*Carya aquatica*).

Fig. 302. Bitternut hickory (*Carya cordiformis*) leaf, male flowers, twig, and fruit.

Fig. 303. Native range of bitternut hickory (*Carya cordiformis*).

Water hickory, Bitter pecan
Carya aquatica (Michx. f.) Nutt. (fig. 300)

Large excurrent tree growing to 150 ft in height. Leaves similar to pecan. Fruit 1–1.5 in. long; somewhat flattened. Husk nearly black; splitting halfway to the base. Nut 4-ribbed; seed bitter. Bark shaggy in long strips; gray. Wood similar to bitternut hickory but not harvested commercially since it has a reputation for ring-shake. Moderately tolerant of shade; grows slowly but reproduces abundantly from seeds and sprouts; good seed crops produced most years; seeds dispersed by water; become established on bare soil or leaf litter. Grows on silt and clay soils in wet first bottoms and the edges of sloughs that commonly flood for moderately long periods. Our most water-tolerant hickory. Grows with overcup oak, American elm, green ash, and red maple. The abundance of water hickory has increased over the last 75 years, because it is usually left after high-grade logging operations have removed the more marketable species. Hybridizes with pecan and black hickory. For range see figure 301.

Bitternut hickory, Bitternut
Carya cordiformis (Wangenh.) K. Koch (fig. 302)

Form. Excurrent or deliquescent tree growing 80–90 ft in height and 2–3 ft in diameter (largest known 140 by 4 ft). Crown often very broad; slender ascending branches.

Leaves. Alternate; pinnately compound; 6–10 in. long. Leaflets 7–11; lanceolate to oblong-lanceolate; slightly curved (falcate); terminal leaflet slightly larger than laterals; hairless above; slightly hairy below. Margin serrate. Rachis slightly hairy.

Fruit. Subspherical; about 1 in. long; 4-winged above the middle. Husk 0.1 in. thick; yellow-green; scattered scurfy yellow scales near base; splitting halfway to base. Nut surface smooth; bitter. Oil pressed from husks formerly used in oil lamps.

Twigs. Rather stout; green to gray-brown. Terminal bud 0.3–0.7 in. long; pointed; sulfur-yellow; scurfy hairy. Scales valvate.

Bark. Firm and smooth; never shaggy; gray; crisscrossing flat ridges forming x-shapes.

Wood. Sapwood white to pale brown. Heartwood brown; very heavy; very hard. Used for furniture, striking tool handles, ladders, skis, charcoal, and fuelwood.

Natural History. Moderately tolerant of shade. Moderately fast growing reaching maturity in 100–120 years (extreme age 200 years). Reproduces from seeds; good nut crops produced every 3–5 years; dispersed by gravity; requires stratification. Reproduces from stump and root sprouts. Deep taproot. Adapted to a variety of sites; generally found on lower slopes and riverside levees but sometimes found on drier uplands. Grows in small pure groves or mixed with sweetgum, white oak, northern red oak, swamp chestnut oak, sycamore, yellow-poplar, and musclewood.

Hybrids. Hybridizes with pecan, pignut hickory, shagbark hickory, and shellbark hickory.

Range. See figure 303.

Pecan, Sweet pecan

Carya illinoinensis (Wangenh.) K. Koch (fig. 304)

Nomenclature. Older manuals generally spell the specific epithet *illinoensis*, but the original spelling is used here.

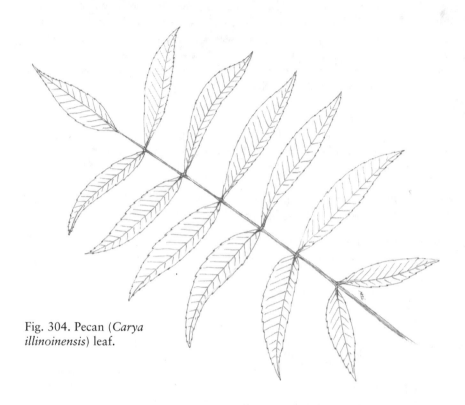

Fig. 304. Pecan (*Carya illinoinensis*) leaf.

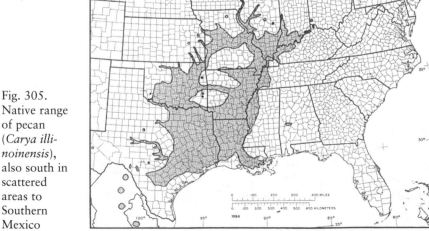

Fig. 305. Native range of pecan (*Carya illinoinensis*), also south in scattered areas to Southern Mexico

Form. Large excurrent to deliquescent tree growing 130–150 ft in height and 3–4 ft in diameter (largest known 180 ft by 7 ft); largest of the hickories. Crowns of open-grown trees wide-spreading.

Leaves. Alternate; pinnately compound; 12–18 in. long. Leaflets 9–17; lanceolate; serrate; slightly curved (falcate); nearly stalkless; approximately the same size.

Fruit. Ellipsoidal; 1–2 in. long. Husk green turning black; 4-winged; splitting from apex to base; sometimes remaining on tree after nut has fallen. Surface of nut smooth; light brown with dark brown splotches. Seed edible; widely used in baking especially in the Southeast. Nuts produced commercially in orchards where cross-pollination between varieties is required; often bearing nuts every other year.

Twigs. Terminal buds 0.2–0.5 in. long; yellow-brown; scurfy.

Bark. Smooth on young trees developing large loose scales with age; light gray. Pecan is sometimes confused with black walnut; the light gray scaly bark of pecan easily contrasts with the black furrowed bark of black walnut.

Wood. Similar to bitternut hickory but heartwood red-brown. Used also for flooring.

Natural History. Intolerant of shade. Growth rate moderately fast; reaches maturity in 120–150 years (extreme age 300 years). Reproduces by seed; nuts mature in fall; dispersed by mammals and floating on water; seeds require stratification. Also reproduces by stump sprouts. Grows on well-drained alluvial soils; absent from poorly drained bottomlands. Grows in mixed stands with sycamore, green ash, boxelder, sweetgum, eastern cottonwood, sugarberry, and American elm. Commonly planted in cities throughout the South.

Hybrids. Hybridizes with water hickory, bitternut hickory, shellbark hickory, shagbark hickory, and mockernut hickory.

Range. See figure 305.

Nutmeg hickory

Carya myristiciformis (Michx. f.) Nutt.

Medium-sized excurrent tree growing 80–100 ft in height. Leaflets 7–9; ovate-lanceolate; not curved; silver or bronze scales below. Fruit ellipsoidal; 4-winged; 1.5 in. long; not flattened. Husk very thin; splitting to the base. Twigs brown; hairless but scaly. Bark shaggy separating into long strips. Intolerant of shade. Grows in second bottoms and on slopes above streams. Nuts eagerly eaten by squirrels. Little is known about this rare hickory. Found in widely scattered populations in southeastern North Carolina, South Carolina, Alabama, Mississippi, Arkansas, Louisiana, Oklahoma, and east Texas.

TRUE HICKORIES (*EUCARYA*)

The seven true hickories in our region are characterized by numerous overlapping bud scales, three to nine leaflets, and essentially nonwinged fruit husks. The terminal leaflet is usually larger than the lateral leaflets.

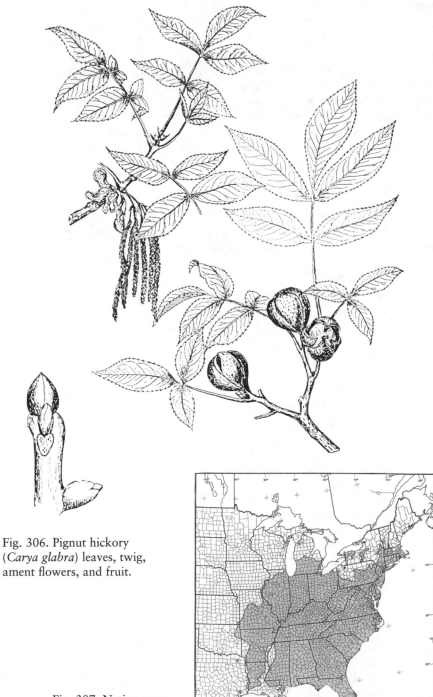

Fig. 306. Pignut hickory
(*Carya glabra*) leaves, twig,
ament flowers, and fruit.

Fig. 307. Native range
of pignut hickory
(*Carya glabra*).

Scrub hickory
Carya floridana Sarg.

Intergrades with pignut hickory and possibly not fully distinct. Large shrub or moderate-sized tree growing 70–80 ft in height. Leaflets 5–7 per leaf; lanceolate to elliptic; not curved; stalkless or nearly stalkless; red-brown scales below. Margin coarsely toothed. Fruit oblong; 1.5 in. long; husk 0.1 in. thick. Terminal buds covered with red-brown granules and hairs. Found on dry hills in central Florida.

Pignut hickory, Pignut
Carya glabra (Mill.) Sweet (fig. 306)

Nomenclature. The appropriate taxonomic treatment for pignut hickory has been discussed for decades. Some authors have argued for a single polymorphic species while others have advocated subdivision into 8 or more taxa. Hybridization with the species noted below adds to the confusion.

Form. Moderate-sized excurrent tree growing 80–90 ft in height and 2–3 ft in diameter (largest known 150 ft by 4 ft). Crown rounded; thick covering one-half to two-thirds of the tree.

Leaves. Alternate; pinnately compound; 6–9 in. long. Leaflets 5 (rarely 7); nearly hairless below; serrate; stalkless; terminal leaflet larger. Tip acute to acuminate. Rachis hairless.

Fruit. 1–1.5 in. long; pear-shaped to obovoid. Husk 0.1 in. thick; 4-parted; often splitting only halfway from the tip of the fruit to the base. Ripens in September and October; released in September to December.

Twigs. Relatively slender; hairless. Terminal buds 0.2–0.5 in. long.

Bark. Gray; hard; smooth with shallow cracks on young trees; on older trees developing narrow flat sharp-edged ridges that crisscross forming diamond and x-patterns; not shaggy.

Wood. Similar to bitternut hickory.

Natural History. Shade tolerance varies by region but generally moderately tolerant. Growth rate slow. Regenerates from seed; good nut crops occur every 2–3 years; nuts require stratification; dispersal by gravity and small mammals; seed viability about 50 percent. Reproduces well from stump sprouts. Taproot long with few laterals. Found most commonly on drier hilltops and upper slopes, but also found occasionally on lower slopes where development is impressive. Grows only in mixed stands with white oak, northern red oak, chestnut oak, post oak, yellow-poplar, blackgum, shortleaf pine, Virginia pine, and loblolly pine. Nut high in crude fat; eaten by turkeys, chipmunks, black bears, foxes, raccoons, and white-tailed deer.

Varieties. Consensus is building for subdivision into 2 varieties, the typical var. *glabra* (described above) and var. *odorata*. Var. *odorata*, commonly called red hickory or false shagbark hickory, has 5–7 leaflets per leaf, a spherical nut, a husk that splits completely from tip to base of the fruit, and bark that becomes slightly shaggy on older trees. No differences between the 2 varieties in wood or natural history are known. Some authors have considered red hickory to be a separate species, *Carya ovalis*.

Hybrids. Pignut hybridizes with bitternut hickory, scrub hickory, sand hickory, and black hickory.

Range. See figure 307.

Fig. 308.
Shellbark hickory
(*Carya laciniosa*)
leaves, twig,
ament flowers,
and fruit.

Fig. 309. Native
range of shellbark
hickory (*Carya
laciniosa*).

Shellbark hickory

Carya laciniosa (Michx. f.) Loud. (fig. 308)

Leaves alternate; pinnately compound; 15–22 in. long. Leaflets 7–9 per leaf; lanceolate to obovate; velvety below; not curved; finely serrate; teeth lacking marginal hair tufts; tips long acuminate. Fruit largest of all hickories; 2–3 in. long; ellipsoid; husk 0.3–0.6 in. thick; nut flattened; 4–6 ribbed. Twigs stout; orange-brown; hairy; terminal bud 0.7–1 in. long; outer scales loose. Bark light gray; developing wide flat ridges that become long shaggy. Very tolerant of shade; seedlings develop under dense canopy shade. Growth slow; reaches maturity in 180–200 years. Reproduces from seeds and stump sprouts. Develops a long taproot; difficult to transplant. Grows in fertile, well-drained soils in bottomlands on levees, terraces, and second bottoms. Common nowhere; found in small groves or more commonly mixed with red maple, sweetgum, American elm, eastern cottonwood, swamp white oak, white oak, swamp chestnut oak, white ash, and green ash. Nuts eaten by humans, wild turkeys, squirrels, chipmunks, deer, fox, raccoons, and mice, but they are hard to crack. Hybridizes with pecan and shagbark hickory. For range see figure 309.

Shagbark hickory

Carya ovata (Mill.) K. Koch (fig. 310)

Form. Moderate-sized excurrent tree growing 70–80 ft in height and 1–2 ft in diameter (largest known 140 ft by 4 ft).

Fig. 310. Shagbark hickory (*Carya ovata*) leaves, twig, ament flowers, and fruit.

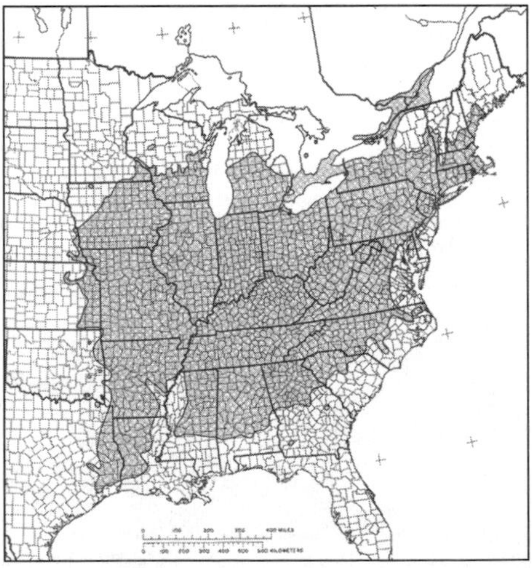

Fig. 311. Native range of shagbark hickory (*Carya ovata*). Also found in scattered areas in Mexico

Leaves. Alternate; pinnately compound; 8–14 in. long. Leaflets 3 or 5 per leaf; obovate; nearly stalkless; slightly hairy below especially on the major veins; terminal leaflet 5–7 in. long; much longer than the laterals; dark green above; yellow-green below. Margin serrate; teeth with marginal tufts of hairs that progressively abscise during growing season.

Fruit. Spherical to ellipsoidal; 1–2 in. long; 4-ribbed; not flattened; shell thick; husk 0.2–0.5 in. thick; completely dehiscent; seed sweet.

Twigs. Stout; gray to red-brown; hairy. Terminal buds 0.5–0.7 in. long; broadly ovoid; hairy; outer bud scales loose.

Bark. Gray; 0.7–1 in. thick; shaggy by developing narrow flat plates 1–3 ft long that separate and curve away from the bole at 1 or both ends.

Wood. Similar to bitternut hickory. Prized for fuelwood and charcoal.

Natural History. Moderately tolerant of shade; able to withstand suppression for many years. Moderate growth rate (but fast among hickories); reaches maturity in 180–200 years (extreme age 300 years). Reproduces by seed and stump sprouts; seed dispersed by gravity and animals. Deep taproot with few laterals. Never found in pure stands; in the North and southern Appalachians, grows on upland sites mixed with northern red oak, white oak, black oak, pignut hickory, yellow-poplar, and black cherry; in the Southeast grows on moist alluvial soils with loblolly pine, sweetgum, boxelder, white ash, swamp chestnut oak, white oak, Shumard oak, sugarberry, and bitternut hickory. Nuts eaten by humans, chipmunks, squirrels, black bears, foxes, rabbits, mice, wood ducks, and turkeys.

Varieties. Divided into 3 varieties but only 2 occur in our area. In addition to the typical variety (var. *ovata*) described above, the var. *australis*, commonly called Carolina hickory or southern shagbark hickory, is recognized. Carolina hickory has hairless leaflets and twigs, smaller leaves and fruits, and terminal leaflets lanceolate to oblanceolate. Some authors consider this variety to be a separate species, *Carya carolinae-septentrionalis*.

Hybrids. Hybridizes with bitternut hickory and shellbark hickory.

Range. See figure 311.

Sand hickory

Carya pallida (Ashe) Engl. & Graebn.

Small tree growing 40–60 ft in height and 1 ft in diameter (largest known 95 ft by 3 ft). Leaves alternate; pinnately compound; 6–8 in. long. Leaflets 5–9; lanceolate to ovate; nearly stalkless; sometimes curved (falcate); abundant silver or brown scales below. Fruit 1–1.5 in. long; brown to red-brown; husk 4-valved; 0.1 in. thick; 1 valve often wider than the others. Twigs red-brown; sparse silver-brown scales. Buds covered with red-brown scales. Bark dark gray not shaggy. Grows on dry sandy or rocky soils on bluffs and sandhills. Found in the Coastal Plain from southern New Jersey to northern Florida, west to eastern Louisiana, and in the Mississippi River valley to southwestern Indiana. Disjunct in Connecticut.

Black hickory
Carya texana Buckl.

Moderately large tree growing 120–130 ft in height and 2–3 ft in diameter. Leaves 8–12 in. long. Leaflets 7 per leaf; ovate, obovate, or elliptic; covered with red-brown scales below. Margin toothed. Fruit spherical to obovoid; 1–2 in. long; green turning red-brown; husk 0.1–0.2 in. thick; splitting to the base. Nut slightly flattened; 4-winged above the middle. Terminal buds covered with scales. Grows on rocky hillsides. Hybridizes with water hickory, pignut hickory, sand hickory, and mockernut hickory. Found from southwestern Indiana to southeastern Kansas, and south to Louisiana and central Texas.

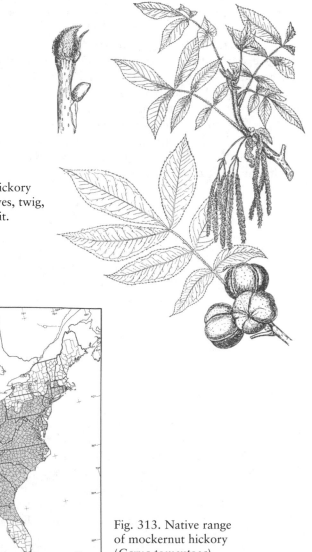

Fig. 312. Mockernut hickory (*Carya tomentosa*) leaves, twig, ament flowers, and fruit.

Fig. 313. Native range of mockernut hickory (*Carya tomentosa*).

Mockernut hickory, Mockernut

Carya tomentosa (Poir.) Nutt. (fig. 312)

Form. Moderate-sized tree growing 50–70 ft in height and 1–2 ft in diameter (largest known 140 ft by 4 ft). Crown broad; open.

Leaves. Alternate; pinnately compound; 8–12 in. long. Leaflets 7–9 (rarely 5); lanceolate to obovate-oblanceolate; yellow-green and hairless above; pale with clusters of hairs below; stalkless or nearly stalkless; terminal leaflet 4–7 in. long; larger than the laterals. Margin finely to coarsely serrate. Rachis covered with resinous pungent hairs.

Fruit. Spherical to obovoid; 1.5–2 in. long; husk 0.2–0.3 in. thick; splitting to the base.

Twigs. Stout; gray to red-brown; hairy. Terminal buds 0.5–0.7 in. long; subspherical; outer scales tan-brown and soon abscising; inner scales light tan and hairy.

Bark. Firm never shaggy; gray; shallow furrows; rounded interlacing ridges forming diamond and x-patterns.

Wood. Similar to bitternut hickory. Preferred wood for smoking hams.

Natural History. Intolerant of shade. Slow-growing; long-lived; reaches maturity in 150–200 years (extreme age 500 years). Reproduces from seed especially when buried in leaf litter; good seed crop produced every 2–3 years; seed viability 50–75 percent. Reproduces prolifically from stump sprouts. Develops a deep taproot with few laterals. Fire, twig girdler, and hickory bark beetle cause the most damage. Found on a wide range of soils and sites but most typical of well-drained upland slopes. Grows only in mixed stands with post oak, blackjack oak, white oak, black oak, blackgum, yellow-poplar, white ash, loblolly pine, shortleaf pine, and Virginia pine. Nuts eaten by squirrels, chipmunks, black bears, foxes, rabbits, beavers, mice, wood ducks, and turkeys.

Hybrids. Hybridizes with pecan, shagbark hickory, and black hickory.

Range. See figure 313. Most common in the Southeastern Coastal Plain and Piedmont.

WALNUT: THE GENUS *JUGLANS*

About 20 species of walnut occur in the world. Six species are native to our region, but only the 2 commercially important eastern species are treated separately here. English walnut (*Juglans regia*), native to southeastern Europe and Asia, is cultivated in California and Oregon for the nut fruits.

Walnut leaves are alternate, pinnately compound, and deciduous. The leaflets fall much sooner than the rachis. Between 9–23 leaflets per leaf are found, and they are nearly stalkless. Male flowers occur in unbranched aments. Female flowers occur in spikes of 2–8 flowers. The fruit is a drupelike, thick-shelled nut encased in a semifleshy, indehiscent husk. It matures in one year. The twigs are stout with a chambered pith. Terminal buds are present. The wood is semi-ring-porous.

KEY TO WALNUTS

1. Leaves with 5–9 (rarely to 13) leaflets; margin entire or nearly entire . . . .
. . . . .English walnut, *Juglans regia*
1. Leaves with 9–29 leaflets; margin toothed . . . . .Go to 2

Fig. 314. Butternut (*Juglans cinerea*) leaves, twigs, twig pith, ament flowers, and fruits.

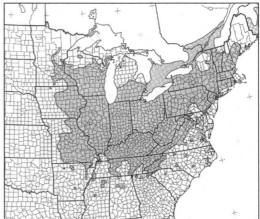

Fig. 315. Native range of butternut (*Juglans cinerea*).

2. Band of pale hairs on twig between leaf scar and lateral bud. . . . .
. . . . .butternut, *Juglans cinerea*
2. No hairs between leaf scar and lateral bud 3
3. Nut 1.5–2.5 in. wide 4
3. Nut less than 1.5 in. wide 5
   4. Surface of nut deeply ridged . . . . .Eastern black walnut, *Juglans nigra*
   4. Surface of nut smooth or faintly grooved; California . . . .
   . . . . .Hinds walnut, *Juglans hindsii*
5. Nut 1–1.5 in. long . . . . .Arizona walnut, *Juglans major*
5. Nut 0.5–0.7 in. long 6
   6. Leaflets 17–23; Oklahoma, Texas, and New Mexico . . . .
   . . . . .little walnut, *Juglans microcarpa*
   6. Leaflets 11–15 (rarely to 19); California . . . .
   . . . . .California walnut, *Juglans californica*

Butternut, White walnut

Juglans cinerea L. (fig. 314)

Form. Moderate-sized tree growing 60–70 ft in height and 1–2 ft in diameter (largest known 110 ft by 4 ft). Crown broad and open.

Leaves. Alternate; pinnately compound; 1–2 ft long. Leaflets 11–17 per leaf; 2–4 in. long; oblong-lanceolate; serrate; nearly stalkless; yellow-green; wrinkled above; hairy below.

Fruit. Oblong-ovoid; 1–2 in. long; solitary or in clusters of 2–5; husk green-brown; glandular hairy and sticky; no natural suture lines; surface of nut deeply corrugated; matures in 1 year. Orange and yellow fabric dyes obtained from green husks.

Twigs. Stout; green to red-brown; leaf scar straight at top with dense hairy stripe. Pith chambered after 1 year; chocolate-brown with thick diaphragms. Terminal bud present; 0.5–0.7 in. long; conical; flattened; hairy. Lateral buds smaller; rusty tomentose.

Bark. Light gray; smooth on young trees becoming shallowly furrowed with broad ridges.

Wood. Very different from black walnut. Sapwood white to gray-brown. Heartwood chestnut-brown; straight grained; moderately lightweight; moderately soft. Used for furniture, cabinets, interior paneling, toys, and novelties; often stained to look like black walnut. West Virginia, Tennessee, Indiana, and Wisconsin produce the most lumber.

Natural History. Intolerant of shade. Fast growing; short-lived; reaches maturity in 60–70 years. Reproduces from seeds; good nut crops produced every 2–3 years; nuts require stratification. Reproduces vegetatively by stump sprouting. Roots release allelopathic compound. Butternut decline causes the most damage virtually eliminating the species from North and South Carolina. Grows on streambanks, stream terraces, slopes, and talus slopes; occupies drier sites than black walnut. Found only in mixed stands with northern red oak, white oak, yellow-poplar, basswood, slippery elm, red maple, sugar maple, eastern hemlock, yellow birch, and sweet birch.

Range. See figure 315.

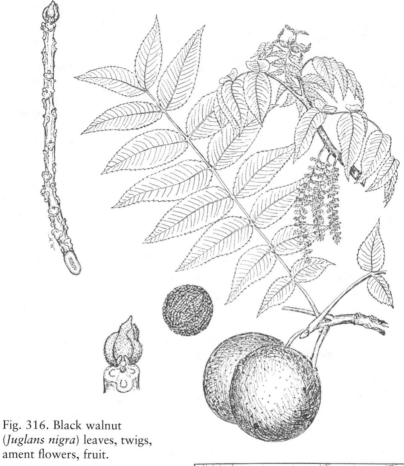

Fig. 316. Black walnut
(*Juglans nigra*) leaves, twigs,
ament flowers, fruit.

Fig. 317. Native range of
black walnut (*Juglans nigra*).

Black walnut, Eastern black walnut, American walnut

Juglans nigra L. (fig. 316)

Form. Excurrent to deliquescent tree growing 90–120 ft in height and 2–3 ft in diameter (largest known 150 ft by 6 ft). Crown broad; open; comparatively few branches.

Leaves. 1–2 ft long; 11–23 leaflets per leaf; leaflets smaller at tip and base. Leaflets 3–4 in. long; ovate-lanceolate; serrate; yellow-green; nearly stalkless; hairless above; hairy below; aromatic.

Fruit. Spherical; 1.5–2.5 in. in diameter; solitary or in clusters of 2–3; covered by indehiscent husk; surface deeply wrinkled; matures in 1 year dropping shortly after the leaves. Husk thick; semifleshy; yellow-green; lacking suture lines; hairy; contains yellow dye that stains fingers. Nuts used in baked goods and ice cream. Ground husks used to clean machinery, provide filler in dynamite and smokestack scrubbers, and as a carrying agent in insecticides.

Twigs. Stout; light brown. Leaf scar obcordate; lacking hairy strip above. Pith chambered after 1 year; tan colored. Terminal bud 0.3 in. long; ovoid; blunt; hairy. Lateral buds smaller; often superposed.

Bark. Dark brown to black; sometimes with slight purple tint; deep interlacing furrows forming triangle and diamond shapes.

Wood. Commercially very valuable; traditionally commanding high prices although the lumber value of individual trees in yards and along roads often overestimated. Prices have dropped lately following declines in demand stemming from increased consumer preference for lighter colored wood. Sapwood white to yellow-brown; sometimes stained to match the heartwood. Heartwood light brown, chocolate brown, or purple-brown; heavy; hard. Used for tables, desks, bookcases, audio-visual cabinets, piano cases, interior paneling, gunstocks, plaques, novelties, and occasionally flooring. The highest quality lumber comes from the Ohio River Valley.

Natural History. Intolerant of shade. Fast growing; reaches maturity in 120–150 years (extreme age 250 years). Reproduces by nuts dispersed by small mammals and rolling downslope; heavy nut crops produced every 3–5 years; nuts require stratification. Also reproduces from stump sprouts. Long taproot with well-developed lateral roots; roots release allelopathic compound. Site demanding; grows well only on fertile, nearly neutral, moist but well-drained soils; common on limestone-derived soils. Found sometimes in small groves but more commonly mixed with yellow-poplar, white oak, northern red oak, basswood, American beech, black cherry, and white ash.

Hybrids. Hybridizes with Hinds walnut. Over 400 cultivars have been named mostly for improved nut production.

Range. See figure 317.

ALLTHORN FAMILY: KOEBERLINACEAE

This family contains only the species listed below (monotypic). The family is sometimes placed within the family Capparaceae.

Allthorn

Koeberlinia spinosa Zucc.

Shrub or small tree occasionally growing to 25 ft in height. Leaves alternate; simple; scalelike; falling quickly leaving a tangled mass of green thorns. Flowers bisexual; small; green-white; petals 4; borne in clusters. Fruit a berry; black; nearly spherical; 0.2–0.3 in. wide. Seed coat wrinkled. Twigs hairless; light green; terminated by stiff thorn. Intolerant of shade. Grows on dry gravelly plains and foothills. Found mostly in Mexico but extending north into southwestern United States.

LAUREL FAMILY: LAURACEAE.

Worldwide the Lauraceae contains about 2,500 species in 31–50 genera. Found mostly in tropical regions of America and Asia, a few species extend into temperate regions. Thirteen species in 9 genera occur in our region, but only 5 species in 4 genera become tree-sized. Among our shrubs in this family, spicebush (*Lindera benzoin*) is widely distributed in the East on moist slopes and bottomlands.

Fig. 318. Camphor-tree (*Cinnamonum camphora*) leaves.

The Laurel Family contains no herbaceous species. The leaves are simple, entire, strongly aromatic, generally alternate, and sometimes evergreen. Stipules are lacking. The flowers are pollinated by insects (usually flies) and either bisexual or unisexual with the sexes found on different trees (dioecious). The perianth usually persists, and it partly surrounds the base of each fruit. The fruits are drupes, mature in one growing season, and dispersed by birds. The fruit stalk is often bright red-colored. The seeds lack endosperm. The wood is either diffuse- or ring-porous. Economically the family provides bay leaves (*Laurus*), spices (*Cinnamomum*), avocados (*Persea americana*), and occasionally lumber prized for its fragrance (*Sassafras* and *Nectandra*).

CINNAMON: THE GENUS *CINNAMOMUM*

About 250 species of cinnamon occur in east Asia and Indonesia, but none are native to our region. The species listed below is cultivated and has become naturalized. Economically the genus provides cinnamon and camphor.

Camphor-tree, Camphor-berry
Cinnamomum camphora (L.) J. Presl (fig. 318)

Formerly known as *Cinnamomum camphora* (L.) Nees and Eber., an identical name published later by different people. Small tree growing to 50 ft in height but often much smaller. Crown sometimes as wide as the tree is tall. Leaves ovate to elliptical; evergreen; smelling strongly of camphor; 2 main lateral veins curve to follow the margin; glands sometimes present in vein axils above. Leaf tip acute. Leaf base rounded. Fruit a blue-black drupe; spherical; 0.3–0.4 in. long. Generally found in disturbed areas: fencerows, waste places, and along roads; occasionally planted as a shade tree. Leaves provide camphor. Native to tropical Asia; planted and naturalized from southern North Carolina to southern Texas; also planted in California.

REDBAY: THE GENUS *PERSEA*

The genus *Persea* contains about 150 species found in subtropical and tropical regions of the Western Hemisphere. Only 3 species occur in our area.

Redbay leaves are alternate, evergreen, strongly aromatic, and often disfigured by psyllid galls. The fruit is a dark drupe. The wood takes a fine polish, but it is only used locally for cabinets and novelties. Silkbay (*Persea humilis*) is found only in central Florida.

KEY TO REDBAYS

1. Leaf undersurface with very short appressed hairs, appearing hairless . . . .
. . . . .redbay, *Persea borbonia*
1. Leaf undersurface with obvious hairs . . . . .Go to 2
   2. Leaf undersurfaces with short erect red hairs   . . . . .swampbay, *Persea palustris*
   2. Leaf undersurfaces with long white or red silky hairs. . . .silkbay, *Persea humilis*

Fig. 319. Redbay
(*Persea borbonia*)
shoot with fruit.

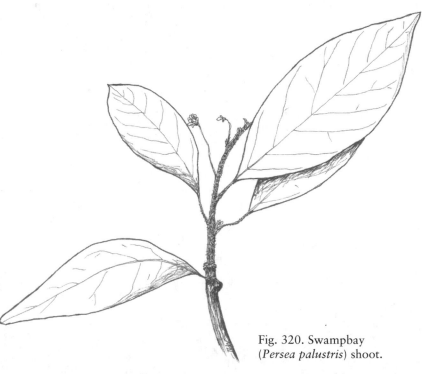

Fig. 320. Swampbay
(*Persea palustris*) shoot.

Redbay
Persea borbonia (L.) Spreng. (fig. 319)

   Differing largely in the amount of hair and length of the fruit stalk, redbay and swampbay are sometimes lumped into a single species. Small to medium-sized tree occasionally growing to 70 ft in height and 3 ft in diameter. Leaves alternate; evergreen; elliptical to lanceolate; 2–5 in. long; often disfigured by psyllid galls; tip leaves often shorter than others; entire; strongly aromatic; nearly hairless; lustrous above; appressed short hairs and white-waxy below. Leaf hairs not evident to the naked eye. Fruit a drupe; oblong; dark blue; often covered with white wax; 0.5–0.7 in. long; borne on red stalks, which are shorter than the subtending petiole. Twigs slender; hairless or with fine appressed hairs; dark green. Terminal bud present; naked; red woolly. Bark brown to red-brown; furrowed with interlacing ridges. Moderately tolerant of shade. Fire causes the most damage. Grows on barrier islands, river bluffs, and lower slopes. Fruit eaten by songbirds, turkeys, quail, black bears. Foliage browsed by white-tailed deer. Dried leaves sometimes used in cooking. Found in coastal areas from North Carolina to Florida, and west to east Texas. Disjunct in Arkansas.

Swampbay
Persea palustris (Raf.) Sarg. (fig. 320)

   Differing largely in the amount of hair and length of the fruit stalk, swampbay and redbay are sometimes lumped into a single species. Small tree growing to 50 ft in height. Often leaning. Leaves ovate to elliptical; 2–6 in. long; often disfigured by galls; tip leaves often shorter than others; strongly aromatic; sometimes slightly curved; lustrous above; white-waxy with erect red-brown hairs below especially on the major veins. Fruit a drupe; blue-black; 0.3–0.4 in. long; spherical; stalk longer than subtending petiole. Twigs with erect red hairs. Leaf and twig hairs easily seen by the naked eye. Bark gray to gray-brown; deep furrows separate interlacing ridges. Grows in wet sandy soils or organic soils in nonalluvial bottomlands and pocosins. Found in mixed stands with loblolly-bay, sweetbay, pond pine, loblolly pine, pond cypress, swamp blackgum, swamp laurel oak, and sweetgum. Fruit eaten by songbirds, turkeys, quail, and black bears. Foliage browsed by white-tailed deer. Found in coastal areas from Delaware to Florida, and west to east Texas; also in the West Indies.

Fig. 321. Sassafras
(*Sassafras albidum*)
leaves twigs, and fruit.

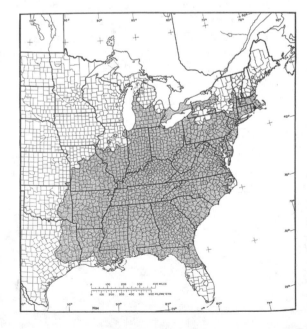

Fig. 322. Native range
of sassafras (*Sassafras
albidum*).

SASSAFRAS: THE GENUS *SASSAFRAS*

Worldwide three species of sassafras occur—one species in our region and two species in Asia. Sassafras is probably the name used by Native Americans.

Sassafras

Sassafras albidum (Nutt.) Nees (fig. 321)

Form. Tall shrub to medium-sized tree growing to 70 ft in height and 2 ft in diameter (largest known 90 ft by 5 ft). The form of this tree is very plastic forming a colony of short stems in fencerows but moderate-sized trees in closed stands.

Leaves. Alternate; simple; deciduous; oval to obovate; aromatic; not lobed (on large trees) or 1–3 lobed (on small trees and juveniles); 3–6 in. long; hairless and white waxy below.

Flowers. Unisexual; each tree produces only 1 sex (dioecious); 0.5 in. long; yellow-green; appearing before the new leaves expand in the spring; corolla absent.

Fruit. Drupe; dark blue; borne on red club-shaped stalk; subspherical; lustrous; 0.3–0.5 in. long.

Twigs. Hairless; yellow-green to olive green; aromatic. Terminal bud present; 0.3 in. long; green; 3–4 scales.

Bark. Thick; red-brown; developing furrows on older trees that separate narrow crisscrossing flat ridges. Adjacent ridges crack at the same height to form distinctive horizontal lines.

Wood. Low commercial value. Sapwood light yellow. Heartwood gray-brown, orange-brown, or dark brown; moderately heavy; ring-porous. Used occasionally for fence posts, furniture, small boats, barrels, and buckets. Sometimes sold as black ash.

Natural History. Intolerant of shade. Moderately fast growing; short-lived. Reproduction from seed sporadic; good seed crops produced every 1–2 years. Reproduction from root sprouts more common, often forming clones that can be difficult to eradicate. Roots produce allelopathic compounds. Fire causes the most damage. Found on a wide variety of sites ranging from dry ridges to fertile coves; most abundant on sandy- or gravelly loams; common pioneer in old fields and along fencerows. Oil of sassafras used to perfume soap distilled from roots and bark. Tea brewed from the roots; leaves used to thicken soup; root beer formerly made from roots.

Range. See figure 322.

CALIFORNIA BAY: THE GENUS *UMBELLULARIA*

Worldwide this genus contains only the species listed below (monotypic).

California-bay, California-laurel, Oregon-myrtle, Myrtle-wood
Umbellularia californica (Hook. & Arn.) Nutt. (fig. 323)

Form. Small to medium-sized tree growing 40–80 ft in height and 1–3 ft in diameter (largest known 175 ft by 13 ft). Bole often forked becoming shrubby on dry sites.

Leaves. Alternate; evergreen; lanceolate to elliptical; 2–4 in. long; leathery; entire; hairless; persistent 2–6 years; spicy-scented; dark green and lustrous above; paler below.

Flowers. Bisexual; yellow-green; 0.6 in. wide; borne in umbels; appearing before the new leaves; corolla absent.

Fruit. Acrid drupe; color at maturity variable, yellow-green, red-purple, or purple-brown; 0.5–1 in. wide; maturing in 1 year; surrounded at base by enlarged lobes of calyx.

Twigs. Slender; yellow-green; hairless; aromatic. Terminal buds present; minute; naked.

Bark. Thin; dark brown; tight scales.

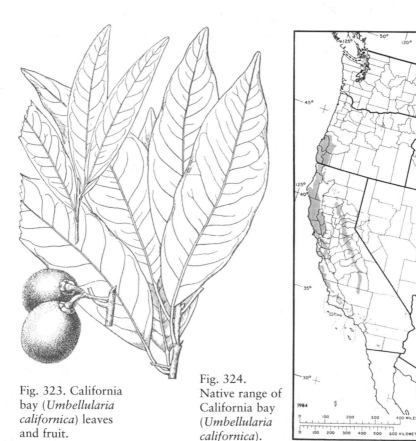

Fig. 323. California bay (*Umbellularia californica*) leaves and fruit.

Fig. 324. Native range of California bay (*Umbellularia californica*).

Wood. Most highly valued hardwood in western United States. Sapwood white to light brown. Heartwood light brown to gray-brown, often with dark streaks; moderately heavy; diffuse-porous; aromatic; grain straight or interlocking. Used for furniture (burls are prized), woodenware, interior trim, paneling, gun stocks, and novelties. Sold as myrtle-wood.

Natural History. Moderately tolerant of shade. Flowering and fruiting abundant; large seed crops produced most years. Seed dispersed by gravity, animals, and water; germination best when seeds are buried. Sprouts from stumps. Leaves may produce allelopathic compounds. Fire, windthrow, and ice breakage cause the most damage. Found on a wide variety of sites as long as moisture is abundant including slopes, coastal bluffs, alluvial flats, and ravines. Grows with Port Orford-cedar, redwood, Douglas-fir, Oregon white oak, canyon live oak, and coast live oak.

Varieties. Known only from Fresno County, California, var. *fresnensis* has hairy leaf undersurfaces.

Range. See figure 324. Elevation: sea level to 5,000 ft.

CORKWOOD FAMILY: LEITNERIACEAE

The Corkwood Family contains only the species listed below (monotypic).

Corkwood

Leitneria floridana Chapm.

Shrub or less commonly a small tree growing to 25 ft in height. Leaves alternate; simple; deciduous; oblong to lanceolate; 3–6 in. long; hairless above; thick silky hairy below especially on veins. Margin entire. Tip and base acute. Flowers unisexual with only 1 sex per plant (dioecious); borne in catkins. Fruit a drupe; ellipsoid; brown; 0.7 in. long; veins netlike and conspicuous. Twigs stout; hairy at first becoming hairless; lenticels large; circular; tan; leaf scars elevated. Pith white. Bark smooth; red-brown. Wood extremely soft; lightest weight of any in our area; formerly used for fishnet floats. Rare and local in swamps, marshes, and stream banks in the Coastal Plain of southern Georgia, northern Florida, and southeastern Texas; also in eastern Arkansas and southeastern Missouri.

MAGNOLIA FAMILY: MAGNOLIACEAE

Found mostly in southeastern Asia and eastern North America, the Magnolia Family contains about 220 species in 6–12 genera in the world. In our region, only 9 species in 2 genera occur naturally.

Our members of this family are small to large trees with alternate, simple, entire, aromatic leaves with circular stipule scars. Most species are deciduous, but a few are evergreen. Pollinated by beetles and bees, the flowers are large and showy. With numerous spirally arranged parts, each flower contains both sexes (perfect). Flowering occurs after or well after the new leaves have expanded in the spring. They are produced singly at the tips of small branches. The fruit matures in a single season, and is either a collection of samaras (*Liriodendron*) or follicles (*Magnolia*). The wood is relatively uniform and diffuse-porous. Members of this family are considered to be among the most primitive of angiosperms.

YELLOW-POPLAR: THE GENUS *LIRIODENDRON*

Worldwide this genus contains only two species—one in east Asia and one in our region.

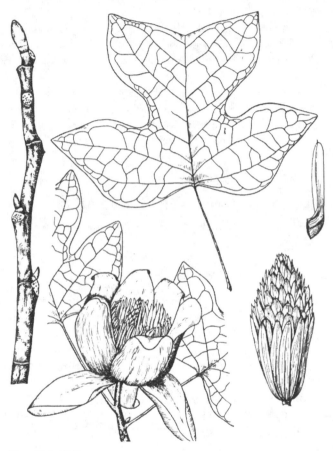

Fig. 325. Yellow-poplar (*Liriodendron tulipifera*) leaf, twig, flower, and fruit.

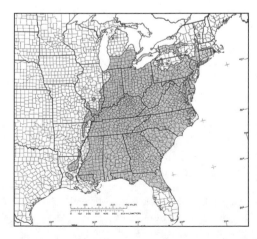

Fig. 326. Native range of yellow-poplar (*Liriodendron tulipifera*).

Yellow-poplar, Tulip-poplar, Tuliptree
Liriodendron tulipifera L. (fig. 325)

Nomenclature. The widely used name yellow-poplar has been a source of irritation to some people, because the true poplars belong to the genus *Populus*. But the other common name tuliptree is even more problematic, because tulips are monocots, an entirely different class.

Form. Large excurrent tree growing 90–120 ft in height and 4–6 ft in diameter (largest known 198 ft by 12 ft). Among the tallest widest trees in eastern North America. Bole extremely straight.

Leaves. Alternate; simple; deciduous; almost round; 3–8 in. long; 4-lobed (2-lobed on juveniles); entire; hairless above; light green to slightly whitened and hairless below. Tip flat or broadly V-shaped. Base flat to rounded.

Flowers. Cup-shaped; yellow-green with orange markings at base; 3 sepals; 6 petals. Source of nectar for honey.

Fruit. Aggregate of overlapping samaras; each samara 1.5 in. long; falling separately at maturity; light brown; wing terminal; wind dispersed.

Twigs. Encircling stipular scar at each node; aromatic; pith diaphragmed; leaf scar round. Terminal bud covered with valvate stipules; 0.5 in. long; flattened resembling a duck bill.

Bark. Smooth and dark green on young trees; developing wide furrows that separate flat ridges. Base of furrows white.

Wood. Commercially valuable especially in the last 15 years as the supply of pine has become strained. Sapwood nearly white. Heartwood variable in color, either yellow, tan, green-brown, dark green, purple, blue, or black; moderately soft. Used for plywood furniture panels, interior plys of pine plywood sheets, fruit and berry boxes, window sashes, blinds, cabinets, coffins, kitchen utensils, pulpwood, and occasionally dimension lumber.

Natural History. Intolerant of shade. Height growth very rapid on suitable sites. Reaches maturity in 200–250 years (extreme age 300 years). Reproduces well in full sunlight from seeds; large seed crops produced most years. Seeds dispersed by wind; viability about 10 percent; remain viable for 4–7 years in the forest floor. Also reproduces well by stump sprouts, which may grow 3–6 ft in height each year for several years. Wildfire, ice breakage, and loss of form by grape vines cause the most damage; not eaten by gypsy moth. When protected from fire found on a wide variety of sites; site-sensitive fast growth limited to concave lower slopes with moist, well-drained, loose soil and northern or eastern aspects; does not tolerate prolonged flooding or droughty soils. Grows in pure stands on the best-quality sites; elsewhere grows in mixed stands with very many associates including white oak, northern red oak, swamp chestnut oak, cherrybark oak, sweetgum, loblolly pine, Virginia pine, eastern white pine, eastern hemlock, red maple, sugar maple, American beech, yellow birch, sweet birch, basswood, and silverbell. Leaves and twigs eaten by livestock and white-tailed deer. Rabbits eat the buds and inner bark of small trees.

Varieties. A form with rounded leaf lobes occurs on organic soils in the South, but no formal name has been accepted.

Range. See figure 326.

MAGNOLIA: THE GENUS *MAGNOLIA*

Worldwide about 120 species of magnolia are known. In our region, 8 species occur naturally, all in eastern North America. These species, Asian species, and their hybrids are commonly planted through the southern part of the United States as ornamentals for their showy flowers. Included in the key below, Ashe magnolia and pyramid magnolia are rarely encountered.

Leaves of magnolias are evergreen or deciduous and never lobed. Some species have earlike flaps at the leaf base (auriculate). Each flower contains 3 sepals and 6–15 petals. Flowers of our native species are white, yellow-white, or green-yellow. The fruit is a large conelike aggregate of spirally arranged follicles. Each follicle contains one or two seeds. At maturity when the follicle splits open, the outer part of the seed becomes fleshy and turns bright red. Each seed falls from the follicle but hangs suspended in the air on a slender thread. Looking and functioning like a berry, the seed is dispersed by birds. The pith of the twig is either homogeneous or diaphragmed.

KEY TO MAGNOLIAS

1. Leaves evergreen . . . . .Go to 2
1. Leaves deciduous . . . . .Go to 3

Fig. 327. Cucumbertree (*Magnolia acuminata*) leaves, twig, flower, and fruit.

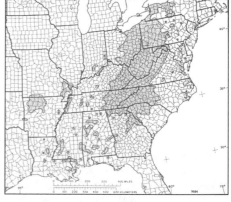

Fig. 328. Native range of cucumbertree (*Magnolia acuminata*).

2. Leaves red or brown hairy below   . . .southern magnolia, *Magnolia grandiflora*
2. Leaves white-waxy below . . . . .sweetbay, *Magnolia virginiana*
3. Leaf base rounded, flat, or pointed 4
3. Leaf base with earlike flaps (auriculate) 6
    4. Leaves white-waxy below . . . . .sweetbay, *Magnolia virginiana*
    4. Leaves light green below 5
5. Leaf base flat to rounded; leaf 5–10 in. long . . .cucumbertree, *Magnolia acuminata*
5. Leaf base pointed; leaf over 10 in. long . . . .umbrella magnolia, *Magnolia tripetala*
    6. Buds, twigs, and leaf undersurfaces hairless 7
    6. Buds, twigs, and leaf undersurfaces hairy 8
7. Found in Coastal Plain; leaves slightly fiddle-shaped . . . .
. . . . .pyramid magnolia, *Magnolia pyramidata*
7. Found in mountains; leaves tapering uniformly to base . . . .
. . . . .Fraser magnolia, *Magnolia fraseri*
    8. Rare in Florida panhandle; leaf 9–18 in. long . .Ashe magnolia, *Magnolia ashei*
    8. Found outside Florida; leaf over 18 in. long . . . .
. . . . .bigleaf magnolia, *Magnolia macrophylla*

Cucumbertree, Cucumber magnolia

Magnolia acuminata L. (fig. 327)

Form. Medium-sized excurrent tree growing 60–80 ft in height and 3–4 ft in diameter (largest known 120 ft by 6 ft). Bole clear and straight with small branches.

Leaves. Deciduous; broadly elliptical to ovate; 5–10 in. long; entire; hairless above; hairless or hairy below. Tip acute to acuminate. Base rounded to broadly wedge-shaped.

Flowers. Usually green-yellow but sometimes yellow; 2–3 in. long.

Fruit. Aggregate of follicles resembling a cone; cylindric to ovoid; 2–3 in. long; hairless. Seeds 0.5 in. long. Young green fruit resemble a cucumber, hence the common name.

Twigs. Moderately stout; lustrous. Pith homogenous. Terminal buds 0.5–0.7 in. long; silver-white hairy.

Bark. Thin; dark brown to gray-brown; divided by shallow furrows into narrow scaly ridges. Similar to yellow-poplar but with smaller ridges.

Wood. Sold as yellow-poplar. Wood use same as yellow-poplar.

Natural History. Moderately tolerant of shade. Short-lived; reaches maturity in 100–120 years. Reproduction sparse; good seed crops produced every 4–5 years; sprouts vigorously from stumps. Wildfire and late spring frosts cause the most damage. Found on moist but well-drained soils; most common on gentle to moderate slopes. Occurs as scattered trees, nowhere abundant; grows with yellow-poplar, northern red oak, white oak, black cherry, sugar maple, red maple, yellow birch, sweet birch, eastern hemlock, basswood, and American beech.

Varieties. As many as 5 varieties have been named, but most authorities recognize none. Var. *cordata* with yellow flowers and hairy twigs is probably best known.

Range. See figure 328. Elevation: to 5,000 ft.

Fraser magnolia, Wahoo

Magnolia fraseri Walt. (fig. 329)

Moderate-sized understory tree growing to 80 ft in height (largest known 110 ft by 3 ft). Bole often crooked or leaning; often 2–3 stems growing in a clump. Leaves broadly obovate to diamond-shaped; tapering uniformly to the base; entire; 8–12 in. long; hairless above and below. Leaf tip acute to obtuse. Leaf base deeply heart-shaped or with earlike flaps (auriculate). Flowers mostly white; the outer petals green-white. Fruit a conelike aggregate of follicles; 3–4 in. long; hairless. Twigs and buds hairless; pith homogeneous. Bark gray to red-brown; smooth except on very large trees, which develop minute round cobbles. Wood used most-

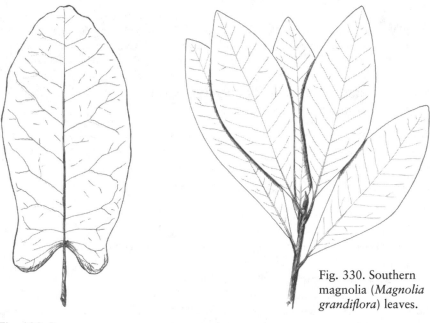

Fig. 330. Southern magnolia (*Magnolia grandiflora*) leaves.

Fig. 329. Fraser magnolia (*Magnolia fraseri*) leaf.

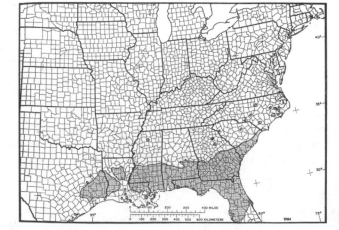

Fig. 331. Native range of southern magnolia (*Magnolia grandiflora*).

ly for pulpwood; sold as yellow-poplar. Moderately tolerant of shade; generally slow growing. Some seed produced every year, but good seed crops produced only every 4–5 years; seed viability only about 15 percent. Most trees become members of the lower canopy by sprouting from saplings or stumps. Wildfire causes the most damage. Generally found on moist well-drained soils in coves; occasional on dry-mesic upper slopes. Grows as scattered individuals in mixed stands with yellow-poplar, yellow birch, sweet birch, eastern hemlock, sugar maple, red maple, basswood, sassafras, black cherry, northern red oak, white oak, and chestnut oak. Pyramid magnolia is sometimes classified as a variety of Fraser magnolia. Pyramid magnolia occurs in the lower Piedmont and Coastal Plain of the deep South, while Fraser magnolia occurs in the Appalachians from West Virginia to northern Georgia.

Southern magnolia, Bullbay

Magnolia grandiflora L. (fig. 330)

Form. Medium-sized tree growing 60–80 ft in height and 2–3 ft in diameter (largest known 120 ft by 6 ft). In the northern part of the range, the bole is short and crooked. In the southern parts, a clear straight bole develops.

Leaves. Evergreen; persisting 2 years; narrowly oval to ovate; 5–8 in. long; entire; thick and leathery; dark green and lustrous above; hairless or red hairy below. Tip acute to acuminate. Base wedge-shaped or rounded. Used in dried floral arrangements.

Flowers. Cream-white; showy; lemon-scented; 6–8 in. in diameter; 6–12 large petals. Produces flowers scattered throughout the crown from late spring to late summer.

Fruit. Conelike aggregate of follicles; ovoid; 3–4 in. long; hairy. Seeds 0.5 in. long.

Twigs. Stout; red; woolly. Pith diaphragmed. Terminal buds 1–1.5 in. long; white or red; woolly.

Bark. Gray to light brown. Smooth on young trees. Old trees becoming somewhat cobbled with small thick blocks about 1 in. in length.

Wood. Sold as magnolia or yellow-poplar. Uses similar to yellow-poplar.

Natural History. Tolerant of shade when young; but becoming less tolerant with age. Fast growing. Reproduces well by seed in shaded understories; large seed crops produced most years; seed viability about 50 percent. Geographic range extending north and west from reproduction of cultivated specimens. Also reproduces by stump and root sprouts; branches resting on the ground develop roots and produce new trees. Resistant to sulfur dioxide; fire and winter drought cause the most damage. Found on moist well-drained bottomlands and lower slopes; will not tolerate prolonged flooding. Found on mesic uplands when protected from fire. Rarely found in pure stands; more commonly found mixed with loblolly pine, slash pine, American beech, sweetgum, yellow-poplar, swamp chestnut oak, white oak, southern red oak, cherrybark oak, sweetbay, and cabbage palmetto. Seeds eaten by squirrels, opossums, turkeys, and quail.

Hybrids. Hybridizes with sweetbay.

Range. See figure 331.

Bigleaf magnolia
Magnolia macrophylla Michx.

Small to moderate-sized tree growing 50–80 ft in height (largest known 105 ft by 2 ft). Leaves deciduous; broadly ovate to obovate; 18–36 in. long; pale green or more commonly chalk-white below. Leaf tip acute to obtuse. Leaf base flat or more commonly with earlike flaps (auriculate). Flowers 12–14 in. wide; cream-white; inner petals blotched with purple at base. Fruit a conelike aggregate of follicles; spherical; hairy toward tip. Twigs and buds silky hairy; pith homogeneous. Bark

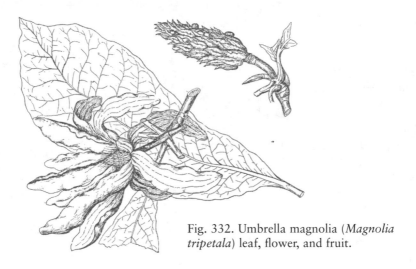

Fig. 332. Umbrella magnolia (*Magnolia tripetala*) leaf, flower, and fruit.

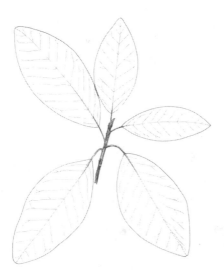

Fig. 333. Sweetbay (*Magnolia virginiana*) leaves.

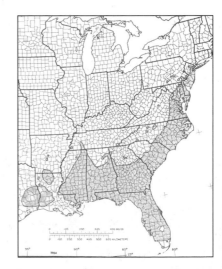

Fig. 334. Native range of sweetbay (*Magnolia virginiana*).

yellow-gray; smooth. Wood has no commercial value. Grows in well-drained bot-tomlands and fertile lower slopes. The relationship between bigleaf magnolia and Ashe magnolia has long been debated. They are considered varieties of 1 species by some authorities. Bigleaf magnolia is a larger tree found in the Piedmont and Appalachian Mountains from Kentucky to Mississippi with disjuncts in southern Ohio, coastal South Carolina, extreme northeastern Arkansas, and Louisiana. Ashe magnolia is limited to 6 counties in the panhandle of Florida.

Umbrella magnolia, Umbrella-tree
Magnolia tripetala L. (fig. 332)

Small deliquescent tree growing to 50 ft in height. Generally found growing in a clump of 2–5 stems. Leaves deciduous; 10–20 in. long; elliptical; often clustered at tips of twigs and looking like an umbrella; light green and hairy below, especial-ly on the midvein. Leaf tip and base long to short pointed. Flowers cream-white; 3–4 in. wide; foul scented. Fruit a conelike aggregate of follicles; 3–4 in. long; hair-less. Twigs and buds hairless; pith homogeneous. Bark light gray; smooth. Wood has no commercial value. Grows in rich woods, steep ravines, and well-drained bot-tomlands. Found from southern Pennsylvania to southern Mississippi; also in Arkansas and extreme southeastern Oklahoma.

Sweetbay, Sweetbay magnolia
Magnolia virginiana L. (fig. 333)

Form. Large spreading shrub growing to 30 ft, north of North Carolina; elsewhere moderate-sized excurrent tree growing to 90 ft in height. Grows tallest in cen-tral Florida.

Leaves. Deciduous in the northern parts of the distribution; evergreen in the south-ern parts; 3–9 in. long; oblong to elliptical; shiny above; white to white-waxy and hairless to hairy below. Tip acute to rounded. Base rounded to wedge-shaped.

Flowers. White; 2–3 in. wide; appearing in late spring and early summer.

Fruits. Conelike aggregate of follicles; 1–2 in. long; elliptical; hairless.

Twigs. Olive-green. Terminal buds silky white.

Bark. Smooth; gray; thin.

Wood. Sold as magnolia or yellow-poplar. Use same as yellow-poplar.

Natural History. Moderately tolerant of shade. Growth rate slow to moderate. Low numbers of seed produced nearly every year; seed viability about 40 percent. Also reproduces from stump sprouts. Fire causes the most damage. Found on poorly drained nonalluvial sandy or organic soils; common in pocosins, Carolina bays, and small backwater rivers. Grows with pond pine, slash pine, loblolly pine, Atlantic whitecedar, pondcypress, loblolly-bay, redbay, titi, swamp blackgum, sweetgum, and laurel oak. Sometimes cultivated; first North American magnolia introduced to Europe. Foliage and twigs eaten by white-tailed deer in winter.

Varieties. Several varieties have been named but none are currently recognized.

Range. See figure 334.

MAHOGANY FAMILY: MELIACEAE

Worldwide the Mahogany Family contains about 550 species in about 50 genera, all either trees or shrubs. The family is widespread in tropical and subtropical regions. Many species are found in the understory of rainforests. No species are native to our region, but Chinaberry has become naturalized in the warmer sections. The family is best known for the valuable wood produced by mahogany

Fig. 335. Chinaberry
(*Melia azedarach*) leaf.

(*Swietenia*), African-mahogany (*Khaya*), and cedar (*Cedrela*); and insecticides and medicines from neem (*Azadirachta*).

Leaves of this family are alternate, compound, and lack stipules. The flowers are usually unisexual, and pollinated by insects mostly bees and moths. The fruit is either a capsule, drupe, or berry.

Chinaberry
Melia azedarach L. (fig. 335)

Small tree growing 30–40 ft in height and 0.5–1 ft in diameter. Often growing in a clump of 2–4 stems. Crown open; spreading. Leaves alternate; deciduous; bipinnately compound; 1–2 ft long. Leaflets 1–3 in. long; oval; toothed or lobed near base; dark green; hairless. Flowers bisexual; fragrant; light purple; appearing after the new leaves are expanded. Fruit a drupe; yellow; 0.5–0.7 in. wide; persisting into winter; poisonous to humans and livestock. Seeds smooth; black; stone ridged. Twigs stout; olive-green; prominent lenticels. Terminal buds absent. Lateral buds appearing naked. Bark gray-brown to gray; nearly smooth on young trees with shallow orange furrows; with age, developing crisscrossing low ridges. Intolerant of shade; short-lived; fast growing. Formerly planted near southern farm houses because farmers believed the tree repelled insects, especially flies. Native to Asia from Iran to China. Naturalized from southeastern Virginia to Florida, and west to Arkansas and central Texas; also in California.

MIMOSA FAMILY: MIMOSACEAE

Sometimes recognized as a separate family, the Mimosaceae is included within the Legume Family (Fabaceae) in this manual. If recognized as a separate family, Mimosaceae would in our region contain acacia (*Acacia*), albizia (*Albizia*), leucaena (*Leucaena*), blackbead (*Pithecellobium*), and mesquite (*Prosopis*).

MULBERRY FAMILY: MORACEAE

The Mulberry Family contains nearly 1,100 species in about 40 genera in the world. Most species are tropical, but some occur in the temperate region. Our region contains 18 species in 7 genera, but only 4 species in 3 genera are tree-sized. Fig (*Ficus*) is one of the largest genera in the world, but only common fig (*Ficus carica*) occurs in our region in cultivation. Native to southwest Asia, common fig may persist at old homesites following cultivation, and it reportedly escapes occasionally in states along both coasts. Some authors include this family within the Nettle Family: the Urticaceae.

The Mulberry Family contains trees, shrubs, or occasionally vines and herbs. The leaves are evergreen or deciduous, alternate, and simple. Stipules are present, and the sap is usually milky. The flowers are minute and unisexual. Trees contain either both sexes (monoecious) or only one sex (dioecious). The flowers are wind pollinated, except for fig, which is pollinated by small wasps. The pollen is allergenic. The fruit is a drupe, often multiple in a small to large head. The wood of our species is heavy and ring-porous, but it has little current commercial value.

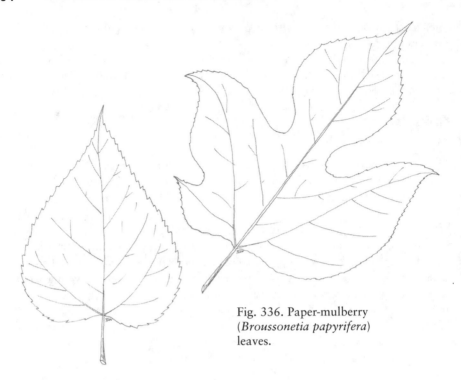

Fig. 336. Paper-mulberry (*Broussonetia papyrifera*) leaves.

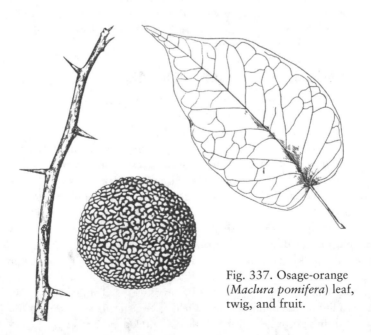

Fig. 337. Osage-orange (*Maclura pomifera*) leaf, twig, and fruit.

PAPER-MULBERRY: THE GENUS *BROUSSONETIA*

The paper-mulberries are all native to Asia where seven or eight species are known. Our region contains only the one species listed below.

Paper-mulberry

Broussonetia papyrifera (L.) Vent. (fig. 336)

Small tree growing to 50 ft in height. Crown broad and rounded. Leaves without lobes or 3–5 lobed; 3–8 in. long; margin serrate; sandpapery above; densely gray hairy below. Tip acuminate. Base flat to heart-shaped. Male and female flowers borne on separate trees (dioecious); apparently most trees are male. Fruit a drupe; spherical; orange-red; partly surrounded by calyx. Twigs hairy. Terminal bud absent (pseudoterminal); slightly hairy. Wood without commercial value; brittle. Bark was formerly used to make paper, rope, and tapa cloth. Native to eastern Asia; found persisting and somewhat spreading from cultivation at old home sites from southern New England to southern Texas.

OSAGE-ORANGE: THE GENUS *MACLURA*

The only species of *Maclura* in the world is the one in our region (monotypic).

Osage-orange, Hedge-apple, Bois d'arc, Bowwood

Maclura pomifera (Raf.) Schneid. (fig. 337)

Moderate-sized deliquescent tree growing 30–50 ft in height 1–2 ft in diameter (largest known 65 ft by 6 ft). Crown rounded; large curving branches; retains dead lower branches. Leaves ovate to oblong-lanceolate; 3–6 in. long; entire; dark green and lustrous above; hairy on the veins below. Tip long acuminate. Base rounded. Fruit a large spherical cluster of drupes; surface consisting of irregular rounded bumps; semiwoody; 3–5 in. in diameter; yellow-green; milky sap. Sexes borne on separate trees (dioecious). Twigs orange-brown; milky sap; some people are allergic to the milky sap; juveniles and sprouts armed with straight axillary thorns; 1–2 in. long; older trees without thorns but with spurlike lateral branchlets. Terminal bud absent. Bark thin; dark orange-brown; divided by shallow furrows into long, flat ridges. Wood with limited commercial value. Sapwood light yellow. Heartwood orange darkening with exposure; decay resistant; heavy; durable; not attacked by termites; yellow-orange dye formerly extracted from the wood with hot water; used for fence posts, insulator pins, machinery parts, and archery bows. Intolerant of shade. Reproduces well in full sun from seeds; large seed crops produced most years; seeds with little internal dormancy. Female trees without males nearby produce abundant fruit with empty seeds. Sprouts vigorously. Grows naturally in small pure stands or mixed with other hardwoods in rich bottomlands. Widely planted throughout the United States and southeast Canada as a living fence before barbed wire was available; later planted as a windbreak and in spoil bank reclamation. Fruit seldom eaten by wildlife. Found naturally in southeastern Oklahoma, extreme southwestern Arkansas, and east Texas. Also disjunct in Brewster County, Texas.

MULBERRY: THE GENUS *MORUS*

The genus *Morus* contains ten species in the world. Only three species occur naturally in our region, the two tree species described below and Texas mulberry (*Morus microphylla*), a tall shrub of south central and southwestern United States and Mexico with leaves only 1–2 in. long. In addition, black mulberry (*Morus nigra*), a native of Asia with dark red or black fruit, is cultivated and may escape locally.

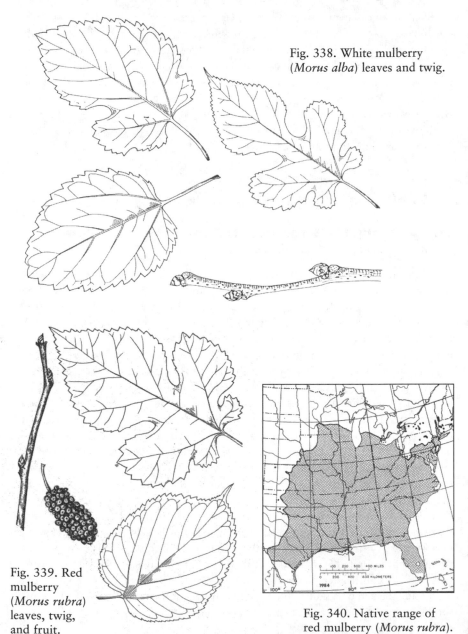

Fig. 338. White mulberry (*Morus alba*) leaves and twig.

Fig. 339. Red mulberry (*Morus rubra*) leaves, twig, and fruit.

Fig. 340. Native range of red mulberry (*Morus rubra*).

KEY TO MULBERRIES AND PAPER-MULBERRY

1. Fruit clusters spherical; leaves gray hairy below . . . .
. . . . .paper-mulberry, *Broussonetia papyrifera*
1. Fruit clusters cylindrical; leaves hairless or green-hairy below . . . . .Go to 2
   2. Leaves shiny above; hairless or hairy only on major veins below . . . .
. . . . .white mulberry, *Morus alba*
   2. Leaves dull above; hairy throughout below . . . . . . .red mulberry, *Morus rubra*

White mulberry
Morus alba L. (fig. 338)

Small to moderate-sized tree growing to 50 ft in height. Leaves ovate; 3–4 in. long; margin crenate; deeply irregularly 1–5 lobed on young trees; not lobed or 1 lobed on older trees; shiny and hairless above; hairless or hairy only on the major veins below. Tip acute. Base flat to heart-shaped. Fruit a drupe; white or dark purple; cylindrical; 0.5–1 in. long; juicy; edible. Twigs orange-brown; hairless or hairy. Bark smooth and orange-brown on young trees; developing shallow fissures on older trees but remaining basically smooth and orange-brown. Wood without commercial value. Found on a wide variety of soils, but generally in disturbed areas and edges of woods. Introduced from China in colonial times to provide a food source more suitable than red mulberry for the silk worm industry. Widely naturalized throughout our region.

Red mulberry
Morus rubra L. (fig. 339)

Small deliquescent tree growing 20–40 ft in height and 0.5–2 ft in diameter (largest known 70 ft by 3 ft). Generally found in the understory. Leaves almost rounded; 3–5 in. long; not lobed on large trees; 1–3 lobed on smaller trees; margins crenate; smooth or slightly sandpapery above; hairy throughout below. Tip acuminate. Base flat to heart-shaped. Each tree producing either both sexes or only one sex. Fruit a drupe; juicy; multiple and resembling a blackberry; 1–1.5 in. long; dark purple; edible. Twigs slender; brown; smooth. Terminal buds absent (pseudoterminal). Bark thin; orange-brown to gray-brown; divided by shallow furrows into long flat ridges; ends of ridges becoming slightly shaggy with age. Sapwood yellow. Heartwood orange-yellow to brown; no current commercial value; formerly used locally for fence posts, barrels, caskets, and agricultural implements. Tolerant of shade. Reproduces well from seeds; large seed crops produced every 2–3 years. A bacterial disease is beginning to cause considerable damage in the central portions of the range, but the disease has not been investigated thoroughly. Grows on moist well-drained soil in bottomlands and coves. Fruit eaten by humans, most birds, hogs, opossums, raccoons, and squirrels. Range shown in figure 340.

BAYBERRY OR WAXMYRTLE FAMILY: MYRICACEAE

Found mostly in subtropical and temperate conditions, the Bayberry Family contains 40–50 species in three genera in the world. Our region contains only *Myrica*, and only southern waxmyrtle is regularly tree-sized.

The Bayberry Family includes shrubs and small trees generally found in either wet or dry soils. The leaves are alternate, simple, and most contain aromatic yellow dots. Stipules are usually lacking. The flowers are reduced and unisexual, and they are borne in axillary aments. Each tree either contains both sexes (monoecious) or only one sex (dioecious). Each flower lacks both sepals and petals but is subtended by bracts. The ovary is inferior (usually) or superior with two carpels.

KEY TO BAYBERRIES

1. Leaves aromatic and leaf undersides with black glands . . . .
. . . . .Pacific waxmyrtle, *Myrica californica*
1. Leaves not aromatic or leaves aromatic with leaf undersides with yellow glands . . .
. . . . .Go to 2
   2. Leaves entire or nearly entire 3
   2. Leaves coarsely toothed 4
3. Leaves not aromatic . . . . .odorless bayberry, *Myrica inodora*
3. Leaves aromatic . . . . .northern bayberry, *Myrica pensylvanica*
   4. Leaves with many yellow glands on both surfaces . . . .
. . . . .southern waxmyrtle, *Myrica cerifera*
   4. Leaves with few or no yellow glands on upper surface . . . .
. . . . .evergreen bayberry, *Myrica heterophylla*

Southern waxmyrtle, Wax-myrtle, Bayberry

Myrica cerifera L. (fig. 341)

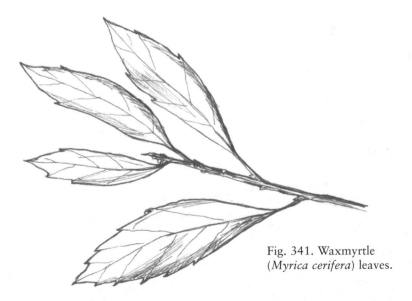

Fig. 341. Waxmyrtle
(*Myrica cerifera*) leaves.

Small multistemmed deliquescent tree growing 20–30 ft in height and 0.3–1 ft in diameter; often leaning and crooked. Leaves oblanceolate; evergreen. Tip blunt pointed; base gradually tapering. Margin with a few coarse teeth above the middle. Fruit a spherical drupe; dark blue; thickly covered with gray-white wax; 0.1 in. in diameter; often persisting into winter. Bark thin; smooth; gray; often covered with white splotches. Wax used in making scented candles. Roots contain nitrogen-fixing bacteria. Leaves thought to repel fleas. Found from southern New Jersey to southern Florida (including the Keys), and west to central Arkansas and central Texas.

MYRTLE FAMILY: MYRTACEAE

Worldwide the Myrtle Family contains 3,000–4,500 species in 130–145 genera. Most are found naturally in Australia and tropical America. None are native to our region, but eucalypt (*Eucalyptus*) is occasionally planted in the southern portions. Blue gum (*Eucalyptus globulus*) and possibly a few additional species have escaped in southern California where eucalypts are grown in plantations for commercial wood and oil production. In the search for fast-growing pulpwood species, much breeding and selection research was formerly conducted in the Southeast to find cold hardiness in tree-sized eucalypt, but these efforts have been abandoned as hopeless. In tropical America, Southeast Asia, South Africa, and Portugal eucalypt plantations have been established for pulpwood, lumber, and fuelwood because they are extremely productive.

Members of this family are either trees or shrubs with simple, alternate or opposite, evergreen leaves. The leaves are highly aromatic with translucent glands, and they lack stipules. The flowers have four to five petals and numerous often brightly colored stamen that sometimes look like a bottlebrush or a pom-pom. They are pollinated by birds, bats, or insects. The ovary is inferior or half inferior. The fruit is a berry or capsule. Economically the family provides Surinam-cherry (*Eugenia*), guava (*Psidium*), oils (*Eucalyptus* and *Melaleuca*), allspice (*Pimenta*), cloves (*Syzygium*), and lumber (*Eucalyptus* and *Eugenia*).

TUPELO FAMILY: NYSSACEAE

In this manual the Tupelo Family is included within the Dogwood Family (Cornaceae).

OLIVE FAMILY: OLEACEAE

Worldwide the Olive Family contains about 615 species in 24 genera found mostly in the Northern Hemisphere. Members of this family are either trees, shrubs, or lianas. The leaves are opposite, simple or compound, and they lack stipules. The flowers are bisexual or unisexual. Each flower usually contains four sepals, four petals, two stamen, and two carpels fused into a single structure. The ovary is superior. The fruit is either a drupe, capsule, or samara. Economically the family provides olive fruit and oil (*Olea*), perfume (*Jasminum*), wood products (*Fraxinus*), and ornamentals from fringetree (*Chionanthus*), forsythia (*Forsythia*), jasminum (*Jasminum*), privet (*Ligustrum*), and lilac (*Syringa*).

FRINGETREE: THE GENUS *CHIONANTHUS*

Worldwide this genus contains three species, two in our region and one in east Asia. Only one of our species is tree-sized.

Fig. 342. Fringetree (*Chionanthus virginicus*) leaves, flowers, and fruit.

Fig. 343. Swamp-privet (*Forestiera acuminata*) leaves.

Fringetree, Old man's beard
Chionanthus virginicus L. (fig. 342)

Shrub or small tree rarely growing to 40 ft in height and 1 ft in diameter. Leaves opposite; simple; deciduous; 4–8 in. long; oval to ovate; entire; slightly hairy below on the veins. Petiole slightly winged near base of leaf. Flowers bisexual; showy; white; borne in drooping clusters (panicles); appearing in the spring before or with the new leaves. Petals 4; linear. Fruit a drupe; oval; blue to nearly black; 0.5 in. long. Twigs with raised round leaf scars. Terminal buds present; scales keeled. Wood with no commercial value. Moderately tolerant of shade; found both in exposed and understory conditions. Grows on a variety of sites from dry-mesic to mesic. Planted as an ornamental for the showy flowers. Found from southern New Jersey to southern Missouri, and south to central Florida and east Texas.

FORESTIERA: THE GENUS *FORESTIERA*

Worldwide this genus contains about 20 species found in North and South America. Our region contains about 9 species, but only 1 is tree-sized.

Swamp-privet
Forestiera acuminata (Michx.) Poir. (fig. 343)

Shrub or small tree growing to 25 ft in height (tallest known 42 ft). Leaves opposite; simple; deciduous; lanceolate to rhombic; 2–4 in. long; 1–2 in. wide; hairless; finely toothed; tip gradually tapering. Flowers functionally unisexual; small; petals lacking; sepals quickly falling; appearing in the spring before the leaves; borne in clusters. Fruit a drupe; oblong; red-purple; sometimes covered with white-wax; 0.4–0.7 in. long; flesh thin. Grows along streams, in swamps, and edges of ponds. Not common. Found mostly in the Coastal Plain from southern South Carolina to northern Florida, west to East Texas, and north in the Mississippi River valley to southwestern Indiana.

ASH: THE GENUS *FRAXINUS*

Worldwide this genus contains about 70 species, scattered through the Northern Hemisphere and extending into the tropical forests of Java and Cuba. In our region, 16 species occur naturally, but fragrant ash (*Fraxinus cuspidata*) and two-petal ash (*Fraxinus dipetala*) are usually large shrubs. Chihuahua ash (*Fraxinus papillosa*) and Gregg ash (*Fraxinus greggii*) occur only along the Mexican border and are seldom encountered. Leaves of different species are often similar, and fruit is often necessary for correct identifications.

Ash leaves are opposite, deciduous, and pinnately compound on most adults. (Leaves of one species and on seedlings are simple.) Stipules are lacking. The flowers are wind pollinated and either unisexual or bisexual. Individual trees either produce flowers of only one sex (dioecious) or produce bisexual flowers and flowers of one sex (polygamo-dioecious). Each flower contains either four sepals or no sepals, four petals or no petals, and 2 carpels. The pollen is allergenic. The fruit is a samara with a terminal wing. Terminal buds are produced, and the wood is ring-porous.

KEY TO ASHES

1. Flowers with petals . . . . .Go to 2
1. Flowers without petals . . . . .Go to 3
   2. Flowers with 4 petals . . . . .fragrant ash, *Fraxinus cuspidata*
   2. Flowers with 2 petals . . . . .two-petal ash, *Fraxinus dipetala*
3. Petioles winged . . . . .Gregg ash, *Fraxinus greggii*
3. Petioles not winged 4
   4. Young twigs 4-angled or 4-winged 5
   4. Young twigs round 7
5. Each leaf with 5–11 leaflets; Eastern . . . . .blue ash, *Fraxinus quadrangulata*
5. Each leaf with 1–5 leaflets; Southwestern 6
   6. Each leaf with 1 leaflet (rarely 3–7) . . . . .singleleaf ash, *Fraxinus anomala*
   6. Each leaf with 3–5 leaflets . . . . .Lowell ash, *Fraxinus anomala* var. *lowellii*
7. Body of fruit flat 8
7. Body of fruit nearly round 9
   8. Leaflets 7–11; lacking stalks .black ash, *Fraxinus nigra*
   8. Leaflets 3–7; stalked . . . . .Carolina ash, *Fraxinus caroliniana*
9. Wing terminal or extending to middle of seed cavity .10
9. Wing extending well below middle of seed cavity 13
   10. Leaflets stalkless or nearly so . . . . .Chihuahua ash, *Fraxinus papillosa*
   10. Leaflets stalked 11
11. Seed wing extending to middle of seed cavity . .green ash, *Fraxinus pennsylvanica*
11. Seed wing terminal, beginning at tip of seed cavity 12
   12. Leaflets 7 (rarely 5–9) per leaf . . . . .white ash, *Fraxinus americana*
   12. Leaflets 5 (rarely 7) per leaf . . . . .Texas ash, *Fraxinus texensis*

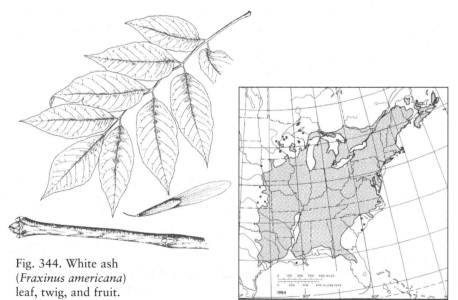

Fig. 344. White ash
(*Fraxinus americana*)
leaf, twig, and fruit.

Fig. 345. Native range of white ash
(*Fraxinus americana*).

13. Fruit 2–3 in. long; Eastern . . . . .pumpkin ash, *Fraxinus profunda*
13. Fruit not over 2 in. long; Western 14
    14. Leaflets usually stalkless; West Coast . . . . .Oregon ash, *Fraxinus latifolia*
    14. Leaflets stalked; Southwestern 15
15. Leaflets hairless below (except for tufts in vein axils) . . . .
  . . . . .Berlandier ash, *Fraxinus berlandierana*
15. Leaflets densely hairy below . . . . .velvet ash, *Fraxinus velutina*

White ash, American ash

Fraxinus americana L. (fig. 344)

Form. Medium-sized tree growing 60–90 ft in height and 2–3 ft in diameter (largest known 160 ft by 7 ft). Crown open.

Leaves. Opposite; pinnately compound; 8–12 in. long. Leaflets 5–9 (mostly 7); ovate to oblong-lanceolate; 3–5 in. long; entire or with rounded teeth; cuticle with minute rounded projections; hairy or hairless below.

Flowers. Unisexual with each tree producing only 1 sex (dioecious); petals absent; borne in loose clusers (panicles); appearing in the spring with or before the new leaves.

Fruit. Samara; 1–2 in. long; wing beginning at end of seed cavity. Seed cavity rounded; plump.

Twigs. Round; rather stout; gray-green; hairy or hairless. Terminal buds small; rounded; dark brown; nearly hairless; uppermost lateral buds located at base of terminal bud.

Bark. Two forms. Light gray with shallow furrows and interlacing ridges that form diamond- and x-shapes. In the South, yellow-brown and corky with deep furrows that separate short pointed ridges.

Wood. Sapwood nearly white; wide. Heartwood gray-brown, light brown or yellow; hard; heavy. High commercial value; used for long tool handles (rakes and hoes), furniture, kitchen cabinets, paneling, flooring, truck and train car parts, and sports equipment (hockey sticks, baseball bats, tennis rackets, and oars).

Natural History. Tolerant of shade when young, becoming intolerant. Initial growth slow but becoming fast growing. Large seed crop produced about every 3 years. Sprouts well from stumps; epicormic branching minimal. Root grafting to other white ash common. Ash decline, air pollution, and oystershell scale cause the most damage. Demanding in site requirements; requires moist well-drained soil with high nitrogen and medium to high calcium content. Grows in mixed stands with eastern white pine, northern red oak, white oak, southern red oak, yellow-poplar, basswood, American beech, black cherry, sugar maple, red maple, and yellow birch. Foliage eaten by white-tailed deer and cattle. Seeds eaten by songbirds and squirrels. Bark eaten by rabbits, porcupine, and beaver. Leaves formerly thought to repel rattlesnakes.

Varieties. Trees with hairy leaves and twigs are sometimes classified as var. *biltmoreana*. Some authors make this variety a distinct species, *Fraxinus biltmoreana*.

Hybrids. Hybridizes and intergrades with Texas ash.

Range. See figure 345.

Singleleaf ash, Dwarf ash

Fraxinus anomala Torr. ex Wats.

Shrub or small tree growing to 25 ft in height. Branches often contorted. Leaves usually with 1 leaflet (rarely 2–3); broadly ovate or suborbicular; 1–2 in. long (smaller if compound); hairless; margins entire or sparingly toothed above middle. Flowers appearing in the spring with the new leaves; bisexual or unisexual by abortion of stamens; petals absent. Fruit a samara; obovate-oblong; 0.5–0.7 in. long; wing rounded or notched at tip; seed cavity flat. Twigs square; slightly winged; orange-brown at first becoming round and ash-gray. Terminal bud ovoid; orange-hairy. Bark dark brown tinged with red; divided by shallow furrows into narrow scaly ridges. Wood with no commercial value. Intolerant of shade. Grows near streams or on dry hillsides. A variety with 5 leaflets is classified as Lowell ash (var. *lowellii*). Some authorities classify this variety as a separate species, *Fraxinus lowellii*. Found from western Colorado to eastern California, and south to Arizona and northwestern New Mexico.

Fig. 346. Carolina ash (*Fraxinus caroliniana*) leaves and fruit.

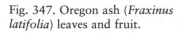

Fig. 347. Oregon ash (*Fraxinus latifolia*) leaves and fruit.

Fig. 348. Native range of Oregon ash (*Fraxinus latifolia*).

Berlandier ash

Fraxinus berlandieriana A. DC.

Small tree growing 25–30 ft in height. Leaves opposite; pinnately compound; 3–10 in. long. Leaflets 3–5; 3–4 in. long; 0.5–1.5 in. wide; hairless above and below. Fruit a samara; 1–1.5 in. long; wing extending along the seed cavity to base; mature in late spring. Found on stream banks and in moist canyons in central and southern Texas, and south into Mexico.

Carolina ash, Water ash, Pop ash

Fraxinus caroliniana Mill. (fig. 346)

Formerly called *Fraxinus pauciflora* Nutt. Small tree growing to 35 ft in height (tallest known 58 ft). Often found in a clump of 2–3 stems. Leaves 5–10 in. long. Leaflets 5–7; hairless or nearly so; long stalked; margin entire to slightly toothed. Flowers unisexual; appearing in the spring before the new leaves. Fruit a samara; obovate to elliptic; 2–3 in. long; wing extending along seed cavity to base; seed cavity flat; occasionally 3-winged. Bark gray with small ridges. Found in sloughs and wet flats long flooded in the growing season. Grows with baldcypress, red maple, water tupelo, swamp blackgum, laurel oak, overcup oak, and American elm. Found in the Coastal Plain from northeastern Virginia to southern Florida, and west to southern Arkansas and southeastern Texas.

Oregon ash

Fraxinus latifolia Benth. (fig. 347)

Nomenclature. Sometimes called *Fraxinus oregona*, a name published later.

Form. Medium-sized tree growing 60–80 ft in height and 2–3 ft in diameter (largest known 100 ft by 6 ft).

Leaves. Opposite; pinnately compound; 5–12 in. long. Leaflets 5–9; ovate to elliptic; 2–4 in. long; stalkless or short stalked; entire or finely toothed; hairy or slightly hairy below.

Flowers. Unisexual with each tree bearing only 1 sex (dioecious); borne in compact clusters (panicles); petals absent; appearing in the spring with the new leaves.

Fruit. Samara; oblong to elliptical; 1–2 in. long; wing extending well below middle of seed cavity. Seed cavity flattened.

Twigs. Round; stout; red-brown hairy. Terminal buds conical; brown; hairy.

Bark. Thick; gray-brown; fissured with flat ridges.

Wood. Similar to white ash but used mostly for fuel.

Natural History. Tolerant of shade as seedlings, becoming moderately tolerant with age. Reaches maturity in 200–250 years. Seeds produced most years; heavy seed crops every 3–5 years. Usually found along streams on poorly drained soil high in organic matter but also found in old fields and along roads. Grows in mixed stands with red alder, bigleaf maple, black cottonwood, Douglas-fir, and grand fir.

Range. See figure 348. The only ash native to the Pacific Northwest.

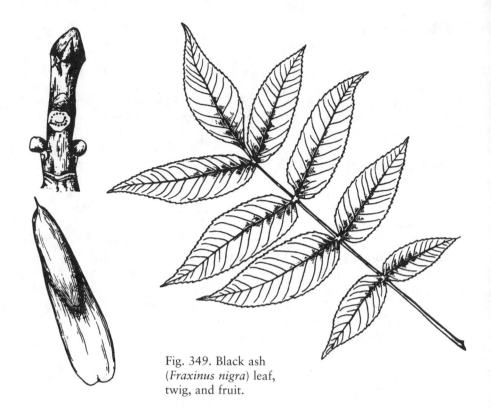

Fig. 349. Black ash
(*Fraxinus nigra*) leaf,
twig, and fruit.

Fig. 350. Native
range of black ash
(*Fraxinus nigra*).

Black ash

Fraxinus nigra Marsh. (fig. 349)

Form. Medium-sized tree growing 60–70 ft in height and 1–2 ft in diameter (largest known 110 ft by 5 ft). Crown open.

Leaves. Opposite; pinnately compound; 12–16 in. long; 7–13 leaflets. Leaflets oblong to oblong-lanceolate; 3–5 in. long; stalkless; toothed; hairless except for tufts at base of each leaflet.

Flowers. Bisexual and unisexual on each tree (polygamo-dioecious); appearing in the spring before the new leaves.

Fruit. Samara; oblong; 1–1.5 in. long; wing completely surrounding the flat indistinct seed cavity; falling early or late.

Twigs. Round; stout; gray; hairless. Terminal buds ovoid-conical; nearly black; nearly hairless; first pair of lateral buds located about 0.2 in. below terminal bud.

Bark. Gray; smooth becoming scaly.

Wood. Wood formerly used for baskets.

Natural History. Intolerant of shade. Growth rate slow. Seed production irregular; heavy crops produced every 4–6 years. Most seed germinates after the second year. Usually found in peat, muck, and wet sand soils along streams and seasonally flooded sloughs and flats. Grows in mixed stands with American elm, yellow birch, American beech, and red maple.

Range. See figure 350.

Green ash, Red ash

Fraxinus pennsylvanica Marsh. (fig. 351)

Form. Medium-sized tree growing 50–120 ft in height and 1–3 ft in diameter (largest known 145 ft by 6 ft). Upper stem often forked repeatedly.

Leaves. Opposite; pinnately compound; 6–10 in. long. Leaflets 7–9; lanceolate to elliptic; 3–5 in. long; usually toothed at least above the middle; hairless or hairy below.

Flowers. Unisexual with only one sex produced on each tree (dioecious); petals absent; appearing in the spring before or with the new leaves.

Fruit. Samara; narrowly oblanceolate; 1.5–2 in. long; wing extending to middle of seed cavity. Seed cavity slender; pointed at both ends.

Twigs. Rounded; rather stout; hairless or hairy. Terminal buds hairy.

Fig. 351. Green ash (*Fraxinus pennsylvanica*) leaf and fruit.

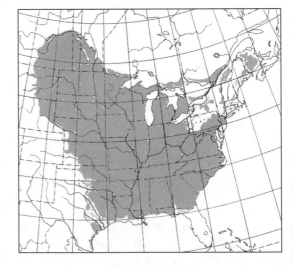

Fig. 352. Native range of green ash (*Fraxinus pennsylvanica*).

Bark. Thin; gray-brown; shallow fissures separate crisscrossing ridges to form x-patterns.

Wood. Similar to and sold as white ash. Planted in bottomlands in the Southeast for pulpwood, owing to the dense wood that provides high yields.

Natural History. Moderately tolerant of shade; tolerant when young in the South. Many female trees produce seed every year. Vigorous first-year seedlings lack side branches. Sprouts vigorously from stumps; 1-year-old seedlings and sprouts root easily and can be planted horizontally or vertically. Oystershell scale causes the most damage. The most site-adaptable ash in our region but found naturally only in alluvial bottomlands; tolerant of flooding for up to 40 percent of the growing season. Tolerant of droughty sites when planted; used on mine spoil banks. Sometimes found in nearly pure stands but more commonly mixed with American elm, boxelder, red maple, silver maple, sugarberry, sweetgum, eastern cottonwood, swamp cottonwood, swamp chestnut oak, swamp blackgum, and sycamore. Seeds eaten by songbirds. Foliage browsed by white-tailed deer. Rabbits and beaver eat the inner bark.

Varieties. Hairy plants were formerly called red ash (*Fraxinus pennsylvanica*) and hairless plants green ash (*Fraxinus pennsylvanica* var. *lanceolata*). This distinction was abandoned after research found that hairy parents produce both hairy and hairless offspring, and vice versa.

Range. See figure 352.

Pumpkin ash
Fraxinus profunda (Bush) Bush

Formerly known as *Fraxinus tomentosa*. Large tree growing 100–110 ft in height and 3–4 ft in diameter (largest known 130 ft by 5 ft). Base often swollen on wet sites, the source of the common name. Leaves opposite; pinnately compound; 10–18 in. long. Leaflets 7–9; lanceolate to elliptical; entire or slightly toothed; hairy below at least on the veins. Fruit a samara; oblong to oblanceolate; 2.5–3 in. long the largest of any native ash. Seed wing extending to base of seed cavity; frequently 3-winged. Seed cavity rounded. Twigs round; stout; gray-brown; hairless to very hairy. Terminal buds; red-brown; outer bud scales with flat tips. Bark thin; light gray with shallow fissures. Wood same as white ash. Tolerant of shade when young but becoming intolerant. Grows faster than green ash and usually managed like green ash but biology little known. Sprouts vigorously from stumps. Wildfire and drought cause the most damage. Found on mineral or muck soils on very wet sites that flood well into the growing season. Grows with baldcypress, water tupelo, swamp blackgum, red maple, Carolina ash, swamp cottonwood, overcup oak, swamp chestnut oak, American elm, and water hickory. Fruits eaten by songbirds. White-tailed deer browse the foliage. Based upon the number of chromosomes, some authorities think that pumpkin ash developed from hybridization between white and green ash. Found from southeastern Virginia to central Florida; in the Mississippi-Ohio River valley from southwestern Indiana to southern Tennessee; disjunct in Ohio, Indiana, central Tennessee, Mississippi, and Louisiana. Local and sporadic throughout its range.

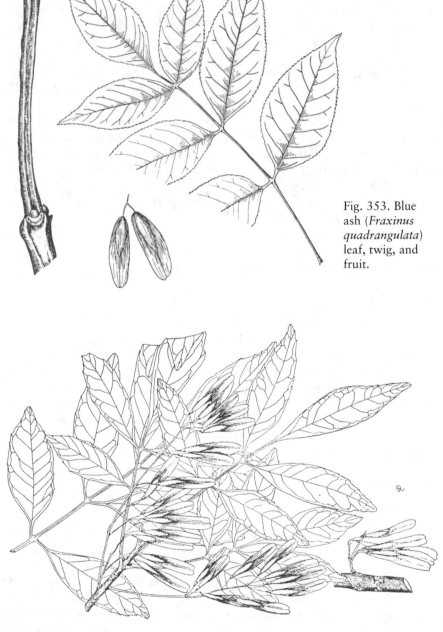

Fig. 353. Blue ash (*Fraxinus quadrangulata*) leaf, twig, and fruit.

Fig. 354. Velvet ash (*Fraxinus velutina*) leaves and fruit.

Blue ash
Fraxinus quadrangulata Michx. (fig. 353)

Medium-sized tree growing 40–50 ft in height and 1–2 ft in diameter (largest known 120 ft by 3 ft). Crown narrow; open. Leaves opposite; pinnately compound; 8–12 in. long. Leaflets 7–11; lanceolate to ovate; 3–5 in. long; coarsely toothed; stalks short; hairless. Flowers bisexual; petals absent; appearing in the spring before the new leaves. Fruit a samara; oblong-obovate; 1–2 in. long; wing completely surrounding the flat seed cavity; falling soon after maturing. Twigs 4-angled or 4-winged; stout; orange-brown; red hairy. Terminal buds rounded; dark red-brown; somewhat hairy. Bark rather thin; gray; divided into platelike scales; often becoming shaggy; inner bark turns blue on exposure and was formerly used for dye. Found from Ohio to extreme southern Wisconsin, and south to northern Alabama and eastern Oklahoma. Disjunct in southern Ontario, southern Michigan, western West Virginia, and northwestern Georgia.

Texas ash
Fraxinus texensis (Gray) Sarg.

Small tree growing to 50 ft in height and 1–2 ft in diameter. Bole and branches often twisted. Similar to and closely related to white ash. Leaves opposite; pinnately compound; 5–8 in. long; hairless or slightly hairy on the veins below and sometimes white-waxy. Leaflets 5 (rarely 7); 1–3 in. long; ovate, obovate, or elliptical; teeth widely spaced above the middle. Twigs round; green, red-brown, or gray; slightly hairy when young, becoming hairless. Buds densely orange-brown hairy. Fruit a samara; wing beginning at tip of seed cavity extending only slightly along the cavity; 0.5–1 in. long; wing tip rounded or notched; seed cavity round. Wood with limited commercial value; used locally for fuel and flooring. Found in southern Oklahoma and Texas.

Velvet ash
Fraxinus velutina Torr. (fig. 354)

Form. Small tree growing 25–50 ft in height and 1–1.5 ft in diameter.

Leaves. Opposite; pinnately compound; 4–6 in. long; stalk long hairy. Leaflets 3–9; elliptic, ovate, or obovate; 1–1.5 in. long; finely toothed above middle; hairy above becoming hairless; very hairy below.

Flowers. Unisexual with each tree bearing only 1 sex (dioecious); petals absent.

Fruit. Samara; oblong-obovate to elliptic; 0.7–1.5 in. long; wing shorter than and extending below middle of seed cavity. Seed cavity round.

Twigs. Rounded; slender; velvet hairy the first year becoming hairless. Buds hairy.

Bark. Thin; furrowed; gray to red-brown.

Wood. Little or no commercial value; used locally for fuel, tool handles, and wagon parts.

Natural History. Intolerant of shade. Grows in mountain canyons and on banks of streams.

Range. Found from southwestern Utah to southern Nevada, and south from western Texas to southern California. The common ash of the Southwest.

PRIVET: THE GENUS *LIGUSTRUM*

Worldwide this genus contains 40–50 species found in Europe, Asia, and Australia. None are native to our region, but several species have become naturalized following cultivation as hedges. Japanese privet (*Ligustrum japonicum*) from Japan; glossy privet (*Ligustrum lucidum*) from China, Korea, and Japan; California privet (*Ligustrum ovalifolium*) from Japan; and Chinese privet (*Ligustrum sinense*) are naturalized across the South. Glossy privet and Chinese privet have become noxious weeds in some bottomlands.

Privets are large shrubs or small trees with multiple stems. The leaves are opposite, simple, and either deciduous or evergreen. The flowers are bisexual and white. The fruits are blue or blue-black drupes sometimes covered with white wax borne in large clusters, and they persist into winter. The bark is smooth and gray. The fruits are eaten by songbirds.

Fig. 355. Devilwood (*Osmanthus americanus*) leaves, shoot and young flowers.

KEY TO PRIVETS

1. Leaves evergreen; shiny . . . . .Go to 2
1. Leaves deciduous; dull . . . . .Go to 3
   2. Leaves with translucent margin . . . . .glossy privet, *Ligustrum lucidum*
   2. Leaves with opaque margin . . . . .Japanese privet, *Ligustrum japonicum*
3. Twigs hairy . . . . .Chinese privet, *Ligustrum sinense*
3. Twigs hairless . . . . .California privet, *Ligustrum ovalifolium*

OSMANTHUS: THE GENUS *OSMANTHUS*

Worldwide this genus contains about 32 species found mostly in east Asia. Our region contains only the 1 species listed below.

Devilwood, Wild olive
Osmanthus americanus (L.) Benth. & Hook. f. ex Gray (fig. 355)

Shrub or small tree growing 25–30 ft in height (largest known 37 ft by 1.7 ft). Leaves opposite; simple; evergreen; oblong, elliptical, or obovate; thick; lustrous; entire; 3–5 in. long. Flowers small; white; bisexual or bisexual and unisexual (polygamous); borne in clusters. Fruit a drupe; oval; blue-purple; 0.5–0.7 in. long. Wood hard; difficult to work with or split, qualities that provide the common name. In central Florida, plants with smaller leaves and larger fruits are sometimes designated var. *megacarpus,* which some authors treat as a distinct species. Found in the Coastal Plain from southeastern Virginia to central Florida, and west to southeastern Louisiana.

SYCAMORE OR PLANE-TREE FAMILY: PLATANACEAE

Worldwide the Sycamore Family contains six to eight species, all in one genus found in our region, Mexico, Guatemala, and Eurasia. Our region contains three native species. In addition, the London plane-tree (*Platanus* x *acerifolia*), the probable hybrid between American sycamore and Oriental plane-tree (*Platanus orientalis*), is sometimes planted. In North America, trees of this genus are called sycamore; elsewhere they are plane-trees.

Sycamores are trees with alternate, simple, deciduous leaves with stipules that leave encircling scars on the twig. Leaves on mature trees have three to seven palmate lobes, but leaves on juveniles are often not lobed. Many young leaves and twigs contain distinctive candelabralike hairs that cause allergic reactions in humans. The highly reduced flowers are wind pollinated and unisexual. They are borne in unisexual spherical heads, but both sexes occur on each tree (monoecious). Also arranged in heads, the fruits are achenes surrounded by bristles (the perianth). The fruits mature in one season and are dispersed by wind and water. The buds are completely enclosed by the base of the petiole. The bark naturally flakes to reveal the lighter undersurface. The wood is diffuse-porous with broad rays.

KEY TO SYCAMORES

1. Leaves with broad L-shaped sinuses ....Go to 2
1. Leaves with deep, U- or V-shaped sinuses ....Go to 3

Fig. 356. American sycamore (*Platanus occidentalis*) leaves, leaf stalk with hollow base, and fruiting heads.

Fig. 357. Native range of American sycamore (*Platanus occidentalis*).

2. Fruit heads single . . . . .American sycamore, *Platanus occidentalis*
2. Fruit heads in clusters of 2–3 . . . . .London plane-tree, *Platanus* x *acerifolia*
3. Summer leaves decidedly hairy below . . . . .California sycamore, *Platanus racemosa*
3. Summer leaves hairless or nearly hairless below 4
    4. Leaf margin coarsely toothed; exotic . . .Oriental plane-tree, *Platanus orientalis*
    4. Leaf margin entire or finely toothed; native . . . .
. . . . .Arizona sycamore, *Platanus wrightii*

American sycamore, Buttonwood

Platanus occidentalis L. (fig. 356)

Form. Large excurrent tree growing 80–120 ft in height and 3–8 ft in diameter (largest known 175 ft by 14 ft). One of the largest eastern hardwoods. Bole prunes well; may be free of branches for 80 ft.

Leaves. Round; 4–7 in. long; 3–5 lobes; sinuses L-shaped; coarsely toothed; light green and hairless above; paler and hairy along the veins below; petiole 2–3 in. long. Stipules large; leafy and persistent on vigorous shoots.

Fruit. Multiple of achenes; borne in heads 1–1.5 in. wide; achenes club-shaped with spur at apex and ring of erect hairs at base. Heads borne singly on stalks 3–6 in. long. Mature in autumn but not falling until late winter.

Twigs. Round; orange-brown; encircled by stipular scars. Pith round; homogeneous. Terminal bud absent; 0.2–0.4 in. long; cone-shaped; brown; covered by petiole base.

Bark. Tan; shallow fissures and small scaly ridges near base. Upper bole mottled with tan, green, and cream from peeling outer layers that expose lighter inner layers.

Wood. Commercially valuable. Sapwood yellow-white to red-brown. Heartwood red-brown to dark brown; moderately heavy; grain interlocked making splitting difficult. Used mostly for pulpwood, furniture drawers, baskets, barrels, paneling, and interior trim.

Natural History. Moderately tolerant of shade. Fast growing throughout life. Reproduces well from seed on bare soil; thick leaf litter prevents seedling establishment. Some seed produced every year; large seed crops produced every 1–2 years. Grown in plantations for pulpwood sometimes in intensive short rotations of 3–12 years. Reproduces well from stump sprouts. Anthracnose and top dieback cause the most damage. Subject to decline and stagnation on infertile or wet sites. Found on streams banks, levees, and small ridges in bottomlands; does not tolerate flooding during the growing season. In the central states, pioneers on old fields; used in mine spoil bank reclamation. Grows in pure stands or mixed with river birch, sweetgum, eastern cottonwood, black willow, boxelder, green ash, sugarberry, red maple, silver maple, and water oak.

Varieties. Trees with deeply lobed leaves with the blade winged along the petiole have been named var. *attenuata*. Trees with smaller leaves that are wider than long have been named var. *glabrata*, found mostly in the western part of the distribution.

Range. See figure 357.

California sycamore
Platanus racemosa Nutt. (fig. 358)

Moderate-sized tree growing 50–80 ft in height. Bole often leaning or partly reclining on the ground. Leaves 3–5 lobed; sinuses U-shaped; lobes longer than wide; margin entire or finely serrated; nearly hairless above; densely hairy below. Fruit a multiple of achenes; borne in heads in clusters of 2–7. Found along streams and in moist canyons in California and south into Baja California.

Arizona sycamore
Platanus wrightii S. Watson

Moderate-sized tree growing to 80 ft in height. Bole upright, leaning, or partly reclining on the ground. Leaves deeply 3–7 lobed; sinuses U- to V-shaped; lobes much longer than wide; margin entire or serrated; nearly hairless above and below. Fruit a multiple of achenes; borne in heads in clusters of 2–4. Common along streams and springs, and in moist canyons. Sometimes considered a variety of California sycamore, *Platanus racemosa*. var. *wrightii*. Found in southwestern New Mexico and Arizona, and south into Mexico.

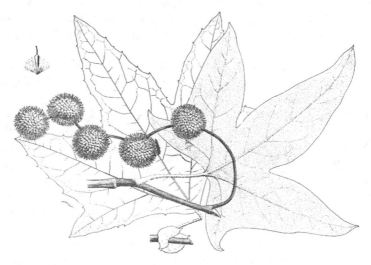

Fig. 358. California sycamore (*Platanus race-mosa*) leaf, fruit clusters (heads), and fruit.

BUCKTHORN FAMILY: RHAMNACEAE

Worldwide the Buckthorn Family contains about 850 species in 45 genera, found in both temperate and tropical areas. In our region about 100 species in 10 genera occur naturally, but only 3 genera—*Ceanothus, Condalia,* and *Rhamnus*—are tree-sized (see below). In addition, common jujube (*Ziziphus jujuba*), a tree native to Europe and cultivated for the edible fruit, occasionally escapes in the warmer areas of our region.

This family contains trees, shrubs, and vines. The leaves are simple and usually alternate with stipules. The flowers are small with four to five petals of various colors and are pollinated by insects. The fruit is basically a drupe, but in some species the flesh is thin and the inner stones split open resembling a capsule. Economically the family provides medicine (*Rhamnus*), dye (*Rhamnus*), and edible fruits (*Hovenia, Rhamnus*, and *Ziziphus*).

CEANOTHUS: THE GENUS *CEANOTHUS*

Worldwide this genus contains about 60 species found principally in California and Mexico. Most species are shrubs, but 3 species in our region occasionally become tree-sized. Of these 3 species, feltleaf ceanothus (*Ceanothus arboreus*) is found only on Santa Rosa, Santa Cruz, and Santa Catalina Islands of California.

Ceanothus leaves are simple, alternate or opposite, 1–3 in. long, and entire or toothed. Leaves usually have three prominent veins that nearly extend the length of the leaf. Some species develop thorns. The flowers are small with five petals and three carpels, and they are borne in clusters (umbels or panicles). The fruit is a three-lobed capsule that falls in three separate parts but often leaves the disklike base. The roots fix nitrogen.

KEY TO CEANOTHUS

1. Branchlets thorny . . . . .greenbark ceanothus, *Ceanothus spinosus*
1. Branchlets lacking thorns . . . . .Go to 2
　　2. Leaves densely short hairy and gray-white below . . . .
　　 . . . . .feltleaf ceanothus, *Ceanothus arboreus*
　　2. Leaves slightly hairy and yellow-green below . . . .
　　 . . . . .blueblossum, *Ceanothus thyrsiflorus*

Greenbark ceanothus, Redheart
Ceanothus spinosus Nutt.

Medium-sized shrub or small tree occasionally growing to 25 ft in height. Stems often leaning. Leaves alternate; simple; oblong to elliptical; entire or finely toothed; 0.5–1.5 in. long; slightly pinnately veined; hairless or nearly so. Flowers light blue to white. Fruit a capsule; resinous; barely 3-lobed. Twigs green-yellow; often with leafy thorns. Found in the Pacific Coast Range of southern California, and south into Mexico.

Blueblossum
Ceanothus thyrsiflorus Eschsch.

Medium-sized shrub or small tree sometimes growing to 25 ft in height. Stems usually upright. Leaves simple; alternate; ovate to elliptical; 3-veined; 0.7–2 in. long; fine glandular teeth; hairless and lustrous above; slightly hairy below on the veins. Flowers blue, rarely white. Fruit a capsule; slightly lobed; glandular and black at maturity. Twigs strongly angled. Found in the Pacific Coast Range from southwestern Oregon to southern California.

CONDALIA: THE GENUS *CONDALIA*

Worldwide this genus contains 18 species, all found in the American tropics or subtropics. Our region contains 5 species. Bitter condalia (*Condalia globosa*), found in southwestern Arizona and adjacent California, may rarely become tree-sized. Bluewood, discussed below, more commonly grows large enough to become tree-sized. The remaining 3 species are shrubs.

KEY TO CONDALIAS

1. Leaves 0.2–0.6 in. long; calyx shed from fruit . . .bitter condalia, *Condalia globosa*
1. Leaves 0.3–1.5 in. long; calyx retained on fruit . . . . . bluewood, *Condalia hookeri*

Bluewood
Condalia hookeri M. C. Johnst.

Long known as *Condalia obovata,* this name was discarded in 1962 because it had been used before for another species in a different family. Shrub or small tree sometimes growing to 30 ft in height. Commonly forming dense thickets. Leaves alternate but in clusters on short lateral branches; leathery; obovate; 0.3–1.5 in. long; entire. Petiole short or lacking. Flowers 0.1 in. wide; borne singly or in clus-

Fig. 359. Carolina buckthorn (*Rhamnus caroliniana*) shoot.

ters of 2–4; axillary. Petals absent. Sepals 5; green. Fruit a drupe; deep red or black; nearly spherical; 0.2–0.3 in. wide; shiny; calyx persistent. Twigs thorny; velvet hairy becoming hairless. Bark gray to brown; smooth on young trees developing deep furrows that separate narrow flat ridges. Sapwood yellow. Heartwood light red; heavy; hard; sinks in water; provides blue dye and fuelwood. Songbirds eat the fruit. Common in dry limestone soil along the Rio Grande in central and southern Texas.

BUCKTHORN: THE GENUS *RHAMNUS*

Between 100 and 150 species of buckthorn occur in the world mostly in the northern temperate region, but also in South America and South Africa. Our region contains 9 native species, and 2 species are naturalized. The taller species are keyed below, and the 4 tree-sized species are described in greater detail.

Buckthorns have simple, evergreen or deciduous, alternate or subopposite leaves with stipules. The small axillary flowers are either bisexual or unisexual. The flowers may produce abundant nectar making some species useful in honey production. The fruit is a one- to few-seeded drupe sometimes called a berrylike drupe. The wood is diffuse-porous.

KEY TO BUCKTHORNS

1. Terminal buds scaly . . . . .Go to 2
1. Terminal buds lacking scales . . . . .Go to 3
   2. Leaves deciduous; fruit black . . . . . .European buckthorn, *Rhamnus cathartica*
   2. Leaves evergreen; fruit red . . . . .hollyleaf buckthorn, *Rhamnus crocea*
3. Leaves evergreen; thick . . . . .California buckthorn, *Rhamnus californica*
3. Leaves deciduous; thin 4
   4. Leaves with 8–9 pairs of lateral veins . . . .glossy buckthorn, *Rhamnus frangula*
   4. Leaves with 8–15 pairs of lateral veins 5
5. Leaves 8–10 pairs of veins; fruit stalk shorter than petiole . . . .
   . . . . .Carolina buckthorn, *Rhamnus caroliniana*
5. Leaves 10–15 pairs of lateral veins; fruit stalk longer than petiole 6
   6. Leaves with 10–11 pairs of lateral veins . . . .
   . . . . birchleaf buckthorn, *Rhamnus betulifolia*
   6. Leaves with 10–15 pairs of lateral veins cascara buckthorn, *Rhamnus purshiana*

Carolina buckthorn
Rhamnus caroliniana Walt. (fig. 359)

Large shrub or small tree growing to 30 ft in height and 0.5 ft in diameter (tallest known 46 ft). Leaves alternate; simple; deciduous; 2–6 in. long; elliptical to oblong; margin nearly lacking teeth; lateral veins parallel except near margin; hairy below becoming less hairy. Leaf tip acute to obtuse. Leaf base rounded. Stipules present but falling quickly. Flowers bisexual; small; green-yellow; borne singly or in small clusters; axillary. Fruit a berrylike drupe; usually with 3 seeds; juicy; lustrous; black. Twigs red-brown and hairy becoming gray and hairless. Bud scales lacking. Grows most often in moist soil. Fruits eaten by songbirds, especially catbirds. Found from North Carolina to Missouri, and south to Florida and Texas.

European buckthorn, Common buckthorn

Rhamnus cathartica L.

Shrub or small tree sometimes growing to 30 ft in height. Leaves alternate or subopposite; deciduous but falling late; 1.5–3 in. long; elliptical to ovate; 3–5 pairs of lateral veins; teeth rounded; base rounded or heart-shaped. Flowers yellow-

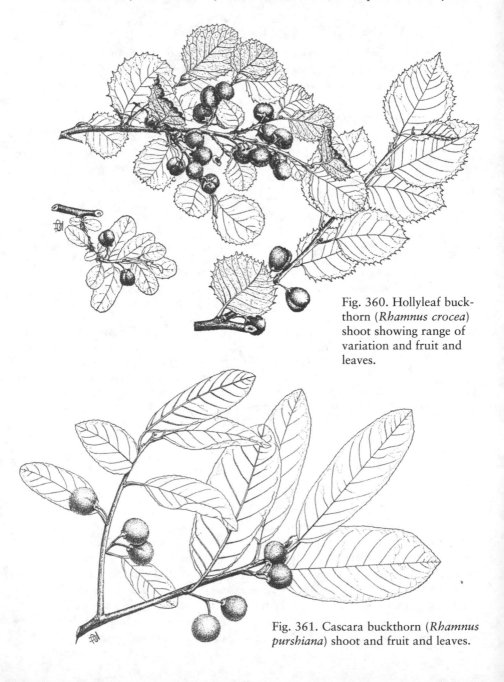

Fig. 360. Hollyleaf buckthorn (*Rhamnus crocea*) shoot showing range of variation and fruit and leaves.

Fig. 361. Cascara buckthorn (*Rhamnus purshiana*) shoot and fruit and leaves.

green; borne in small axillary clusters. Fruit a drupe; black; spherical; 0.2–0.3 in. wide. Twigs gray; often terminated by a small thorn. Terminal bud lacking. Lateral buds black; often angled. Found in disturbed habitats: roadsides, fencerows, and edges of woods. Fruits eaten by songbirds. Native to Europe and western and northern China. Cultivated in our region sometimes as a hedge, and now widely naturalized on upland sites in the Lake States, northeastern United States, and southeastern Canada.

Hollyleaf buckthorn
Rhamnus crocea Nutt. (fig. 360)

Shrub or small tree rarely growing to 30 ft in height and 0.5 ft in diameter. Crown round; branches stout. Leaves alternate or subopposite; evergreen; simple; oval or round; 1–1.5 in. long; margin spiny dentate; leathery; yellow-green and hairless above; hairy below and often golden. Flowers bisexual and either male or female on the same tree (polygamo-dioecious); borne in small axillary clusters; petals absent. Fruit berrylike drupe; obovoid; 0.2 in. wide; red; flesh thin and dry. Twigs slender; round; rigid; often spiny; red-brown; hairless. Terminal bud 0.1 in. long; scaly; scales hairy fringed. Bark thin; dark gray; slightly roughened by small bumps; bitter. Wood with low commercial value; hard and heavy. Intolerant of shade. Produces abundant fruits. Grows on hot dry hillsides; in small groves or scattered among other species. Found from northern to southern California, east into Arizona, and south into Mexico.

Cascara buckthorn
Rhamnus purshiana DC. (fig. 361)

Large shrub or small tree growing 30–40 ft in height and 1–1.5 ft in diameter (largest known 60 ft by 3 ft). Crown wide; numerous stout branches. Leaves alternate or subopposite; simple; broadly elliptical to obovate; 2–6 in. long; thin; lateral veins straight; hairy on the veins above and below. Margin undulate; finely toothed. Petiole stout; hairy; 0.5–1 in. long. Stipules minute; deciduous. Flowers bisexual; small; in axillary clusters; long stalked. Petals green; 5-lobed. Fruit a berrylike drupe; nearly spherical; 0.3–0.5 in. wide; blue-black; remnants of style persistent; not edible. Twigs slender; round; hairy becoming hairless; yellow-green or red-brown; lacking thorns. Terminal bud lacking bud scales (naked); red-brown hairy. Bark thin; gray to dark brown, often with irregular white patches; scaly. Wood with little commercial value; sapwood yellow-white. Heartwood yellow-brown tinged with red; heavy; hard; used locally for posts. Tolerant of shade; reproduces best in shade on moist or mucky litter. Produces abundant fruits. Sprouts prolifically from the stump. Found on a wide variety of sites ranging from moist bottomlands to gravelly soils. Found in small groves or mixed with Douglas-fir and western hemlock. Bark collected in Pacific Northwest to manufacture laxatives; trees with a diameter of 0.5 ft provide 12–15 pounds of bark. Found from southwestern British Columbia to northern California; also in southeastern British Columbia, western Montana, northern Idaho, and eastern Washington.

ROSE FAMILY: ROSACEAE

Worldwide the Rose Family contains between 2,000 and 3,000 species in 95–100 genera. The family is found throughout the world, but eastern Asia, Europe, and North America contain most species. In our area, about 900 species in 62 genera occur, but only 9 genera have members that regularly become tree-sized. In addition, 2 western species, cliffrose (*Cowania mexicana*) and Torrey vauquelinia (*Vauquelinia californica*), may occasionally become tree-sized under favorable conditions.

In our region, only black cherry is important for wood production although apples, pears, peaches, serviceberries, some plums, and some cherries provide valuable edible fruits. Many other trees in this family, known only to cultivation, are also important economically. For fruit production, quince, loquat, medlar, almond, apricot, some plums, and some cherries are valuable. For ornamental plantings, flowering cherries, crab apples, and pears are valuable. Many shrubby and nonwoody plants in this family are economically important, notably blackberry, raspberry, rose, and strawberry.

The Rose Family contains trees, shrubs, and herbs, some of which form thorns or prickles on leaves or twigs or both. The leaves are almost always alternate, but may be either simple, pinnately compound, or palmately compound. The margin is usually serrate, and stipules may or may not be present. Generally bisexual, the flowers have five sepals and five petals, and they are usually colorful and showy. The base of the sepals, petals, and stamens are fused into a cuplike structure (the floral cup or hypanthium), and the flowers are therefore perigynous and the ovary superior. In one subfamily (Maloideae), the cup completely encloses the ovary, and the ovary is inferior. Depending upon the genus, the fruits are either drupes, follicles, achenes, or pomes. Little or no endosperm forms in the seeds.

The family is divided into four subfamilies based upon ovary and fruit characteristics. The Amygdaloideae (which contains *Prunus*) has a superior ovary with one carpel that develops into a drupe. The Maloideae (which contains *Amelanchier*, *Crataegus*, *Malus*, *Pyrus*, *Sorbus*, and others) has an inferior ovary with two to five fused carpels that develop into a pome. The Rosoideae (which has few trees) has a superior ovary with numerous usually distinct carpels that develop into drupes or achenes. The Spiraeoideae (which contains no trees) has a superior ovary with two to five usually distinct carpels that develop into follicles.

SERVICEBERRY: THE GENUS *AMELANCHIER*

Worldwide the genus *Amelanchier* contains 16–33 species. Most species are large shrubs, but 4 species occasionally become tree-sized in our area. Only downy serviceberry, the species most often tree-sized, is discussed below. Serviceberries hybridize, and the characters separating the species are few and relatively minor. These situations make identification to species sometimes difficult, and most non-specialists identify individuals only to genus.

The leaves of serviceberry are alternate, simple, and deciduous. The margin is completely or partly toothed. The flowers are white, bisexual, borne in clusters, and appear in the spring before or with the new leaves. Each flower contains five petals. The fruit is a pome (apple) that matures in a single growing season. The twigs are slender, and the terminal buds green, slender, and about 0.5 in. long. The bark is smooth and gray. The wood is diffuse-porous.

KEY TO SERVICEBERRIES

1. Leaves with small teeth spaced much closer than 0.1 in. . . . .
   . . . . .downy serviceberry, *Amelanchier arborea*
1. Leaves with coarse teeth spaced at least 0.1 in. apart . . . . .Go to 2
   2. Leaf margin toothed from tip to base; eastern species . . . .
   . . . . .roundleaf serviceberry, *Amelanchier sanguinea*
   2. Leaf margin toothed from the tip to the middle of the leaf; western species . . .3
1. Leaves hairless or nearly so below; fruit hairless . . . .
   . . . . .western serviceberry, *Amelanchier alnifolia*
1. Leaves woolly below; fruit sometimes hairy . . . .
   . . . . .Utah serviceberry, *Amelanchier utahensis*

Downy serviceberry, Shadbush, Sarvis, Juneberry

Amelanchier arborea (Michx. f.) Fern. (fig. 362)

Form. Large shrub or small tree growing 25–40 ft in height and 0.5–1 ft in diameter (largest known 70 ft by 2 ft). Often leaning and growing in a clump of 2–3 stems.

Leaves. Oblong, ovate, or oval; 2–4 in. long; finely serrate from the tip to the base;

Fig. 362. Downy serviceberry
(*Amelanchier arborea*) leaf, twig,
and flower and fruit clusters.

each tooth about the same size; hairy below becoming hairless. Leaf tips acute. Leaf base rounded or heart-shaped. Petiole hairy.

Flowers. Held erect in crowded racemes; white; appearing with the new leaves; calyx tube persistent on fruit.

Fruit. Pome; spherical; 0.3–0.5 in. wide; dark red to purple; more or less white-waxy; flesh sweet. Seeds 5–10; dark chestnut-brown.

Twigs. Slender; round; red-brown to dark gray; bundle scars 3. Terminal bud 0.2–0.5 in. long; slender; green turning red-brown; pointed.

Bark. Thin; smooth; gray; developing dark gray vertical lines that develop into shallow fissures.

Wood. Little or no commercial value. Heartwood light brown; heavy; hard; close grained.

Natural History. Moderately tolerant of shade. Slow growing. Reproduces from seeds or stump sprouts. Found on a wide variety of soils ranging from stream banks to dry slopes, but not tolerant of flooding. Occurs as scattered individuals in mixed stands. Fruits eaten by songbirds and humans.

Varieties. Called Allegheny or smooth serviceberry, trees with hairless leaves and petioles are separated as var. *laevis*. This variety is sometimes made a distinct species, *Amelanchier laevis*.

Range. Nova Scotia to eastern Minnesota, south to northwestern Florida and eastern Oklahoma, but absent from most of the southeastern Coastal Plain and the Mississippi River valley south of extreme southern Illinois. Disjuncts in Newfoundland and Louisiana.

MOUNTAIN-MAHOGANY: THE GENUS *CERCOCARPUS*

Worldwide about ten species of mountain-mahogany occur, all in western North America and Mexico. Keyed below, three species of this generally shrubby genus are widespread and occasionally reach tree-size. In addition, Catalina mountain-mahogany (*Cercocarpus traskiae*) sometimes becomes tree-sized, but it is found only on Santa Catalina Island in California and not encountered by most people. Widespread but generally shrubby, alderleaf mountain-mahogany (*Cercocarpus montanus*) becomes tree-sized only in Utah.

The leaves of mountain-mahogany are alternate, simple, and either evergreen or deciduous. Lacking petals, the flowers are small and borne in axillary clusters on short lateral twigs. The fruit is an achene terminated by a long persistent style, which has the appearance of a long curly tail. The wood is diffuse-porous.

KEY TO MOUNTAIN-MAHOGANIES

1. Leaf margin rolled under (revolute) . . . .
. . . . .curlleaf mountain–mahogany, *Cercocarpus ledifolius*
1. Leaf margin flat . . . . .Go to 2
   2. Leaves entire or toothed only near the tip . . . .
. . . . .hairy mountain-mahogany, *Cercocarpus breviflorus*
   2. Leaves with numerous teeth above the middle . . . .
. . . . .birchleaf mountain-mahogany, *Cercocarpus betuloides*

Fig. 363. Curlleaf mountain-
mahogany (*Cercocarpus ledifolius*)
shoot and fruit with long curly tails.

Birchleaf mountain-mahogany
Cercocarpus betuloides Nutt.

Large shrub or small tree growing to 40 ft in height. Leaves alternate; evergreen or deciduous; thick; obovate to oval; 0.5–1.5 in. long; serrated above the middle; dark green and hairless above; paler and slightly hairy below. Fruit an achene; enclosed by silky hairy or nearly hairless calyx tube that often splits along one side; terminated by a long (2–4 in.) tail (the style). Twigs red-brown or gray; slightly hairy. Bark gray; smooth on young trees becoming scaly. Wood heavy; sometimes used for fuelwood, bowls, and novelties. Found along the Pacific coast from southern Oregon to Baja California; also disjunct in central Arizona.

Curlleaf mountain-mahogany, Curlleaf cercocarpus
Cercocarpus ledifolius Nutt. (fig. 363)

Form. Large shrub or small tree rarely growing to 40 ft in height and 2 ft in diameter. Bole short; crooked. Crown round; compact. Branches crooked; twisted.

Leaves. Alternate; lanceolate to lanceolate-elliptic; 0.5–1 in. long; thick; leathery; resinous odor; dark green and lustrous above; paler and slightly hairy below. Margin entire; rolled under (revolute).

Fruit. Achene; linear-oblong; 0.2 in. long; completely enclosed by silky calyx tube; chestnut-brown; tipped with hairy tail 2–3 in. long. Seeds solitary; linear.

Twigs. Stout; red-brown or silver-brown; hairy at first becoming hairless; spurlike lateral branches common. Terminal buds minute; scaly; hairy.

Bark. Red-brown or gray-brown; divided by furrows into scaly ridges.

Wood. Little or no commercial value. Heartwood red to dark brown; exceedingly heavy and hard sometimes sinking in water; close grained taking a high polish. Long-burning fuelwood; often used to smoke meat.

Natural History. Intolerant of shade. Slow growing. Found in small groups or thickets on dry, gravelly, windswept slopes. Foliage eaten by deer and elk. Animals find protection in the tangled thickets from weather and hunters.

Range. Found from western Montana to extreme southeastern Washington, and south to western Colorado, northern Arizona, and southern California.

HAWTHORN: THE GENUS *CRATAEGUS*

Hawthorn is an extremely large and reproductively complex genus. Some specialists consider the genus taxonomically unstable. Due to hybridization and the ability to form viable seeds without fertilization (apomixis), identification to species is difficult even for specialists. Most nonspecialists identify hawthorns to genus only and that procedure is followed here. It is not surprising that estimates of the number of species of hawthorn in the world vary greatly from 135 to over 3,000. In our area, roughly 65 species become tree-sized.

Fig. 364. Sample range of leaf shapes found in hawthorn (*Crataegus* sp.).

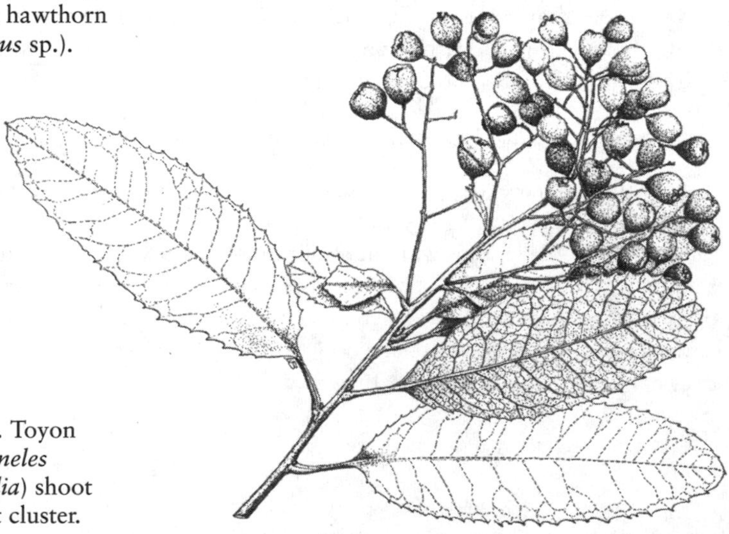

Fig. 365. Toyon (*Heteromeles arbutifolia*) shoot and fruit cluster.

Hawthorn, Haw
Crataegus sp. (fig. 364)

Form. Large shrubs or small trees growing to 40 ft in height and 1–2 ft in diameter. Sometimes forming thickets.

Leaves. Alternate; simple; deciduous; margin serrate or dentate; more-or-less lobed on some species. Stipules present; may persist on vigorous shoots. The range of possible leaf shapes shown in figure 364.

Flowers. White or pink; 5 petals; borne in flat-topped clusters (corymbs), each with few to many flowers; borne at the tips of small branches.

Fruit. Pome; spherical or pear-shaped; 0.3–1 in. wide; generally red or red-orange but also orange, blue, or black. Edible but usually dry and tasteless.

Twigs. Slightly zigzag. Thorns found above some leaves. Thorns stiff; straight or slightly curved; smooth; sharp; 1–3 in. long; not branched. Terminal buds present.

Bark. Smooth and gray when young. With age, turning red-brown, red-gray, or gray and developing shallow fissures that separate scaly ridges; the ridges sometimes becoming loose and thereby shaggy.

Wood. Little or no commercial value. Diffuse-porous. Sapwood light brown. Heartwood red-brown; heavy. Formerly used for tool handles; currently used occasionally for carving or turning stock.

Natural History. Moderately tolerant to intolerant of shade depending upon species. Generally slow growing. Found on a very wide variety of sites and conditions depending partly on species. A few species grow in standing water in sloughs but most species grow in first bottoms or in uplands. Common pioneer in disturbed areas, pastures, old fields, and along roads. Songbirds, upland game birds, and small mammals eat the fruit, especially in winter. Good nesting tree for songbirds because the thorns provide protection. Jelly made from the fruit of some species.

Range. Found essentially throughout our region.

TOYON: THE GENUS *HETEROMELES*

Worldwide this genus contains only the one species listed below (monotypic).

Toyon, Christmas-berry
Heteromeles arbutifolia (Lindl.) M. J. Roem. (fig. 365)

Formerly classified as *Photinia arbutifolia*. Large shrub or small tree rarely growing to 30 ft in height. Branches held erect. Leaves alternate; simple; thick; glossy; oblong to elliptical; sharply serrated; evergreen; 3–4 in. long. Flowers small; white; bisexual; borne in terminal leafy clusters (panicles) 4–6 in. wide. Fruit a pome; red to yellow; 0.2–0.3 in. long; partly covered by persistent sepals; remaining on branches until late winter. Twigs tan, hairy when young, becoming dark red and hairless. Terminal buds 0.2 in. long; acute; scales loose. Bark smooth; light gray. Wood with no commercial value; hard; heavy; close grained; heartwood dark red-brown. Intolerant of shade. Reproduction vigorous, often forming groves. Fruit-covered branches used for Christmas decorations. Grows in chaparral, dry-mesic slopes, and canyons. Found on west coastal islands, Coast Ranges, Sierra Nevada foothills, and south into Mexico.

APPLE AND CRAB APPLE: THE GENUS *MALUS*

This genus contains about 55 species scattered through the Northern Hemisphere. In addition, over 300 hybrids and cultivars have been developed for landscaping. In our region, 4 native species sometimes become tree-sized. A Eurasian species, the common apple, was introduced in colonial times and has become widely naturalized. A second exotic, Siberian crab apple (*Malus baccata*), is doubtfully naturalized. Species of *Malus* hybridize making identification difficult. Some authorities combine apples and pears into a single genus, *Pyrus*. See additional comments provided under pear (*Pyrus*).

Most apples and crab apples are large shrubs occasionally small trees. The leaves of this genus are alternate, simple, and either deciduous or semi-evergreen. Leaves of native species are more-or-less lobed with stipules free from the petioles.

Fig. 366. Sweet crab apple (*Malus coronaria*) leaf, twig, flowers, and fruit.

The flowers are bisexual, borne in small clusters on spurlike branches, and they appear with or after the new leaves. The petals are white to red. The calyx has five lobes, and it sometimes persists on the fruit. The ovary is inferior usually with five carpels, and it develops into a pome (apple). The wood is heavy, diffuse-porous, and not commercially valuable.

KEY TO APPLES AND CRAB APPLES

1. Leaves not lobed; exotic . . . . .Go to 2
1. Leaves lobed at least on vigorous shoots; native .Go to 3
   2. Leaves hairy below . . . . .common apple, *Malus sylvestris*
   2. Leaves hairless below . . . . .Siberian crab apple, *Malus baccata*
3. Calyx deciduous on fruit . . . . .Oregon crab apple, *Malus fusca*
3. Calyx persistent on fruit 4
   4. Mature leaves and calyx woolly . . . . .prairie crab apple, *Malus ioensis*
   4. Mature leaves and calyx hairless 5
5. Leaves on vigorous shoots lobed . . . . .sweet crab apple, *Malus coronaria*
5. Leaves on vigorous shoots with large teeth . . . .
  . . . . .southern crab apple, *Malus angustifolia*

Southern crab apple

Malus angustifolia (Ait.) Michx.

Small tree. Leaves elliptical to lanceolate; 1–3.5 in. long; margin crenate to serrate; hairy below at first but becoming hairless. Flowers pink turning white. Fruit spherical; green; waxy. Twigs hairy at first becoming hairless. Grows along fencerows, roadsides, and edges of woods. Found from North Carolina to Mississippi; also in disjunct areas farther north from New Jersey to east Texas.

Sweet crab apple, wild crab apple

Malus coronaria (L.) Mill. (fig. 366)

Large shrub rarely a small tree. Leaves ovate to triangular; 2–4 in. long; margin sharply toothed, becoming lobed at base; hairless below. Petiole often glandular near the middle. Flowers white to pink. Fruit nearly spherical; yellow-green; waxy; persisting through the winter. Twigs thorny. Grows along roads, in fencerows, old fields, and edges of woods. Sometimes forms thickets from root sprouts. Found in central Michigan, Ontario, and New York; and south to Kentucky and West Virginia; also found in small disjunct areas in surrounding states.

Oregon crab apple, Pacific crab apple

Malus fusca (Raf.) Schneid.

Large shrub or small tree sometimes reaching 35 ft in height. Leaves ovate to lanceolate; 1–3 in. long; 3-lobed on vigorous shoots; red hairy below. Flowers white. Fruit oblong; red-yellow. Twigs sometimes thorny. Grows in wet woods and on stream banks along the western coast from Alaska to northern California.

Prairie crab apple, Wild crab apple

Malus ioensis (Wood) Britt. (fig. 367)

Large shrub or small tree sometimes growing to 35 ft in height. Leaves ovate to elliptical; 2–4 in. long; margin coarsely toothed or lobed especially on vigorous shoots; very hairy below at least on the veins. Petiole very hairy. Fruit nearly spherical; green; waxy. Grows in abandoned pastures, fencerows, and edges of woods. Found in southern Wisconsin and Minnesota; Illinois, Iowa, and Missouri; also in disjunct areas in surrounding states and Texas and Louisiana.

Common apple

Malus sylvestris (L.) Mill.

Medium-sized tree. Leaves elliptical to ovate; 2–4 in. long; not lobed; dull; margin serrate, crenate, or entire; white hairy below. Petiole slightly white hairy. Nectar used in honey production. Native to Eurasia; parent of most cultivated apples, over 3,000 varieties have been developed; introduced to our region during colonial times for fruit and now widely naturalized in North America; often found at home sites persisting from cultivation.

CHERRIES AND PLUMS: THE GENUS *PRUNUS*

Worldwide between 200 and 400 species of *Prunus* are known mostly in northern temperate regions. In our region, about 30 species are native. Most species are thicket-forming shrubs; only 16 species become more-or-less tree-sized. Two species have tiny distributions. Desert apricot (*Prunus fremontii*) occurs only in extreme

Fig. 367. Prairie crab apple (*Malus ioensis*) leaf.

southern California and Baja, while Catalina cherry (*Prunus lyonii*) is limited to several islands of southern California and a disjunct population in Baja. Six exotic species are sporadically naturalized or may persist from cultivation: mazzard (*Prunus avium*), sour cherry (*Prunus cerasus*), garden plum (*Prunus domestica*), Mahaleb cherry (*Prunus mahaleb*), peach (*Prunus persica*), and sloe or blackthorn (*Prunus spinosa*). Commonly planted only recently, Japanese apricot (*Prunus mume*) is adventive in the South, and may become thoroughly naturalized.

Cherry leaves are alternate, simple, deciduous or evergreen, and usually serrated. Stipules are produced, and the petiole or lower leaf blade usually contains glands. The flowers are usually bisexual, showy, and pollinated by insects. They appear before, with, or after the new leaves. The flowers may be single or in clusters (racemes, corymbs, or umbels). Each flower contains five petals usually white or pink. The ovary consists of a single carpel that matures in one growing season. The fruit is a dry or fleshy drupe containing one seed. The fruit of several species is important food for humans and wildlife. The twigs often contain hydrocyanic acid and smell of bitter almond. Lateral twigs are often thornlike. Terminal buds are present or absent. The bark is generally marked with horizontal lines of lenticels. The wood is diffuse-porous, but only black cherry produces commercially valuable lumber on a large scale.

KEY TO CHERRIES AND PLUMS

1. Fruit usually over 0.5 in. in diameter; grooved from tip to base . . . . .Go to 2
1. Fruit less than 0.5 in. in diameter; smooth not grooved . . . . .Go to 13
  2. Terminal bud present; fruit hairy . . . . .peach, *Prunus persica*
  2. Terminal bud absent; fruit hairless 3
3. Flowers single or in clusters of 2; naturalized 4
3. Flowers in clusters of 3 or more; native 5
  4. Twigs hairless . . . . .garden plum, *Prunus domestica*
  4. Twigs hairy or woolly . . . . .sloe, *Prunus spinosa*
5. Leaves round-ovate; western Oregon and California . . . .
  . . . . .Klamath plum, *Prunus subcordata*
5. Leaves ovate to lanceolate; east of Pacific Coast 6
  6. Leaves with pointed teeth 7
  6. Leaves with rounded teeth 10
7. Fruit purple; often covered with white wax 8
7. Fruit red to yellow 9
  8. Pit of fruit curved . . . . .Allegheny plum, *Prunus alleghaniensis*
  8. Pit of fruit flattened . . . . .flatwoods plum, *Prunus umbellata*
9. Leaves hairy below; twigs hairy . . . . .Mexican plum, *Prunus mexicana*
9. Leaves nearly hairless below; twigs hairless . . . .American plum, *Prunus americana*
  10. Leaves coarsely or doubly toothed . . . . .Canada plum, *Prunus nigra*
  10. Leaves finely toothed 11
11. Leaves 1–2.5 in. long; calyx not glandular . .Chickasaw plum, *Prunus angustifolia*
11. Leaves 2.5–6 in. long; calyx glandular 12
  12. Leaves oblong to obovate . . . . .hortulan plum, *Prunus hortulana*
  12. Leaves elliptic to lanceolate . . . . .wildgoose plum, *Prunus munsoniana*

13. Flowers 10 or more in elongated racemes 14
13. Flowers single or 2–6 in umbels or corymbs 18
  14. Leaves deciduous 15
  14. Leaves evergreen 16
15. Calyx shed from fruit . . . . .chokecherry, *Prunus virginiana*
15. Calyx persistent on fruit .black cherry, *Prunus serotina*
  16. Southeastern . . . . .Carolina laurel cherry, *Prunus caroliniana*
  16. California 17
17. Leaves spiny toothed . . . . .hollyleaf cherry, *Prunus ilicifolia*
17. Leaves entire or minutely toothed . . . . .Catalina cherry, *Prunus lyonii*
  18. Calyx persistent on fruit 19
  18. Calyx shed from fruit 20

Fig. 368. American plum
(*Prunus americana*) shoot
and flower and fruit clusters.

19. Leaves thin; hairy below at least along veins . . . . . . .mazzard, *Prunus avium*
19. Leaves semileathery; hairless below . . . . .sour cherry, *Prunus cerasus*
  20. Leaves round to broad-ovate; naturalized . . . .
    . . . . .Mahaleb cherry, *Prunus mahaleb*
  20. Leaves lanceolate, oblong, or obovate; native 21
21. Leaves oblong to obovate . . . . .bitter cherry, *Prunus emarginata*
21. Leaves lanceolate .pin cherry, *Prunus pensylvanica*

American plum

Prunus americana Marsh. (fig. 368)

Form. Shrub or small tree growing to 30 ft in height and rarely to 1 ft in diameter. Bole short usually dividing near the ground. Spreading by root sprouts to form dense thickets.

Leaves. Ovate to lanceolate; sometimes obovate; 3–4 in. long; 1–1.5 in. wide; sharply and often doubly serrate; teeth not tipped by glands; dark green above; pale and hairless below. Tip acuminate. Base rounded. Petiole 0.5–0.7 in. long; glandless.

Flowers. Borne in clusters (umbels) of 2–5. Stalk slender; hairless; 0.5–0.7 in. long. Appearing before or with the new leaves; ill scented. Calyx tube narrow; bright red outside; green and hairy inside. Petals white.

Fruit. Drupe; subspherical; 1 in. in diameter; orange to red often spotted with yellow; thick skinned; nearly free of white wax. Flesh bright yellow; juicy; acidic; used for jelly. Pit oval; rounded at tip; 0.7–1 in. long.

Twigs. Hairless; often thornlike; bitter almond odor; green at first turning orange-brown; marked by small round lenticels. Terminal bud absent; acute, chestnut-brown.

Bark. Gray or brown tinged with red; divided by shallow furrows into scaly plates.

Wood. No commercial value. Sapwood light brown. Heartwood dark brown tinged with red.

Natural History. Intolerant of shade. Found on a variety of sites: moist bottomlands, banks of intermittent streams, dry uplands, and mountain slopes. Often found in old pastures and edges of woods.

Range. Found from Vermont to Montana, and south to northeast Florida and Oklahoma; also in the Rocky Mountains from Montana to New Mexico.

Mazzard, Mazzard cherry

Prunus avium (L.) L.

Moderate-size excurrent tree growing 50–80 ft in height and 1 ft in diameter. Leaves ovate to obovate; doubly serrated; 2 large glands at base of blade; dull green above; slightly hairy below. Flowers white; borne in umbellike clusters of 2–4. Fruit a drupe; dark red; 1 in. wide; sweet. Spur shoots common. Terminal bud brown; lustrous. Bark smooth even on large trees; gray to red-gray; prominent horizontal lines of lenticels. Widely cultivated for the fruit. Native to Asia Minor, naturalized throughout North America.

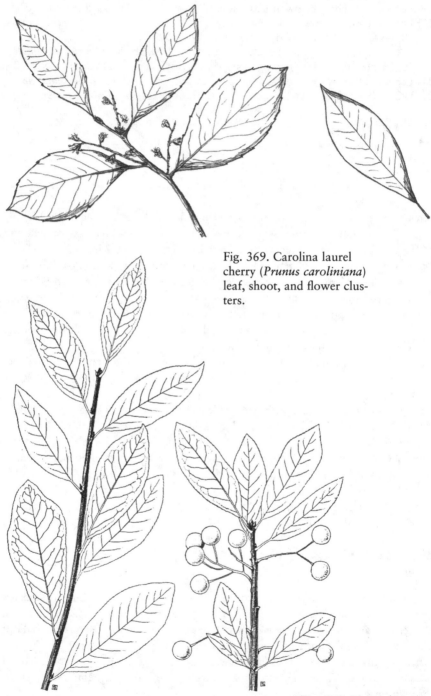

Fig. 369. Carolina laurel cherry (*Prunus caroliniana*) leaf, shoot, and flower clusters.

Fig. 370. Bitter cherry (*Prunus emarginata*) shoot and fruit clusters.

Carolina laurel cherry

Prunus caroliniana (Mill.) Ait. (fig. 369)

Large shrub or small tree growing to 40 ft in height and 1 ft in diameter (largest known 44 ft by 3 ft). Bole often crooked or leaning or both; commonly found in clumps of 2–4 stems. Leaves oblong elliptical to oblanceolate; 2–4.5 in. long; evergreen; lustrous; hairless above and below; 1–2 glands appearing as black dots below near base of blade. Margin with numerous spinelike teeth on seedlings and small trees; margin entire or slightly serrate on larger trees. Flowers white; borne in short racemes. Fruit a drupe; black; nearly spherical; 0.2–0.5 in. wide; often persisting over winter. Bark gray to black; smooth becoming slightly warty. Wood with little or no commercial value. Commonly cultivated in the South. Found originally in coastal maritime forests with waxmyrtle, swamp bay, loblolly pine, longleaf pine, eastern redcedar, and yaupon. Found naturally from southeastern North Carolina to central Florida, and west to east Texas. Becoming widely naturalized elsewhere from cultivated specimens.

Bitter cherry

Prunus emarginata Dougl. ex Eaton (fig. 370)

Shrub to small tree growing in ideal conditions to 40 ft in height and 1 ft in diameter. May form dense thickets. Leaves oblanceolate, obovate, or oval; 1–3 in. long; 0.3–1.5 in. wide; finely serrated or finely crenated; teeth glandular; sometimes with small notch at tip; dark green and hairless above; hairy below becoming hairless. Petiole hairy; glandular near blade. Flowers white to green-white; 0.3–0.5 in. wide; open when the new leaves are half expanded; borne in clusters (racemes or corymbs) of 3–12 flowers; small leaves occur at base of cluster. Fruit a drupe; red turning black; 0.2–0.5 in. wide; bitter; skin translucent. Twigs red-brown turning gray; hairy becoming hairless. Bark smooth; light brown or gray; horizontal yellow-orange lenticels. Overall similar in appearance to pin cherry. Moderately tolerant of shade. Grows on stream sides and moist slopes. Found from British Columbia to Montana and south to California, Arizona, and New Mexico.

Hortulan plum

Prunus hortulana Bailey

Large multiple-stemmed shrub or small tree growing to 35 ft in height. Leaves ovate to oblong-obovate; 4–6 in. long; finely glandular serrated; lustrous and hairless above; hairless or slightly hairy below. Petiole with glands near base of blade. Flowers white; 0.7–1 in. wide; in clusters (umbels) of 2–3. Fruit a drupe; yellow-red to red; covered with white dots; 0.7–1 in. wide; lustrous. Twigs hairless or hairy; red-brown; lateral twigs somewhat thorny. Bark brown, peeling in thin sheets. Not common in the wild; several cultivated forms have been developed. Found in southwestern Ohio, Indiana, Illinois, Missouri, and eastern Kansas.

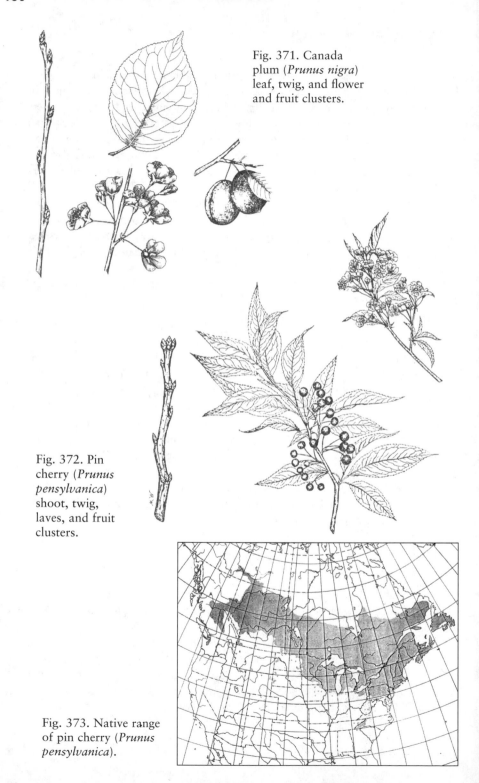

Fig. 371. Canada plum (*Prunus nigra*) leaf, twig, and flower and fruit clusters.

Fig. 372. Pin cherry (*Prunus pensylvanica*) shoot, twig, laves, and fruit clusters.

Fig. 373. Native range of pin cherry (*Prunus pensylvanica*).

Canada plum
Prunus nigra Ait. (fig. 371)

Small deliquescent tree rarely growing to 30 ft in height. Leaves oval to obovate; doubly serrate; teeth rounded often gland tipped; 2–4 in. long. Petiole with large dark glands near blade. Flowers white to pink; 0.5–1 in. wide; on red stalks; in clusters of 2–4; opening before or with the new leaves. Fruit a drupe; 1–1.5 in. long; slightly elongated; yellow or red; sour. Lateral twigs often thorny. Bark gray to black; splitting and curling vertically. Found in moist soil, especially in bottomlands. Similar to American plum and sometimes classified as a variety of it, *Prunus americana* var. *nigra*. Found from New Brunswick to southern Manitoba, and south to New York, Indiana, Iowa, and Illinois.

Pin cherry, Fire cherry
Prunus pensylvanica L. f. (fig. 372)

Form. Large shrub or small tree growing 30–40 ft in height and 1 ft in diameter (largest known 80 ft by 2 ft).

Leaves. Lanceolate; sharply and finely serrate; light green and hairless above; paler and hairless below; lacking orange hairs along the midvein; 3–4 in. long; 1–2 in. wide. Tip acuminate. Base rounded. Petiole with glands.

Flowers. White; 0.5–0.6 in. wide; in clusters (umbel-like) of 2–5; opening when the new leaves are half grown. Stalks 1 in. long.

Fruit. Drupe; spherical; 0.2–0.3 in. wide; red; quite sour; occasionally made into jelly. Pit oblong; pointed; ridged.

Twigs. Slightly hairy becoming hairless; light red at first becoming dull red; marked by orange lenticels; bitter almond odor; pith brown. Terminal buds 0.2 in. long; red-brown; pointed; often clustered.

Bark. Thin; red-brown; smooth sometimes peeling in thin sheets; marked by horizontal lines of orange lenticels.

Wood. Low commercial value; occasionally used for pulpwood. Sapwood yellow; heartwood light brown; soft.

Natural History. Very intolerant of shade. Fast growing; short-lived; reaches maturity in 30 years; quickly replaced by other species. Reproduction in disturbed areas abundant from seed stored up to 50 years in the leaf litter and soil; fruit production begins at age 3–4 years; large numbers of fruits produced most years. Sprouts from stumps and roots forming small colonies. Grows on a wide variety of soils; often in rocky or sandy soil but also in fertile loams. Songbirds and upland game birds eat the fruit. Foliage eaten by white-tailed deer. Beavers eat the inner bark sometimes felling entire stands. Leaves poisonous to livestock. Sometimes used as grafting stock for sour cherry.

Range. See figure 373.

Black cherry, Wild black cherry

Prunus serotina Ehrh. (fig. 374)

Form. Medium-sized excurrent tree growing 60–80 ft in height and 1–3 ft in diameter (largest known 150 ft by 7 ft). Size varies greatly with geographic region. Bole clear of branches.

Leaves. Oval to oblong-lanceolate; 2–6 in. long; finely serrate with incurved teeth;

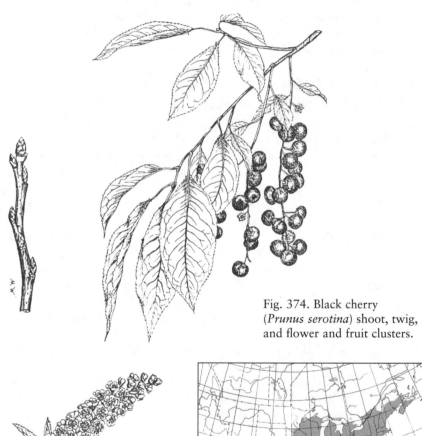

Fig. 374. Black cherry (*Prunus serotina*) shoot, twig, and flower and fruit clusters.

Fig. 375. Native range of black cherry (*Prunus serotina*).

dark green and lustrous above; paler and hairless below except sometimes for red-brown hairs along base of midvein. Tip acute to acuminate. Base rounded. Petioles usually with 2–4 black glands near blade.

Flowers. White; borne in many-flowered racemes 4–5 in. long; appearing in the spring with the new leaves. Calyx persistent on fruit.

Fruit. Spherical; 0.3–0.5 in. wide; nearly black when ripe; juicy; edible but bitter.

Twigs. Slender; hairless; red-brown; bitter almond odor; spur shoots common on older twigs. Terminal buds 0.2 in. long; ovoid; scaly; green and brown turning all brown.

Bark. Thin; on young trees, smooth, red-brown or gray; marked by lines of horizontal lenticels. On older trees, scaly or flaky with upturned edges; red-brown (in the North) or gray to nearly black (in the South).

Wood. Commercial value varies tremendously by region owing to variation in tree size and wood quality. Extremely valuable in the Cumberland Plateau and sometimes the southern Appalachians; value sporadic and usually much lower in other areas. Sapwood nearly white to light red-brown. Heartwood light to dark red-brown; moderately heavy; semi-ring-porous to diffuse-porous; traumatic gum canals sometimes present. Prized for furniture, cabinets, interior trim, professional and scientific instruments, piano actions, woodenware, and novelties.

Natural History. Intolerant of shade. Reproduces well from seed; some seed produced most years; heavy seed crops every 2–3 years; seeds remain viable in the litter layer for 3–5 years. Seedbed requirements not exacting as long as moisture is present continuously. Regeneration greatest under light shade but full sunlight is required after 2–3 years. Regeneration inhibited by allelopathy from some asters and goldenrods, oatgrass, and bracken fern. Also reproduces well from seedling and stump sprouts. Wildfire, breakage by ice or snow, browsing by white-tailed deer and rabbits, defoliation by eastern tent caterpillar, and wood degrade by beetles cause the most damage. Found on a wide variety of soils especially those cool and moist in summer. Does not tolerate flooding in summer. Grows in closed stands, fencerows, old fields and pastures, and edges of woods. Best development occurs on the Allegheny Plateau and at about 4,500 ft in the southern Appalachians. Grows in pure stands or more commonly mixed with sugar maple, northern red oak, white oak, black oak, white ash, beech, red maple, eastern white pine, loblolly pine, yellow-poplar, basswood, yellow birch, and eastern hemlock. Fruits eaten by many wildlife species especially songbirds, squirrels, white-tailed deer, turkeys, and small mammals. White-tailed deer browse the shoots. Leaves, twigs, and bark contain cyanogenic glycoside, which converts to cyanide in wilted foliage. Livestock are poisoned from eating wilted foliage. Fruit used to make jelly and wine; formerly used to flavor brandy or rum producing cherry bounce.

Varieties. Several varieties have been named but 3 are widely recognized. Var. *exima* (escarpment black cherry) of Texas has smaller leaves and fruit. Var. *alabamensis* (Alabama black cherry) of eastern Georgia, northeastern Alabama, and northwestern Florida is a small tree with hairy leaf undersides. Var. *rufula* (southwestern black cherry) occurs in the Southwest and Mexico.

Range. See figure 375.

Chokecherry

Prunus virginiana L. (fig. 376)

Large shrub to small tree barely growing to 35 ft. Forming thickets from root sprouts. Leaves oval to obovate; 1–4 in. long; sharply serrate; sometimes hairy on the veins below but lacking red hairs along the midvein. Petiole usually with 2

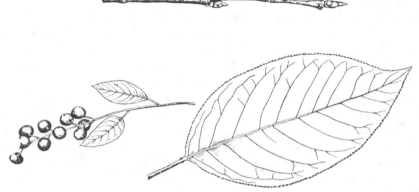

Fig. 376. Chokecherry (*Prunus virginiana*) leaf, twig, and fruit cluster.

Fig. 377. Common pear (*Pyrus communis*) shoot.

glands near the blade. Flowers white; borne in a raceme 3–6 in. long. Fruit a drupe; 0.2–0.3 in. wide; scarlet, dark red, or nearly black; lustrous; juicy but bitter; calyx quickly shed from fruit. Twigs red-brown to orange-brown; hairless. Moderately tolerant of shade. Found on a wide variety of soils but usually in disturbed areas and open woods. Very hardy in cold northern regions and frost pockets. Fruit used in jelly and jam; eaten by songbirds and bears. Inner bark used in flavoring cough syrup. Several varieties have been named. Most notably var. *melanocarpa* of the western United States with nearly black fruit and var. *demissa* of the Pacific Coast with heart-shaped leaf bases and hairy twigs. Very widely distributed; found in the northern and central United States, Rocky Mountains, Washington, Oregon, and California; transcontinental in Canada except for western British Columbia.

PEAR: THE GENUS *PYRUS*

Worldwide about 20 species of pear are known, but none are native to our region. The common pear and cultivars of callery pear are naturalized in our area. Pears are similar in general characteristics to apples and crab apples (*Malus*), and the two genera are sometimes combined. Key differences lie in the flowers and fruit. Pears have flower styles that are not fused at the base and produce grit cells in the fruit. Apples and crab apples have flower styles fused at the base and form few or no grit cells in the fruit. Pears are also sometimes combined with *Sorbus*.

KEY TO PEARS

1. Fruit spherical . . . . .callery pear, *Pyrus calleryana*
1. Fruit wider at one end (pear-shaped) . . . . .common pear, *Pyrus communis*

Callery pear
Pyrus calleryana Decne.

Small to moderate-sized tree growing to 60 ft in height. Leaves ovate to broadly ovate; 2–4 in. long; hairless above and below; tip acute; base rounded; margin crenate. Fruit spherical; 0.5 in. wide; brown; dotted. Twigs hairless; buds short hairy. Native to China and Korea. Introduced in 1908 for use in breeding disease resistance to fire blight in common pear. About 20 cultivars have been developed and planted widely, most notably Bradford pear, which has shorter nearly round leaves. The tree has recently escaped, especially in pastures, edges of woods, and roadsides, but the escapes revert to the wild form of callery pear.

Common pear
Pyrus communis L. (fig. 377)

Moderate-sized tree. Leaves broadly ovate to elliptical; 1–3 in. long; lustrous; hairless except in the early spring. Fruit top shaped to nearly round; green to yellow-green. Twigs hairless or slightly hairy; spur branches present. Buds hairless or slightly hairy; becoming sharp pointed at tip. Eurasian species widely cultivated for the fruit; found persisting from cultivation and occasionally naturalized locally.

MOUNTAIN-ASH: THE GENUS *SORBUS*

Found in the northern temperate zone, this genus contains 80–100 species in the world. Four species occur in our area, 2 in the east and 2 in the west. In addition, 1 European species is naturalized. Only the eastern and European species regularly become tree-sized. Formerly sometimes lumped with the genus *Pyrus*. Not to be confused with the true ashes (*Fraxinus*), which have opposite leaves.

Mountain-ash are shrubs or small trees. The leaves are alternate, pinnately compound with 9–17 leaflets, and deciduous. The margin is usually serrated, and small stipules are present. The flowers are small, white, bisexual, borne in flat-topped clusters (cymes) at the ends of twigs, and pollinated by insects. The fruit is a small red or orange pome (apple) that develops in a single growing season. The bark is smooth with prominent lines of horizontal lenticels. The wood is light brown, diffuse-porous, and generally not valuable commercially.

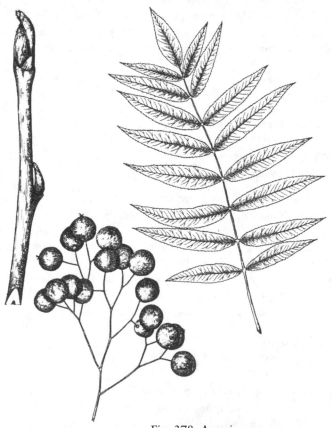

Fig. 378. American mountain-ash (*Sorbus americana*) leaf, twig, and fruit cluster.

KEY TO MOUNTAIN-ASHES

1. Winter buds densely covered with long white hairs . . . .
. . . . .European mountain-ash, *Sorbus aucuparia*
1. Winter buds hairless or nearly hairless . . . . .Go to 2
   2. Small tree of eastern North America 3
   2. Shrub or small tree of western North America (including South Dakota) 4
3. Leaflets serrated nearly to the base . . . .American mountain-ash, *Sorbus americana*
3. Leaflets serrated only above the middle . . . . .showy mountain-ash, *Sorbus decora*
   4. Leaflets with rounded or blunt tips . . . . .Sitka mountain-ash, *Sorbus sitchensis*
   4. Leaflets sharp pointed at tip . . . . .Greene mountain-ash, *Sorbus scopulina*

American mountain-ash

Sorbus americana Marsh. (fig. 378)

Form. Shrub to small tree seldom exceeding 30 ft in height and 1 ft in diameter.

Leaves. Alternate; pinnately compound; 6–8 in. long. Leaflets 7–17; nearly stalk-less; oblong-oval to lanceolate; 2–4 in. long; 0.5–1 in. wide; serrated nearly to the base; hairless above and below. Petiole grooved above.

Flowers. Cream-white; 5 petals; borne in broad flat cymes 3–5 in. across; appearing after the new leaves.

Fruit. Pome; nearly spherical; 0.2–0.3 in. in diameter; bright orange-red; acrid. Borne on hairless stalks. Seeds 1–2 in each cell; 0.1 in. long; ovoid; brown.

Twigs. Stout; round; red-brown; hairy becoming dark brown and hairless; pith large; leaf scars large; lenticels oblong. Terminal bud 0.3–0.7 in. long; acute; dark red; hairy; sticky with gummy exudate.

Bark. Light gray to red-gray; smooth or slightly roughened by scales; inner bark fragrant.

Wood. Little or no commercial value. Sapwood yellow-brown. Heartwood light brown; lightweight; soft.

Natural History. Moderately tolerant of shade. Slow growing; short-lived. Prefers moist sites but also found on rocky hillsides. Always found growing in mixed stands. Fruit eaten by songbirds.

Range. Found from Newfoundland to western Ontario, south to New Jersey and northern Illinois, and in the Appalachians from West Virginia to northern Georgia.

Showy mountain-ash

Sorbus decora (Sarg.) Schneid.

Small tree growing to 45 ft in height. Leaves alternate; pinnately compound; blue-green above; paler and slightly hairy below, at least when young. Leaflets 13–17; 1.5–2.5 in. long; serrated above the middle. Fruit red; lustrous; 0.4–0.5 in. wide. Twigs red-brown to gray; hairless. Terminal bud cone-shaped; red-brown; shiny; crooked at tip. Grows on rocky shores of rivers and lakes. Found in eastern Canada, New England, and the Lake States; also in scattered disjunct areas in New York.

VAUQUELINIA: THE GENUS *VAUQUELINIA*

Worldwide this genus contains about eight species, all found in either Mexico or the southwestern United States. Our region contains two species, Torrey vauquelinia, the tree-sized species listed below, and fewflower vauquelinia (*Vauquelinia pauciflora*), normally a shrub that is possibly only a variety of Torrey vauquelinia.

Torrey vauquelinia

Vauquelinia californica (Torr.) Sarg.

Shrub or small tree rarely growing to 25 ft in height. Leaves simple; evergreen; lanceolate; 1–3 in. long. Margin with small, widely spaced, glandular teeth. Flowers small; bisexual; white; borne in leafy woolly panicles. Fruit a 5-celled capsule;

Fig. 379. Common buttonbush
(*Cephalanthus occidentalis*) shoot
with flower and fruit clusters (heads).

ovoid; 0.2 in. long; woolly; subtended by the remnants of the flower; long persistent on the branches. Found in southern Arizona, southwestern New Mexico, and northern Mexico.

MADDER FAMILY: RUBIACEAE

The Madder Family contains about 9,000 species in 500–600 genera. Most species are trees or shrubs of tropical or subtropical areas, especially South America. Our region contains about 300 species in about 60 genera, but only 2 species in 2 genera are tree-sized.

Leaves of this family are simple, opposite or whorled, and entire (usually) with stipules. The flowers are bisexual with four to five petals fused into a tube or funnel and usually two carpels. The fruit is either a capsule, berry, or drupe. Economically the family provides coffee (*Coffea*), ipecac (*Cephaelis*), dye (*Rubia* and *Uncaria*), quinine (*Cinona*), and ornamentals (*Gardenia*).

BUTTONBUSH: THE GENUS *CEPHALANTHUS*

Worldwide this genus contains about six species found mostly in tropical areas. Our region contains two species, but willowleaf buttonbush (*Cephalanthus salicifolius*) is usually a shrub found only in extreme south Texas.

Common buttonbush

Cephalanthus occidentalis L. (fig. 379)

Form. Shrub or moderate-sized tree growing to 50 ft in height and 1–2 ft in diameter. Sometimes forming thickets.

Leaves. Opposite or whorled; simple; ovate, lanceolate, or elliptical; 3–8 in. long; margins entire; deciduous; hairless above; hairy below at least on the veins. Tip pointed to long pointed. Base rounded or wedge-shaped. Stipules triangular; quickly deciduous. Stalk stout; grooved; hairless; 0.5–0.7 in. long.

Flowers. Bisexual; cream-white; 4–5 lobed slender tube with expanded tip. Borne in spherical clusters (heads); 1–1.5 in. wide; terminal or lateral.

Fruit. Nutlike capsule; splitting from base into 2–4 sections. Borne in heads in small terminal clusters; green tinged with red turning dark red-brown.

Twigs. Stout; hairless; marked by raised dots (lenticels); light green becoming red-brown. Terminal bud absent. Lateral buds minute nearly imbedded in the twig.

Bark. Thin; dark brown to nearly black; divided into broad, flat, scaly ridges; contains tannin.

Wood. No commercial value. Moderately heavy and hard; fine grained; diffuse-porous; light red-brown.

Natural History. Moderately tolerant of shade. Found on wet sites; often in shallow water at the edge of rivers and ponds.

Range. Found from Nova Scotia to southeastern Nebraska, and south to southern Florida and central Texas; also in California, Arizona, and Mexico.

PINCKNEYA: THE GENUS *PINCKNEYA*

This genus contains only one species in the world, pinckneya (*Pinckneya pubens*). This species has awl-shaped stipules, trumpet-shaped flowers, a petal-like sepal, and a two-valved papery capsule about 1 in. long. Rare in nature, pinckneya is found in the southeastern Coastal Plain from South Carolina to north Florida.

RUE FAMILY: RUTACEAE

Worldwide the Rue Family contains about 1,800 species in about 150 genera. Nearly all species are shrubs or trees, found mostly in South America, southern

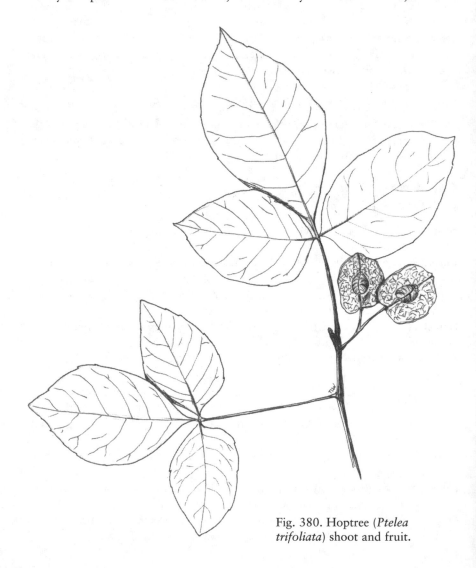

Fig. 380. Hoptree (*Ptelea trifoliata*) shoot and fruit.

Africa, or Australia. In our region, 4 genera are native, but only 2 species in 2 genera become tree-sized. Several other genera are cultivated and rarely escape, notably orange, lime, lemon, grapefruit, and tangerine (all *Citrus*), cultivated in the warmer areas for the fruits, honey, and flowers; cork-tree (*Phellodendron*); hardy-orange (*Poncirus*); and rue (*Ruta*).

The leaves of this family are alternate (occasionally opposite) and simple (unifoliate) or compound. The leaves contain oil cells, which appear as translucent dots and are usually aromatic when crushed. No stipules are produced. The flowers are bisexual or unisexual, and usually pollinated by flies or bees. Each flower has four to five sepals, four to five petals, and two to five carpels. The type of fruit is variable either a leathery berry (hesperidium), capsule, drupe, or samara. The seeds lack endosperm. No species of this family provides wood products in our region.

HOPTREE: THE GENUS *PTELEA*

This genus contains three species; two occur in our region and the third occurs in Mexico. Only one of the species in our region becomes tree-sized. The other species, California hoptree (*Ptelea crenulata*), is a tall shrub of California. Hoptree wood is heavy and ring-porous.

Hoptree, Wafer-ash

Ptelea trifoliata L. (fig. 380)

Large shrub or small tree growing occasionally to 30 ft in height. Bole usually branching close to the ground. Leaves alternate, rarely opposite; 4–7 in. long; trifoliate rarely pinnately compound with 5 leaflets. Leaflets ovate; entire, crenulate, or serrate; stalks short; with translucent dots below. Petiole long. Flowers bisexual and unisexual on the same tree (polygamous); borne in terminal clusters (cymes or umbels). Fruit a samara; waferlike; 1 in. wide; borne in drooping clusters; thin; may persist into winter. Seeds 0.3 in. long; oblong; dark red-brown. Twigs slender; round; dark brown; lustrous; large lenticels; ill-scented. Terminal bud absent; lateral buds naked; pale; very hairy. Bark smooth or scaly; thin; bitter; ill-scented; brown. As many as 8 intergrading geographical varieties have been proposed. Found in 2 broad bands: Virginia to Florida and west to eastern Mississippi; and southern Michigan to central Texas. Also found in numerous disjunct areas from Quebec to New Jersey and southwest to eastern Mexico and western Arizona.

PRICKLY-ASH: THE GENUS *ZANTHOXYLUM*

The genus is sometimes spelled *Xanthoxylum,* which is orthographically correct but not the original spelling. Worldwide this genus contains about 250 species, found mostly in tropical and subtropical areas. Our region contains 4 species, but only the 1 species described below is tree-sized. A second clonal species, prickly-ash (*Zanthoxylum americanum*), only rarely grows into a tree. Some tropical species provide lumber from the wood, medicine from the bark, and condiments from the seeds.

KEY TO PRICKLY-ASHES

1. Young twigs with paired spines at most nodes . . . .
. . . . .prickly-ash, *Zanthoxylum americanum*
1. Twigs and bole with scattered prickles not paired at each node . . . .
. . . . .Hercules-club, *Zanthoxylum clava-herculis*

Hercules-club, Toothache tree, Prickly-ash

Zanthoxylum clava-herculis L. (fig. 381)

Small deliquescent tree growing 30–35 ft in height (largest known 40 ft by 2 ft in diameter). Bole usually crooked and irregular. Leaves alternate; slowly deciduous; pinnately compound with a terminal leaflet; sometimes with prickles. Leaflets 7–19; ovate; curved; leathery; crenate with a gland; dark green and lustrous above; translucent glands above and below. Flowers unisexual with 1 sex per tree (dioecious); clustered. Fruit a follicle; brown; ovoid. Seeds black; hanging from the capsule by a thread. Twigs with scattered prickles. Bark smooth; white to light gray; with cone-shaped corky growths. Grows on forested sand dunes, shell middens, and fencerows. The bark, buds, and fruits produce a numbing effect when chewed; formerly used to treat toothache. Found in coastal regions from Virginia to Florida, and coastal and interior regions from Alabama to east Texas, and north to Arkansas.

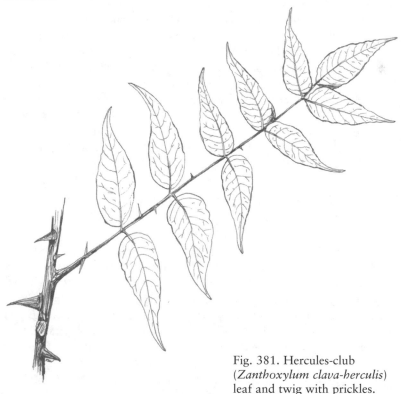

Fig. 381. Hercules-club
(*Zanthoxylum clava-herculis*)
leaf and twig with prickles.

WILLOW FAMILY: SALICACEAE

Worldwide the Willow Family contains between 400–500 species in three genera, but only *Populus* and *Salix* occur in our region. The family is characterized by fast-growing, often clonal, trees and shrubs most commonly found in north temperate and subarctic regions.

The leaves in this family are alternate, simple, and deciduous. Stipules are produced, sometimes quite large, but they often fall in the spring after the new leaves have expanded. The flowers are unisexual, highly reduced, borne in aments, subtended by bracts, insect or wind pollinated, and either lack petals or have their petals modified into disks or glands. Each tree produces only one sex (dioecious). The ovary consists of two to four carpels, and it matures into a two- to four-valved capsule that produces numerous seeds.

COTTONWOOD AND POPLAR: THE GENUS *POPULUS*

The genus *Populus* includes about 35 species scattered over the Northern Hemisphere and in northern Africa. Eight species and several hybrids are native to our region, and 3 European species are naturalized in some places. Many *Populus* species are interfertile and produce natural hybrids. In addition, some hybrids have been artificially produced for wood production, shelterbelts, and ornamental plantings.

Members of this genus have ovate to deltate leaves. The petioles are rather long and often laterally compressed, a characteristic that causes the leaves of some species to flutter in the wind. The flowers are wind pollinated and subtended by fringed bracts. The ovary contains two to four carpels, and the fruit is a two- to four-part capsule containing numerous seeds tufted with silky hairs. Terminal buds are present and covered by several overlapping scales. The wood is soft and diffuse-porous.

KEY TO COTTONWOODS AND POPLARS

1. Leaf undersides white; planted or naturalized . . . . .Go to 2
1. Leaf undersides green or yellow-green . . . . .Go to 3
   2. Leaves palmately 3–5 lobed; base round or flat . . . .white poplar, *Populus alba*
   2. Leaves toothed but not lobed; base heart-shaped . . . .
   . . . . .gray poplar, *Populus x canescens*
3. Petiole round in cross section 4
3. Petiole flattened in cross section 8
   4. Leaves broadly ovate nearly deltate . .swamp cottonwood, *Populus heterophylla*
   4. Leaves lanceolate to ovate 5
5. Petiole length shorter than blade length . . . .
   . . . . .narrowleaf cottonwood, *Populus angustifolia*
5. Petiole at least as long as leaf blade 6
   6. Leaf margin finely toothed; buds very resinous and aromatic 7
   6. Leaf margin coarsely toothed; buds slightly resinous but not aromatic . . . .
   . . . . .lanceleaf cottonwood, *Populus x acuminata*

7. Capsule 3-valved; hairy; Pacific region . . . .black cottonwood, *Populus trichocarpa*
7. Capsule 2-valved; hairless; northern North America . . . .
. . . . .balsam poplar, *Populus balsamifera*
   8. Leaves broadly ovate to nearly round; buds almost nonresinous 9
   8. Leaves deltate to rhombic-ovate; buds resinous 11
9. Leaf margin with 30 teeth per side; buds hairless . . . .
. . . . .trembling aspen, *Populus tremuloides*
9. Leaf margin with fewer than 25 teeth per side; buds hairy or hairless 10
   10. Leaf margin with 10 large teeth per side . . . .
. . . . .bigtooth aspen, *Populus grandidentata*
   10. Leaf margin with 20 teeth per side . . . . .Smith aspen, *Populus* x *smithii*
11. Leaves rhombic-ovate (rarely deltate); base wedge-shaped or rounded; naturalized
. 12
11. Leaves deltate; base flat; native 14
   12. Leaves as long as wide; margin finely toothed 13
   12. Leaves longer than wide; margin coarsely toothed . . . .
. . . . .Carolina poplar, *Populus* x *canadensis*
13. Tree with broad crown . . . . .black poplar, *Populus nigra*
13. Tree with columnar narrow crown . . .Lombardy poplar, *Populus nigra* var. *italica*

Fig. 382. White
poplar (*Populus alba*)
leaf, twig, and ament.

14. Leaves with glands at point where petiole and blade meet 15
14. Leaves without glands at point where petiole and blade meet 16
15. Buds hairless; leaves moderately toothed; East . . . .
. . . . .eastern cottonwood, *Populus deltoides*
15. Buds slightly hairy; leaves coarsely toothed; Great Plains to Rocky Mountains . . .
. . . . .plains cottonwood, *Populus deltoides* var. *occidentalis*
16. Pedicel longer than capsule; leaves with no more than 10 teeth per side;
Colorado, New Mexico, west Texas, Mexico . . . .
. . . . .Rio Grande cottonwood, *Populus fremontii* var. *wislizeni*
16. Pedicels shorter than capsules; leaves with more than 10 teeth per side; New
Mexico west to California . . . . .Fremont cottonwood, *Populus fremontii*

White poplar
Populus alba L. (fig. 382)

Moderately large tree growing 60–80 ft in height and 1–2 ft in diameter. Leaves alternate; simple; round to ovate; 2.5–5 in. long; dark green above; white feltlike hairs below. Leaf margin with coarse teeth or small lobes; sometimes maplelike with 3–5 lobes. Twigs and buds covered with white hairs. Bark smooth; white with black markings; base of tree turning black with small tight ridges. Sprouts from the roots and forms clones. Silver poplar and Boleana poplar are horticultural selections of white poplar. Hybridizes with bigtooth aspen. Sometimes erroneously identified as silver maple, which has opposite leaves. Native to Eurasia; planted in our region as an ornamental. Found persisting and spreading from cultivation.

Narrowleaf cottonwood
Populus angustifolia James

Form. Medium-sized tree growing 50–70 ft in height and 1–2 ft in diameter. Crown pyramidal with slender erect branches.

Leaves. Alternate; simple; lanceolate to ovate-lanceolate; 2–5 in. long; 0.5–1.5 in. wide; bright yellow-green above, paler below. Tip long-tapering. Margin finely to coarsely serrate. Petioles shorter than length of blade; slender; somewhat flattened on upper side.

Fruit. Capsule; broadly ovoid; 0.2 in. long; 2-valved.

Twigs. Slender; round; yellow-green becoming ash-gray. Buds 0.2–0.7 in. long; slender; long pointed; chestnut-brown; very resinous and somewhat aromatic.

Bark. Light yellow-green; 0.1–1 in. thick; smooth except near base where it divides into shallow furrows.

Wood. Used locally for fence posts and fuelwood.

Natural History. Grows in moist soil along stream banks and in bottomlands.

Hybrids. Hybridizes with eastern cottonwood to form lanceleaf cottonwood, *Populus* x *acuminata*. Also hybridizes with balsam poplar and Fremont cottonwood in the Davis Mountains in Texas.

Range. Mountains from southern Alberta to Mexico; disjunct populations in South Dakota, Nebraska, Texas, Nevada, Oregon, and California.

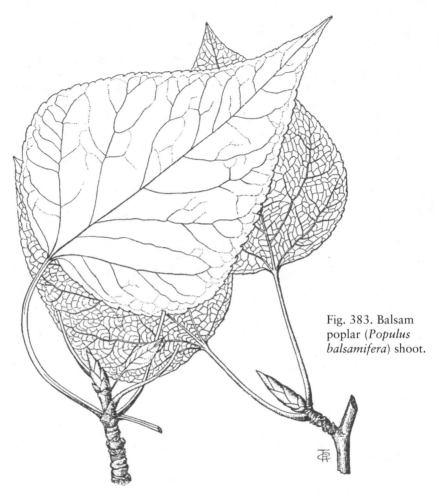

Fig. 383. Balsam poplar (*Populus balsamifera*) shoot.

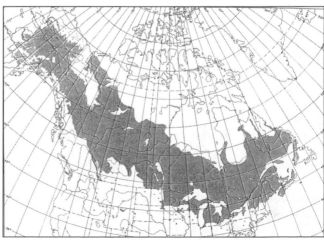

Fig. 384. Native range of balsam poplar (*Populus balsamifera*).

Balsam poplar

Populus balsamifera L. (fig. 383)

Nomenclature. The correct scientific name for balsam poplar has long been debated. For many years called *Populus balsamifera*, some authors switched to *Populus tacamahacca* in 1919, and switched back to *Populus balsamifera* in 1946. Balm-of-Gilead is a clonal selection of the hybrid between this species and eastern cottonwood. See the Balm-of-Gilead entry below.

Form. Medium-sized excurrent tree growing 70–90 ft in height and 1–3 ft in diameter (largest known 130 ft by 5 ft); becomes deliquescent with age and on infertile sites. Crown open; narrow.

Leaves. Alternate; simple; broadly ovate to ovate-lanceolate; 3–6 in. long and 2–4 in. wide; dark green above paler below with brown splotches. Tip acute to acuminate. Base rounded or cordate; Margin finely crenate or serrate. Petioles round; slender; long.

Fruit. Ovoid; 0.2–0.3 in. long; 2-valved; hairless; short stalked. Seeds light brown; 0.1 in. long.

Twigs. Moderately stout; round; red-brown. Terminal buds 1 in. long; ovoid; chestnut-brown; saturated by fragrant amber-colored resin. Winter buds heated in oil to relieve congestion.

Bark. On young trees, smooth; green-brown. On older trees, deeply furrowed; gray-black.

Wood. Sapwood white; heartwood gray-white to gray-brown not clearly distinguished from the sapwood; straight grained; moderately lightweight. Used for pulpwood used in making high-grade book and magazine paper, the central core of hardwood plywood, berry boxes, crates, ironing boards, poultry and apiary supplies, and log cabins.

Natural History. Intolerant of shade. Fast growing; reaches maturity in 80–120 years (extreme age 200 years). Reproduces from wind and water dispersed seeds; requires bare mineral soil; germination occurs within 1–5 weeks of dispersal; seeds lose viability after about 5 weeks. Seed production prolific. Reproduces also from stump and root sprouts as well as severed branches that root. Root system multilayered on flood plains with successive layers of deposited sediment. Found along rivers and in river flood plains; colonizes new sand and gravel bars; also colonizes sites after severe fires or mining. Grows farther north than any other tree in our region; northernmost stands occur around warm springs in the Brooks Range of Alaska. Occurs in even-aged pure stands or mixed with balsam fir, subalpine fir, white spruce, trembling aspen, paper birch, and jack pine. Twigs eaten by beavers; ruffed grouse eat the buds in winter.

Hybrids. Hybridizes with narrowleaf cottonwood, eastern cottonwood, and trembling aspen. Forms a hybrid swarm with black cottonwood where their ranges overlap causing some authors to classify black cottonwood as a subspecies of balsam poplar.

Range. See figure 384.

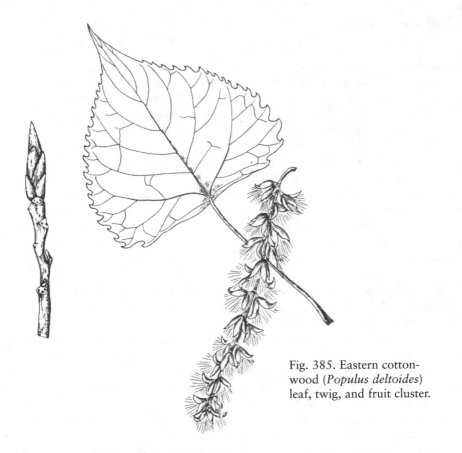

Fig. 385. Eastern cotton-
wood (*Populus deltoides*)
leaf, twig, and fruit cluster.

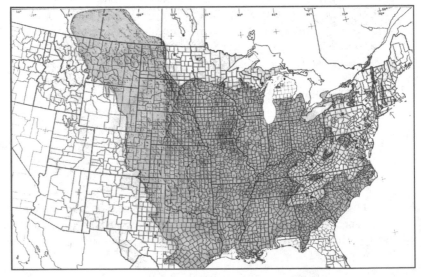

Fig. 386. Native range of eastern cottonwood (*Populus deltoides*).

Gray poplar
Populus x *canescens* (Ait.) Sm.

Hybrid between white poplar (Populus alba) and European aspen (*Populus tremula*). Small to moderate-sized tree. Leaves alternate; simple; lacking lobes. Leaves on long shoots ovate; dark green above; gray-white below. On short shoots nearly round; gray-white to light green below. Margin with narrow translucent border; irregularly dentate. Young twigs gray hairy. Native to Eurasia; known to cultivation for centuries; often persists and spreads at abandoned home sites.

Eastern cottonwood
Populus deltoides Bartr. ex Marsh. (fig. 385)

Form. Large excurrent to deliquescent tree growing 80–100 ft in height and 3–5 ft in diameter (largest known 190 ft by 11 ft). Crown broad; open; large, spreading branches.

Leaves. Alternate; simple; broadly deltate; 3–6 in. long; hairless. Tip acuminate. Base flat to heart-shaped. Margin crenate to serrate; teeth glandular; 20–25 teeth per side. Petiole flat; 1–3 in. long; 2 glands near leaf base.

Fruit. Capsule; ovoid; 0.3 in. long; borne in catkins 8–12 in. long. Seeds light brown; hairy; about 0.1 in. long.

Twigs. Stout; yellow-brown; angular; hairless. Buds 0.7 in. long; conical; acute; lustrous; green-brown; resinous.

Bark. Yellow-green and smooth on young trees; developing rectangular ridges separated by deep furrows; ash-gray.

Wood. Similar to balsam poplar; but in addition interest exists in using eastern cottonwood in intensively managed plantations for energy biomass.

Natural History. Very intolerant of shade. Growth rate rapid among the highest in the South; total heights of 40 ft at age 3 years and 100 ft at age 9 years have been recorded on excellent sites; reaches maturity in 70–100 years. Reproduction by seeds adequate; good seed crops produced nearly every year; seed viability high but brief; requires moist bare mineral soil. Reproduces by stump sprouts and occasionally by root sprouts. Plantations established by pushing long twigs into moist ground. Root growth slow; seedlings easily dislodged. Best growth occurs on moist, well-drained, fine sandy loams or sandy silt loams. Requires abundant moisture when young. Found in pure even-aged stands or mixed with black ash, American elm, red maple, river birch, sycamore, sweetgum, willow oak, sugarberry, and boxelder. Used in shelterbelt plantings. Beavers eat the twigs.

Varieties. The plains cottonwood (var. *occidentalis*) with wider leaves and fewer teeth extends from Texas and New Mexico north to Alberta and Saskatchewan. Some manuals make var. *occidentalis* a distinct species, *Populus sargentii*.

Hybrids. Hybridizes with narrowleaf cottonwood and balsam poplar. The widely planted Carolina poplar (*Populus* x *canadensis*) is the hybrid between eastern cottonwood and black poplar.

Range. See figure 386.

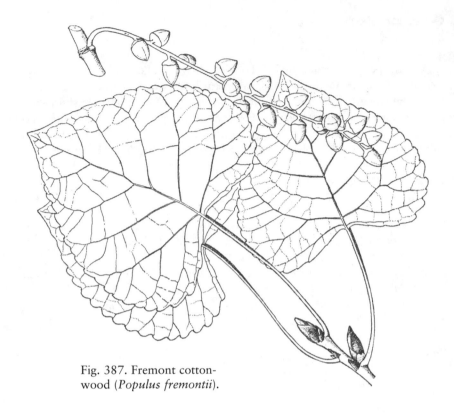

Fig. 387. Fremont cotton-
wood (*Populus fremontii*).

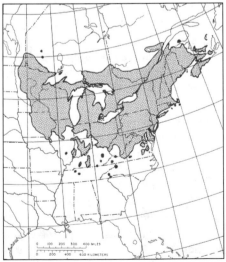

Fig. 388. Bigtooth aspen
(*Populus grandidentata*) shoot.

Fig. 389. Native range of bigtooth
aspen (*Populus grandidentata*).

Fremont cottonwood

Populus fremontii Wats. (fig. 387)

Form. Medium to large tree growing 50–60 ft in height and 1–2 ft in diameter (largest known 100 ft by 6 ft). Crown open.

Leaves. Alternate; simple; deltate to reniform; 2–3 in. long; 2–3 in. wide; coarsely serrate to crenate; yellow-green; hairless; lacking glands where blade and petiole meet. Tip short pointed. Petiole flat; yellow; 1.5–3.5 in. long.

Fruit. Capsule; ovoid; 0.2–0.3 in. long; brown; thick walled; 2–4 valves. Seeds light brown; hairy; 0.1 in. long.

Twigs. Stout; yellow-gray; sometimes drooping. Buds 0.3–0.5 in. long; ovoid; acute; green; resinous.

Bark. Gray-brown and smooth on young trees; becoming gray to dark brown and deeply furrowed.

Natural History. Commonly found along streams. Grows with sycamore and willow. Foliage eaten by mule deer and cattle.

Varieties. Two varieties are recognized. Var. *mesetae*, meseta cottonwood, occurs along the Mexican border from Texas to Arizona. Some older manuals classify meseta cottonwood as a separate species, *Populus arizonica*. Var. *wislizeni*, Rio Grande cottonwood, ranges from southern Colorado and Utah to New Mexico and Texas. It has slender pedicels and ellipsoid capsules. Rio Grande cottonwood is sometimes classified as a separate species, *Populus wislizeni*.

Hybrids. Hybridizes with narrowleaf cottonwood and black cottonwood.

Range. Found from southern and eastern Colorado to California, and south into Mexico. Elevation: sea level to 7,000 ft.

Bigtooth aspen

Populus grandidentata Michx. (fig. 388)

Medium-sized excurrent tree growing 60–70 ft in height and 1–2 ft in diameter. Leaves alternate; simple; nearly round to ovate; 2–5 in. long. Margin coarsely sinuate toothed with 10 teeth per side. Buds slightly hairy; dusty gray; 0.1 in. long. Fruit similar to trembling aspen. Bark golden-brown to green-brown. Wood and natural history similar to trembling aspen except for the following differences: smaller distribution, grows on a narrower range of site conditions, and flowers and fruits produced about 10 days later. Hybridizes with trembling aspen and white poplar. For range see figure 389.

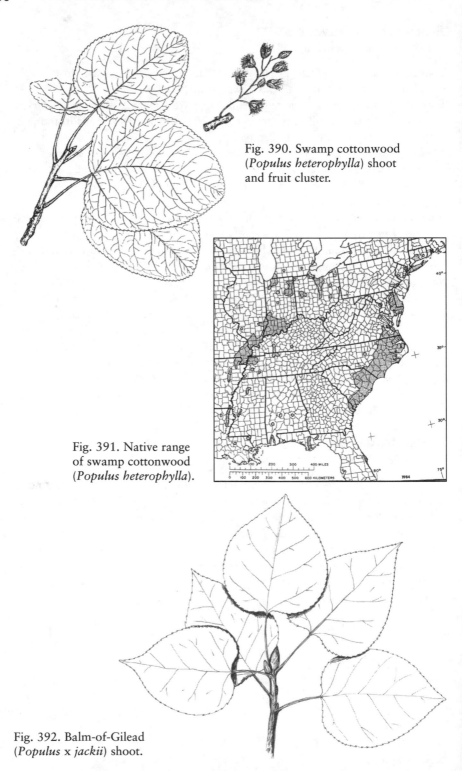

Fig. 390. Swamp cottonwood
(*Populus heterophylla*) shoot
and fruit cluster.

Fig. 391. Native range
of swamp cottonwood
(*Populus heterophylla*).

Fig. 392. Balm-of-Gilead
(*Populus* x *jackii*) shoot.

Swamp cottonwood
Populus heterophylla L. (fig. 390)

Excurrent medium-sized tree growing 80–100 ft in height and 2–3 ft in diameter (largest known 130 ft by 6 ft). Leaves alternate; simple; broadly ovate; 4–7 in. long; 3.5–6 in. wide; serrate to crenate; at least 15 teeth per side; white hairy below when young, becoming hairless. Petiole round in cross section; 2.5–6 in. long. Base round or heart-shaped. Buds not sticky. Bark with rectangular flat ridges, separated by deep furrows; gray to gray-brown; white inner bark visible in furrows. Wood similar to balsam poplar but heartwood usually darker. Intolerant of shade; short-lived; reaches maturity in 80 years. Reproduces by seeds that germinate shortly after release in the spring; seeds lose viability after 1–3 weeks; requires bare mineral soil; dispersed by wind and water. Reproduces also by stump sprouts. Found on silt, clay, or muck soils, in sloughs, back swamps, and first bottoms flooded for moderately long periods of time. Our most water-tolerant *Populus*. Almost always found in mixed stands with baldcypress, swamp blackgum, water tupelo, water hickory, overcup oak, laurel oak, red maple, American elm, and Carolina ash. For range see figure 391.

Balm-of-Gilead, Balm-gilly
Populus x *jackii* Sarg. (fig. 392)

A sterile clone selected from hybrids between balsam poplar and eastern cottonwood. Some authors report the clone is female while others claim it is male. Older manuals classify this species as *Populus candicans* or *Populus* x *gileadensis*. Medium-sized excurrent tree growing 60–90 ft in height and 1–2 ft in diameter. Leaves alternate; simple; broadly ovate; 4–6 in. long; 3.5–4.5 in. wide; dark green above; white-green below with brown veins; hairy on the veins below. Tip acuminate. Base cordate. Margin coarsely serrate to crenate; at least 15 teeth per side. Petiole round; hairy. Twigs stout; slightly angled in cross section. Terminal buds large; hairy; viscous; aromatic. The buds, which essentially contain aspirin, were boiled to relieve pain and sinus congestion. Cultivated from New England to the southern Appalachians; persisting and slightly spreading vegetatively from abandoned homesites.

Black poplar
Populus nigra L.

Moderate-sized excurrent tree. Leaves alternate; simple; deltate; lustrous; narrow translucent border. Base rhombic forming a very wide V-shape. Margin serrate to crenate. Petiole flat; lacking glands at tip. The form almost always encountered is Lombardy poplar (*Populus nigra* var. *italica*), a horticultural selection from black poplar with a narrow columnar crown and ascending branches. Widely planted; persisting and locally spreading from root sprouts.

Smith aspen, Hybrid aspen

Populus x *smithii* Boivin

The natural hybrid between trembling aspen and bigtooth aspen. Intermediate in characteristics between the 2 parental species. Usually recognized by the leaves, which typically contain 20 teeth on each side. Found on disturbed sites and roadsides in the Lake States.

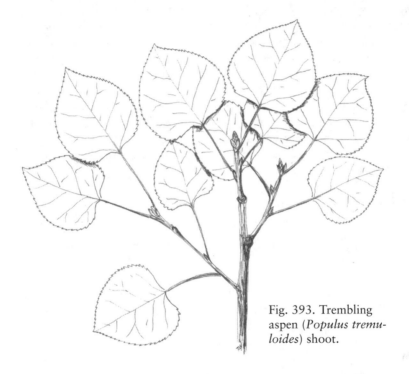

Fig. 393. Trembling aspen (*Populus tremuloides*) shoot.

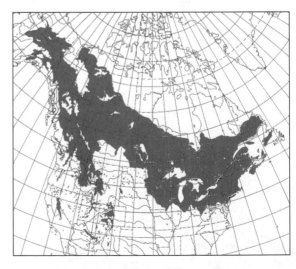

Fig. 394. Native range of trembling aspen (*Populus tremuloides*).

Trembling aspen, Quaking aspen, Popple

Populus tremuloides Michx. (fig. 393)

Form. Small excurrent tree growing 50–60 ft in height and 1–2 ft in diameter (largest known 120 ft by 4 ft). Crown open.

Leaves. Alternate; simple; nearly round to broadly ovate; 1–3 in. in diameter; yellow-green; crenate to serrate with about 30 glandular teeth per side; hairless. Petiole flat; 1–3 in. long. Tip acute; base rounded.

Fruit. Capsule; narrowly conical; 0.2 in. long; curved; 2-valved; gray hairy. Seeds light brown; 0.05 in. long.

Twigs. Slender; lustrous; red-brown becoming gray. Terminal buds 0.2–0.5 in. long; conical; sharp pointed; red-brown; slightly resinous.

Bark. Thin; on younger trees smooth; green-white to white. On older trees becoming tightly furrowed; gray to black.

Wood. Sapwood white; heartwood light brown but the difference between sapwood and heartwood not clearly defined; disagreeable odor when wet; soft; straight grained; lustrous; moderately light. Used mostly for pulpwood, fiberboard, and matches but also for shingles, log cabins, clothespins, core of plywood panels, lumber, outdoor play furniture, and novelty items.

Natural History. Very intolerant of shade. Fast growing; individual stems reach maturity in 50–80 years (extreme age 225 years) but the clone itself may persist by repeated root sprouting for thousands of years. Reproduction from seed rare; heavy seed crops produced every 4–5 years; seeds released in spring; germination occurs on bare mineral soil 1–2 days after release. Reproduction vigorous from root sprouts on disturbed areas forming large clones occupying as much as 100 acres. Responds well to intensive management, particularly thinning and fertilization. Fire, shoot blight, hypoxylon canker, forest tent caterpillar, western tent caterpillar, and gypsy moth cause the most damage. Owing to the large distribution, found on a very wide variety of soils. The best sites generally found in the Lake States are well-drained loams high in organic matter and fertility. Pioneers in old fields in New England; successional in the Lake States; forms a fire climax in the central Rocky Mountains. When young, found in pure stands; when old, mixed with white spruce, balsam fir, Douglas-fir, lodgepole pine, white fir, and Engelmann spruce. Browsed heavily by white-tailed deer, mule deer, elk, moose, cattle, and sheep. Beaver eat the young bark and twigs. Grouse eat the buds. Sapsuckers commonly feed on the stems. White-tailed deer, mule deer, elk, and moose rub their antlers on small trees.

Hybrids. Hybridizes with many other *Populus* especially bigtooth aspen, forming Smith aspen.

Range. See figure 394. Elevation: sea level to 11,500 ft. The most wide-ranging tree in North America.

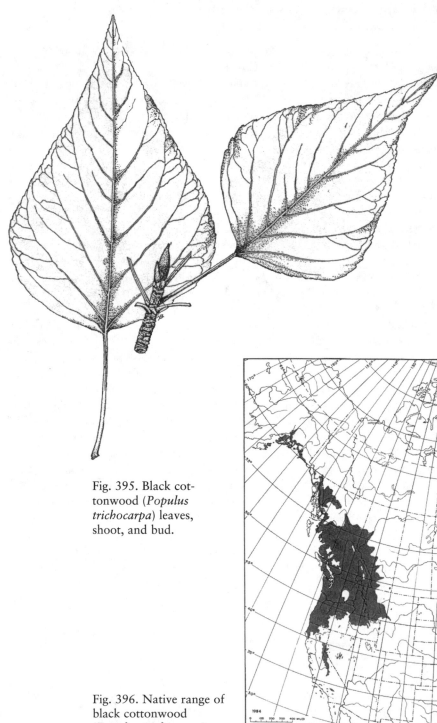

Fig. 395. Black cottonwood (*Populus trichocarpa*) leaves, shoot, and bud.

Fig. 396. Native range of black cottonwood (*Populus trichocarpa*).

Black cottonwood

Populus trichocarpa Torr. & Gray (fig. 395)

Form. Large excurrent tree growing 120–150 ft in height and 5–6 ft in diameter (largest known 200 ft by 10 ft); the largest angiosperm in the Pacific Northwest and the largest cottonwood in North America. Crown long; open; rounded.

Leaves. Ovate to ovate-lanceolate; 3–6 in. long; 2–4 in. wide; leathery; dark green above; silver-white to pale green below with rusty markings. Tip acute to long acuminate. Base rounded or slightly cordate. Margin finely crenate or entire. Petioles 1.5–3 in. long; round or slightly flattened in cross section.

Fruit. Capsule; subspherical; 0.3 in. long; 3-valved; hairy.

Twigs. Moderately slender; slightly angled; red-brown becoming dark gray. Terminal bud 0.7 in. long; ovoid; orange-brown covered by fragrant yellow-brown resin.

Bark. Smooth and gray-brown on young stems; developing small flat ridges; dark gray; 1–2 in. thick; deeply and sharply furrowed.

Wood. Similar to balsam poplar. Mostly used for pulpwood; plantations established in the Willamette Valley in Oregon as early as 1901 to supply the paper mill in Oregon City.

Natural History. Very intolerant of shade. Fast growing; short-lived reaching maturity in 60–70 years (extreme age 200 years). Reproduces by seed; abundant seed crops produced almost every year; seed released in spring; dispersed by wind and water; requires moist bare soil; seed viability high but lasting only 2–4 weeks. Also regenerates vegetatively from stump sprouts, fallen branches that root, and occasionally from root sprouts. Ice storms and browsing by mammals cause the most damage. Generally found on silt, sand, and gravel alluvial soils associated with river floodplains; occasionally found on upland clay soils. Forms extensive, even-aged, pure stands, but may also be found in mixed stands with red alder, Douglas-fir, western hemlock, western redcedar, Sitka spruce, bigleaf maple, grand fir, white fir, western larch, Engelmann spruce, and black willow.

Hybrids. Hybridizes freely with balsam poplar where their ranges overlap. Also hybridizes with Fremont cottonwood and eastern cottonwood, some of which grow very rapidly and have been tested in plantations for pulpwood production.

Range. See figure 396. Elevation: sea level to 7,000 ft.

WILLOW: THE GENUS *SALIX*

This genus contains roughly 400 species scattered throughout the Northern Hemisphere, but only about 90 species are native to our region. In addition, 4 Eurasian species occasionally escape cultivation. Although 27 native species occasionally grow tall enough in a portion of their range to be considered trees only 5 species are consistently treelike. The largest willows are keyed below, and the 8 most treelike species are described in greater detail below. Identification of willows is often difficult even for experts, because the leaves are similar in size and shape, the flowers and fruits are minute, and the species hybridize.

Some willows are trees, but most are shrubs sometimes growing only 1 ft tall. Willow leaves are usually linear to lanceolate. The flowers are either wind or insect pollinated. Individual flowers are subtended by hairy bracts. Female flowers contain two carpels fused into a single structure. The fruit is a two-valved capsule containing small seeds tufted with long silky hairs. The twigs easily break at junctions with larger branches, and they root easily after falling and contacting bare soil. Terminal buds are absent. Each lateral bud is covered by a single scale. Bark was the original source of aspirin. The wood is lightweight and diffuse-porous.

KEY TO WILLOWS

1. Stamens 3–12 . . . . .Go to 2
1. Stamens 2 . . . . .Go to 6
    2. Leaves green below; large tree . . . . .black willow, *Salix nigra*
    2. Leaves white or blue-green below; shrubby tree 3

Fig. 397. Peachleaf willow
(*Salix amygdaloides*) leaf.

3. Petioles with glands at base of leaf . . . . .Pacific willow, *Salix lasiandra*
3. Petioles without glands at base of leaf 4
    4. Flower bracts toothed . . . . .Bonpland willow, *Salix bonplandiana*
    4. Flower bracts entire 5
5. Leaves 4–5 in. long . . . . .coastal plain willow, *Salix caroliniana*
5. Leaves 2–4 in. long .peachleaf willow, *Salix amygdaloides*
    6. Naturalized ornamentals; usually trees 7
    6. Native; seldom planted; usually shrubby 9
7. Branchlets drooping; capsule stalkless . . . . .weeping willow, *Salix babylonica*
7. Branchlets not drooping; capsule short stalked 8
    8. Leaves white hairy on both sides; twigs green or yellow . . . .
    . . . . .white willow, *Salix alba*
    8. Leaves nearly hairless; twigs brown . . . . .crack willow, *Salix fragilis*
9. Flower bracts deciduous; filaments slightly hairy 10
9. Flower bracts persistent; filaments hairless 11
    10. Leaves 0.3–1.3 in. long . . . . .yewleaf willow, *Salix taxifolia*
    10. Leaves over 2 in. long . . . . .sandbar willow, *Salix exigua*
11. Ovary and capsule hairless 12
11. Ovary and capsule hairy 13
    12. Leaf tip acute or rounded . . . . .arroyo willow, *Salix lasiolepis*
    12. Leaf tip acuminate . . . . .Mackenzie willow, *Salix mackenzieana*
13. Flower bracts green-yellow with red tips . . . . .Bebb willow, *Salix bebbiana*
13. Flower bracts black with white hairs . . . . .Scouler willow, *Salix scoulerana*

White willow
Salix alba L.

Medium-sized tree growing 70–80 ft in height. Leaves alternate; simple; lance-olate; 2–4 in. long; acuminate; finely toothed; white-waxy with white silky hairs below. Petioles with minute glands near the leaf base. Bark gray; furrowed. Intolerant of shade; fast growing; adapted to a wide variety of sites. The weeping willow of cooler areas in our region is often *Salix alba* var. *tristis*. Native to Europe, northern Africa, and western and central Asia. Planted and escaped in the East and locally in Colorado.

Peachleaf willow, Almond willow
Salix amygdaloides Anderss. (fig. 397)

Small tree growing 40–50 ft in height and 2 ft in diameter (largest known 70 ft). Leaves alternate; simple; lanceolate to ovate-lanceolate; 2–6 in. long; 0.7–1.2 in. wide; acuminate; finely serrate; light green above; hairy when young, becoming hairless; white-waxy below. Petiole twisted; lacking glands. Fruit a capsule; spheri-cal-conic; 0.2 in. long; long stalked; hairless; light yellow-red; valves 2–3; recurved when open. Seeds minute; hairy tufted. Bark red-brown; 0.5–0.7 in. thick; divided by furrows into interconnecting irregular flat ridges. Intolerant of shade; fast grow-ing but short-lived. Grows in moist sites along streams and lakes. Found from New York to eastern Washington, and southwest to New Mexico.

Fig. 398. Weeping willow
(*Salix babylonica*) leaf.

Fig. 399. Crack willow
(*Populus fragilis*) leaf.

Fig. 400. Pacific willow
(*Salix lasiandra*) shoot.

Weeping willow
Salix babylonica L. (fig. 398)

Large tree growing 90–100 ft in height with characteristic long, slender, drooping branches. Leaves narrowly lanceolate; 3–6 in. long; finely toothed; hairless; dark green above; white-waxy below; sometimes with silky hairs. Tip long acuminate. Petiole with glands near base of blade. Bark gray-brown; rough; fissured. Intolerant of shade; fast growing; short-lived. Often confused with weeping cultivars of other species. Native to China; planted as an ornamental in warmer areas; occasionally naturalized.

Bonpland willow
Salix bonplandiana H. B. K.

Small tree growing 50 ft in height and 1–2 ft in diameter. Leaves alternate; simple; narrowly lanceolate to broadly linear; 4–5 in. long; 0.5–0.7 in. wide; green above; silver-white below. Tip long acuminate. Petiole stout; grooved. Fruit a capsule; ovoid; yellow or red. Bark dark brown to black; divided into broad flat ridges. Intolerant of shade; generally found in well-drained soil. Cattle eat the twigs. Found from southwestern Utah to northern California, and south from southwestern New Mexico to southern California; also in Mexico and Central America.

Crack willow
Salix fragilis L. (fig. 399)

Large tree growing 100–120 ft in height. Leaves alternate; simple; lanceolate to oblong-lanceolate; white-waxy below. Tip long acuminate. Margin serrate; teeth tipped with glands. Petiole with glands near leaf base. Branches often breaking, falling, and rooting in moist soil, a characteristic that provides the common and scientific names. Native from Turkey to Iran; occasionally planted and escaped in the East.

Pacific willow
Salix lasiandra Benth. (fig. 400)

Large shrub or small tree growing to 60 ft in height and 2–3 ft in diameter. Leaves alternate; simple; lanceolate to broadly lanceolate; 2.5–4.5 in. long; 0.5–1.5 in. wide; dark green above; white-waxy below. Margin finely serrate; teeth tipped with glands. Petiole 0.5 in. long; glands near leaf base. Fruit a capsule; 0.2 in. long; light brown. Twigs stout; lustrous; yellow-brown to purple-brown; often white-waxy; hairy to very hairy when young. Bark brown to red-brown; broken into flat scaly ridges. Grows in sandy soil along streams. Found from Saskatchewan to central Alaska, and south to the Black Hills of South Dakota, New Mexico, and southern California.

Black willow
Salix nigra Marsh. (fig. 401)

Form. Large tree growing 90–100 ft in height and 2–3 ft in diameter (largest known 140 ft by 4 ft). Bole often divided. Crown broad; open.

Leaves. Alternate; simple; lanceolate; 3–6 in. long; acuminate; finely serrate; thin; bright green above; paler beneath; petiole short.

Fruit. Capsule; ovoid-conic; 0.2 in. long; short stalked; hairless. Seeds minute; hairy tufted.

Bark. Gray-brown to nearly black; divided into furrows separating scaly ridges.

Wood. The largest native willow and the only one important for wood products. Used for lumber, veneer, pulp, charcoal (preferred species for making black gun powder), and artificial limbs.

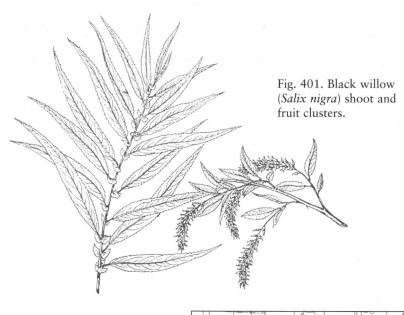

Fig. 401. Black willow (*Salix nigra*) shoot and fruit clusters.

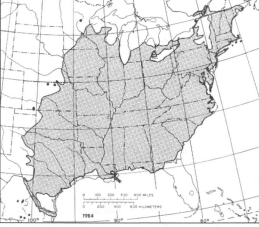

Fig. 402. Native range of black willow (*Salix nigra*); also in disjunct areas in Mexico

Natural History. Intolerant of shade. Fast growing but short-lived; reaches maturity in 50–70 years. Reproduces by seed on bare mineral soil; requires abundant moisture; good seed crops produced almost every year; dispersed by wind and floating on water; seeds germinate shortly after release; seed viability short, only 1 week. Reproduces vegetatively from stump and root sprouts; broken branches root easily; planted by pushing large twigs into moist soil; branches as large as 3–5 in. in diameter still root successfully. Found on almost any soil type as long as abundant water is present. Found on stream banks, lake shores, wet flats, and river islands. Best development is in the lower Mississippi River valley and Gulf Coastal Plain. Grows in pure stands or mixed with river birch, sycamore, eastern cottonwood, sweetgum, American elm, red maple, boxelder, and swamp blackgum. Favorite choice for river bank stabilization projects.
Range. See figure 402.

Yew-leaf willow
Salix taxifolia H. B. K.

Large shrub or small tree growing to 50 ft in height and 1–2 ft in diameter. Leaves alternate; simple; lanceolate to oblanceolate; 0.3–1.3 in. long; 0.1 in. wide; slightly curved; entire or sometimes toothed above the middle; hairy above and below. Leaves stalkless or with very short petioles. Fruit 0.2 in. long; red-brown; silky hairy becoming hairless. Twigs red-brown; densely hairy becoming hairless. Found on creek banks and in canyons. Cattle eat the twigs. Bundles of twigs are sometimes tied into brooms. Found mostly in Mexico, but disjunct populations occur in west Texas, New Mexico, and southeastern Arizona.

SOAPBERRY FAMILY: THE SAPINDACEAE

With trees, shrubs, and sometimes vines, the Soapberry Family contains 1,500–2,000 species in 130–140 genera worldwide, found mostly in tropical and subtropical areas. Our region contains only 2 native genera that become tree-sized. In addition, goldenraintree (*Koelreuteria paniculata*) native to China, Japan, and Korea is a popular ornamental. Tropical species akee (*Blighia*), lychee (*Litchi*), and Spanish-lime (*Melicoccus*) provide edible fruits. The Maple Family (Aceraceae) and Buckeye Family (Hippocastanaceae) are sometimes placed in the Soapberry Family.

SOAPBERRY: THE GENUS *SAPINDUS*

Worldwide the genus *Sapindus* contains about 12 species found in tropical America, southeast Asia, Hawaii, and other Pacific islands. Our region contains 2 species, the one described in detail below and wingleaf soapberry (*Sapindus saponaria*) found in scattered localities in Florida and coastal Georgia.

KEY TO SOAPBERRIES

1. Leaves with 6–13 leaflets each . . . . .wingleaf soapberry, *Sapindus saponaria*
1. Leaves with 11–19 leaflets each . . . . .western soapberry, *Sapindus drummondii*

Western soapberry

Sapindus drummondii Hook. & Arn. (fig. 403)

Small tree growing to 50 ft in height and 1–2 ft in diameter. Branches held erect. Leaves alternate; pinnately compound; semi-evergreen. Leaflets 11–19; alternate or subopposite; lanceolate; 2–3 in. long; margins entire; yellow-green; hairless above; hairy below. Flowers unisexual and bisexual on the same tree; white; minute; borne in many-flowered clusters 6–9 in. long. Fruit a berry; translucent; 0.5 in. wide; yellow turning black; shriveling and persisting until spring; formerly used as soap. Seeds obovoid; dark brown; smooth. Twigs moderately stout; yellow-green and hairy becoming slightly hairy and gray. Terminal bud absent. Lateral buds small; spherical; stacked in pairs. Bark thin; red-brown; furrowed into long scaly plates; bitter and astringent. Heartwood light brown tinged with yellow; heavy; hard; ring-porous; no commercial value. Found from southwestern Missouri to southeastern Colorado, and south from Louisiana to southern Arizona; also in Mexico.

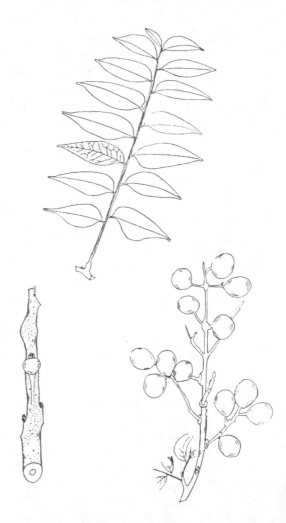

Fig. 403. Western soapberry (*Sapindus drummondii*) leaf, twig, and fruit cluster.

This genus contains only the one species listed below.

Mexican-buckeye
Ungnadia speciosa Endl.

Large shrub or small tree growing to 35 ft in height. Leaves alternate; deciduous; 5–12 in. long; pinnately compound. Leaflets 5–7 per leaf; ovate-lanceolate; serrate or crenate; 3–5 in. long; thick; lustrous and dark green above; paler and hairy or hairless below; lateral leaflets nearly lacking stalks. Flowers about 1 in. wide; light red; petals 4–5; stamen much longer than the petals; appearing in the spring with the new leaves. Fruit a capsule; leathery; broadly ovoid; 3-valved; red-brown; 2 in. wide. Seeds black; shiny; about 0.5 in. long; reputedly poisonous. Bark thin; smooth; gray to brown; developing shallow furrows on old trees. Grows on moist limestone soils on stream banks and in canyons. Leaves and fruits poisonous to livestock. Found in south Texas, New Mexico, and south into Mexico.

SAPODILLA FAMILY: SAPOTACEAE

Worldwide this family contains about 1,100 species in 53 genera found mostly in the tropics in lowland and montane rain forests. Our region contains only the genus *Bumelia*.

The Sapotaceae contains trees and shrubs that produce milky sap. The leaves are alternate, simple, leathery, and entire. Most members lack stipules. The flowers are usually bisexual, white, insect or bat pollinated, and small with four to eight fused petals and usually four to five carpels. The fruit is a berry containing one to a few large hard seeds, each with a large white spot (hilum). Economically the family provides chicle for chewing gum (*Manilkara*), rubberlike compounds, star-apple (*Chrysophyllum*), sapodilla (*Manilkara*), and edible oil from seeds. It also provides durable lumber from bullet-wood (*Manilkara*), cherry-mahogany (*Mimusops*), and ironwood (*Sideroxylon*).

This genus contains 25–50 species in the world, found mostly in the New World tropics. Our region contains 6 species. The tallest species are keyed below, but only 2 occasionally become tree-sized.

KEY TO BUMELIAS

1. Leaves evergreen; thick and leathery . . . . .saffron-plum, *Bumelia celastrina*
1. Leaves deciduous; thin . . . . .Go to 2
    2. Leaves hairless or nearly so below . . . . .buckthorn bumelia, *Bumelia lycioides*
    2. Leaves hairy below 3
3. Leaves with dull brown hairs below . . . . .tough bumelia, *Bumelia tenax*
3. Leaves with lustrous red-brown hairs below . . . .gum bumelia, *Bumelia lanuginosa*

Gum bumelia, Gum elastic

Bumelia lanuginosa (Michx.) Pers. (fig. 404)

Shrub or small tree growing 40–50 ft in height and 1–2 ft in diameter. Leaves alternate; simple; 1–3 in. long; 0.4–1 in. wide; oblanceolate to obovate; margins entire; thin; dark green above; shiny red-brown hairy below; tardily deciduous. Leaf tip rounded; base long tapering. Flowers bisexual; white; minute; bell-shaped; borne in axillary clusters; appearing in summer. Fruit a 1-seeded drupelike berry; oblong; 0.5 in. long; black; flesh thick; borne singly or in clusters of 2–3. Seeds 0.5 in. long; shiny. Some lateral twigs modified into stout thorns; red-brown to gray-brown hairy. Bark thin; dark red-brown; divided into scaly ridges. Wood heavy; not strong; close grained; ring-porous; light brown; produces clear viscid gum; low commercial value. Found from Georgia to central Florida, west to southeastern Arizona, and north in the Mississippi River valley to southern Illinois.

Fig. 404. Gum bumelia
(*Bumelia lanuginosa*) shoot.

Buckthorn bumelia
Bumelia lycioides (L.) Pers.

Large shrub or small tree occasionally growing to 25 ft in height. Leaves alternate; simple; narrowly elliptical to oval; 2.5–4 in. long; 1–2 in. wide; entire; light-brown hairy below at first becoming hairless. Flowers like gum bumelia. Fruit a drupelike berry; black; nearly spherical. Twigs hairy becoming hairless; short thorns present and some branches thorn tipped. Bark gray-brown; developing scaly plates that fall to expose the red-brown inner bark. Found in bottomlands or on adjacent slopes; often on slightly acidic or neutral soils. Found mostly in the Coastal Plain from southeastern Virginia to northern Florida, west to southeastern Texas, and north in the Mississippi River valley to southern Indiana.

THE FIGWORT FAMILY: SCROPHULARIACEAE

Worldwide this family contains 3,000–5,000 species in about 300 genera. Most species are herbs, but a few are shrubs or trees. Found throughout the world but most common in the north temperate regions. Our region naturally contains about 850 species in 73 genera, but none are tree-sized. An exotic species native to China, *Paulownia* is planted and has escaped in our region.

Members of the Figwort Family have simple alternate or opposite leaves that lack stipules. The flowers are bisexual, usually showy, insect pollinated, and bilaterally symmetrical with two carpels and four to five petals fused into bells or tubes. The fruit is usually a multiseeded capsule enclosed by persistent sepals. Economically the family provides heart medicines (*Digitalis*) and popular ornamental herbs, particularly snapdragon (*Antirrhinum*) and foxglove (*Digitalis*).

PAULOWNIA: THE GENUS *PAULOWNIA*

Worldwide *Paulownia* contains 6–17 species all native to eastern Asia, but the genus has been repeatedly introduced to Europe, Australia, and North America. Several species have been planted in our region, but currently only the species listed below is naturalized. Some authorities place this genus in the family Bignoniaceae.

Paulownia, Princess-tree, Royal paulownia
Paulownia tomentosa (Thunb.) Sieb & Zucc. ex Steud. (fig. 405)

Form. Moderate-sized tree growing 40–50 ft in height and 1–2 ft in diameter (largest known 60 ft by 4 ft); Often with wide-spreading branches.

Leaves. Opposite; simple; deciduous; heart-shaped; 6–16 in. long but 2–3 ft long on sprouts; entire with occasional large tooth; hairy below.

Flowers. Light purple; tubelike; 1.5–2.5 in. long; borne in many-flowered terminal clusters (panicles); appearing in the spring before or with the new leaves.

Fruit. Capsule; 2-parted; ovoid; 1.5–2 in. long; woody; beaked; borne in terminal clusters; persisting through the winter. Seeds tiny; winged; white; released slowly from autumn to spring.

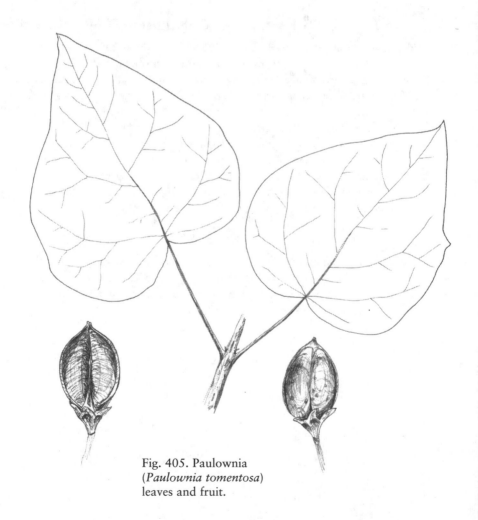

Fig. 405. Paulownia
(*Paulownia tomentosa*)
leaves and fruit.

Twigs. Stout; terminal bud lacking; pith hollow after 1 year. Flower buds appearing in autumn; spherical; brown hairy.

Bark. Brown; marked with diamond- and triangle-shaped depressions when young; developing small ridges with age.

Wood. Variable commercial value. Well-formed trees eagerly purchased by Japanese; traditional wood in Japan for chests, furniture, picture frames, musical instruments, clogs, bowls, toys, and pulp. Lightweight; splitting and cracking minimal.

Natural History. Intolerant of shade. Growth rate rapid; growing up to 8 ft in 1 growing season; some reports of rapid growth are from sprouts. Seeds lack dormancy. Requires bare soil for seedling establishment. Sprouts prolifically from stumps and roots. Winter dieback causes the most damage. Found on a wide variety of upland sites, but most abundant on rocky hillsides. Usually found in fencerows, disturbed places, along roads, and in rocky road cuts. Sometimes regenerating in open forest understories after fire or disturbance. Planted on mine spoil banks. Considered a weed by some, and a candidate for short-rotation intensively managed plantations by others.

Range. Native to China. Planted in the East from Massachusetts to Missouri, and south from central Florida to southern Texas; also planted in Pacific Coast states. Naturalized from New York to eastern Missouri, and south from northern Florida to southern Texas.

QUASSIA FAMILY: SIMAROUBACEAE

Worldwide the Quassia Family contains about 120 species in 20 genera, found mostly in tropical and subtropical areas. Our region contains 2 native genera (*Castela* and *Holacantha*), but they are tall shrubs. The only naturally occurring tree in our region is tree-of-heaven, an exotic from China.

Leaves of this family are alternate and usually compound but sometimes simple. Stipules are usually lacking. The flowers are small, radially symmetrical, and bisexual and unisexual on the same tree (polygamo-dioecious). They are pollinated by birds or insects. The fruit is usually a samara or capsule, but sometimes a berry or drupe. The bark is often very bitter. The wood is ring-porous. Overall, the family is similar to the Rutaceae, but it lacks translucent dots.

AILANTHUS: THE GENUS *AILANTHUS*

Worldwide ailanthus contains about ten species found naturally in Asia and Australia. No species are native to our region, but tree-of-heaven is widely naturalized.

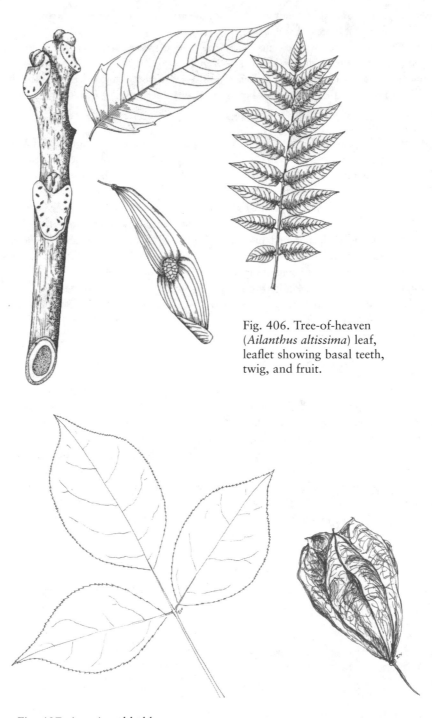

Fig. 406. Tree-of-heaven (*Ailanthus altissima*) leaf, leaflet showing basal teeth, twig, and fruit.

Fig. 407. American bladdernut (*Staphylea trifolia*) leaf and fruit.

Tree-of-heaven, Ailanthus
Ailanthus altissima (Mill.) Swingle (fig. 406)

Moderate-sized tree growing 50–70 ft in height and 1–2 ft in diameter. Crown open. Leaves alternate; deciduous; 1–3 ft long; pinnately compound with or without a terminal leaflet; aromatic smelling like peanut butter. Leaflets 13–41 per leaf; ovate or lanceolate; 3–6 in. long; entire except for 1–4 glandular teeth at the base. Flowers appearing after the new leaves have expanded. Fruit a samara; oblong; twisted; 1–2 in. long; seed in center. Twigs very stout; velvet hairy becoming hairless; red-brown. Terminal bud absent. Lateral buds small; nearly round; brown. Bark thin; gray; smooth at first developing shallow furrows with age. Wood with no commercial value; soft; weak; pale yellow. Intolerant of shade. Very fast growing; short-lived. Reproduces easily from seed; abundant seed produced most years. Reproduces aggressively from root sprouts forming large colonies. Tolerant of a wide range of conditions. Usually found growing in disturbed urban areas especially along railroad tracks, roadsides, abandoned city lots, and large cracks in sidewalks; occasionally found as scattered trees in natural oak-hickory stands. Usually considered a weed. Native to China. Formerly planted and now naturalized from Massachusetts to Iowa, and south from northern Florida to Texas; also from New Mexico to southern California, and north to Washington.

BLADDERNUT FAMILY: STAPHYLEACEAE

Worldwide this family contains about 60 species in five genera, all either trees or shrubs found mostly in Asia. Our region contains 2 species in one genus (*Staphylea*), but only the species discussed below is tree-sized. The other species, Sierra bladdernut (*Staphylea bolanderi*), is a tall shrub infrequently found in the interior mountains of California.

KEY TO BLADDERNUTS

1. Leaflets hairless below; California . . . . .Sierra bladdernut, *Staphylea bolanderi*
1. Leaflets hairy below at least along the veins; eastern North America . . . .
. . . . .American bladdernut, *Staphylea trifolia*

American bladdernut
Staphylea trifolia L. (fig. 407)

Large shrub or rarely a small tree growing to 35 ft in height. Usually found in a clump of several stems. Leaves opposite; pinnately compound. Leaflets 3 per leaf (rarely 5); ovate; finely toothed. Stipules present but falling quickly. Flowers bisexual; green-white to cream; bell-shaped; petals 5; borne in few-flowered clusters. Fruit a capsule; papery; 3-parted; looking like a Japanese lantern; persisting into the winter; seeds poisonous. Twigs olive-green turning brown; dotted with lenticels. Bark smooth with short vertical furrows; gray to black. Found on moist fertile sites or bottomlands where flooding is brief. Found from New Hampshire to southeastern Minnesota, and south from northwestern Florida to eastern Oklahoma.

STERCULIA FAMILY: STERCULIACEAE.

Worldwide this family contains about 700 species in about 60 genera found mostly in tropical areas. In our region, the family contains about a dozen native species in six genera, but only fremontia contains trees. In addition Chinese parasol tree (*Firmiana simplex*) with alternate entire leaves with 3en5 palmate lobes is planted and sometimes escapes in the warmer parts of our region.

FREMONTIA: THE GENUS FREMONTODENDRON

This genus contains only 2 species, the one listed below and Mexican fremontia (*Fremontodendron mexicanum*) a large shrub found only in San Diego County, California and in Baja California.

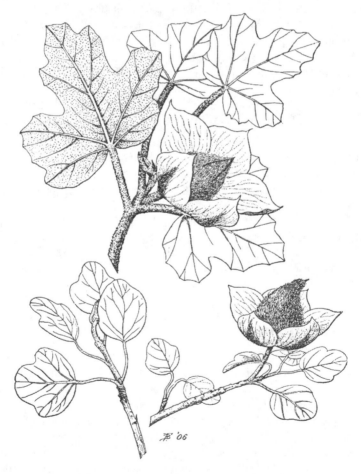

Fig. 408. California fremontia (*Fremontodendron californicum*) shoots and blooms.

KEY TO FREMONTIAS

1. Leaves with 1–3 palmate veins . . . .
. . . . .California fremontia, *Fremontodendron californicum*
1. Leaves with 5–7 palmate veins   Mexican fremontia, *Fremontodendron mexicanum*

California fremontia, slippery elm, flannelbush
Fremontodendron californicum (Torr.) Cov. (figure 408)

Formerly called *Fremontia californica*. Large shrub or small tree occasionally growing to 25 ft in height and 0.5 ft in diameter. Leaves simple; alternate; evergreen but sometimes falling during dry periods; nearly round; not lobed to 3-lobed; 0.5–2 in. long; dull green and slightly hairy above; densely rusty-hairy below. Flowers mostly bisexual; large and showy; subtended by 3 bracts. Sepals 5; yellow. Petals absent. Fruit a 4-5 parted capsule; wooly.   Forms large thickets or grows mixed with various scrub oaks and mountain mahogany. Found on dry gravelly slopes mostly in the Coast Ranges and Sierra Nevada of California, but also south into Baja California and in central Arizona.

STORAX OR SNOWBELL FAMILY: STYRACACEAE

Worldwide this family contains about 160 species in 11 genera. Our region contains 2 genera, tree-sized silverbells (*Halesia*) and shrub-sized snowbells (*Styrax*).

SILVERBELL: THE GENUS *HALESIA*

Worldwide this genus contains four species. Our region contains three species, and the fourth occurs in China. Little silverbell (*Halesia carolina*, formerly called *Halesia parviflora*) occurs locally in widely scattered localities from South Carolina to northern Florida, and west to Mississippi.

KEY TO SILVERBELLS

1. Fruit with 2 longitudinal wings . . . . .two-wing silverbell, *Halesia diptera*
1. Fruit with 4 longitudinal wings . . . . .Go to 2
    2. Leaf margin entire to slightly toothed . . . . . . .little silverbell, *Halesia carolina*
    2. Leaf margin with rounded teeth . . . . . . .Carolina silverbell, *Halesia tetraptera*

Two-wing silverbell
Halesia diptera Ellis

Small tree growing to 40 ft in height (tallest known 55 ft). Leaves alternate; simple; oval to broadly obovate; margin with widely spaced glandular teeth; slightly hairy above and below. Flower petals united at base only. Fruit a dry drupe with 2 longitudinal wings. Grows in mesic uplands to well-drained bottomlands. Found from extreme southern South Carolina to east Texas; disjuncts in northern Alabama and southern Arkansas.

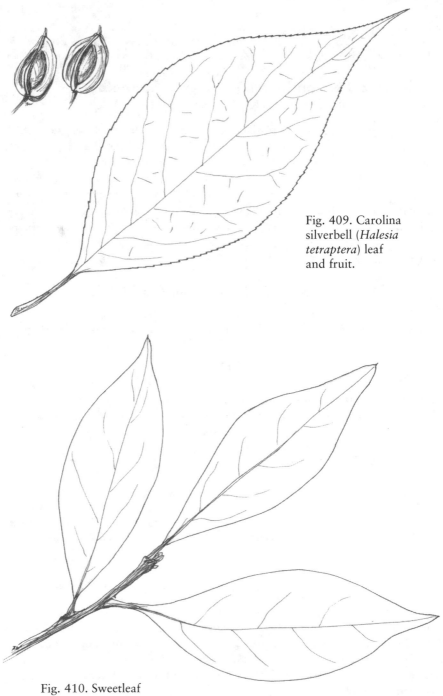

Fig. 409. Carolina silverbell (*Halesia tetraptera*) leaf and fruit.

Fig. 410. Sweetleaf (*Symplocos tinctoria*) shoot.

Carolina silverbell, Silverbell
Halesia tetraptera Ellis (fig. 409)

Formerly known as *Halesia carolina* and *Halesia monticola*. Moderate-sized tree growing 40–80 ft in height and 1 ft in diameter (largest known 100 ft by 3 ft). Leaves alternate; simple; deciduous; 4–7 in. long; 2–3 in. wide; obovate to elliptical; margin toothed; hairy below. Tip acuminate; base rounded. Flowers bisexual; white rarely pink; showy; bell-shaped; petals united above the middle; borne in drooping axillary clusters of 2–5; appearing in the spring before the leaves. Fruit a drupe; dry; oblong; 4-winged; 1–2.5 in. long. Twigs slender; terminal bud absent. Bark gray to purple-gray; developing furrows that separate scaly ridges. Grows on a wide variety of sites from ridge tops to lower slopes. On upper slopes, occasionally found in pure stands, but more commonly found on middle and lower slopes in mixed stands with yellow-poplar, northern red oak, white oak, white ash, yellow birch, sweet birch, sugar maple, and red maple. Found from southern Ohio to extreme southern Illinois, and south from northern Florida to Alabama; also local in Arkansas and southeastern Oklahoma. Most common below 4,000 ft in the southern Appalachians of North Carolina and Tennessee.

SWEETLEAF FAMILY: SYMPLOCACEAE

Worldwide this family contains about 500 species in two genera— *Cordyloblaste* and *Symplocos*—found mostly in the tropics and subtropics. Our region contains only *Symplocos*.

SWEETLEAF: THE GENUS *SYMPLOCOS*

Worldwide this genus contains about 350 species found mostly in tropical and subtropical areas. Our region contains only the 1 species described below.

Sweetleaf, Horse-sugar
Symplocos tinctoria (L.) L'Her. (fig. 410)

Shrub or small excurrent tree growing to 30 ft in height (largest known 55 ft by 1 ft). Leaves simple; alternate but clustered at the tips of short axillary twigs; elliptical to obovate; entire to slightly scalloped; thick; falling slowly or semi-evergreen in mild climates; 3–5 in. long; often tasting slightly sweet; hairless or hairy above; hairy below. Flowers bisexual; yellow-white; fragrant; found in dense axillary clusters; petals 5; stamen numerous; appearing in the spring before the new leaves. Fruit a drupe; green; oblong; dry; 0.4–0.6 in. long. Twigs brown hairy becoming gray and hairless; chambered. Bark smooth; gray; larger stems marked with short white depressions. Grows on a wide variety of sites from moist bottomlands and flatwoods to dry mountain ridges. Found in the Coastal Plain from Delaware to Florida, west to Texas, and north in the Mississippi valley to Arkansas.

TAMARISK FAMILY: TAMARICACEAE

Found in salty and droughty habitats in temperate and subtropical areas, this family contains 70–120 species in four genera in the world, all found in Eurasia and Africa.

TAMARISK: THE GENUS *TAMARIX*

Worldwide about 54 species of tamarisk occur in western Europe, the Mediterranean, and east to India and northern China. All are halophytes capable of growing in salt-laden soil by excreting salt through specialized glands. Several species are cultivated in our region especially for windbreaks, erosion control, and ornamental purposes; 3 species are naturalized. French tamarisk (*Tamarix gallica*),

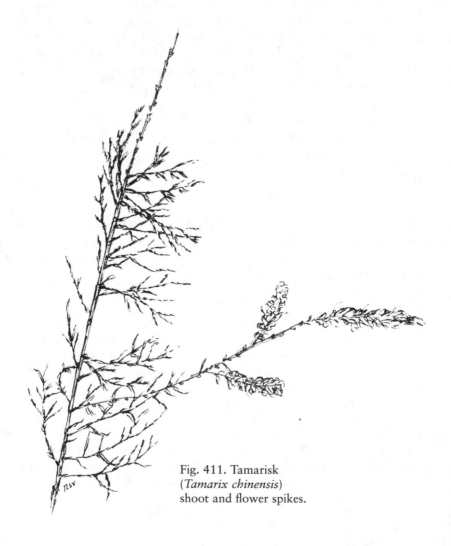

Fig. 411. Tamarisk (*Tamarix chinensis*) shoot and flower spikes.

native to southern Europe, is locally naturalized in southern Louisiana and Texas. Small-flower tamarisk (*Tamarix parviflora*) of the Mediterranean region with four petals is locally naturalized in southern California. Tamarisk (*Tamarix chinensis*) described in detail below and native to Asia and southeastern Europe is widely naturalized in the West.

Tamarisks are either slender trees or shrubs with minute appressed scale leaves. In foliage they resemble junipers. Individual flowers are small, but they occur in large showy clusters. The flowers are bisexual, white or pink, with four or five petals; they are insect pollinated. The fruit is a three- to five-parted capsule usually producing seeds with a terminal tuft of hairs. The various species look similar, and, as noted below, they are easily confused.

Tamarisk, Saltcedar

Tamarix chinensis Lour. (fig. 411)

For years this species was misidentified as *Tamarix gallica*. Many older manuals still reflect this mistake. Large shrub or small tree occasionally growing to 45 ft in height. Leaves scalelike; alternate; crowded and appressed. Flowers pink; petals 5; crowded into showy terminal clusters. Fruit a capsule; 3–5 valves. Seeds minute. Twigs slender; purple; shed with the leaves. Bark red-brown. Transpires large amounts of water lowering local water tables. Flowers provide nectar for honey. Wood sometimes used for fuel. Native from southeastern Europe to northern China. Extensively naturalized along streams throughout the central and southern parts of the western United States where it is often considered a weed.

TEA FAMILY: THEACEAE

Worldwide this family contains 500–600 species in about 28 genera. Most members are found in tropical or subtropical areas especially in America and Asia. Our region contains about a dozen species in 7 genera, but only loblolly-bay becomes tree-sized. Franklinia (*Franklinia alatamaha*), a shrub, was discovered in 1765 by John and William Bartram in McIntosh County, Georgia. Last found growing wild in 1790, franklinia is currently known only in cultivation from materials collected in and before 1790. Virginia stewartia (*Stewartia malacodendron*) and mountain stewartia (*Stewartia ovata*) are native shrubs sometimes cultivated for the showy white flowers. Various cultivars of *Camellia*, native to China and Japan, are grown for ornamental purposes in the warmer areas of our region.

Members of this family are either trees or shrubs with alternate simple leaves that lack stipules. The flowers are bisexual, showy, usually borne singly, subtended by bracts, and pollinated by insects. The flowers usually have five petals and numerous stamen. The fruit is a capsule with a persistent central column. Economically the family provides tea leaves and oil from *Camellia sinensis*.

GORDONIA: THE GENUS *GORDONIA*

Worldwide the genus *Gordonia* includes about 30 species, but our region contains only the 1 species listed below.

Loblolly-bay, Gordonia

Gordonia lasianthus (L.) Ellis (fig. 412)

Form. Medium-sized excurrent tree growing 60–75 ft in height and 1–2 ft in diameter. Crown narrow; compact; conical.

Leaves. Alternate; simple; evergreen; 3–6 in. long; lanceolate to elliptic; toothed; dark green turning scarlet before falling.

Fig. 412. Loblolly-bay
(*Gordonia lasianthus*)
leaf and fruit.

Flowers. Bisexual; showy; white; fragrant; 2–3 in. wide; appearing over a long period from early to late summer. Pollinated by insects and hummingbirds.

Fruit. Capsule; woody; 5-parted; long stalked. Seeds 0.1 in. long; flat; nearly square; winged.

Twigs. Slender; dark brown; rough. Terminal bud present; 0.2 in. long; acute.

Bark. Red-brown turning gray; deeply furrowed into long flat ridges. Formerly used to provide tannin.

Wood. Light-brown; soft; fine grained. Low commercial value; sometimes used for pulpwood and cabinets.

Natural History. Tolerant of shade but usually becoming established in openings with bare soil. Moderate to slow growing. Reproduces by wind-blown seeds and stump sprouts. Wildfire causes the most damage. Studied as a possible pulpwood species, but growth too slow. Grows on poorly drained mineral or organic soils; common in pocosins, wet flats, and bays. Found in small groves or mixed with pond pine, loblolly pine, Atlantic whitecedar, red maple, redbay, sweetbay, swamp blackgum, sweetgum, and pondcypress. White-tailed deer browse the foliage. Occasionally planted but difficult to cultivate.

Range. Found in the Coastal Plain from eastern North Carolina to central Florida, and west to southern Mississippi.

BASSWOOD OR LINDEN FAMILY: TILIACEAE

Worldwide this family contains about 680 species in about 50 genera, found most abundantly in southeast Asia and Brazil. Our region contains three genera, but only basswood (*Tilia*) is tree-sized.

BASSWOOD OR LINDEN: THE GENUS *TILIA*

Basswood contains 40–50 species in the world, but our region contains only 3 species all native to eastern North America. Little-leaf linden (*Tilia cordata*), native to Europe with leaves only 2–3 in. long, is sometimes planted in our region. Classification of our basswoods has varied greatly over the years. Based largely upon geographic range and the number and type of hairs, authorities have recognized as few as 1 species and as many as 20. The treatment here recognizes 3 traditional species even though the recognition of a single variable species has considerable merit. When all of our basswoods are considered to constitute but a single species, the correct name is *Tilia americana*.

KEY TO BASSWOODS

1. Leaf undersurfaces (except for tufts in axils of veins) and fruit stalks hairless or nearly so . . . . .American basswood, *Tilia americana*
1. Leaf undersurfaces and fruit stalks hairy . . . . .Go to 2
   2. Leaf undersurfaces white; Appalachian . . . .white basswood, *Tilia heterophylla*
   2. Leaf undersurfaces gray, brown, or red-brown; Southeastern Coastal Plain . . . . .Carolina basswood, *Tilia caroliniana*

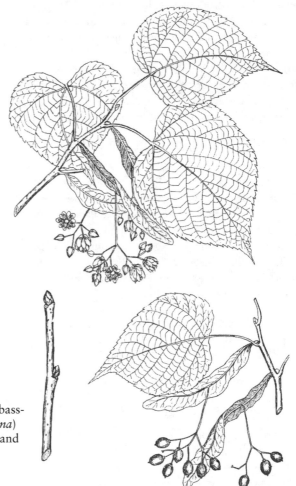

Fig. 413. American basswood (*Tilia americana*) shoots with flowers and fruits, and twig.

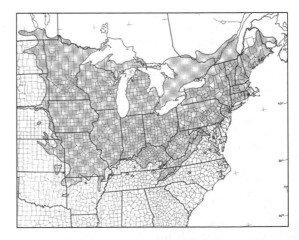

Fig. 414. Native range of American basswood (*Tilia americana*).

American basswood, American linden

Tilia americana L. (fig. 413)

Form. Large excurrent tree growing 80–130 ft in height and 2–3 ft in diameter (largest known 125 ft by 4 ft).

Leaves. Alternate; simple; deciduous; 4–6 in. long; broadly ovate; sharply serrate; green and hairless (or nearly so) above and below except for tufts of hairs in vein axils. If present, hairs not branched. Base unequally heart-shaped. Petioles slender; 1–2 in. long; stipules falling early.

Flowers. Bisexual; 0.5–0.6 in. wide; yellow-white; fragrant; petals 5; borne in loose clusters of 3–8 (cymes); appearing in the spring after the leaves are fully expanded. Stalk long; attached to a straplike bract. Pollinated mostly by bees and flies during the day and moths at night.

Fruit. Drupe or nutlet; spherical; gray hairy; 0.2–0.4 in. wide; attached to straplike bract; mature in autumn.

Twigs. Generally rather stout; green to red; stipule scars large. Terminal bud absent. Lateral buds acute; red; lopsided; 0.2–0.3 in. long; mucilaginous when crushed and rubbed; 2–3 scales visible externally.

Bark. Smooth and gray-green on young trees; on older trees becoming light brown or gray and developing furrows that separate crisscrossing flat ridges. Inner bark (bast) used for rope and weaving.

Wood. Commercial value high especially in the Lake States. Sapwood white to cream. Heartwood light brown sometimes with red tinge; lightweight; soft; after drying will not warp or crack; decays quickly. Used for plywood, drawer panels, mirror backings, trunks and valises, dairy and apiary supplies, coffins, venetian blind slats, shade rollers, piano keys, novelties, woodenware, and carving.

Natural History. Tolerant of shade; reproduces well under a light canopy. Fast growing; reaches maturity in 200 years. Abundant seed produced every other year; germination slow owing to thick seed coat; seed viability about 25 percent. Sprouts vigorously from stumps. Girdling of young trees by mice and rabbits and wildfire cause the most damage. Grows mostly on sandy loam, loam, and silt loam soils; common on limestone soils; requires abundant moisture and nitrogen. Found rarely in pure stands; more commonly found in mixed stands with sugar maple, red maple, white ash, yellow birch, American beech, yellow-poplar, northern red oak, black cherry, American elm, eastern hemlock, and eastern white pine. Prized for nectar used in honey production.

Varieties. Some authors classify the 2 species listed below as varieties of American basswood.

Range. See figure 414.

Carolina basswood
Tilia caroliniana Mill.

Includes trees formerly classified separately as *Tilia floridana*. Small tree growing 40–60 ft in height. Leaves alternate; simple; 2–4 in. long; broadly ovate; margin sharply toothed; green above; brown, gray- or red-brown hairy below; hairs branched. Leaf base usually lopsided sometimes heart-shaped. Fruit a drupe or nutlet; nearly spherical; gray or brown; hairy to very hairy; borne in clusters (cymes) on a long hairy stalk; subtended by a strap-shaped bract. Grows on mesic flatwoods, lower slopes above rivers, and in sinkholes. Overall similar to American basswood differing in geographical location and by the hairy leaf undersurfaces. Sometimes considered to be a variety of American basswood, *Tilia americana* var. *caroliniana*. Found in the southeastern Coastal Plain from North Carolina south to Florida, and west to Texas and Oklahoma.

White basswood, Beetree linden
Tilia heterophylla Vent.

Moderately large tree growing 100–125 ft in height. Often found growing in clumps of 2–4 stems. Leaves alternate; simple; sharply toothed; 3–5 in. long; white hairy below; hairs branched. Base lopsided or heart-shaped. Fruit a drupe or nutlet; spherical; gray to red-brown hairy; borne in clusters (cymes) of 4–6 on a long hairy stalk; subtended by a strap-shaped bract. Tolerant of shade. Sprouts vigorously from stumps. Wildfire causes the most damage. Grows on mesic slopes with abundant humus in coves of the southern Appalachians. Found in mixed stands with yellow-poplar, northern red oak, white oak, black oak, white ash, black cherry, American beech, yellow buckeye, yellow birch, sweet birch, eastern white pine, and eastern hemlock. Leaves and twigs browsed by livestock and white-tailed deer. Prized for nectar used in honey production. Overall very similar to American basswood differing in geographical location and the white hairy undersurfaces. Sometimes considered a variety of American basswood, *Tilia americana* var. *heterophylla*. Found from southwestern Pennsylvania to central Missouri, and south from northwestern Florida to northern Arkansas.

ELM FAMILY: ULMACEAE

Naturally occurring in the tropics and north temperate regions, the Elm Family contains about 150 species in about 18 genera in the world. Our region contains 3 genera—*Celtis, Planera,* and *Ulmus.*

All members of the Elm Family are woody. The leaves are simple, deciduous, often sandpapery, and generally alternate. The leaves usually lie in a single plane, have inequilateral bases, stipules, and a toothed margin at least on juveniles. Borne on axillary branches, the flowers are very small, wind pollinated, and, with few exceptions, appear with or before the leaves. In hackberry and planertree, the flowers are unisexual, but each tree contains both sexes (monoecious). In elms the flowers are bisexual. Each flower generally contains four to eight sepals, but the petals are always absent. The ovary is superior and consists of two carpels. The fruit is either a samara, drupe, or nutlet each containing one seed with little or no endosperm. True terminal buds are lacking (pseudoterminal). The wood is ring-porous and often difficult to split.

HACKBERRY: THE GENUS *CELTIS*

The genus *Celtis* contains 60–80 species in the world, but only 6 species occur in our area. Two of our species are shrubs and beyond the scope of this manual. Another species, Lindheimer hackberry (*Celtis lindheimeri*), is rare with a small distribution in eastern Texas. Distinct with white hairy leaf undersides and light brown fruits, Lindheimer hackberry is seldom encountered. The taxonomy of hackberries is not settled, and additional study is needed. The treatment here is traditional.

Hackberries produce spherical drupe fruits with very little flesh that ripen in the fall, but they may persist into winter after the leaves have fallen. Dispersal is accomplished by birds, small mammals, and water.

KEY TO HACKBERRIES

1. Fruit dark purple; leaves sharply serrate with numerous teeth . . . .
. . . . .hackberry, *Celtis occidentalis*
1. Fruit orange, red, red-black, or light brown; leaves entire or sparingly toothed
. . . . .Go to 2
    2. Fruit stalks longer than leaf petioles 3
    2. Fruit stalks shorter or about the same length as the leaf petioles 4
3. Fruit red to red-black; leaves yellow-green below . . . .
. . . . .netleaf hackberry, *Celtis reticulata*
3. Fruit light brown; leaves white hairy below . . . .
. . . . .Lindheimer hackberry, *Celtis lindheimeri*
    4. Leaves 2–3 times longer than wide . . . . .sugarberry, *Celtis laevigata*
    4. Leaves 1–1.5 times longer than wide . . . . . . .dwarf hackberry, *Celtis tenuifolia*

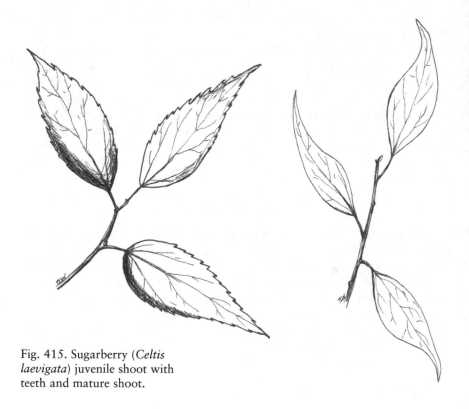

Fig. 415. Sugarberry (*Celtis laevigata*) juvenile shoot with teeth and mature shoot.

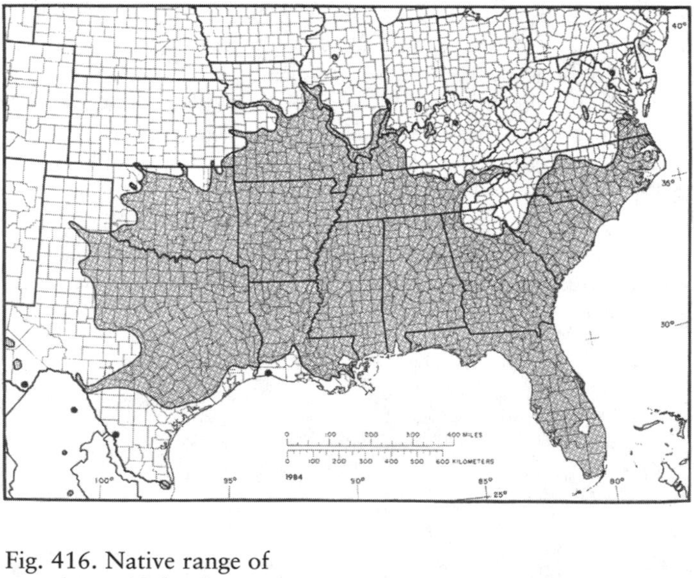

Fig. 416. Native range of sugarberry (*Celtis laevigata*).

Sugarberry, Southern hackberry

Celtis laevigata Willd. (fig. 415)

Form. Medium-sized excurrent to deliquescent tree growing 70–80 ft in height and 2–3 ft in diameter (widest known 5 ft).

Leaves. Alternate; simple; ovate to lanceolate; 2–5 in. long; smooth or slightly sand-papery above; smooth below. Margin entire on mature trees but serrated on juvenile trees. Tip acuminate to long acuminate. Base asymmetrical; rounded.

Fruit. Drupe; subspherical; 0.2–0.4 in. long; dull orange; borne on stalks shorter or slightly longer than leaf petioles; sweet to the taste, hence the common name. Style absent on mature fruit; skin smooth when dry.

Bark. Pale gray; smooth between raised, corky warts. Inner bark formerly used to treat sore throats.

Wood. Sapwood light yellow or green-yellow, frequently discolored with blue stain. Heartwood yellow-gray to light brown streaked with yellow; moderately heavy. Sometimes sold as hackberry but more commonly as elm. Used for steam-bent arms in furniture.

Natural History. Moderately tolerant of shade. Fast growing; reaches maturity in 150 years. Reproduces well from seeds; large seed crops produced most years; also reproduces from stump sprouts. Fire and ice breakage cause the most damage. Leachate from the leaves inhibits the growth of grasses. Grows on a wide range of sites; sometimes found on uplands but more typical of bottomland levees and terraces. Common on limestone soils in central Alabama. Found in mixed stands with sweetgum, eastern cottonwood, boxelder, overcup oak, willow oak, water oak, red maple, American elm, green ash, and sycamore.

Range. See figure 416.

Fig. 417. Hackberry (*Celtis occidentalis*) shoot, twig, twig pith, and fruit.

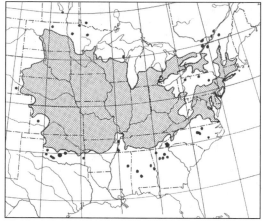

Fig. 418. Native range of hackberry (*Celtis occidentalis*).

Fig. 419. Netleaf hackberry (*Celtis reticulata*) shoot and fruit.

Hackberry, Northern hackberry
Celtis occidentalis L. (fig. 417)

Form. Shrub to moderate-sized excurrent to deliquescent tree growing 40–60 ft in height and 1–2 ft in diameter (largest known 130 ft by 4 ft). Crown rounded; spreading branches.

Leaves. Alternate; simple; ovate to ovate-lanceolate; 2–4 in. long; coarsely serrate; sandpapery above; hairy along veins below. Tip acuminate. Base asymmetrical; rounded.

Fruit. Drupe; subspherical; 0.2–0.4 in. long; dark green to purple; bitter to the taste; skin wrinkled when dry.

Twigs. Slender; light brown; hairless or hairy; marked by pale oblong lenticels; pith often finely chambered at nodes. Terminal buds 0.2 in. long; hairy; chestnut-brown.

Bark. Gray; smooth when young; with age, becoming covered by irregular black warts or long ridges.

Wood. Use same as sugarberry.

Natural History. Intermediate in tolerance to shade. Fast growing; reaches maturity in 150–200 years. Good seed crops produced most years. Sprouts from small stumps. Adapted to a wide variety of upland and lowland sites; grows largest in bottomlands; tolerates flooding for several months in the growing season. Often found on limestone soils and outcrops. Fruit eaten by quail, ringneck pheasants, turkeys, cedar waxwings, mockingbirds, and fox squirrels.

Range. See figure 418.

Netleaf hackberry
Celtis reticulata Torr. (fig. 419)

Shrub or small tree occasionally growing to 30 ft in height and 1 ft in diameter. Crown open; stout ascending branches. Leaves broadly ovate; 1–3 in. long; thick; margin entire or with a few teeth above the middle; dark green and sandpapery or smooth above; paler below with conspicuous netlike small veins. Tip acute to acuminate. Base rounded, heart-shaped, or asymmetrical. Fruit 0.2–0.4 in. long; red to red-black; subspherical. Fruit stalk longer than leaf petiole. Bark brown to gray; rough with corky ridges. Moderately intolerant of shade. Found on dry, rocky hillsides; often on limestone. Sometimes classified as a variety of hackberry, *Celtis occidentalis* var. *reticulata*. A variable species with several named varieties previously considered distinct. Found from central Kansas to eastern Washington, and south from Texas to southern California; also in Mexico.

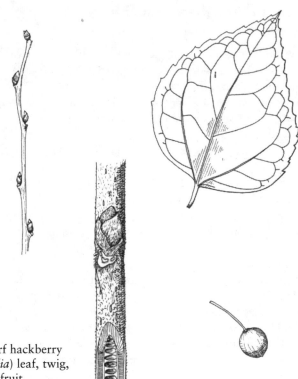

Fig. 420. Dwarf hackberry (*Celtis tenuifolia*) leaf, twig, twig pith, and fruit.

Fig. 421. Planertree (*Planera aquatica*) shoot.

Dwarf hackberry, Georgia hackberry
Celtis tenuifolia Nutt. (fig. 420)

Sometimes classified as a variety of hackberry, *Celtis occidentalis* var. *georgiana*. Shrub to small tree growing occasionally to 30 ft in height (tallest known 60 ft in Georgia). Crown compact with numerous small branches. Leaves alternate; simple; ovate; 2–3 in. long; margin entire to serrate. Tip acuminate. Base rounded to asymmetrical. Fruit a drupe; 0.2–0.3 in. long; orange to brown; stalk about as long as the leaf petiole; style persistent on mature fruit; skin smooth when dry. Bark gray; smooth with small warts. Found in open woods from Pennsylvania to Indiana, Missouri, and eastern Kansas, and south from northern Florida to Oklahoma.

PLANERTREE: THE GENUS *PLANERA*

Worldwide this genus contains only the species found in our region (monotypic). The leaves resemble elm, but the fruit is a nutlet with irregular hornlike projections.

Planertree, Water-elm
Planera aquatica J. F. Gmel. (fig. 421)

Small tree growing to 35 ft. Leaves alternate; simple; ovate to elliptical; elmlike; 1–3 in. long; margin crenate to serrate; teeth gland tipped. Fruit slightly hairy; compressed with hornlike projections. Wood weak and brittle; no commercial value. Grows in swamps and along the margins of rivers and lakes often forming thickets. Found in the Coastal Plain from North Carolina to north Florida, west to Texas, and north in the Mississippi River valley to southern Illinois.

ELM: THE GENUS *ULMUS*

This genus contains 20–40 species of trees scattered through the Northern Hemisphere especially Eurasia. Many are important ornamental shade trees. Six species are native to eastern and central North America. Four exotic species commonly planted in our region are included in the key. Only Siberian elm, widely naturalized through much of the United States, is discussed in detail. The remaining 3 exotics are only locally naturalized. The genus *Zelkova*, cultivated but not naturalized in our region, is sometimes mistaken for elm, but the fruit of *Zelkova* is an asymmetrical drupe, not a samara.

Leaves of elms are strongly pinnately veined, simply or more commonly doubly serrate, and with short petioles. The fruit is an oblong to round samara that matures in spring (usually) or autumn of the first year. The remnants of the sepals persist at the base of each fruit. The seed is surrounded by a thin papery wing commonly notched at the apex and tipped with the remnants of the style. Native elm populations have been severely reduced especially in the Lake States and New England by the Dutch elm disease, a fungus native to Europe and first discovered in North America in the 1930s. The exotic elms listed below have varying degrees of disease resistance and have been widely planted as replacements.

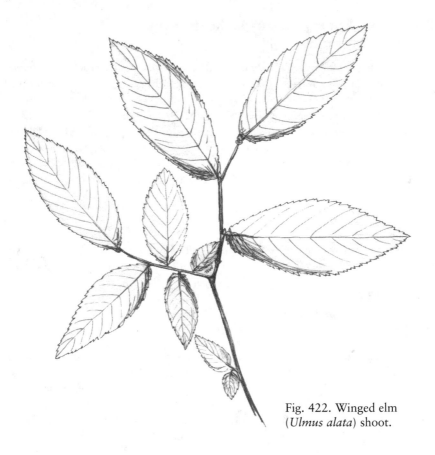

Fig. 422. Winged elm (*Ulmus alata*) shoot.

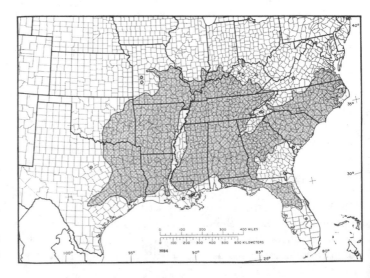

Fig. 423. Native range of winged elm (*Ulmus alata*).

KEY TO ELMS

1. Leaf margin singly serrated; leaf base symmetrical . . . . .Go to 2
1. Leaf margin doubly serrated; leaf base asymmetrical . . . . .Go to 3
   2. Leaf tip rounded to acute; fruit mature in autumn . . . .
   . . . . .Chinese elm, *Ulmus parvifolia*
   2. Leaf tip acuminate to acute; fruit mature in spring . . . .
   . . . . .Siberian elm, *Ulmus pumila*
3. Leaves very sandpapery above 4
3. Leaves smooth above on mature trees, slightly sandpapery on juveniles 6
   4. Leaves 2–3 in. long . . . . .English elm, *Ulmus procera*
   4. Leaves 3–7 in. long 5
5. Leaf base strongly asymmetrical, 1 side overlapping the petiole . . . .
   . . . . .Wych elm, *Ulmus glabra*
5. Leaf base asymmetrical, but neither side overlapping the petiole . . . .
   . . . . .slippery elm, *Ulmus rubra*
   6. Buds and young twigs pale hairy . . . . .rock elm, *Ulmus thomasii*
   6. Buds and young twigs hairless or nearly so 7
7. Leaf 2–3 in. wide 8
7. Leaf 0.5–1 in. wide 9
   8. Fruits mature in fall; leaves yellow hairy below . . . .
   . . . . .September elm, *Ulmus serotina*
   8. Fruit mature in spring; leaves hairless below . .American elm, *Ulmus americana*
9. Fruit mature in spring; leaf tip acute . . . . .winged elm, *Ulmus alata*
9. Fruit mature in fall; leaf tip rounded or obtuse . . . . . . .cedar elm, *Ulmus crassifolia*

Winged elm

Ulmus alata Michx. (fig. 422)

Small excurrent to deliquescent tree growing to 60 ft in height (tallest known 90 ft). Leaves alternate; simple; lanceolate to oblong; 1–3 in. long; doubly serrate; smooth or sandpapery above; hairy below on veins and in vein axils. Tip acute. Base heart-shaped or asymmetrical. Petiole hairy. Fruit gray-brown; narrowly winged; 0.3 in. long; margin slightly hairy; mature in spring. Twigs hairless or hairy; winged on young trees and sprouts. Buds slightly hairy. Bark gray or light brown; divided by shallow furrows into short narrow ridges. Wood has little or no commercial value. Moderately tolerant of shade. Dutch elm disease and phloem necrosis cause the most damage. Found on a wide variety of soils and conditions ranging from silty bottomlands to moderately dry uplands; the most site adaptable native elm. Common in fencerows and disturbed areas. May become troublesome on range lands where it survives grazing by repeated sprouting. Grows in mixed stands with post oak, blackjack oak, white oak, black oak, northern red oak, swamp chestnut oak, cherrybark oak, sugarberry, American elm, and green ash. For range see figure 423.

American elm, White elm

Ulmus americana L. (fig. 424)

Form. Large deliquescent tree growing 80–100 ft in height and 3–6 ft in diameter (largest known 120 ft by 10 ft). Bole commonly forks several times forming a vase-shaped crown.

Fig. 424. American elm (*Ulmus americana*) shoot and fruit clusters.

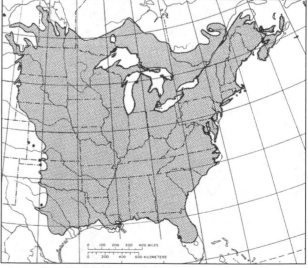

Fig. 425. Native range of American elm (*Ulmus americana*).

Leaves. Oblong-obovate to oval; 4–6 in. long; doubly serrate; smooth above on mature trees; somewhat sandpapery on juveniles and sprouts. Base asymmetrical.

Fruit. Samara; oval; 0.2–0.4 in. long; hairy on margins; deeply notched at tip; seed cavity distinct; mature in spring.

Twigs. Slender; round; red-brown; hairy at first becoming hairless; never winged. Terminal buds chestnut-brown; hairless or with scales hairy fringed.

Bark. Ash-gray to dark brown; divided by fissures into small irregular ridges; cross section of outer bark shows alternating light and dark layers.

Wood. Low commercial value but the most valuable of the elms. Sapwood gray-white to light brown. Heartwood brown often with a red tinge; moderately heavy. Used for the steam-bent parts of furniture especially arms and rockers, farm vehicles, agricultural implements, hockey sticks, and poultry and apiary supplies. Prized for staves and hoops of barrels used in storing solids. Interlocking grain makes splitting difficult.

Natural History. Moderately tolerant of shade. Reaches maturity in 175–200 years (extreme age 300 years). Reproduces well by seed; prolific seed crops produced most years. Sprouts well from stumps and possibly from roots. Forms root grafts with other elms. Wildfire, Dutch elm disease, and phloem necrosis provide the most damage. Most common on silt and clay loams in bottomlands on levees, first bottoms, and terraces, but also found in uplands. May colonize old fields. Formerly found in both pure and mixed stands, but Dutch elm disease has eliminated pure stands. Currently found in mixed stands where disease transmission is slower with red maple, boxelder, silver maple, sugarberry, hackberry, green ash, sycamore, sweetgum, swamp chestnut oak, cherrybark oak, Shumard oak, swamp white oak, pin oak, overcup oak, and cottonwood. Buds, flowers, and fruits eaten by squirrels. Fruits eaten by mice, opossum, grouse, and quail. Several disease-resistant cultivars have recently been developed.

Range. See figure 425.

Cedar elm

Ulmus crassifolia Nutt.

Moderate-sized tree growing to 80 ft in height and 2–3 ft in diameter (tallest known 100 ft). Leaves ovate to elliptical; 1–2 in. long; margin crenate or doubly serrate; rough sandpapery above; soft hairy below. Tip obtuse. Base rounded to asymmetrical. Petiole hairy. Fruit a samara; oval; green to tan; 0.2–0.4 in. long; hairy; mature in late fall. Twigs red-brown; often with corky wings. Terminal buds hairy. Wood use similar to other elms. Dutch elm disease causes the most damage. Found on moist or dry limestone soils. Grows in mixed stands with Ashe juniper, live oak, willow oak, overcup oak, hackberry, sweetgum, pecan, red maple, eastern cottonwood, and boxelder. Hybridizes with September elm and Chinese elm. Found from southern Arkansas to central Texas, and south from central Louisiana to southern Texas.

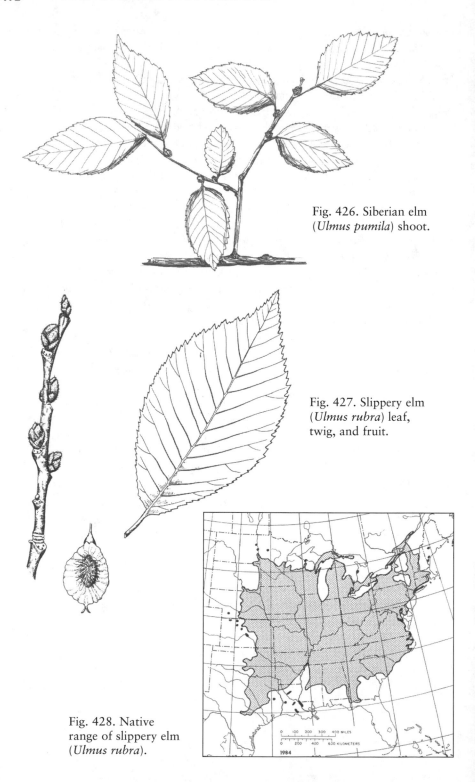

Fig. 426. Siberian elm (*Ulmus pumila*) shoot.

Fig. 427. Slippery elm (*Ulmus rubra*) leaf, twig, and fruit.

Fig. 428. Native range of slippery elm (*Ulmus rubra*).

Siberian elm
Ulmus pumila L. (fig. 426)

Moderate-sized deliquescent tree growing 50–80 ft in height. Branches weak, commonly breaking. Leaves narrowly elliptical; 1–3 in. long; singly serrate; hairless above; hairy in vein axils below. Tip acute. Base symmetrical. Fruit a samara; yellow; round; 0.4 in. long; hairless; terminal notch present; mature in spring. Twigs gray-brown; never winged. Lateral buds dark brown to black, spherical; shiny. Bark gray or brown; divided by shallow fissures into small irregular flat ridges. Native to Asia; sometimes planted for windbreaks and commonly escaping. Sometimes confused with Chinese elm, which has smooth or scaly orange to red-brown bark and fruit mature in autumn.

Slippery elm, Red elm
Ulmus rubra Muhl. (fig. 427)

Nomenclature. Formerly known as *Ulmus fulva*.

Form. Medium-sized tree growing 60–70 ft in height and 2–3 ft in diameter (largest known 130 ft by 6 ft).

Leaves. Obovate to oval; 4–7 in. long; coarsely doubly serrate above the middle; singly serrate toward the base; thick and firm; always very sandpapery above; hairy below with tufts of white hairs in vein axils. Tip acute to acuminate. Base asymmetrical. Often confused with juvenile leaves of American elm, which are slightly sandpapery above.

Fruit. Samara; nearly round; 0.5–0.7 in. long; seed cavity distinct and hairy on body; wings hairless; tip with shallow or no notch; matures in spring.

Twigs. Ash-gray; hairy when young; never winged. Buds nearly black at base; sometimes red hairy at tip.

Bark. Dark red-brown; furrows nearly parallel; cross section lacking alternating light and dark layers. Inner bark mucilaginous; used to treat sore throats.

Wood. Low commercial value; considered inferior to American elm.

Natural History. Tolerant of shade; generally a member of the subcanopy. Juvenile growth rapid; faster than American elm. Dutch elm disease, elm yellows, and phloem necrosis cause the most damage. Found on a wide variety of sites and soils: lower slopes, terraces, and uplands; absent from sites frequently flooded and long flooded. Frequent on limestone soils. Grows mixed with red maple, silver maple, boxelder, white oak, black oak, chinkapin oak, river birch, sycamore, shagbark hickory, bitternut hickory, pignut hickory, white ash, American elm, and hackberry. Bark eaten by white-tailed deer.

Hybrids. Hybridizes with rock elm and Siberian elm.

Range. See figure 428.

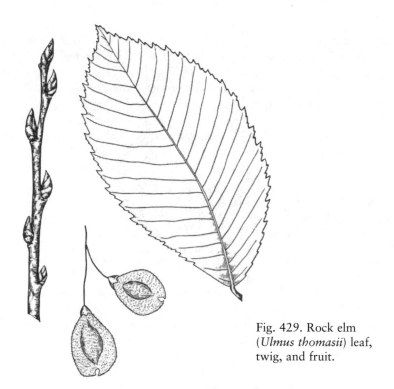

Fig. 429. Rock elm
(*Ulmus thomasii*) leaf,
twig, and fruit.

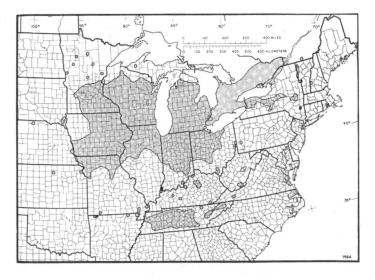

Fig. 430. Native range of
rock elm (*Ulmus thomasii*).

September elm, Red elm
Ulmus serotina Sarg.

Small to medium-sized tree growing to 60 ft in height. Leaves alternate; simple; oblong to obovate; 3–4 in. long; margin doubly serrate; hairless above; yellow-hairy below. Tip acuminate. Base asymmetrical. Petiole hairless or hairy. Fruit a samara; light brown; 0.4–0.5 in. long; wing narrow; white-hairy on margin; deeply notched at tip; matures in fall. Twigs brown to gray; hairless or hairy; slightly drooping; irregular corky wings common. Wood red-brown; polishes well; heavier than American elm. Tolerant of shade. Grows rapidly in open areas. Very susceptible to Dutch elm disease. Found on well-drained clay loam or sandy loam soils in bottomlands and coves; absent from poorly drained soils. Also found on dry limestone soils. Grows with river birch, sweetgum, white ash, northern red oak, and American elm. Generally thought to be an uncommon species, but possibly overlooked and confused with other elms. Found in small scattered areas in Kentucky, Tennessee, northwestern Georgia, northern Alabama, northern Mississippi, Arkansas, and eastern Oklahoma.

Rock elm, Cork elm
Ulmus thomasii Sarg. (fig. 429)

Medium-sized excurrent tree growing 60–80 ft in height and 2–3 ft in diameter (largest known 100 ft by 5 ft). Crown narrow with drooping lower branches. Leaves alternate; simple; obovate to oval; 2–5 in. long; coarsely doubly serrate; thick and firm; dark green and usually hairless above; paler and slightly hairy below. Base nearly symmetrical. Fruit a samara; obovate to oval; 0.4–1 in. long; hairy; seed cavity not distinct; tip with shallow or no notch; matures in spring. Twigs red-brown; usually developing irregular corky wings. Buds brown; acute; downy ciliate. Bark dark gray-brown; deeply and irregularly furrowed; cross section with alternating light and dark layers. Wood heavier and more shock resistant than American elm; formerly used for furniture and ship timbers but overcutting has almost eliminated the supply. Moderately tolerant of shade. Does not reproduce well from seeds even though large seed crops produced every 3–4 years and the species is self-fertile. Sprouts from stumps and roots, but vegetative reproduction is also scarce. Dutch elm disease causes the most damage. Found on a wide variety of sites ranging from loamy wet-mesic soils to dry limestone outcrops. Grows in mixed stands with red maple, sugar maple, black ash, white ash, northern red oak, yellow birch, American beech, eastern hemlock, and American elm. Seeds eagerly eaten by chipmunks, ground squirrels, and mice. For range see figure 430.

GLOSSARY

Aborted. Imperfectly developed or not developed.

Achene. A dry indehiscent small fruit.

Acicular. Needle-shaped.

Acuminate. Gradually tapering to the tip; longpointed.

Acute. Quickly tapering to a point of less than 90 degrees.

Adnate. organs or parts fused together.

Aggregate. A compound fruit developing from separate ovaries of the same flower.

Allelopathy. Growth inhibition of one species from chemicals released from the roots, leaves, or fruits of a second species.

Alternate. Scattered singly along an axis; one part (usually a leaf or scale) per node.

Ament. A scaly flexible spike usually containing unisexual flowers and falling as a unit; catkin.

Angiosperms. Plants with seeds borne in an ovary.

Anther. The pollen-bearing part of the stamen.

Anthesis. The time when pollination takes place or a flower expands.

Apetalous. Lacking petals.

Apex. Tip.

Apophysis. The part of a cone scale that is exposed when the cone is closed.

Appressed. Lying close and flat against.

Arborescent. Attaining the size or character of a tree.

Arcuate. Leaf veins moderately curved.

Aril. An appendage or outer covering (usually fleshy) that partly or completely overgrows a seed.

Attenuate. Slender tapering; acuminate.

Auriculate. Furnished with an earlike appendage.

Awl-shaped. Tapering from the base to a slender and stiff point.

Axil. The upper angle formed by a leaf or branch with the stem.

Axillary. Located in the axil of a leaf.

Berry. A fruit fleshy or pulpy throughout with immersed seeds.

Blade. The expanded flat portion of a leaf.

Bloom. A powdery or waxy substance easily rubbed off.

Bole. The main stem of a tree; the trunk.

Boss. A raised projection, usually pointed.

Bract. A modified leaf usually subtending a flower, a scale, or part of an inflorescence.

Bud. An unexpanded branch, flower, or flower cluster.

Bud scales. Modified leaves covering a bud.

Bundle scar. The exposed tip of fibrovascular tissue (xylem and phloem) found in a leaf scar.

Calyx. All of the sepals.

Campanulate. Bell-shaped.

Canescent. Gray-pubescent and hoary.

Capitate. Shaped like a head; in dense head like clusters.

Capsule. A dry fruit with more than one carpel that splits open along two or more lines at maturity.

Carpel. The basic unit of the gynoecium.

Catkin. Another name for ament.

Caudate. Furnished with a tail or a slender tip.

Cell. The unit of structure of living things; a cavity in an ovary.

Chambered. A pith that is regularly interrupted by hollow spaces.

Ciliate. Fringed with hairs on the edge.

Clone. A group of genetically identical individuals; in nature, usually arising from root sprouts or rooted cuttings.

Compound. Composed of several parts, usually leaflets or carpels.

Cone. A reproductive structure, usually papery or woody, composed of overlapping scales.

Connate. Similar tissues fused together.

Coppice. Sprouts arising from the root collar or roots.

Cordate. Heart-shaped.

Coriaceous. Of the texture of leather.

Corolla. All of the petals.

Corymb. A flat-topped flower cluster with the flowers opening from the outside inward.

Crenate. With rounded teeth.

Crenulate. With small, rounded teeth.

Crown. Upper part of a tree, containing the living branches with leaves.

Cuneate. Wedge-shaped.

Cuspidate. Tipped with a sharp, rigid point.

Cylindrical. Shaped like a cylinder.

Cyme. A flat-topped flower cluster, the flowers opening from the center outward.

Deciduous. Not persistent; falling away, usually referring to the leaves of a tree in autumn.

Decurrent. Running down as the blades of leaves extending down their petioles.

Decussate. Opposite, with alternate pairs rotated 90 degrees.

Dehiscent. Opening or splitting naturally at maturity.

Deliquescent. Tree stem (trunk) that divides repeatedly into branches of equal size; vase-shaped.

Deltoid. Delta-shaped; triangular.

Dentate. Toothed with the teeth pointing outward.

Denticulate. Minutely toothed with the teeth pointing outward.

Diaphragmed. A solid pith with regularly spaced disks of hardened tissue.

Diffuse-porous. Wood in which the water-conducting pores show little difference in size.

Dimorphic. Occurring in two shapes.

Dioecious. Unisexual flowers or cones with the sexes borne on different trees.

Dissemination. Release and spreading mature seeds from the parent plant.

Divergent. Spreading apart; pointing away.

Dorsal. Relating to the back or outer surface of an organ; the lower surface of a leaf.

Downy. Clothed with a coat of soft, fine hairs.

Drupaceous. Resembling a drupe, usually containing more than one stone.

Drupe. A fleshy fruit containing a single stone or pit in the center.

E-. A Latin prefix meaning without or lacking.

E-glandular. Without glands.

Ellipsoidal. Of the shape of an elliptical solid.

Elliptic. Of the form of an ellipse.

Emarginate. Notched at the tip.

Entire. Leaf margin without teeth.

Erose. A cone scale that is jagged at the tip.

Excrescences. Warty outgrowths or protuberances.

Excurrent. Main stem (trunk) of tree extending from the base to the top of the tree without forking.

Exfoliate. To peel off in thin layers.

Exserted. Extending beyond the surrounding tissues.

Exstipulate. Without stipules.

Falcate. Sickle-shaped; curved.

Fascicle. A cluster, usually a cluster of leaves in pines.

Fibrovascular. Consisting of woody fibers and ducts.

Filament. The stalk of an anther.

Fluted. Regularly marked by alternating ridges and depressions.

Foliaceous. Leaflike in texture or appearance.

Follicle. A dry fruit with one carpel that opens naturally along one line (suture).

Fruit. Mature or ripened ovary.

Fulvous. Tawny; dull yellow with gray.

Funiculus. The stalk of an ovule.

Furrowed. With channels or grooves.

Glabrate. Nearly hairless.

Glabrous. Smooth, without hairs.

Gland. A secreting pore or structure.

Glandular. Furnished with glands.

Glaucous. Covered or whitened with white wax.

Globose. Spherical in form or nearly so.

Gymnosperms. Plants with naked seeds (seeds not enclosed in an ovary).

Habit. The general appearance of a plant, best seen from a distance.

Habitat. The place where a plant naturally grows.

Hilum. The scar or place of attachment of a seed.

Hirsute. Covered with coarse, long hairs.

Hispid. With rigid or bristly hairs.

Hoary. Covered with short, white or gray-white hairs.

Hybrid. A cross usually between two related species.

Hybrid swarm. Hybridization between two species followed by repeated back-crossing to both parents so that the differences between the original two species are obscured by a continuous series of intermediates.

Imbricate. Overlapping like shingles on a roof.

Imperfect (flower). Containing one sex but not the other.

Indehiscent. Not splitting open; remaining closed.

Inferior ovary. Appearing to occur below the calyx.

Inflorescence. Flowers appearing in clusters.

Inserted. Attached to or growing out of; shorter than surrounding structures.

Intolerant. Not capable of growing well in shade.

Involucre. A circle of bracts surrounding a flower cluster.

Irregular flower. Bilaterally symmetrical; similar parts of different shapes or sizes.

Keeled. With a central ridge like the keel of a boat.

Laciniate. With long, narrow, pointed lobes.

Lanceolate. Lance-shaped.

Lateral. Situated on the side.

Leaf scar. Scar left on twig by the falling of a leaf.

Leaflet. One of the small blades of a compound leaf.

Legume. A dry fruit with one carpel that often opens naturally at maturity along two lines (sutures). Found only in the Legume Family, Fabaceae.

Lenticel. Specialized corky opening on young twigs or bark that admits air to the interior. On bark, several lenticels often found in a horizontal row.

Liana. A woody vine.

Linear. Long and narrow, with parallel edges.

Lobe. A somewhat rounded division of an organ.

Lobulate. Divided into small lobes.

Lustrous. Glossy, shining.

Membranaceous. Thin and somewhat translucent.

Midrib. The central vein of a leaf or leaflet; midvein.

Midvein. The central vein of a leaf or leaflet; midrib.

Mixed stand. A group of trees in which no one species comprises at least 80 percent of all individuals.

Monoecious. Unisexual flowers or cones with both sexes found on each plant.

Mucro. A small and abrupt tip to a leaf.

Mucronate. Furnished with a mucro (bristle-tipped).

Multiple. A compound fruit developing from ripened ovaries of separate flowers.

Naked buds. Buds without scales.

Nonporous. Wood that lacks vessels, specialized water-conducting pores; found in nearly all wood produced by gymnosperms.

Nut. A hard and indehiscent large fruit.

Nutlet. A small nut.

Ob-. Latin prefix signifying inversion.

Obconic. Inverted cone-shaped.

Obcordate. Inverted heart shape.

Oblanceolate. Lanceolate but with the broadest part toward the tip.

Oblique. Slanting or with unequal sides.

Oblong. About three times longer than broad with nearly parallel sides.

Obovate. Ovate with the broader end toward the tip.

Obovoid. An ovate solid with the broader part toward the tip.

Obtuse. Blunt or rounded at the apex.

Odd-pinnate leaf. Pinnately compound with a terminal leaflet.

Opposite. Two leaves emerging at opposite sides from the same place on the twig.

Orbicular. A flat body circular in outline.

Oval. Broad elliptic, rounded at ends, and about one time as long as broad.

Ovary. The bottom part of the carpel contains the ovules.

Ovate. Shaped like the longitudinal section of an egg, with the broad end at the bottom.

Ovoid. Solid ovate or solid oval.

Ovule. An immature seed.

Palmate. Radially lobed or divided; often veins arising from one point.

Panicle. A loose, compound, or branched flower cluster.

Papilionaceous. Butterflylike; typical flower shape of legumes.

Pectinate. Comblike with narrow, closely inserted segments.

Pedicel. Stalk of a single flower in a compound inflorescence.

Pedicellate. Borne on a pedicel.

Peduncle. A general flower stalk supporting either a cluster of flowers or a solitary flower.

Peltate. Shield- or mushroom-shaped and attached by its lower surface to the central stalk.

Pendent. Hanging downward.

Pendulous. More or less hanging or declined.

Penniveined. Having the form of a feather; secondary veins arranged parallel to each other and arising from a main vein.

Perfect. Flower with both stamens and pistil.

Perianth. The calyx and corolla of a flower considered as a whole.

Persistent. Remaining attached; not falling off; evergreen.

Petiolate. Having a petiole.

Petiole. Stalk of a leaf.

Petiolule. Stalk of a leaflet.

Pilose. Hairy, with soft and distinct hairs.

Pinna. One of the main divisions of a pinnately compound leaf.

Pinnae. Plural of pinna.

Pinnate. Featherlike; often used to describe parallel veins that regularly branch from both sides of the midvein, or compound leaves with leaflets arranged along each side of the rachis.

Pistil. Female organ of a flower, consisting of ovary, style, and stigma.

Pistillate. Female flowers; descriptive of unisexual flowers.

Pith. The central part of a twig.

Pollen. The fecundating grains borne in the anther.

Polygamo-dioecious. Flowers bisexual and either male or female flowers on the same tree.

Polygamo-monoecious. Flowers bisexual and male and female flowers on the same tree.

Polygamous. Flowers bisexual and unisexual on the same tree.

Pome. A fleshy fruit with an inferior ovary enclosed in thick flesh; an apple.

Prickle. A stiff, sharp hair.

Prostrate. Lying flat on the ground.

Puberulous. Minutely pubescent.

Pubescent. Clothed with soft, short hairs; or hairy.

Pungent. Terminating in a rigid, sharp point; acrid.

Pure stand. Group of trees in which one species comprises at least 80 percent of all individuals.

Pyramidal. Shaped like a pyramid.

Pyriform. Pear-shaped.

Raceme. A group of stalked flowers borne on a more or less elongated axis. Each stalk of similar length.

Racemose. In racemes; resembling racemes.

Rachis. An elongated axis bearing leaflets, flowers, or fruits.

Receptacle. The more-or-less expanded tip of a flower stalk.

Recurved. Curving downward or backward.

Reflexed. Abruptly turned downward.

Regular flower. Radially symmetrical; similar parts of the same shape and size.

Remotely. Scattered, not close together.

Reniform. Kidney-shaped.

Repand. With a slightly wavy margin.

Reticulate. Netted; netlike.

Retrosely. Directed backward or downward.

Revolute. Rolled backward, margin rolled toward the lower side.

Rhombic. Having the shape of a diamond.

Ring-porous. Wood in which the water-conducting pores formed in the early spring are much larger than those formed later.

Rufous. Red-brown.

Rugose. Wrinkled.

Salverform. Tubular corolla with a spreading limb.

Samara. An indehiscent winged fruit.

Scabrous. Rough to the touch, sandpapery.

Scarious. Thin, dry, membranaceous; not green.

Scurfy. Covered with small scales.

Sepal. The lowest part of a flower, usually green, that usually protects the flower in bud; one division of the calyx.

Serotinous. Late in bearing or opening.

Serrate. Toothed, teeth pointing upward or forward.

Serrulate. Finely toothed.

Sessile. Without a stalk.

Sheath. A tubular envelope, or enrolled part or organ.

Shrub. A woody plant with multiple branches arising at or near the base and usually less than 25 feet in height.

Simple. Consisting of or containing a single part.

Sinuate. With a wavy margin.

Sinus. The space between two lobes.

Spatulate. Spatula-shaped.

Spike. A simple inflorescence of stalkless flowers arranged on a common, elongated axis.

Spine. A leaf or leaf part modified into sharp-pointed needlelike structure.

Spinescent. With short, rigid, thorny branches.

Spinose. Furnished with spines.

Spur shoot. A very short, lateral branch often growing only 0.1–0.2 in. each year.

Stamen. The pollen-bearing organ of the male flower.

Staminate. Male flowers; provided with stamens but without functional carpels.

Stellate. Star-shaped.

Sterigmata. Peglike outgrowths of the twig that support the leaves of some conifers, especially spruce and hemlock.

Stigma. The tip of the carpel that receives pollen.

Stipe. The stalklike support.

Stipule. Leafy or hairlike appendages (usually) found in pairs at the base of the petiole or at the node.

Stoloniferous. Having lower branches that bend to contact the soil and root at the tip.

Stoma. A specialized opening in the epidermis of a leaf used to connect internal cavities with the outside air.

Stomata. Plural of stoma.

Stomatiferous. Furnished with stomata.

Strobile. A cone or conelike structure.

Strobili. Plural of strobilus.

Strobilus. A cone or conelike structure.

Style. The attenuated portion of a carpel between the ovary and the stigma.

Sub-. A Latin prefix denoting somewhat or slightly.

Suborbicular. Nearly round.

Subtend. Found below or under.

Subulate. Awl-shaped.

Succulent. Juicy; fleshy.

Superior ovary. An ovary that occurs above and free from the calyx.

Superposed. Placed above, as one bud above another at a node.

Suture. A junction or line of dehiscence.

Syncarp. A multiple fleshy fruit.

Taproot. The primary descending root, which may be either very large or absent at the maturity of the tree.

Taxa. Plural of taxon.

Taxon. A taxonomic category of any rank, such as a variety, a species, a genus.

Terete. Circular in traverse section.

Terminal. Situated at the end of a branch.

Ternate. In groups of three.

Thorn. A twig modified to become pointed and sharp-tipped.

Tolerant. Capable of enduring shade and other understory conditions.

Tomentose. Densely hairy with matted wool or tomentum.

Tomentulose. Slightly hairy with matted wool.

Tree. A woody plant with one to four stems arising at ground level, and growing at least 25 ft in height and 3 in. in diameter.

Truncate. Ending abruptly, as if cut off at the end.

Tubercle. A small tuber or excrescence.

Turbinate. Top-shaped.

Twig. A young woody stem; more precisely, the shoot of a woody plant representing the growth of the current season.

Umbel. A group of flowers with stalks all arising from the same point.

Umbo. A boss or protuberance found on the apophysis of a cone scale.

Undulate. With wavy surface or margin.

Unisexual. With one sex.

Valvate. Bud scales that meet at the edges, not overlapping.

Valve. One of the pieces into which a capsule splits.

Veins. Threads of fibrovascular tissue in a leaf or other flat organ.

Ventral. Belonging to the anterior or inner face of an organ; the upper surface of a leaf.

Vernal. Appearing in the spring.

Vesicle. A little bladder or cavity.

Villous. Hairy with long and soft hairs.

Viscid. Gluey or sticky.

Whorled. Three or more organs arranged in a circle around an axis.

Wing. A membranous or thin and dry expansion or appendage of an organ.

Woolly. Covered with long matted, or tangled hairs.

INDEX